O9-CFS-927

Political Commentators in the United States in the 20th Century

Political Commentators in the United States in the 20th Century

A Bio-Critical Sourcebook

Dan Nimmo
Chevelle Newsome

Greenwood Press
Westport, Connecticut • London

Library of Congress Cataloging-in-Publication Data

Nimmo, Dan D.
    Political commentators in the United States in the 20th century : a bio-critical
sourcebook / Dan Nimmo, Chevelle Newsome.
      p. cm.
    Includes bibliographical references and index.
    ISBN 0–313–29585–9 (alk. paper)
    1. Mass media—political aspects—United States. 2. Journalists—
United States—Biography. 3. United States—Politics and
government—20th century. I. Newsome, Chevelle. II. Title.
P95.82.U6N57   1997
302.23'092'273—dc20   96–28069

British Library Cataloguing in Publication Data is available.

Copyright © 1997 by Dan Nimmo and Chevelle Newsome

All rights reserved. No portion of this book may be
reproduced, by any process or technique, without the
express written consent of the publisher.

Library of Congress Catalog Card Number: 96–28069
ISBN: 0–313–29585–9

First published in 1997

Greenwood Press, 88 Post Road West, Westport, CT 06881
An imprint of Greenwood Publishing Group, Inc.

Printed in the United States of America

The paper used in this book complies with the
Permanent Paper Standard issued by the National
Information Standards Organization (Z39.48–1984).

10 9 8 7 6 5 4 3 2 1

To
Linda R. Cobbs
Access Services Librarian, Baylor University

Authors frequently overuse a trite phrase in acknowledging the contributions of others to their works, namely, "without whom this book could not have been written." In this instance the phrase is not trite, but accurate and sincere. Without Linda Cobbs' competent and gracious understanding and assistance, this book literally could not have been written.

Joseph Addison on Commentary

"I . . . recommend . . . my speculations to all well-meaning families that set apart an hour in every morning for tea and bread and butter; and advise . . . [they] be looked on as part of the tea equippage."

"The Aims of the Spectator"
The Spectator, March 12, 1711

CONTENTS

INTRODUCTION

As the closing decade of the twentieth century directed Americans toward a new millennium, a complex coupling as old as the ancients—that between politics and communication—came under highly critical scrutiny. Political leaders, scholars, journalists, media critics, and rank-and-file spokespersons complained that the practices of political discourse were seriously flawed. Such claims by politicians were scarcely new. Such elected public officials as U.S. presidents have routinely condemned their opponents for ''ducking the issues'' for decades; politicians' condemnations of press coverage of politics date back to the founding of the republic.

Criticism from other quarters, however, is a more recently tailored fashion. Political scientists, who until the 1970s largely dismissed the role of communication media in politics as marginal, with ''limited effects,'' were by the 1990s competing with popular writers to place their scholarly volumes, claiming that practices of political discourse were ''out of order,'' on airport book stalls (see Patterson, 1993). Political journalists, baring their newly searched souls before the world, attacked their colleagues as either ''a generation of vipers'' so entrapped by cynicism that they ascribed sinister motives to all politicians, thus contributing to widespread disillusion with all government (Starobin, 1995), or as more committed to entertaining the public than engaging it, as courting celebrity at the expense of performing a requisite informational role (Fellows, 1996).

Media critics became hypercritical. *Washington Post* media critic Howard Kurtz, examining the plethora of radio and television political talk shows, concluded that America had become a shouting-head society of electronic court jesters who are loud, angry, smug, and poorly informed rumor mongers (1996). Alan Bennett, a noted playwright, producer, and social commentator who is no stranger to the entertainment world, offered his own severe judgment of the massive imbalance in the relationship between political action and discourse. Speaking of political commentator David Frost (and by implication all contemporary show business cum political commentators), Bennett wrote, "Not that Frost isn't highly respectable, but his rise as a political commentator is in direct proportion to the decline in respect for politicians" (1996, 35).

In light of contemporary criticism of the state of political discourse, it is useful to pause and look back at the state of the art of one form of such discourse as it was during the early decades of the century, namely, *political commentary*. Although political commentary as implicit in all political philosophy has existed since the ancients, its development as a fact of popular life, in which it is distributed and consumed via the mass media by all segments of society, is a phenomenon of the twentieth century spawned by the unfolding of successive radical socioeconomic shifts, the industrial revolution, and the revolution in communication and popular culture (Carey, 1969). The purpose of *Political Commentators in the United States in the 20th Century: A Bio-Critical Sourcebook* is to portray the careers of key political commentators of the era and, through their lives and works, to illustrate the rise and decline of political commentary across the century.

THE POLITICAL COMMENTATOR AS A POLITICAL COMMUNICATOR

As long as there have been human conflicts, and people have endeavored to regulate those disputes short of mutual annihilation, there has been political communication. As a form of communication, the political variant has consequences for the creation, maintenance, enhancement, and even disruption of the social order (Duncan, 1968). If one answer to the continuing philosophical query, "What makes society possible?," is politics, then political communication is the essence of the process.

Once limited to face-to-face interactions in forums, marketplaces, public assemblies, and street corners, political communication evolved to include ever wider audiences and participants. Interpersonal venues typical of political discourse in the city-state yielded to the geographical expanse of the nation-state and empires; exchanges in intimate settings of small groups, such as the council of George Washington's first presidential cabinet, yielded to the vast bureaucratic complexes of the twentieth century. Thus the impersonality of organizational communication supplemented, and often replaced, the immediacy of face-to-face discourse. With the arrival of the mass media of communication—newspapers, telegraphy, wire services, telephones, radio, film, television, and satellite communications—political communication combined interpersonal, organizational, and mass communication means.

With respect to each of its three variants, political communication has always possessed two types of participants. One is the dabbler in politics, the political amateur who joins and leaves the political fray, who perhaps has a vested interest in the outcome of a particular conflict, but whose vocation lies elsewhere: the grape grower, artisan, or merchant who joins the political dialogue of the forum, then retires to a commercial enterprise; the labor union member who hands out leaflets for a political candidate, then returns to duties as a shop foreman in an industrial organization; or the celebrity movie star, home run slugger, quarterback, or rock singer who endorses a political candidate or testifies at a televised congressional hearing, then courts again the spotlight of popular adulation.

The other type of political communicator is committed to political affairs full-time; to this person, politics is a vocation, a lifetime career occupying the talents of the political professional. In a later era they would be known as "pols" (and amateur politicians as "vols"), but many of the Greek Sophists were as committed to careers in politics through their face-to-face instruction of the rhetorical arts as were nineteenth-century political bosses through the intimacy of their ward petty graft. The organizational age gave rise to career government bureaucrats. Although political scientist Woodrow Wilson's distinction between "administration" and "politics" implied that bureaucrats were above partisanship, they were scarcely as "non-political" as he sought to portray them (Wilson, 1887, 197). Finally, the advent of mass communication yielded a new type of pol, the career political-media consultant, a derivative of the rise of the public relations industry and a variant of the professional communicator.

Communication scholar James W. Carey coined the label "professional communicator" to describe

> one who controls a specific skill in the manipulation of symbols and who utilizes this skill to forge a link between distinct persons or differentiated groups [i.e.,] a broker in symbols, one who translates the attitudes, knowledge, and concerns of one speech community into alternative but suasive and understandable terms for another community (1969, 27).

The role of the professional communicator, or "pro," is a distinct social role brought about by the specialization of labor, which accompanied the industrial revolution, and the emphasis placed on symbol manipulation—especially through mass persuasion, advertising, and propaganda—as a derivative of the revolution in communication and popular culture that followed industrialization. Representative of that social role are all manner of journalists (including reporters, editors, and editorial writers), artists (for example, painters and photographers, actors and actresses, musicians, dancers, and architects), writers of fiction and nonfiction (novelists, poets, science and technical writers, speech writers, and sundry others), and, in an age of mass communication, teachers.

The term "professional communicator" Carey regards as "accurate but unfelicitous [sic]" (23). It is accurate in the sense that professional communicators possess specialized skills, perform specialized brokering functions, and adhere to widely shared conventions of acceptable performance. However, in the stricter sense that one designates, for example, physicians, as professionals, the accuracy of the term "professional communicator" is problematic. Philosopher Alfred North Whitehead took pains to distinguish between a profession and a craft. The professional's work is "subjected to theoretical analysis" and "modified by theoretical conclusions derived from that analysis. . . . foresight based upon theory and theory based upon understanding the nature of things, are essential to a profession" (1933, 72). By contrast, a craft consists of what Whitehead labeled "customary activities" which are modified by the "trial and error of individual practice" (73).

If Whitehead's more rigorous standard for professional conduct is applied, professional communication is less of a profession and more of a craft. Certainly the current state of the communication arts and sciences, not to speak of that of political communication and journalism, falls far short of Whitehead's "theoretical analysis," and the conduct of professional political communicators is far more likely to be modified by trial and error than by "theoretical conclusions derived from that analysis." Calls by political communication scholars for "explicit theorizing" by "the use of formal models, experiments, and large-scale content analysis to study the effects of political communication" (Simon & Iyengar, 1996, 32), well intentioned though they may be, are unlikely to result in a theory of political communication to guide professionals.

To the degree that an overriding logic drives the professional communicator, it is the logic of what Jacques Ellul called *la technique*. The logic of technique is the logic that drives all endeavor in the modern world. It impels people to seek and discover ever more efficient means to achieve ever more controlled and complete results in all matters—politics and communication included. *La technique* converts means to an end, the end of action itself. The standard to judge the technician's performance, including the broker of symbols, is that of efficiency, not theoretical understanding.

Nonetheless, as Michael Schudson has written, political journalists prefer to regard themselves as professionals, not craftsmen (1995). In doing so they rationalize and dignify their calling as something it is not. Such conventions of journalistic performance as objectivity, filling the news hole, deadline pressures, and keeping an eye on the bottom line provide, respectively, excuses for serving as a shill for political news sources, manufacturing stories when there is nothing to report, failing to present well-rounded reports, and pandering to popular tastes rather than instructing them. As the entries in this volume attest with respect to many in the contemporary generation of political commentators, the craft's conventions for evaluating commentary are so elastic in application and so grounded in entertainment criteria that caveat emptor is required of any discerning citizen.

Carey distinguishes between "the writer, novelist, scholar and others who produce messages" and the professional communicator on the grounds that the message produced by the professional communicator "has no *necessary* relation to" the communicator's "own thoughts and perceptions"; the professional "operates under the constraints or demands imposed on one side by the ultimate audience and, on the other side, by the ultimate source'' (1969, 28; emphasis in original). However, in the more than a quarter of a century of the revolution in popular culture that has taken place since Carey made that distinction, the line has become increasingly blurred.

On the one hand, writers and novelists certainly are constrained by the demands imposed by the necessity to produce best-selling works in the mass marketplace; and in an age when scholars are under scrutiny by students, administrators, and colleagues at every turn, they too face constraints from an ''ultimate audience'' and ''ultimate source.'' On the other hand, in the highly politicized and dramatized world of electronic journalism, correspondents bent on projecting celebrity personae routinely sort themselves from their competitors by fashioning messages that do bear a ''necessary relation'' to their ''own thoughts and perceptions.'' This is especially so of one particular type of professional political communicator, namely, the political commentator.

Although ''commentator'' is a designation first associated primarily with the ''golden age of radio'' that covered the two decades from 1929 to 1948, it is more appropriate to trace the heritage of the role to events surrounding America's entry into World War I. The journalistic conventions of the inverted pyramid and the ''Four Ws and an H'' (i.e., packing the who, what, when, where, and how of a news account into the opening paragraph, then supplying details in successive paragraphs) was an admirable device for accomplishing several ends. One was technical and economic—telegraphic wire services carried the essential facts surrounding events in a short, economic passage that newspapers could print without incurring the costs of using the detailed materials. Another was circulation—by sticking to the ''facts,'' news organizations appealed to large, heterogeneous audiences and alienated nobody.

However, the convention also played into the hands of news sources bent on manipulating the content of news accounts. Indeed, there is evidence that it was President Abraham Lincoln's secretary of war, Edwin M. Stanton, who invented the inverted pyramid as a means of keeping a tight control over the release of information regarding Lincoln's assassination (Mindich, 1993). The device remained useful to politicians for that purpose throughout the ensuing decades. With America's entry into World War I, President Woodrow Wilson recognized that basic facts alone would not sustain popular support behind his war aims. To supply the ''why'' behind unfolding events, putting matters into a perspective to serve America's interests, Wilson turned in a new direction and created America's first propaganda agency, the Committee on Public Information (CPI). Commentary was a principal propagandistic device and the CPI director, George Creel (q.v.), was the organizer of political commentary on a scale heretofore unheard of in the nation's history.

Following World War I, vehicles of political commentary multiplied, diversified, and became increasingly entrepreneurial. Edward L. Bernays (q.v.) pioneered in public relations. Walter Lippmann (q.v.) invented the syndicated political column, a means by which the individual, independent journalist wrote

signed commentary and, to recall and perhaps dispute Carey's phrase, produced
messages that had a "necessary relation to his own thoughts and perceptions."
Soon Lippmann had his imitators; the political commentator as a columnist,
distinct from the editorial writer serving as the ghosted voice of a news organization, was born (Fisher, 1944; Cohen, 1989). With the arrival of radio, H.
V. Kaltenborn (q.v.) pioneered political commentary on that medium; he too
had his imitators, as did Eric Sevareid (q.v.) on television after World War II
(Fang, 1977).

The evolution of political commentary in the twentieth century passed through
four overlapping phases. The four phases shade into one another with vestiges
of early stages remaining throughout; the process has been one of accretion
rather than replacement. The first phase coincided with the monopoly of mass
circulation newspapers as a popular medium of political information. This phase
extends roughly from 1914 to 1928. As E. J. Dionne argued, it was the Progressive Era when journalism reinvented itself (1996). It was the time of telegraphy, wire services, the Four Ws and an H, and—with the origin of a "Fifth
W" (why) and the political column—syndication. The earliest political columnists, such as David Lawrence, restricted themselves to interpreting what the
news meant and did not express their opinions about it (Rivers, 1967). When
Walter Lippmann's column in the *New York Herald Tribune* added the opinion
dimension, it personalized commentary even more than did the use of a byline.

The column of opinion, however, was still basically a *news* column; it informed readers of events, what they meant, and what the particular columnist
thought. Hence, its approach was essentially didactic. As the readership of political columns increased, politicians quickly recognized the public relations
value of taking prominent columnists into their confidences, thus enlisting the
columnists—sometimes consciously, more often unconsciously—on behalf of
their programs. President Franklin D. Roosevelt was a master of the art; Walter
Lippmann, Arthur Krock (q.v.), Roosevelt's ex-aide Raymond Moley (q.v.), and
others often thought they had an inside track to the president's thinking, only
to be disappointed and subsequently fall out with FDR. Still the leader-columnist
exchange was to the mutual benefit of both parties: politicians publicized their
views and columnists publicized themselves as having the ear of politicians.
Thus, political commentary during the period was essentially elite driven; both
political leaders and columnists talked down to audiences in a didactic manner.

The arrival of radio on the scene in the 1920s did not at first substantially
change the nature of political commentary per se; it merely shifted the didactic
approach to a different medium. The first radio commentator, H. V. Kaltenborn,
delivered commentaries standing before a microphone in the fashion of a lecturer
declaiming to an audience. Nor did another medium that reached its maturity
during this second phase, the newsreel, alter the pace of political commentary
in the early 1920s. Political commentator Lowell Thomas (q.v.) approached the
newsreel as he had his lecture/slide presentations—a mixture of information and
showmanship.

When the golden age of radio, from 1929 to 1948, hit full stride, political reporting and commentary entered a new phase. Firsthand, eyewitness accounts of the Spanish Civil War, the *anschluss* in Austria, the Sudetenland and Munich crises all carved out a unique role for broadcast news. It was Edward R. Murrow (q.v.) who recognized the full potential of that role and exploited it. For Murrow, radio became an *interpretive* medium par excellence, even more so than a didactic medium. His accounts of the London blitz, symphonies that blended his artistic imagery with the sounds of a populace girding itself for survival, expanded political commentary from solely an elite-driven columnist's format on the op-ed pages of newspapers to a populist-driven account of the responses of ordinary people to their fate conveyed by radio to ordinary people in their own living rooms.

Insofar as political commentary on television was concerned, television after World War II was simply radio with pictures, and few pictures at that. The influence of the Chicago School marked television's effort to strike out on its own as an independent force. The partnership of Edward R. Murrow and Fred W. Friendly resulted in the groundbreaking documentary effort, "See It Now." That CBS production opened up a whole new forum of political commentary. Eric Sevareid, a veteran of radio commentary, shifted his efforts to television; his commentaries on "CBS Evening News" made him a popular icon of political wisdom, visually the bust of Pericles scowling at the world.

But, whether it was Murrow, Sevareid, John Chancellor (q.v.), or a host of other political commentators that populated the television airways in the third phase of commentary's evolution, from 1949 to 1980, they all understood—many to their chagrin—that political commentators must not only be didactic and interpretive, but also entertaining. If elitist and populist tendencies had marked commentary in earlier phases, now performance values counted—the ability to project an appealing dramatic persona.

In the last two decades, popular communications have undergone striking changes in technology (e.g., cable and satellite TV, cellular communication, and cyberspace networking), organization (e.g., the fragmentation of public affairs programming beyond terrestrial networks, locally published and distributed national newspapers), and venues for political talk and commentary. Political talk and commentary shows pervade local, regional, and national radio and television programming. The celebrity interview is now a feature of prime-time over-the-air and cable television. Politicians confront, and are confronted by, political commentators in sedate settings, for example, William F. Buckley, Jr. (q.v.); adversarial modes, including David Brinkley (q.v.) and Ted Koppel (q.v.); and stroking sessions, notably Larry King (q.v.). Political commentators debate one another in raucous displays of one-upmanship, like John McLaughlin (q.v.); play Falstaff to the powerful, like Rush Limbaugh (q.v.); and submit leaders to public verbal floggings, like Phil Donahue (q.v.). This is an era less of opinion commentary that informs, interprets, even entertains, than opinionated commentary that incites expressive behavior among audiences.

Throughout these unfolding phases, political commentators have performed the generic role attributed by Carey to the professional communicator: they devote technical skills to manipulate words and pictures bridging distinct persons, differentiated groups, and conflicting interests. Different political commentators employ different styles depending in part on the links they seek to forge. Some stand above the crowd, talking down to readers/listeners/viewers, and offer priestly absolutions originated by elites as beneficial to the masses (see Lessl, 1989). William Buckley, George F. Will (q.v.), and Dorothy Thompson (q.v.) exemplify the priestly style and tradition. Others, including Walter Lippmann and James "Scotty" Reston (q.v.), wrap themselves in the cloaks of sages and imply that they alone know what others simply cannot know. A great many claim to have the ear of the high and mighty, and they purport to offer inside dope on why things are as they are; these are personified by Fulton Lewis, Jr. (q.v.), Drew Pearson (q.v.), and Corrine "Cokie" Roberts (q.v.). Still others pose as "one of us" and perform the bard's role of spinning tales of, by, and for the masses. Paul Harvey (q.v.) has done so for over half a century, and Lowell Thomas and Walter Winchell (q.v.) did so even earlier; Phil Donahue invented a new forum for such commentary.

Whether the political commentator employs one of these or one of the numerous other styles of political commentary currently in vogue, the task of placing raw, newsworthy events into a digested perspective is paramount. In the formative days of political commentary, that task was often performed without the commentator's offering solutions, taking partisan stands, or advocating lines of action. That is rarely the case today. Contemporary political commentators trade in what Alvin Goldman has called epistemic paternalism. By placing events in a selected perspective, a commentator forecloses possible competing interpretations: "I shall think of communication controllers as exercising epistemic paternalism whenever they interpose their own judgment rather than allow the audience to exercise control" (1991, p. 119). The caveat emptor for any consumer of political commentary is, thus, to heed not only what a commentator says but also what is *not* said, indeed is impossible to say in light of the commentator's interpretation.

Of course, with so many avenues of political commentary now available it is possible to argue that what one commentator forecloses a competing commentator discloses. Yet, as many of the contentions undergirding the views of such political commentators as Noam Chomsky (q.v.), John Dewey (q.v.), and others suggest, even in the face of disagreement, the commentator's paternalistic political function is not necessarily diminished. Indeed the cacophony, to the degree that it is taken by citizens as an accurate reading of a politics that contains so many conflicting solutions that no problem has any clear-cut solution, may render political commentary in the next decade more illusory than elucidating.

THE SELECTION OF KEY POLITICAL COMMENTATORS

Any volume that offers a guide to leading political commentators in the twentieth century must of necessity be highly selective. During World War II on radio alone there were more than 600 local, regional, and national commentators. Add columnists, and the body of commentary was of staggering size. Today radio commentary is but a ghost of its former self; yet, with the advent of "talk radio" shows one suspects that the number 600 pales by comparison. This volume provides bio-critical profiles for forty-two political commentators across America's century (Steel, 1980); thirty-eight chapters are devoted to a single commentator, and two chapters each consider a team of commentators, namely, Robert MacNeil and James Lehrer of the "MacNeil/Lehrer Newshour," and Martha Rountree and Lawrence E. Spivak of "Meet the Press." It is well to set forth the basis for the selection of those forty-two representatives of political commentary.

There is a vast array of types of political commentary. There are the obvious ones: newspaper and news magazine columnists, radio broadcasters, and television broadcasters. There are others not so obvious: political media consultants, press agents, information officers, spin doctors; special and public interest spokespersons; religious leaders; and so on. There are also political humorists, political and entertainment celebrities, academicians, innumerable freelance writers, and cyberspace commentators on the Internet.

Solely because of the limitations of space, the largest number of political commentators discussed in this volume consists of columnists and radio and television broadcasters. Because of their roles as political persuaders and influential interpreters of politics, we have included the father of American propaganda commentary, George Creel; the father of public relations, Edward Bernays; and academic scholars who have stepped outside the classroom to play influential roles as political commentators, Noam Chomsky and John Dewey. Of necessity we had to resist the temptation to include such political humorists as Will Rogers, Mort Sahl, Art Buchwald, and Mark Russell; political cartoonists such as Bill Mauldin, Walt Kelley, and Garry Trudeau; and freelancers such as David Halberstam, Samuel Lubell, Kevin Phillips, and Upton Sinclair.

Each of the forty-two commentators selected made a key contribution to the development of political commentary during the twentieth century. The nature of the contribution we spell out in each bio-critical entry. This is not to suggest that the political commentators excluded failed to make unique contributions to the development of the art form. Many certainly did, be they bardic columnist Mike Royko; the father of confrontational television, Joe Pyne; or the first television broadcaster to be labeled a "communicator," Dave Garroway; or Pauline Frederick, NBC's pioneering United Nations correspondent; social confidants to the High and Mighty, Rich and Well Born, such as syndicated columnists Stewart and Joseph Alsop; or translators of the arcane findings and technical jargon of political science into conventional wisdom, such as the *Washington Post*'s

David Broder. Instead it is to urge that the world of political commentary in the United States alone, let alone in other nations, in this century has been so richly populated as to elude all but a minimal sampling.

Each bio-critical essay in this volume situates the selected political commentator in the communication environment of the commentator's life, describes the commentator's background and career, and analyzes the commentator's contributions to the development of the art in twentieth-century America. As a guide to source material, each entry lists references in three categories: selected works by the commentator, selected works about the commentator, and selected general works that situate the commentator within the more general area of political communication. With the exception of the Pulitzer Prize in journalism, and the political and professional implications it carries, we have not listed the special awards and honors, including honorary academic degrees, received by each political commentator during her or his respective career; there are so many such awards and honors meted out by so many different groups that few command sufficiently broad professional or political prestige to warrant a detailed inventory.

For the most part, the source material for each political commentator included in this volume is specific to that commentator. There are also general source directories that prove useful to those interested in exploring political commentators as a general category beyond the limits of this volume. Among the serial volumes or specialized volumes deserving of mention here, and frequently cited in individual chapters, are

> *The Annual Obituary* (Detroit: St. James Press).
>
> *Benet's Readers Encyclopedia* (New York: Harper & Row).
>
> *Celebrity Register* (New York: Simon and Schuster).
>
> *Current Biography Yearbook* (New York: H. W. Wilson Co.).
>
> *Dictionary of American Biography* (New York: Charles Scribner's Sons).
>
> *National Cyclopedia of American Biography* (New York: James T. White).
>
> *Newsmakers* and *Contemporary Newsmakers* (Detroit: Gale Research, Inc.)
>
> *New York Times Obituary Index* (New York: The New York Times Co.).
>
> *Political Profiles* (New York: Facts on File, Inc.).
>
> *World Authors* (New York: H. W. Wilson Co.).

Among the key works that devote entries or essays to one or more specific types of political commentators, readers will find useful Charles Fisher's *The Columnists* (1944), David Bulman's *Molders of Opinion* (1945), William Rivers' *The Opinionmakers* (1967), D. H. Culbert's *News for Everyone* (1976), Irving Fang's *Those Radio Commentators!* (1977), William Howard Taft's *Encyclopedia of Twentieth-Century Journalists* (1986), J. P. McKerns' *Biographical*

Dictionary of American Journalism (1989), and S. G. Riley's *Biographical Dictionary of American Newspaper Columnists* (1995).

This volume can be consulted in two ways. First, it serves readers as a bio-critical source book to key political commentators, listed alphabetically, in America's twentieth century. Second, in many instances, the contributions of a selected political commentator involved contact with, or the influence of, another commentator included in the volume. The commentators within each chapter are cross-referenced to facilitate pursuing those contacts and influences. Third, bearing in mind the four phases in the development of political commentary in the United States, we invite readers to follow that chronological development by consulting successively the commentators in each of the four eras outlined above. Readers can then judge whether the art of political commentary has been elevated in tone and quality over successive generations. Or, instead, if it has declined to a state akin to that of Babel when the builders of a temple rising to the heavens were forced to abandon their project by a God (in the case of America, its citizens) who found the chatter of so many languages confusing, hence, debilitating.

REFERENCES

Bennett, A. "The Diary of Alan Bennett." *The Weekly Telegraph* (London, England), January 24–30, 1996, 35.

Bulman, D., ed. *Molders of Opinion.* Milwaukee: Bruce Publishing, 1945.

Carey, J. W. "The Communications Revolution and the Professional Communicator." In *The Sociology of Mass Communications*, edited by P. Halmos, 23–38. Staffordshire, England: University of Keele, 1969.

Cohen, R. "The Syndicated Columnist." *Gannett Center Journal* 3 (Spring 1989): 9–16.

Culbert, D. H. *News for Everyone.* Westport, CT: Greenwood Press, 1976.

Dionne, E. J. *They Only Look Dead: Why Progressives Will Dominate the Next Political Era.* New York: Simon & Schuster, 1996.

Duncan, H. D. *Communication and the Social Order.* New York: Oxford University Press, 1968.

Ellul, J. *The Technological Society.* New York: Vintage Books, 1964.

Fang, I. E. "The Excess Prophets." In *Those Radio Commentators!*, 3–14. Ames: Iowa State University Press, 1977.

Fellows, J. *Breaking the News: How the Media Undermine American Democracy.* New York: Pantheon, 1996.

Fisher, C. *The Columnists.* New York: Howell, Soskin, 1944.

Goldman, A. "Epistemic Paternalism: Communication Control in Law and Society." *Journal of Philosophy* 85 (March 1991): 113–31.

Kurtz, H. *Hot Air: All Talk, All the Time.* New York: Times Books, 1996.

Lessl, T. M. "The Priestly Voice." *Quarterly Journal of Speech* 75 (May 1989): 183–97.

McKerns, J. P., ed. *Biographical Dictionary of American Journalism.* New York: Greenwood Press, 1989.

Mindich, D.T.Z. "Edwin M. Stanton, the Inverted Pyramid, and Information Control." *Journalism Monographs* 140 (August 1993): 1–28.

Patterson, T. E. *Out of Order*. New York: Alfred A. Knopf, 1993.

Riley, S. G. *Biographical Dictionary of American Newspaper Columnists*. Westport, CT: Greenwood Press, 1995.

Rivers, W. *The Opinionmakers*. Boston: Beacon Press, 1967.

Schudson, M. *The Power of News*. Cambridge: Harvard University Press, 1995.

Simon, A. F., and S. Iyengar. "Toward Theory-Based Research in Political Communication." *PS: Political Science and Politics* 29 (March 1996): 29–33.

Starobin, P. "A Generation of Vipers: Journalists and the New Cynicism." *Columbia Journalism Review* (March/April 1995): 25–32.

Steel, R. *Walter Lippmann and the American Century*. Boston: Little, Brown and Co., 1980.

Taft, W. H. *Encyclopedia of Twentieth-Century Journalists*. New York: Garland Publishing, 1986.

Whitehead, A. N. *Adventure of Ideas*. New York: Macmillan, 1933.

Wilson, W. "The Study of Administration." *Political Science Quarterly* 2 (Summer 1887): 197–222.

EDWARD L. BERNAYS

(November 22, 1891–March 9, 1995)

Political Commentary as Consulting

By the mid-1970s the typical American could purchase an inexpensive watch, strap it on his or her wrist, and then, when the battery went dead, add to the nation's accumulating trash by throwing the watch away and buying a replacement. That was not the case in the early days of the twentieth century. Watches were relatively expensive. To purchase one was to make a long-term commitment; watch repair shops thrived along with jewelers who supplied the new article. There was, however, one "dollar watch" manufacturer, Ingersoll, who priced a product for mass purchase. One of its jewelry items, particularly popular with women, was the wristwatch. It was not customary for men to wear wristwatches: pocket watches were masculine, wristwatches feminine. Ingersoll wanted to change that image and sell wristwatches to the untapped male market.

Ingersoll turned to an Austrian-born immigrant whose family had come to the United States when he was one year old, Edward L. Bernays. (The "L." stood for nothing; the last name, as a ditty that became popular after Bernays became a celebrity said, "rhymes with her ways, starts a new craze, finds that it pays" [Block, 1942, 79]). Bernays' profession was advising people how to deal with image problems; he was the first professional public relations counsel. To solve Ingersoll's dilemma, Bernays undertook research. He discovered, through contacts with the U.S. Department of War, that American combat troops in Belgium and France during World War I, true to the male custom, carried pocket watches. To read their watches at night, they struck matches to cast sufficient light to see the dials. This proved a dangerous practice; the light could draw enemy sniper fire. Bernays approached U.S. Army officials and argued that the lives of American troops could be saved if they were issued wristwatches with luminous dials. There would then be no need for the hazardous practice of reading by match light. The Army acted on Bernays' proposal and issued wristwatches as standard equipment. Thus, a government agency, acting at a consultant's behest, solved Ingersoll's problem: if wristwatches were the fashion of necessity for rugged fighting men, they were thereby fashionable for all men.

In Bernays' long career as a public relations consultant, his clients came from the arts, business and financial industries, communication, education, labor organizations, public interest groups, transportation, trade, and, notably, politics and government. The 1950s witnessed a marriage of politics and public relations that has been consummated with ever more passionate intensity with each passing decade. Election campaigns at all levels of government, advocacy campaigns for and against specific public policies, and campaigns of both special and public

interest groups routinely employ legions of professional counsels: campaign or-
ganizers, managers, fund-raisers, press liaisons, media consultants, "spinmeisters," advertisers, pollsters, issue researchers, and many more.

As a result of their successful legerdemain, many mercenaries achieved over-
night celebrity as political gurus: Matt Reese, Bill Roberts, Stu Spenser, Clem
Wittaker, and Tony Schwartz in the 1960s; Pat Caddell, David Garth, Doug
Bailey, John Deardourff, and Joe Napolitan in the 1970s; Roger Ailes, Bob
Goodman, Ray Strother, and Richard Viguerie in the 1980s; and James Carville,
Stanley Greenberg, Dick Morris, and Bob Squier in the 1990s. It is no exaggeration to say that each such political communication consultant walks in the
pioneering footsteps trod by Edward Bernays during his career which spanned
almost nine decades. They but dot his I's and cross his T's. Perhaps "all his
contributions may have been inevitable, but it was he who made them" (Blumenthal, 1980, 26). To say political commentary is political consulting is to say
Bernays.

THE FOUNDING OF A PROFESSION

A century and a year after his birth in Vienna, on November 22, 1891, Edward
Bernays told an interviewer

> Today's politicians are like doctors who haven't gone to medical school. They
> know only what they know and won't listen to other people. Personally, I think
> that if people use the modern day strategies and tactics which are based on the
> social sciences—we've got psychology, sociology, statistics, public opinion
> research—they would be more effective. . . . I think they use the polls to get
> elected, but they could use many more fundamental concepts and views. (Zgor-
> ski, 1992, 22)

The assessment is perhaps not surprising from a man who was one of five
children of a mother, Anna, whose brother was Sigmund Freud. Bernays told
Bill Moyers (q.v.) in a television interview for "The Image Makers," a program
in Moyers' "A Walk through the Twentieth Century" (1984), that he remembered little from his youth about Freud himself, but he recalled many a family
dinner when the conversation turned on matters of the ego, id, and unconscious,
as well as other Freudian ideas.

After Eddie's high school graduation, his father, Ely, who became a successful grain merchant after he immigrated to New York with the family, sent him
to the College of Agriculture at Cornell University to learn to become a farmer.
Eddie stuck it out and graduated from Cornell in 1912. He had an apprenticeship
as a grain merchant on the New York Produce Exchange, but that was the last
thought he ever gave to becoming a farmer. Instead he turned to journalism.
For the salary of $25 a week, Bernays was a jack-of-all-trades for two forgettable
health-oriented publications—he was editor, copy reader, and office boy, and

he did the makeup and promoted the journals. His editorials advocated that people take regular showers and instructed children in sex education.

It was all mundane except for one thing; it was his first experience as a public relations counsel. When an actor wanted to produce a stage play about venereal disease, a risky topic in those days, Bernays' publications supported the venture. Moreover, Bernays organized a Sociological Fund; anyone who joined the fund for a $4 fee to support the cause of sex education received a free first-night ticket to the play. Through Bernays' efforts, socially prestigious people joined, giving lesser lights the courage to do so. The play was a success and Bernays turned to publicity as a career.

The Sociological Fund was a forerunner of a publicity tactic that Bernays would return to repeatedly in other cases: use an "overt action" as a gimmick to draw attention, especially of the news media. Through press coverage, a public relations counsel thus gave a "publicity direction" to a cause (Bernays, 1965, 187–205). In contemporary political communication jargon Bernays' overt actions and publicity directions have acquired new names—"pseudo events," "media events," "spin doctoring"—but it is Bernays' seminal principle that is being applied (Zgorski, 1992, 21–22).

In the years before America's entry into World War I, Bernays worked as a publicity agent for theatrical productions, including the Diaghilev Russian Ballet and opera star Enrico Caruso. He also worked on behalf of Fox Film Corporation, now at a fee of $150 a week, promoting the film *Cleopatra*. On the day the United States declared war, Bernays volunteered for the army through a letter to the adjutant general, only to be ignored. When selective service came, Bernays was again passed by for the army, this time because of defective vision; he tried volunteer work for his local draft board: "I thought this might help me get into the war, but the U.S. wasn't taking anyone who didn't have 20/20 vision" (Bernays, 1965, 147). Finally, in 1917, he persuaded the Committee for Public Information (CPI), the U.S. war propaganda organization, to accept him as a staff member.

His CPI service, consisting of working in the foreign press bureau in New York, then in Paris, and writing leaflets for distribution behind German lines, convinced him that victory had come as a result of words as much as armaments, and that the words that had won the war should be used to secure the peace. This viewpoint put him at loggerheads with the chair of the CPI (see George Creel [q.v.] and Mock & Larson, 1939). In any event, Bernays felt that the long-term result of the CPI propaganda effort would result in a publicity revolution. When he returned to the United States after the peace conference, Bernays acted on his conviction. In 1919 he and Doris Fleishman, whom he married three years later, set up a joint business to provide what was first called "publicity direction," then retitled "counsel of public relations."

As the business got off the ground, it proved Bernays' war contacts an asset. A first key client was the U.S. War Department; it hired Bernays' firm to mount a national campaign on behalf of the rehiring of ex-servicemen. Clients from outside the government soon followed. Most notably they included a manufac-turer of women's hair nets. Since the style was to wear short hair, the manu-facturer's sales were low. Bernays' publicity direction was two-pronged: first, he recruited social and fashion leaders willing to endorse long rather than bobbed hairstyles; second, seemingly in contradiction but not so, he sought out health experts to comment on the hazards of long hair in factories, restaurants, and other workplaces. The plan worked: long hair became the fashion, and several states, which deemed the fashion hazardous in the workplace, passed regulatory legislation requiring female workers to wear hair nets.

There were other noteworthy coups. To promote the sales of Ivory soap, Bernays organized a National Small Sculptural Committee (with a prestigious membership) to award prizes for the best sculptures created out of Ivory; news-papers publicized the contest and, thereby, Ivory sales. In the depression year of 1929, Bernays organized a national overt action on behalf of General Electric: "Light's Golden Jubilee" commemorating Thomas Edison's invention of the lightbulb. For newspapers, radio broadcasts, and newsreels Edison himself rec-reated the moment of his invention, timed precisely to coincide with the turning on of light switches across a darkened America. Bernays recruited economic luminaries Henry Ford and John D. Rockefeller, Jr., to take part, and even President Herbert Hoover put his imprimatur on the publicity stunt by making a public address. The electrical industry profited accordingly.

For other business clients Bernays was equally active; for example, he pro-moted the rights of women to smoke cigarettes in public (the American Tobacco Company), the fashionable practice of women on weekend trips to take along at least three sets of clothing (on behalf of the luggage industry), and beer as the alcoholic drink of "moderation" (for the brewing industry). It is difficult to measure the number of popular mores and customs, for good or ill, in vogue in America between the two world wars that derived from Bernays' publicity di-rection.

BERNAYS' POLITICAL CLIENTELE

As a counsel on public relations in the employ of political clients, Bernays exploited research, overt actions, media manipulation, and publicity direction as a pathfinding pioneer in the manipulation of political commentary. Through a series of published books and articles, he codified his political experience. A few examples are sufficient to summarize his approach to creating and refur-bishing the political images of politicians, causes, groups, and nations.

A typical application of Bernays' exploitation of the overt action to improve the public perception of a politician was his work on behalf of President Calvin Coolidge. Coolidge had a reputation for being cold, dry, frugal, and taciturn. In a widely reported put-down of the president, Alice Roosevelt Longworth quipped that Coolidge looked like he had been "weaned on a pickle" (Bernays, 1965, 340). At the behest of the Non-Partisan League for Coolidge, Bernays accepted the challenge of transforming the president's public persona into that of a warm, sympathetic human being. Challenge it was: days before Bernays accepted it Coolidge had reinforced his Scrooge image by publicly rebuking a Secret Service agent who had dared walk with the president's wife in the woods.

Bernays met the challenge by orchestrating a media event. He recalls, ''I racked my brain for some association that would reverse the impression of coldness. I decided that stage people symbolized warmth, extroversion and Bohemian camaraderie and that if they breakfasted at the White House they would dissipate the impression'' of Coolidge as cold, aloof, and humorless (Bernays, 1965, 340). After theater performances closed on Broadway one evening, Bernays boarded a party of forty stage stars on the midnight train to Washington. Among them were Al Jolson, Ed Wynn, the Dolly Sisters, and Buddy de Sylva. The party arrived at the White House to find the president and first lady awaiting them. Bernays introduced each celebrity to the president. Then, the president asked Bernays his name. Bernays replied that his own name was ''not important'' since he was but the publicity man for the party. The president quickly displayed his political and showbiz savvy, ''Not unimportant either,'' Coolidge chided. ''The publicity man—your name?'' (Bernays, 1965, 341). Although Coolidge remained largely expressionless during the breakfast, he chatted amiably, especially with the starlets. Newspaper accounts of the breakfast appeared on the front pages; the *New York Times* headlined, ''Actors Eat Cakes with the Coolidges'' and ''President Nearly Laughs'' (Blumenthal, 1980, 24).

Coolidge's successor also turned to Bernays for consultation. For Herbert Hoover, Bernays organized a Non-Partisan Fact-Finding Committee that telegraphed national leaders for support in the president's 1932 reelection campaign. The work of the committee, although impressive and well publicized, was a failure. Hoover lost in a landslide. Nevertheless, six decades after Hoover's loss, Bernays remained upbeat about his advice, even if he was speaking tongue in cheek. Asked to list his proudest career accomplishments, one of the three he ticked off was ''Advising Herbert Hoover to promise 'A chicken in every pot' '' (Zgorski, 1992, 22).

Bernays made other consulting forays into the politics that surround the Oval Office. For example, in 1930, while promoting the cause of credit expansion to ease burdens on agriculture during the Great Depression, Bernays met an Iowa newspaper editor, Henry Wallace. In 1933, after Franklin Roosevelt's elevation to the presidency, Bernays organized a luncheon of bankers, financiers, and financial editors and writers to support Wallace's candidacy for secretary of agriculture in the FDR cabinet. Held at the posh Bankers Club in New York City, the get-together allayed fears of financial leaders that Wallace was a wild radical; moreover, the press commentary on Wallace's speech was positive. Whether the Bernays' overt action swayed FDR only the president could say. However, Wallace was appointed secretary.

Through his consultation with other presidents, Bernays promoted causes with varying success. He met with President Dwight Eisenhower to promote a people-to-people public relations campaign in international affairs. The president grinned, said he agreed, and made off for the golf course, seemingly without having heard a word. In 1957 Bernays advocated a variation of his people-to-people approach to improve U.S.–British relations. In a meeting with Lyndon Johnson, then U.S. Senate majority leader ("his arm around my shoulder and in an animated discussion"), Johnson sufficiently grasped the essentials of the proposal that Bernays would later write, "President Johnson understands the problem fully, which is more than can be said for some of our recent presidents" (Bernays, 1965, 793–94).

Aside from his association with U.S. presidents, either as his clients or as targets of his political commentators, Bernays consulted for other politicians. For example, in 1932 he was public relations counsel to George Z. Medalie in his race for the U.S. Senate in New York. In that campaign, Bernays gave a boost to the political career of a future governor of New York and twice-defeated Republican presidential candidate—Thomas E. Dewey. (Bernays chose Dewey to serve as liaison to Medalie's office and to write speeches, press releases, and mailings.) Bernays also consulted in William O'Dwyer's race for mayor of New York City in 1941. Bernays' advice (i.e., survey first what people expect of a mayor and second what issues voters associate with each candidate) is standard fare in contemporary elections. A half century ago it was a revelation.

One of Bernays' earliest political clients was not a politician but a nation. After World War I Lithuania had been detached from Russia and declared itself a republic. England had granted diplomatic recognition; U.S. recognition was vital to the republic's status. The Lithuanian National Council of the United States engaged Bernays' services. Bernays first researched in detail what aspects of Lithuanian culture appealed to specific target groups in the United States—Lithuanian music to music lovers, Lithuanian drama to playgoers, Lithuanian sports to sport fans, and so on. He then wrote short features about each interest: one on Lithuanian embroidery for women, one on Lithuanian exports for businessmen, even one on prohibition in Lithuania to interest imbibers and non-imbibers! Woven into each feature was the subtle message that the little Baltic republic warranted liberty and freedom. Bernays distributed the prefabricated news features to newspapers, magazines, trade journals—any potential publisher.

Bernays also exploited pathos. He found an attractive twenty-year-old daughter of a Lithuanian-born coal miner: "We called her the 'Joan of Arc of Lithuania,' and her face, with its distinctly Lithuanian features—high cheekbones and slightly slanted eyes—became widely known through the country [United States] as a result of newspaper publicity" of her speeches, interviews, public appearances, and appealing looks (Bernays, 1965, 189). Finally, when a rumor circulated that Poland was planning to invade Lithuania, Bernays publicized a mass protest against Polish imperialism and the slaughter of Lithuanian Jews. In 1922 Lithuania received U.S. recognition.

The victory convinced Bernays of the effectiveness of his public relations approach to international affairs. Foreign nations around the globe now routinely hire public relations firms to manage their images within the United States and with other nations. Extensive research confirms Bernays' conviction that there are "consistencies in the timing and direction of image changes associated with public relations activities" on behalf of nations (Manheim, 1994, 147). Successful image enhancement sometimes backfires. Ivy Lee counseled Adolf Hitler how to improve the image of Nazi Germany in the United States in the 1930s. Newspapers publicized Lee's pro-Nazi contract; he had to explain it to a congressional committee. The ordeal wrecked his health and he died shortly thereafter (Hiebert, 1966).

BERNAYS' CONTRIBUTIONS TO POLITICAL COMMENTARY

To grasp fully Edward L. Bernays' contributions to political commentary, it is necessary to go beyond his pioneering tactics, techniques, and practices. One must explore his unique view of the character of persuasive campaigns. Although he was the first to bill himself as a counsel on public relations, he was not the first to advise others how to conduct persuasive campaigns. The ancient Greeks had their Sophists and the teachings of Aristotle, the Romans their Cicero. Nor was Bernays the first publicist. There were, for instance, Matthew, Mark, Luke, and John of the *New Testament*; the court heralds of medieval monarchs; and the *Congregatio de Propaganda Fide* of Pope Gregory XV. Bernays was not even the first freelance, for-a-fee public relations specialist. He himself grants that "the public relations counsel is the lineal descendant, to be sure, of the circus advance man" (1923, 56). Moreover, in Bernays' youth there had been Ivy Lee and CPI chair George Creel.

What set Bernays apart from his predecessors in the art of public persuasion was the assumptions he brought to the craft of public relations. For one thing, sophists, carnival hucksters, press agents, propagandists like Creel, and publicists like Lee typically assumed persuasion to be a one-way process. Lee, for example, viewed the public relations agent as one who *reports* clients' actions to the public. Even before becoming a professional counsel, however, "I tried to evaluate my audience by hunch and insight" and adjust the message to the beliefs to which they were already predisposed (Bernays, 1965, 82). The public relations counsel's task is, then, to "interpret the client to the public and the public to the client" (1923, 14). Interpretation is the defining craft of political commentary.

In thinking this Bernays was influenced, in part, by his familial association with Freudian psychology. He also was much impressed by Walter Lippmann's (q.v.) 1922 analysis that how people behave depends not on their directly experienced realities but on the "pictures in our heads," pictures that can be exploited for persuasive purposes. Moreover, he pondered how to make everyday use of Gustave Le Bon's (1960) theories of the "crowd mind" first published in 1895. The views of individuals are hard to sway, argued Le Bon, but once they surrender their identities to the crowd, the emotional state of the mass is contagious. Finally, as the social sciences developed increasingly sophisticated measures of tapping human convictions, Bernays recognized that scientific research could replace his earlier dependence on hunch and insight. Campaign messages could truly be crafted to match audience views; audience views could then, and only then, be given a publicity direction toward a client's view.

A second feature that distinguished Bernays' public relations from those of his predecessors was the insight that conventional, pre-twentieth-century propaganda was being replaced by a "new propaganda" that takes the inarticulate, vague, and amorphous fears and desires of people and gives them a focus to act upon, in other words, the overt action. This is particularly the case in political affairs. Scientific measurement reveals that voters, for example, faced with competing political claims are drawn every which way; unable to act with clarity, they voluntarily agree to let an "invisible government" step in and "organize chaos" and create a public opinion "necessary to orderly life." That invisible government consists not of formal institutions, but of propaganda: "Propaganda is the executive arm of the invisible government," an arm stimulated by a "small group of persons" who "can, and do, make the rest of us think what they please about a given subject" (Bernays, 1928, 25–27).

Finally, it was Bernays who, as early as his CPI years, went beyond the likes of Lee or Creel, each of whom was as much a combination of semi-journalist and semi-promoter as a full-time public relations counsel, and called for a public relations *profession*. For decades he argued for professional training, licensing, and a code of ethics. Historian Eric Goldman, reviewing Bernays' *Crystallizing Public Opinion* (1923), observed that public relations had reached a third stage of development: the public was not to be fooled as the press agent sought to do in stage one, not merely to be informed of a client's side of issues as Ivy Lee practiced in stage two, but to be *understood*, by an expert using scientific means, as made up of an intricate network of group relationships, an expert with ethics and a professional social view—a two-way street in a good neighborhood (1948). Involving the audience in the politician's, spokesperson's, or news analyst's political commentary was the key to Bernays' pioneering approach.

REFERENCES

Selected Works by Edward L. Bernays

Crystallizing Public Opinion. New York: Liveright, 1923.
An Outline of Careers: A Practical Guide to Achievement. New York: George H. Doran, 1927.
Propaganda. New York: Liveright, 1928.
Speak Up for Democracy. New York: Viking Press, 1940.
Take Your Place at the Peace. New York: International Press, 1945.

Public Relations. Norman: University of Oklahoma Press, 1952.

The Engineering of Consent. Norman: University of Oklahoma Press, 1955.

Biography of an Idea: Memoirs of Public Relations Counsel Edward L. Bernays. New York: Simon and Schuster, 1965.

Selected Critical Works about Edward L. Bernays

Block, M. ed. "Bernays, Edward L." In *Current Biography 1942*, 76–79. New York: H. W. Wilson, 1942.

Blumenthal, S. "The Interpretation of American Dreams: Edward L. Bernays." In *The Permanent Campaign: Inside the World of Elite Political Operatives*, edited by S. Blumenthal, 11–26. Boston: Beacon Press, 1980.

Goldman, E. *Two Way Street: The Emergence of the Public Relations Counsel*. Boston: Bellman Publishing, 1948.

Moritz, C. ed. "Bernays, Edward L." In *Current Biography 1960*, 32–34. New York: H. W. Wilson, 1961.

Zgorski, L. "He Stated It All." *Campaign*, November 1992, 21–22.

Selected General Works

Boorstin, D. *The Image: A Guide to Pseudo Events*. New York: Atheneum, 1973.

Combs, J., and D. Nimmo. *The New Propaganda*. New York: Longman, 1993.

Hiebert, R. E. *Courtier in the Crowd: The Story of Ivy Lee and the Development of Public Relations*. Ames: Iowa State University Press, 1966.

Le Bon, G. *The Crowd*. New York: Viking, 1960.

Lippmann, W. *Public Opinion*. New York: McGraw-Hill, 1922.

Manheim, J. B. *Strategic Public Diplomacy and American Foreign Policy*. New York: Oxford, 1994.

Mock, J. R., and C. Larson. *Words That Won the War*. Princeton, NJ: Princeton University Press, 1939.

DAVID (MCCLURE) BRINKLEY

(July 10, 1920–   )

Political Commentary from the Wry Perspective

An op-ed columnist with a sense of wry humor and wit recently wrote via a tribute, "Some media scientist should have had David Brinkley cloned" (Sherrod, 1996, 23 A). A comic flair for political analysis is usually reserved for professional comedians—Will Rogers in the 1930s, Mort Sahl in the 1950s and 1960s, and Mark Russell in the 1980s and 1990s. Rare is the journalist who is willing to take the risk of being charged with making trivial the tragic business of politics by, instead, finding it funny (Combs & Nimmo, 1996). David Brinkley is a major exception. For that reason, and for others, perhaps he should be cloned.

FROM DAVID MCCLURE BRINKLEY TO HUNTLEY-BRINKLEY

Although David McClure Brinkley, the son a North Carolina railroad worker named William Graham Brinkley and his wife Mary MacDonald West Brinkley, was born in 1920, it was almost four decades later, in 1956, when his name became almost a household word for most Americans. Even then they thought his first name was "Huntley." The distance, as the crow flies, may be relatively short between David Brinkley's birthplace and boyhood home, Wilmington, North Carolina, and where he achieved fame as a political commentator on NBC-TV News' "Huntley-Brinkley Report," in Washington, D.C., but it took him a while to travel it.

David Brinkley, who was considerably younger than his two brothers and two sisters, developed few friends as a child. His father died when David was eight years old. His mother, called "Mama," displayed "rare moments of warmth and humanity":

> None of us could anticipate when Mama could or would let down enough, give enough of herself to show some small sign of kindness or generosity, since she seemed to love babies, dogs and her flower garden but nothing or no one else. (Brinkley, 1995, 11–12)

So, without many friends and with no parental warmth, David turned to reading books and writing for companionship. Mama, however, showed no warmth for that either. One day David wrote a "little story" and showed it to his mother. She glanced at it, threw it back in his face, and demanded, " 'Why are you wasting your time on this foolishness.' It was another scar slow to heal'' (Brinkley, 1995, 15).

David Brinkley persisted. While he was in Hemenway grade school, a local radio station ran an essay contest, awarding a handsome $5.00 for the best entry that answered the question of what the station meant to Wilmington. "With a cynicism I had never known I possessed," young David wrote a tongue-in-cheek essay about how, by selling ads, the station provided Wilmington with "free" entertainment and "information no one . . . should miss" (Brinkley, 1995, 16). He won the contest and, to students at Hemenway grade school, he was now a famous writer. At New Hanover High School, Brinkley became involved in various extracurricular activities, including the band, school newspaper, English club, and rifle team, but he kept his sights on writing: "I have always liked to write, and I've always been reasonably good at it. [While in high school] I went to work on the local paper [the *Star News*] free, found that I loved it. And I have never done anything else since" ("The View from the Trenches," 1982, 95).

By the time Brinkley entered the University of North Carolina at Chapel Hill in 1940, he had decided to prepare for a career in journalism. But, along came World War II. Brinkley's college days were interrupted when he entered the U.S. Army for active military duty, hoping to perform his service, then return to college. He served as a supply sergeant at Fort Jackson, South Carolina, and was discharged for a kidney ailment. Upon his discharge, Brinkley returned to the Wilmington *Morning Star*, the morning edition of the *Star-News* paper he worked for awhile in high school.

In 1941 David Brinkley moved to Atlanta to work for the United Press, later United Press International (UPI), coincidentally the same news service with which one of Brinkley's major rivals as a political commentator, Walter Cronkite (q.v.), worked for years. Brinkley's experience included an interview with Georgia's governor (who accused the cub reporter of being a "foreigner" for being a native North Carolinian), writing for the UP's radio service, covering Montgomery and Nashville for UP, and becoming the manager of UP's Nashville bureau at the age of twenty-two. While working for UP, Brinkley resumed his academic career and enrolled as a part-time English student at Emory University in Atlanta and Vanderbilt University in Nashville. "I have a somewhat checkered and incomplete academic career," he recalls ("Nobody Does It Better," 1986, 119).

One of Brinkley's tasks at Nashville was to fulfill a commitment made by UP to a local radio station, 50,000-watt WLAC. UP rented an office in the station's building and kept the rent down by ordering its staffers, in this instance David Brinkley, to work for the station for free. So, under the tutelage of a WLAC woman staff member, Brinkley began broadcasting on the radio. It was from her that Brinkley acquired the unique clipped, wry broadcasting style that later made him famous. "I still talk as she taught me to talk," he said of his tutor's lessons (Brinkley, 1995, 46). The style was parodied in the 1960s in a ditty sung to the tune of "Love and Marriage" (Hickey, 1995, 51):

> Huntley-Brinkley,
> Huntley-Brinkley.
> One is gloomy,
> And the other is twinkley.

David Brinkley moved with UP from Nashville to Charlotte, North Carolina, again working for the news service and for one of UP's client-landlords, radio station WBT. Brinkley successfully persuaded the news director at WBT to lobby the Columbia Broadcasting System (CBS), to get him a job in Washington, D.C. However, when he arrived in Washington to start his job, there was some apparent confusion, and he was informed that there was no job. The head of the Washington CBS bureau refused to see Brinkley. Brinkley, in return, sent the bureau chief a terse message, "Go to hell," walked four blocks to the offices of the National Broadcasting Company (NBC), was immediately hired, and remained with NBC for thirty-eight years (Brinkley, 1995, 48). CBS saw a great deal of Brinkley in that time, looking up in the Nielsen television ratings at the "Huntley-Brinkley Report" which outdistanced the "CBS Evening News" for years.

David Brinkley's combined UP wire and radio experience had taught him to write for print in a style that, when read, his words could be smoothly spoken. It was much the same style Edward R. Murrow (q.v.) had learned to write. Brinkley began his first NBC assignment as a writer producing news scripts for staff radio announcers; in addition, he was assigned as the reporter for the White House and Capitol Hill. He commented, with typical directness, about his early days at NBC, "It was tough because announcers then read the words, not the meanings. If you read a sentence one way, you can change the whole meaning of it. I had to work hard to see that they didn't screw up" ("Nobody Does It Better," 1986, 119).

In the late 1940s, television crossed a barrier to becoming a widely used medium. During the 1948–1949 broadcast season, coaxial cables provided a link between the eastern United States and the Midwest. Simultaneous live broadcasting to different regions of the country became possible. Yet, even with these advances, the television medium still had a limited audience due to the expense of purchasing a television set. Therefore, the medium did not yet attract ambitious journalists wanting to advance their careers. Brinkley profited from these years. He was able not only to write his own news material, as well as supplying two fifteen-minute scripts for other newscasts, but also to practice the scripts' proper delivery on television since other news correspondents shied away from the novelty. He perfected his writing while he honed his speaking skills before a small television audience.

In February 1949, John Cameron Swayze, an NBC radio newscaster, became the newscaster (actually the British term "news reader" is more apt) for NBC's new nightly fifteen-minute "Camel News Caravan." NBC hoped to compete with the "CBS News with Douglas Edwards." Swayze took the job reluctantly; if he had not, NBC would have requested his resignation. Like the CBS newscast, the "Camel News Caravan" was a "rip and read" broadcast: Swayze either memorized his copy or read from a script when not on camera. The newscast was filled with film footage, featuring staged and frivolous events, such as fashion shows, ship launchings, and politicians' photo opportunities (Goldberg & Goldberg, 1990). From 1951 to 1956, David Brinkley briefly reported from Washington on the events of the day in the nation's capital on the "Camel News Caravan."

During those years NBC began to see the promise in building television news and moved quickly to establish its television staff and film operations. In most major American cities and in several foreign capitals, NBC placed correspondents. The network was fast developing a news organization to rival its major competitor, CBS. By 1956, in order to attract new viewers, NBC executives decided that their telecast of the national political party conventions for the year required a strong, dynamic approach. CBS had used Walter Cronkite in 1952 as "anchor" of its coverage with considerable success. NBC needed someone to compete with Cronkite's rating. A virtual "non-choice" by NBC executives was the making of David Brinkley and Chet Huntley. The executives did not have a consensus for a single correspondent they were willing to trust alone to compete against CBS's Walter Cronkite. So they decided to use both Huntley and Brinkley to cover the conventions.

On his father's side, Chet Huntley, born in 1911 and reared in Montana, was descended from U.S. presidents John Adams and John Quincy Adams; on his mother's side, he was the grandson of a pioneer who crossed the plains in a covered wagon. Huntley grew up on a ranch near the Canadian border, played football and basketball in high school, and entered Montana State College with a scholarship because of his outstanding record as a high school debater and student. He won a national oratorical contest while at Montana State which yielded a scholarship to the Cornish School of Arts in Seattle. So, he transferred to the University of Washington and graduated with a B.A. in 1934.

Huntley was still a student at the University of Washington when he got a broadcasting job at a Seattle radio station, KPCB. He worked, among many tasks, as announcer, writer, and disk jockey. Two years later, he joined Spokane's KHQ as writer and announcer, then worked at KGW in Portland, Oregon, and KFI in Los Angeles. By 1939 Chet Huntley was in broadcasting to stay, and he joined CBS as a member of its Los Angeles affiliate. His coverage of conditions of minority citizens on the West Coast during World War II earned him numerous awards. In 1951 he moved from CBS to ABC and broadcast daily radio and television newscasts on KABC. His efforts to air all sides on controversial issues won him the praise and enmity of several pressure groups while he was with KABC in Los Angeles and at the NBC TV affiliate when he joined in 1955.

In 1956 Chet Huntley moved to New York City with NBC on a seven-year contract; he broadcast a Monday through Thursday ten-minute commentary on radio, "Chet Huntley Reporting," gave news roundups on NBC's Sunday television series, "Outlook," and served as a newscaster for WRCA-TV. Huntley's view of reporting combined news, analysis, and commentary:

> I don't mean simply reading a bulletin which says "Senator So-and-So declares that farmers do not want a Congressional bill that will arbitrarily jack up farm prices." Given alone, that statement can mislead. It doesn't give any insight into the whole issue. After I tell what the Senator said, I'll relate what the opposition had to say, and, to the best of my ability, give latest developments on the matter. (Torre, 1956, 7)

NBC executives were pleased with the performance of the tall, handsome, serious, and deep-voiced newscaster. He might be, they hoped, NBC's answer to CBS' legendary Edward R. Murrow, but it was not clear that he alone could sustain the continuing on-air, potentially round-the-clock, coverage of two national political party conventions. Nor did he have sufficient experience with politics and politics in the nation's capital to do so. Hence, there came the pairing with David Brinkley. It proved a fortuitous move. Chet Huntley's straight-faced and straight-from-the-shoulder account of unfolding events, combined with Brinkley's humorous, tension-easing commentary, won critical acclaim.

Although CBS' Walter Cronkite received the highest ratings for coverage of the conventions in 1956, as in 1952, NBC's research indicated that their new team attracted a new audience not previously loyal to any particular network. Thus, it came as no surprise when NBC announced that Huntley and Brinkley would replace John Cameron Swayze on a revamped nightly newscast. On October 29, 1956, the "Camel News Caravan" ceased to roll. "NBC News," later renamed the "Huntley-Brinkley Report" with Huntley's news reported from New York and Brinkley's wry commentaries coming from Washington, opened a pioneering and ratings grabbing run. By the end of 1956, the newscast had full sponsorships, and by 1958, it was the top-rated news program in the United States. The show, extended to thirty minutes in 1963 in response to CBS' lengthened nightly newscasts the same year, remained number one in the ratings until it ended a fourteen-year run. In an interview for *Time* magazine, Brinkley stated, "We sort of set the form of TV news as it persists to this day. A story or two, or three; somebody setting them up and then switching away to somewhere and coming back to do a commercial or two" ("David Takes on Goliath," 1980, 61).

FROM "GOOD NIGHT, CHET" AND "GOOD NIGHT, DAVID" TO "THIS WEEK"

The two anchors' identification with their newscast, each other, the audience, and complementing political commentary contributed to the success of the "Huntley-Brinkley Report." Once Chet Huntley was asked, "Are you Huntley or Brinkley?" His deadpan response was, "I'm not sure. Sometimes it's hard even for me to keep us straight" (Huntley, 1973, 246). For the first time, according to Brinkley, television journalists treated news as a serious business. He said, with an ironic air, "It was the first real news program. Prior to that, news programs were essentially jokes . . . It worked and we got very good reviews. In those days, news executives didn't believe their own people were any good until the *New York Times* said so" ("Nobody Does It Better," 1986, 119). Despite their success, neither Huntley nor Brinkley appeared pompous; they were simply a balance of skepticism and wit.

In addition to the "Huntley-Brinkley Report," David Brinkley was involved with a weekly NBC public affairs program that aired from October 1961 to August 1963. On "David Brinkley's Journal," he appeared live with taped segments related to a topic or issue under discussion. It was an NBC version, lighter in tone, of CBS' "See It Now" and "CBS Reports." The series gave Brinkley an opportunity to present commentary on issues that were on the social agenda and won him a host of television broadcasting awards.

In July 1970, Chet Huntley retired. For the last time, he bid farewell to David Brinkley with the signature closing of the fourteen-year-old nightly newscast: "Good Night, David," to Brinkley's "Good Night, Chet." Although the team had constituted a magic formula for television news dominance for years, its members had not always seen eye to eye on political matters. For example, in 1967 when the American Federation of Television and Radio Artists went on strike, Brinkley refused to cross the picket lines; Huntley did so and carried on the evening report alone. During the Vietnam War, Brinkley was a dove, Huntley a hawk.

In a quandary as to what to do with the evening news, NBC executives experimented with rotating anchors on its "NBC Nightly News." David Brinkley, Frank Magee, and John Chancellor (q.v.) rotated nightly, two on and one off, for thirteen months following Huntley's departure. The experiment failed; NBC sacrificed first place in the ratings to the "CBS Evening News with Walter Cronkite." Brinkley remembered the experiment as the "worst excuse for a news program. . . . People got confused; they didn't know what program they were looking at" ("Nobody Does It Better," 1986, 119).

In August 1971, John Chancellor became the sole anchor and, until 1976, David Brinkley appeared on the evening newscast as a commentator. Changes were occurring in Brinkley's personal, as well as professional, life during these years. On June 10, 1972, Brinkley married his second wife (having divorced Ann Fischer, the mother of his three sons), Susan Melanie Benfer, a professional woman with a daughter. In June 1976, NBC inaugurated another experiment in a drive to overtake CBS and Walter Cronkite. Brinkley returned to coanchoring the "NBC Nightly News" with John Chancellor, and he remained coanchor until October 1979. But NBC fell even farther behind in the news ratings, now trailing ABC as well as CBS. Brinkley was growing restless with the grind of a nightly newscast. In the fall of 1980 he became the host, although he preferred the title of "lead correspondent," of a weekly public affairs program entitled "NBC Magazine with David Brinkley." In promoting the series Brinkley said, "Mostly, the program will be ad lib. We are going to let the correspondents pretty much pick their own stories" ("David Takes on Goliath," 1980, 61). Designed to compete with CBS' "60 Minutes" and ABC's "20/20," the program suffered from scheduling woes and failed to capture a respectable market share in its time slot.

Brinkley grew disillusioned with NBC after his experience with "Magazine." Not only had his series been denied a competitive time, he also had problems with the NBC News president, William Small. Brinkley said he "could not stand and refused to work for [Small]. The worst disaster that NBC News ever had was Bill Small. . . . I said: 'Either Small or me' " ("Nobody Does It Better," 1986, 119). The network informed Brinkley that it could not fire Small, and, in 1981, David Brinkley moved from NBC News to ABC News.

Brinkley characterized his departure from NBC as a divorce: "It was extremely difficult. I have many friends there . . . and I shed a few tears. But I really wanted to get out and I was really happy to get out" ("The View from the Trenches," 1982, 97). On September 4, 1981, Brinkley announced that he was leaving NBC.

David Brinkley signed a four-year contract with ABC News to assume several assignments, including anchoring an hour-long weekly news and discussion show, doing the political commentary for "World News Tonight," and covering the 1982 and 1984 elections ("TV Tremors," 1981, 62). On Sunday, November 15, 1981, ABC News launched an hour-long weekly show, "This Week with David Brinkley." According to Brinkley, conventional Sunday morning news programs were "very tired, and had been for a long time" ("The View from the Trenches," 1982, 96). "This Week with David Brinkley" offered a new format for its viewers. It opened with a short newscast by Brinkley, followed by a correspondent's report with background on the main topic of the telecast. The correspondent's report set the stage for a panel interview with invited guests and then a roundtable discussion by Brinkley, *Washington Post* and *Newsweek* columnist and political commentator George F. Will (q.v.), ABC correspondent Sam Donaldson, and, joining in 1988, Corrine "Cokie" Roberts (q.v.) of ABC News and National Public Radio. Within less than a year, "This Week with David Brinkley" captured a larger market share than its competitors on Sunday morning, NBC's "Meet the Press," founded by Martha Rountree and Lawrence E. Spivak, (q.v.), the longest continuously aired program on radio or television, and CBS' "Face the Nation."

ABC producers, and Brinkley as well, are aware that "This Week with David Brinkley" is successful because it *makes* news, not because it covers it. The program seeks well-known guests who respond to rigorously put questions on timely topics—all in the hopes of generating a newsy tidbit that will be covered by other news programs. With candor and humor, Brinkley explained the reason why the program's names and graphics are prominently displayed in the background as a means of letting viewers know where other news organizations "swiped" ABC's news: "And that accounts for the small, round 'bug' in the lower right corner on your screen showing the initials of the network originating the picture. If you want to take our picture, you have to take our bug and show it on your screen" (Brinkley, 1995, 240). Politicians know what ABC's "This Week" is about; hence, they appear as guests with their newsworthy sound bites all prepared, as though "thought up on the spur of the moment, apparently. So it is that political speech has become a manufactured commodity, like sausage. And as with sausage, it includes some dubious and invisible ingredients best not described" (1995, 241).

His celebrity notwithstanding, Brinkley's penchant for witty commentary sometimes is awry rather than wry. For example, in 1970, while speaking to a nationwide conference of 6,000 teachers, Brinkley prophesied the end to televised political ads: "People just can't be fooled by those sly, tricky, cute little clips of film. I think they're dead because they didn't work. I'm sick of looking at these things," and dismissed television political spots as quickly as "Mama" had once dismissed his short stories (Dye, 1970, A-3). And, proving experience does not always teach lessons about being too quick to wit, in 1995, when *Heterodoxy*, a magazine of popular culture, ran a parody about a fictitious hiker being prosecuted by animal-rights activists for eating squirrels to stay alive when lost in the Adirondacks, two political commentators took the hoax as fact and broadcast it as fact: Paul Harvey (q.v.) on his daily newscast and David Brinkley on "This Week." It was an egregious error ("The Furry Critter Setup," 1995, 2 A).

CONCLUSION: A COMMENTATOR ON COMMENTARY

Objectivity in its strictest sense, argues David Brinkley, refers to a computer: "You put something in it and push the button you get back precisely what you put in, with no coloring, shading, changing or anything. To put that same requirement on a news broadcaster . . . I think would probably be dangerous to society." But, Brinkley does not provide news "heavily larded with editorial comments" like the journalists did when he started in broadcasting, including H. V. Kaltenborn (q.v.), Morgan Beatty, and Fulton Lewis, Jr. (q.v.) ("The View from the Trenches," 1982, 95). Although he believes he is impartial in his political journalism, Brinkley's critics cannot make up their minds where his partisanship lies; they have placed him at all points on the political spectrum, from a left-wing radical to a right-wing reactionary. His supporters, in response, simply describe him as "an iconic figure in our culture" who provides a "stately and predictable observance and analysis of the events. . . . Brinkley, to be sure, is a consistently intelligent validation of the immense sums of money poured into network news" (McConnell, 1991, 196).

In his years as a broadcast journalist and political communicator, David Brinkley has brought a level of political sophistication and literary craftsmanship to his work as a journalist. He has a lively sense of humor that comes across on television, a trait often lacking in political commentators who take themselves all too seriously while on the air. Brinkley's distinctive delivery, a wry wit marked with simple declarative sentences characteristic of his news-writing style, became a trend in the news industry and one that new journalists have tried to emulate. They are probably making a mistake: "I can't be anything, but myself. If I start trying to act, I am lost right away. I can't talk any way but the way I talk. I am physically unable to read (on the air) anything written by someone else" ("David Takes on Goliath," 1980, 61). According to John Chancellor, "As a writer, [Brinkley] is simply the best. As a stylist, he is impossible to imitate" ("TV Tremors," 1981, 62).

Since he and Chet Huntley first sat down together in an anchor booth at the Democratic National Convention in Chicago in 1956, David Brinkley has revealed the wry side of America, its politics, and its politicians. In 1996, four decades after first appearing with Chet Huntley, David Brinkley revealed that that year's political party conventions would be his last. Perhaps, he might have thought wryly, it was time for both party institutions and himself as another to go out together.

REFERENCES

Selected Works by David Brinkley

Washington Goes to War. New York: Alfred A. Knopf, 1988.
David Brinkley: A Memoir. New York: Alfred A. Knopf, 1995.

Selected Critical Works about David Brinkley

"David Takes on Goliath." *Time*, September 8, 1980, 61.
Dye, R. M. "Brinkley Predicts End to TV Ads." *Kansas City Star*, November 6, 1970, p. A-3.
Hickey, N. "This Epoch with . . . " *Columbia Journalism Review* 34 (November/December 1995): 51–55.
Lichenstein N., ed. "Brinkley, David." In *Political Profiles: The Kennedy Years*, 49–50. New York: Facts on File, 1976.
McConnell, F. "Sunday with David: A Sabbath of Sorts." *Commonweal*, March 22, 1991, pp. 195–96.
Moritz, C. ed. "Brinkley, David (McClure)." In *1987 Current Biography Yearbook*, 67–70. New York: H. W. Wilson, 1987.
"Nobody Does It Better." *Broadcasting*, November 10, 1986, p. 119.

"TV Tremors." *Time*, September 6, 1981, p. 62.

"The View from the Trenches." *Broadcasting*, 103, November 15, 1982, pp. 95–99.

Selected General Works

Candee, M. D., ed. "Huntley, Chet." In *Current Biography 1956*, 290–91. New York: H. W. Wilson, 1956.

Combs, J. E., and D. Nimmo. *The Comedy of Democracy*. Westport, CT: Praeger, 1996.

"The Furry Critter Setup." *Dallas Morning News*, September 26, 1995, 2 A.

Goldberg, R., and G. J. Goldberg. *Anchors*. New York: Birch Lane Press, 1990.

Hirsch, A. *Talking Heads: Political Talk Shows and Their Star Pundits*. New York: St. Martin's Press, 1991.

"Huntley, Chet." In *Celebrity Register*, 246. New York: Simon and Schuster, 1973.

Sherrod, B. "Of Departing Congressmen, Rats and Sinking Ships." *Dallas Morning News*, April 11, 1996, 23 A.

Torre, M. "Chet Huntley Profile." *New York Herald Tribune*, March 29, 1956, 7.

WILLIAM F. (FRANK) BUCKLEY, JR.

(November 24, 1925–)

Commentator of a Political Movement

Following three decades of Franklin Roosevelt's New Deal and Harry Truman's Fair Deal, many political observers wrote epitaphs to conservatism as a political movement. Even the election of a Republican, Dwight Eisenhower, to the presidency in 1952 did little to remove the impression that political conservatism, if not dead, was certainly moribund. Yet, in the 1950s, there emerged occasional voices bent on reawakening the political conservative movement. Among these were intellectuals Peter Viereck, Russell Kirk, Clinton Rossiter, Willmore Kendall, and others; so out of place did they seem that one liberal spokesman labeled them "Scrambled Eggheads on the Right" (MacDonald, 1956, 367).

No conservative commentator, however, was so outspoken, relentless, versatile, and enduring as William F. Buckley, Jr. Indeed, the triumph of the conservative movement with the election of Ronald Reagan in 1980 owed much to the political commentaries of Buckley. George F. Will (q.v.), a leading conservative pundit of the last two decades, summed up in the *National Review* (December 31, 1980, 164) conservatism's debt to Buckley:

> All great Biblical stories begin with Genesis.... Before Ronald Reagan there was Barry Goldwater and before Barry Goldwater there was *National Review* and before there was *National Review*, there was Bill Buckley, with a spark in his mind, and the spark in 1980 had become a conflagration.

BECOMING A CONSERVATIVE GADFLY

William F. Buckley, Jr., descends from a paternal great-grandfather who migrated to Canada from Ireland; Buckley's paternal grandfather migrated to Texas in 1879 and became a successful rancher and local sheriff. Buckley Senior struck it rich in oil. He and his wife, Aloise Steiner of New Orleans, had ten children. The sixth, William, Jr., was born in New York City on November 24, 1925. As the son of an oil tycoon, Bill Buckley, Jr., did not want for comfortable surroundings or an aristocratic education. As a youth he divided his time between private tutoring at the family home in Sharon, Connecticut, and exclusive Roman Catholic schools in England (St. Thomas More in London and St. John's Beaumont Windsor) and France. In 1943 young Bill Buckley graduated from Millbrook School in upstate New York, a college prep school. After a brief time at the University of Mexico, he entered the U.S. Army as an infantry private in 1944. Two years later, he was discharged as a second lieutenant. He returned to college at Yale University and graduated with honors in 1950. The same year he married Patricia Austin Taylor, a Canadian by birth who had been educated at Vassar; their son, Christopher, was born in 1954. ''By all accounts,'' writes a Buckley biographer, the marriage ''has been happy and decorous'' (Winchell, 1984, 8).

William Buckley, Jr., had by this point in his life demonstrated himself to be an outspoken young man. At the age of six he wrote to the king of England and demanded that Great Britain repay its World War I debt. At the age of ten Buckley, two days after having had enrolled in school, remonstrated to his British prep school's headmaster the deficiencies of the place. Upon entering the U.S. Army he wrote to his commanding general, again only two days after his arrival on the army base, detailing the deficiencies of camp operations. Fortunately, a friend interceded and Buckley did not send the insubordinate letter, thus avoiding what would have undoubtedly been severe disciplinary action in the army of that era. It was not surprising, therefore, that when he arrived at Yale, there too he discovered matters that, in his mind, required correction. He was well on his way to becoming ''a gadfly and a dilettante who practices a conservative version of the politics of joy'' (Winchell, 1984, 1).

At Yale he concentrated on history, political science, and economics; he was on the debate team; he became class orator; he taught Spanish; and he was the chairman of the *Yale Daily News*. Through his chairmanship he developed a taste for journalism; through his close association with Professor Willmore Kendall and a friend, L. Brent Bozell (later his brother-in-law), he sharpened his conservative views. Based upon his Yale experience and associations, Buckley published, in 1951, *God and Man at Yale: The Superstitions of Academic Freedom*, the first of what would be a shelf of conservative volumes that would bring him an enduring following as well as widespread criticism.

Buckley's argument was that Yale's teaching was irreligious and collectivist, when instead it should stress Christian and individualist values. He argued that Yale operated in an open marketplace where consumers—the parents and alumni of the school—should be able to secure for students, the product their financial contributions were underwriting, the kind of education those consumers demanded. A teacher is like any other tradesman, a seller of goods; if the goods have no market (''goods'' such as socialist, collectivist views), the teacher, like any other tradesman, should suffer the consequences. Unable to compete with more popular products, the teacher should go out of business. Academic freedom was, Buckley argued, thus the freedom of the marketplace (Burner & West, 1988).

After remaining at Yale for a year after his graduation to continue teaching Spanish, Buckley became an agent for the Central Intelligence Agency (CIA) in Mexico. (His superior at the CIA, E. Howard Hunt, would later play a major role in the Watergate scandal that brought about the resignation of President Richard Nixon in 1974.) In 1952 Buckley returned to the United States and joined the staff of *American Mercury* as associate editor. The *Mercury* had once been an influential conservative voice under its cofounder, H. L. Mencken (q.v.), and later under its editor and publisher, Lawrence E. Spivak (see Martha Rountree and Lawrence E. Spivak). Following World War II, however, the magazine declined in appeal and preached a political doctrine verging on intolerance. Buckley's tenure with the *American Mercury* was brief; when the magazine's editorial policy took an anti-Semitic tone, Buckley resigned to undertake freelance writing and lecturing. However, his *Mercury* experience convinced Buckley that there was a market for a more respectable journal of conservative opinion, a conviction he acted on in 1955 when he founded the *National Review*.

In 1954 William Buckley, Jr., published a second book, this one in collaboration with L. Brent Bozell, *McCarthy and His Enemies*. In spite of its title, ''it is not a book about McCarthyism, an event that had a character of its own, quite distinct from the character of both the technical and the philosophical issues it happened to intersect'' (Burner & West, 1988, 46). Buckley and Bozell criticized McCarthy's excesses in tracking down alleged subversives in governing positions, excesses that contributed to fashioning an anticommunist conformity in official and popular opinion. Yet, argued the coauthors, some conformity is essential to the body politic as a means of weighing an inexhaustible supply of opinions, giving priority to those vital to a society's survival. The book's mixed review of McCarthy's performance, critical yet concluding that his movement could rally people of good will and morality, did little to enhance the coauthors' reputation among liberal establishment members.

BUCKLEY'S VEHICLES FOR MOVEMENT COMMENTARY

In 1955 Buckley founded the *National Review*, a biweekly magazine of politics and letters that became the vanguard of conservative commentary in the ensuing decades. With another conservative spokesman, William Rusher, as publisher and himself as editor, William Buckley, Jr., designed a magazine to reach opinion makers rather than the rank-and-file citizenry. The contents of the *Review* consisted of signed commentaries by Buckley, unsigned commentaries and editorials by Buckley and colleagues, and political and literary writings by notable conservatives and talented authors.

At the time of the founding of the *National Review*, the conservative movement in American politics consisted of disparate and distinct philosophies coalesced around a common opponent—liberalism. In this respect the movement was similar to other twentieth-century social movements; it was a loose coalition of diverse interests united in their resistance to, or support of, change. Frequently the uniting vehicle for such a movement is a rhetorical agent; for example, Carrie Nation, who galvanized the temperance movement, and Martin Luther King, Jr., who sparked demands for civil rights (Simons & Mechling, 1981; Stewart, Smith, & Denton, 1984). William Buckley, commenting via *National Review* and later through other media, was such an agent.

The principal elements of the 1950s conservative movement were, according to Buckley biographer Mark Royden Winchell, economic libertarianism, cultural traditionalism, and messianic anticommunists (1984). The libertarians espoused views opposed to federal intervention in private matters, especially in economic concerns. They consisted of both those who viewed all government with suspicion, sharing Henry David Thoreau's admonition that the best government is one that does not govern at all, and proponents of economic laissez-faire, former liberals driven to conservative views when the designation "liberal" adhered to advocates of the welfare state. Cultural traditionalists shared the libertarian preference for limited government and for individual and property rights in the face of collectivist pressures. However, traditionalists grounded their conservatism not in an uncritical devotion to corporate capitalism, but in the permanence of standing religious and cultural values. Finally, the anticommunist strain was dominated by disaffected radicals, once supporters of revolutionary change, now staunch defenders against Soviet influences at home and abroad.

It was William F. Buckley's task at the *National Review* to mediate the persistent disputes among adherents of the libertarian, traditionalist, and anticommunist viewpoints. In several respects, he was ideally suited to the task. By birth and upbringing, he was libertarian and traditionalist; although he had been isolationist prior to World War II, Buckley's acute awareness of the threat of tyranny moved him to the anticommunist camp. In disputes between libertarian and traditionalist staffers on the *National Review*, Buckley steered a middle course; in conflicts between libertarians and traditionalists and the anticommunist camp, he sided with the latter. Gifted with a ready wit and intelligence, convinced that conservative views could prevail, and a prescient judge of talented thinkers and writers, William Buckley built a solid following for *Review* positions. Circulation multiplied tenfold from 1957 to 1964 and leveled off at 100,000 by the time of Ronald Reagan's successful 1980 campaign. More important than circulation figures was the fact that the views espoused in the *National Review* increasingly set the agenda for debate on the national scene.

In their comprehensive analysis of the *National Review* under Buckley's tutelage, David Burner and Thomas West (1988) summarize the magazine's evolving role in the national political debate. A leading principle espoused by the magazine's editorial policy was preservation of property rights. The argument echoed libertarian themes: welfare programs transfer wealth from the advantaged, be they conservative or liberal, to the less privileged. Permitting property to be taken from one's control evidences not only defects of character; it is a violation of liberty, for "it is the right of individuals to dispose of their property, to use it charitably or keep it, according to their own wishes and free of governmental policies of redistribution" (Burner & West, 1988, 46).

On the burning social issue of the 1950s and 1960s, desegregation of public schools, Buckley and his colleagues contributed unique commentary to the controversy, yet came down on what proved to be the losing, and wrong, side of the issue. Buckley's magazine opposed implementation of the 1954 Supreme Court decision in *Brown v. Board of Education*. Here the argument picked up on conservatism's strain of cultural conservatism. Southern values embodying segregationist customs were organic to the community itself. Modern liberalism, however, is not organic but rationalist. In words reminiscent of H. L. Mencken at the 1925 Scopes trial over the right to teach evolution in public schools, when Mencken *defended* rationalist attacks on communal values, the *National Review* defended the organic in a commentary on September 22, 1956 (p. 6). Liberalism "rejects custom, revelation and tradition, in order to base its doctrine and program exclusively on reason. . . . The cult of reason divorced from tradition and faith ends in brute appeal to force," and, hence, federal troops to force integration. The "organic, historic, traditional" recognizes, and checks, the fallible tendencies in pure reason with the wisdom embodied in custom, institutions, and common sense. Years later, Buckley modified his views on racial change, opting for a version of preferential treatment for black Americans. In doing so, he again enlisted the concept of the evolving, organic community opposed to the rationalist, mechanical society, on behalf of his shift.

The *National Review*'s anticommunist strain of thought remained staunch throughout the magazine's development. The bête noire of many commentaries was the naive, in the editorial view, compulsion of liberals to view global politics as fraught with increasing complexity after World War II. What was at issue, however, was not complexity but evil. *Review* commentaries viewed Soviet-led international communism as an evil force (President Ronald Reagan would ultimately speak of it as an "Evil Empire") set out to destroy Western democracy. Summing up *Review* commentaries over three decades, Burner and West (1988, 58) drew a sharp, critical contrast between the view of complexity, attributed to liberals by the *National Review*, and the magazine's own editorial stance:

> The liberal response [to global complexities] has been activist, to the extent of sustaining the Cold War and two hot ones. *National Review* discovered complexity in South Africa, the American South, in the problem of poverty; and its response was passive: to recommend that everyone go on contemplating complexity.

In 1959 William F. Buckley published a third book that would place him at the forefront of the resurgence of a conservative political movement. *Up from Liberalism* argued that liberalism, in spite of the power of its doctrinal views, was decadent. It must be brought down. Conservatism, much weaker but more viable, must replace it. Liberalism's decadence, asserted Buckley, resided in liberals' mindless tolerance for all schools of thought, a relativism that denies absolute belief in anything. To tolerate all and believe in nothing renders even tolerance itself impotent, incapable of taking a convincing position regarding why all positions should be voiced. Conservatives believe; because they believe, they practice tolerance through more than lip service.

In 1962 Buckley added another form of political commentary to his conservative arsenal. He began to write a weekly newspaper column, "A Conservative Voice" (later titled "On the Right," also extended to thrice weekly). The column enlarged Buckley's audience by over 7 million readers and appeared in over 300 newspapers by 1980. Periodically, Buckley's columns have been reprinted in booklength volumes, including *The Jeweler's Eye* (1968), *The Governor Listeth* (1970), *Inveighing We Will Go* (1972), *Execution Eve* (1975), and *A Hymnal* (1978). Each volume of topical columns, not always political, is sometimes strikingly uneven in quality; that is, perhaps, to be expected under the pressures of writing three columns a week. Each is also guilty of one of Buckley's severe strictures of liberalism. Namely, with no weighing of priorities between essentially equally important short essays, a distinct conservative thrust is sometimes absent.

William Buckley expanded his audience in 1966 with the weekly television series, "Firing Line," on WOR-TV in New York City. Five years later "Firing Line" became part of the program lineup of the Public Broadcasting System. The program's format is suited to Buckley's commentary style and his showmanship. His guests include political leaders, sports figures, entertainers, publishers, scientists, and educators—all persons of celebrity and, often, achievement. Before their presidencies both Jimmy Carter and Ronald Reagan appeared on "Firing Line" to tilt with Buckley's celebrated acid wit, polysyllabic meanderings, and sharp debating style. Buckley is an unrelenting interrogator, unlike Larry King (q.v.) who often seems a patsy by contrast. Buckley is also a master of the entrapping question; however, he is never as loud as John McLaughlin (q.v.), convivial as Phil Donahue (q.v.), or somber as Barbara Walters.

Buckley's television style frequently appears overly erudite; he dotes on the apt phrase, pertinent pause, and bon mot. That commentary, not simple questions and answers, is his aim surfaces in his approach to inquiry:

> Buckley's questions tend to be long, comprised of introductory and background statements of fact and opinion, starting slowly in a deep, cultured voice, picking up tempo and losing volume until they degenerate into a rapid faint mumble, leaving the interviewee frequently leaning out of the chair to catch the gist of the final, interrogatory portion. (Garner, 1976, 77)

Buckley confesses to only one grossly egregious television appearance, which was not on "Firing Line." In 1968 ABC-TV featured live commentary at the Democratic and Republican national conventions, employing a modified debate format, between novelist and liberal Gore Vidal and columnist and commentator William F. Buckley, Jr. Since Vidal also possesses an acid tongue, it was no surprise when the debate turned poisonous. Vidal accused Buckley of being a crypto-Nazi. Buckley responded by calling Vidal a "queer," threatening to "sock" Vidal in the "goddamn face and you'll stay plastered" (Winchell, 1984, 119). Each made public apologies, sued each other, then dropped the lawsuits.

Although he has never actually been in a physical sparring match with detractors—unlike notable political commentator Drew Pearson (q.v.) was with Senator Joseph McCarthy—William Buckley has been a political activist as well as commentator. In 1960 Buckley helped found the Young Americans for Freedom, partly to recruit youth to the conservative cause, and partly to blunt the edge of the extreme rightist John Birch Society whose widely publicized claims that America was threatened by conspiratorial politics were making inroads on young Americans. A year later Buckley joined others to form the New York Conservative party. In 1965 William Buckley was the Conservative candidate for mayor of New York City. His campaign style—detailed position papers rather than pressing of the flesh and television advertising—was no match for the tactics of liberal Republican John V. Lindsay. Buckley received less than 14 percent of the vote. Thus, Buckley, who once quipped that he would rather be governed by the first 2,000 names in the telephone directory rather than by 2,000 members of the Harvard faculty, missed out on public office, perhaps because there were more than ten score names ahead of him (Winchell, 1984). The Conservative party, however, survived. James L. Buckley, William Buckley's brother, was elected to the U.S. Senate on the party's ticket in 1970.

During President Richard Nixon's first term, William F. Buckley, Jr., became a member of the five-person advisory board to the United States Information Agency (USIA). The USIA's mission has always been a source of political controversy. Every political commentator who has been enlisted to work in some capacity associated with the agency has been frustrated by the infighting. These commentators include Elmer Davis (q.v.), Edward R. Murrow (q.v.), and John Chancellor (q.v.). By 1972 William Buckley suffered the same frustration and resigned from the advisory committee. A year later Buckley was appointed a member of the U.S. delegation to the United Nations General Assembly. There Buckley chafed over the anti-Americanism rampant in the Assembly, yet defended U.S. membership in the organization (Buckley, 1974).

Throughout Richard Nixon's career, William Buckley's relationship with the controversial political leader was mixed. For his part, Nixon credited Buckley with being instrumental in exposing the sham behind the John Birch Society in the 1960s: ''Buckley's articles cost the Birchers their respectability with conservatives. I couldn't have accomplished that. Liberals couldn't either'' (Moritz, 1983, 59). For Buckley's part, the political commentator was never quite secure with Nixon's credentials as a conservative. Buckley easily supported Nixon in the 1968 presidential campaign, yet he had a falling out over USIA policies. In 1971 Buckley suspended his support for Nixon on the grounds that the president had turned his back on conservative principles by imposing price and wage controls, opening the door to Communist China, and relaxing tensions with the Soviet Union. When Ohio Republican Congressman John Ashbrook's challenge to Nixon for the Republican nomination in 1972 collapsed, Buckley, who had supported Ashbrook, again endorsed the president. Two years later, however, in the wake of the Watergate scandal, both columnist William Buckley and Senator James Buckley called for the president's resignation.

Beginning in the 1970s, William Buckley began to diversify his writing interests, and he became not only a conservative commentator but also a man of letters. This was especially true in his book-length works. He wrote novels, specifically espionage fiction. In a series of spy novels set in the 1950s and beyond, Buckley created his own fictional hero, his "Walter Mitty image of himself" as his biographer put it (Winchell, 1984, 122). His fictional creation, Blackford Oakes, is a young, handsome, CIA agent. Through a sequence of adventures, Oakes foils a plot against the British monarchy, is involved with a Soviet agent in an assassination intrigue, gets caught up in a U.S.–Soviet competition to exploit outer space, and uncovers a CIA mole. The overriding message of the espionage tales parodies Buckley's anticommunist conviction— unsavory practices are often justified to defeat the evil enemy.

CONCLUSION: THE TIMES, THEY ARE A CHANGIN'

As America approached the end of the 1990s, William F. Buckley's life had spanned almost two-thirds of the twentieth century, his career as a conservative commentator almost half of it. By its nature, political commentary focuses on events in the here and now. It is not, therefore, surprising that as events unfolded over Buckley's career, political observers detected "ideological gyrations" in his views (Winchell, 1984, 137). He has upset many conservatives by seeming to soften his stand on the decriminalization of marijuana, prostitution, and homosexual rights. Once solidly opposed to the welfare state and steeped in the belief that it could be repealed, Buckley came to modify his opposition to federally financed welfare measures. His support for Jimmy Carter's Panama Canal treaty seemed to many conservatives the sellout of an American birthright (Moritz, 1983).

Yet, as Burner and West note, "No sudden break in philosophy exists to account for this" mellowing; "neither is there a measured and continuing development modification" (1988, 58). Rather, Buckley adjusted to new conditions; for example, a welfare state accepted as the status quo by a series of presidential administrations including those of Nixon, Reagan, and Bush; the end of the Cold War; and the admission three times by a Democratic president, Bill Clinton, in his 1996 State of the Union address, that "the era of Big Government is over" (*Washington Post* National Weekly Edition, January 29–February 4, 1996, 11).

Conservative commentary is no longer guided by the writings and television appearances of William F. Buckley, Jr. Other voices predominate: the neo-Toryism of George Will, the populist outrage of Rush Limbaugh (q.v.), the Barnum-like promotions of John McLaughlin, and the opportunistic pandering of television commentator cum presidential candidate, Patrick Buchanan. William F. Buckley's conviction a half-century ago that conservatism would replace liberalism was, perhaps, validated. It remains to be seen whether in the twenty-first century the decline of political commentary will validate a different judgment on the two political doctrines, namely, a "plague on both houses."

REFERENCES

Selected Political Works by William F. Buckley, Jr.

God and Man at Yale. Chicago: Henry Regnery, 1951.

McCarthy and His Enemies. With L. Brent Bozell. Chicago: Henry Regnery, 1954.

Up from Liberalism. New York: Obolensky/McDowell, 1959.

The Committee and Its Critics: A Calm Review of the House Committee on Un-American Activities. Editor. Chicago: Henry Regnery, 1963.

Rumbles Left and Right, A Book about Troublesome People and Ideas. New York: Putnam, 1963.

Dialogues in Americanism. Chicago: Henry Regnery, 1964.

The Jeweler's Eye. New York: Putnam, 1968.

Did You Ever See a Dream Walking? American Conservative Thought in the Twentieth Century. Editor. Indianapolis, IN: Bobbs-Merrill, 1970.

Odyssey of a Friend: Whittaker Chambers' Letters to William F. Buckley, Jr., 1954–1961. Editor. New York: Putnam, 1970.

The Governor Listeth. New York: Putnam, 1970.

Inveighing We Will Go. New York: Putnam, 1972.

Four Reforms: A Guide for the Seventies. New York: Putnam, 1973.

United Nations Journal: A Delegate's Odyssey. New York: Putnam, 1974.

Execution Eve. New York: Putnam, 1975.

"Essay on Hayek." In *Essays on Hayek*, edited by F. Machlup, 95–106. New York: New York University Press, 1976.

The Galbraith Viewpoint in Perspective. Stanford, CA: Hoover Institution Press, 1977.

The Unmaking of a Mayor. New York: Arlington House, 1977.

A Hymnal. New York: Putnam, 1978.

"Human Rights and Foreign Policy: A Proposal." *Foreign Affairs* 58 (Spring 1980): 775–96.

Overdrive: A Personal Documentary. New York: Doubleday, 1983.

Right Reason: A Collection. New York: Doubleday, 1985.

Selected Critical Works about William F. Buckley, Jr.

Burner, D., and T. R. West. "William F. Buckley, Jr. and *National Review*." In *Column Right: Conservative Journalists in the Service of Nationalism,* edited by D. Burner and T. R. West, 39–64. New York: New York University Press, 1988.

Garner, P. "Backstage on Firing Line." In *Authors in the News*, edited by B. Nykorak, vol. 1, 76–77. Detroit: Gale Research Company, 1976. Originally published in the *Atlanta Journal & Constitution*, March 3, 1974, C-4.

Lichtenstein, N., ed. "Buckley, William F(rank), Jr." In *Political Profiles: The Johnson Years*, 76–77. New York: Facts on File, 1976.

———."Buckley, William F(rank), Jr." In *Political Profiles: The Kennedy Years*, 73–74. New York: Facts on File, 1976.

MacDonald, D. "Scrambled Eggheads on the Right." *Commentary*, April 1956, 367–73.

Markman, C. L. *The Buckleys: A Family Examined.* New York: William Morrow, 1973.

Merritt, F. E. "William F. Buckley, Jr.: Spokesman for Contemporary American Conservatism—A Classical-Weaverian Analysis." Ph.D. diss., Ohio State University, 1973.

Moritz, C., ed. "Buckley, William F(rank), Jr." In *Current Biography Yearbook 1962*, 58–60. New York: H. W. Wilson, 1963.

———. "Buckley, William F(rank), Jr." In *Current Biography Yearbook 1982*, 57–61. New York: H. W. Wilson, 1983.

Riley, S. G. "Buckley, William Frank, Jr." In *Biographical Dictionary of American Newspaper Columnists*, 47–48. Westport, CT: Greenwood Press, 1995.

Schoenebaum, E. W., ed. "Buckley, William F(rank), Jr." In *Political Profiles: The Eisenhower Years*, 57–58. New York: Facts on File, 1977.

Winchell, M. R. *William F. Buckley, Jr.* Boston: Twayne, 1984.

Selected General Works

Hart, J. *The American Dissent: A Decade of Modern Conservatism.* Garden City, NY: Doubleday, 1966.

Nash, G. H. *The Conservative Intellectual Movement in America since 1945.* New York: Basic Books, 1976.

Ross, M. S. *The Literary Politicians.* Garden City, NY: Doubleday, 1978.

Simons, H., and E. W. Mechling. "The Rhetoric of Political Movements." In *Handbook of Political Communication*, edited by D. Nimmo and K. Sanders, 417–44. Beverly Hills, CA: Sage, 1981.

Stewart, C., C. A. Smith, and R. E. Denton, Jr. *Persuasion and Social Movements.* Chicago: Waveland Press, 1984.

Wills, G. *Confessions of a Conservative.* Garden City, NY: Doubleday, 1979.

JOHN (WILLIAM) CHANCELLOR
(July 14, 1927–July 12, 1996)

A Golden Mean for the Golden Years of Political Commentary

Robert Campbell titles his volume celebrating a half-century of radio and television for the National Broadcasting Company (NBC) *The Golden Years of Broadcasting* (1976). A close reading of his account of news and special events programming at NBC reveals, however, that those golden years were tarnished by emerging tensions in political reporting, especially after World War II. There had always been a tension between what could properly be labeled reporting versus editorializing. The postwar years blurred the distinctions between what was the legitimate correspondents' news-gathering function and what was news making.

Also, correspondents, once obscure, faceless voices crying in the wilderness, became national, even global, celebrities; if they were not larger than life, then certainly they were larger than the stories they covered. As television became an all-pervasive medium, competing values drove political news coverage, namely, the information-driven values of news versus the market-driven values of entertainment programming. In the almost quarter of a century that has followed Campbell's celebration of NBC news, political commentary has become less golden than gold plated. Editorializing, newsmaking, and celebrity commentators have erased the distinction between news and entertainment.

The career of NBC political commentator John Chancellor exemplifies the competing values in political commentary that arose in the half-century following World War II. Chancellor's effort to find a golden mean between news and entertainment, news commentary and news making, and the contrasting roles of the reporter as both working journalist and as a public persona is unique. That the mean he fashioned has largely been discarded by political commentators approaching the millennium reflects not Chancellor's failure sui generis, but that of political communication in general.

THE CHICAGO SCHOOLS OF REPORTING AND PERFORMING

The city of Chicago has been a breeding ground for political commentators. Mike Wallace (q.v.), Georgie Anne Geyer (q.v.), and Phil Donahue (q.v.), to name a few, cut their political teeth in the turbulent winds of Chicago. John Chancellor, born in the Windy City on July 14, 1927, acquired his own streetwise sense of politics in his native town. He lamented in a 1974 interview that one of the problems of contemporary journalism derived from the vanishing of a Chicago-like experience among cub reporters:

> Journalism is a loose, unlicensed fraternity of men who get paid for their curiosity. Too many have lost the sense of fun and anger I saw in Chicago in the later 1940s and early '50s. In the words of an old Chicago [*Sun*] *Times* editor, "It's the newspaper's duty to print the news and raise hell." (Drew, 1974, 625)

Chancellor was the only child of E.M.J. and Mollie (Barett) Chancellor. Early on he developed an inclination to gain an education through work experience rather than formal study. He left DePaul Academy at the age of fifteen and became a jack-of-all-trades by working in a hospital, carpentry, chemical testing, trucking, a job agency, and on a riverboat. At the age of eighteen he joined the U.S. Army; there he acquired an early taste for writing by working in public relations. Following his discharge from the army in 1947, Chancellor attended briefly an undergraduate branch of the University of Illinois in Chicago. Within a year, he had again departed formal study to join the Chicago *Sun Times* as a copyboy, then reporter, rewrite man, and feature writer.

In 1950, "in one of those self-indulgent exercises of City Editor as King that so color Chicago's newspapering," Chancellor was fired as a newspaperman. He took "the only job he could get and joined the staff of the Chicago NBC affiliate, WNBQ (Frank, 1991, 99). In what he later termed the happiest years of his career, John Chancellor chased down police calls in an unmarked mobile unit sporting a whirling red light—shades of a political commentator who was trained in crime reporting during the early days of broadcasting: Walter Winchell (q.v.). In 1955 his taped coverage of a street shootout between Chicago police and a killer brought him a national reporting award. A broadcast in the midst of an oil refinery fire, a documentary on the mistreatment of Southern white migrants in Northern cities, and other unconventional displays of journalistic initiative caught the eye of NBC network officials.

By 1956 Chancellor covered both national political party conventions as a television floorman for the network, then traveled the campaign of Adlai Stevenson as an NBC correspondent. A year later Chancellor reported nightly for eight weeks from Little Rock, Arkansas, as the struggle over the end of segregation at Central High School unfolded. John Chancellor was the only national television reporter of any network present on the morning Governor Orval Faubus sent Arkansas National Guard troops to Central High when nine black teenagers sought admission to the school. Because of a technical problem, Chancellor's nightly reports for NBC originated not in Little Rock, but in Oklahoma City. For two weeks Chancellor shuttled between the two locales via chartered plane (Frank, 1991).

Throughout these early years as a television correspondent, Chancellor fashioned an appealing broadcast style and on-air presence. He combined the reporting of an on-the-scene observer with a subtle, almost wink-of-the-eye humor. Although it was not yet the avuncular, colloquial style he would perfect in his news anchoring and commentary of later years, it was a "cool" manner suited to the Eisenhower era of the 1950s—calm, deliberate, detached, and slightly impudent. In 1958 Chancellor's streetwise education moved abroad. He successively worked with the NBC bureau in Vienna, where he covered a revolt in Algeria that brought Charles de Gaulle to power in France, and a civil war in Lebanon; London, where he reported the wedding of Princess Margaret; and Moscow, where he reported Yuri Gagarin's space flight.

During the 1960 presidential campaign, NBC returned Chancellor to the United States. He had the distinction of being one of the journalists selected to ask questions of John F. Kennedy and Richard Nixon in their historic presidential debates. As correspondent for the Midwest during NBC's election night coverage, Chancellor won critical acclaim as "outdoing Huntley and Brinkley in sagacity and . . . one of the few commentators who kept saying all night long that the result would be close" ("Portrait: John Chancellor," 1961, 72). From his perspective, however, Chancellor's critical success brought him close to his undoing. He considered himself a professional journalist, not an entertainer, performer, or even a "commentator." Yet, his evolving on-camera style, which mixed detached cordiality, dry humor, and a trace of impudence, appealed to NBC executives in 1961 when they sought a permanent host for their showpiece daily program, "Today."

From its inception in 1952, "Today" provoked a collision between competing sets of values in television programming: information versus entertainment. Although its format featured regular segments of news, "Today" was considered to be entertainment and was produced within the NBC Program Department. Whereas John Chancellor's streetwise journalistic approach derived from a vital Chicago tradition of ambulance-chasing, on-the-spot reporting, the "Today" approach flowed from a different Chicago tradition. That was the Chicago School of radio and television that "encouraged performers to treat their audiences as if they were only a few feet distant" (Campbell, 1976, 112). In the Chicago market, at least in the 1950s, the two traditions coexisted; neither encroached on the other. As John Chancellor told a radio/television critic in 1975 regarding Chicago reporting:

> It's a good news town. They've always had lively journalism, with plenty of initiative and a sense of competition. And there was some very imaginative Chicago television—*Garroway at Large*, Studs Terkel—before *Kukla, Fran and Ollie*.
>
> There was no network line when we went to work there. We produced for Chicago, with no network competitive pressures, no rules. (Ryan, 1975, 504)

In short, the Chicago School, be it in news or entertainment, encouraged imagination and ingenuity in an atmosphere of low pressure.

The ancestry of "Today" can be traced to "Garroway at Large," a variety show of music, comedy, and the musings of its host, David Garroway. Garroway epitomized "cool" television performance—unpretentious, understated, diffident, and comforting, with a shy confidence and a smile in the fashion of the nation's hero, Dwight Eisenhower. Like Eisenhower, Garroway was an empty vessel into which viewers could pour any quality they wanted to find. Whether the manner was calculated or not, it was credible.

When, in 1951, the critically acclaimed "Garroway at Large" lost its commercial sponsorship, NBC proposed that Dave Garroway return to network headquarters—where he had started as a $16-a-week page in 1938 and had studied at the NBC announcers' school in the late 1930s—to help develop a two-hour early morning television show. "Today" aired for the first time on January 15, 1952. In its early days, the show seemed more shambles than innovative entertainment. Gradually, however, it established itself as a stable mix of news, weather reports, drama and book reviews, interviews with popular celebrities, music, and variety. Garroway became the first "communicator," a designation for his role as host coined by an NBC executive. The word entered the lexicon of broadcasting to describe one who makes all things "common" in a variety of senses: common as in shared by everyone, common as in ordinary, and common as in the lowest common denominator. (In the early years of "Today," Garroway's on-camera sideman was J. Fred Muggs, a banana-chomping chimpanzee—as common a denominator as one could possibly conceive.)

After a decade David Garroway decided to leave his role of communicator on "Today." In pondering a successor, NBC president Robert Kintner recalled how well John Chancellor had ad-libbed on camera for over an hour, describing things he could not see from the residence compound of John F. Kennedy, while awaiting the official outcome of the 1960 presidential election. When he was offered the job, Chancellor was not enthusiastic about the prospect. He reluctantly accepted on the grounds that the network must be in trouble and, as a loyal company man, he had no choice but to go to NBC's aid in its hour of need. As Garroway's successor in 1961 and 1962, John Chancellor, like Garroway, sported horn-rimmed glasses and was, in a less calculated way, cool. In other respects, however, Chancellor was scarcely Garroway's replacement:

> "Today" is going to be a news game, supervised by newsmen, produced by newsmen, and interpreted by newsmen. Though they call me Garroway's replacement, the concentration will not be on one dominant personality but on a corporate personality, [newsmen] Edwin Newman, Frank Blair and me. I think this is all to the good. I don't mean to knock Garroway, but the new format will have the look of a younger generation—the New Frontier, if you will. (Moritz, 1963, 83)

Chancellor's borrowing of John F. Kennedy's metaphor of the "new frontier," brought significant, although not all permanent, changes to "Today." NBC News, not the NBC Program Department, produced the program. The show moved to two hours of live, rather than prerecorded, broadcasting, from 7:00 A.M. to 9:00 A.M. EST, Monday through Friday. When events warranted, Chancellor covered breaking national and international stories at the scene rather than from the NBC studio. And Chancellor, unlike his predecessor, refused to do product commercials, arguing that he was not a salesman.

John Chancellor's effort to strike a golden mean between the demands of informative and entertainment programming played to mixed reviews. On the one hand, "Today" became regular viewing for public officials, especially for Washington, D.C., insiders. The chairman of the Federal Communications Commission, Newton Minow, who had labeled television a "vast wasteland," when asked to name any television programming that did not conform to that metaphor, immediately responded with Chancellor's "Today." On the other hand, informative programming was bought at the price of not being entertaining. One critic wrote that the show was "a rather somber affair" and watching was a "chore" (Bennetts, 1975, 503).

By 1962 John Chancellor recognized that he was a political reporter and commentator, not a performing communicator, and he departed from the show. In the ensuing period of more than three decades, the "Today" pendulum moved back and forth between news and entertainment. Some hosts were journalists (e.g., Frank Magee, John Hartz, and Tom Brokaw), and others came from the entertainment industry, including a former quiz show host, a so-so baseball catcher, and a sportscaster. By the 1990s, however, news and entertainment had merged. To be the host or cohost of "Today," no matter what one's professional background, carried sufficient celebrity to allow any incumbent to perform as a political commentator or communicator.

THE ANCHOR AS COMMENTATOR

When John Chancellor departed "Today," it was to work on special projects for NBC News. Among these were documentaries, including "A Country Called Europe" in 1963 for which he wrote the script and served as reporter. The program, a report on the Common Market, won critical acclaim from prestigious newspapers, most notably the *New York Times*. Basically, however, Chancellor had returned to his primary love, being a correspondent with the freedom to do commentary. As Chancellor practiced it, "commentary" was a version of "interpretive" reporting as advocated by such notable journalists as Marquis W. Childs (q.v.) and James "Scotty" Reston (q.v.), and the "elucidation" of meaning as practiced by Eric Sevareid (q.v.). "Commentary is different from opinion," Chancellor later explained. "You give the thought process you went through rather than the conclusion, and let people draw their own judgment. I don't think it comes through as editorializing. People have to give the news, we're all human, and that does come through" (Bennetts, 1975, 503).

As a reporter giving commentary, John Chancellor achieved fame, a fame that he wished had come from something else, at the 1964 Republican National Convention. That convention was contentious enough, what with the severe moral judgments liberal and conservative Republicans were leveling at one another from the rostrum. It was made more so, however, when President Dwight Eisenhower lashed out at "sensation-seeking columnists and commentators" (Frank, 1991, 221). The charge released a storm of indignities aimed at floor reporters, the press gallery, and anchor booths by delegates. During the ruckus, John Chancellor attempted to interview a delegate, only to be arrested by uniformed police officers for disrupting convention business. The entire episode of the officers, one on each of Chancellor's arms, forcing the correspondent from the floor was covered by television cameras. As he was led out, Chancellor continued to report, thus broadcasting his own arrest: "I formally say this is a disgrace," he protested. Then, with a touch of humor as he was forced out, he signed off, "This is John Chancellor, NBC News, somewhere in custody." A few minutes later, a convention official in tow, Chancellor returned to the convention floor. He resumed his interview, "As I was saying, . . ." (Campbell, 1976, 100).

In 1965, again with considerable reluctance and at the urging of NBC superiors, John Chancellor accepted an appointment as the first journalist to become director of the Voice of America (VOA). "It was involuntary—like being drafted a second time," Chancellor said later (Ryan, 1975, 504). "I took the job kicking and screaming. Two Presidents, Lyndon Johnson and NBC's [Robert Kintner] twisted my arm. I did it for two years on a nonpolitical basis and got out of it with my whole skin and reputation intact. I didn't have to shill" (Drew, 1974, 625).

VOA radio, which came into existence during World War II, broadcast twenty-four hours a day to Europe. Although at the time the VOA's mission was primarily to broadcast pro-Allied, anti-Nazi messages, even then there was disagreement over that mission. Some government authorities, most notably the director of the Office of War Information, Elmer Davis (q.v.), argued that the VOA should concentrate on providing newscasts and features that were factual and informative rather than, as his detractors insisted, serve as a propaganda agency. When the war ended and the Cold War began, the debate continued over the VOA's proper role. By the time of Lyndon Johnson's presidency, and the escalation of the Vietnam War, critics charged that the VOA was nothing more than a mouthpiece for the administration's policies.

Chancellor came down on the side of accurate, factual reporting at the VOA, including broadcast coverage of civil rights issues and conflicts within the United States over Johnson's Vietnam policy. He concurred with a view voiced by Edward R. Murrow (q.v.) during his tenure as head of the United States Information Agency (USIA). The VOA should be a "radio mirror" reflecting the considerable diversity of culture and opinion in America. In the manner of one striving for a golden mean between news commentary and news management, Chancellor's view was that "Selling America was a matter of being truthful. The persuasiveness of the commentaries stemmed from the credibility of the news" (Shulman, 1990, 198). As VOA director, Chancellor introduced new programming techniques to give VOA broadcasts a pointed, incisive, yet pleasantly cool rather than bombastic, propagandistic style. Looking back later on his VOA experience, Chancellor said he had "learned how the government works from the inside and how much attention it pays to the press" (Drew, 1974, 625). That lesson taught him, once back at NBC, to exploit the telephone as a conduit to news sources he otherwise had no contact with as a reporter, a technique perfected long before by political commentator James Reston.

Back at NBC News in 1967, Chancellor continued as he had before his departure. However, in 1970, Chet Huntley, coanchor with David Brinkley (q.v.) on NBC News' highly successful "Huntley-Brinkley Report," decided to retire. The Huntley-Brinkley duo had come into existence in 1956 as a successor to NBC's first nightly newscast, the "Camel News Caravan." Through the 1960s Huntley-Brinkley had easily outdistanced the competition at CBS and ABC in television ratings. With Huntley's departure the "one-horse race," as the executive producer of "Huntley-Brinkley," Reuven Frank, called it, could well become a two- or three-horse race (Goldberg & Goldberg, 1990, 33). Casting about for a means to cope with potential threats to his newscast, Frank gave it a new name, "NBC Nightly News." Then, in an experiment that failed, Frank split the anchoring chores among three newsmen: David Brinkley, John Chancellor, and Frank McGee. Coanchoring would be rotated, two anchors each night, across seven nights a week. "In retrospect, it was obviously stupid," wrote Frank in his memoirs (1991, 315).

In 1971 McGee departed the rotation to become host of the "Today" show: "Chancellor was best fitted to anchor alone by intellect and the universality of his curiosity and was unencumbered by Brinkley's [penchant] for the ridiculous or low boredom threshold, but he did not have the aspect of a star performer and would be a gamble," wrote Frank (1991, 316). Frank took the gamble.

Although John Chancellor relished the challenge of anchoring the "NBC Nightly News," it was not because he coveted the prestige and celebrity attached to the position. Indeed, throughout his eleven-year tenure in the position, Chancellor admitted to being embarrassed by the public attention (Bennetts, 1975). Rather, he enjoyed the latitude of combining straight political reporting with commentary that his position provided, both in his anchor position and on NBC radio three times per week. Moreover, he enjoyed, after a career of being on the road, the opportunity to remain at home (he was able to walk from his home to the NBC News studios). In 1958 Chancellor had married Barbara Upshaw. It was his second marriage; the first marriage to Constance Herbert had ended in divorce. In addition to a daughter from his first marriage, Mary Catherine, Chancellor had two younger children, Laura Campbell and Barnaby John, from his second. Being permanently based in New York City permitted him finally to get to know them all.

To the degree that it proved to be a long-term solution regarding who would anchor "NBC Nightly News," Reuven Frank's gamble was only partially successful. Throughout the 1970s, the "CBS Evening News with Walter Cronkite" dominated the ratings. NBC executives fretted about how to respond. The network president, Herbert Schlosser, admitted in 1976 that he respected an anchor who was "responsible," "experienced," and had "wisdom and depth"; however, "let's face it, what we're also looking for in an anchor man . . . are performance qualities" (Goldberg & Goldberg, 1990, 302). So the network, in 1976, paired Chancellor with David Brinkley. After a year and a half, no ratings boost came. Chancellor returned to being the sole anchor. There he remained until April 1982, when "Chancellor was squeezed out by a combination of [Tom] Brokaw and Roger [Mudd] (Goldberg & Goldberg, 1990, 339). Wrote Reuven Frank, "Chancellor's contract, which did not protect him from summary treatment, did ensure that he would continue on the program as a commentator—three or four times a week *on his own initiative*, with virtually no say from the editorial hierarchy of the program" (1991, 381). Chancellor exercised that initiative until his retirement from NBC after four decades of serving the network.

POLITICAL COMMENTARY AS REASSURANCE

Although he was not able to provide what NBC executives wanted—"What the bosses want are numbers," he said after leaving the anchor's job (Goldberg & Goldberg, 1990, 302)—he did establish a distinctive style of commentary, one that struck a golden mean between the dividing tensions in broadcast news. Unlike Walter Lippmann (q.v.) and Eric Sevareid, who directed philosophical commentaries to members of a ruling elite, or Paul Harvey (q.v.), whose bardic appeal is to populist politics, Chancellor assumed his audience was neither politically brilliant nor stupid, neither an anonymous "it" nor a conspiratorial "they."

Instead, for Chancellor, television viewers were merely ignorant members of a pluralist citizenry, an ignorance to be corrected by explaining the news and the thought processes for understanding it in straightforward, colloquial, didactic figures of speech. If that meant, for instance, in reporting the social and political crisis that was Three Mile Island in 1979 by comparing a nuclear power plant to a "big tea kettle," Chancellor did so (Nimmo & Combs, 1985, 76). In a similarly low-keyed fashion, John Chancellor commented on television pictures and interviews with American businessmen hiding in a hotel in Panama during the 1989 U.S. invasion to depose Manual Noriega: "They're watching American TV in those hotels, and they have people working for NBC and other networks reporting on TV that they were trapped in the hotel, presumably being watched by the people who have trapped them. . . . We live in a strange world" (Goldberg & Goldberg, 1990, 375).

As a result, perhaps of his years as a working reporter chasing police cars in Chicago and politicians across convention floors, Chancellor's analyses of politics were rarely, if ever, pontificatory like Eric Sevareid's (q.v.), preachy like

Bill Moyers' (q.v.), sensationalist like Drew Pearson's, or biting like H. L. Mencken's (q.v.). His golden mean was, to be sure, to sound an alarm if need be, be professorial in analysis when called upon, and be morally concerned when appropriate. But, more than any other quality in Chancellor's political commentary was the one of reaffirmation. No matter how bad politics may seem, he told Americans, it can still be tolerated with a proper leavening of wisdom and droll humor.

Probably no example illustrates Chancellor's distinctive political commentary as well as his 1974 broadcast pertaining to the resignation of President Richard Nixon in the wake of the Watergate coverup. "It was my job at NBC to come on when he finished," he later told the story. "While he was talking I kept thinking, 'What the hell am I going to say when he's done?' What could possibly be said at a time like that?" Finally, Nixon stopped speaking.

> And when the red light came on, I looked into the camera and said one word, with a sort of sigh of relief, "Well." I paused for a couple of seconds, and then, in a very business-like way, got on with the rest of the coverage. . . . It was the best thing I could have done. . . . Knowing when to shut up is sometimes as important as knowing when to talk. (Chancellor, 1983, 94)

John Chancellor was a rare commentator who let silence teach his political lesson.

REFERENCES

Selected Works by John Chancellor

Peril and Promise: A Commentary on America. New York: Harper and Row, 1990.
The News Business. With W. R. Mears. New York: Harper and Row, 1983. Harper/Collins ed., 1995.

Selected Critical Works about John Chancellor

Bennetts, L. "John Chancellor: The Studious Uncle Bringing Us News." *Biography News* 2 (June 1975): 503. Reprinted from Philadelphia *Bulletin*, May 11, 1975.

Drew, M. H. "Ambulatory Anchorman." *Biography News* 1 (June 1974): 625. Reprinted from Milwaukee *Journal*, April 28, 1974.

Lichtenstein, N., ed. "Chancellor, John W(illiam)." In *Political Profiles: The Johnson Years*, 101. New York: Facts on File, 1976.

Moritz, C., ed. "Chancellor, John (William)." In *Current Biography Yearbook 1962*, 81–83. New York: H. W. Wilson, 1963.

"Portrait: John Chancellor." *Time*, July 14, 1961, 72–73.

Ryan, B. H. "John Chancellor: NBC's Chancellor One Cool Guy in Red-Hot Profession." *Biography News* 2 (May/June 1975): 504. Reprinted from Denver *Post*, April 27, 1975.

Selected General Works

Barnouw, E. *The Image Empire*. New York: Oxford University Press, 1970.

Campbell, R. *The Golden Years of Broadcasting*. New York: Charles Scribner's Sons, 1976.

Frank, R. *Out of Thin Air*. New York: Simon and Schuster, 1991.

Goldberg, R., and G. J. Goldberg. *Anchors*. New York: Birch Lane Press, 1990.

Lewis, T. *Empire of the Air*. New York: Harper/Collins, 1993.

Nimmo, D., and J. E. Combs. *Nightly Horrors: Crisis Coverage in Television Network News*. Knoxville: University of Tennessee Press, 1985.

Rothe, A. ed. "Garroway, Dave." In *Current Biography Yearbook* 13 (May 1952): 18–20.

Shulman, H. C. *The Voice of America*. Madison: University of Wisconsin Press, 1990.

Wicker, T. *On Press*. New York: Viking Press, 1978.

MARQUIS W. (WILLIAM) CHILDS

(March 17, 1903–June 30, 1990)

Political Commentary and Interpretive Reporting

On February 10, 1950, a relatively unknown junior member of the U.S. Senate from Wisconsin announced in a minor preliminary speech to the featured speaker's address at a Lincoln Day fund-raising dinner in Wheeling, West Virginia, that the junior senator possessed a list of 205 officials in the U.S. Department of State who were Communists actively engaged in shaping American foreign policy. Although the featured speaker's remarks went largely unreported, the junior senator's charge electrified the press. As weeks passed the senator's count of alleged State Department Communists fluctuated from news briefing to news briefing—sometimes eighty-one, sometimes sixty-one, sometimes fifty-seven. Still, "if Senator Joseph McCarthy of Wisconsin said that there were over one hundred card-carrying Communists in the State Department, out it would go on the wires regardless of whether or not what the Senator said was true" (Reston, 1967, 16).

As a result of press coverage, McCarthy emerged from obscurity to become a political force. Eventually, the senator spent his force, came under political and press scrutiny, received censure from his senatorial colleagues, and died a defeated man. Throughout the rise and fall of McCarthyism, a growing number of journalists engaged in considerable hand-wringing. How, they asked themselves, could they have been so readily manipulated as to aid and abet a politician in constructing a massive edifice of untruths? (Bayley, 1981).

Ironically enough, one of their own members of the Fourth Estate had already provided an answer in an address to a small audience at the University of Oregon weeks before Senator McCarthy gave his speech at Wheeling, West Virginia. However, unlike McCarthy's sensational charges, Marquis Child's careful analysis of the state of American journalism, voiced in the fourth annual Eric Allen Memorial Lecture, captured no headlines, stirred no emotional interest. Months later it appeared as an article in a journal read by mostly "stuffy" academics, the *Journalism Quarterly* (Childs, 1950). Yet, Child's analysis capsulized a view of the reporter's role that has had far more impact on the development of political communication and commentary in the twentieth century than all of Joseph McCarthy's not-so-subtle news manipulation ever did.

THE INTERPRETIVE POLITICAL REPORTER

"I was seventeen," wrote Marquis Childs, "when I first discovered the power of the printed word" (*Witness to Power*, 1975, 1). The event occurred at a county fair a short distance from Clinton, Iowa, a Mississippi River town where Childs had been born on March 17, 1903. A barnstorming pilot was selling adventurous souls a ride for $5 each. Childs was at the fair with his father, lawyer William Henry Childs, who was campaigning for county attorney. Mark Childs boarded the aircraft carrying a bundle of handbills advertising his father's candidacy. While the plane circled the fairgrounds, Mark scattered the leaflets from the open cockpit to the amazement of his father William and mother Lilian Melissa (Marquis) Childs. William won the election.

Whether that was the formative influence in Marquis Child's later becoming a political correspondent, he never ventured to say. But growing up in the Midwestern part of America as an heir to forbearers who, until his father, had been farmers for generations, did shape Child's attitude toward politics: "As an outlander . . . I have a deep suspicion of big government and big business. I have never been able to see how we could have a democracy if all the orders came from a few men in one city on the Eastern seaboard, whether that city was Washington or New York" (*I Write from Washington*, 1942b, 9).

After leaving Clinton, Marquis Childs attended the University of Wisconsin and graduated with his B.A. in 1923. He then worked for the United Press (UP) in several cities in the Midwest, including Chicago. Although Walter Lippmann (q.v.) published *Public Opinion* a year before Childs' college graduation, it would be a long period before Lippmann's argument, namely, that the press should deliver audiences more than stereotyped bulletins of reality, influenced newsgathering. United Press, like other wire services and news agencies, was wed to an early version of objective reporting emphasizing the who, what, when, where, and how of events, but largely to the exclusion of the why. It was that "why" that would later set Marquis Childs' brand of reporting apart from what he practiced during his early days with UP.

Childs interrupted his reporting career to return to college at the University of Iowa. There he taught English composition and met his first wife, Lue Prentiss, whom he married in 1925, the year after he received his M.A. (Lue Childs, the mother of Childs' two children, died in 1968; a year later, Childs married Jane Neyland McBain who survived his death on June 30, 1990). Childs rejoined United Press in New York where he was shifted, in typical wire service routine, from one assignment to another, never staying with one sufficiently long to develop expertise in any given area. However, in 1926, Childs joined the Saint Louis *Post-Dispatch* as a feature writer specializing in what peers derided as "cornfield murders" and weird happenings—including a story about a baby in Tennessee allegedly born with a tail. Childs went from those features to political reporting, literally "by the back door" when he "managed to insinuate" himself into the bedroom of Louisiana Governor Huey Long in the "new executive mansion in Baton Rouge, where he was holding court as a monarch in cornpone style" (Childs, 1975, 2). Childs' account of the antics of the governor was duly noted, and applauded, by his newspaper superiors.

After four years with the *Post-Dispatch*, Childs took a leave of absence to

attend a housing exposition in Sweden. That and subsequent visits resulted in
his well-received book, *Sweden: The Middle Way* (1936), which provoked the
administration of President Franklin Roosevelt to send a special commission to
Sweden to explore the nature of the Swedish cooperative movement as an alternative to fascist and communist doctrines sweeping other parts of Europe.
After Childs' return from another visit to Sweden in 1934, the managing editor
of the *Post-Dispatch* summoned the young reporter ostensibly, hoped Childs, to
appoint him the newspaper's movie critic. But the editor had a different thought,
one that was the turning point in Childs' career: "Three weeks later I was on
my way to Washington as the third man in the small bureau the *Post-Dispatch*
then maintained. I could hardly have been happier. It was what I scarcely hoped
for" (1975, 4). For it was as a Washington correspondent for the *Post-Dispatch*
(his home throughout the remainder of his journalistic career), that Childs developed a sense of interpretive versus objective reporting:

> To my way of thinking the *Post-Dispatch* is about the best newspaper you can
> work for. Few if any prejudices are superimposed from the top. And you have
> latitude to move around, to explore on your own initiative, and to write what
> you see and hear. That is rare. (Childs, 1942b, 9)

For the *Post-Dispatch*, Marquis Childs, using his skill at "observation knowledge" gained largely from the perspective of the nation's capital, was a "witness
to power" in the New Deal, World War II, the postwar reconstruction, the
nuclear age, the McCarthy era, and every presidential administration from FDR's
through Richard Nixon's (retiring, coincidentally, in 1974, the same year that
Nixon, who placed Childs on the infamous White House "Black List," resigned
the presidency). Beginning in 1944, Childs started a syndicated column, "Washington Calling," which appeared in the *Washington Post* and more than 200
other newspapers across the nation. In the golden eras of radio and television,
Childs appeared on "Meet the Press" and "Who Said That" (see Martha
Roundtree and Lawrence E. Spivak). Childs also was host of his own discussion
forum, "Washington Spotlight," in the early 1970s. In 1969 Marquis Childs
won a Pulitzer Prize for his political analysis and commentary.

Childs did not restrict his reporting solely to politics in the national capital.
In addition to writing from and about Sweden, Childs was a war correspondent
during the Spanish Civil War and covered the siege of Madrid and Valencia.
He also wrote a series of articles from Mexico that resulted in a U.S. Senate
investigation of oil expropriation in Mexico, a denunciation on the U.S. Senate
floor of Childs by Pennsylvania senator Joseph Guffey, a Childs' suit of
$100,000 against Guffey when the senator made the same remarks off the Senate
floor, and a public apology from the senator which resulted in the suit's being
dropped. In 1943, during World War II, Marquis Childs made a three-month
tour of European battlefronts. After the war, Childs interviewed such world

leaders as India's Pandit Nehru, China's Zhou Enlai, Germany's Konrad Adenauer, and Britain's Anthony Eden.

Marquis Childs also served, albeit indirectly, as both campaign and war propagandist. Unlike other notable twentieth-century political commentators—George Creel (q.v.), Raymond Moley (q.v.), or Elmer Davis (q.v.)—Childs was not drawn into the web of federal bureaucracy as a result of his propaganda experience. During Franklin Roosevelt's 1936 campaign for reelection, Childs traveled over 15,000 miles covering the president. Childs' *They Hate Roosevelt* (1936), originally written as a magazine article, became a pamphlet distributed by the president's campaign organization. In 1942 Childs contributed *This Is Your War* to the U.S. effort during World War II, a slim book that explained to Americans the likely effects of war on their lives, the sacrifices they would be asked to make, and the contributions they could make as volunteers, guardians against waste, and morale builders. And, to make certain that his writing career left little time for leisure, Marquis Childs also published four political novels.

After Childs' retirement in 1974 he looked back on the years that had intervened between his discovery of the power of the printed word at the Clinton County Fair in 1920 and the unfolding of his career. "The press," he wrote, "plays a part in the brokerage of power." Theoretically, reporters and commentators "are in the bleachers keeping an objective eye on the field, but, impelled by a sense of righteousness or merely by the love of the game, they become participants" (1975, 1). But what kind of participants? If not "objective," then what role do reporters play? Childs called it "interpretive," a role shared by newspaper journalists like himself and such others as Arthur Krock (q.v.) or James "Scotty" Reston (q.v.); radio commentators such as Elmer Davis, Edward R. Murrow (q.v.), and Eric Sevareid (q.v.); and columnists such as Walter Lippmann.

Marquis Childs characterized the interpretive reporter as "one who tries sincerely and honestly to give not merely the news but the meaning of the news as he sees it"; that is what, he said, "I conceive to be my role" (1950, 134–35):

> The interpretive reporter expands the horizons of the news. He explains, he amplifies, he clarifies. Often he does this within a framework of opinion, trying honestly to make the reader understand where opinion ends and interpretation and exposition begin. In my opinion the interpretive reporter is a phenomenon too little understood and explored.

In the last decade of the twentieth century, it might seem that every journalist is an interpretive reporter, that Childs' midcentury insights no longer remain a contribution to political communication and commentary. That presumption is in error: what passes for interpretation at the century's close is *not* what Childs advocated.

Childs recognized that in politics the shelf life of a political story is frequently brief. For every Watergate there are numerous short-lived scoops; as Childs knew, headlines burst forth overnight, sensation follows sensation. Frequently the underlying facts do not bear out the sensational claims made in journalistic accounts. For example, during Childs' tenure in Washington, a U.S. Air Force officer claimed to have expedited lend lease shipments to the Soviet Union, an outrageous act in light of the growing tensions during the Cold War. The officer claimed that former presidential aide Harry Hopkins and former vice president Henry Wallace had been behind the clandestine aid to Russia. Fulton Lewis, Jr. (q.v.) broke the story. It proved to be without foundation. Just as members of the press would later fret over their reporting of Joseph McCarthy's fabrications regarding dozens of Communists in the State Department, they agonized over (a) how "irresponsible" journalists could report such news and (b) the growing disillusion of Americans with press and radio journalists who help fuel a false sensation.

For Childs the problem resided in contemporary, contradictory conventions of the journalistic craft. On the one hand, sensationalist seeking reporters and commentators reported groundless charges in hopes of attracting an audience; on the other hand, skeptical reporters did not probe, amplify, and clarify for fear of not being "objective." There are dangerous consequences in both tendencies. Sensational reporting has diminishing returns: "as the bubble of sensation is blown larger and larger, it becomes more and more incredible and less likely to be accepted" by the public. As practiced in postwar America, objective reporting was too often a transmission of half-truths and untruths.

Childs set down guidelines for how interpretive reporters could check the dangers inherent in sensational and objective reporting tendencies. In keeping with his characterization of interpretation, Childs argued that the interpretive reporter expands the "horizons" or "peripheries" of the news. This occurs in two ways. First, one does not take at face value the official government release, politician's handout, prepared statement, or orchestrated response in a press conference. This does not mean that one should cynically reject all news releases as, by definition, untrue. It means instead that one must meticulously check and recheck in minute detail *what is claimed* in the handout, prepared statement, or politician's response and, frequently more important, *what is not claimed*. To do this a reporter must possess substantive background knowledge about news topics and skills for acquiring relevant information, not simply a bag of clever verbal and nonverbal tropes for reporting: "The interpretive reporter must be able to judge the value of the information and to use it in the best way to inform the reader" (Childs, 1950, 137). Note that Childs' "value" is not sensational appeal; "inform" is not to titillate or entertain the reader.

Second, peripheral expansion of the news places on the interpretive reporter the obligation to present differing points of view "which might be otherwise excluded" (1950, 137). Childs does not simply trot out the shopworn "there are two sides to every story." His extension is greater: there are *many* sides to any story. Conventional reporting of what Childs called the "press associations" (i.e., wire services) typically uncovers the pro and con; objective reporting does not detect the subtle variation and interplay of vested interests not captured by Republican versus Democrat, conservative versus liberal, state versus local, and national versus international. Teasing out subtle variations and interplays of political interests, again, demands substantive background knowledge well beyond the superficial acquaintance afforded the correspondent—or staff member in the case of contemporary television tabloid journalism—who rushes from sensation to sensation searching for sound bites and visual packages.

Childs did not, as did many contemporary critics of journalistic objectivity, attack the convention as useless, only as misapplied and incomplete. For example, British commentator Auberon Waugh has written, "It is a grand old tradition of American newspapers—led by the *New York Times*, the most boring and uninformative newspaper in the world—that nothing should be printed until it has been checked out or confirmed by an official source. This is what they call their ethics" (1995). Childs would not concur with Waugh's assessment; rather cross-checking with and without official sources should be the accepted practice. If sufficiently comprehensive, that practice need not, indeed will not, result in boring reporting.

For Childs interpretive reporting rests on a "framework of opinion." Opinion, however, does not mean a doctrinal overlay, or spin, for each story. Rather, Childs is concerned with the interpretive reporters' "privilege of independence of opinion" (Childs, 1950, 138). This implies only partially the right to express one's opinion—with the obligation to label it as such. It also implies a purpose behind that expression, namely, to express opinion to the degree that doing so assists a citizen to formulate a judgment of the correspondent's accuracy in reporting and soundness in drawing conclusions. The interpretive reporter expresses opinions not for expressive purposes, and not solely for judgmental ones, but to inform. And, there is a final implication in the phrase, "privilege of independence of opinion." The interpretive reporter's "independence" includes a sufficient maturity of judgment to prevent the correspondent from becoming a captive of her or his own "framework of opinion." This demands continuous, self-conscious appraisal of each reporter's views, not slavish, conditioned acceptance of any doctrine. By so doing, the interpretive reporter earns the trust of editors and contributes to a "mature editor-reporter relationship" essential to responsible communication.

THE INTERPRETIVE OR CYNICAL POLITICAL REPORTER?

The fact that Marquis Childs was arguing a role for interpretive reporting before McCarthyism was born indicates that the objective versus interpretive journalism debate (Lindstrom, 1953; Markel, 1953) at midcentury predated the senator's exploitation of the news media. Yet, the McCarthy experience did fuel a growing disillusion with objective reporting: "For decades the American press has worshipped the god of objectivity," wrote Ronald May in the *New Republic*. "This seemed to keep voters informed," at least until it became clear that "the big lie" by objective standards was simply "reported straight" (1953, 10–12). Two generations after McCarthyism, journalists were still lamenting their craft's inability to deal with the senator's daily doses of false sensationalism. In 1987 David Broder, a syndicated columnist of the *Washington Post*, called McCarthyism a time when journalists were "personally and professionally debauched by the experience" (1987, 137) . In 1991 James Reston wrote, "No journalistic memoir of my day in Washington would be complete without an attempt to explain, however painful, the role of the press during McCarthy's anticommunist crusade" (1991, 214).

What was too easily ignored at midcentury in the objective versus interpretive controversy, and remains obscure at the century's end, is that interpretive reporting is not a substitute for objective reporting; it is the *essential ingredient* in objective reporting. The skeletal who, what, where, when, and how possess no objective being beyond bare bones until fleshed out with the "why." Left to flesh out "why" the Soviet Union had become a coequal power with the United States in the postwar world, "why" the Republic of China had become the People's Republic, or "why" America had not become the postwar utopia that victory promised, Joseph McCarthy put the red meat of communist conspiracy on the skeletal bones. In the absence of a journalistic rendering, in the dictionary sense of "to melt down [fat] by heating," McCarthy's meat poisoned the nation.

The challenge that Marquis Childs issued his colleagues was to become responsible, disciplined interpreters. Such reporting required rigor—the rigor imposed by substantive expertise, not superficial acquaintance, in researching politicians' sins of omission as well as commission; the rigor imposed by a catholic understanding that there are many, not just two, sides to every story; and the rigor imposed by a brutal honesty not only with one's audience but with one's editor and one's self in exercising the privilege of independent judgment as a correspondent. As professional political communication reaches the century's end, Childs' challenge no longer remains such; it is a utopian dream. For objective reporters have not been fortified with the rigor of Childs' interpretive correspondents; instead, they have been replaced by cynical reporters (Starobin, 1995), adversaries not only of politicians but of citizens' needs to know rather than be entertained (Olson, 1994).

In extending the horizons of news, Marquis Childs charged interpretive reporters with the task of going beyond both the words and actions of politicians. The interpreter judges the face "value of information to use it in the best way to inform his reader" (Childs, 1950, 137). The cynical reporter makes no such judgment—by definition the cynic has "a prejudice against the face-value explanation bordering on disbelief, accompanied by a ready willingness to ascribe base motives" (Starobin, 1995, 26). Whereas the difference between the objective and interpretive reporter, at its best, was one of degree, that between the interpretive and cynical reporter is one of *kind*.

If sensational and objective reporting respectively jeopardized citizens' civic knowledge at midcentury, so too does contemporary cynical reporting. A cynic's penchant for dismissing all political utterances as self-serving gimmicks may blind reporters to what is actually happening rather than reveal politicians' alleged hidden agendas. For example, in 1994, reporters quick to dismiss the Republicans' "Contract with America" as merely a run-of-the-mill campaign ploy, cloaked from news coverage of the 1994 elections a story of substantial consequence—the radical overhaul of government seriously proposed and, subsequently, imposed. Moreover, cynical reporters, always reluctant to take seriously what politicians themselves claim to take seriously, either as office holders or aspiring officials, too eagerly sensationalize instances when politicians' deeds fall short of words. For instance, there is a "knee-jerk media assumption that presidents and other politicians do not keep their promises" (Starobin, 1995, 27). Yet, politicians (both Democratic president Bill Clinton and the Republican-controlled 104th Congress being recent cases in point) often do keep their promises. That their efforts are often thwarted by other political interests trying to keep their own promises is more a mark of ineffectiveness than insincerity.

The blithe, jaded contempt for politics and politicians that underlies the cynical reporter's approach is a far cry from the interpretive reporter's rigorous probing, amplification, and clarification of politics. If Childs' interpreter accepts that "politics is politics, to be valued as itself," the contemporary cynic by contrast reduces politics to a "troublesome obstacle" that stands in the way of scoundrels achieving selfish goals (Crick, 1962, 12). There is nothing to probe, amplify, or clarify because, for the cynical reporter, politics itself is nothing.

Marquis Childs' career exemplified the fulfillment of the tasks and the standards that he set out for interpretive reporting. He did so in the belief that, as he said, "This kind of independent and responsible reporting can bring to the American people a clearer, sharper, and more intelligent understanding" (1950, 140). The interpretive reporter's replacement, the cynical, by contrast "has not served the cause of journalism well"; instead, it is "a lazy substitute for curiosity" that in its worst form "can damage readers and viewers and thus, democracy" (Starobin, 1995, 31).

Although he did not shape actions among the powerful who often confided their views to him in interviews, in the title of his partially autobiographical work, he was a "witness" (1975); he certainly had their ear. Perhaps therein resides the fundamental difference between Childs, the interpretive reporter of the mid-twentieth century, and the cynical reporters who had replaced him by the century's end. Bertrand Russell's generalization is apt for the latter: "Cynicism such as one finds very frequently amongst the most highly educated young men and women of the West results from the combination of comfort with powerlessness" (1930, 149).

REFERENCES

Selected Works by Marquis Childs

Sweden: The Middle Way. New Haven, CT: Yale University Press, 1936. Original publication date, 1936; revised and enlarged, 1947.

They Hate Roosevelt! New York: Harper and Brothers, 1936.

This Is Democracy: Collective Bargaining in Scandinavia. With W. T. Stone. New Haven, CT: Yale University Press, 1938.

Towards a Dynamic America: The Challenge of a Changing World. New York: The Foreign Policy Association, 1941.

This Is Your War. Boston: Little, Brown, 1942a.

I Write from Washington. New York: Harper and Brothers, 1942b.

"The Interpretive Reporter's Role in a Troubled World." *Journalism Quarterly* 27 (Spring 1950): 134–40.

The Farmer Takes a Hand: The Electrical Power Revolution in Rural America. Garden City, NY: Doubleday, 1952.

Ethics in a Business Society. With D. Cater. New York: Harper, 1954.

The Ragged Edge: Diary of a Crisis. Garden City, NY: Doubleday, 1955.

Eisenhower, Captive Hero: A Critical Study of the General and the President. New York: Harcourt Brace, 1958.

Walter Lippmann and His Times. Edited with J. Reston. New York: Harcourt, 1959.

Witness to Power. New York: McGraw-Hill, 1975.

Sweden: The Middle Way on Trial. New Haven, CT: Yale University Press, 1980.

Selected Critical Works about Marquis Childs

Andrews, D., ed. "Marquis Childs." In *The Annual Obituary 1990*, 348–49. Chicago: St. James Press, 1991.

Block, M., ed. "Childs, Marquis W(illiam)." In *Current Biography, 1943.* 126–28. New York: H. W. Wilson, 1944.

"Childs, Marquis." In *Celebrity Register*, 103. New York: Simon and Schuster, 1973.

Kunitz, S. J., ed. "Childs, Marquis William." In *Twentieth Century Authors First Supplement*, 196. New York: H. W. Wilson, 1955.

Riley, S. G., "Childs, Marquis William." In *Biographical Dictionary of American Newspaper Columnists*, 57–58. Westport, CT: Greenwood Press, 1995.

Selected General Works

Bayley, F. R. *Joe McCarthy and the Press.* Madison: University of Wisconsin Press, 1981.

Broder, D. *Behind the Front Page.* New York: Touchstone Books, 1987.

Cater, D. *The Fourth Branch of Government.* Boston: Houghton Mifflin, 1959.

Crick, B. *In Defense of Politics.* Chicago: University of Chicago Press, 1962.

Lindstrom, C. "By What Right Do We Interpret or Explain?" *ASNE Bulletin*, January 1, 1953, 2–3.

Markel, L. "The Case for 'Interpretation.' " *ASNE Bulletin*, April 1, 1953, 1–2.

May, R. "Is the Press Unfair to McCarthy?" *New Republic*, April 20, 1953, 10–12.

Nimmo, D. *Newsgathering in Washington.* New York: Atherton Press, 1964.

Olson, K. M. "Exploiting the Tension between the News Media's 'Objective' and Adversarial Roles: The Imbalance Attack and Its Use of the Implied Audience." *Communication Quarterly* 42 (Winter 1994): 36–56.

Persico, J. E. *Edward R. Murrow: An American Original.* New York: Dell, 1988.

Phillips, E. B. "Approaches to Objectivity: Journalistic versus Social Science Perspectives." In *Strategies for Communication Research*, edited by P. Hirsch and P. Miller, 63–77. Beverly Hills, CA: Sage, 1977.

Reston, J. *The Artillery of the Press.* New York: Harper and Row, 1967.

———. *Deadline: A Memoir.* New York: Random House, 1991.

Russell, B. *The Conquest of Happiness.* New York: Liveright, 1930.

Starobin, P. "A Generation of Vipers: Journalists and the New Cynicism." *Columbia Journalism Review* 33 (March/April 1995): 25–32.

Waugh, A. "Why Nobody Cares." *The Weekly Telegraph* (London, England), November 8, 1995, 35.

Zelizer, B. "Journalists as Interpretive Communities." *Critical Studies in Mass Communication* 10 (1993): 219–37.

(AVRAM) NOAM CHOMSKY

(December 7, 1928–   )

Propaganda Analysis and Analysis as Propaganda

In the 1980s political scientists took note of a "linguistic turn" that serious analyses of government and public affairs appeared to be taking. A rash of scholarly approaches—rhetorical, interpretive, structural, poststructural, deconstructionist, and postmodernist—were reorienting the way in which specialists and analysts conceived of the relationship between language and politics (Combs & Nimmo, 1993). Many scholars began "to confront the epistemological implication that language is neither a mirror of nature nor a potentially perfectible tool of representation and analysis." Instead, "language—what we *do* with language—is *implicated* in action." Language "is not merely a channel or medium for carrying out thought and action; it also constitutes the form of consciousness that identifies interests, objects of study, choices, and appraisals" (Corcoran, 1990, 67; emphasis in original).

The linguistic turn in political analysis actually originated at least a half-century earlier. The British political commentator, George Orwell, had remarked on the threats to the politics of an open society posed by the decline in the English language: As "the decline of a language must ultimately have political and social causes," so too does English, as it "becomes ugly and inaccurate," the "slovenliness of our language makes it easier for us to have foolish thoughts" (1946, 163). The dangers of sloppy language were all the greater, thought Orwell, because they were so charmingly seductive. As he put the point in the final passage of an untitled poem, he dreamed he dwelled in marble halls, and awakened to find it true that he was not born for the age in which he lived, then asked,

Was Smith? Was Jones? Were You?

(1947, 318)

From the mid-1960s, Noam Chomsky, Ferrari Ward Professor of Modern Languages and Linguistics at Massachusetts Institute of Technology, has fashioned twin careers as a scholar of language and as a scholar of politics. Although he regards his dual careers as parallel rather than overlapping, his active role as a political commentator for more than three decades has made him a trendsetter for a loyal band of followers (see, for example, issues of the quarterly publication *Propaganda Review*) who employ *communication analysis* as a prelude to *political advocacy*. Whereas another college professor in the 1920s, John Dewey (q.v.), derived a model of public opinion as a defense against what he regarded as deceptive news accounts of politics, Noam Chomsky a half-century later fashioned a propaganda model to accomplish the same goal. Whether Chomsky's model will be more enduring than Dewey's is problematic; however, like Dewey he is a key aspect of the heritage of political commentary in the twentieth century.

THE LINGUISTIC CAREER

Noam Chomsky's father, William, came to the United States from Czarist-ruled Eastern Europe in 1913 for the expressed purpose of avoiding conscription into the Russian army. William was a member of a Jewish-Zionist culture that prized traditional teachings over books and reading. Yet, the elder Chomsky taught himself Russian and Hebrew and became a noted scholar of Hebrew; he was the author of an edition of a medieval Hebrew grammar, a work that ten-year-old Noam proofread; it was Noam's first encounter with the complexities of grammar. William's wife, Elsie Simonofsky, had come to America from Lithuania when she was a year old. The couple settled in Philadelphia, Pennsylvania, and it was there that Avram Noam Chomsky was born on December 7, 1928, barely a year before the United States entered the Great Depression and thirteen years before the nation's entry into World War II.

Noam Chomsky's earliest memories were of the disastrous economic times—rag peddlers, picket lines, and terrorist police strikebreaking tactics. By the time he was a teenager, he was already familiar with the socialist-anarchist leanings of the Jewish intellectual community in New York City through his aunts and uncles. Later Noam Chomsky claimed that much of his political education came at one uncle's newsstand; it was the setting for lively round-the-clock intellectual discussions. By his own admission, Chomsky recalls that his basic political views, although becoming more sophisticated, did not change after age twelve: "I can't really say how I came to be influenced by anarchist ideas; I can't remember a time when I was not so influenced" (Chomsky, 1988b, 133).

In spite of growing up in the depression era, Noam Chomsky's youthful educational opportunities were rewarding. For ten years, from the ages of two to twelve, he attended an experimental progressive school that followed many of John Dewey's tenets: the Oak Lane Country Day School. The school took for granted that every student was outstanding; hence, it eschewed rankings and tracking of students, promoted individual creativity, and encouraged students to focus on what interested them. A few weeks before his tenth birthday, Chomsky displayed an interest in politics; he published an editorial in the school news-paper about the fall of Barcelona during the Spanish Civil War. By compari-son, his subsequent days at Central High School in Philadelphia did little to pique his intellectual or political curiosity. He was skeptical of the war fever surrounding World War II, badly shaken by the use of an atomic bomb on Hi-roshima, opposed to the postwar notion of a Jewish state in Palestine, and supportive of Arab-Jewish cooperation. He even considered emigrating to a life in an Israeli kibbutz in order to work on behalf of such cooperation.

In 1945 Noam Chomsky enrolled at the University of Pennsylvania. Although in the next ten years he received a B.A. (1949), M.A. (1951), and Ph.D. (1955) from the University of Pennsylvania, the chronology typical of many a college professor's resumé was anything but conventional in the case of Chomsky's education. Chomsky matriculated to the university with enthusiasm and high expectations about the intellectual worlds that might unfold. Within two years, the enthusiasm was dead, the expectations dashed. Chomsky entered college with no particular career in mind but with an interest in numerous subjects. Yet, each time he took a course in a particular subject the stifling classwork killed the interest.

Chomsky gave serious consideration to becoming a college dropout to pursue his political interests in Arab-Jewish cooperation. Yet, it was through those interests that Chomsky met Zellig Harris, a professor of modern linguistics who also supported the cause of Arab-Jewish cooperation. Chomsky enrolled in Harris' courses and, just as he had for his father, proofread Harris' book-length treatise of methods in structural linguistics. Unlike his experience with other subjects and courses, Chomsky's interest in linguistics intensified through his association with Harris: "So the problem in my case was not how the linguist became a radical, but rather the opposite. It was how the radical student became the linguist sort of by accident" (Chomsky, 1988b, 167).

After two years at Pennsylvania, Chomsky ceased taking courses in a formal manner. His "classes" were all-day and late evening sessions in Harris' apartment or in a local restaurant. Although Chomsky had almost no contact with the university, he nonetheless received his B.A. in 1949, the year he married Carol Doris Schatz. He then served as an assistant instructor in linguistics in 1950 and adapted an undergraduate thesis as the basis for his master's thesis on the morphophonemics of modern Hebrew. From 1951 to 1955 Chomsky was a Junior Fellow of the Society of Fellows at Harvard University. In 1955 he met the technical requirements for his Ph.D. at the University of Pennsylvania by submitting for his dissertation a chapter of a book he was writing, later published as *The Logical Structure of Linguistic Theory* (1975).

In 1955, when Chomsky petitioned the University of Pennsylvania for his Ph.D. degree, it had been four years since he had had any contact with the school. His research had been conducted at Harvard, punctuated in 1953 with a trip to Europe. He wanted to reestablish his contact with Pennsylvania to delay his being drafted into the military for the Korean War. As it turned out, he had no draft to fear. His local draft board took his name, "Avram Noam," to be a misspelling of a woman's name. Hence, a clerk crossed out the entry on his birth certificate and substituted "Arvane Naomi" (Rai, 1995).

Given his unconventional professional training, Noam Chomsky's claim to be taken seriously by linguists at first fell on deaf ears. Although he had published his first journal article in 1953 and had completed the first version of *The Logical*

Structure of Linguistic Theory, the article was only a first step toward a career, and the book would await publication for two decades. However, with the assistance of a member of the faculty at the Massachusetts Institute of Technology, Chomsky received an MIT appointment—conducting research in an electronics laboratory. He persisted in his linguistic research and, in 1957, published *Syntactic Structures*. Positive reviews won Chomsky acclaim and, while working with his colleagues, he developed a graduate program at MIT that reoriented the field of linguistics in major ways.

Frequently, observers of Noam Chomsky's work as a political commentator since the mid-1960s have remarked upon the "duality" between his scholarly work as a linguist and his activist pronouncements as a popular lecturer and writer. A few speak of the "Chomsky problem," or the task of reconciling Chomsky's abstract and highly technical modeling of language phenomena, accessible only to experts in the field, with his political analyses which, although maddeningly difficult to follow at times, could as easily be undertaken by any serious, persistent, informed citizen. Since he sees the two undertakings as separate, he denies any problem exists (Rai, 1995, 2–6). Be that as it may, no consideration of Chomsky's contribution to twentieth-century political commentary can ignore altogether his linguistic work, no matter how simplified the summary.

One of the most controversial problems facing linguists has been both methodological and epistemological. It concerns whether the human language facility is innate or acquired, a problem of nature or nurture. Cartesian theories argue for innate language capacities, structures, and laws; Lockian based views subscribe to the notion of the natural mind as a blank tablet on which human experience inscribes all knowledge, including language. Chomsky's work on language broke with the prevailing either-or assumptions about language acquisition. He maintained that humans are born with a genetically determined capacity to acquire language—an innate mechanism to acquire language. Hence, language is indeed learned in response to experience, but learning itself is made possible because of innate language competence. The mechanism consists of "an underlying structure of 'linguistic competence' generically inherent in human intelligence and physiology enabling an individual to acquire and use language" (Corcoran, 1990, 57).

Linguistic competence comprises the innate capacities which allow humans to master the underlying rules, or grammar, of language (Eagleton, 1983). In *Syntactic Structures* (1957), Chomsky outlined a system of generative, transformational grammar. The sounds and words of a sentence constitute the "surface" structures of grammar; the meaning of a sentence, however, resides in the "deep" structures of grammar. The meaning in deep structure is converted by a transformation, following any of an ordered set of rules, to a surface structure. Conversely, confronted with a surface of sounds and words, an analyst might dig beneath it to uncover deep layers of meaning that have been transformed through generative principles.

Viewed in this light, *if* an analyst were inclined to apply Chomsky's notions of language competence and generative grammar to political analysis, there is an obvious, albeit perhaps superficial, lesson to be drawn: any literate citizen, regardless of professional training or background in politics, possesses the political competence to apply the age-old maxim that "things are not always as they seem" (Combs & Nimmo, 1993, 217–20). It pays to probe political messages for deeper meanings not apparent on the surface, even searching for meanings at variance with surface messages. In fact, Chomsky advocates such an application of a "common sense" comparison of political facts as they are with the manner in which communication presents them: "With a little industry and application, anyone willing to extricate himself from the system of shared ideology and propaganda will readily see through the modes of distortion developed by substantial segments of the intelligentsia. Everybody is capable of doing this" (Chomsky, 1979, 4). Simple as it may seem, this is Chomsky's means for arming citizens to protect themselves against political propaganda.

THE PROPAGANDA MODEL

Whether language competence is natural or nurtured remains controversial among scholars. However, the linguistic turn in political communication forged a consensus on another matter: language itself is decidedly *not* neutral. Critic Kenneth Burke argued (1969) that human vocabularies as reflections of reality are inevitably selections of reality, hence deflections of reality. To name phenomena is not to take an objective stance toward them but to activate a linguistic bias, to assume an attitude toward the named. Words have meanings, but they also have uses. As John Dewey stressed, "Words are so loaded with associations derived from a long past that instead of being tools for thought, our thoughts become subservient tools of our words" (Dewey, 1939, 817; see also Weldon, 1953).

Few enterprises exemplify the logocentric quality of human action as does news coverage of politics. Both the syntax, or logic, and the semantics, or words and pictures, of political news are laden with representative, selective, and deflective bias (Altheide & Snow, 1979). Noam Chomsky's Propaganda Model (formulated with his coauthor, Edward Herman) argues that entrenched political and corporate interests have routinely exploited the logocentric character of the news media to realign the nature of democratic rule. As a result, American political communication practices have more in common with totalitarian ways than observers might think; they protect entrenched political interests at the expense of fostering popular self-government (Chomsky, 1991a; Chomsky [& Herman], 1988c).

The Propaganda Model purports to account for how the U.S. (and, by extension, the Western) news media cover politics. The model challenges the conventional view of the news media as independent, impartial, devoted to reporting truth, and performing in the public interest. For Chomsky the news media are not, in the words of Edmund Burke, a "Fourth Estate" (Burns, 1977, 176) defiant of power and exposing the errors and crimes of public officials, but a "manufacturer of consent," complying with power by mobilizing popular approval for politicians' failings and offenses (Chomsky, 1991a, 10).

Received theories of democracy emphasize the role of citizen participation in politics, popular accountability of politicians, and a free flow of impartial political information. Viewed superficially, American politics meet these criteria. However, Chomsky argues that an "alternative conception of democracy" actually prevails below the surface, namely, "that the public must be barred from management of its own affairs, and the means of information must be kept narrowly and rigidly controlled" (Chomsky, 1991a, 9). Although Chomsky recognizes that the alternative conception of democracy is an old one, he argues that it reached dominance in the United States through twentieth-century practices of political communication. Specifically, it began "with the first modern propaganda operation," the Committee on Public Information, chaired by George Creel (q.v.), in the presidential administration of Woodrow Wilson during World War I. Through its saturation of political media with propaganda, the Creel Committee successfully turned pacifist Americans into anti-German warmongers; then, following the war, it made citizens antilabor and antiunion and made them victims of the Red Scare of the 1920s.

The rationale for government's manufacturing of consent—for government *of*, rather than *by*, public opinion—was, according to Chomsky, provided by political columnist Walter Lippmann (q.v.), who had served the Wilson administration as a propagandist. In his widely read and, with the exception of John Dewey's review, widely acclaimed *Public Opinion* (1922), Lippmann argued that the process of generating public opinion was too vital for governments to leave to chance. "A revolution is taking place," wrote Lippmann, wherein "the knowledge of how to create [public] consent will alter every political calculation and modify every political premise." The "manufacture of consent is capable of great refinements"; hence, it no longer need be trusted solely to "intuition, conscience, or the accidents of casual opinion" (1922, 248–49).

This reasoning, argues Chomsky in a critical vein, artificially constructs two classes of citizens. The majority of citizens are in a lower class, a "bewildered herd" of people confused and afraid who must be protected from the whirl of threatening public affairs. An upper, "specialized class" consists of a small group of involved, informed, and active citizens who discern the public interest and act accordingly. The function of the specialized class is to manufacture consent; of the bewildered, to support the specialists in doing so. Chomsky notes an irony: Lippmann's view of manufactured consent is remarkably like the Marxist/Leninist view that "a vanguard of revolutionary intellectuals should take state power using popular revolutions as the force that brings them the state power, and then drive the stupid masses towards a future they're too dumb and incompetent to envision for themselves" (Chomsky, 1991a, 10). The crumbling of the communist empire in the late 1980s may, thus, have reflected an end of an economic management system, but the Marxist/Leninist political communication system had triumphed well in advance of that crumbling. Or, as Lippmann wrote, "A revolution is taking place infinitely more significant than any shifting of economic power" (1922, 248).

Key to the Propaganda Model are compliant news media organizations whose social purposes are "protecting privilege from the threat of public understanding and participation" (Chomsky, 1989, 14). As private, profit-making concerns of corporate conglomerates that grow in size daily, mass circulation newspapers and magazines, radio, television, films, and other popular political media are wed to the very privilege their news reporting protects. Hence, the "Propaganda Model is a 'guided-free-market' model in which thought control is the product not of violence and terror, but of market forces in a highly unequal society." The guide to the market is provided by "the government, the leaders of the corporate community, the top media owners and the executives, and the assorted individuals and groups who are assigned or allowed to take constructive initiatives" (Chomsky, 1988c, xii).

Writes Chomsky, "The logic is clear—propaganda is to a democracy what a bludgeon is to a totalitarian state" (1991a, 11). The strokes of that velvet-gloved bludgeoning consist of the techniques of public relations, techniques pioneered by another member of the Creel Committee, Edward Bernays (q.v.). As envisioned by the Propaganda Model, these techniques are the reliable ploys of using a compliant news media to construct and create a sense of crisis rallying the bewildered in support of the privileged regime, to construct enemies as the source of the crisis, to convert the enemies into scapegoats to be offered as sacrifices to alleviate the crisis, and—most important—to preserve for privileged interests throughout the crisis the "Right to Lie" (Rai, 1995, 30).

One of the unique aspects of Chomsky's model of manufactured consent is his argument that propaganda feeds on the very freedom of thought and expression that is alleged in democratic theory to provide a defense against it. In a paradoxical fashion, news propaganda is almost transparent and readily detectable, yet its victims still are unaware of the manipulation. The bewildered are victims of an invisible control that sets the "boundaries of thinkable thought" and insulates unspoken underlying political principles from scrutiny (Rai, 1995, 35). Thus, for instance, the lesson that news coverage of the Watergate crisis during the presidency of Richard Nixon was *not* that a political process that aided and abetted political lying, intimidation, and corruption was seriously flawed; instead, the lesson of Watergate, the framework for thinkable thought after Nixon's resignation, was that "the system worked."

So long as the boundaries of "thinkable thought" protect privilege, it is to the advantage of established interests to encourage debate and discussion of issues. No matter how hostile on the surface critics may appear in their attack on established policy, by accepting the premises of thinkable thought, "The more vigorous the debate, the better the system of propaganda is served, since the tacit, unspoken assumptions are more forcefully implanted" at a deeper level

(Chomsky, 1982, 81). Therefore, in Chomsky's view, a useful defense is, "If you want to learn something about the propaganda system, have a close look at the critics and their tacit assumptions. These typically constitute the doctrines of the state religion" (Chomsky, 1987, 126).

CONCLUSION: POLITICAL COMMENTARY AS PROPAGANDA CRITICISM

One of Noam Chomsky's colleagues has written, "On first sight, the Propaganda Model is a difficult theory to take seriously. The idea that the media systematically distort the news in the interests of the powerful is a very difficult one to accept" (Rai, 1995, 32). Yet, well before the linguistic turn taken by political analysis, there were ample grounds for questioning the news media as sources of reliable reflections of reality. The shrewd French observer of Jacksonian democracy, Alexis de Tocqueville, ever mindful of the potential "tyranny of the majority," clearly foresaw the likelihood that newspapers might be required to manufacture consent long before Walter Lippmann urged it or Noam Chomsky condemned it. "The more equal men become and more individualism becomes a menace," wrote de Toqueville, "the more necessary are newspapers. We should underrate their importance if we thought they just guaranteed liberty; they maintain civilization" (de Tocqueville, 1969, 517).

Over a century later, another French observer, Jacques Ellul, foreshadowed the Propaganda Model in far more encompassing terms than even Chomsky envisions. Propaganda, wrote Ellul, is the ruling *technique* of our times, the overriding method of "the totality of methods . . . having absolute efficiency in every field of human knowledge" (Combs & Nimmo, 1993, 84). Propaganda both agitates and integrates, constructs conflicts, and manufacturers consent— all in the name of protecting privileged, technologically based interests. Propaganda is total and ubiquitous in every medium, not only in the printed or spoken word, but in architecture, clothing, and all public displays. Human beings in the modern world, thought Ellul, could no more live without propaganda than they could live without oxygen.

So it is not hard to "take seriously" the Propaganda Model in light of the earlier versions of it. What makes Noam Chomsky's claim to being taken seriously unique is his indefatigable thirty-year effort in lectures and written works to put his model to a social scientific test. He has tested individual cases by analyzing claims of news media independence, paired examples of historical events, and rituals of mainstream media discourse. Repeatedly Chomsky and his colleagues have found the Propaganda Model a valid explanatory tool—that media independence is a chimera. "By the standards of the social sciences," argues Chomsky, the model is "well confirmed and its predictions are often considerably surpassed. . . . I would hazard a guess that it is one of the best-confirmed theories in the social sciences" (Rai, 1995, 23).

There may, however, be a separate sense in which it is difficult to take the

Propaganda Model seriously. Although the model serves as a starting point for conducting political commentary not as propaganda but as propaganda analysis, it is only a start. For, in one respect, it goes not too far but not far enough. Resting as it does on the tacit acceptance of privileged interests' "right to lie," the model implies that propaganda is limited to intentional manipulation, deception, and deceit. Chomsky repeatedly stresses, however, that his Propaganda Model is not driven by "conspiracy theories" in the sense that propaganda is a weapon used by conspirators to wrap base motives in layers of self-serving rhetoric. Rather it is driven by imperatives inherent in the institutional pressures of a guided free market combined with pressures for self-censorship by media organizations operating to maximize profits within that market. Profit, not conspiracy, is the overriding intention of the manufacturers of consent.

There are propaganda analysts who argue that the defining characteristic of propaganda is not deliberate, intentional manipulation, deception, and deceit—whether for reasons of profit, conspiracy, or anything else. Instead propaganda derives from the suasive consequences of any suggestible message regardless of the persuasive intent of the communication's source. Viewed in this way propaganda versus nonpropaganda is not a pairing of truth versus falsehood, manipulation versus education, or persuasion versus information. Propaganda is *phony*; it is neither true nor false in substance but is instead a derivative of communication *techniques* that court, beguile, seduce, please, entice, and charm. Like a forged painting or a facsimile document, the phony message may, indeed, possess more allure than "the real thing" (Combs & Nimmo, 1993).

So conceived, any political commentary possesses potential for propaganda consequences, even messages that otherwise purport to unmask and analyze propaganda (Norton, 1993). The complexities of propaganda are not limited to surface and deep structures. The geological metaphor does not suffice. One from horticulture is more appropriate, namely, the simple complexity of the onion. Each time a surface layer is peeled away, there is another, and another, and another. The analyst peels away until nothing remains, thus leaving the analyst peering through tears at what Kenneth Burke regarded as the insurmountable dilemma of logocentric humans: while any tyro can say nothing about something it takes real genius to say something about nothing. Noam Chomsky, the linguist, expressed the dilemma differently: "It may be beyond the limits of human intelligence to understand how human intelligence works" (Chomsky, *Celebrity Register*, 1973, 103).

REFERENCES

Selected Works in Linguistics by Noam Chomsky

Syntactic Structures. The Hague: Mouton, 1957.
Current Issues in Linguistic Theory. The Hague: Mouton, 1964.
Aspects of the Theory of Syntax. Cambridge: MIT Press, 1965.

Cartesian Linguistics: A Chapter in the History of Rationalist Thought. New York: Harper and Row, 1966.
Topics in the Theory of Generative Grammar. The Hague: Mouton, 1966.
Language and Mind. New York: Harcourt Brace Jovanovich, 1972.
Studies on Semantics in Generative Grammar. The Hague: Mouton, 1972.
The Logical Structure of Linguistic Theory. New York: Plenum Press, 1975.
Reflections on Language. New York: Pantheon, 1975.
Rules and Representations. New York: Columbia University Press, 1980.
Knowledge of Language: Its Nature, Origin, and Use. New York: Praeger, 1986.
Generative Grammar: Its Basis, Development and Prospects. Kyoto, Japan: University of Foreign Studies, 1987.

Selected Works in Politics by Noam Chomsky

American Power and the New Mandarins. Harmondsworth, England: Penguin Books, 1969, 1971.
At War with Asia. London: Fontana/Collins, 1971.
Problems of Knowledge and Freedom. London: Barrie and Jenkins, 1972.
The Backroom Boys. London: Fontana/Collins, 1973.
For Reasons of State. London: Fontana/Collins, 1973.
Peace in the Middle East? Reflections on Justice and Nationhood. New York: Pantheon, 1974.
Language and Responsibility, Based on Conversations with Mitsou Ronat. Hassocks, England: Harvester Press, 1979.
Towards a New Cold War: Essays on the Current Crisis and How We Got There. London: Sinclair Brown, 1982.
The Fateful Triangle: The United States, Israel and the Palestinians. London: Pluto, 1983.
Turning the Tide: US Intervention in Central America and the Struggle for Peace. London: Pluto, 1985.
The Chomsky Reader. Edited by J. Peck. London: Serpent's Tail, 1987.
The Culture of Terrorism. London: Pluto, 1988a.
Language and Politics. Edited by C. P. Otero. Montreal: Black Rose Books, 1988b.
Manufacturing Consent: The Political Economy of the Mass Media. With E. Herman. New York: Pantheon, 1988c.
Necessary Illusions; Thought Control in Democratic Societies. London: Pluto, 1989.
"20th Century American Propaganda." *Propaganda Review* 8 (Fall, 1991a): 8–11, 37–44.
Deterring Democracy. London: Verso, 1991b.
Letters from Lexington: Rethinking Propaganda. Edinburgh: AK Press, 1993.
Rethinking Camelot: JFK, the Vietnam War, and US Political Culture. Boston: South End Press, 1993.
World Orders, Old and New. London: Pluto, 1994.

Critical Works about Noam Chomsky

"Chomsky, Noam." In *Celebrity Register*, 103–4. New York: Simon and Schuster, 1973.
Haley, M. C., and R. F. Lansford. *Noam Chomsky*. New York: Twayne, 1994.
Herman, G., ed. *On Noam Chomsky: Critical Essays*. Garden City, NY: Doubleday/Anchor, 1974.

Leiber, J. *Noam Chomsky: A Philosophic Overview*. Boston: Twayne, 1975.

Lyons, J. *Noam Chomsky*. New York: Viking Press, 1970.

Modgil, S., and C. Modgil. *Noam Chomsky: Consensus and Controversy*. New York: Folmer Press, 1987.

Rai, M. *Chomsky's Politics*. London: Verso, 1995.

Salkie, R. *The Chomsky Update*. Boston: Unwin Hyman, 1990.

Sampson, G. *Liberty and Language*. Oxford: Oxford University Press, 1979.

Selected General Works

Altheide, D., and R. Snow. *Media Logic*. Beverly Hills, CA: Sage, 1979.

Burke, K. *A Grammar of Motives*. Berkeley: University of California Press, 1969.

Burns, T. *The BBC: Public Institution and Private World*. London: Macmillan, 1977.

Combs, J. E., and D. Nimmo. *The New Propaganda*. New York: Longman, 1993.

Connolly, W. E. *The Terms of Political Discourse*. London: D. C. Heath, 1974.

Corcoran, P. E. "Language and Politics." In *New Directions in Political Communication*, edited by D. Swanson and D. Nimmo, 51–85. Newbury Park, CA: Sage, 1990.

Dewey, J. "The Unity of the Human Being." In *Intelligence in the Modern World*, edited by J. Ratner, 817–35. New York: Modern Library, 1939.

Eagleton, T. *Literary Theory*. Minneapolis: University of Minnesota Press, 1983.

Ellul, J. *Propaganda*. New York: Random House, 1965.

Herman, E. S. *Beyond Hypocrisy: Decoding the News in An Age of Propaganda*. Boston: South End Press, 1993.

Lippmann, W. *Public Opinion*. New York: Macmillan, 1960.

Norton, A. *Republic of Signs*. Chicago: University of Chicago Press, 1993.

Orwell, G. "Politics and the English Language" (1946). In *A Collection of Essays by George Orwell*, edited by G. Orwell, 162–77. Garden City, NY: Doubleday & Company, 1954.

———. "Why I Write" (1947). In *A Collection of Essays by George Orwell*, edited by G. Orwell, 313–20. Garden City, NY: Doubleday & Company, 1954.

Shapiro, M., ed. *Language and Politics*. New York: New York University Press, 1984.

Tocqueville, A. de. *Democracy in America*. Garden City, NY: Doubleday/Anchor, 1969.

Weldon, T. D. *The Vocabulary of Politics*. London: Penguin, 1953.

GEORGE (EDWARD) CREEL

(December 1, 1876–October 2, 1953)

Political Commentary as Centralized War Propaganda

The entry of the United States in the Great War in 1917, a war that later generations would call World War I, meant that political communication would never be the same again. What had been primarily the province of politicians became increasingly a craft of communication specialists; what had been the idiosyncratic art of entrepreneurial individuals became the administrative task of organized functionaries. The transformation would intensify trends toward today's thriving industries of strategic communication—public relations, political advertising, image management, and thought control.

The shift in emphasis was in large measure due to the political and administrative skills of a man less a political commentator himself than a coordinator of political commentary for an entire nation, George Creel. Creel took to heart a dictum that a student of World War I propaganda, Harold Lasswell, a decade later, used to sum up the era: "In the Great Society it is no longer possible to fuse the waywardness of individuals in the furnace of the war dance. . . . Talk must take the place of drill; print must supplant the dance" (Lasswell, 1977, 227). Shooting warfare would be supplemented on a gigantic scale by Talkwar.

THE MAKING OF A PROGRESSIVE

George Creel was born in the year that witnessed the biggest political deal consummated to date in the United States. It was 1876. That year the Democratic presidential candidate, Samuel J. Tilden, was denied the presidency itself despite receiving majorities of the popular and electoral vote. An Electoral Commission, voting along partisan lines, awarded disputed electoral votes of four states to the Republican candidate, making Rutherford B. Hayes president. What Democrats received as a quid pro quo was the withdrawal of federal troops from the Southern states and an end to Reconstruction. Of course, the dispute meant nothing to the newborn George; yet it is interesting to note that Creel would become, first, a muckraking reporter who unmasked political deals, then a federal administrator who continuously defended his president, Woodrow Wilson, against charges of deal making.

Creel was born on December 1 in a Missouri county, Lafayette, which now is an ecology of bedroom communities for the commuting population of Kansas City. His father, Henry, had been a Confederate officer during the Civil War. In his autobiography, *Rebel at Large* (1947), George Creel writes that his father, realizing that his native Virginia's recovery from the war's devastation would be difficult, decided to migrate to Lafayette County, close to the home of Creel's mother, Virginia. Henry invested $10,000 in a Missouri farm. However, he was more successful at siring sons on that farm (George and brothers Wylie and Richard Henry) than tilling the soil. Henry was, writes George, "a flop from the first" and turned to "diligent drinking as an escape from his failure" (1947, 10). Henry then tried cattle raising in Hickory County. That too flopped, so the Creel family moved to Independence, Odessa, and finally Kansas City, where George's mother ran a boardinghouse and he attended public schools.

While he was growing up, George Creel acquired his first progressive sentiments. "If I came to voting age," he wrote later, "with a passionate belief in equal suffrage, it was because I *knew* [Creel's emphasis] my mother had more character, brains, and competence than any man that ever lived." Through "toil and sacrifice" she raised three sons, "imbuing them with something of her own indomitability and pride," all the while with a husband "that during the years that came under my seeing eye he never lifted a useful hand" (1947, 17).

Creel quit high school early, performed odd jobs, and became a $4.00-a-week reporter for the Kansas City *World*. Looking back on that employment a half-century later, Creel marveled that he was ever hired; his qualifications, he said, would not have gained him admission to the kindergarten class in a modern school of journalism and he had "fought off every effort to provide me with a well-rounded education" (1947, 35). Although the job did not last long (Creel got the "boot" after a falling out with his city editor), it whetted his appetite for a reporting career. In search of a position on another paper, Creel gathered his meager savings and, in 1897, set off for New York City; in exchange for free transportation, he worked on a cattle train from Chicago to New Jersey.

Like a Midwestern contemporary who would also become a pioneering twentieth-century political commentator, H. V. Kaltenborn (q.v.), Creel found end-of-the-century New York City an expensive city with few jobs for aspiring journalists. However, fortune smiled in the form of a heavy snowfall; Creel earned enough shoveling snow to tide him over. Finally, he landed a job, not as a reporter, but as a joke and verse writer selling his work to the New York *Evening Journal*, *Puck*, *Judge*, *Truth*, and *Life*. He also worked on the staff of the comic supplement for the New York *American*, writing jokes for "The Katzenjammer Kids," "Foxy," "Grandpa," and "Buster Brown." As Creel later noted, such writing scarcely challenged the reputation of Mark Twain for humor. Yet, Creel learned the persuasive value of the humorous cartoon series with a patriotic message; during World War I, the propaganda machine over which Creel presided created 287 cartoons on behalf of the U.S. war effort.

Creel built his income to $40 a week. Yet, he was unhappy: "Twenty-two years old, and nothing more than a penny-a-liner. Life half gone and a failure!" (Creel, 1947, 42). When a colleague broached the idea of jointly beginning publication of a weekly literary newspaper, Creel jumped at the opportunity. He returned to Kansas City to found the *Independent*. By 1903 he was the sole owner, editor, and publisher. Creel's contributions to the *Independent* as a writer were diverse—articles, verse, stories, dramas, reviews, even popular songs (including the commercial success, "Every Jack Must Have His Jill'').

Moreover, he covered politics. Kansas City was a Democratic party monopoly. The party was split into two factions, the Rabbits and the Goats. "The turn of the century was an ideal time for my advent as a 'reformer'," wrote Creel; he joined with the "muckrakes" and "dynamic progressives," exposing corruption and demanding responsive government (Creel, 1947, 50). Creel supported the Rabbits, in part because the Goats, under Jim Pendergast, were controlled by special interests, and, in greater measure, because noted progressive lawyer Franklin Walsh stood with the Rabbits. In the end, the Rabbit faction "dehorned" the Goats and elected a reformer as governor of Missouri.

With a political victory in hand, Creel looked for new reform battles to fight, but not in Missouri. In 1908 he gave the *Independent* away and moved to Colorado where he worked as an editorial writer for the Denver *Post*. He soon had a falling out with the newspaper's owners over endorsements for candidates of a citizens' party that Creel had helped organize. However, by 1911, he was editor of the *Rocky Mountain News*, where he again challenged special interests, exposed corruption, and called for political reform. (One such reform was his editorial call that eleven state senators be "lynched," a term he claimed in a libel trial against him he did *not* use as a figure of speech.) In 1912 reformers won office in Denver's elections; and Creel became police commissioner, only to be fired by his fellow reformers when he stepped on too many toes!

Creel did not desist in reform politics and civic activities in Colorado. He was particularly incensed with the working conditions in the coal fields. During a miner's strike in 1913–1914 there was a bitter effort on the part of mine ownership to break the strike. It even included the Ludlow Massacre (April 20, 1914), when troops and mine guards opened machine-gun fire on a tent city of striking miners and their families. The resulting carnage attracted national attention. For his part, Creel took on the leading power of mining interests in Colorado, John D. Rockefeller, Jr., and all state officials under his control, and branded them all as "accessories to the murders of babes." Creel organized a 10,000-strong mass meeting on the statehouse lawn to protest the massacre. The Rockefeller interests countered Creel's attacks by hiring Ivy Ledbetter Lee, a former journalist turned press agent, to flood the state and nation with *Facts*, a pamphlet publicizing the owners' version of events. Although Creel would later dismiss Lee's publicity campaign as a failure, it is noteworthy that in organizing propaganda in World War I, the distribution of 75 million pamphlets played a key role. Others were not so quick to scoff at Lee's contributions to the development of professional political communication. Political commentator and documentarian Bill Moyers (q.v.), for example, devoted a long segment of a one-hour documentary in his "A Walk through the Twentieth Century" to the success of Lee's pro-Rockefeller image building, crediting Lee and Edward Bernays (q.v.) with founding professional public relations.

Creel's progressive reputation became national in scope. He was contributing articles on Woodrow Wilson's "New Freedom" to national magazines, muck-raking features to magazines such as *Cosmopolitan* and *Harper's Weekly*, and writing widely read books, including *Children in Bondage* (1914), exposing the evils of child labor, and *Wilson and the Issues* (1916) in defense of the president. His marriage to Blanche Bates, a well-known actress, brought him in contact with key figures in the entertainment industry—contacts that would assist him in enlisting the aid of movie moguls in World War I propaganda efforts in shifting popular sentiment from pacifist to pro-belligerent via popular movies.

Upon his reelection as president in 1916, Woodrow Wilson invited Creel to join the president's official family. Creel declined. However, entry of the United States into the Great War changed his mind.

GEORGE CREEL IN THE GREAT TALKWAR

America's entry into the war raised serious concerns in official circles re-garding what newspapers and other publications should and should not be per-mitted to print about U.S. war preparations, plans, and movements. Many military leaders called for a hard and fast censorship law and for centralized clearance of news, and Woodrow Wilson appeared to favor the move (Creel, 1947; Heckscher, 1991). George Creel, however, appealed to the president along different lines. He argued on behalf of voluntary censorship by the press and urged the creation of an official agency that would not suppress information but would, instead, make it available: *"expression,* not *suppression* was the real need"* (Creel, 1947, 157; emphasis in original). Although subsequent legislation did not go as far as Creel advocated in making each news publication its own censor, as a member of the Censorship Board he continued to argue against efforts to judge the loyalty of every published item. Moreover, as chairman of the Committee on Public Information (CPI), he worked to choke all channels of political information with "official, approved news and opinion, leaving little freeway for rumor or disloyal reports" (Mock & Larson, 1939, 11).

On April 13, 1917, a scant week after America's entry into the war, the president created the CPI by executive order. The CPI consisted of the chair, Creel; and the secretaries of state, war, and the navy. Thus began "the world's greatest adventure in advertising" (Creel, 1920, 4; Vaughn, 1980, 141). Thus also began George Creel's seminal contribution to the evolution of political commentary as controlled propaganda in the twentieth century.

The story of Creel's stewardship of the CPI on behalf of the U.S. war effort and, not so coincidentally, Woodrow Wilson, has been related many times. Creel himself reported it in his candidly titled *How We Advertised America* (1920), his official chairman's report summarizing CPI activities at the war's conclusion, and his memoirs, *Rebel at Large* (1947). His, along with other accounts (Mock & Larson, 1939; Vaughn, 1980), stress the multimedia, multipersonnel, and multiaudience nature of the propaganda campaign. The advertising figures are staggering: 75 million pamphlets, 6,000 press releases, and 14,000 drawings;

75,000 speakers, called Four Minute Men, presenting over half a million lectures to more than 300 million people in 5,200 communities, several thousand more youths as "junior" minute men, 4,000 fact-checking historians, and numerous filmmakers; and news, books, and films exported to Latin America, the Orient, and Europe. In all, more than 150,000 men and women devoted "their highly specialized abilities to the work of the Committee, as faithful and devoted in their service as though they wore the khaki" (Creel, 1920, 5).

Equally important as the sheer magnitude of the CPI output in assessing George Creel as a coordinator of U.S. political commentary was the philosophy he brought to his task. From the outbreak of war in August 1914, until America's entry, the job of informing, educating, and persuading Americans about the war was fragmented throughout separate, disparate agencies. Creel sought to bring all propaganda efforts under the control of the CPI, "not by imposing unwanted views on the general public," but by "vitalizing convictions already held and toward developing the will to fight for ideas already familiar" (Mock & Larson, 1939, 10). The organizational challenge, Creel later wrote, "was like asking the Babylonians to build a threshing machine, for there was no chart to go by" (1947, 160).

In keeping with the philosophy of not imposing doctrines on Americans, Creel did not impose an organizational plan on the propaganda campaign: it was "inspirational rather than planned," going "from day to day" (Creel, 1947, 162). Thus, for example, an artist entered Creel's office to contribute a poster; the artist departed with the job of organizing a Division of Pictorial Publicity. A young man suggested a plan to put public speakers in Chicago's movie houses; he left with instructions to form the Four Minute Men, trained speakers to deliver the government's message throughout the nation. A spin-off led to coast-to-coast speakers' tours. In similar fashion, improvising all the way, Creel and his associates spawned divisions and bureaus for news dissemination, for the publication of an official U.S. government newspaper (the *Official Bulletin*), for the publication of foreign language newspapers, for civic and education services, for film, for pictures, for pictorial publicity, for cartoons, for advertising, for war expositions, for state fair exhibits, for industrial relations, for labor relations, for women's war work, and for working with the foreign born. And, that was only the domestic side of the Creel committee. A foreign section consisted of a wireless and cable service, a foreign press bureau, and a foreign film division.

All this took place well before the electronic age of radio or television, but not before the age of film. Capitalizing on the popularity of newsreels, short subjects, and feature films, the CPI went into the motion picture business. In newsreels, the CPI coordinated distribution in the United States of the *Official War Review*, a propaganda newsreel prepared by the British, French, and Italian governments. CPI cameramen and the Signal Corps filmed short subjects that carried a war message, yet did not compete with private film producers. Typical titles, such as *Submarines*, *The Second Liberty Loan*, or *Ship Building* suggest the content. Finally, the CPI produced patriotic feature films, such as *Pershing's Crusaders*, and *America's Answer*.

One of George Creel's key accomplishments was his successful recruitment of Hollywood's support for the war effort. The CPI's Scenario Department, for instance, wrote plots for private producers to film as short subjects and features. Most Hollywood producers, given the emotional climate of the time, needed no prodding to churn out patriotic war movies:

> Given the frame of assumptions that guided American film propaganda during World War I . . . enterprising filmmakers could fulfill both their commercial and political functions. . . . these films contained a recurrent theme of Americans overcoming their moral and political doubts and their domestic ties and duties to throw themselves enthusiastically into the war. . . . For the first time, many millions of people saw a war and believed that what they were seeing was in some sense true. (Combs & Combs, 1994, 31–33)

In keeping with George Creel's view that the CPI should not impose popular views, only exploit them, within twenty-four hours after the signing of the Armistice on November 11, 1918, his orders were to cease all operations of the committee. But ceasing the controversies that surrounded the CPI and its long-term impact on political communication was not to prove so simple as shutting down its programs.

CREEL'S CONTRIBUTIONS

Throughout his tenure as CPI chair, George Creel had to defend himself against charges in the press, Congress, and the federal bureaucracy that he was an empire-building tyrant dictating public opinion. Although he claimed no desire to impose convictions on Americans, there is little question that Creel possessed a master's touch when it came to orchestrating the overall advertising of America. Creel treated political communication, in this case propaganda, as an administrative function that required centralized organization and management, administrative action coordinated with the overall war aims of the Wilson administration. Although he recruited a plethora of communication specialists and gave them freedom to be creative and to follow through on their ideas, he frowned on staff members who acted as private entrepreneurs. He sought overall loyalty to the committee's tasks and to the president. Two decades later, Joseph Goebbels, Nazi Germany's propaganda minister, accepted Adolf Hitler's verdict that Germany had lost the Great War in large measure because it had forfeited the propaganda war. Goebbels studied the CPI's efforts, took Creel seriously, and formulated his own dictum that all Nazi domestic and foreign propaganda must be planned and executed by only one authority (Doob, 1950).

Creel's efforts to coordinate all U.S. propaganda during World War I embroiled him in controversies with other notable political commentators of his time. One, for example, was Walter Lippmann (q.v.). At the juncture of America's entry into the Great War, Lippmann was already an established and influential journalist. George Creel had already felt Lippmann's ire; in a 1915 *New Republic* editorial, Lippmann, criticizing Creel's work as a muckraking reporter in Colorado, had charged Creel with being "reckless and incompetent" and "determined to make a noise no matter what canons of truthfulness he violates" (Steel, 1980, 143). Creel did not appreciate, or forgive, the attack. Nor, in 1917, did Creel appreciate Lippmann's charge, as a special assistant to Secretary of War Newton D. Baker, that Creel was intolerant of a free press. With Creel clearly in mind, Lippmann appealed to Colonel Edward House, the president's chief advisor. Censorship, he wrote, should "never be entrusted to anyone who is not himself tolerant, not to anyone who is unacquainted with the long record of folly which is the history of suppression" (Steel, 1980, 125).

The stage was set for a confrontation when, in 1918, Secretary Baker authorized U.S. Army Captain Lippmann to serve as an emissary to European allies in conducting a leaflet campaign that would appeal directly to the German enemy over the head of the Allies and the CPI. When he arrived in London, Lippmann found to his displeasure that the lines of responsibility for propaganda had been changed while he was en route. Lippmann's Military Intelligence Branch (MIB) would *not* prepare and distribute pamphlets behind enemy lines; it would instead be limited to distributing leaflets at the front. Creel's CPI had the responsibility and authority to coordinate everything else. Lippmann and his colleagues ignored the administrative edict. Moreover, Lippmann wrote to Colonel House claiming that the CPI's European operation was "very bad," that the committee's reputation among the British was "very low," and that a propaganda unit should be established independent of Creel's.

President Wilson sided with Creel in the dispute; hence, although jurisdictional lines for propaganda remained confused, Creel achieved a Pyrrhic victory. It was not the first time, nor would it be the last, that Wilson defended Creel, even when Creel's efforts to use humor, a remnant of his cartoon penny-a-line days, in dealing with congressional and press critics backfired. Once asked if he knew what was going on in the minds of Congress, Creel quipped, "I do not like slumming, so I won't explore into the hearts of Congress for you" (Mock & Larson, 1939, 61). Wilson defended him. A Wilson biographer speculates that "Creel gave form to the side of Wilson that was at home in the rough and tumble of practical politics"; Wilson's own silences "were complimented by the crude drumbeat of that propaganda machine" (Heckscher, 1991, 466–67).

Wilson also sided with Creel in Creel's skirmish with another pioneering figure in twentieth-century political communication, Edward Bernays. Bernays joined the CPI in 1917 as a director for news in Latin America, part of the Wireless-Cable Service. Following the Armistice, Bernays went to Paris with the CPI delegation to the peace conference. An issue arose regarding whether members of the delegation should respond to reporters who were clamoring for news about the conference. Bernays thought a response was appropriate; he even thought that President Wilson should meet with the press. When Creel arrived in Paris, he was displeased with Bernays' handling of publicity. The CPI, he felt, should cease its publicity role with the end of hostilities; moreover, although Creel had implored the president to brief the press, a heavy schedule had made it impossible. According to Bernays, "I believe that Creel's failure to insist on effective handling of Peace Conference press relations—that is, to maintain liaison with the public—lost the peace for us" (Bernays, 1965, 177). And, according to Creel:

> When it is charged . . . that the failure [of the peace] is the fault of the Committee on Public Information because we did not conduct a "vigorous campaign," I disagree absolutely and unalterably. Nothing would have been more instantly attacked, and *justly* attacked, than the use of governmental machinery and public funds for any such purpose. . . . As for the Committee on Public Information, its duties ceased automatically when fighting ceased. (Creel, 1920, 401)

Creel had good reason to take the position that propaganda should be under his control and should not be " 'press-agenting' with the people's money" (Creel, 1920, 401). For, no matter where the press agentry on behalf of the president originated, the CPI got the blame. Better to have jurisdictions clear than to take the blame for unauthorized publicity efforts. This said, however, Creel recognized that his committee's work on behalf of America also made it the promotional agency of the White House. In fact, Woodrow Wilson told him as much and warned of the future dangers of an orchestrated presidency, albeit naively in light of Wilson's close scrutiny of Creel's public speeches (Carpenter, 1989). While en route to the peace conference, Wilson said to Creel, "It is a great thing you have done, but I am wondering if you have not unconsciously spun a net for me from which there is no escape." Creel's success left the world looking to America and to Wilson to solve all its problems "with terrible urgency." But, Wilson continued, "You know, and I know, that these ancient wrongs, these present unhappinesses, are not to be remedied in a day or with a wave of the hand." So, "What I seem to see—with all my heart I hope I'm wrong—is a tragedy of disappointment" (Creel, 1947, 206).

In 1919 Creel returned to private life. He moved to San Francisco to write numerous books and magazine articles, to serve as chair of the anticensorship Committee of Art and Literature, to chair the San Francisco Regional Labor Board, to chair the national advisory board of the Works Progress Administration, and to act as consultant to the United Mine Workers. Two years after the 1941 death of his wife, he married Alice Rosseter.

Creel remained steadfast in his belief that wartime propaganda must be a centralized, coordinated, orchestrated effort as it was during World War I. Reflecting on the travails of Elmer Davis (q.v.) as head of the Office of War

Information (OWI) during World War II, who inherited three existing official information programs and had to compete with a plethora of others, he judged that his own "starting from scratch" in 1917 was "my salvation" (Creel, 1947, 160). In spite of Davis' likable and "brilliant" leadership, no efforts were made by the OWI to "bring together everything under one tent" as had been the case with the Creel committee; "administrative blundering persisted to the very end" (1947, 321–22). Moreover, the seeds of controversy sown in Creel's time over the proper mission of the CPI, whether propagandistic or informative commentary, littered not only Davis' path with OWI in World War II, but also, decades later, the paths of Edward R. Murrow (q.v.) as director of the U.S. Information Agency, Murrow's successor, Carl T. Rowan (q.v.), and John Chancellor (q.v.) as director of the Voice of America.

Although Woodrow Wilson hoped "with all my heart . . . I'm wrong," he was not wrong. The "war to end all wars" foreshadowed other wars. George Creel was witness to World War II and the Korean War. But never again was he a talkwar belligerent in such a conflict. He had long since made his singular contribution to political commentary. He died on October 2, 1953.

REFERENCES

Selected Works by George Creel

Quatrains of Christ. New York: D. Elder, 1908.
Children in Bondage. With Edwin Markham and Benjamin B. Lindsey. New York: Hearst's International Library, 1914.
Wilson and the Issues. New York: Century, 1916.
How We Advertised America. New York: Harper and Brothers, 1920.
The War, the World, and Wilson. New York: Harper and Brothers, 1920.
War Criminals and Punishment. New York: M. McBride, 1944.
Rebel at Large: Recollections of Fifty Crowded Years. New York: G. P. Putnam's Sons, 1947.

Selected Critical Works about George Creel

Bean, W. E. "George Creel and His Critics." Ph.D. diss., University of California, Berkeley, 1941.
Carpenter, R. H. "Woodrow Wilson as Speechwriter for George Creel." *Presidential Studies Quarterly* 19 (1989): 117–26.
"Creel, George." In *National Cyclopedia of American Biography* 41, 575–76. New York: James T. White, 1956.
Leonard, T. C. "Creel, George." In *Dictionary of American Biography*, Supplement Five, edited by J. A. Garraty, 141–43. New York: Charles Scribner's Sons, 1977.
Mock, J. R., and C. Larson. *Words That Won The War.* Princeton, NJ: Princeton University Press, 1939.
Rotha, A., ed. "Creel, George." In *Current Biography 1944.* New York: H. W. Wilson, 1945: 120–123.

Vaughn, S. *Holding Fast the Inner Lines: Democracy, Nationalism, and the Committee on Public Information.* Chapel Hill: University of North Carolina Press, 1980.

Selected General Works

Bernays, E. *Biography of an Idea: Memoirs of Public Relations Counsel Edward L. Bernays.* New York: Simon and Schuster, 1965.

Combs, J. E., and S. T. Combs. *Film Propaganda and American Politics.* New York: Garland, 1994.

Combs, J. E., and D. Nimmo. *The New Propaganda.* New York: Longman, 1993.

Doob, L. "Goebbels' Principles of Propaganda." *Public Opinion Quarterly* 14 (1950): 419–442.

Heckscher, A. *Woodrow Wilson.* New York: Charles Scribner's Sons, 1991.

Lasswell, H. D. "The Wartime Propaganda Front." In *Harold D. Lasswell on Political Sociology,* edited by D. Maverick, 223–28. Chicago: University of Chicago Press, 1977. Originally published as a chapter in Lasswell's Ph.D. diss., "Propaganda Techniques in the World War," University of Chicago, 1927.

Pratkanis, A. and E. Aronson. *Age of Propaganda.* New York: W. H. Freeman, 1991.

Steel, R. *Walter Lippmann and the American Century.* Boston: Little, Brown, 1980.

WALTER (LELAND) CRONKITE (JR.)

(November 4, 1916–   )

Political Commentary from Wire Service to Wired Nation

At the close of the twentieth century, it is hard to conceive what a technological marvel Alfred Vail, a business partner of Samuel B. Morse, had achieved a century and a half earlier on May 1, 1844. Sitting in a makeshift office near a railroad station in Annapolis, Maryland, Vail learned from a recently arrived passenger that Henry Clay had just been nominated by the Whig party for president of the United States. Using an experimental telegraph line to Washington, D.C., Vail relayed the news. Newspapers ignored the report, but political insiders did not. Clay's nomination was literally the talk of the town. Newspapers learned their lesson. Soon they were exploiting the newfangled telegraph to transmit their own dispatches; moreover, they created "wire services" to distribute news to subscribing newspapers across the country. Electronic political commentary had been born.

As Americans prepared to enter the twenty-first century, they had long since witnessed the closure of prestigious metropolitan daily newspapers across the country and the end of the benevolent hegemony of news organizations at the major television networks that had marked early post–World War II America. The information age centered instead on cyberspace. In spite of extraordinary technological breakthroughs in communication, critics soon fretted over a persistent decline in the levels of political knowledge across the mass of citizens. Thus, Walter Cronkite opined, "We've got a great percentage of our population that, to our great shame, either cannot or, equally unfortunate, will not read. . . . Those people are suckers for the demagogue" (Rottenberg, 1994, 36). It is ironic that one who was part of the rapid movement away from an era when Americans relied on wire services for the bulk of their political information to an age of cyberspace satellites and cable hookups should be at the forefront of current media criticism. However, from wire service to wired nation, Cronkite's streetwise experience in political journalism has qualified him to make judgments that few other political commentators would dare to utter.

In 1942 Walter Cronkite's superiors at United Press (UP), the wire service, sent him to London as a war correspondent. He covered bombing missions of the U.S. Eighth Air Force. It was often a hazardous assignment because of the intense warfare and heavy casualties. Cronkite's ease at winning the confidence of military authorities and his cool, accurate reporting under fire caught the attention of Edward R. Murrow (q.v.), who was quietly building a pioneering news organization for the Columbia Broadcasting System (CBS). Murrow offered Cronkite an opportunity to leave the grind of wire service news reporting and join the CBS radio bureau; an impressive salary increase would have accompanied the move. At first Cronkite welcomed the opportunity to join Murrow, but after speaking with his superiors at UP he declined the offer.

It was a decision that Cronkite questioned several years later, for being one of "Murrow's Boys," would have advanced his career. For his part, Murrow later regretted making the offer. Years later, when Cronkite did join CBS, Murrow thought Cronkite "talked too much" and personified the generation of "comfortable" television correspondents (Schroth, 1995, 326). In any event, during World War II, Cronkite remained with United Press and relished the hustle and bustle of wire service reporting. As a child Cronkite had craved a career that would allow him to travel, see the world, and experience adventure and excitement; one of the reasons he stayed at UP was to be energized by the fierce competition and intense pressure of covering breaking stories for the news organization (Gates, 1978). Working for the wire service was the fulfillment of his need to work hard and do what he deemed was important.

From 1946 through 1948, Cronkite was the chief correspondent for the United Press in Moscow; he spent these years covering the political activities of the Soviet Union. In 1948 he again faced a decision of whether to leave the United Press. This time he chose to leave for financial reasons, and he returned to Kansas City, Missouri, where he became the Washington correspondent for several radio stations in Missouri, Kansas, and Nebraska. At heart, however, he remained a wire service reporter throughout a distinguished and rewarding career as America's most trusted journalist.

BECOMING WIRED FOR ADVENTURE AND NEWS

Cronkite did not always have the burning desire to work as a journalist. His family background would not have suggested it. Cronkite's paternal ancestors were among the original New Amsterdam settlers who built up communities along the Hudson River in the seventeenth century. His maternal ancestors were mid-nineteenth century German immigrants, one of the first families to own a cigar factory west of the Mississippi River (Gates, 1978, 82). Walter's father was a physician. Neither cigar manufacturing nor medicine held much allure for Cronkite. He considered a career as a mining engineer. As a young boy, he gave serious, albeit fleeting, consideration to becoming an Episcopalian minister in Houston, Texas.

The only son of Dr. Walter Leland and Helen Lena (Fritsche) Cronkite, Walter Leland Cronkite, Jr., was born on November 4, 1916, in Saint Joseph, Missouri. Three-quarters of a century before, Saint Joseph had been the eastern terminus of the Pony Express. Long before the information superhighway existed, Pony Express riders set their own records for spreading political information. By horseback, riders delivered news of Abraham Lincoln's election as president of the United States to Sacramento, California, in a scant eight days in 1860, and news of his inaugural address in a record seven days and seventeen hours. Ironically, the Pony Express was in business only sixteen months, when it was muscled out by the expansion of the telegraph wire service.

Walter Cronkite grew up in Kansas City, Missouri, and Houston, Texas. His family lived in Kansas City until he was ten years old, when they moved to Houston, where his father converted from Lutheranism to become a founder of a Unitarian church. The younger Cronkite joined the Boy Scouts, and through his troop scoutmaster, who was a minister at an Episcopal church, Cronkite became very involved in a religious denomination like his father. After converting from a Lutheran to an Episcopalian, he became an acolyte. In deciding to become the editor for the church newspaper, Cronkite joined his religious convictions and his love for writing. Although he considered a life in the ministry, his passion for writing and politics prevailed over his desire to be a leader of a religious mission ("Covering Religion," 1994).

Walter Cronkite was also involved as a member of the yearbook staff, in student government, and on the track team while he attended San Jacinto High School in Houston. A high school journalism teacher encouraged Walter to develop his talent for news reporting. Upon graduation in 1933, Cronkite entered the University of Texas to study economics and political science. He continued his involvement in student government and intramural sports and added the Curtain Club, a drama organization on campus, and the Chi Phi fraternity to his list of social activities. His direction toward news reporting continued when he became a campus correspondent for the *Houston Press*. Cronkite was also an announcer for a local sports radio station.

Walter Cronkite impressed several of his professors in college by having the inside story of the events at the Texas state capitol. In the mornings, Cronkite attended classes at the university, and in the afternoons he would cover the events of the state legislature. While his professors provided the theories of the governmental system, Cronkite reported tangible information about the operations of the state's rough-and-tumble politics.

He gained valuable experience while a reporter at the capital in Texas, but in 1936 Cronkite left the *Houston Press* to join KCMO radio in Kansas City. While there, he was a news and sports editor and a broadcaster for the radio station. A year later he joined the United Press and opened its news bureau in El Paso, Texas. In 1937 he also was a football broadcaster at WKY in Oklahoma City, worked briefly with Braniff Airways in Kansas City, then rejoined the United Press, the move that would eventually result in his World War II assignments after reporting stints with various UP bureaus in the United States and abroad.

Cronkite was one of the first reporters accredited to cover American forces after the America's entry into World War II following the attack on Pearl Harbor. Soon he was providing eyewitness accounts of U.S. bombing raids over Germany. Throughout the remainder of his career, if a breaking story occurred,

Cronkite preferred the scene of the event as his vantage point, rather than safely interviewing key military personnel in remote headquarters. In an attempt to give his readers a nonmilitary viewpoint of the events, Cronkite risked his life to be in the middle of military combat. He was the first reporter on the scene during the invasion of Normandy; he jumped with the 101st Airborne Division into the Netherlands; he was with the Third Army during the Battle of the Bulge; and he covered the German surrender of northwest Europe. His feats as a reporter provided him the excitement he yearned for during his youth in Houston; his newsgathering tactics earned him the label "daredevil" (Rowe, 1992, 63).

These wartime assignments not only allowed Cronkite to fulfill his childhood desires for adventure and excitement, they also helped him earn a professional reputation for his firsthand accounts of events as they unfolded. After the war, he reestablished the UP bureaus in Belgium, the Netherlands, and Luxembourg; covered the Nuremberg war trials; and, in 1946, went to Moscow, a choice assignment for an important byline correspondent. However, due to rising tensions in U.S.–Soviet relations, Cronkite decided to return to the United States. By this time, he was thirty-one years old. He and his wife, Mary Elizabeth (Betsy) Simmons, were planning to add children to their family. He sought a more lucrative salary and a more secure working environment.

"AND THAT'S THE WAY IT IS"

Walter Cronkite returned from the Soviet Union to report via radio for a group of stations in the Midwest from his base in the nation's capital. As he had when working in the Texas state capital while a university student, Cronkite enjoyed the excitement and pandemonium of Washington politics. Then in July 1950, Edward R. Murrow again approached Cronkite. Would he *now* be interested in working for CBS News, this time as a correspondent covering the Korean War? There was no hesitation; Cronkite joined the network's Washington news staff. In preparation for the trip to Korea, Cronkite began to give nightly reports on the war on WTOP, the network's Washington television outlet.

True to his background as a factual, wire service reporter, Cronkite's telecasts were informational segments that employed charts and graphs (no film footage was available) to describe troop movements and operational details in an illuminating, not ponderous, way. Drawing upon his years as a wire service war correspondent, Cronkite displayed an uncanny ability to explain the complicated strategies of war to a largely untutored civilian audience. The broadcasts were so successful that CBS executives decided not to send Cronkite to Korea; instead, they wanted him to continue his reports from home. This outraged Cronkite; he felt like he had been duped, but he continued to broadcast for the network. The decision to keep him in Washington would prove to be most beneficial to his career as a political commentator, for his influence in the news business would continue to grow.

By the spring of 1951, he was the reporter on the live television broadcast of

General Douglas MacArthur's return from Korea after being relieved of command of the Allied forces in Korea by President Harry S. Truman. In his broadcast of MacArthur's return, Cronkite illustrated his most promising talent, an ability to ad-lib intelligently about political events and figures. This ability had been a hallmark of another former CBS political commentator of note, H. V. Kaltenborn (q.v.). What the talent did for Kaltenborn on radio, it did for Cronkite on television.

For years Cronkite had been an important political commentator on war, legislation, and the political officials in Washington as a reporter for the United Press and a correspondent for a Midwestern radio group, but now he had a far more popular and powerful forum to display his talents—television. Cronkite's ability to ad-lib on almost any topic gave him a reputation as the "reporters' reporter." He simply picked up the microphone and gave an extemporaneous commentary on events (Rottenberg, 1994). The talent did not go unnoticed by the head of the television division at CBS, Sig Mickelson. In the fall of 1951, the industry was acquiring the technology to deliver telecasts from coast to coast. The television set was about to become the principal source of news and entertainment in this country, and Mickelson wanted to establish the CBS network as a primary entity in the industry. Mickelson was looking for a broadcaster to serve as the network's centerpiece of coverage of the 1952 national political party nominating conventions.

In his quest to find the right personality for television, Mickelson considered Edward R. Murrow and Eric Sevareid (q.v.), but both still looked down their noses on the fledgling television news industry and wanted no part of the job (Gates, 1978). Cronkite was Mickelson's choice by default. Despite Cronkite's inexperience in television, he was a respected journalist and had demonstrated his ability to ad-lib intelligently. The decision to assign Cronkite to the convention coverage met with some opposition, but in the end, Mickelson convinced the CBS executives that Cronkite was the natural choice. Cronkite's performance during the summer of 1952 at the Republican and Democratic national conventions in Chicago was flawless and entertaining. The contests for both party's nominations involved conflict, acrimony, and high drama, virtually the last such conventions in American politics. Cronkite smoothly shifted from calling in CBS correspondents for reports to extemporaneous commentary to studio commercials. In effect, he was the "anchor" of the spectacle. A CBS producer, Don Hewitt, who later reinvented the career of political commentator Mike Wallace (q.v.), borrowed the term "anchor" from relay races to designate the correspondent in the CBS news booth regarded as the one in charge (Goldberg & Goldberg, 1990). As anchor, Cronkite was much more visible to millions of Americans than any single politician could ever be over the two weeks of convention coverage. The network surpassed competitors in both radio and television ratings, and the label "TV anchor" entered the vernacular of political commentary.

His anchoring of the 1952 conventions propelled Cronkite into a position that would lead him to become one of America's most trusted political commentators. He had become a major attraction for the network, and CBS was determined to utilize his popularity. In 1953 Cronkite began as the narrator for the show "You Are There," which featured dramatic recreations of historical events (Metz, 1975). This show increased his popularity with the public, but it did not provide him with an opportunity to utilize his journalistic skills. Cronkite later undertook a documentary series, "Air Power," that lead to the highly popular CBS series, "The Twentieth Century." Both series gave Cronkite latitude to wed commentary with visual news footage while concentrating on historical events.

When Cronkite's popularity continued to rise, CBS executives deemed the time opportune to fashion him as a television personality-entertainer. Cronkite became host in 1954 of the "Morning Show," an informational news program designed to compete with NBC's "Today" (see John Chancellor, q.v.). Although Cronkite came across to critics as an engaging host, the role of comedian and entertainer did not fit "wire service Walter" very well. He wanted to be considered a journalist and a commentator, not a comedian who occasionally conducted on-air chats with a puppet named Charlemagne the Lion. Within months of his debut, Cronkite eagerly yielded his role to Jack Paar, who would later go on to celebrity as host of NBC's "Tonight Show"; CBS' struggle to program a competitor to "Today" has gone through a plethora of variations and hosts, each a television ratings failure.

During his stint on the "Morning Show," Cronkite managed to continue working on CBS's "Sunday News Special" and "The Twentieth Century." In addition to the regular shows and news assignments, Cronkite was still the anchor for network television coverage of quadrennial political conventions and election night returns. The network utilized him to narrate many important live news events, including dedication ceremonies for military facilities and the President and Mrs. Harry S. Truman's tour of the White House.

During the 1960 national political party conventions, CBS executives paired Walter Cronkite and Edward R. Murrow as coanchors for network convention coverage, an effort to compete with NBC's popular Chet Huntley and David Brinkley (q.v.). The respected CBS duo proved no match for Huntley and Brinkley. Murrow was uncomfortable at ad-libbing and was not used to sharing the limelight with a partner; tensions mounted and the poor chemistry produced a sharp decline in television ratings for CBS convention coverage. The disaster helped provoke a shake-up in the news staff at CBS. In 1961 Murrow left CBS, and Cronkite became the network's premier correspondent.

Cronkite had established himself as exclusively a journalist by the time he became the host of the network's evening newscast when he replaced Douglas Edwards in April 1972. Once again Cronkite found himself matched against NBC's popular duo, Huntley and Brinkley. To grab an edge in the air wars, on September 2, 1963, CBS lengthened its nightly television newscast from fifteen to thirty minutes and called it "The CBS Evening News." It was a bold move that forced NBC to follow suit. In his first, historic, half-hour telecast, Cronkite conducted an exclusive interview with President John F. Kennedy. It was one of the last interviews for the president; Kennedy was assassinated eighty-one days after the telecast.

Neither the introduction of Cronkite as anchor nor the switch to a new half-hour format yielded a ratings superiority over NBC. In the spring of 1964 Walter Cronkite received an unsettling surprise. In the battle to reclaim their banner of top news organization in television, CBS executives decided to replace Cronkite as anchor of the network's coverage of the Democratic national convention. The decision was based on his poor ratings performance at the 1964 Republican convention held in San Francisco. Cronkite had employed his talent of ad-lib to excess, according to his colleagues (Gates, 1978), who accused him of hogging airtime and not allowing correspondents on the convention floor time to report more current and pertinent facts. By contrast, rival NBC's correspondents not only reported news, they *made* it; for example, NBC's John Chancellor's broadcast of his own ejection from the floor of the convention. Executives at CBS replaced Cronkite with the team of Robert Trout and Roger Mudd for coverage of the upcoming 1964 Democratic convention.

When CBS announced its decision, the network received numerous calls and letters of complaint. The public's outrage encouraged Cronkite who felt that he was being unfairly treated. In a power play, Cronkite decided to telecast "The Evening News" from the convention each night, even though he was no longer a part of the convention news team. The ploy proved ingenious. By reporting each night from the convention site, Cronkite kept his name and image prominently displayed. Also, Cronkite helped to fuel rumors that rival networks were interested in hiring him away from CBS. These conditions, coupled with the lukewarm response to the Trout-Mudd pairing, brought CBS executives to their knees. Once again Cronkite had the preeminent position as the top CBS correspondent.

As a journalist, he had a knack for identifying the hard facts and presenting them with clarity. Setting the social agenda is part of the task of a political commentator. Cronkite was criticized for not being an intellectual, for not being as glibly erudite as Edward R. Murrow, Eric Sevareid, Howard K. Smith, and other political commentators. Cronkite had never finished college. As a former wire service reporter, he focused primarily on the daily fact-finding tasks of news journalists and less on the analysis. He had an image of being more grunt than grand. However, Cronkite had a facile talent for identifying salient issues regarding business, economics, social matters, and the environment long before they became politically controversial. He was able to create an image as a credible public figure whom people could respect, more like "us" than "them."

In 1969 Walter Cronkite anchored the CBS coverage of the momentous landing of astronauts on the surface of the moon. It was a story he had worked on since 1957, when the Soviet satellite *Sputnik* was launched into space. At that point in history, Cronkite foresaw that space exploration would be an important phase in history. His careful, meticulous, tedious efforts to acquire a knowledge of the techniques of astrophysics—all attributable to lessons he had learned as a cub wire journalist—made him far more conversant than any rival correspondents. When *Eagle* touched down on the surface of the moon, Cronkite gave a gasp of relief all Americans could share, then presented a commentary that was intelligible and informative. He exuded a confident conversational style that made people believe what he was saying. He was *the* credible source of news information for a generation of citizens (Gates, 1978).

In the early 1970s, while safely at the pinnacle of his field, Cronkite decided in his role of managing editor and anchor of "The CBS Evening News," that the show's staff needed to conduct a series of reports on threats to the environment (Gates, 1978). During the early 1970s, environmental issues were not at the top of the political agenda. Yet, Cronkite had begun researching the effects of pollution on our air and water supplies. According to him, his goal in reporting the news and in presenting investigative stories was to provide viewers with enough information to stir their interest and intrigue them so that they would further investigate the topic (Walker, 1984). He viewed his role as one of an instigator. His job was to report the facts, and the public's job was to analyze.

Walter Cronkite became known as "the only honest face on television" (Rottenberg, 1994, 34). He anchored the network's evening newscast for nineteen years. His signature sign-off phrase, "And that's that way it is," became more familiar to many Americans than the Lord's Prayer (Rottenberg, 1994). Cronkite influenced what Americans thought about world events, and when he spoke out against the Vietnam War, his actions had an impact on American presidential politics. In 1968 he had a half-hour news special to express his "disillusionment" with the Vietnam War. No longer was he solely an investigator; now he was analyst. Perhaps the story is apocryphal, but, after watching the news special, President Lyndon Johnson supposedly turned to his press secretary and exclaimed that if he as president had lost Walter Cronkite, he had lost Mr. Average Citizen (Rowe, 1992, 63). "Cronkite's reporting did change the balance; it was the first time in American history that a war had been declared over by a newsman" (Halberstam, 1979, 514).

THE CONCERNS OF A RETIRED ANCHOR

Often referred to as "Uncle Walter" because of his avuncular style and the abiding trust placed in him, Cronkite became an icon of national importance. Years after his 1981 retirement from CBS as news anchor, Walter Cronkite remained one of America's most respected and trusted broadcasters, perhaps the most respected newsperson in the journalism industry (Rottenberg, 1994).

In 1992 Cronkite signed a contract that marked his full journey from wire service to the wired nation. He joined the Discovery Network, a cable television network, to produce a series of shows, including one entitled "Walter Cronkite's

World'' and, later, the ''Cronkite Report.'' He frequently uses CATV as a forum for his examination of the tensions between news designed to please audiences and news as unbiased coverage of current events. A wire service newspaper correspondent in a wired age, Cronkite grew fearful that Americans rely too heavily on television to gain information. He often reminded audiences to read newspapers if they wanted the story behind television's mere headline news service. When CBS News, in a Draconian retrenchment, closed down eight foreign bureaus, Cronkite spoke out against the action as a travesty in American journalism that would have a negative impact on the depth of information gained and reported to the American public. He learned his lessons as a wire service journalist well—a commitment to getting the news firsthand—and closing news bureaus is a step backward that renders news secondhand.

Cronkite abhors the sensationalist trend in television news. Tabloid journalism, junkdog journalism, or trash journalism—whether in print or on television—does nothing to elevate the human spirit or to elevate the level of public political discourse. He has been sharply critical of the trend toward ''politics by talk show,'' the phenomenon popularized in the 1992 and 1996 presidential elections by such political commentators as Larry King (q.v.), Rush Limbaugh (q.v.), and John McLaughlin (q.v.). ''It's a phenomenon of the moment,'' he urged; ''*It will not stand!*'' (Range, 1992, 16).

Yet, just as the Pony Express met its demise at the hands of wire service telegraphy, and radio journalism succumbed to television, Americans have grown accustomed to satellite, cellular, minicam technology. The adventurers of wire service journalism have long since, as Walter Cronkite's career evidenced, yielded the way to electronic wraparound, wall-to-wall spectacles anchored from a glitzy studio. He was more than solely a news anchor, he was an ''institution'' (Slater, 1988, 288). As such, Walter Cronkite kept alive in the electronic age the values that drove wire service political commentary. Whether those values survive in the wired nation remains to be seen. The outlook is not good.

REFERENCES

Selected Political Works by Walter Cronkite

The Challenge of Change. Washington, DC: Public Affairs Press, 1971.
Eye on the World. New York: Crowles Book Co., 1971.
Eyes on an Era: Four Decades of Photojournalism. New York: Rizzoli, 1995.

Selected Critical Works about Walter Cronkite

Candee, M., ed. ''Cronkite, Walter (Leland, Jr.).'' In *Current Biography 1956*, 130–32. New York: H. W. Wilson, 1957.
Flint, J. ''Discovery Finds Cronkite.'' *Broadcasting*, December 21, 1992, 32.
Goodman, W. ''The Cronkite Report: The Drug Dilemma: War or Peace?'' *New York Times*, 144, June 20, 1995, C24(L).

Range, P. R. "Walter Cronkite Is Mad as Hell." *TV Guide*, July 11, 1992, 15–18.
Rottenberg, D. "And That's the Way It Is." *American Journalism Review* 16 (May 1994): 34, 36–37.
Rowe, C. "Seventeen Years with Uncle Walter." *Washington Journalism Review* 14 (March 1992): 63.
Walker, S. "Cronkite on the Changing Media." *Christian Science Monitor*, March 7, 1984, 16.

Selected General Works

Boyer, P. J. *Who Killed CBS?* New York: Random House, 1988.
"Covering Religion." *Christian Century*, 111, December 14, 1994, 12.
Gates, G. P. *Air Time: The Inside Story of CBS News.* New York: Harper & Row, 1978.
Goldberg, G., and G. J. Goldberg. *Anchors.* New York: Birch Lane Press, 1990.
Halberstam, D. *The Powers That Be.* New York: Alfred A. Knopf, 1979.
Metz, R. *CBS: Reflections in a Bloodshot Eye.* Chicago: Playboy Press, 1975.
Nimmo, D. "Politics and the Mass Media: From Political Rule to Postpolitical Mediarchy." *Current World Leaders* 36 (April 1993): 303–320.
Schroth, R. A. *The American Journey of Eric Sevareid.* South Royalton, VT: Steerforth Press, 1995.
Slater, R. *This . . . Is CBS.* Englewood Cliffs, NJ: Prentice-Hall, 1988.

ELMER (HOLMES) DAVIS

(January 13, 1890–May 18, 1958)

Missionary for Free Expression

When the Great War began in Europe in 1914, Henry Ford, the pioneer American automobile manufacturer, was vexed. He wanted the killing to end. By November 1915, Ford had launched a project to get the soldiers out of the trenches by Christmas of that year. His plan was to send a Peace Ship filled with a passenger list of luminaries, idealists, and statesmen, from New York to Oslo (then called Christiania), Norway. It was a dramatic gesture he believed would be applauded by one and all and provoke the world into demanding an end to the conflict.

To cover the news of the voyage, the *New York Times* dispatched a twenty-five-year-old cub reporter who had been with the newspaper for only one year. In his brief tenure, he had displayed a gift for objective, sardonic reporting, the ideal attributes for awakening readers to the realities of power politics in an age of modern warfare. The young reporter managed to keep his contempt for Ford's foolish project out of the wireless dispatches he sent back to the *Times* from the Peace Ship. But on board bickering among passengers developed over whether America should prepare for the eventuality of war, a prospect that was anathema to Henry Ford. The *Times* correspondent felt obligated to report the wrangling without slant or comment. Ford, who was not pleased, censured the cub reporter, and soured on the whole project well before docking in Oslo.

In 1939, when the Columbia Broadcasting System (CBS), required a calm, even-handed style of radio commentary in the days leading up to Nazi Germany's invasion of Poland, CBS selected the same objective, sardonic correspondent. On December 7, 1941, shortly after broadcasting the news of the Japanese attack on Pearl Harbor, CBS turned again to the calming, analytical voice that had come to the network in 1939. With the entry of the United States into World War II, President Franklin Roosevelt, casting about for a trusted person to head up America's domestic and foreign propaganda campaign, came to the same choice that the *Times* and CBS had made on earlier occasions and appointed the CBS commentator director of the Office of War Information (OWI). As soon as the war ended, the journalist with a Midwestern twang returned to radio, with the American Broadcasting Company (ABC), and, when the political witchcraft called McCarthyism swept the United States in the 1950s, once again the same calming voice softened the anger and advised Americans, ''Don't let them scare you.''

The *New York Times* reporter, CBS commentator, U.S. propaganda chief, and voice of free expression in the 1950s was Elmer Davis. In an open society, one would hope that *any* political communicator would always insist upon free speech and free press for *every* political communicator. However, in times of war, real or imagined threats to national security, and political crises, that is not always the case. The contribution of Elmer Davis to political commentary lies precisely in his consistent role as a missionary for free expression. Whereas the crusader campaigns for a personal, partisan, or doctrinal cause in the name of an unquestioned TRUTH—for example, Fulton Lewis, Jr. (q.v.)—the missionary's task is to educate audiences to adhere to a different conviction, namely, that truth is not engraved in capital letters, that, indeed, truth is so complex and multisided as to require constant testing and reformulation.

The American philosopher, Charles Sanders Peirce, put the assumption that guided Elmer Davis' career succinctly when he wrote,

> Upon this first, and in some sense this sole, rule of reason, that in order to learn you must desire to learn, and in so desiring you must not be satisfied with what you already incline to think, there follows one corollary which itself deserves to be inscribed upon every wall of the city of philosophy.

Peirce's "corollary" consistently motivated Davis' political communication:

> Do not block the way of inquiry. (Thorson, 1962, 120)

PURSUING TRIDIMENSIONAL TRUTH THROUGHOUT A QUADRIDIMENSIONAL CAREER

Like another major figure in political commentary in the twentieth century, Walter Lippmann (q.v.), Elmer Davis drew a sharp distinction between news and truth: "Too much of our news is one-dimensional, when truth has three dimensions (or maybe more)" (R. L. Davis, 1964, 177). Davis believed that the unidimensional quality of news produces accounts of the world from a single viewpoint, usually one derived from the routines, rituals, conventions, and encrusted habits of the news business. By contrast, truth has many dimensions, far more even than envisioned in Protagoras' ancient belief that there are two sides to every issue. Davis' convictions about the multidimensionality of truth came naturally to a man who, in his three score and eight years of life, pursued a career possessing at least four dimensions of its own.

Elmer Davis was the only child of a bank cashier, Elam Davis, and a high school teacher and principal, Louise, Elam's second wife. Born Elmer Holmes Davis in Aurora, Indiana, on January 13, 1890, Davis eschewed his middle name early. Aurora was a short distance from Cincinnati, one of the hotbeds of baseball in the Midwest at the century's turn. Indeed, the Cincinnati Reds were reborn themselves as a franchise after a decade's hiatus in the year of Davis' birth. Small wonder that as a youth Davis came to love baseball, a game that attracted other political commentators of the century, including James "Scotty"

Reston (q.v.) and George F. Will (q.v.). When young Elmer could not make his high school team as a result of his ungainliness, he became the team manager and scorekeeper. Had Davis not developed avid political interests his love of sports might well have led him to a career as a sports journalist.

Although he was not a high school athlete, Davis did excel in the classroom. He also was a skillful rebel, one who questioned received wisdom (of which there was a great deal in the Baptist stronghold of Aurora) with a dry wit touched with an appreciation of the ironic. The word high school classmates often used to describe Davis was "droll" (Burlingame, 1961, 24). Drollery turned out to be a hallmark of the Davis style of writing and broadcasting throughout his career. Decades later, a colleague who admired Davis as a mentor, political commentator Edward R. Murrow (q.v.), frequently recalled something that Davis had said that fully captured the latter's droll sense of irony: "A filthy mind is a great consolation" (Persico, 1988, 167).

At the age of sixteen, Elmer Davis enrolled in Franklin College. He continued his excellent scholarly record, concentrated on Greek and Latin, and graduated magna cum laude with a B.S. degree; he obtained a master's degree shortly thereafter. When Davis applied for a Rhodes scholarship, he had no problems whatsoever with the rugged qualifying exam; his classical education served him well. But, another of the Rhodes' requirements was a "fondness for and success in manly outdoor sports." Since Davis had no athletic record to speak of, it was fortunate that "fondness" alone was enough. In the six-year existence of the scholarship program, 397 Rhodes Scholars had been named. Elmer Davis in 1910 became the 398th student to win a Rhodes scholarship to Queen's College, Oxford.

To defray the costs of getting to England, Davis proposed a scheme to a steamship company. In exchange for his rounding up all forty-eight Rhodes Scholars embarking from New York to travel on the same ship, the company gave Davis free passage. So, coincidentally, a decade after another future twentieth-century political commentator, H. V. Kaltenborn (q.v.), worked his way across the Atlantic from New York to Liverpool on a cattle boat, Davis sailed on the *Haverford*, a cattle boat, to Liverpool. His plan was to take full advantage of three years of study and travel. However, when word came that his father had suffered a financial disaster, Davis sandwiched a three-year program into two. Still, on his examinations for a degree, he barely missed achieving highest honors.

Elmer Davis returned from Oxford a skilled and polished writer, so much so that his aim was to make a career as a freelance writer, rather than as a teacher as his widowed mother wished. He became neither freelance writer nor salaried teacher. Instead he joined the editorial staff of *Advantage* magazine, then in 1914 he obtained a job as a *New York Times* reporter. He thus began the first phrase of his career, that which gave him a newspaper reporter's perspective of the world. On general assignment, he viewed a world from the vantage point of chasing fire engines; scenes of brutal murders, accidents, and sporting events; and even the deck of Henry Ford's Peace Ship of quarreling peacemakers.

Through it all, Davis managed to sharpen his skill at turning phases in a droll but realistic fashion. Moreover, he made money at it. In that era reporters' salaries were minimal. Newspaper correspondents worked on a "space system" whereby a column earned an established number of dollars, a feature a little more, an exclusive story even more, and so on. For a reporter to earn a livable wage it was necessary to write in an appropriate style, neither terse nor prolix. If terse, the account would be too few column inches to earn dollars; if prolix, copy editors would prune the excess away leaving, again, minimal income. Davis' solution was to exploit his "facility with the English language [that] made it possible for him to write a long story so phrased that a copy-reader couldn't cut it much" (Burlingame, 1961, 67).

Davis was especially inventive in this respect in his coverage of national political party conventions. In 1920 he created for readers of the *Times* a fictional character, Godfrey G. Gloom. Gloom was correspondent for a nonexistent newspaper, the *Grapevine Telegraph* of Amity, Indiana. As the "oldest living conventioneer," Gloom allegedly had been an eyewitness to national political party conventions since the Civil War. Davis' convention coverage took the form of interviews with Gloom, reporting the seasoned convention watcher's views of parties, issues, candidates, the times, political philosophy—always in several hundred words. Davis dispatched Godfrey G. Gloom to conventions even after departing the *Times* as a staff member in 1924. However, on June 28, 1936, in a "special to the *New York Times*" under Davis' byline, Davis dispatched Gloom altogether. Davis reported Gloom's death while crossing a street outside the convention center where the Democrats had just renominated Franklin Roosevelt for the presidency. "The convention system and I have both outlived our time," Davis quotes Gloom as saying just before expiring; "and I know it even if the national committees don't" (Burlingame, 1961, 129).

In a ten-year period at the *Times*, Davis mastered journalism with hands-on experience as a sports writer, political analyst, foreign correspondent, editorial writer, and political humorist. He did not, however, give up his desire to be a freelance writer. In fact, while he was at the *Times*, he published two novels, several short stories and essays, and the *History of the New York Times* (1921). His motivation was a thirst for writing and a necessity to support his family (he married Florence MacMillan in 1917 after a four-year courtship; they had two sons). In 1924 Davis left the *Times* as a full-time reporter and undertook a second phase of his career as a freelance author. In the next fifteen years came ten more novels, several short stories, and light essays for *Harper's*, *The Saturday Review of Literature*, and *The New Yorker* and editorials for *Life*, a weekly magazine published before the photo magazine of the same name that was popular in the 1930s and 1940s. (At one point there was an effort to contact the freelancing Davis and inform him that he had won a writing contest; Davis was at a baseball game, did not get the message until too late, and the prize went to another contestant.)

One of the appeals of freelancing for Davis was that it liberated him from the restrictions of straight, objective reporting implied by the motto of the *New York Times*: "all the news that's fit to print." As an independent author he could draw upon his scholar's knowledge of ancient history, Greek, and Latin to analyze current events. For instance, Davis could scarcely in his day at the *Times* (even using the guise of Godfrey G. Gloom) make the scathing observation about the 1924 political conventions that he was able to write in *Harper's*: "The only visible difference of any sort is that the Republican party seems to contain a slightly higher percentage of crooks, and the Democratic party of fools" (Fang, 1977, 179), a judgment worthy of caustic political observer H. L. Mencken (q.v.).

A freelance perspective allowed Elmer Davis to broaden the definition of politics to include arts, tastes, and customs beyond the narrow confines of laws, political conventions, and politicians' rhetoric. Thus, in an essay, "On Being Kept by a Cat" (R. L. Davis, 1964, 185–98), Davis drew an analogy between alley cats' fierce independence and liberals' rugged individualism; conservatives prefer docile dogs. And, as an opera fan, Davis had a fancy for Richard Wagner's *Ring* cycle. In a review of the cycle, "The Imperfect Wagner" (R. L. Davis, 1964, 216–31), Davis compared the mythic world of the *Ring* to Adolf Hitler's Nazi Germany, a comparison copied by numerous political observers thereafter.

In 1939 Elmer Davis began a third phase of his career, one interrupted by World War II. CBS' noted radio commentator, H. V. Kaltenborn was on vacation. There were ominous signs that war was about to break out in Europe and the network did not want to get caught shorthanded in its New York studios in Kaltenborn's absence. On repeated occasions Ed Klauber, who was in charge of news operations at CBS and a former *New York Times* colleague of Davis' as well as the best man at Davis' wedding, had tried to lure Davis to CBS. Although he had appeared on CBS as early as 1930, discussing "What is College For?" (Davis, in Culbert, 1976, 132) and had replaced Kaltenborn on a part-time basis in 1937 on routine broadcasts, Davis was reluctant to enter broadcasting full-time under crisis conditions (Halberstam, 1979). His Midwestern twang seemed unsuited to the medium; one listener complained he had a "voice as lousy and monotonous as [Hollywood gossip commentator] Luella Parsons" (Davis, in Culbert, 1976, 131). Moreover, his essayist style might not fit the time limits imposed on radio newscasts. Still, when Kaltenborn went on holiday, Klauber convinced Davis to substitute. Davis broadcast the evening news for five minutes at 8:55 P.M. EST (Slater, 1988).

Ever the lover of baseball, Elmer Davis recalled his eighteen-hour days for CBS in the prelude to World War II as Kaltenborn's replacement as "a little like trying to play center-field in place of Joe DiMaggio" (Burlingame, 1961, 154). A more apt baseball analogy is Lou Gehrig's subbing for Wally Pipp and playing 2,130 consecutive games for the New York Yankees as Pipp's career declined and ended. Davis' capacity for combining the essentials of the day's news with objective commentary in a candid, witty style presaged Kaltenborn's departure from the network:

> From the first five minutes of that [Davis'] voice Hans Kaltenborn's immense reputation began to fade.... When Kaltenborn spoke one never felt his immediate presence. He was always talking from afar: one could picture the environment: the soundproof studio, the controls, the meticulously prepared script. Elmer Davis was right in your room ... telling you in the fewest possible words what you wanted to know. The why of it was partly in the words, partly in the inflection. In that flat, even voice, the impact of the slightest up and down was stunning. And, hearing it, you could almost see facial expressions: the slight raising of eyebrows, the slighter twist of the mouth toward the smile that never quite came. (Burlingame, 1961, 154–55)

His role as a radio commentator opened up yet another perspective on political truth for Elmer Davis. It brought home to him the immediacy of radio's coverage of breaking events. In the days leading up to Germany's invasion of Poland and England's declaration of war on Germany, working in the CBS New York studios Davis monitored the reports of CBS correspondents from Europe. He did not leave the block containing the CBS offices and his hotel for nine straight days before September 1, 1939 (Hosley, 1984). Davis proved adept at distilling large quantities of information in a minimum of time, adding a single commentary to give listeners a sense of new insights, identifying his sources, but keeping his own political views to himself (Shulman, 1990).

Correspondents' live reports, especially Edward R. Murrow's, impressed Davis. As he later wrote in his introduction to a volume of Murrow's memorable broadcasts from London, like any news broadcaster reporting live from the site of breaking events, Murrow "talks under no instructions from the home office in New York except to find the news and report it," even if it be reporting an air raid from a roof top as "a good way to get the news, but perhaps not the best way to make sure you will go on getting it" (Davis, in Murrow, 1941, viii). In late April 1940, Davis joined Murrow in England and witnessed the devastation of Coventry, Plymouth, Bristol, Southampton, and other areas. In his five-minute evening broadcasts, he faithfully reported his observations to listeners in America, an audience of 12.5 million.

Elmer Davis developed a unique style in his early days at CBS. Unlike most newscasters, he never tore teletype reports from the machines. Instead, he read the teletype as it came in, jotted notes on a ruled notepad to fix key news points in his memory, and then constructed his broadcast from his notes. No longer was he Elmer Davis, *New York Times* reporter writing to maximize the number of column inches for which he would be paid; now he was Elmer Davis, radio newscaster reporting and commenting while economizing words to fit a five-minute broadcast. Although Davis made it look easy, his style required maximum concentration. He was the very opposite of the apocryphal letter writer who apologized to a friend for sending a verbose, long letter on the grounds that there was no time to write a short one (Burlingame, 1961, 170).

From the vantage point of a radio broadcaster, Elmer Davis reinforced his belief in the sanctity of free expression, a right that a reporter should not abuse. The policy of CBS News was that broadcasters should help listeners understand, weigh, and judge information but not do the judging themselves. Davis reformulated that code:

> Radio news analysts have their opinions like everybody else, but those opinions ought to be kept out of sight as far as possible . . . the essence of this job is to try to straighten out the record so that the public can form its own opinions. (Fang, 1977, 186)

This same view guided Elmer Davis not only as a radio analyst but in the next phase of his career as a political communicator, that of government administrator.

At 2:25 P.M. EST, Sunday, December 7, 1941, a CBS broadcaster read a terse announcement over the network informing listeners of the Japanese attack on Pearl Harbor. Thirty-six minutes later Elmer Davis was on the air with direct news from Honolulu, reporting eyewitness accounts relayed to CBS of fire and smoke at U.S. facilities. Davis also discussed the political background of the attack and the possible motives of the Japanese ruling clique (Slater, 1988, 95; Burlingame, 1961, 180). Six months later, on June 13, 1942, President Franklin Roosevelt issued Executive Order No. 9182 to create the Office of War Information (OWI) with the responsibility of channeling war information from government to the news media and public (Solely, 1989). During World War I, that responsibility had been the task of the Committee on Public Information (CPI), which was directed by a former journalist, George Creel (q.v.). Two months after its inception, President Roosevelt appointed as director of the OWI a journalist, Elmer Davis.

In one aspect the choice of Davis to head the OWI was felicitous. In many respects Davis as a *New York Times* reporter, freelance writer, and radio broadcaster had remained the rebel of high school days, developing a unique communication style. Rebels thrive on free expression, and in the first three phases of his career Elmer Davis had done just that. Davis viewed America's war effort as a rebellion against tyranny, one that could succeed only through free expression and a free flow of war information. He envisioned a "propaganda of information"; that is, one to tell the truth both to Americans and to America's enemies "as closely and as objectively as possible" (Shulman, 1990, 170). Given such views it is not surprising that Davis' colleagues in the news business rejoiced that a respected journalist would coordinate the government's wartime propaganda; here was one who understood the needs of journalists.

Not everyone at the OWI shared Davis' view of propaganda. Others favored a "propaganda as weapon" approach—an approach that would selectively shape messages to boost Americans' morale, weaken the enemy's resolve, and advance U.S. military and diplomatic aims. Therein was the source of a conflict—propaganda of information versus propaganda as weapon—that plagued the OWI throughout the war. It also plagued the directors of the OWI's successor agencies during the Cold War, namely, Edward R. Murrow of the United States Information Agency (USIA), Carl T. Rowan (q.v.) who followed Murrow at the USIA, and John Chancellor (q.v.), director of the Voice of America.

Whatever view of propaganda prevailed, it must be adhered to by each of the plethora of fragmented agencies responsible for information, publicity, and censorship at home and abroad—a vast, complex bureaucracy of more than 2,300 persons and a $20 million budget. During World War I George Creel handled a similar problem at the CPI by an administrative imposition of his propaganda aims and the enlistment of President Woodrow Wilson's aid in subduing any rebellion within the organization.

Creel's approach, however, was not an option available to Elmer Davis. For one thing, the fragmentation within the OWI was far greater than anything experienced at the CPI. Furthermore, as a lifelong rebel, Elmer Davis had no stomach for stamping out dissent and the free expression that nourishes it. Even had he been so inclined, Franklin Roosevelt's administrative style was to encourage conflict among administrative subordinates, not to override it, as was the case with Woodrow Wilson. And, whereas there was a personal intimacy between George Creel and Wilson, there was none between Elmer Davis and Roosevelt. Added was one other crucial complicating factor. Elmer Davis came to the OWI without any administrative experience. As the biographer of the Voice of America, the postwar offspring of the OWI, assessed Davis' role:

> Davis gave the new agency an immediate national respectability. He understood journalism and public relations, and he knew the members of the press corps and worked easily with them, but he was completely inexperienced as an administrator. Despite his efforts, his integrity, and his self-assurance, he lacked the know-how to take an issue and push it through a bureaucratic obstacle course. He was not aggressive enough to fight his way through the thickets of Washington politics. His ignorance of Washington politics was . . . enormous. (Shulman, 1990, 36)

Throughout the existence of the OWI, Elmer Davis was in the midst of running battles that must have reminded him of the quarrels on Henry Ford's Peace Ship in 1915. Among many struggles were those with congressional critics over budgets, with military leaders who wanted their own information programs, with news versus advertising specialists regarding information versus sloganizing approaches to propaganda, and with the Domestic Branch versus the Overseas Branch concerning control of overall OWI policy. The battle for policy control brought Davis into direct confrontation with the head of the Overseas Branch, playwright Robert Sherwood, a speechwriter and close confidant of President

Roosevelt. Davis prevailed with the help of a newly appointed associate director of the OWI, old friend and CBS executive Ed Klauber. With Klauber, Davis reorganized the Overseas Branch, relieving Sherwood. Sherwood appealed to the president. Reluctant to settle the issue, Roosevelt lectured Davis and Sherwood and instructed them to settle their own differences. The two managed a face-saving compromise.

With the end of World War II, the OWI was liquidated in September 1945. One of Davis' final struggles at the agency was, typically, on behalf of a free flow of information. After Germany's defeat, the Allies secretly made plans to prohibit American and other newspapers, magazines, and wire services from entering occupied Germany. When Davis scuttled the plan by exposing the secret, he received a rebuke from President Harry Truman, budget-cutting threats from Congress, and editorial criticism from hostile news organizations. (A similar Allied effort had been made to keep the press out of Germany after World War I; Lowell Thomas (q.v.), then a CPI correspondent, was instrumental in blocking that effort.)

Elmer Davis resumed his career as a radio broadcaster in December 1945, but not with CBS. Davis accepted a position with ABC. At first he broadcast a fifteen-minute program of news and analysis at 7:15 P.M. EST Mondays and Tuesdays, and at 3:00 on Sunday afternoons. In January 1947, Davis occupied the 7:15 P.M. time slot five nights a week. He continued until ill health required him to retire from nightly newscasts in 1953.

Versions differ over why he departed CBS. Davis maintained there was a difference over ''working conditions'' with CBS president William Paley. Davis' agent attributed the departure to a breakdown of communications between CBS and Davis (Sperber, 1986). Another possibility was ABC's offer, which increased Davis' salary from $1,000 per week to $3,500 per week. Finally, after fighting with missionary zeal for freedom of information under wartime conditions, it is entirely likely that Davis was reluctant to return to CBS with its guidelines that demanded newscasters keep their opinions to themselves.

Regardless of his reasons for switching networks, in his years at ABC Elmer Davis was increasingly staunch in advocating Peirce's Corollary that the way of inquiry should not be blocked. In postwar America the anticommunist sentiment, the Korean War, and McCarthyism erected many such barriers. When Senator Joseph McCarthy enlarged his search for Communists, seeking them not only in the State Department but also on college campuses, Davis spoke out for academic freedom. In his radio analysis, Davis noted that McCarthy's claim that the senator ''would rather'' be ''looking for Communist thinkers than for Communists'' was a ''conventionally vague phrase'' that could but produce outcries ''about interference with academic freedom'' (Burlingame, 1961, 324). When President Dwight Eisenhower was criticized by a member of his own political party for urging Americans not to ''join the book burners,'' Davis defended Eisenhower's attitude as the same ''toward freedom of thought and freedom of speech as the men who wrote the Declaration of Independence and the Constitution'' (Burlingame, 1961, 331–32). And, when a Davis broadcast defended a political meeting that self-styled ''patriots'' sought to end with violence, a listener castigated Davis for being ''inconsistent''; Communists break up meetings too. Davis was not persuaded. As far as Davis was concerned, that Communists behave like Communists and try to break up other people's meetings was no reason why the other democrats should behave like Communists.

Elmer Davis' clearest defense of free expression opposed those who sought to prevent Henry Wallace, a 1948 presidential candidate, from speaking; Wallace was too leftist. Said Davis,

> Now listeners to these broadcasts know that I yield to none in my conviction that Henry Wallace is wrong. But wrong or not, he has just as much right to express his opinions as I have or anybody else. Free speech means free speech for everybody, not merely for those you happen to approve personally. (Burlingame, 1961, 288)

CONCLUSION: DEATH OF A LION

After high blood pressure forced Elmer Davis to discontinue his nightly newscasts in 1953, he made lecture tours, spent a brief time as a television commentator on Sunday afternoons in 1954, and published volumes of his collected writings. Two such volumes repeat his never ceasing mission on behalf of free expression: *But We Were Born Free* (1954) about the McCarthy era and *Two Minutes till Midnight* (1955) about the nuclear age. Hypertension, paratyphoid fever, a stroke, and pneumonia all took their toll. In the last month of his life, he could not speak or swallow.

In one of his later essays, ''Grandeurs and Miseries of Old Age,'' he summed up the mission of his quadridimensional career and its lessons for all political commentators in any age:

> We have got to defeat this attack on the freedom of the mind; and I think we can defeat it if enough of us stand up against it—enough of all kinds of people, rich and poor, young and old. . . . At any age it is better to be a dead lion than a living dog—though better still, of course, to be a living and victorious lion. (Davis, in R. L. Davis, 1964, 29)

Whether Elmer Davis was victorious as a lion awaits the course of future political commentary. The lion himself succumbed to increasing frailties and died on May 18, 1958.

REFERENCES

Selected Political Works by Elmer Davis

History of the New York Times. New York: New York Times, 1921.
Not to Mention the War. Indianapolis, IN: Bobbs Merrill, 1940.

Introduction. In E. R. Murrow, *This Is London*, vii–ix. New York: Schocken Books, 1941.

"War Information." In *War Information and Censorship*. Washington, DC: American Council on Public Affairs, 1943.

But We Were Born Free. Garden City, NY: Garden City Books, 1954.

Two Minutes till Midnight. Indianapolis, IN: Bobbs Merrill, 1955.

Selected Critical Works about Elmer Davis

Block, M., ed. "Davis, Elmer." *Current Biography 1940*, 224–26. New York: H. W. Wilson, 1940.

Burlingame, R. *Don't Let Them Scare You*. Philadelphia: J. B. Lippincott, 1961.

Culbert, D. H. "Elmer Davis: Radio's Hoosier." In *News for Everyman*, 125–152. Westport, CT: Greenwood Press, 1976.

"Davis, Elmer (Holmes)." In *National Cyclopedia of American Biography*, 13. New York: James T. White, 1968.

Davis, R. L., ed. *By Elmer Davis*. Indianapolis, IN: Bobbs Merrill, 1964.

Downs, R. B., and J. C. Downs. "Elmer Holmes Davis." In *Journalists of the United States*, edited by R. B. Downs and J. C. Downs, 107–8. Jefferson, NC: McFarland, 1989.

Fang, I. E. "Elmer Davis." In *Those Radio Commentators!*, 175–97. Ames: Iowa State University Press, 1977.

Schoenbaum, E. W., ed. "Davis, Elmer H(olmes)." *Political Profiles: The Truman Years*, 117–18. New York: Facts on File, 1978.

Selected General Works

Halberstam, D. *The Powers That Be*. New York: Alfred A. Knopf, 1979.

Hosley, D. H. *As Good as Any: Foreign Correspondence on American Radio, 1930–1940*. Westport, CT: Greenwood Press, 1984.

Persico, J. E. *Edward R. Murrow: An American Original*. New York: Dell Publishing, 1988.

Schroth, R. A. *The American Journey of Eric Sevareid*. South Royalton, VT: Steerforth Press, 1995.

Shulman, H. C. *The Voice of America: Propaganda and Democracy, 1941–1945*. Madison: University of Wisconsin Press, 1990.

Slater, R. *This Is . . . CBS*. Englewood Cliffs, NJ: Prentice-Hall, 1988.

Solely, L. C. *Radio Warfare*. New York: Praeger, 1989.

Sperber, A. M. *Murrow: His Life and His Times*. New York: Freundlich, 1986.

Thorson, T. L. *The Logic of Democracy*. New York: Holt, Rinehart and Winston, 1962.

JOHN DEWEY

(October 20, 1859–June 1, 1952)

The Philosopher as Democracy's Communicator

The values that underlie politics, values that politicians seek to secure for themselves and their constituents through conflict and compromise, include well-being, wealth, respect, moral repute, affection, and control over others. In achieving their ends, politicians also value skill—"proficiency in any practice whatever, whether in arts or crafts, trade or profession"—and enlightenment, "knowledge, insight, and information concerning personal and cultural relations" (Lasswell & Kaplan, 1950, 55).

In large measure, the key commentators who have made notable contributions to political communication in the twentieth century have done so by exercising polished technical skills: Edward L. Bernays (q.v.) as a public relations counsel, George Creel (q.v.) as an administrator of propaganda, Theodore H. White (q.v.) as a chronicler, and Arthur Krock (q.v.) and James "Scotty" Reston (q.v) as news bureau administrators. Walter Lippmann (q.v.), Dorothy Thompson (q.v.), Carl T. Rowan (q.v.), and George F. Will (q.v.), used their writing skills as columnists. Walter Cronkite (q.v.), H. V. Kaltenborn (q.v.), Bill Moyers (q.v.), Edward R. Murrow (q.v.), and Eric Sevareid (q.v.) exploited broadcasting techniques as commentators. That is not to say that these technicians failed to inform, elucidate, or impart insight in exercising their skills. Their expertise, however, was more stylistic than substantive; the *meaning* of their message resided in the *means* they used to convey it rather than in its intrinsic content (McLuhan, 1964).

John Dewey, "the most influential figure in American philosophical thought in the first half of the twentieth century" (Sidorsky, 1977, vii), contributed to political communication in a markedly different way. By all accounts, his method of communicating was not impressive: "He had none of the tricks or gifts of the effective lecturer" (Edman, 1938, 138). Although he wrote a column of opinion for a political magazine for two decades, his writing often seemed obscure. His penchant for staring off into space while talking would render him a poor candidate for success alongside a Corrine "Cokie" Roberts (q.v.) or Rush Limbaugh (q.v) of electronic politics; his solemn facial expressions, lightened by a rare chuckle, would be no match for a Ted Koppel (q.v.). Surely Dewey's frequent meanderings would vex the most skilled television producer's efforts to extract a ten- or twenty-second sound bite.

Nevertheless, John Dewey was the forerunner of an important cadre of professionally trained academic intellectuals who have left their mark on twentieth-century political commentary. Some, such as Raymond Moley (q.v.), former Secretary of State Henry Kissinger, or former U.N. Ambassador Jeane Kirkpatrick, have done so through government service. Others are members of "think tanks," institutions engaged in policy analysis, research, and advocacy, such as the Brookings Institution, the American Enterprise Institute, and the Heritage Foundation. Numerous academics act as freelance entrepreneurs who appear on radio and television public affairs programs, newscasts, and panel shows; Kathleen Hall Jamieson, of the Annenberg School of Communications, University of Pennsylvania, and Larry Sabato, of the University of Virginia, exemplify academics whose business cards read, "Have Insights, Will Travel." A few scholastics, notably John McLaughlin (q.v.) and George Will, flee the classroom for the television studio and op-ed pages; they become media and political celebrities in their own right (Nimmo & Combs, 1992).

Although heirs to the Dewey legacy, few such intellectuals have managed, as did Dewey, to retain a consistent focus on enlightenment as the end of political commentary rather than a display of skilled legerdemain—Noam Chomsky (q.v.) is a notable exception. Unlike Dewey, who regarded the intellectual as a creative thinker, his heirs act more in keeping with historian/critic Jacques Barzun's derisive use of the term "intellectual": an intellectual is anyone "who carries a briefcase," set off from others by being "aware of the world of opinions, of-isms, schools of thought, sides of questions, movements of ideas"; one "who reads journals, books, reports, memoranda," hence, "obviously carries a briefcase" (Barzun, 1954, 201). Like many of the philosophers who were courtiers in the salons of the French Enlightenment, contemporary claimants to Dewey's legacy are frequently charmed more by the manner than by the material of their arguments. Dewey, however, was not so easily seduced:

> To attend a lecture of John Dewey was to *participate* in the actual business of thought. Those pauses were delays in creative thinking, when the next step was really being considered, and for the glib dramatics of the teacher-actor was substituted the enterprise, careful and candid, of the genuine thinker. (Edman, 1938, 143)

THE PHILOSOPHER APPROACHES THE ARENA OF THE CONCRETE

John Dewey, born on October 20, 1859, lived four decades of his life in the nineteenth century, occupied with philosophical contemplation of what human beings know and how they know it. By the date of his death, on June 1, 1952, he had lived five decades in the twentieth century, occupied increasingly with, as one of his former pupils put it, "the [political] arena of the concrete, himself interpreting current life" (Westbrook, 1991, 195).

John Dewey was born in the same year that Charles Darwin's *Origin of the Species* and John Stuart Mill's *On Liberty* were published, two volumes that would reconstruct received views about the human condition. Dewey's philosophy would in later years do the same. It was also the year before the outbreak of the Civil War. Young John Dewey later recalled with sadness the devastation of the Virginia countryside, where the family joined his father who was serving as an army quartermaster. War too would be a subject of John Dewey's writings in the twentieth century.

Born in Burlington, Vermont, John was the third of four sons of Archibald and Lucina (Rich) Dewey. His father was a grocer, and John grew up in relative comfort. The young Dewey delivered newspapers for $1 a week and earned $6 more per week in a lumber yard. He was a so-so student easily bored by the stultifying tedium of memorizing and reciting in the local school. "I remember how glad we were whenever vacation time rolled around," he later recalled, "We would sing, 'Goodbye school, goodbye teacher, old fool' " (Schuessler, 1979, 56). Archibald Dewey expected his son to become a mechanic, but the University of Vermont was nearby and John decided to give it a try. Average at most subjects yet adept at science, he graduated from college at the age of eighteen.

After graduation, John's cousin offered him a job in Oil City, Pennsylvania, a small boomtown in the early days of petroleum exploration. The job was teaching high school. Like college John gave it a try; he taught for three years, from 1879 to 1882, in Oil City and, again, after he returned to Burlington. He also wrote his first philosophical article, was pleased when a scholarly journal published it, wrote another scholarly essay that was also published, and decided to attend Johns Hopkins University for advanced study in philosophy. Johns Hopkins was a young institution; it was also unique. Its model was the German university, one that concentrated on graduate study, seminar teaching, and original research. At Johns Hopkins Dewey encountered as teachers the challenging Charles Sanders Peirce and George S. Morris, both of whom influenced his later scholarship. In 1884 John Dewey received his Ph.D.

In the next decade, Dewey's prolific scholarship brought him praise as a brilliant philosophic scholar. He began his college teaching at the University of Michigan, then moved to the University of Minnesota, for 1888 and 1889, before returning to the University of Michigan to head the philosophy department from 1889 to 1894. However, his life was not all writing and teaching, despite students' characterizations of him as "cold, impersonal, psychological, sphinxlike, anomalous and petrifying to flunkers" (Westbrook, 1991, 35). One of his students, Alice Chipman, found him not such a bad sort after all. Alice, an orphan, had been raised by her grandparents. Alice and John Dewey were married in 1886. Throughout their marriage, until her death in 1927, the keen intelligence of Alice was a major influence on John's social, political, and religious views. (In 1946 John Dewey was married again, this time to Roberta Grant Lowitz.)

A major professional move came in John Dewey's career in 1894 when he became chair of philosophy, psychology, and pedagogy at the University of Chicago. Few universities have experienced the bubbling intellectual ferment that excited the University of Chicago, founded in 1891, during and in the years following Dewey's residence there. The intellectual community was a gathering of a remarkable set of scholars that distinguished Chicago from other universities. Harvard philosopher William James, who would have a formative influence on Walter Lippmann, summed up the climate: "At Harvard we have plenty of thought but no school. At Yale and Cornell, the other way about." But "the Chicago School of Thought," James wrote, "is splendid stuff, and Dewey is a hero. A real school and real thought" (Perry, 1936, vol. 2, 501). James had reason to be impressed; in addition to Dewey, the university's faculty included such luminaries as George Herbert Mead, James Rowland Angell, Edward Scribner Ames, Addison Webster Moore, and, from 1895 to 1896, Arthur F. Bentley, with whom Dewey would later collaborate in a seminal volume, *Knowing and the Known* (1949), which acknowledged the influence of linguistics on Anglo-American philosophy.

One of John Dewey's major contributions to Chicago's intellectual ferment was the Laboratory School. There he began to develop ideas for educational reform which carried major implications for the conduct of democratic politics. Perhaps in part because of the tedium of the schooling he had undergone as a child, John Dewey rejected the view that education is simply a preparation for living. Learning, he urged, *is* living—an active process of inquiry involving students as *participants* not passive spectators. Educators should not take students as empty vessels, fill them with the liquid of learning, then test to see if they have soaked up their lessons. There is no separation of theory from practice, ideas from doing, knowing from known, or learning from thinking, reflection, and problem solving.

By the same token, John Dewey recognized that a nation's schools are major institutions in formulating a climate of cultural freedom, individual freedom, and active citizen participation in democracy. He understood well Niccolò Machiavelli's maxim, "It is true that men are more or less virtuous in one country or another according to the nature of the education by which their manners and habits have been formed" (Combs & Nimmo, 1984, 196). Schools that teach a *spectator* view of knowledge breed a passive citizenry; schools that teach a *participatory* view (i.e., what later became "progressive education") breed an active citizenry.

Dewey's theories of education derived from his enlarging application of the views of the pragmatic movement in American philosophy contained in the thoughts of Charles Sanders Peirce, William James, George Herbert Mead, and many others of Dewey's colleagues of "the Chicago School." Dewey's version of pragmatism, referred to as instrumentalism, made pragmatism a philosophy of everyday life and experience. Dewey taught that actions have consequences; theories and concepts have consequences, thus are actions and tools to guide action; intelligent action is fundamentally an experimental process of trial and error, "knowing" and "learning" each act's meaning—including ideas as acts—by its consequences; and finally, knowledge and morals are not fixed lessons to be drummed into people in advance of inquiry, but constitute, instead, a continuous *process* of self-correction through practical, intelligent reflection. Thus stated, Dewey's pragmatic theories could, and did, have profound consequences for political actions.

Communities, even scholarly communities, are susceptible to political infighting and bureaucratic bungling. The University of Chicago proved to be no exception. In 1901 the university's School of Education absorbed the Chicago Institute, a training ground for teachers. As a result the university had two elementary schools, one associated with the training school, the other with the "Dewey (Laboratory) School." Although the missions, and certainly the approaches, of the two schools differed in striking ways, that did not deter Dewey's superiors from attempting to achieve every university administrator's dream: consolidate units, cut costs, and extend imperial domain. Unfortunately, one condition for the 1903 merger of the two schools provided that, after a year, Alice Dewey, the principal of the consolidated school, would lose her job. When John Dewey discovered that stipulation, after not having been consulted on the matter, the president of the University of Chicago learned that actions do indeed have consequences, albeit unanticipated: Dewey's unexpected and immediate resignation. He departed Chicago and moved to Columbia University in 1905 where he remained for twenty-six years.

THE CONCRETE FOUNDATION OF POLITICAL COMMENTARY

Throughout his first decade at Columbia University, John Dewey continued his work in educational philosophy. He published scholarly articles, books on education as a lived experience, and his seminal *Democracy and Education* (1916). These early years in New York City coincided with Dewey's increased participation in civic, national, and international affairs. In the process, he endeavored to make his philosophy a guide to political action. For example, he led educators at Teachers College, Columbia, in a program of educational reform and adoption of progressive education throughout the nation and in foreign countries as well.

Dewey also became involved in political commentary. His first major forum was a magazine of popular political opinion founded in 1914, the *New Republic*. The magazine, coedited by Walter Lippmann, defined its mission in ways that Dewey used to describe the politically active philosopher, namely, "social education" and "opinion formation" but not manipulation of public sentiments. The *New Republic* had a two-pronged agenda that espoused elements of the nation's progressive political movement: to professionalize the administration of governmental programs, and to make those professionally trained experts accountable as public servants. As a regular contributor to the *New Republic*, John Dewey formulated and expressed his views on national politics until he resigned from the journal in 1937.

Early on in the pages of the *New Republic*, Dewey supported women's suffrage; he also gradually warmed to the presidency of Woodrow Wilson (Dewey had voted for socialist Eugene V. Debs in 1912). He endorsed the incumbent president in 1916 and opposed U.S. entry into the Great War; wars, he maintained, were not an efficient means for resolving social conflicts because their violence was costly in terms of human lives. However, like many other progressives, Dewey switched his stance to support the war with America's entry— much to the consternation of many of his critics who argued that he was turning his back on the basic premises of his philosophy. At war's end, Dewey opposed President Woodrow Wilson's pet project, American membership in the League of Nations, maintaining that the League was simply another forum for airing outdated nationalistic interests rather than promoting a global community. Instead, Dewey supported the outlawing of war.

In later years, Dewey's commentaries in the *New Republic* expressed impatience with the New Deal's cautious approach to economic reform; he even encouraged the development of a third party in the 1930s. In 1937 he resigned from the *New Republic* because of the magazine's treatment of the Stalinist purge trials in the Soviet Union; he was especially upset about the journal's implicit acceptance of the guilt of the defendants. However, Dewey did not cease political commentary. In other forums he continued arguing his political views, including opposition to U.S. entry in World War II, steadfast rejection of bigotry in all forms, and unwavering support of science in the face of charges that the use of the atomic bomb in Hiroshima in 1945 was uncontrovertible evidence that science was evil.

To many critics of John Dewey, his political stances often appeared capricious and vacillating, even a denial of the philosopher's underlying thinking. Such criticism rarely troubled Dewey. "It is less important," he said, "that we all believe alike, than that we all alike inquire freely, and put at the disposal of one another such glimpses as we may attain of the truth for which we are in search" (Schuessler, 1979, 56). For Dewey, democracy was a way of life, not merely a form of government. In an address before the National Education Association in 1937, Dewey gave voice to his philosophy of democracy:

> Democracy is much broader than a special political form, a method of conducting government, of making laws and carrying on governmental administration by popular suffrage and elected officers. It is that, of course. But it is something broader and deeper than that. . . . It is, as we often say, though perhaps without appreciating all that is involved in the saying, a way of life, social and individual. The keystone of democracy as a way of life may be expressed, it seems to me, as the *necessity for the participation of every mature human being in formation of the values that regulate the living of men together.* (Ratner, 1939, 400; emphasis added)

Democracy involves people trying to make their way in the world, people who should be unrestrained by, on the one hand, intellectual timidity, or, on the other, outmoded habits, rigid disciplines, received wisdom, fixed ideas, or oppressive routines. Intelligent political action, like all intelligent action, must be instrumental and experimental, looking to the consequences of choices, embracing those that help people make their way, and discarding those that do not.

Joining John Dewey's seemingly shifting, sometimes contradictory, poles on specific political matters stood a single philosophical cornerstone for politics, and for political communication, that he outlined in systematic fashion in the 1920s, especially in *The Public and Its Problems* (1927). Although a brief, succinct volume (barely more than 200 pages), as most treatises on political philosophy, and certainly most of Dewey's, go, the work has justly been appraised as "a maddeningly difficult book" (Carey, 1982, 25). A free rendering of his argument states that whenever people are in direct social intercourse, the interactions of those individuals directly involved have consequences for other persons; these other persons constitute a "public." There is the "objective fact," wrote Dewey, "that human acts have consequences for others." Moreover, "some of these consequences are perceived" and "their perception leads to a subsequent effort to control action" that will secure some consequences and avoid others. Two categories of consequences result: "those which directly affect the persons engaged in a transaction, and those which affect others beyond those immediately concerned" (Dewey, 1927, 12).

Thus, every member of a social community, either by being directly affected through immediate interaction, or indirectly via being benefited or victimized by the immediate intercourse of other people, is in fact part of the public. "The members of a social community, as a public, develop rules or norms or standards of social interaction [i.e., political communication] applicable to all members of the community in order to control the public effects of social intercourse" (Morris, 1970, 94). To the degree that such rules, norms, or standards are maintained by force, they constitute a set of laws—in political communication, for example, the laws privileging or discouraging open expression—a subject of prime concern to such political commentators as Elmer Davis (q.v.). And, "the persons to whom these laws are applicable are members of the political community; the persons who enforce the laws constitute a government" (Morris, 1970, 94).

Public issues, be they pro or con regarding entry into warfare, redistribution of wealth, provision of physical well-being, separation of church and state, equal opportunities, and so on, center in conflicts that extend beyond the parties immediately concerned with the disagreements. The question that arose for Dewey was what means of communicating about politics is most efficient—efficient using Dewey's instrumentalist and experimental tests—for the members of a political community resolving social conflicts and trying to make their way in the world? Dewey hinted at his answer in 1925 in *Experience and Nature*, "Of all affairs, communication is the most wonderful"; for, "when communication occurs, all natural events are subject to reconsideration and revision; they are readapted to meet the *requirements of conversation*, whether it be public discourse or that preliminary discourse termed thinking'' (1925,166–67; emphasis added).

Portions of *The Public and Its Problems* had appeared before the publication of Dewey's book in lectures he gave in response to Walter Lippmann's 1922 work, *Public Opinion*. Although Lippmann's work was widely acclaimed, Dewey labeled it as ''perhaps the most effective indictment of democracy as currently conceived ever penned'' (Dewey, 1922b)—a judgment echoed by a key critic of propagandistic commentary in the 1960s and beyond, Noam Chomsky. Lippmann argued that the pictures in people's heads of the world outside shape their actions. Since the political world is not readily accessible to citizens, they rely on media—most notably the press—for information. Newspapers, however, are not up to the task of presenting accurate pictures on which citizens can act. Lippmann asserted that they picture only selected truths from an ocean of possible truths; moreover, the news media are incapable of *discovering* truth. Lippmann's answer to the question of what means of communicating about politics are effective was to give up on participatory democracy, turn instead to qualified elites, a few in number, who could effect the ''organization of intelligence'' and no longer ''burden every citizen with expert opinion on all questions, but to push that burden away from him towards the responsible administrator'' (Lippmann, 1922, 250–51).

Thus, Lippmann's approach to political communication was one of ''democratic elitism'' (Westbrook, 1991, 299), one that recommended holding popular participation in political affairs and communication about them to an absolute minimum. Dewey disagreed strongly. Harkening back to his view that efficient communication meets the ''requirements of conversation,'' Dewey returned to an old theme: to meet democratic requirements, effective political communication must be direct, face-to-face dialogue; it must be personal and social; and it must be local. Newspapers, magazines, or any other form of print—media that Lippmann would professionalize in order to present a more representative picture of reality—will not suffice. Dewey makes the point adamantly and forcefully in the closing passages of *The Public and Its Problems*. Public problems can be addressed ''only in the relations of personal intercourse in the local community'':

> The connections of the ear with vital and outgoing thought and emotion are immensely closer and more varied than those of the eye. Vision is a spectator; hearing is a participator. Publication is partial and the public which results is partially informed. . . . We lie, as Emerson said, in the lap of an immense intelligence. But that intelligence is dormant and its communications are broken, inarticulate and faint until it possesses the local community as its medium. (218–19)

Dewey here is not a Johnny-One-Note returning to a single theme: the spectator versus the participant. When he says publication is partial and the resulting public is partially informed, he is using "partial" in its conventional sense of incompleteness, and also in its sense of being partisan. Partial communication is partisan communication, messages biased on behalf of a cause, not on behalf of intelligent action; "it does not contain a well-rounded frame within itself," hence, partial/partisan communicating can "be used for the ends of wisdom only insofar as we provide the ways for making allowances for it" by actively testing claims rather than merely viewing them (Burke, 1959, 55).

John Dewey died in 1952, the year that television threatened publication's dominance as a visual political medium. That year's presidential election campaign introduced televised national nominating conventions on a much larger scale than ever before, televised political advertising to nationwide audiences, and a visual self-exoneration by a vice-presidential nominee caught up in an alleged financial scandal. In the ensuing decades, that nominee would use the videopolitical innovations of the year of John Dewey's death to win the presidency, open his reelection bid from the Great Wall of China, justify widening a war in Southeast Asia, attempt to justify his actions in the far wider and more severe Watergate scandal, announce his breach of the people's faith, picture his fall from power, and resurrect his reputation as an international political sage and statesman.

By his good fortune, John Dewey missed all of that. In the era of Richard Nixon, Dewey's notion of politics as the *public* life, of political communication as dialogue for the ear, and as citizenship constituting participation in a community of inquirers, seems a quaint holdover of Athenian democracy out of touch with twentieth-century America. Whether the growing fashion for political commentary to occur in other visual, albeit localized, settings—"virtual communities"—will restore citizenship as a participatory rather than spectator activity is problematic. The legacy of John Dewey's career lies not in his political stances but in the consistency of his message: the effective function of commentary is to confront and solve human problems, not to mask them from ear *and* eye in a "silent" fog of propaganda.

REFERENCES

Selected Politically Relevant Works by John Dewey

Democracy and Education. New York: Macmillan, 1916.
Human Nature and Conduct. New York: Holt, Rinehart, 1922a.
"Public Opinion." *New Republic,* May 3, 1922b.
Experience and Nature. Chicago: Open Court Publishing, 1925.
The Public and Its Problems. New York: Holt, Rinehart, 1927.
Individualism, Old and New. New York: Minton, Balch, 1930.
Liberalism and Social Action. New York: Minton, Balch, 1935.
German Philosophy and Politics. New York: G. P. Putnam's Sons, 1942.
Knowing and the Known. With Arthur F. Bentley. Boston: Beacon Press, 1949.

Freedom and Culture. New York: Putnam/Capricorn, 1963.
Philosophy of Education. Totowa, NJ: Littlefield, Adams, 1975.

Selected Edited Compilations of Works of John Dewey

Ratner, Jr. ed. *Intelligence in the Modern World: John Dewey's Philosophy*. New York: Modern Library, 1939.
Sidorsky, D., ed. *John Dewey: The Essential Writings*. New York: Harper and Row, 1977.

Selected Critical Works about John Dewey

Carey, J. W. "The Mass Media and Critical Theory: An American View." In *Communication Yearbook 1981*, edited by M. Burgoon, 18–33. Beverly Hills, CA: Sage Publications, 1982.
Damico, A. J. "Dewey, John." In *The Blackwell Encyclopedia of Political Thought*, edited by D. Miller, 122–24. New York: Basil Blackwell, Inc., 1987.
Kunitz, S. J., ed. "Dewey, John." In *Twentieth Century Authors: First Supplement*, 279. New York: H. W. Wilson Co., 1955.
Morris, C. *The Pragmatic Movement in American Philosophy*. New York: George Braziller, 1970.
Schuessler, R. "He Taught by Acts—Not Facts." *NRTA Journal* (March-April 1979): 54–56.
Westbrook, R. B. *John Dewey and American Democracy*. Ithaca, NY: Cornell University Press, 1991.

Selected General Works

Barzun, J. *God's Country and Mine*. Boston: Little, Brown, 1954.
Burke, K. *Attitudes toward History*. Berkeley: University of California Press, 1959.
Combs, J. E., and D. Nimmo. *A Primer of Politics*. New York: Macmillan, 1984.
Commager, H. S. *The American Mind*. New Haven, CT: Yale University Press, 1950.
Edman, Irwin. *Philosopher's Holiday*. New York: Viking, 1938.
Lasswell, H. D., and A. Kaplan. *Power and Society*. New Haven, CT: Yale University Press, 1950.
Lippmann, W. *Public Opinion*. New York: Macmillan, 1960.
McLuhan, M. *Understanding Media*. New York: Signet, 1964.
Nimmo, D., and J. E. Combs. *The Political Pundits*. Westport, CT: Praeger, 1992.
Perry, R. B. *The Thought and Character of William James*. 2 vols. Boston: Little, Brown, 1936.

PHIL (PHILLIP) DONAHUE

(December 21, 1935–   )

Audience Participation and Political Commentary

Television genres change and evolve with the times. As one genre reaches popularity, another one is created, reshaped, or molded to fit our ever changing times. The people who take part in shaping and molding a particular genre are as much affected by its life as the receivers of the genre. The talk show genre in television is no exception to the rule. The 1960s were years marked by growing social turmoil—dissent over the Vietnam War and civil rights and mounting concern over the outburst of violence and economic recession. These volatile social conditions were the impetus for a shift in television programming. Whereas television shows were once either solely entertainment or wholly news and information staples, the line between entertainment and news gradually disappeared. Mix portions of "The Price is Right," "The Tonight Show," "Firing Line," and "Meet the Press," and there is the hybrid that propagated a perennial crop of talk television. Certainly the most celebrated and inventive of the hybrids was "The Phil Donahue Show."

Programs that allowed the viewers to escape from the harsh realities of life were still broadcast, but a portion of the audience also wanted more "reality" based, albeit frequently a provocative peepshow, reality. Conventional television networks did not produce enough shows to fill all of the time slots available to local television outlets, especially during the daytime. So producers encouraged local stations to experiment with innovative local programming formulas and develop appealing shows to fill the open time slots. The new genre of the television talk show, again led by "The Phil Donahue Show," proved to be just what the doctors of advertising sales wanted—entertaining, informative, glib, popular, controversial, and money making. Put the right talk host in the right talk format and, *Voila*!, television programming would never be the same.

PHIL DONAHUE, MADALYN MURRAY O'HAIR, AND A THREE-DECADE RUN

Phil Donahue's career in journalism and broadcasting began during the summer before his senior year at Notre Dame University, while he was working at a commercial station owned by the university, WNDU-TV. Born on December 21, 1935, in Cleveland, Ohio, he was the son of an Irish Catholic furniture salesman, also named Phillip, and a department store shoe clerk, Catherine McClory Donahue. A "good glove, no hit" man, young Phil could only dream of becoming what he would have liked, a major league baseball player, a child-

hood dream he shared with other youths who also became political commentators instead; for example, Elmer Davis (q.v.) and George F. Will (q.v.). At St.
Edward's High School, Donahue was a largely mediocre student, a better actor
in class dramas, a passable cartoonist for the school paper, and a so-so clarinet
player. As a business major at Notre Dame, he improved his scholarship several
fold, worked on the public information committee of the student senate, and
acted in the university theater.

In 1957, after graduating from Notre Dame, Donahue worked as the summer
replacement announcer for a radio and television outlet on Cleveland's KYW-
AM and KYW-TV. He found it a tedious and insipid job, but he returned to it,
in 1958, after a brief stint in Albuquerque, New Mexico, where he worked in
a bank sorting checks. The young college graduate had two goals: to be a success
in broadcasting and to marry Marge (Marquette) Cooney. On February 1, 1958,
he achieved his second wish; he married Marge. But he had to wait much longer
for his success in broadcasting.

Throughout the summer of 1958, Donahue auditioned for numerous jobs in
the Midwest, but to no avail. In September 1958, his stint with KYW ended,
and he was back in banking, counting money at a bank in Cleveland. A few
weeks later, he was hired as the Program/News Director at WABJ, a 250-watt
radio station in Adrian, Michigan. From this experience in Adrian, Donahue
learned that "it's not so much the nature of the material you are dealing with
as the nature of the egos involved" (Donahue, 1979, 49). In 1959 Donahue left
Adrian for WHIO-AM-TV in Dayton, Ohio. He started out by reading the morning radio news reports every half-hour. Then he became a street reporter for the
station's daily television news program. At this post, he obtained two exclusive
interviews, which both would later be aired nationally. He interviewed Jimmy
Hoffa, the controversial head of the International Brotherhood of Teamsters,
Chauffeurs, Warehousemen, and Helpers of America; and Billy Sol Estes, an
influential Texas businessman who would soon be the center of a major scandal
involving business fraud.

Phil Donahue sent audition tapes, an eight-by-ten-inch glossy picture, and a
resumé to CBS News after the interviews in hopes of obtaining a position with
the network in New York; the response or lack thereof indicated that the network
was not ready to offer him a position. In 1963, he honed his skills as an investigative reporter and as a tenacious interviewer and put them to work as host
for "Conversation Piece," the daily radio phone-in talk show with a predominantly female audience. This experience was the catalyst for his career as a
major social and political commentator in the burgeoning venue of talk show
television.

As he learned the trade of journalist and talk show commentator, Donahue
developed a distrust for business leaders, politicians, judges, and the clergy. He
wrote, "Within broadcasting I had discovered this terribly exciting cerebral pursuit which was satisfying and adventuresome—and it had power" (Donahue,
1979, 50). Although Donahue despised, or at least criticized, powerful person-

ages with whom he rubbed elbows in his quest to get the news, he also enjoyed the power it yielded him when he discovered he was able to make these same power wielders answer his questions. It was a process of power brokering he had come to learn and appreciate as an interviewer.

He began his career as what he termed a dedicated journalist in search of the real story; he later discovered that he was unwittingly playing a role in the perpetuation of war propaganda. While at WHIO-TV, he was host of a show highlighting Wright Patterson Air Force Base, Dayton's largest employer. The show was "Technology for Tomorrow." On the surface, "Technology for Tomorrow" was a public service series designed to show the people of Dayton the innovative technologies that were being created, tested, and maintained at the facilities in their area. Each program featured a different division of the base and the work being performed by it. Donahue interviewed base commanders, Pentagon officials, and enlisted airmen, as well as civilian personnel. The capital outlay and the expense involved in hardware development never raised a question in the mind of the naive, albeit tenacious, reporter and commentator Phil Donahue.

In hindsight Donahue wrote, "It was only years later, with the war and Nixon and Johnson and the lies and the government and the military-industrial complex and the sudden recognition that I worked for Avco, which made bombs . . . and helicopter engines, that my head started to turn" (Donahue, 1979, 59). So, at the time, Donahue thought he was simply reporting on the system that provided jobs to the people in Dayton; in retrospect, he would say that he was not the critical reporter asking enlightening questions, but was instead collaborating in a "half-hour commercial for the civilian contractors who developed the new weapons systems and the military bosses who managed the projects" (Donahue, 1979, 56).

In the midst of his interviewing, and being identified with, Pentagon officials, presidential candidates, and presidents, Phil Donahue was becoming a star at WHIO. Yet, while his professional life was thriving, his personal life was deteriorating. His wife, Margie, was raising their four boys and baby girl essentially without the support and assistance of her husband. By 1967 he was producing and moderating a radio show five days a week, coanchoring the 6 and 11 o'clock news, and hosting a daily television business program. He had achieved the pinnacle of success at WHIO, and there was nowhere else for him to go except out. He wrote about this point in his life, "I wanted out [of WHIO]. I wanted out and up" (1979, 73). In June 1967, Donahue quit his job at WHIO and left broadcasting to work for E. F. MacDonald, an incentive and trading stamp company in Dayton, as a salesperson.

During his time at WHIO, Donahue had reached sufficient celebrity status in the Dayton area that he assumed the contacts that he had made over the years in broadcasting would help him sell his sales-incentive plans to businesses. Much like the successful college football star who finds himself unsuited for the professional ranks and moves on to making commercials for automobile dealerships, Donahue's celebrity status helped him to secure a place on a top sales team, but it did not bode well for him in the sales market. He found himself less suited for sales than he had been for a baseball career as a young man. Fortunately, while he was making visits to company executives trying to sell the incentive plans, Don Dahlman, the station manager for WLWD-TV in Dayton was preparing to make a presentation to Donahue about a job with the station hosting a new talk show.

BECOMING A SOCIAL AND POLITICAL COMMENTATOR

In 1967 the conventional and highly popular talk show format was patterned after NBC's "Tonight Show." It employed a host who interviewed several guests and had a band to entertain on the side and an announcer to pitch commercials. The format was also used by nationally syndicated talks shows with hosts like Merv Griffin and Mike Douglas. WLWD's George Resing, working with Don Dahlman, conceived an idea for a format similar to one created by the programmer for the Westinghouse group of stations, Squire Rushnell (Haley, 1992). Featuring a host interviewing a single guest, it was designed as the lead-in to the local late evening news. Resing wanted a host who could ask the pointed questions and who could moderate the conversations between the guest and callers who were watching the show. Donahue, who could moderate as well as instigate open debate and discussion, was chosen to be that host.

On November 6, 1967, four months after he started selling sales-incentive programs, Donahue quit his day job to become the host of a morning interview program, "The Phil Donahue Show," which debuted on Dayton's WLWD-TV the same day. The first week of shows included Madalyn Murray O'Hair, the atheist who championed the cause to rid the public schools of prayer; a panel of men discussing what they liked about women; a Dayton obstetrician and a film of a live childbirth; a funeral director explaining the etiquette of coffin display; and a promoter for the anatomically correct "Little Brother" doll.

With Madalyn Murray O'Hair as a guest, Phil Donahue was just settling down to launch his version of the couch-and-desk format when suddenly a studio audience appeared. They were there to attend the variety show usually aired at Donahue's time; apparently no one had bothered to get the word out that the variety show had been canceled, and the station management felt obliged to honor the ticket holders with a show to view. When Donahue struggled to find questions that would elicit responses from O'Hair of interest to viewers, he invited the audience to ask their own questions. Although not unique in the history of broadcasting— H. V. Kaltenborn (q.v.) began the first such audience participation show on radio decades earlier—the technique of inviting questions from audience members was scarcely common. Donahue's producers decided to keep an audience present, but they were not yet moved to bring them into the act.

Hence, for six weeks, a studio audience was not an integral part of the basic program format. Although present, audience members simply chatted with Donahue and the guest, frequently feeding them questions to be asked during the televised show. One day, Gunilla Knudsen, a Swedish model, was the guest, and during a commercial break, an audience member had begun to show Knudsen how to braid her hair. The show resumed and Donahue allowed the audience members to continue their interaction with the guest (Haley, 1992). This simple action by a woman in the audience helped to convince the producer, the director, and the host to allow the audience to participate in the show. It proved to be a fortuitous decision. The audience's participation provided an important ingredient to keep the discussion on the show lively and entertaining.

Throughout the formative days of "The Phil Donahue Show" the host proved himself a master of turning the unexpected into a triumph. The ratings for that November of the show were spectacular, a 15 rating/50 share (Haley, 1992). Donahue was inventing the audience-participation talk show for television, his major contribution as a twentieth-century social and political commentator, and becoming a successful celebrity in the process. The topics discussed and the format of "The Phil Donahue Show" on WLWD-TV were dictated by the fact that celebrities were unwilling to travel to Dayton. According to Donahue, "The show's style had developed not by genius but by necessity. The familiar talk-show heads were not available to us in Dayton, Ohio" (Donahue, 1979, 100). So, the production staff worked with the unconventional format of one guest and one issue per show. Allowing the audience to take part was actually, therefore, a substitute for not having more guests available.

By the end of 1969, "The Phil Donahue Show" was syndicated and aired on many of the Avco-owned stations throughout the country. The station manager at WLWD began to solicit stations outside the Avco Broadcasting network to air the show. Station WJR-TV in Cleveland was the first station outside the Avco network to do so; thereafter, stations in Atlanta, Detroit, Toledo, and Milwaukee licensed the show. By the end of the fall of 1971, more than forty stations were airing the show, mostly in the Midwest. As the program developed, its producers hit upon a winning formula to produce friction and attract viewers, namely, to match a liberal guest line-up with a conservative, predominantly female studio audience. The combination provided an open forum of dialogue on matters of social and political import.

Yet by late 1973, four fewer stations were carrying the program. Many of the audience members had been to see the show several times in Dayton, and the interest and novelty of being in the studio audience were beginning to wane. In order for the show to become a national success, changes were required. Phil Donahue advised the executives at Avco that, in order for his show to survive in syndication, the show would have to move to a city with a larger population. Walter Barlett, the senior vice president for television at Avco Broadcasting started looking for a new station to serve as the flagship for "The Phil Donahue Show." Even though the show had been a top seller in syndication, and was garnering top share and ratings in its home market, Barlett had trouble convincing station managers that Donahue's show was a viable commodity. Barlett finally persuaded WGN-TV, an independent station in Chicago with "superstation" status on satellite television, to become the home for "Donahue," as the show became known after the transition. It premiered on WGN-TV on April 29, 1974.

Donahue cut an important professional tie in moving from small-market Dayton to large-market Chicago. He cut a long-standing personal tie as well. In the late summer of 1973, Marge Donahue left her husband and moved to Albuquerque with two of their children. Phil Donahue later wrote in his biography, "When at age 39, I became legally and spiritually 'sundered', I thought of my professional ambition and how costly it had been to my family. I thought of how I had been married to my job instead of my wife" (1979, 104). The man who had been a television crusader for women's rights and equality had not, in fact, been practicing at home the rules and virtues he was extolling on his program.

The move to Chicago was not only a professional awakening, but also a personal wake-up call. For the first time in his life, Donahue had to be both the primary caretaker for his children and the professional talk show host in a competitive market. The first week on WGN-TV "Donahue" received an average rating of 1! Gradually, however, matters began to right themselves. In the beginning the show, unable to draw a local audience, brought people in by bus from Wisconsin and other surrounding areas where the show had name recognition and an audience base. Slowly "Donahue" built a larger audience in the Chicago area. The busses stopped rolling.

In 1976 Avco Broadcasting encountered financial hardship and decided to sell its radio and television stations to the more financially stable Multimedia Incorporated. Phil Donahue had the opportunity to purchase "Donahue" himself. He did so and decided to link up with Multimedia as syndicator in hopes of using its financial resources to help build his show's ratings and break into the major markets (Los Angeles and New York) through syndication. Without the support of viewers in these markets, Donahue had a limited chance of getting the national coverage he wanted. A year later, "Donahue" got the break it needed when the 9:00 A.M. slot at WNBC-TV in New York City opened. By the late 1970s, "Donahue" had become one of the most popular shows in syndication, with more than 200 stations carrying the show.

Donahue attributes his success to women members of his studio audience. Their honesty and assertiveness helped create controversy and attract viewers. During the early days of his format, television executives frequently commented on the intelligent women Donahue found as audience members. Intelligence aside, Donahue believes that his show provides women with an outlet through which to express their opinions. In offering women a relief from soap operas, game shows, and sitcom reruns in the daytime programming line-up, Donahue's focus on controversial social topics made him a symbol of America's social and political conscience.

From May 1979 to November 1980, Donahue appeared on NBC's "The To-day Show" with a thrice-weekly commentary. During this time, he was also the cover story of numerous magazines, including *Esquire* and *People*. He married television actress Marlo Thomas. Donahue had, at last, become a sex symbol and the major creator of a social phenomenon. The Notre Dame graduate, who was once told that journalism was a profession unworthy of his time, had not only made his name recognizable, but also had perfected a talk show format emulated by many in the not so distant future. In January 1982, with a move to WBBM-TV in Chicago, Phil Donahue further penetrated the realm of super stardom, now as a recognized political commentator and moderator of discussions on political and social issues on a television outlet noted for political discussion programs.

In his twenty-nine-year talk show career, spanning from 1967 to 1996, when he announced he would cease his long-running issue-driven talk show at season's end to devote his time to television specials and new projects in broadcasting and cable television, Phil Donahue was part of a television genre that made political history. Among the political figures Donahue interviewed over the years were Jane Fonda, actress and Vietnam War protester; David Duke, active in the Ku Klux Klan and a controversial politician; Ross Perot, Texas business tycoon and political candidate; and, in a 1992 debate on his show, candidates for the Democratic presidential nomination, Jerry Brown and Bill Clinton. Yet, perhaps Phil Donahue's most interesting guests were the people with personal stories that have an impact on the political and social agenda in this country. For example, Donahue interviewed a wheelchair-bound woman who had visited many of our national parks and monuments. She wrote a book about handicapped access to these public facilities and ignited a political debate on handicap accessibility to public facilities.

"Donahue" was a forum to discuss what the host and his staff deemed interesting and politically and socially relevant topics. As moderator of the fractious talk on his show, Donahue used the audience members' energy to coax, probe, and challenge controversial guests, all in a quest to reveal the hidden agendas of politicians and ignite a fervor of debate. Donahue was quick to assure that the pendulum of discussion swung both ways; guests could respond to questions to reveal the illogicality of a perspective. Phil Donahue did not attack or harass his guests, but he was never reluctant or uncomfortable when expressing his own viewpoint (Haley, 1992). His appeal was in his commitment to his moral obligation to be a decent human being regardless of disagreements on specific issues.

Donahue used his show as a place to engage in dialogue about political issues relevant to the social agenda. His program served as an electronic town hall meeting well before the same format gained popularity with presidential candidates in the early 1990s. That being the case, "Donahue" was a required campaign stop for major political candidates during and beyond the 1970s. From Ronald Reagan in 1977 to Bill Clinton in 1992, politicians have regularly exploited the format to get their messages across without being required to answer questions from "working journalists" who travel with presidential candidates.

Phil Donahue takes umbrage at not being viewed as a "working journalist," as more entertainer than reporter. One reason is that he has covered breaking news, for example, from inside the Ohio State Penitentiary. He endeavored to air an execution; critics of his attempt argue that Donahue, who is an opponent of the death penalty, hoped that viewers might revoke their support of state executions after viewing the gore on television (Goodman, 1994). Donahue lost a court battle over whether airing an execution was a free speech issue. Lawyers for the California inmate who wanted his execution televised argued that it was, but the judge and many opponents disagreed. Donahue suffered a defeat in the courts, but he had once again raised the public consciousness on a volatile political issue.

Another reason lies in his view that it is a badly shopworn view of journalism to assume that entertainment programming is not also information programming. In a televised debate before a forum of journalists, Donahue proclaimed, "I do not apologize for wanting to draw a crowd"; moreover, "I believe there is a great deal of information in talk shows" (Who's a Journalist?, 1989).

Donahue's influence on the political agenda extended well beyond presidential politics and controversial domestic issues to international matters as well. Donahue teamed with Soviet radio and television commentator Vladamir Pozner in December 1985 for the first-ever live discussion between an American and a Soviet audience. The two audiences, one in Seattle, Washington, and the other in the Soviet Union, discussed political relations and their everyday lives in their respective countries. This event was followed by another show commenting on the Soviet people. In 1987 "Donahue" became the first U.S. talk show to tape inside the Soviet Union.

THE END OF AN ERA?

Phil Donahue taped the last of the syndicated talk shows that had made him a household name on May 2, 1996. That the end might be in sight, however, had been foreshadowed a decade earlier. In 1986 "Donahue," at the top of the television talk show ratings charts for years, encountered competition. "The Oprah Winfrey Show" successfully imitated the talk show format Donahue made famous. In its first season, Winfrey's show beat Donahue in the ratings in several large markets, and the onslaught of other talk show clones featuring Geraldo Rivera, Sally Jesse Raphael, and others began to diminish Donahue's uniqueness. Despite his move to New York in 1985 to WNBC, the NBC network's New York affiliate, and in spite of winning twenty national Emmy awards, a prestigious Peabody broadcasting award, and critical accolades, "Donahue" was reaching the end of its tether. As ratings sank in the tide of ever wilder, younger talk show hosts and topics, Phil Donahue struggled to keep up with the competition. As he explained, clearly with tongue in cheek, in an interview with Ted Koppel (q.v.), "We thank the strippers [a show on male strippers] for what they have given us"; he was referring to the ratings points for sensationalist shows ("Nightline," 1996).

Pandering, however, was not Donahue's style. He contends that his shows were designed to enlighten the people and encourage public discussion. He claims "Donahue" gave rise to what he calls his "bastard children" ("Nightline," 1996). Many observers agree:

> Phil Donahue managed to find something we could relate to in every program, every story, some way to connect us, some common thread. He showed us how to identify with people with whom we had nothing in common. He practiced respect, tolerance, acceptance, and he always thanked the caller for waiting. His departure marks the end of an era. (Henson, 1996, 43)

The genre of issue-driven, audience participation, talk television that Phil Donahue created has undergone many metamorphoses with his not so respectful, tolerant, accepting imitators. Yet, Donahue's influence upon the television talk show and the discussion of political issues in the United States for almost three decades remains undeniable. Reminiscent of a tennis match gone awry, Donahue's flair and style of journalism were appropriately satirical, candid, and explicit; he was a creator and crusader who, as a political commentator, converted housewives from mere consumers to citizens with an active voice in the political and social process.

REFERENCES

Selected Works by Phil Donahue

My Own Story. New York: Simon & Schuster, 1979.
The Human Animal. New York: Simon & Schuster, 1985. Based on a five-part television series hosted by Phil Donahue.

Selected Critical Works about Phil Donahue

Barron, J. "Their Day on *Donahue*: Dirty Linen on the Air." *New York Times,* January 15, 1993, B4.
Flint, J. "Donahue Bolts NBC for Multimedia." *Variety,* May 29, 1995, 25.
Goodman, W. "Viewing an Execution from the Sofa." *New York Times,* June 13, 1994, B4.
Haley, K. "From Dayton to the World: A History of the *Donahue Show.*" *Broadcasting,* November 2, 1992, S 7–12.
Henson, J. "A Tribute to the Father of All Talk Shows." *TV Guide,* February 3–9, 1996, 43.

Moritz, C., ed. "Donahue, Phil." In *Current Biography 1980*, 75–78. New York: H. W. Wilson, 1981.

"Nightline with Ted Koppel." Donahue. Aired January 12, 1996, KXTV-10, Sacramento, CA.

Wadler, J. *Phil Donahue: A Man for All Women*. New York: Jove, 1980.

Selected General Works

Fellows, J. *Breaking the News: How the Media Undermine American Democracy*. New York: Pantheon, 1996.

Hitchens, A. *Talking Heads: Political Talk Shows and Their Star Pundits*. New York: St. Martin's Press, 1991.

Kurtz, H. *Hot Air: All Talk, All the Time*. New York: Times Books, 1996.

Nimmo, D., and J. E. Combs. *The Political Pundits*. New York: Praeger, 1992.

Who's a Journalist? Talk Show Sensationalism. Public Affairs Video Archives, Purdue University, 1989.

GEORGIE ANNE GEYER

(April 2, 1935–   )

The Political Commentator as Courier Between Cultures

"Susceptibility to a disabling emotionalism was the charge that newspapermen long levied against women of the press and used, along with alleged physical limitations and vulnerabilities, to keep them in largely subordinate roles" (Kluger, 1989, 438). Georgie Anne Geyer, who in a "willful" and "blindly determined" act named herself "Gee Gee" while still a baby, is a striking refutation of the newsman's canard about women journalists. In that respect she is heiress to an honorable tradition of female political communication professionals who have proved their mettle not only in reporting domestic politics but in the far more demanding world of overseas correspondence.

Margaret Fuller, the first woman to serve on the editorial staff of a prominent American newspaper—the *New York Herald Tribune* in 1844—was also probably the first woman to act as a newspaper's foreign correspondent. After Fuller came a trickle of other women correspondents reporting from overseas. Among the most notable was Elizabeth Cochrane of the *New York World*. In 1889 the *World* sent Cochrane, writing under the name "Nellie Bly," to retrace the footsteps of Jules Verne's fictional Phineas Fogg. Her published accounts generated considerable popular interest and boosted the *World*'s circulation; and, although it took Fogg eighty days to go around the world, Cochrane did it in seventy-two!

There was also Ellen Browning Scripps, whose brothers Edward and James developed a chain of metropolitan dailies in the 1870s. Ellen, writing as "E.B.S.," filed filler paragraphs, short items, and features, based on firsthand observations and interviews, from Europe, North Africa, Mexico, and Cuba from 1881 through 1889 (Desmond, 1978).

During World War I Peggy Hall pioneered a war correspondent style that Ernie Pyle would make famous in World War II—candid accounts about the daily lives of ordinary doughboys. These stories she supplied to the *Chicago Tribune*. Rival male correspondents' protests prevented her accreditation as a war correspondent even though, in fact, that is the role she performed better than they. Martha Gellhorn provided vivid coverage of the Spanish Civil War. Years later, in a series of articles on the conditions in orphanages, she exposed the havoc U.S. military involvement was imposing on South Vietnam. Since no American newspaper would publish the searingly critical series, Gellhorn had to turn to British publication. When she sought to return to Vietnam, she was repeatedly denied a visa (Knightley, 1975).

Another Geyer predecessor was Marguerite Higgins of the *New York Herald*

Tribune. As a war correspondent during World War II, Higgins was instrumental in liberating prisoners at the Dachau concentration camp. Her eyewitness account described liberated prisoners beating one SS guard to death. When the prisoners were confined for typhus screening, "in a suicidal protest against the quarantine edict" the prisoners threw themselves against the charged fences "electrocuting themselves before our eyes" (Higgins, 1955, 95). Just prior to the Korean War, Higgins worked for the *Herald Tribune* in Tokyo. When word came that war had begun, she and her office mate, Keyes Beech of the *Chicago Daily News,* arrived in Seoul, covered the invasion of the city by the North Koreans, then barely escaped. She and Beech were separated and, had he not found and rescued her, she would have perished.

To return to Korea to cover the war, Higgins had to play second fiddle to another *Herald Tribune* correspondent, Homer Bigart. (In 1965 Georgie Anne Geyer, who spoke fluent Spanish, would find herself playing second fiddle to a male correspondent of the *Daily News* while covering a revolution in the Dominican Republic, a male reporter who knew no Spanish!) Higgins' eyewitness account of the first U.S. soldier to die in battle, frantic U.S. retreats and withdrawals, and troops ill-prepared for combat made her "the most famous newspaperwoman in the world" (Kluger, 1989, 442). She shared the 1951 Pulitzer Prize for international reporting with, among others, Keyes Beech and Homer Bigart. Higgins later covered the Vietnam War for *Newsday,* but she contracted a fatal tropical disease and died, a forty-five-year-old victim of the Vietnam War buried in Arlington National Cemetery.

"War," wrote Carl von Clausewitz, "is a mere continuation of policy by other means" and all wars "may be regarded as political acts" (1968, 119–20). Georgie Anne Geyer is in the tradition of women who have made notable contributions commenting about political acts, acts of war, quasi-war, and peace, as a foreign correspondent. What has made Geyer distinctive in her career as a foreign correspondent and columnist is her unique approach to the contributions overseas reporting can make to cultural understanding, an approach that derives from her family background and professional experience.

GEE GEE: FROM CHERUB TO COURIER

Georgie Anne Geyer, a native of Chicago's South Side, was born on April 2, 1935. Scholars in the arcane field of "intercultural communication" differ over precisely what it is they study: the art of understanding and being understood by persons of another culture, communication between parties of differing experiential backgrounds, communication between people of contrasting languages and customs, or simply exchanges between different cultures themselves (Saral, 1977). Such scholarly subtleties are unnecessary and unwarranted to anyone growing up on the South Side of Chicago in the 1930s and 1940s. *Life* was intercultural. As Geyer recalls it, "we had 'old countries' and 'old neighborhoods' . . . in this basically tribal milieu" (1983, 30). There were the "old" and "new" neighborhoods within tribal cultures—among the Germans, Poles, Czechs, Irish, Africans, and so on. Politically, there were the "machine" ethnic groups, like the Irish, and the "outsiders," like the Germanic Geyers. Cross-cultural understanding, whether via negotiation, bribes, or warlike "enforcers," was part of the South Side heritage.

Gee Gee was herself a cross-cultural product. Both her parents were German. Her father, Robert George, was a "mountain man" from southern Germany—a huge, hard-working, silent, brooding man not given to emotional displays. Her mother, Georgie Hazel, was a cultural contrast; she was of Rhinelander stock—sensitive, affectionate, and curious, a woman "who created neighborhoods wherever she went" (Geyer, 1983, 27). She had taught Gee Gee to read and write by the age of four.

The Geyers—father, mother, daughter, and brother Glen—realized the American Dream by achieving modest prosperity as the owners of a dairy in the early days of the Great Depression. White Castle, a chain of white-brick hamburger stands constructed in the manner of small castles, opted to buy its milk from Geyer's Dairy. Family legend had it that the president of White Castle was so impressed with the honesty of Robert Geyer, who stated flatly that he would offer no bribe to secure the White Castle contract, that he signed with Geyer on the spot. In exchange, White Castle received chocolate milk so thick that simply whipping it made tasty milk shakes to go with the stand's five-cent hamburgers.

The Geyer tribal expectation was that Gee Gee would grow up, marry, have two children, and pursue the normal housewife's life. She, however, thought otherwise. While still young, she would lie awake in her bed and wonder what would happen if only one person knew the truth and that person were a woman. The world would be denied that truth because, realized Gee Gee, the women she knew did not speak out. Surely, pondered Gee Gee, truth should not be silent simply because it is a woman who utters it. Years later, she articulated her view in other ways: "Even from the beginning I didn't want to change things so that women would become like men; I wanted to change things so that what was female would be respected for both men and women" (1983, 35). Free choice, for male or female, carries responsibility. Anyone starting out on a cause or crusade is accountable to those who depend upon her as well as to herself. As recently as 1995 Georgie Anne Geyer wrote, pertaining to a female who started a crusade to break the gender barrier at an all-male military academy, won a legal victory in doing so, then quit the academy,

> No one asks you to be a pioneer; nobody out there is demanding that you thrust your spear into historic prejudice. So if you are going to put yourself forward and try to become a standard-bearer for the underprivileged or the oppressed (or the left out), you had better have a little of the Valkyrie in you. For once you start, you deliberately have involved others with you. (1995a, 25A)

Upon high school graduation, Geyer enrolled in Northwestern University; she studied journalism at the Medill School of Journalism where she earned her B.S. in 1956. Her choice, she writes in her autobiography, derived from her belief that in journalism "truths" would be concrete and approachable rather than abstract and theoretical. She found "J-school," as do so many students, a mixed blessing. The strictly professional courses—reporting, copyediting, typesetting—were tedious and dull. She enjoyed what humanities and political science she could work into her program, but still regrets having taken no course in philosophy, sociology, or anthropology.

Gee Gee, along with a few other Medill students, took courses in Mexico during the winter quarter of her junior year. That experience, combined with a Fulbright scholarship year at the University of Vienna, sparked and intensified her desire for travel and an "addiction" to learning foreign languages. In Austria she polished her German; during her career, she added fluency in Spanish, Portuguese, and Russian.

There was, however, a downside to Austria; she returned to Chicago in 1957 with a severe case of hepatitis that hung on for a full year; then followed an agonizingly slow recovery. Plans for a journalism career were stymied. So, it was not until the winter of 1960 when Geyer joined the staff of the *Chicago Daily News*. It was a newspaper well suited to training cub reporters in how to deal with the ecology of diverse cultures that constituted the neighborhoods of Chicago. Unfortunately, her initial wish to work on the city desk was denied: the *Daily News* already had its quota of two women on the city desk. Her banishment to the women's and society desks, however, was relatively brief. When Geyer's talent was recognized the paper abandoned the two-women-on-the-city-desk rule and appointed her as a third.

Geyer's break at the *Daily News* came when Gee Gee assumed the role of "Irene Hill." A reporter on the Mafia beat had arranged to place a waitress, a nonexistent Irene Hill, to serve drinks at a Mafia member's wedding. Proving herself an adept actress, Geyer improvised her way through the assignment; her front-page story, accompanied by a picture of Gee Gee in her waitress uniform, was a scoop. In other coveted assignments that followed she covered race relations and Saul Alinsky's reformist political methods, and, in the process, she grew ever more streetwise about Chicago's neighborhood cultures.

In the 1960s the *Daily News* had an impressive staff of foreign correspondents, including Keyes Beech; they were all men. Geyer wanted to join them, much to the amusement of her male colleagues. In his introduction to Geyer's biography, popular columnist and humorist and political analyst Mike Royko wrote, " 'She's nuts' we all laughed, in our basso voices, when Gee Gee made clear her intentions to become a foreign correspondent" (Geyer, 1983, xii). However, Gee Gee got the last laugh. She won a small grant that allowed her to work in Latin America for six months. The *Daily News* editor asked Geyer to accept the grant but continue on the payroll, work for the paper in Latin America, and return at the end of the grant. Geyer agreed and traveled to Peru.

There she worked on her Spanish, acquired a knack for discovering news sources, and wrote dispatches based upon interviews with Peruvian leaders. Her success put the lie to an accepted aphorism of American journalism, attributed to political commentator James "Scotty" Reston (q.v.), that Americans would do anything for Latin America except read about it. They read Geyer's columns.

Gee Gee, the one time cherub, also accomplished something else in Peru: she formulated a definition of herself and staked out her career role as a political commentator—one who would explain different cultures to U.S. readers. "If we correspondents are anything," she wrote later, "we are couriers between cultures, carrying messages from people to people" (1983, 56).

A DECADE AS FOREIGN CORRESPONDENT

There was one remaining obstacle to Georgie Anne Geyer's transition to becoming a full-fledged overseas correspondent, namely, editorial foot dragging. When revolution broke out in Santo Domingo in the Dominican Republic in 1965, Geyer assumed she would be the *Chicago Daily News* reporter on the scene. The editor assigned someone else. Geyer protested. The editor tried to strike a compromise, telling her Santo Domingo was too dangerous; instead, he would send her to Vietnam where she would be safe in Saigon. Geyer refused. The editor relented, at least partially; she went to Santo Domingo as the second-string correspondent to a male reporter unversed in Spanish.

Once there, however, there was never again any doubt that she was a foreign correspondent. Over the course of the next decade, Georgie Anne Geyer went well beyond "good reporting"; she successfully sought to incorporate in her writing from all parts of the globe "an implicit understanding of the different truths that other cultures are living by—and dying by" (1983, 156). Although she acquainted herself with the [extra]ordinary lives of the common people, she also interviewed and interpreted the thoughts for Americans of a striking number of world and cultural leaders. This despite her view that leaders were, by and large, "boring," tending to be "egomaniacs" who issue "tiresome pronouncements about what the 'public' want when they are talking about what they want" (1983, 208). Among Geyer's interviews were Juan Bosch, the Dominican revolutionary leader, then hiding in Puerto Rico; Cuban dictator Fidel Castro (her 1966 stories based on the interview put the lie to a widely circulated rumor of his death); Guatemalan rebel leader Luis Turcios (she was the first American correspondent to travel to the dangerous mountains of that nation); Chile's Salvadore Allende in his rise and fall from power; Walter Rauff, the German government's second-most-wanted Nazi war criminal, in his hideaway in Tierra del Fuego; French radical Regis Debray, imprisoned in Bolivia; Argentine writer Jorge Luis Borges; Archbishop Oscar Romero of El Salvador; Yasser Arafat of the Palestine Liberation Organization; Libyan president Muammar el Qaddafi; Iran's Ayatollah Khomeini; Anwar Sadat, president of Egypt; and Shimon Peres, president of Israel. Long before he would become a thorn in the side of a series of U.S. presidents in the 1990s, Geyer in 1973 interviewed Iraq's Saddam Hussein.

On several occasions, Geyer sailed in harm's way. In 1966, in her pursuit of the exclusive interview with Luis Turcios that appeared in newspapers across the globe, there were several times when, held incommunicado in the dim light of a small, dirt-floor hut, she had cause to regret her primary rule of dealing with revolutionary movements: put yourself in their hands and demonstrate every kind of trust. Yet, even after she ceased being a foreign correspondent and had turned to writing a syndicated column, Geyer continued a dangerous reporting style. In 1976, while traveling in Angola to examine the regime of Marxist leader Agostinho Neto, she was imprisoned by supporters of the minister of the interior for refusing to divulge the sources for a column claiming that the minister opposed Neto. She remained undaunted, interviewed her captors, and published another revealing report on Angolan politics from those sources.

Although Geyer had turned down Vietnam as an assignment in 1965, she eventually traveled there, in part to be with Keyes Beech (the same Beech who had befriended Marguerite Higgins in Korea) with whom Geyer had a romantic relationship at the time. Geyer wrote a series of articles on "The GI Who Wants to Know Why." The series foreshadowed a theme that later would become recurrent in the reports of the Vietnam War filed by other correspondents. The American soldier, as Geyer understood, was no longer a mindless cog in a military machine, as had been characteristic in other wars. Instead, the soldier was becoming an autonomous person unwilling to follow blindly the direction of superiors unfamiliar with the realities of Vietnam combat. In 1967 Geyer took a side trip to Cambodia, where once again, she achieved a coup denied to other correspondents. She managed to interview Prince Sihanouk at a time when he denied entry to all other Western correspondents.

Geyer's work in Latin America, the Soviet Union, and the Middle East produced examples of cultural journalism, both as news accounts and book-length publications. However, for Geyer's systematic viewpoint of the reporter's role as a cultural courier, one must turn to her autobiography, *Buying the Night Flight* (1983). There Geyer distinguishes the type of straight reporting she learned as a young journalist on the *Chicago Daily News* from the interpretive journalism required of the cultural courier. As objective journalists, commentators did not insert personal interpretations on the news pages. However, by the time of her work in Santo Domingo, Geyer "began to see my job not only as reporting the day-to-day news but also interpreting the deeper sense of what is going on— not only political analysis but psychological interpretation" (67). Thus Geyer became a full-time interpretive commentator in the manner of Marquis Childs (q.v.), James Reston, and other political analysts.

Intercultural journalism, interpreting one culture to another, follows a distinct rule, according to Geyer: "avoid the cliche of your time" (234). Too many accounts of foreign wars, revolts, and revolutions, argues Geyer, are not only "unreadable"; they also fail to capture the great social, political, and cultural movements of history that stimulate conflict. Instead of explaining what is happening now, too many journalists retroactively apply the lessons of the last war, revolution, moral conflict. Hence, Geyer concentrated on covering *trends*, trying to pull together social movements, conceptualize them, get to their roots, and explain them in a cross-national fashion. This, according to Geyer, was merely following the advice of noted British journalist Alistair Cooke, namely, to accept the fact that, although a domestic reporter begins a career in general reporting, then increasingly specializes, the foreign correspondent has the "stimulating duty" of making all knowledge the reporter's province, of returning "to the origins of things every day" (55).

The foreign correspondent is in a unique position. On the one hand, she is a stranger in a strange land, unknown and unknowable to its natives. The correspondent in this position is "anonymous." On the other hand, as Geyer herself did, the foreign correspondent must make "myself 'one' with a new place—rather like a puppy or a cat scratching into his bed." The foreign correspondent resolves the tensions between anonymity in and blending into a strange place by "creating a reality out of pieces—and it, of course, was creating me" (105).

THE COURIER RETURNS HOME

After a decade on the road, Geyer was growing weary of constant travel; she needed, she said, a "home." In the summer of 1975 Georgie Anne Geyer left the *Chicago Daily News*. (She would return only in 1978 for a sad farewell party, the closing of the 102-year-old *Daily News*). She moved to Washington, D.C., and began a new career as a columnist under a five-year contract for the Los Angeles Times Syndicate. She moved to Universal Press Syndicate exclusively in 1981. As Mike Royko has pointed out, however, being based in Washington did not make her merely the typical Washington columnist who covers cocktail parties, dinner parties, press briefings, and the press clubs. Home or no home, she still found herself catching night flights to other lands.

Because of her store of cultural knowledge, gleaned from a lifetime of interpreting people to one another, Geyer's commentaries are unique in their informed focus on topics and issues about which few of her rivals have any firsthand understanding. For example, when President Bill Clinton decided in 1995 to deploy U.S. troops in Bosnia to enforce the Dayton Accords, it was Geyer's column that stood alone in probing the considerable ambiguities that would plague an armed force now called upon to shift from a "war mission to a peace mission. Well, this had better be a war mission, at least initially ... a watershed mission in which the Clinton administration finally hammers out a long-term U.S. strategy in the world" (Geyer, 1995b, 25A).

Since becoming a columnist, she has also undertaken other roles as a political commentator. She has been a regular panelist on PBS-TV's *Washington Week in Review*, a lecturer for the International Communication Agency, a radio commentator for the *Voice of America*, and a member of the panel of journalists questioning candidates Ronald Reagan and Walter Mondale in the 1984 presidential debates. She has taught journalism at Syracuse University and has been a Woodrow Wilson scholar as well.

As did her involvement as a domestic reporter and her career as a foreign correspondent, Geyer's experience as a columnist has sharpened her views of the journalist as political commentator. To the reporter she attributes the qualities of accuracy, fairness, and contextual understanding. The foreign correspondent too must be accurate and fair, but must have a deep understanding of cultural nuances and the ability to interpret them. The columnist/commentator must be accurately perceptive, informed, and opinionated, and ever cognizant of the effect one's words can have on people and events (Geyer, 1983, 328).

Buying the Night Flight is the stuff out of which novels and films are crafted. Yet, if a fictional work were based on the life of Georgie Anne Geyer, a new stereotyping of the foreign correspondent would be required. Fiction, reports Howard Good, offers distinct caricatures—the foreign correspondent as knight errant, as fool and liar, and as witness to history. "Gee Gee: The Docudrama" would break new ground, ground she set out to break: the foreign correspondent as cultural courier.

REFERENCES

Selected Works by Georgie Anne Geyer

The New Latins: Fateful Change in South and Central America. New York: Doubleday, 1970.
The New 100 Years War. New York: Doubleday, 1972.
The Young Russians. Chicago: ETC Publications, 1975.
Buying the Night Flight: The Autobiography of a Woman Foreign Correspondent. New York: Delcorte Press/Seymour Lawrence, 1983.
"Is Faulkner a Heroine or a Quitter?" *Dallas Morning News*, August 23, 1995a, 25A.
"Ambivalence Clouds U.S. Role in Bosnia." *Dallas Morning News*, December 6, 1995b, 25A.

Selected Critical Works about Georgie Anne Geyer

Moritz, C., ed. "Geyer, Georgie Anne." In *1986 Current Biography Yearbook*, 171–74. New York: H. W. Wilson, 1987.
Riley, S. G., "Geyer, Georgie Anne." In *Biographical Dictionary of American Newspaper Columnists*. Westport, CT: Greenwood Press, 1995, 99.

Selected General Works

Clausewitz, C. V. *On War*. Baltimore: Penguin, 1968.
Desmond, R. W. *The Information Process: World News Reporting in the Twentieth Century*. Iowa City: University of Iowa Press, 1978.
Good, H. "The Image of War Correspondents in Anglo-American Fiction." *Journalism Monographs* 97 (July 1986).

Higgins, M. *News Is a Singular Thing*. New York: Doubleday, 1955.

Kluger, R. *The Paper: The Life and Death of the New York Herald Tribune*. New York: Vintage, 1989.

Knightley, P. *The First Casualty*. New York: Harcourt Brace Jovanovich, 1975.

Saral, T. B. "Intercultural Communication Theory and Research: An Overview." In *Communication Yearbook I*, edited by B. Rubin, 389–96. New Brunswick, NJ: Transaction Books, 1977.

PAUL HARVEY (AURANDT)

(September 4, 1918–   )

Bardic Political Commentary

In "The Loop," the energizing sinew of what poet Carl Sandberg called "The City of Big Shoulders," Chicago, are monuments to a bygone media era. Here stand the Wrigley Building and the *Tribune* Tower, homes to fabled radio stations and newspapers. Jutting off Michigan Avenue runs a small boulevard whose name bears tribute to a broadcaster whose career began as the Golden Age of Radio had reached its full glow, Paul Harvey. The golden age may have faded, but the golden sound of "Paul Harvey, Gooood Dai," his signature sign-off, reminds observers that the unique style of political commentary that Harvey pioneered after World War II is as popular a half century later as it was when he first became the Voice of Middle America.

A BARD STEPS OUT OF THE HEARTLAND

To understand Paul Harvey's stature among political commentators of the twentieth century, one must understand his distinctive role as a communicator and his preparation for playing that role before an equally distinctive audience in America's heartland. For half a century his role has been that of a bard; his audience has been a populist one reluctant to slip away quietly either into a past its members find ever so comforting or a future they regard with foreboding.

The original bards were Celtic poets who composed and recited epic and heroic tales for the instruction and entertainment of Irish, Welsh, Breton, and Scottish audiences. The honorific title, "The Bard," bestowed on William Shakespeare recognizes that he composed bardic narratives without peer. Like any bardic compositions, those of Shakespeare confined themselves "to the world of common sense experience already integral to its audience's identity . . . when bards talk, it is our own voice that we hear" (Lessl, 1989, 184). To the degree that the bard's appeal is grounded in the real world as the populace perceives it, the bard's role in discourse differs substantially from that of the priest. Reality for the priest consists of how established elites view the world. Priests communicate views that derive from what governors, not the governed, see as real; it is "a reality that the audience can only superficially hope to approach" (Lessl, 1989, 183). Thus when priests talk, it is the voice of God we hear.

Whereas the tie between bard and populace is close, that between priest and populace is remote. Numerous twentieth-century political commentators have evoked the priestly voice; Walter Lippmann (q.v.), Edward R. Murrow (q.v.),

Eric Sevareid (q.v.), and Bill Moyers (q.v.) have been notable examples. By comparison, relatively few commentators speak in bardic tones. Most who have aspired to bardic commentary have been humorists—Mark Twain, Will Rogers, Mort Sahl, Art Buchwald, and Mark Russell. Even Walter Winchell's (q.v.) bardic pose before a microphone, shirt sleeves rolled up, tie askew, and hat jauntily perched like any *working* journalist, or Rush Limbaugh's (q.v.) Falstaffian style, privilege a seriocomic style; Winchell and Limbaugh become caricatures of themselves.

Of all commentators Paul Harvey stands preeminent in his consistent refinement and perfection of a bardic voice interpreting American politics in this century. It has proved a very popular voice. In 1985 alone national ratings of the most popular radio programs were, one through four, "Paul Harvey News" (broadcast each weekday morning), "Paul Harvey News" (the weekday noontime edition), the Saturday "Paul Harvey News," and Harvey's weekday afternoon series, "The Rest of the Story." Career politicians have long recognized Harvey's bardic popular appeal. Frank Mankiewicz—political consultant to 1972 Democratic presidential candidate George McGovern, political columnist, and former head of the Corporation for Public Broadcasting—ranked Harvey as one of "the ten most powerful voices" in each decade from the 1940s through the 1980s (Mankiewicz, 1989).

It is but a minor exaggeration to say that Paul Harvey's assumption of the role of Bard of America's Heartland resulted less from training than natural selection. Although the priestly voice metaphor evokes religious associations— the divine speaking to the faithful through devout priests—those connections are primarily with "high" Christian religions, especially the Catholic or Anglican faiths. On the other hand, the Baptist faith has been and remains grounded in populist traditions and identities. Baptist preaching is far more bardic than priestly. Paul Harvey's heritage is Baptist. Although his father, Harry Harrison Aurandt, was in law enforcement, Harvey (born Paul Harvey Aurandt) is a descendent of five generations of Baptist preachers. His tie to the bardic tradition via religious faith is thereby solid.

The bond is strong in another respect. Paul Harvey Aurandt was born on September 4, 1918, in Tulsa, Oklahoma. Oklahoma had been a state only a little over a decade, since 1907; it had been less than three decades (1889) since the former "Indian Territory" was opened via land rushes and lotteries to homesteading by white settlers. The land's populist history, traditions, and values were contained more in the memories of its residents, passed along in bardic tales, than in the stale pages of books. Harvey's success as a commentator in telling "the rest of the story," brief narratives about the humble, populist backgrounds of composers, inventors, artists, sports heroes, arch criminals, novelists, and so on, as well as presidents, prime ministers, and monarchs, has its origins in a culture that took pride in spinning yarns, parables, and apocryphal stories.

Today Tulsa is a thriving metropolitan area of almost three-quarters of a million people, a port city in America's heartland, home to universities, the

renowned Gilcrease Museum, and other cultural attractions. In 1918 it was neither so sophisticated nor so civilized. It was still a frontier town with less than
2,000 people. Legend, the "documentary evidence" of a bardic people, has it
that Harry Aurandt, assistant to the Tulsa police commissioner, died at the hand
of outlaws' gunshots. (A less romantic version of the death of Harvey's father
claims it came about as the result of a hunting accident.) Paul was a toddler at
the time, left to be raised by his mother, Anna Dagmar Christiansen Aurandt,
and a sister.

Family finances were tight, yet Paul thrived. It was in high school that his
bardic bent, a leaning spawned by the natural selection of a convergence of
family religious tradition and a populist environment, was stimulated through
training. Under the tutelage of his English teacher he excelled at oratory. However he was never to affect the pretensious manner of expression of The Bard,
Shakespeare, that his teacher insisted he adopt, saying later, it "sounded pretty
funny in Oklahoma" (Moritz, 1987, 205). Yet, he polished his delivery to the
flawless perfection that has become his trademark. He took another lesson from
his English teacher. As a child in frontier Tulsa, Harvey had become fascinated
with a remarkable invention introduced in the United States when he was two
years old—radio. In fact, he was so fascinated at the prospect of hearing radio
broadcasts in remote backwater Tulsa that he, like many a child of the era
throughout the Midwest, built his own crystal sets out of cigar boxes. When his
teacher-mentor urged him to take his speaking talents into broadcasting as a
career, Harvey eagerly did just that.

While he was still in high school, Harvey's teacher escorted him to KVOO,
a radio station still very much a part of the Tulsa scene. "This boy should be
on the air," she insisted (Miller, 1983, 45). The station's management gave
Harvey a job—as a sweeper, cleaner, and errand boy. Occasionally he filled in
for broadcast personnel, reading spot ads and news off the wire, even playing
a guitar on the air. By the time of his high school graduation, and subsequent
enrollment as a speech and English major at the University of Tulsa, Harvey
was a staff announcer at KVOO. The lure of speech and English in the classroom
paled in comparison to speaking English on the air; Harvey did not complete a
degree (although he now holds diverse honorary degrees from numerous universities).

Here, then, was a young man, reared in a young state, pursuing a career in a
young communication medium. Harvey's combination of background, youth,
and ambition proved a natural fit for broadcasting. From KVOO Harvey moved
to KFBI in Abilene, Kansas, where he served as station manager; then it was
back to Oklahoma, to KOMO in Oklahoma City as a newscaster; by 1940 he
was news and special events director at a Saint Louis station, KXOK. It was at
KXOK that he met and married Lynne Cooper, a student teacher who came to
the station to deliver school announcements. In subsequent years "Angel," as
Harvey called her, would often be mentioned in newscasts by Harvey; she would

also figure prominently in editing and publishing Harvey's collected broadcasts as books under the family label, Paulynne Productions.

From 1941 to 1943 Harvey was program director at WKZO in Kalamazoo, Michigan. At that small station, he worked with colleagues who, like Harvey, would later become broadcast legends, for example, Hall of Fame major league baseball radio and television broadcaster, Harry Carey. While in Kalamazoo, Harvey also was news director for the Office of War Information's (OWI) Michigan and Indiana region. Elmer Davis' (q.v.) OWI consisted of a domestic and an international branch. The former, of which Harvey was a part, was charged during World War II with the dissemination of information relating to the war effort within the United States. The OWI was Harvey's first, and only, brush with governmental bureaucracy in a broadcast capacity. It had little impact on his development as a political broadcaster or commentator. After all, the OWI was an extensive operation blanketing the continent and routinely drew its personnel from individuals already employed in the news media. As with other OWI regional news directors, Harvey's duties were mostly routine.

Harvey's military service during World War II was brief. He enlisted in December 1943 in the U.S. Air Corps only to be assigned to the infantry. While he was running an obstacle course during basic training he gashed his heel so severely that the laceration led to an honorable medical discharge in March 1944. Following his discharge Harvey returned to broadcasting, this time with a new name and new radio station. He shortened Paul Harvey Aurandt to Paul Harvey, a more harmonious succession of sounds, and joined WENR in Chicago to broadcast a fifteen-minute, twice each weekday, program of news and commentary. That program, over one radio outlet or another, has anchored Harvey's entire career as a political commentator.

Harvey's news commentaries moved quickly to the top of the ratings lists in the Chicago area. Coincidentally a major change was taking place in radio broadcasting. In 1943 the U.S. Supreme Court upheld a ruling of the Federal Communications Commission that the National Broadcasting Company (NBC) divest itself of one of its two networks (NBC consisted of a Red and a Blue Network). NBC's parent company, Radio Corporation of America, sold the Blue Network to an investor who had made a fortune in Life Saver candies. By the time the deal had been consummated, the fledgling network, the American Broadcasting Company (ABC), was in the market for appealing programming. Harvey's wife, Lynne, lobbied with an advertising firm to secure a sponsor for Harvey's news commentaries on ABC. Paul Harvey began airing nationally over ABC in 1951. Coincidentally, during the same period, another young broadcaster was launching what would become an illustrious career as a political commentator a few doors away at the NBC Chicago affiliate, namely, John Chancellor (q.v.).

A BARDIC VOICE, A POPULIST MESSAGE

In a career that spans over four decades of broadcasting news and commentary twice daily, Paul Harvey's bardic style has produced a consistent fundamentalist, populist message befitting his perceptions of what a broadcaster's role is and what his audience's concerns are. He sums up the broadcaster's role succinctly: "Every man worth his salt has opinions. We have to be for and against, if only in our selection of news. The only difference between me and those who pose as objective is that I let it all hang out" ("Paul Harvey," 1973, 225). Terse and straightforward though that view may seem, it masks a more subtle, complex understanding of the broadcast journalist's task.

Writing in 1993, syndicated columnist Georgie Anne Geyer (q.v.) described how dissidents in the Soviet Union and Eastern Europe had, during the era of Soviet tyranny, become "internal exiles" (Geyer, 1993, 13A). Forbidden to voice openly in public their protests against totalitarian regimes, the dissidents, such as Vaclav Havel in Czechoslovakia or Andrei Sakarov in Russia, lived as exiles in their own lands, refraining from public discussion, drawing instead into "one's own private life." The role of the internal exile, however, is not restricted to totalitarian regimes; Geyer argued that in democratic nations too people may live as exiles. They are not prohibited from speaking out in public; they do so. However, when they speak, it is in what Paul Harvey in the 1960s had called "hushed tones." In the face of overwhelming racial, social, and ecological problems breeding deep animosities and cleavages in America, said Harvey, matters are "so monumental you don't dare raise your voice" loudly (*Current Biography*, 1986, 206).

Early in his career as a national political commentator, Harvey had not experienced such exile. For example, while some political commentators—notably Marquis Childs (q.v.), Elmer Davis, and Edward R. Murrow—condemned Senator Joseph McCarthy's exposé of alleged Communists in high governmental positions in the 1950s, Harvey resoundingly endorsed the effort. He later justified that support for McCarthyism as based on a belief that "it took a roughneck in those days to do a very dirty job, focusing attention on the vulnerability of our country in its internal security" (Steinmetz, 1976, 38).

However, as McCarthy became increasingly vociferous and reckless in charging that the U.S. State Department and the U.S. Army were littered with Communist "dupes," Harvey came in for criticism. Subsequently he lowered his voice in commentaries regarding McCarthyism. As the relatively placid Eisenhower 1950s yielded to the tumultuous 1960s, Harvey continued to speak in hushed tones. In words akin to Geyer's description of internal exiles, Harvey described himself as "a displaced person" who had never left his homeland. He later told an interviewer, "I am a native-born American. I never left my country. It left me" (Steinmetz, 1976, 38).

Although his voice was lowered in the 1960s, it remained bardic. It is not surprising. In many respects the bard's role is one of internal exile. The bard is akin to the social role that social thinker Georg Simmel defined in his seminal essay, "The Stranger." Like a stranger, a bard is not simply a "wanderer who comes today and goes tomorrow," but is "the person who comes today and stays tomorrow . . . the *potential* wanderer: although he has not moved on, he has not quite overcome the freedom of coming and going" (Simmel, 1950, 402; emphasis in original). As wanderer the bard–stranger–internal exile is detached from the community of residence, yet is intimately familiar with the identities of the community's populace. So intimate, in fact, that the bard can speak as one of them without *being* one of them.

Simmel's prototype of the stranger is the historical role of the trader who travels from one land to another to buy and sell necessities, then settles in the land where the trading occurs. The necessities of Harvey's trade consist of bardic commentaries, entertaining tales revealing the identity of Americans *to* Americans. Consider, for example, how Harvey, during the "let it all hang out" decade of the 1960s, instructed Americans that they were not "hippies" but "squares": one "who doesn't want to stop at the bar and get all juiced up," preferring instead one's "own home" and one's "own bed" (Moritz, 1987, 206). Consider, as well, his tribute to America's business community in a syndicated column, "Mr. Businessman, We Owe You an Apology." Why? Because the businessman converts raw materials into salable products, advertises and sells them; he invests his earnings, pays others to work, and "pays out in taxes three times what you pay yourself." And what does the businessman get in return? "Government mandates, restrictions, regulations, and constraints"; legal fees for liability lawyers because "somebody says your coffee is too hot or your product fell on somebody's foot"; expenses to "build a firebreak to protect your property—unless it will damage the habitat of the kangaroo rat." Instead of being extolled by the news media, the businessman is vilified: "For my part in a nonproducing profession that more often castigates, ridicules, or ignores you, I apologize. I wish I could promise it's going to be different. I can't" (Harvey, 1995, 6).

In spite of using a lowered voice, and perhaps because of his bardic presence, Paul Harvey's national popularity increased in the 1960s as he endeavored to introduce America to Americans. In 1969 the Gallup Poll reported that Harvey was the second most admired man in the nation, runner-up to Walter Cronkite (q.v.). Although Harvey himself shied away from political labels, conservatives regarded his commentaries as especially resonant with their views. So much so that in 1968, although he never sought it, Harvey was frequently put forward by his avid supporters to run for vice president with third-party candidate George Wallace (General Curtis LeMay became Wallace's running mate).

On the major issue of the 1960s and 1970s, the Vietnam War, Harvey shifted his views. He began in public support of U.S. involvement in the struggle; by 1966 he was urging that it was a "win-less" war on behalf of an "unworthy government." When the presidential administration of Richard Nixon sought to expand the war into Cambodia in 1970, three days before the tragic demonstrations at Kent State University on May 4, Harvey commented, "Mr. President, I love you . . . but you're wrong" and he urged the United States to pull out of Vietnam (Moritz, 1987, 206). As later events indicated, Harvey had been prescient in detecting Americans' feelings and in dictating to them. In the remainder of the 1970s and through the 1980s, Harvey turned his critical commentaries to a myriad of concerns—opposing governmental regulations that stifle individual initiative, urging the discovery of alternative energy sources, heaping scorn on the social welfare system, rebuking politicians for petty ambitions and corruptions, supporting supply-side economics of the presidency of Ronald Reagan, but opposing Reagan's views on the Equal Rights Amendment.

In gauging the populist leanings of his audience on these and all other topics, Harvey applies his "Aunt Betty" test: what would his sister-in-law, a Missouri housewife, think of the story? The test usually produces news capsules and commentaries, no matter how serious their topical content, that are upbeat, celebrate the quotidian existence of the ordinary citizen, and pay due reverence to divine providence in human affairs. For his twice-a-day broadcasts of news and commentary, he writes his own copy, including the sponsoring commercials. In instances when the English language is too limited to convey Harvey's bardic passion and aphorisms, he coins words like a trader in novel goods in the same manner that political commentators like H. L. Mencken (q.v.) and Walter Winchell once did. Such words as "guesstimate," "trendency," and "snoopervision" are Harveyisms that now are part of the language.

The outlets for Harvey's bardic populism extend well beyond his flagship newscasts. Harvey has been particularly successful at polishing one broadcasting format that dates back to such bardic forerunners as sports commentator Bill Stern and the peripatetic radio and television broadcaster, Lowell Thomas (q.v.). Harvey's daily series, "The Rest of the Story," like the ground-breaking broadcasts of Stern and Thomas, consists of five-minute human interest anecdotes revealing little known facets of the lives of legendary figures. These biocapsules include persons both inside and outside politics. In addition, Harvey has syndicated commentaries for television, served as a regular commentator for ABC's "Good Morning America," written a three-times-weekly syndicated news column, recorded anecdotes and commentaries for phonograph albums, prepared videotapes for home distribution, and published books; he is also an indefatigable public speaker. As a trader in bardic political commentary, Paul Harvey is no stranger to entrepreneurial success.

CONCLUSION: THE OUTSIDER AS INSIDER

The stranger, wrote Georg Simmel, is "fixed within a spatial group, or within a group whose boundaries are similar to spatial boundaries." As a bard or trader, the stranger imports qualities into the group "which do not and cannot stem from the group itself"; the stranger's membership in the group "involves both being outside it and confronting it" (Simmel, 1950, 402–3). Paul Harvey has always possessed a strong sense of the group and its boundaries of which he as bard is outside, yet confronts.

Over his career as a national broadcaster, Harvey has relentlessly resisted all efforts to move his broadcasting home from Chicago to New York City. His argument has recognized the essential nature of the bardic role, that it imports opinion from outside while remaining on the inside. The vantage point of Manhattan would, in his view, place Harvey so far outside he would no longer be inside his populace heartland; he would be "myopic."

By remaining true to his bardic style and Mid-America grassroots, Paul Harvey Aurandt has proved remarkably popular and successful in a unique career of political communicating that has spanned almost half a century on the national scene. So unique, in fact, thinks Harvey himself, that America may not see the likes of such a fiercely bardic, grassroots commentator again.

REFERENCES

Selected Works by Paul Harvey

Paul Harvey's The Rest of the Story. New York: Doubleday, 1977.
More of Paul Harvey's The Rest of the Story. New York: Morrow, 1980.
You Said It. Chicago: Paulynne Productions, n.d.
Autumn of Liberty. Chicago: Paulynne Productions, n.d.
Remember These Things. Chicago: Paulynne Productions, n. d.
Paul Harvey's For What Its Worth. New York: Bantam, 1991.
"Mr. Businessman, We Owe You an Apology." Syndicated column, *Daily Oklahoman*, June 19, 1995, 6.

Selected Critical Studies about Paul Harvey

Bowen, R. "Paul Harvey." In *Newsmakers 1995*, edited by G. J. Speace, 76–79. New York: Gale Research, 1995.
"Harvey, Paul." In *Celebrity Register*, 225. New York: Simon and Schuster, 1973.
King, L. Interview with Paul Harvey. "Larry King Live," Cable News Network, August 16, 1991, Transcript no. 367.
Miller, H. G. Interview with Paul Harvey. *Saturday Evening Post*, 255, October 1983: 42–45.
Moritz, C., ed. "Harvey, Paul." In *Current Biography 1986*, 205–8. New York: H. W. Wilson, 1987.
Steinmetz, J. Interview with Paul Harvey. *New York Times*, June 6, 1976, 38.

Selected General Works

"Geyer, G. A. Our 'Internal Exile.' " *Dallas Morning News*, December 7, 1993, 13A.
Lessl, T. M. "The Priestly Voice." *Quarterly Journal of Speech* 75 (1989): 183–97.
Mankiewicz, F. "From Lippmann to Letterman: The Ten Most Powerful Voices." *Gannett Center Journal* 3 (Spring 1989): 81–96.
Simmel, G. "The Stranger." In *The Sociology of Georg Simmel* edited and translated by K. H. Wolff, 402–8. New York: Free Press of Glencoe, 1950.

H. V. (HANS VON) KALTENBORN

(July 9, 1878–June 14, 1965)

A Vocal Chorus of Political Commentary

The Columbia Broadcasting System (CBS) publicized H. V. Kaltenborn's Friday night CBS radio series in 1935, "Kaltenborn Edits the News" as the voice of "authority." In 1938, when Orson Welles' "Mercury Theater" broadcast of the "War of the Worlds" (one month after the Munich Crisis) provoked a small panic among listeners, Kaltenborn's wife contrasted the Welles' fantasy with her husband's voice of "reality." "Anyone would have known it was not a real war," she said. "If it had been the broadcaster would have been Hans" (Fang, 1977, 28). In the 1939 Frank Capra film classic, *Mr. Smith Goes to Washington*, Kaltenborn had a cameo appearance speaking the voice of "integrity" (Smith, 1990, 191). In the same year his was the voice of the "World of Tomorrow" in the New York World's Fair Perisphere. And, for those Americans who grew up listening to radio, wrote historian Eric Goldman, Kaltenborn's voice was "news incarnate to a generation" (Clark, 1968, 310), the sound of an "oracle" (Egan, 1945, 48). All these voices burst forth from the larynx of a man who, like such early broadcast commentators as Elmer Davis (q.v.) and Lowell Thomas (q.v.), did not even face a radio microphone until his career seemed already at its peak.

In this one-man vocal choir there was another voice, a pioneering voice, one that brought numerous innovations to political communication via broadcast journalism during the Golden Age of Radio in the 1920s through the 1950s. H. V. Kaltenborn was the first news analyst, the first reporter of a "living room war," the first instant analyst of politics, and the first man-on-the-street interviewer from a foreign capital. He was a forerunner of the contemporary news anchor, audience participation host, defender of free expression on the airways, and the invented broadcast persona. Small wonder that even a former CBS colleague who often had tilted with him, Edward R. Murrow (q.v.), spoke of Kaltenborn as the "Dean of Commentators" during a "Person to Person" interview with the retired broadcaster on January 13, 1956.

"SPIDERLEGS KALTY" AND PERIPATETIC JOURNALISM

In the opening of his memoirs, *Fifty Fabulous Years: 1900–1950* (1950), H. V. Kaltenborn recalls with affection the name his friends called him as a youth, "Spiderlegs Kalty." The reference was only partially to the appearance of his legs, only partially to his movements as a runner and bicycle rider who often celebrated "centuries" by riding 100 miles in ten hours. For, like any spider,

Kaltenborn liked to move about freely, spinning (in his case news accounts rather than webs) wherever he went. During his career, Spiderlegs contributed to the rise of a peripatetic journalism the likes of which has been matched by few political commentators, even ever-gallivanting Lowell Thomas and the well-traveled Georgie Anne Geyer (q.v.).

Kaltenborn was born in Milwaukee, Wisconsin, on July 9, 1878, the second child of German parents. Milwaukee attracted a large number of immigrants from Germany in those days, one of whom was Kaltenborn's father, Rudolph von Kaltenborn, a Hessian. In Hesse the Kaltenborn family had ties to nobility dating back to the fourteenth century; Rudolph was a lieutenant in the Hessian Guards. When Hesse lost its separate identity by absorption into Prussia, it was too much for the noble Rudolph. He came to the United States in 1866 as an act of protest, and he settled in Milwaukee where he resided as Baron Rudolph von Kaltenborn. Unfortunately, the noble bearing brought little financial success in Milwaukee for the baron, so when Hans was thirteen years old the Kaltenborn family moved to Merrill, Wisconsin. There the father, who became an alcoholic, barely made ends meet by selling building materials.

It was no longer the same family into which Hans had been born. His mother, Betty, died at his birth. Two years later Rudolph remarried and had two sons and a daughter by his second wife to add to Hans and his older sister, Bertha. Although Hans' youth was scarcely grim, the Kaltenborn home was an unhappy one. Spiderlegs contributed to the meager family income, first by selling newspapers in downtown Milwaukee, then by doing odd jobs in Merrill. His schoolwork was, at best, marginal; ironically, as his later career would attest, geography was one of his poorest subjects. After his freshman year in high school, he dropped out to work in his father's business full-time.

He also entered journalism, albeit indirectly. During each winter the kitchen water faucet in the Kaltenborn house froze. To obtain water, family members pumped it from a backyard well. That, however, made no difference to the water company; the company billed the family despite not supplying water. Hans wrote a letter protesting the billing to the weekly Merrill *Advocate*. The editor, Christian Johnson, liked the letter, printed it, and urged Kaltenborn to furnish other copy, without pay. Kaltenborn did so. Johnson liked Hans' articles and soon hired him as a reporter for $5 a week. For Spiderlegs Kalty, Johnson became teacher (from whom he learned the news business), mentor (from whom he acquired a taste for reading books), and advocate (from whom he received support for striking out on his own).

By the age of nineteen, the wanderlust was provoking Hans' spiderlegs to move on. At the outbreak of the Spanish-American War, Kaltenborn enlisted in the army, but only after a regimen of bananas and milk put enough weight on his skinny frame so he could pass the physical. In addition to becoming an army sergeant, Kaltenborn was a "war correspondent." He signed on with the Merrill *Advocate* and Milwaukee *Journal* to supply news dispatches in English on local boys in the 4th Wisconsin Volunteer Infantry, and with the Lincoln County

Anzeiger to file dispatches in German. Although his eight months in the army saw him filing numerous dispatches, it brought him no closer to war than a training camp in Alabama. Yet, the firsthand military experience taught him a journalistic lesson. Writing a half-century later in *Fifty Fabulous Years* he would insist:

> It is dangerous to form opinions secondhand. A responsible publicist should always try to check his opinions by firsthand contacts and observations. For many years I have done my best to do this as much as possible by personal contact with the men, places, and events that dominate the news. (Kaltenborn, 1950, 147)

At war's end Kaltenborn returned to Merrill to become city editor of the *Advocate*. However, a life in Merrill did not appeal to his peripatetic nature. Off he went to work in a lumber camp, spending the long winter evenings reading Shakespeare and old copies of the *New York Sun*. Both provoked his restlessness. Reading in the *Sun* an account of the World's Fair in Paris, scheduled for the summer of 1900, Kaltenborn gathered up his savings, his bicycle, and an agreement with the Merrill *Advocate* to publish his travel dispatches for $1.00 each. Kaltenborn hopped a freight train to New York City, then a cattle boat to Liverpool, cycled on to London, and finally reached Paris.

Kaltenborn traveled two years in France (with visits to Germany to stay with aristocratic relatives) as a salesman-journalist, peddling stereoscopes on commission, and sending dispatches back to the *Advocate*. Adding mastery of the French language, he became trilingual. In 1902 he returned to New York City, serious about pursuing a journalistic career: "From early youth there had been no doubt in my mind about my vocation. I wanted to work on a newspaper" (Kaltenborn, 1950, 31). As with his first entry into newspapers via the Merrill *Advocate*, Kaltenborn's success at finding employment was indirect. Having no luck landing a job, Kaltenborn submitted a poem about the Brooklyn Bridge to the Brooklyn *Daily Eagle*, a nationally known newspaper. Not only did the *Eagle* publish the poem, the editor gave Kaltenborn a clerical job. Over almost three decades with the *Eagle* he served as city hall reporter, Washington correspondent, drama critic, assistant managing editor, associate editor, and—most significantly—editorial writer and commentator.

In 1905 Kaltenborn took a year off from the *Eagle* to enter Harvard as a special student. He decided to remain for an A.B. degree, tutoring himself to pass the entrance exams (including one in algebra that he passed only two weeks before being named a Phi Beta Kappa). Before graduating *cum laude* in political science in 1909, Kaltenborn won prizes as an orator and debater, edited the *Harvard Illustrated Magazine* (where he rejected an article submitted by fellow-student Walter Lippmann (q.v.) on women's suffrage), helped organize the Harvard Dramatic Club, and made numerous social contacts. During Kaltenborn's junior year at Harvard he traveled to Berlin as secretary to the Harvard-Berlin

Professional Exchange. On his return voyage to the United States he met a German baroness, Olga von Nordenflycht, the daughter of a German consul general, whom he would soon marry. Following his graduation he went to work for John Jacob Astor as a tutor for Astor's son.

To support himself as a student (he had a journalist's fellowship his first year and won a $250 scholarship as a senior), he worked as a secretary for a faculty member; as a stringer for the Brooklyn *Daily Eagle*, New York *Post*, and Boston *Transcript*; and spoke before civic groups. In addition he won a $60 Boylston Prize for elocution. Winning the prize taught him a valuable lesson. Although he had memorized a short dramatic speech for the competition, when he began to speak, his mind went blank. So, he extemporized. Much to his surprise he won the contest: "This undetected bit of extemporaneous oratory helped develop a confidence in extempore speaking which has been a great asset ever since," he later wrote in what was a vast understatement (Kaltenborn, 1950, 46–47). It was a skill that he exploited as a political communicator for more than a half-century.

Once Kaltenborn had fulfilled his tutorial obligations for John Jacob Astor, successfully won the hand of Olga, and returned full-time to the *Eagle*, his prospects for advancement brightened (Kaltenborn, 1950, 62). Beyond his assignments as a working reporter for the *Eagle*, Kaltenborn undertook other duties. One was to organize travel tours, sponsored and conducted by the *Eagle* to promote the paper. The tours throughout North and South America and the mid-Pacific not only satisfied Kaltenborn's wanderlust, they also made him knowledgeable about political and social issues on an unrivaled scale. He used this knowledge, along with that acquired in his visits to Europe, to advantage in another *Eagle* promotion, "Talks on Current Times." These were public lectures given to audiences of as many as 1,600 in the *Eagle* auditorium. By the time the possibility of U.S. involvement in World War I became a hotly debated issue, Kaltenborn's public persona and stature had grown far beyond that of a mere editorial writer.

In the Great War Kaltenborn served as *Eagle* war editor. Throughout the war anti-German sentiment was directed at the *Eagle* for the alleged pro-German views of its war editor "with the Hun name" (Fang, 1977, 23). When he had first left Merrill, Wisconsin, for the *Eagle* in 1902 he had switched his name to Hans V. Kaltenborn; but when he entered Harvard, the school's officials insisted on imposing on him the "von" regardless of his wishes. Now, to make his name sound less German, Kaltenborn dropped both the "Hans" and "von" and became H. V. Kaltenborn.

One innovation he brought to the task of war editor was to maintain a map of the European war zone, using pins to mark positions of military units. His meticulous charting of the battle lines made him skeptical that an armistice had actually been reached, as reported by all other newspapers, on November 7, 1918. In spite of charges that the newspaper was withholding the "truth," the *Eagle* held off, on the basis of Kaltenborn's claims, any premature announcement of the war's end. The once mediocre geography student proved to be correct; four days later, when the armistice was official, only the *Eagle* had reported the story accurately.

ELECTRONIC POLITICAL ANALYSIS COMES OF AGE

As a high school dropout, Kaltenborn had taken on Harvard at the age of twenty-seven. He won. As a newspaper reporter, he took on electronic journalism at the age of forty-three. He won again. In 1921, as yet another promotion, Brooklyn's *Daily Eagle* participated in a special radio night organized by the Chamber of Commerce. As guest speaker Kaltenborn spoke, in person, to the chamber audience. He then traveled to Newark, New Jersey, to WJZ, an experimental radio station of Westinghouse. There Kaltenborn transmitted via radio the same speech he had delivered in person to the chamber. This time the chamber audience in Brooklyn heard it over a loudspeaker. When he returned to the banquet room, he received an enthusiastic ovation. The stunt profoundly changed Kaltenborn's career.

Radio was in its infancy, part experiment, part novelty, part entertainment medium, and part public affairs forum. The *Eagle* forum that had proved such a success during the Great War was continued after hostilities ceased. On April 4, 1922, the *Eagle*, in a single broadcast, put the forum on radio over WVP, a U.S. Signal Corps station. On that day, Kaltenborn inaugurated the first analysis of current news on radio, commenting on a miner's strike from three viewpoints—those of a miner, a mine owner, and an average citizen. He called his work a "spoken editorial" (Kaltenborn, 1950, 110). Shortly thereafter, WEAF, an American Telephone and Telegraph (AT&T) station, agreed to accept *Eagle* programs. From October 1922 through May 1923, Kaltenborn broadcast a weekly thirty-minute commentary over a station that, admittedly with difficulty, could be heard a thousand miles away.

In his first year of broadcasting, Kaltenborn was not only a pioneer in news analysis and commentary, but a trailblazer in provoking political controversy. When he criticized a judge who was scheduled to process an AT&T rates case, he was cautioned by station ownership. He was cautioned again when he criticized a labor strike as not being in the public interest. Finally, when he admonished U.S. Secretary of State Charles Evans Hughes for refusing even to entertain the possibility of diplomatic recognition of the Soviet Union, WEAF threatened to cancel the commentaries. As a compromise, Kaltenborn's commentaries were pulled off a Washington, D.C., hookup to please Hughes, but remained on WEAF in New York.

In each case, Kaltenborn's defense was that, as a radio analyst, he was taking a position consistent with that he had already taken as an editorial writer for the *Eagle*. If rights of free expression could not be denied to the editorial writer, how could they be forfeited by a radio commentator? Throughout his career Kaltenborn would continue to uphold the rights of free expression for radio commentators. In 1942 he founded the Association of Radio News Analysts, an organization that promoted free speech and integrity in objective news broadcasting.

WEAF made it clear it was reluctant to accept Kaltenborn's commentaries even though the *Eagle* was willing to pay to air them. Hence, Kaltenborn departed WEAF. He returned to peripatetic journalism in a pioneering role again. He was the first lecturer to travel from community to community airing radio commentaries—Chicago and Kansas City in the Midwest, San Francisco and Los Angeles in the west, and so on. In addition, over New York's WOR, he conducted "The Kaltenborn Digest" on a weekly basis and was billed "The Wandering Voice of Radio." As a forerunner to the likes of Phil Donahue (q.v.) and other late twentieth-century studio talk show hosts, Kaltenborn also inaugurated an audience-participation program on radio, a quiz show for young people.

For the remainder of the 1920s, Kaltenborn combined three professional activities—his work for the *Eagle*, his radio analysis for WOR, and his unrelenting travel. He circled the globe. In China he was even captured by a guerilla band. Among the talents he had acquired over the years was juggling. So he entertained his captors by keeping three oranges in the air while balancing a stick on his toe and a straw on his nose. His captors were so amused that they set him free.

By 1929 Kaltenborn's commentaries had been added to the nineteen stations of CBS. A year later Kaltenborn ended his long affiliation with the *Daily Eagle* and became a full-time CBS reporter. He left his affiliation with WOR with warm regards: "I have always had a feeling of gratitude for this station because it was the first to provide 'the stormy petrel of air,' as I have been called, with a permanent home" (Kaltenborn, 1950, 114). For the next decade, spiderlegs, now "stormy petrel," would have a swirling influence on news and commentary at CBS, in the United States, and around the world. At first he was combination news reader and commentator, the commentaries being carried irregularly in "fringe time" and without commercial sponsorship (Hosley, 1984, 24; Smith, 1990, 163). It was not until 1935 that CBS provided Kaltenborn with a regular Friday evening time slot for a series called "Kaltenborn Edits the News."

In 1932 he became the news analyst for CBS coverage of the Democratic National Convention, working alongside Ted Husing doing a running description. Since there was no commercial sponsorship of convention coverage in 1932, and since Husing and Kaltenborn understood that few listeners cared about the politicians' speeches, the broadcasters filled the air with interviews, special features, and analysis. Thus they established a pattern that, with the exception of C-SPAN's gavel-to-gavel convention coverage, became the radio and television norm. Kaltenborn continued an unbroken skein of coverage of national political party conventions through 1956 for CBS and NBC. With Franklin Roosevelt's victory in the 1932 presidential election, Kaltenborn broadcast FDR's inaugural ceremonies. He was so moved by the inaugural address that he "delivered a ten minute extemporized editorial before getting back to my real job of describing the drive back to the White House" (Kaltenborn, 1950, 171).

As impressed as Kaltenborn was with FDR, he was unimpressed after a 1932 interview with Adolph Hitler at the Nazi leader's retreat in Berchtesgaden. Although Kaltenborn recognized Hitler's undeniable will to power, he commented that Hitler lacked the capability of decisive action, seemed illogical, was self-absorbed, had a resourceful but inflexible mind, and was not in control of his own operations. "He suggests failure rather than success," Kaltenborn said, "a plebeian Austrian of limited mentality" who would never "gain the allegiance of a majority of Germans" (Kaltenborn, 1950, 186). Later Kaltenborn would recant, confessing that he had underestimated Hitler's hold on the German population.

In his global travels Kaltenborn did not restrict his interviews to political leaders. In his coverage of the London Economic Conference in 1933, for example, he sought the British public's reaction by importing a staple of American broadcasting never before used in foreign reporting, the man-on-the-street interview (Hosley, 1984). At Piccadilly Circus, for instance, he interviewed a hairdresser who moonlighted as an "amusement girl" in the evening, and a tipsy bon vivant who thought the conference "marvelous, simply marvelous" but could not explain why. Thus, Kaltenborn's efforts foreshadowed Edward R. Murrow's CBS interviews with Londoners during the Blitz in World War II.

However, it was not Kaltenborn's news reading, commentaries, and interviews with global leaders and passersby that propelled him into a position of esteem at CBS. There were two key incidents. Both changed the face of broadcast news. The first was Kaltenborn's on-the-ground (literally) coverage of the Spanish Civil War in September 1936. Kaltenborn set a precedent by bringing the first live radio battlefield report to American homes, the first example of "living room war" reporting. From a haystack located in a corner of France that jutted into Spain, Kaltenborn saw, heard, and reported a play-by-play account of a battle raging in front, to the right, and to the left of him. From his cineramic position, Kaltenborn spoke into a microphone that carried his voice via cable to a telephone line to Bayonne, then to Bordeaux to Paris to London to a shortwave station in Rugby; by shortwave, his voice reached New York and the entire CBS network. When he first got through to CBS, he was put on hold; he had to await the completion of CBS commercial programming. After eleven hours of trying, Kaltenborn finally aired a fifteen-minute report to the sound of shells and machine-gun fire. From the rooftops of London in World War II Edward R. Murrow would win fame for an identical technique.

The second event was a result of CBS' coverage of the Munich Crisis in 1938. While Germany's Adolph Hitler, England's Neville Chamberlain, France's Edouard Daladier, and Italy's Benito Mussolini bargained for the ceding of Czechoslovakia's Sudeten Germans to Hitler to meet the Fuhrer's demands, Edward R. Murrow and his staff of CBS correspondents filed multiple bulletins from Munich over a three-week period. It was H. V. Kaltenborn's task at CBS headquarters in New York City to analyze and bring perspective to the disparate broadcast dispatches. For twenty days Kaltenborn scarcely left CBS Studio 9, sleeping on an army cot with his microphone beside him. No matter what the hour, whenever a bulletin arrived Kaltenborn interrupted CBS network feeds to 115 stations, read it over the air, and provided instant, in-depth analysis of its meaning. During the crisis coverage, the fifty-nine-year-old peripatetic journalist, now anchored in one place, made 102 such broadcasts. If necessary Kaltenborn gave running translations of speeches, followed by impromptu analysis. As *Time* reported, "Before the hysterical roar at the end of [Hitler's] speech died away . . . Kaltenborn has translated and distilled a 73-minute speech, and for 15 minutes proceeded extempore to explain its significance and predict (correctly) its consequences" (Fang, 1977, 31). Thus did H. V. Kaltenborn bring to broadcast politics both instant analysis and the news anchor role.

Kaltenborn had become an important presence at CBS, but after the Munich Crisis his tenure at the network would prove short. Although he was a key member of the most prestigious broadcast news organization ever assembled, not everyone at CBS was pleased with him. For one thing, there was his ego, one that frequently seemed insensitive to sharing airtime with broadcast colleagues. Although he said it with good nature, one such colleague hinted at the ego factor. Lowell Thomas, like Kaltenborn, had joined CBS in 1930. Although Thomas had many more listeners, he recalls times when, upon passing Kaltenborn after a broadcast, the latter would say, "You are the cocktail, I am the main course" (Thomas, 1977, viii).

Another colleague, Edward R. Murrow, was more critical. Murrow joined CBS in 1935. Younger than Kaltenborn, Murrow was put off by Kaltenborn's seemingly pompous, didactic style and ego. For example, on his broadcasts, Kaltenborn was introduced as "H. V. Kaltenborn, here with a keen analysis." Murrow and other critics at CBS, not paying homage to Kaltenborn, coined a single word, "keenanalysis." During the Munich Crisis, Kaltenborn added to Murrow's irritation. In tones that Murrow found querulous and commanding, Kaltenborn contacted Murrow in London for reports; "Calling Ed Murrow, Calling Ed Murrow," shouted H. V. into his mike (Persico, 1988, 144).

However, what really irritated Murrow was a specific issue. On the eve of the outbreak of World War II, Kaltenborn predicted in a broadcast shared with Murrow, that England would accede to Hitler's demands regarding Poland. Kaltenborn went so far as to analyze Murrow's report as added proof that another Munich sellout was in the offing. Murrow was furious and broadcast a directly contradictory view, ticking off point by point his own earlier remarks that Kaltenborn had analyzed: "At the end of that broadcast you were told that my remarks might have created the impression that appeasement was in the air"; Murrow then flatly denied Kaltenborn's interpretation (Sperber, 1986, 141).

Clashes between talented persons with strong egos are not new to successful enterprises. Although collegial tension may have influenced Kaltenborn to leave

CBS, it was not the only factor. For one, commentator Elmer Davis, who substituted for Kaltenborn on newscasts during the latter's absence for travel on the eve of the Nazi invasion of Poland in 1939, made a positive impression on CBS executives and listeners. Kaltenborn did not feel threatened, but he was no longer certain of being the "main course." Moreover, Kaltenborn felt restrained by the CBS injunction that news correspondents should be totally objective, and never express a point of view. As a sign of his irritation, Kaltenborn named his country house, "Point of View," on the grounds that that was the only place he could have one.

Finally, there was a problem with CBS' allocation of time slots for Kaltenborn's broadcasts. Shortly after the Munich Crisis, the Pure Oil Company offered to sponsor Kaltenborn's newscasts. The financial arrangement was substantial, there was an attractive travel budget, and Kaltenborn would not be restricted in the views he chose to express. Under the arrangement, Kaltenborn aired two fifteen-minute programs a week, on Tuesday and Saturday. Subsequently his broadcast ratings led not only all other newscasts, but all fifteen-minute programs on radio. Pure Oil offered to sponsor Kaltenborn five nights per week. CBS scheduled Kaltenborn in a time slot unsatisfactory to Pure Oil. So, Kaltenborn at the age of sixty-two, in 1940, departed CBS for the National Broadcasting Company (NBC) for a three-nights-per-week commentary, a series of regional commentaries on Sundays, and, in 1942, daily commentaries on NBC. He remained with NBC for the remainder of his career, ceasing regular broadcasting in 1953, but doing occasional radio and television commentaries until 1958.

THE KALTENBORN STYLE AND LEGACY

H. V. Kaltenborn's approach as political commentator for NBC both in World War II and in covering domestic and foreign politics in the postwar and Cold War eras was, as always, peripatetic, analytic, and often wrong but never lacking in confidence. As Kaltenborn once remarked, "I would say whatever came into my head. However, I had my head trained so that I didn't get into too much trouble" (Clark, 1965b, 381). That is an overstatement; "in fact, after moving to NBC in May 1940, his rough drafts consisted of teletype reports glued on sheets of paper with penciled comments added" (Culbert, 1976, 84). Yet, without overriding confidence, the hallmark of his style, it is hard to conceive of how this radio wanderer and commentator could have continued to dominate the radio age as he did. The same confidence that led him to assert (incorrectly) that the Maginot Line was impregnable, helped him predict (correctly), on his December 6, 1941 broadcast, a surprise Japanese attack on the United States. The same confidence that led him (incorrectly) to predict FDR would not seek a third term in 1940 permitted him to castigate as bigots (correctly) those who denied Japanese-Americans their constitutional rights during World War II.

Kaltenborn's confidence was spoken with a voice that combined his German heritage, Midwestern pacing, and a Harvard-acquired accent. The result was a distinctive style. He spoke rapidly, moving in a typical broadcast from 150 words per minute at the opening, to 175, then to a close of 200 words per minute. His gentle sign-on, "Good Evening," contrasted sharply with his forceful sign-off, "Good Night." A Goliath in the Golden Age of Radio, he would appear a caricature of himself in contemporary television journalism. Indeed, one of his crowning moments of fame was as a caricature—when Harry Truman, after his successful 1948 presidential reelection, mimicked Kaltenborn's election-night analysis that Truman, even though leading in the early returns, would go down to defeat. Kaltenborn took it all in good humor: "The United States and 'Spiderlegs Kalty' have come a long way in fifty years. . . . As for 'Spiderlegs,' he has lived long enough to be imitated by the President of the United States"; after all presidents never make fun of "nonentities" (Kaltenborn, 1950, 297).

On July 14, 1965, Kaltenborn's chorus of voices was stilled by death. During his career he pioneered formats of political communication that, although novel when he first created them, have outlived him to become standard fare in what he called the "bastard art" of television ("I Hate TV," 1958, 56). What has not outlived him, in an age when political commentary has become an end in itself rather a means of analysis, is his admonition defining the basic task of the analyst: "to write footnotes to history in the making" and not to make history itself (Fang, 1977, 39).

REFERENCES

Selected Works by H. V. Kaltenborn

We Look at the World. New York: Rae D. Henkle, 1930.
Kaltenborn Edits the News. New York: Modern Age Books, 1937.
I Broadcast the Crisis. New York: Random House, 1938.
Kaltenborn Edits the News. New York: E. P. Dutton, 1942.
Europe Now: A First Hand Report. New York: Didier, 1945.
Fifty Fabulous Years: 1900–1950. New York: G. P. Putnam's, 1950.

Selected Critical Works about H. V. Kaltenborn

Block, M., ed. "Kaltenborn, Hans Von." In *Current Biography 1940*, 446–48. New York: H. W. Wilson, 1940.
Clark, D. G. "The Dean of Commentators: A Biography." Ph.D. diss., University of Wisconsin, 1965a.
———. "H. V. Kaltenborn and His Sponsors." *Journal of Broadcasting* 12 (Fall 1968): 309–21.
———. "H. V. Kaltenborn's First Year on the Air." *Journalism Quarterly* 42 (Summer 1965b): 373–81.
Culbert, D. H. "H. V. Kaltenborn: The Gentle Art of Self-Publicity." In *News for Everyman*, 67–96. Westport, CT: Greenwood Press, 1976.

Egan, L. "Oracle of the Airwaves." In *Molders of Opinion*, edited by D. Bulman, 48–58. Milwaukee: Bruce Publishing, 1945.

Fang, I. E. "H. V. Kaltenborn." In *Those Radio Commentators!*, 17–43. Ames, IA: Iowa State University Press, 1977.

Giraud, C. "The Radio Commentaries of H. V. Kaltenborn: A Case Study in Persuasion." Ph.D. diss., University of Wisconsin, 1947.

"I Hate TV." *Newsweek*, June 2, 1958, p. 56.

"Kaltenborn, Hans Von." In *National Cyclopedia of American Biography*, vol. 51, 457–58. New York: James T. White, 1969.

McKerns, J. P., ed. "Kaltenborn, Hans Von." In *Biographical Dictionary of American Journalism*, 166–68. New York: Greenwood Press, 1989.

Selected General Sources

Desmond, R. W. *Tides of War: World News Reporting, 1931–1945*. Iowa City: University of Iowa Press, 1984.

Hosley, D. H. *As Good as Any: Foreign Correspondence on American Radio, 1930–1940*. New York: Greenwood Press, 1984.

Persico, J. E. *Edward R. Murrow: An American Original*. New York: Dell Publishing, 1988.

Schramm, W., and R. Huffer. "What Radio Means to Middleville." *Journalism Quarterly* 23 (June 1946): 173–81.

Slater, R. *This Is . . . CBS*. Englewood Cliffs, NJ: Prentice-Hall, 1988.

Smith, S. B. *In His Glory: The Life of William S. Paley*. New York: Simon and Schuster, 1990.

Sperber, A. M. *Murrow: His Life and Times*. New York: Freundlich Books, 1968.

Thomas, L. Introduction. In *Those Radio Commentators!*, by I. E. Fang, vii–vix. Ames, IA: Iowa State University Press, 1977.

LARRY KING
(LAWRENCE HARVEY ZEIGER)
(November 19, 1933–   )

The Political Commentator as Talk Show Host

The legendary Edward R. Murrow (q.v.), often credited as the father of political broadcasting in the Golden Age of Radio and Television, pioneered not only in broadcast journalism. He also, beginning on October 3, 1953, was a pioneer in expunging the line between electronic news and show business (Slater, 1988). The premier program in Murrow's televised series of interviews with celebrities from film, high society, sports, the arts, and music, as well as politics, "Person to Person," devised a format that helped erase the demarcation between news and entertainment programming. Over three decades later, on June 3, 1985, "Larry King Live" adapted, perfected, and exploited that eraser to obliterate forever the boundary between politics and celebrity.

In anticipation of the tenth anniversary of his weekly Cable News Network show, "Larry King Live," King told a *Television Guide* interviewer, "Hey, I'm an infotainer. I never said I was a journalist" (Range, 1995, 17). King's vehicle for "infotainment"—the marriage of informative broadcasting with popular entertainment—is not that of Lowell Thomas (q.v.), whose show-and-tell lectures foreshadowed infotainment. Rather, King's vehicle is the Murrow-like celebrity interview.

King first spoke over a radio microphone on May 1, 1957. In the thiry-eight years before May 1, 1995, he had conducted more than 35,000 celebrity interviews (Bark, 1995). Over the course of that career he has formulated a simple, straightforward view of politics, one that makes the celebrity interview an ideal tool for political commentary: *politics is talk*. Once a politician, or wannabe political leader, says something in a broadcast interview, there is no turning back.

The February 20, 1992, edition of "Larry King Live" proved the point in a dramatic, telling way. The guest was Ross Perot, often courted by supporters as a presidential candidate. Perot, however, proved reluctant. King repeatedly sought to get Perot to commit himself. Finally, in a seemingly offhand, throw-away question to close the show, King inquired if there was any scenario under which Perot would seek the presidency. Perot's response, that if his supporters would on their own initiative qualify him as an independent on a sufficient number of state ballots he would seek the office, changed the face of presidential politics in 1992. Whether it was a permanent change, however, proved problematic. For, when Ross Perot returned to "Larry King Live" in September 1995, to announce the launching of the Independence party, later called the Reform party, it caused little movement on the Richter scale of politics.

After having responded to King in his 1992 appearance, Perot concluded "This is all just talk." Talk, however, is precisely King's view of politics: "I think politics is people, and, Boy!, can they talk" (King, "The Best of Larry King Live," 1995). Larry King is scarcely the first to take seriously the talk-based nature of politics. Verbal and nonverbal discourse saturates the actions of politicians, in executive, legislative, judicial, and electoral venues. The very word "parliament" derives from the French verb *parler*, to talk. Moreover, politics is not only talk, it is talk about talk—debates and discussions about policy proposals couched in persuasive language and other symbols. And, to the degree that rational deliberation demands full, public, unfettered consideration of initiatives, political talk keeps the deliberative process open to talk itself: politics is talk to preserve talk (Roelofs, 1967).

So Larry King is correct; talk is vital to the essence of all politics—an evolving discourse of power, influence, authority, and conflict regulation (Nimmo, 1978). King, however, adds yet another dimension to the talk-based nature of politics—the political talk of "the Stoop." To understand that aspect, one must consider King's background.

CROSSING THE LINE FROM LARRY ZEIGER TO LARRY KING

In a 1995 program, aired on the Arts & Entertainment cable network, "Biography," "Larry King: Talk of Fame," the man called the world's "talkmeister" says that what he brings to broadcasting in general, and to political broadcasting in particular, is "natural" and not learned. Be that as it may, it is nonetheless clear that King's youth, at least indirectly, taught him lessons that he would later apply successfully to his career. King was born on November 19, 1933, as Lawrence Harvey Zeiger in the borough of Brooklyn in New York City. He seldom passes up an opportunity, on the air or off, to remind people of those ties to Brooklyn and what they mean to him. (The title of one of his *seven* autobiographical books, *When You're from Brooklyn Everything Else Is Tokyo*, extols his affection for his boyhood Brooklyn, not dislike of the Japanese capital.)

Brooklyn in the 1930s, like many other urban areas in America's cities of that period, consisted of neighborhoods of ethnic immigrants and their offspring. King's parents, Jennie and Eddie Zeiger, were Russian-Jewish immigrants. They had three boys, one of whom died shortly before King's birth. The 1930s comprised a decade of slow economic recovery from the Great Depression, and slow acceptance that a major war would soon be in the offing. Eddie Zeiger's bar-and-grill experienced both the economic recovery and the fact of war. Although the business became successful, when World War II erupted, Eddie Zeiger sold the bar so he could work in a defense plant in New Jersey. On June 10, 1944, when Larry was returning from the local library under the weight of ten borrowed books, he reached home to find a policeman. The news was bad: Eddie Zeiger had died of a heart attack. Larry still remembers spending the rest of that day riding around Brooklyn in a squad car, working through his grief by asking innumerable questions of the thoughtful policeman.

Before the death of his father, Larry had done well as a student, even skipping two grades in elementary school. However, after the loss of his father, he turned from his studies to other pursuits—playing "Spauldeen" against "the Stoop" (a game using a Spaulding ball—"Spaulding" was the brand name of the ball, and the front steps of apartment dwellings in the neighborhood where Jennie moved her family); hanging out at "the Corner" (86th and Bay Parkway) with the "Warriors," a social club, not a gang; going to the afternoon baseball games of the Brooklyn Dodgers and pretending to broadcast play by play through a rolled-up scorecard; becoming a devoted fan of Red Barber, the Dodger's play-by-play radio announcer; listening to his favorite radio luminaries, Arthur Godfrey, Bob (Eliot) and Ray (Goulding), and political commentator Walter Winchell (q.v.); skipping off to Manhattan to see radio broadcasts; and developing an interest in girls. All this inattention to school earned him a reputation as a troublemaker in junior high. He was but one point above the minimum average to graduate from high school in 1951.

For four years after high school, Larry Zeiger bounced around odd jobs in Brooklyn—working as a delivery boy and a mail clerk among others. But his youthful fascination with radio instilled in him an ambition to embark on broadcasting as a career. The question was How. Fortunately, Zeiger met an agent who hired on-air announcers for the CBS radio network. The agent had no job for the kid from Brooklyn, but he advised Zeiger to go to Miami, Florida. It was a growing area with a large number of small wattage radio stations that were always looking for promising talent.

In 1957 Zeiger traveled to Miami by bus. Speaking in 1995 on A&E's "Biography," "Larry King: Talk of Fame," King said of his departure from Brooklyn, "I left it, but never left it." In Miami he landed a job with WAHR, a 5,000-watt AM station, a job sweeping floors. His services as a janitor, however, did not last long. On May 1, 1957, the day that the station's morning disk jockey unexpectedly departed, Larry Zeiger ceased to exist and Larry King became a replacement disk jockey (DJ). A scant fifteen minutes before assuming his duties as a 9:00 A.M.–noon musical host, the WAHR station manager summoned Zeiger. The manager asked Zeiger what his on-air name would be. Befuddled, Zeiger responded, "Larry Zeiger." That, said the station manager, would not work: Zeiger was too ethnic; listeners would not be able to spell it or remember it. The name must be changed. On the station manager's desk was a newspaper bearing an advertisement for King's Wholesale Liquors. "How about "Larry King?," asked the manager. Thus was born the persona who would go on to log more on-the-air time than any other broadcaster in history.

Such an accomplishment did not seem so likely at the time. Before the microphone Larry King froze with mike fright. Every time the musical volume faded to allow for a DJ voice-over, King increased it. Again the station manager intervened; sticking his head into the studio the manager said, "Remember this is a communicating business" (emphasis on both "communicating" and "business"). King got the message, told his audience what had happened, and never suffered from mike fright again (Pekkanen, 1980, 49).

The next fourteen years witnessed the gradual ascendence of Larry King as a radio personality in the Miami market, and a much more rapid fall. He continued at WAHR for a year, then moved in 1958 to WKAT for a "drive-time" slot and an increase in salary. There King added to his DJ patter fictional characters of his own creation (in the tradition of his beloved radio humorists, "Bob and Ray" from Brooklyn days). King's growing popularity at WKAT spurred a local restaurant to hire him to broadcast a four-hour morning show from the eatery. The gimmick was for King to promote the breakfast trade by interviewing the restaurant's patrons. Since business was slow King started off by interviewing waitresses and visitors in town for a convention. On the fourth day at the restaurant, he landed the first of what would become thousands of celebrity interviews in King's career. Bobby Darin, a popular singer and movie star came to the restaurant, apparently intrigued by King's innovative format of unplanned, unrehearsed interviews. All went well, the show garnered public attention, both for Darin and King, and other celebrities began to patronize the restaurant, less for food than to feed on the potential publicity.

By 1963 King had himself become a media celebrity, at least a local one. He changed radio stations again (having moved to WIOD a year earlier) and the venue of his celebrity interviews. He broadcast in the evenings from a houseboat that was the setting for an ABC-television adventure series, "Surfside 6." He was also WIOD's color commentator for games of the Miami Dolphins of the National Football League. He entered television as well, first with a late-night talk show on WLBW-TV, then by moving to WTVI-TV for a weekend show. Moreover, he became a newspaper columnist, starting with the *Miami Beach Sun-Reporter*, then the Miami *Herald* and the Miami *News*.

With increased notoriety in the "communicating business" came increased earnings, and expensive tastes—for the most fashionable clothes, rental Cadillacs, and betting on the horses. By the mid-1960s King, according to his statement to an A&E "Biography" interviewer, was "borrowing from Peter to pay Paul": "I didn't handle money well." While doing his radio show from "Surfside 6," King interviewed a young politician in the presidential administration of John F. Kennedy, a politician who himself would ultimately develop a reputation as a skilled political commentator and master of the celebrity interview. Bill Moyers (q.v.) went on King's show to promote Kennedy's Peace Corps. Aside from the fact that both King and Moyers would both rise to national, even international, media stardom, there are other ironies. Moyers, who had been sponsored politically by powerful U.S. Senator, and Kennedy's vice president, Lyndon Johnson, would later become disappointed in his sponsor. The increasingly debt-ridden King was also about to encounter disappointment with a powerful sponsor, one also with interests in the Kennedy administration.

In 1966 King met financier Louis Wolfson at Hialeah racetrack. Wolfson loaned money to King so the broadcaster could meet his growing debts. In 1968 Wolfson gave King $5,000; King was to give the money to a New Orleans district attorney, Jim Garrison, for Garrison's use in investigating the 1963 assassination of John Kennedy. The money did not reach Garrison. Despite his expressed belief that Wolfson had agreed to permit King to use the money to defray his own debts, Wolfson believed otherwise. Later sentenced to prison for stock market violations, Wolfson brought grand larceny charges against King (refusing to accept King's cashier's check that would repay the undelivered $5,000). Although arrested in December 1971 on Wolfson's charges, King was not convicted; the charges were dropped, however, only because the statute of limitations had run out.

Still, the charges by King's former sponsor proved disastrous for King. His career and his financial standing were ruined. He lost his radio, television, and newspaper jobs. From 1972 to 1978 King bounced around, taking work where he could get it. He worked as a freelance broadcaster and writer for two years; in public relations for a horse-racing track, Louisiana Downs (1974); and as a color commentator for radio broadcasts of the Shreveport Steamers (the World Football League). In 1975 he took a job as an announcer for the University of California football games; however, when WIOD in Miami offered to rehire him, King decided to forego the job announcing football games.

When he returned to WIOD, King resumed his radio interviews with celebrities, adding call-ins from the listening audience. In the ensuing years he returned to television, color commentary for the Miami Dolphins, and to writing a newspaper column. Yet the steady income from these jobs did not help him pay off his debts. He declared bankruptcy in 1978. He eventually was able to put his financial house in order. Although his income since 1978 has become substantial ($3.8 million in 1994), accountants handle his finances and permit him only a weekly allowance for his personal expenses.

NATIONAL POLITICS VIA NATIONAL TALK

Given a second opportunity at a comfortable broadcasting career, Larry King has made the most of it. Once merely a local celebrity, King is now international in his appeal. Once largely confined to show business and sports, he now is a major figure in U.S. politics. Two vehicles have broadened his appeal and have thrust him into serious political commentary. The first was a national radio talk show, "The Larry King Show," which began in 1978, the year of his bankruptcy. The second has been "Larry King Live," his international television interview show since 1985. His role as a high priced, and much sought, public speaker; as a radio commentator for the Westwood One network; as the author of a stream of books; and as a columnist for *USA Today* derive from his reputation as a national interviewer on radio and television.

The idea of a nightly live, multihour, nationally broadcast radio show of lively interviews and commentary had appealed to radio executives well before the 1970s. The Golden Age of Radio had spawned numerous programs of fifteen-minute news and analysis, giving rise to an era of political commentary by noted broadcasters. The commentary was not limited solely to broadcast journalists such as Elmer Davis (q.v.), H. V. Kaltenborn (q.v.), Edward R. Murrow, Drew Pearson (q.v.), and Paul Harvey (q.v.). Gossip columnists, including Walter Winchell, and showmen, such as Lowell Thomas, became popular political commentators as well. Yet, attempts at late-night, interview-commentary programming had been sporadic, controversial, and short lived. The Mutual Broadcasting System, for example, had made two unsuccessful forays into the late-night talk territory. Undaunted, Mutual approached Larry King in 1978 and proposed that he leave Miami and adapt his WIOD format to late-hour, early-morning talk radio. Although King understood the risks involved in such a venture, his precarious financial situation left him with little to lose. He accepted Mutual's offer.

On January 30, 1978, "The Larry King Show" had its debut on Mutual, from midnight to 5:30 A.M., EST. Early broadcasts originated from WIOD, but in April King moved to the Mutual studios in Arlington, Virginia, which afforded producers the opportunity to snare political leaders as guests. From the time of its inception in 1978 until 1980, the Washington political scene became a truly national one when the Mutual Broadcasting Network extended "The Larry King Show" from its original 25 stations to more than 250 affiliates and a late-night audience averaging from 3 to 5 million. As King carefully polished his original WIOD formula, he nationalized political talk. All of America became "the Stoop," a gathering place for chatting about politics from the nation's front steps, Washington, D.C. In a three-part format, King would, each evening, first interview a celebrity guest, for instance, New York Governor Mario Cuomo, controversial Reverend Jerry Falwell, or outspoken Phyllis Schlafly. The hour-long interview would then be followed by two hours of listeners' calls directed to the guest. The final portion of the show, "Open Phone America," consisted of Larry King alone fielding questions and comments (political "Spauldeens") from listeners.

One late-night guest caller on "The Larry King Show" was Ross Perot, long before his quixotic 1992 presidential bid. As a regular listener, Perot was puzzled by why talk shows seemed more effective on radio than on television. King explained: on radio the listener's brain becomes the television tube and generates pictures specific to each person, unlike the television set that generates pictures shared by members of a mass audience. King's appeal to the brain tube proved successful. At its zenith, "Open Phone America" reached 365 stations in the United States and abroad. Moreover, as live programming, "The Larry King Show" was particularly suited to reporting breaking news stories in the wee hours—the failed hostage rescue attempt in Iran in 1980 was one of the most notable.

"The Larry King Show" on radio proved so successful that the Cable News Network (CNN) approached its host to undertake a one-hour prime-time interview/call-in show, "Larry King Live." From its debut on June 3, 1985, the CNN effort nationalized politics on television as King's Mutual show had on radio. It soon served as "the National Stoop," offering political leaders an ongoing forum for debating issues, promoting causes, and celebrating candidacies. Certainly one of the most notable of such debates occurred on November 9, 1993, between Vice President Albert Gore and Ross Perot over the U.S. approval of the North American Free Trade Agreement (NAFTA). The Clinton administration claimed, rightly or wrongly, that Gore's triumph over Perot in that confrontation sealed passage of the treaty.

The short four-block walk separating CNN's studios from the U.S. Capitol carries the footprints of virtually every influential political figure in the nation as they hasten to be interviewed on "Larry King Live." That Larry King had a key impact on the presidential election of 1992 is now conventional wisdom. Ross Perot dubbed King's venue America's "electronic town hall." From Perot's February 20 bombshell announcement that, under certain conditions, he would be an independent candidate, to President George Bush's appearance on October 30, presidential and vice-presidential candidates have paid regular visits to "Larry King Live." (George Bush's October 30 appearance, his second on the show, was the first time an incumbent president ever took phone calls on live television.)

It was more than the popularity of Larry King that made his CNN venue a favorite for 1992 candidates. It was also the way in which King treated them on the air, the freedom he gave each to make appeals in a friendly setting. It was a forum wherein the candidates talked *to* the audience, not *with* its members, and always over the heads of reporters covering the campaign. Said Democratic candidate Bill Clinton to the Radio and Television Correspondents Association, "You know why I can stiff you on press conferences? Because Larry King has liberated me by giving me to the American people directly" (Bark, 1995, 4 C). In 1994 President Bill Clinton was less charitable about talk shows. He complained to a Saint Louis talk show audience on KMOX, "Look at how much radio is a constant, unremitting drumbeat of negativism and criticism. . . . Rush Limbaugh [q.v.] will have three hours to say whatever he wants, and I won't have any opportunity to respond, and there's no truth detector" (Hickey, 1996, 53).

One study of "Larry King Live" (Nimmo, 1994), based on an analysis of fourteen shows aired during the campaign that had presidential or vice-presidential candidates as guests, revealed that a total of only 102 questions came from viewers. For every caller's question, King asked candidates from eight to ten. King's questions were frequently leading, inviting each candidate to stake out broad, not specific, positions: "Would a President Clinton submit a balanced budget soon?'' ''Why is foreign policy hardly ever discussed in this campaign?'' ''Couldn't a good, forceful effective leadership president change things?'' Hence, in 1993, ''Larry King Live'' admirably served the purposes of the candidates. Small wonder, then, that more than a year before the 1996 presidential election, nine aspirants for the Republican nomination had appeared on King's television show to air their candidacies; moreover, the incumbent, Bill Clinton, ever mindful of the role King's show had played in his 1992 campaign, ''honored'' ''Larry King Live'' by devoting an hour to answering questions live from the White House during the week of the show's tenth anniversary, on June 7, 1995.

The first ten years of ''Larry King Live'' unfolded during a period of hyperactivity in King's career. In May 1985 he had agreed to a five-year contract extension for radio's ''The Larry King Show.'' He also agreed to act as a color commentator on a pay-television channel for the Baltimore Colts (National Football League) and the Washington Capitals (National Basketball Association), to conduct a two-and-a-half hour daily interview for Mutual, to conduct a monthly interview program for the Voice of America, to write a weekly *USA Today* column and a weekly *Sporting News* column, and to do a weekly ''Larry King: Let's Talk'' on a Washington, D.C., television station. However, on February 4, 1987, a heart attack slowed King to a halt. Quintuple bypass surgery, losing more than ten pounds, ending his [chain] smoking, and undertaking a strict exercise regimen resulted in severe cutbacks in King's commitments. Although ''Larry King Live'' remains (seen in 200 countries), most notably, ''The Larry King Show'' on Mutual is no more.

CONCLUSION: POLITICS ON "THE STOOP" AND A STYLE OF CURIOSITY AND LISTENING

Larry King's influence as a political communicator is now global. In many nations, the former Larry Zeiger is known by one word, ''larryking.'' A considerable portion of that influence derives from King's style. Although King argues that the basic elements in that style, curiosity and listening, are natural abilities, and not teachable, they are nonetheless elements that he *learned*. In an interview for A&E's ''Biography'' (June 2, 1995) King says, ''I was always a 'Why?' kid.'' But, would he have been a ''Why? kid'' had it not been for his formative days on ''the stoop''? In an era without air conditioning, long, hot summer evenings—lasting well into the wee hours before apartments cooled down—consisted of conversations on the front steps, asking questions and listening to answers. Neighborhoods were ethnic, made up of people with unfamiliar customs one could explore by asking questions, people with strange accents one could understand only by listening.

Teachable or not, Larry Zeiger learned to question and listen on the stoop. Larry King is more emphatic about the style: ''Every good questioner is a good listener'' (''Larry King Live,'' June 7, 1995). King's easygoing (in shirt sleeves, colorful tie, and suspenders leaning across a table toward his guest) style of deferential questioning and listening wins praise from politicians. For example, Ross Perot told A&E's "Biography," "Larry does not try to be the dominant factor in the interview." It also wins respect among other political communicators. Thus, Dan Rather (q.v.) says, "You'll probably get the tough questions from Larry King, but they're going to be put in a civil way" (Bark, 1995, 4 C).

Yet, that very style has its critics. Some accuse King of asking "softball questions." For example, Mike Wallace (q.v.) phoned "Larry King Live" on the evening of September 30, 1992; the show's guest was Ross Perot. Wallace charged King with "softball" journalism. That charge set up an October 10, 1992, segment of CBS's "60 Minutes" in which Wallace gave King a chance to respond. "Basically, my style is one of utter, it's almost, I'd say, naivete. I'm serious. I want to know why." Moreover, King said later,

> I don't know what a softball question is. I ask good questions, incisive questions. I care about people. The person to me counts more than the event. That's essential to me. I'm more interested in the fireman than the fire. ("Larry King: Talk of Fame," June 2, 1995)

Tied to the "softball" criticism, as if King interrogated guests like he played Spauldeen as a boy, is a second, namely, that King does not do his homework before an interview. King rebuts that criticism on three grounds. First is his claim that, although he may sometimes do journalism, he is an "infotainer" not a journalist. Second, he argues that to possess too much factual knowledge in advance of an interview deprives the setting of spontaneity: "That's not me. I try to just stay this regular guy. I'm not an intellectual. I don't know more than the average guy" (Bark, 1995, 4 C). Finally, King complains that critics too often confuse homework with having an agenda, a doctrinal position used to pin people to the wall who dare to disagree. Of terms like "left" or "right," says King, "neither one has great appeal to me" ("Larry King: Talk of Fame," June 2, 1995). That nondoctrinal stance makes King critical of talk show hosts who are laden with an agenda, such as G. Gordon Liddy or Rush Limbaugh. Of Limbaugh he has said, "He's got a gimmick going. He's got an agenda. The thing about bullies is they can't take it. They dish it out, but if you knock them, they go crazy" (Bark, 1995, 5C).

Larry King's contract with CNN extends into the next century. Whether his influence as a political communicator will extend as long remains to be seen. In any event, his impact on nationalizing, even globalizing, politics by bringing the stoop of Depression America to a wired world, and thereby rendering political infotainment the reigning format of political commentary, will be his legacy for good or ill.

REFERENCES

Selected Works by Larry King

Larry King. With E. Yoffe. New York: Simon and Schuster, 1982.
Tell Me More. With P. Occhiogrosso. New York: G. P. Putnam's, 1988.
Tell It to the King. With P. Occhiogrosso. New York: G. P. Putnam's, 1990.
When You're from Brooklyn, Everything Else Is Tokyo. with M. Appel. Boston: Little, Brown, 1992.
On the Line: The New Road to the White House. New York: Harcourt Brace, 1993.
The Best of Larry King Live: The Greatest Interviews. Atlanta: Turner Publishing, 1995.

Selected Critical/Background Sources about Larry King

Bark, E. "The King & Why." *Dallas Morning News*, June 4, 1995, 1 C, 4–5 C.
Moritz, C., ed. "King, Larry." *Current Biography 1985*, 230–33. New York: H. W. Wilson, 1986.
Pekkanen, J. "Larry King." *People*, March 10, 1980, 49–50.
Range, P. R. "The King Am I?" *TV Guide*, June 3–9, 1995, 10–17.

Selected Critical Radio/Television Broadcasts

"The Best of Larry King Live." "Larry King Live." Cable News Network, June 4, 1995 (60 minutes).
"Larry King: Talk of Fame." "Biography." Arts & Entertainment Network, June 2, 1995 (60 minutes).

Selected General Works

Fellows, J. *Breaking the News: How the Media Undermine American Democracy*. New York: Pantheon, 1996.
Hickey, N. "The Good, the Bad, the Insidious, the Dangerous, and the Appallingly Banal." *Columbia Journalism Review* 34 (March/April 1996): 52–54.
Hume, E. "Tabloids, Talk Radio and the Future of News." Internet monograph at //www.annenberg.nwu.edu./pubs/tabloids/, 1996.
Kurtz, H. *Hot Air: All Talk, All the Time*. New York: Times Books, 1996.
Nimmo, D. "The Electronic Town Hall in 1992: Interactive Forum or Carnival of Buncombe?" In *The 1992 Presidential Campaign: A Communication Perspective*, edited by R. Denton, 207–26. Westport, CT: Praeger, 1994.
Nimmo, D. *Political Communication and Public Opinion in America*. Santa Monica, CA: Goodyear, 1978.
Roelofs, M. *The Language of Modern Politics*. Homewood, IL: Dorsey Press, 1967.
Slater, R. *This . . . Is CBS*. Englewood Cliffs, NJ: Prentice-Hall, 1988.

TED (EDWARD JAMES) KOPPEL

(February 8, 1940–   )

America's Late Night Political Analyst

The most radical shift in political commentary in the twentieth century came in its closing three decades. Television's role in, and influence on, news gathering and news making was firmly established. But within the television industry, the race among the three over-the-air networks to enlarge their audiences in a fierce competition for advertising dollars produced a search for ever more appealing programming formats. This was especially the case with respect to entertainment television. But public affairs television, especially news programming, also succumbed to the urge to invent new ways to attract viewers, to become more entertaining. In the process, political commentary became entertainment as well.

Among the inventions—TV news magazines, talk shows, and tabloid news—was a unique one stumbled on more by chance than by design. In 1977 the American Broadcasting Company (ABC) named Roone Arledge head of ABC News. Arledge, who had pioneered ratings successes in entertainment, "NFL Monday Night Football" and "Wide World of Sports," as head of ABC Sports was called upon to do the same with news programming. "Sports and news have a common challenge, dealing as they do with the transmission of events," said ABC's president, Fred Pierce, upon Arledge's appointment (Sanders & Rock, 1988, 170). Arledge revamped ABC's nightly newscast, "World News Tonight" in the manner of "Wide World of Sports"—a wraparound format with three anchors, fast paced, dramatic, even sensational by conventional news standards (Westin, 1982).

Then, on November 4, 1979, protestors stormed the U.S. Embassy in Teheran, capturing sixty-six persons, releasing thirteen in a month, another in 1980, and the remainder after 444 days of captivity on January 20, 1981. The political philosopher, Niccolò Machiavelli, argued that political sagacity resides in seizing the moment and using it to one's advantage. Roone Arledge did precisely that with what was popularly known as "The Iranian Hostage Crisis." Arledge expanded his coverage of the crisis beyond ABC's "World News Tonight," by adding a late night news and interview program, "The Iran Crisis: America Held Hostage," a ratings success competing against late-night talk shows on the other networks. The host of "America Held Hostage" was Frank Reynolds, one of ABC's nightly news anchors.

When the crisis continued to drag on, Arledge, whose invention was slowly becoming as successful in holding late-night viewers hostage from 11:30 to midnight (EST) and beyond as Iranians were with their American prisoners, was also reluctant to turn his viewers loose. So, in March 1980, he replaced "The

Iran Crisis: America Held Hostage'' with a late-night program with a similar format—a planned twenty minutes of news, interviews, and commentary—revolving about newsworthy topics, issues, and personalities. Frank Reynolds continued to host the new program, ''Nightline.'' On November 29, 1980, Reynolds, who was tiring of the fifteen-hour-a-day work pace, received a holiday; ABC's State Department correspondent during the hostage crisis, Ted Koppel, filled in for Reynolds. Soon, as Reynolds tired of the effort and CBS' Dan Rather (q.v.) could not be enticed to ABC, Koppel became the permanent host of ''Nightline.'' Both a new format for political commentary and one of the twentieth century's most respected political commentators had arrived.

A FOUR-DECADE JOURNEY INTO THE NIGHT

Aware that fame often gets in the way of a reporter's commitments to his or her craft, a problem that has plagued such political commentators as Dan Rather, Ted Koppel has said, ''Fame is only an offshoot of what I've always really wanted: to be one of the best'' (Moritz, 1984, 216). If critics of Koppel's work are correct, he is one of the best: ''Ted Koppel is certainly the most universally respected newsman, especially inside the television news business'' (Goldberg & Goldberg, 1990, 341).

Ted (Edward James) Koppel is the only child of a German couple who fled Nazi Germany in 1938. His father, who manufactured rubber tires in his native land, was invited by the British government to open a factory in Lancashire, England. His mother was an artist, singer, and pianist. However, when the couple arrived in England, Koppel was interned by the British government as an enemy alien. Ted Koppel, born in Lancashire on February 8, 1940, later reported that he ''spent the first year of [his] life in a camp on the Isle of Man, where they took all German nationals''; it ''was an extraordinarily difficult time for my mother because she spoke very little English,'' and her husband had been interned as a prisoner (Collins, 1984, 23).

After the war his parents returned to Germany to try to regain some of their possessions and property, but ''they couldn't accept the idea of taking me back to Germany and putting me in a German school,'' Koppel said in an interview (Collins, 1984, 23). Young Ted was left behind in England to attend a boarding school for three years. The boarding school imposed a rigid hierarchical system; underclassmen were servants for upperclassmen. Koppel recalled the experience with mixed feelings, ''It was all considered part of toughening you up, learning self-control . . . in retrospect, there is a lot I gained from that experience. I got self-control the hard way'' (Collins, 1984, 23).

Koppel's family immigrated to the United States in 1954 and settled in the New York City area. Ted Koppel, already fluent in German, French, and English, attended McBurney School, a private preparatory school, and completed the four-year curriculum in three years. Koppel's interest in becoming a journalist had been sparked long before arriving in the United States. He and a contemporary political commentator, born two months after Koppel, Bernard Shaw (q.v.), were directed toward broadcasting by the same political communicator. While growing up in Britain, Koppel listened to the radio broadcasts of Edward R. Murrow (q.v.); while growing up in Chicago, Shaw was an avid consumer of Murrow's broadcasts as well. So, in the fall of 1957, Ted Koppel enrolled in Syracuse University, where his interest in television pointed him to major in speech, take courses in speech, drama, and radio, and work with the campus radio station. Following his graduation in 1960 with a B.A. degree in speech, Koppel enrolled in Stanford University where he obtained a master's degree in journalism in 1962.

Ted Koppel discovered that entering the journalism profession in New York was not an easy feat. For six months, after failing the Associated Press broadcasting exam, Koppel taught English and sociology at his former school, McBurney. Then came a modest beginning in broadcasting as a copyboy at WMCA-AM, a radio station in the New York area. He earned promotions until he was about to conduct on-air radio interviews. At that point, the American Federation of Television and Radio Artists (AFTRA) demanded that Koppel join the union if the station planned to employ him as a reporter; however, after Koppel joined the union, AFTRA demanded higher fees be paid the reporter by the radio station for his work. So, "WMCA did the honorable thing—they took me off the air. And that, and the fact that I asked for a $10 raise after a year, and did not get it, convinced me that my future did not rest with WMCA" ("Right Fit for His Format," 1984, 111).

In 1963 he became a naturalized U.S. citizen. The same year he received a tip from a friend that WABC radio was hiring on-air people for a new program called "Flair Reports." Koppel was required to write two scripts and present them during the interview. He and his wife went to the beach where he wrote the scripts, but upon his return home, he discovered that he had left the scripts at the beach, and he had to rewrite them. The next day he went in and presented the scripts. Three days later, the producers called him and said he was good, but he was too young to hire. As a consolation, they offered him a position as a writer in the news department. Koppel declined. Several days later the producers called him back and said, "It's radio and no one will know how old you are, so come on in" (Collins, 1984, 25).

While working on "Flair Reports," Ted Koppel developed his writing and reporting skills, particularly his own flair for on-air ad-lib when once called on to fill ninety minutes of airtime when he was reporting a delayed motorcade bearing President Lyndon B. Johnson. The talent he displayed during that broadcast earned him a reporting spot at the 1964 Democratic National Convention, then as the anchor of a nightly ABC Radio newscast. Although Koppel won repute as a journalist on radio, he longed to be on television. "Eventually radio news started sending us out in the street as reporters"; for example, Koppel's coverage of the civil rights movement from Selma, Alabama. "But I still knew

I wanted to make it into television, because in 1963, television, not radio, was the class act'' (Collins, 1984, 25).

Ted Koppel's opportunity to get into television news came in 1967 when ABC-TV News called to offer a correspondent posting in Vietnam. At the time, the network did not have a television camera crew on staff, and their cadre of reporters was small. ABC was far behind its competitors, the Columbia Broadcasting System (CBS) and the National Broadcasting Company (NBC). In fact, ABC was the last to expand its nightly newscast from fifteen to thirty minutes, doing so four years after its rivals. Koppel contends that he enjoyed the challenge of being the underdog: "One of the great joys of being a foreign correspondent for ABC was when you kicked the crap out of CBS,'' who had more correspondents, better equipment, and more capital outlay than ABC Television (Blonsky, 1988, 115).

Ted Koppel reported from ABC's Saigon bureau from January to October 1967, and from January 1969 through the summer of 1971. Following his first assignment overseas, he returned to the United States as ABC's Miami bureau chief. In the summer of 1968, Koppel covered Richard Nixon's presidential campaign and political developments in Latin America, then went back to the Far East as the network's Hong Kong bureau chief starting in January 1969. During his time abroad, he covered the news from Hong Kong to Australia and developed a keen interest in foreign affairs that has persisted throughout his career in television journalism. His efforts won him the Overseas Press Club award for best television commentary on foreign news in 1971.

Despite his interest in foreign policy and issues abroad, Koppel was tiring of the traveling and long separations from his family. While still a graduate student at Stanford in 1960, Ted Koppel had met Grace Anne Dorney; they married in 1963, despite reservations from family members because Koppel is Jewish and his wife Catholic. The Koppels were interested in having a family (they have four children), and, hence, his desire at that point was to accept an assignment that did not require travel. He had paid his dues with stints in Vietnam, Miami, and Hong Kong. It was time for more permanence. By 1971 Koppel had been with ABC for eight years. Two assignments were open at the time for someone of his experience either as the White House or State Department correspondent. Due to the travel schedule of the president, he ruled out the White House assignment; Koppel decided on the reputable assignment of chief State Department correspondent.

The appointment as the chief diplomatic correspondent for ABC was a mark of the respect Koppel had earned from his colleagues and the management of the network. But any hopes of a more sedentary life at home with his family proved short lived. Secretary of State Henry Kissinger was one of the most traveled secretaries in the twentieth century. Where the secretary traveled so did the diplomatic correspondents. However, the trips with Kissinger had their compensations. The experience proved important to Koppel's future as a political commentator. During his years covering the State Department, he forged a friendship with Henry Kissinger. From Kissinger, a Harvard professor, Ted Koppel learned the nuances of foreign policy. In 1975 Kissinger offered Koppel a job as his spokesperson at the State Department. Koppel responded, "I was fascinated by the prospect. Also terrified because I don't happen to believe that journalists ought to go into government and then come back to journalism again" (Collins, 1984, 26).

Often criticized for his relationship with Henry Kissinger, Ted Koppel responds,

> I admire his lucidity, the agility of his mind. . . . It doesn't do any good to say
> I sometimes lean over backwards to be a little tougher on him, because that's
> wrong too. I like him. I'm not going to surrender the friendship. But I've also
> made sure that I haven't gotten into that kind of relationship with anyone else.
> (Gareffa, 1989, 260)

He also said, "My years at the State Department taught me to listen very carefully because diplomats are very good at misleading you. Language can be manipulated in wonderful ways" ("Right Fit for His Format," 1982, 111).

From 1971 through 1979, Ted Koppel traveled around the world and reported on foreign policy in his capacity as chief correspondent for the State Department. He traveled with President Richard Nixon on his historic trip to the People's Republic of China in 1972. Subsequently Koppel returned there for a two-month assignment making a 1973 television documentary that explored the daily lives of people in the People's Republic. In 1975 Koppel returned yet again to China, this time with President Gerald Ford. That same year another plum fell Koppel's way; he became anchor for ABC's "Saturday Night News," while continuing his position as the network's State Department correspondent.

In 1976 Ted Koppel was thirty-six years old; he had a steady career at the network. When his wife entered law school, Koppel took a nine-month leave of absence from his duties at ABC News to care for their four children. In an interview Koppel's colleague, Barry Dunsmore, said, "Ted has enormous self-confidence and, because of that, he's not neurotic or paranoid. He's not afraid of someone else doing well, because he knows what he can do" (Waters, Howard, & Hackett, 1981, 75). Koppel's own remarks on the risks of leaving television news at the peak of his career to that point echo that confidence. Asked about the courage of his decision, Koppel responded, "It was not that gutsy. The gutsy thing is when you do that not really knowing if you're ever going to be hired again. There was no doubt in my mind that I would come back after nine months" (Collins, 1984, 27).

Although he did not report every day, during his sabbatical from his regular duties, Koppel provided radio commentary every day, and he continued to fly to New York each weekend to do the "Saturday Night News." He also wrote a novel with another foreign correspondent, Marvin Kalb, as coauthor, *In the National Interest*. In the spring of 1977 Koppel returned to ABC News, then under the helm of a new president. During most of the 1970s, ABC's news division suffered from a major problem. Its ratings were far below those of its competitors. In spite of ABC's efforts to improve the division, little progress had been made in the ratings race in the decade since the network switched to thirty-minute evening newscasts. Roone Arledge, brought to the news division to improve ratings and the quality of news programming, was quickly making personnel changes. Koppel was uncomfortable with the changes. He was especially concerned when Arledge fired the executive producer of the "Saturday Evening News" while Koppel, still its anchor, was away on vacation.

Furious over what he perceived to be a lack of respect for him as an ABC news anchor, Koppel tendered his resignation, and he announced his departure from "Saturday Evening News." Arledge refused to accept the resignation. After a month, Koppel was invited to the network office to discuss the matter. At that point in his career, Koppel wanted more respect than he believed was being given him at ABC News: "I wanted to be an important part of ABC News" (Collins, 1984, 28). The situation was resolved; Koppel did not return as anchor of the Saturday newscast, but he did continue as State Department correspondent.

NIGHTLY POLITICAL COMMENTATOR

Koppel remained unhappy. From 1977 to 1979, he felt that he did not have the role in domestic news coverage that he should; moreover, as a commentator on foreign issues, he was limited to his reports from the State Department. He had been with the network for approximately fifteen years, and in his opinion, the network was ignoring him as a talented and viable asset. Then the Iranian hostage crisis broke upon the domestic and foreign scene. Koppel's role as State Department correspondent took on added stature as he became a vital element in reporting on "ABC World News Tonight" on prospects for resolving the crisis. ABC's nightly coverage imparted credibility to ABC News and contributed to higher ratings and market share.

The coverage of the hostage crisis on "ABC World News Tonight" portrayed a nation and its leadership in a state of chaos, frustration, and panic on how to free its citizens from the U.S. Embassy in Iran. Ted Koppel never failed to underscore the tenor of ABC's approach: on November 4, the day of the seizure of the embassy, Koppel commented, "The State Department is doing what it can, but for the moment, at least, that doesn't appear to be much." Two days later, Koppel's gloom increased: "Since the crisis began, the U.S. government hasn't had a great deal of leverage in Iran. Now it has even less." Another two days, and Koppel's commentary found that " U.S. diplomatic leverage in Iran seems to be diminishing by the hour." ABC's teledrama of pending disaster played well, and Ted Koppel left his mark (Nimmo & Combs, 1985, 144–51).

With the launching of "America Held Hostage" and its successor "Nightline," Koppel had the vehicle for political commentary that he had been waiting for: "Yes, there was no question in my mind. I had put in sixteen and half years with the network. . . . If ever I was going to do something new and different, this was it" (Collins, 1984, 28). At first, however, Roone Arledge was not convinced that Koppel was the person to anchor "Nightline." He was unsure that a scholarly looking diplomatic correspondent could attract an audience away from "The Tonight Show with Johnny Carson." In the end, the naming of Koppel as anchor was not a firm decision made by Arledge, but rather was a gradual adjustment to shifting circumstances. Koppel proved that he could moderate, keeping the dialogue going between guests in a manner his audience members could follow.

Ted Koppel had spent numerous years covering the State Department, and his long tenure there made him familiar with the politicians who made the news on foreign policy and state matters. From Koppel's perspective, his experience as a reporter at the State Department provided him with the knowledge and skills to handle difficult personalities and explore complex subjects as a journalist.

> My abilities come from years of doing battle with very smart diplomats, who tend to deal in nuances, so that I learned to listen very carefully to what people said. And so I learned to probe, perhaps a little more precisely than I might have if I'd been covering HEW [the Department of Health, Education and Welfare]. ("Right Fit for His Format," 1984, 111).

With the success of "Nightline," Ted Koppel surfaced as one of the most respected political commentators on television. The format of the show is flexible to allow for discussion of breaking news stories. The show has a loyal group of viewers, but the ratings for the show increase during a crisis (Alter, 1987). The topic for a given evening is discussed during a morning conference call, and then individual staff members undertake the tasks of researching and arranging for guests. The issues or direction of a show can change as late as an hour before airtime. The flexible schedule creates unpredictable pressures on the correspondents. Introductory segments that chronicle the issues of the evening's focus are often shot and edited on the day of the broadcast to keep abreast of breaking developments, yet the program demands that correspondents also provide analytical reporting, different in tone than their regular reports on newscasts.

The program's innovative moments have received numerous plaudits. In 1985 "Nightline" featured Foreign Minister R. F. Botha and Bishop Desmond Tutu talking directly to one another via a satellite from South Africa. In 1986 a telecast featured Ferdinand Marcos and Cory Aquino in separate interviews on the eve of a Philippines election that changed that nation's political direction (Alter, 1987).

From April 1983 to February 1984, "Nightline" expanded from thirty minutes to an hour. The expanded format was not successful. Critics speculate that many of the topics covered on the shows were too narrow for an hour's probing, that for other topics the number of guests should have been enlarged. Koppel speculates that topics and the time of night were factors in the decision to return the show to its original time format. He concludes, employing a metaphor that renders filling citizens' information needs the functional equivalent of selling Cabbage Patch dolls, "Anytime you are selling a product, you're better off leaving the customer wanting more" (Collins, 1984, 30). The format's return to thirty minutes in length provides approximately fifteen minutes for interviews after the introductory background material and the mandatory commercial ads.

Koppel does not conduct preshow briefings with his guests. According to Koppel, such briefings and personal contacts, no matter how professional in tone, build relationships with respondents that may diminish the spontaneity of the on-air exchange. However, he has violated that standard. In 1988 Gary Hart wanted to return to the race for the Democratic presidential nomination after withdrawing because of published evidence of an extramarital affair. He contacted Koppel and arranged a "Nightline" interview (Koppel, 1996). Hart "negotiated the first face-to-face interview on a program that preferred the mystique of keeping the guests at remote locations, even if it was just down the hall" (Kurtz, 1996, 67).

Koppel's on-air focus is the issue of the day: "I like to be very familiar with the subject that we're going to be talking about"; yet, he also contradicts himself, "All I need to do is know enough about a subject to ask reasonably intelligent questions, and that does not require a great deal of background" (Gareffa, 1989, 260). In any case, "very familiar" or not a "great deal of background," Koppel's level of intimacy with the subject matter, rather than the targets of his queries, permits an air of objectivity in his interview-commentaries. Yet, sometimes the guests *make* the telecast: if there are tensions between guests, "then you kind of hold those two wires together, and let the sparks fly" ("Right Fit for His Format," 1984, 111).

In addition to not briefing his guests, Koppel does not prepare questions for the interviews. His rationale is twofold. First he claims, "I'm a procrastinator. What can I say? . . . My parents and teachers used to be exasperated by the fact that I would wait until the last minute, and now people are fascinated by it. I need the pressure" (*People Weekly*, 1982, 89). Second, he contends that prepared questions may narrow the scope of an interview and result in missing the important issue. Without the prepared questions, he simply listens to the introduction from the correspondent, and relies on whatever information he brings to the telecast.

ANCHOR AS STATESMAN

Koppel honed his skills as a listener and interviewer during his 30 years in network news. When he was a child, says Koppel, "the ultimate concept of magic was Sinbad the Sailor finding a crystal globe and being able to see and hear the voices and faces of people who were thousands of miles away. We produce that kind of magic every single night" (*People Weekly*, 1982, 89). Koppel has the authority to set the stage for political discussion. He helps decide the topics that will be covered, and he influences the choice of which guests will appear and how long they will speak. As moderator, he requires that each guest be fitted with an earpiece that pipes his voice into their ears—a tactic he uses to control guests who talk too long or who try to avoid his direct questions (Alter, 1987). "Nightline" is Ted Koppel's forum, not any guest's.

Koppel's ability to appear neutral and impartial, be tenacious, and be seemingly confident when interviewing a variety of people, including heads of states, is the key to his success as a political commentator. He has linked that success to his surrogate role, "I fulfill a symbolic role on television. I am a surrogate for the audience at home" (Cohen, 1988, 16). Not every critic agrees that Koppel is neutral, impartial, tenacious, or confident. For example, after conducting a six-week analysis of "Nightline," Michael Massing (1989) concluded that neutrality is only an illusion on the program. According to Massing, the show needs fresh ideas and voices. Other critics stress that, after a decade and a half on the air, "Nightline" needs to enlarge its perspective—to get outside the Washington beltway and reach out to other guests for political comment (Katz, 1991; Massing, 1989).

Koppel admits that there is only so much a live interview can accomplish on television. The relationship between the television viewer and the interviewer is very subtle. The task of the interviewer is "to keep the viewer with you." A principal way to do that is to let the person being questioned have a full say at first; if the interviewee is evading or avoiding the question, "Everyone at home gets it." Hence, the interviewer can grow more aggressive. If the person questioned remains evasive, "The best you can do is leave the audience with the impression that the person just doesn't want to answer the question." It comes down to the interviewers performing a mental editing of answers, "The essence of journalism is editing," says Koppel; and "editing while you are on the air is extremely tough" (Rosenstiel, 1995, 26–27). Koppel himself evades the principal question: Is edited reality, in journalism or interviewing, still reality, or, as Walter Lippmann (q.v.) has argued, but one of many versions of it?

So long as he is moderator, and he assures one and all that it is his intention to remain so (Gunther, 1995), Ted Koppel will be the focal point of late-night political commentary, just as the Cable News Network's Larry King (q.v.) is earlier in the evening. Koppel ignores his critics and, instead, bites the hands that feeds him—the television industry and politics in general.

What is largely missing in American life today is a sense of context, of saying or doing anything that is intended or even expected to live beyond the moment . . . the trivial displaces the momentous. . . . We have become so obsessed with facts that we have lost all touch with truth. (Koppel 1986, 19)

And, in an address to the International Radio and Television Society, he said, "As broadcast journalists, it's easy to be seduced into believing that what we're doing is just fine.... But money, fame and influence without responsibility are the assets of the courtesan. We must accept responsibility for what we do, and [what] we think, occasionally in the future" (Koppel, 1986, 19).

Speculation that Ted Koppel will depart "Nightline," either because ABC lures a popular nighttime talk show into his 11:35 P.M. EST time slot, or because he will unseat ABC's Peter Jennings or CBS' Dan Rather as a nightly news anchor, remains mere speculation. (President George Bush once called Koppel "Dan" in a "Nightline" interview, thus giving his endorsement to Koppel as anchor material.) "Can I see anything on the horizon that would cause me to leave? The answer is no. I'm clearly aging, but I'm not dead yet" (Gunther, 1995, 42).

REFERENCES

Selected Works by Ted Koppel

The Wit and Wisdom of Adlai Stevenson. Compiler. New York: Hawthorn, 1965.
In the National Interest. A novel with M. L. Kalb. New York: Simon and Schuster, 1977.
"Media Courtesans." *Harper's Magazine*, 272, January 1986, 18–19.
"What Passes and What Lasts." *Vital Speeches of the Day*, 60, July 15, 1994, 583–85.
Nightline: History in the Making and the Making of Television. With K. Gibson. New York: Times Books, 1996.

Selected Critical Works about Ted Koppel

Alter, J. "America's Q&A Man." *Newsweek*, June 15, 1987, 50–56.
Blonsky, M. "Ted Koppel's Edge." *New York Times Magazine*, August 14, 1988, 14, 115.
Cohen, R. "Ted Koppel." *Life*, 11, October 1988: 15–18.
Collins, N. "The Smartest Man on TV." *New York*, August 13, 1984, 22–33.
Gareffa, P. M., ed. "Ted Koppel." In *Newsmakers*, 258–61. Detroit, MI: Gale Research, 1989.
Gunther, M. "I'm Staying Put, Says Late-Night King Koppel." *TV Guide*, October 7–13, 1995, 41–42.
Katz, J. "Anchor Monster." *Rolling Stone*, January 10, 1991, 61–62.
Kurtz, H. "The Night Stalker." *Columbia Journalism Review* 35 (May/June 1996): 65–68.
Massing, M. "Ted Koppel's Neutrality Act." *Columbia Journalism Review* 27 (March-April, 1989): 30–34.
Moritz, C., ed. "Koppel, Ted." In *Current Biography 1984*, 216–20. New York: H. W. Wilson, 1984.
"Right Fit for His Format, Right Man for His Times." *Broadcasting*, May 21, 1984, 111.
"Ted Koppel." *People Weekly*, December 27, 1982, 84–85, 89.

Waters, H., L. Howard, and G. Hackett. "The Unflappable Koppel." *Newsweek*, February
    16, 1981, 75.

Selected General Works

Goldberg, R., and G. J. Goldberg. *Anchors*. New York: Birch Lane Press, 1990.
Nimmo, D., and J. E. Combs. *Nightly Horrors: Crisis Coverage in Television Network
    News*. Knoxville: University of Tennessee Press, 1985.
Rosenstiel, T. "Yakety-Yak: The Lost Art of Interviewing." *Columbia Journalism Re-
    view* 32 (January/February 1995): 23–27.
Sanders, M., and M. Rock. *Waiting for Prime Time: The Women of Television News*.
    New York: Harper and Row, 1988.
Westin, A. *Newswatch*. New York: Simon and Schuster, 1982.

ARTHUR KROCK

(November 16, 1886–April 12, 1974)

Political Commentary and the Personal Touch

The simple fact that the craft involves proficiency in making a living by communicating political information, misinformation, and disinformation between one another and to one's fellow citizens makes much of political commentary highly personal. All political commentators depend upon personal contacts for professional survival. Just as physicians demand patients, political consultants must have patrons, public relations specialists require clients, professors of politics rely on students and colleagues, political columnists cultivate news sources, and broadcast commentators seek out political insiders. However, few political commentators in the twentieth century have so assiduously and proudly cultivated personal contacts in their careers as Arthur Krock. One of his younger peers, and the man to whom Krock passed along the mantle of "the Washington Correspondent" of the *New York Times*, James "Scotty" Reston (q.v.), wrote of Krock, "He was always seeking the favor of famous people, many of whom were not worthy of his esteem" (1991, 122). In his search for contacts and courtiers, Arthur Krock made the cultivation of personal and social intimacy in political communication a fine art.

THE ART OF CULTIVATING CONTACTS

Arthur Krock was the last Washington correspondent of the *New York Times* to be born in the nineteenth century, on November 16, 1886. His birthplace was Glasgow, Kentucky, a small railhead community near the Tennessee line, "with many large houses surrounded by large lawns" (Krock, 1968, 8). Krock's father, Joseph, was a bookkeeper by trade, but hardly a prosperous one. Joseph's relatively meager earnings were depleted when Arthur's mother, Caroline, was stricken with blindness at her son's birth. Arthur grew up with his maternal grandparents when Joseph was forced to take employment in Chicago, and later he moved Caroline with him to be treated by a specialist who restored her eyesight.

Yet, even if Arthur was not born or reared in aristocratic surroundings, his birth located him in a time (two decades after the Civil War) and space (the American South) that left a mark on him throughout his life. If he was not raised with the advantages of a Southern gentleman, Krock nonetheless devoted his life to being one: "I cannot recall when I did not feel myself to be a Jeffersonian Democrat, after I had read enough history to make a choice," Krock wrote in his *Memoirs* (1968, 8).

Krock's paternal grandfather, although having minimal formal education, possessed an impressive library. There Arthur read a great deal, having learned his "letters" by age four, and he developed a healthy appetite by age seven for the great authors of the English language. He went to Glasgow's "town schools" and a secondary school misnamed Liberty College. By age twelve Arthur joined Joseph and Caroline in Chicago where he completed high school.

In 1904 Krock entered Princeton, but his finances were soon gone. He returned to Chicago and attended the Lewis Institute. At Lewis, Krock made one of the first of the many influential contacts that would shape his career as a political commentator. As he put it, "I encountered one of the richest experiences of my life" taking English courses from, grading papers for, and teaching a poetry course for Professor Edwin Herbert Lewis (Krock, 1968, 25). Krock took an associate of arts degree in 1906. (Two years later Dorothy Thompson [q.v.] enrolled at the Lewis Institute; Professor Edwin Herbert Lewis also had a profound formative influence on her career as a political commentator.)

Upon returning to Kentucky, Krock "feloniously pretended to be a seasoned reporter" and applied for a job at the *Louisville Herald* (Krock, 1968, 26). Although able to fake it for a short time, Krock's city editor grew increasingly conscious of the obvious—that the *Herald*'s young reporter was no journalist at all. Krock admitted to being a fraud, whereupon the editor rewarded him for "trying hard" by retaining Krock on the *Herald* and raising his salary from $15 to $18 a week.

In 1908, while still employed by the *Herald*, Krock had the good fortune also to be hired as a legman by the political correspondent of the Cincinnati *Enquirer*; Krock tracked down stories at the Democratic and Republican National Conventions. Added good fortune came when Krock was able to turn up an exposé about West Virginia's national committeeman ousting a member of the state's delegation. He made another key contact, with a coowner of the *Louisville Courier-Journal* and the *Louisville Times*. Krock's breaking of the West Virginia story established him as a *political* reporter; his contact with the Louisville news magnate got him a job, first, with the Associated Press, then, as correspondent with the Washington, D.C., bureau of the *Louisville Times* (which merged with the *Courier-Journal* bureau under Krock's direction).

In his capacity as Washington correspondent, Krock proposed to the other coowner of the Louisville *Courier-Journal* and *Times* that the newspapers' coverage of the 1910 off-year congressional races center on a field survey in key states. Krock's technique—involving interviews with party bosses, candidates, and local newspaper reporters—accurately anticipated a split in the Republican party between its progressive and conservative wings: "The election forecasts I supplied *The Courier-Journal* in 1910 pleased [coowner] Watterson, and he adopted me as his professional protege" (Krock, 1968, 36). Krock had thus made another professional and personal contact he later exploited successfully; five years later, Krock returned to Kentucky as general editorial and news manager of the *Courier-Journal* and *Times*.

Near the end of World War I, Arthur Krock went to France as a war correspondent for the two Louisville newspapers. He remained to cover the peace conference in Paris and Versailles. Although Krock later acknowledged that the experience scarcely made him an authority on international affairs, it did provide him the opportunity to expand his newsworthy connections and use to advantage a technique that he had exploited throughout his career as a political commentator—the exclusive interview. Through contacts with military liaisons, Krock obtained the only interview that Marshall Ferdinand Foch, Supreme Allied Commander, gave at the peace conference. Moreover, Krock served as one of three Americans on the Inter-allied Press Council, a body that lobbied on behalf of press representatives' admission to sessions of the conference. In light of the controversies surrounding access by U.S. reporters to peace conference proceedings—see George Creel (q.v.) and Edward L. Bernays (q.v.)—Krock's Press Council role was important.

Krock returned to the *Louisville Times* after the peace conference and served as editor in chief. In 1923 Krock broke with his editorial superiors over their support for national prohibition and women's suffrage, and he left Kentucky for good. In the 1920 presidential election, Krock had worked, on a leave of absence from his editorial duties, as an assistant to the chair of the Democratic National Committee. It was Krock's only experience in active politics; it was essentially public relations—to keep the chair from revealing the dismal prospects for victory of the Democratic ticket. In 1923 he used his public relations experience and connections to obtain a position with the Motion Picture Producers' Association, headed by an old friend and former chair of the Republican National Committee, Will Hays.

However, when Krock had the opportunity to rejoin journalism as assistant to the publisher of the *New York World*, he did so. In addition to his tasks as publisher's assistant—critics labeled him the publisher's "spy" (Reston, 1991, 132)—Krock contributed editorials to the *World* and filled in for Walter Lippmann (q.v.), who was on a leave of absence. Lippmann proved to be one contact with whom Arthur Krock never found favor, and vice versa. The reasons differ depending upon whether one accepts Lippmann's or Krock's version of their relationship. Lippmann criticized Krock for Krock's admiration of Bernard Baruch, a Wall Street financier often labeled "adviser to presidents." Krock had made Baruch's acquaintance years earlier, when seeking financial assistance for tobacco farmers in Kentucky and when Baruch attended the 1918–1919 peace conference.

What cooled the Lippmann-Krock relation permanently was an incident involving Baruch. While at the *World*, Krock offered "private counsel on a matter of public relations" at Baruch's request to a financial company, counsel that, according to Krock's version, "in no way infringed on any professional obligation or involved *The World*" (Krock, 1968, 62). Lippmann thought otherwise. Upon overhearing Krock on the telephone giving financial advice to Baruch's office, apparently about a future *World* editorial likely to affect the price of key stocks, Lippmann accused Krock of giving advance financial information. Krock denied Lippmann's accusation, offering evidence that the editorial in question had already been published. Lippmann, who remained unconvinced, insisted that Krock not be allowed to be even a part-time contributor to the editorial page under Lippmann's direction.

In the end, both Krock and Lippmann left the *World*: Krock to join the editorial staff at the *New York Times* in 1927, and Lippman, after the *World* folded, to become a successful political columnist for the *New York Herald Tribune* beginning in 1931. When Lippmann's *Tribune* column became an overnight sensation, Krock wrote, disapprovingly, "To read, if not to comprehend, Lippmann was suddenly the thing to do" (Steel, 1980, 280). When Krock began to write his own political column in the *New York Times*, Lippmann responded in kind: "Arthur used to quote Baruch once a week in his column as if he were the wisest man in America. Actually Baruch was not very wise. In fact he was rather uneducated. He was a character manufactured by public relations" (Steel, 1980, 200).

Now that both Walter Lippmann and Arthur Krock have passed from the political commentary scene, each having made contributions that are a matter of record, the lifelong clash of the prima donnas appears almost childish. Be that as it may, their feud, as well as those between other pairs of professional political commentators, such as that between H. V. Kaltenborn (q.v.) and Edward R. Murrow (q.v.) and that between Drew Pearson (q.v.) and Walter Winchell (q.v), proves a point. Professionals disagree not only on the profound, but on the petty as well.

THE WASHINGTON CORRESPONDENT

For his first four years with the *New York Times*, Arthur Krock wrote political editorials. At the end of 1931, the newspaper's political correspondent who was working in the nation's capital died. Arthur Krock much preferred the New York lifestyle and had no desire to leave it. He reluctantly agreed to become the manager of the *New York Times*'s Washington bureau, but only with the title, "The Washington Correspondent" (Krock, 1968, 78). Although the title was professionally and socially prestigious, it was far more than merely honorific. As *the* Washington correspondent of the *New York Times*, Krock, and his successors, had access to news sources frequently, even routinely, denied to journalists of other news organizations. For almost three decades, Arthur Krock capitalized on the contacts that automatically accrued to the Washington Correspondent.

One of his first tasks as *Times* bureau manager was transitional—to move the bureau's staff from thinking of themselves as essentially independent entrepreneurs free to choose their own assignments to a reorganized staff whose members were given individual assignments by the bureau's editor and a wordage limit on every story written. All this was, of course, working with the approval of the Washington Correspondent. Under the system that prevailed prior to Krock's arrival, *Times* correspondents would often cover identical stories, even interviewing the same officials, thus annoying the news sources and reducing the *Times'* prestige: "It was difficult to reconcile some of the free-wheeling veterans to this mechanization of the report," recalled Krock, "but it was accomplished, and the procedure has since been maintained" (1968, 79).

In 1933 the Washington Correspondent entered the *New York Times* on another transition. Arthur Krock began a column, "In the Nation," that appeared on the editorial page three times a week. Krock had full liberty to express his own views in the column, an unprecedented license for as strict and staid a news organization as the *Times*. The newspaper, whose motto is "All the News That's Fit to Print," wanted straight reporting and nothing else from its correspondents. In fact, some old hands at the *Times* considered even the existence of an editorial page suspect. Allowing the Washington Correspondent freedom to write a column of political opinion and publish it on the editorial page, thus implying that Krock's views were the *Times'* as an institution, was as radical a departure in 1933 as Coca Cola's tampering with its basic formula in 1985 to produce "New Coke."

There were apparently two reasons for inaugurating Krock's column. In part, Krock had been reluctant to move to Washington because he had aspirations to become the editor of the *New York Times'* editorial page. His acceptance of the position as the Washington Correspondent hinged to some degree on his understanding that, when the editorial page post came open, he would receive it. When Krock did not get the appointment and the publisher gave as a reason, "It's a Jewish paper," but "in all the years I've been here we have never put a Jew in the showcase," Krock, whose father was Jewish, was bitterly disappointed (Halberstam, 1979, 216–17). "In the Nation" served as Krock's consolation prize (Krock, 1968, 81; Talese, 1969, 185–86).

It was a consolation prize that worked to the *Times'* benefit as well. The phenomenal success of Walter Lippmann's political column, first published with the *New York Herald Tribune* in 1931, had not gone unnoticed at the *Times*. The "follow-the-leader behavior of the *Times*" thus gave "Arthur Krock a column for political commentary two years after Lippmann" (Kluger, 1989, 289). (The follow-the-leader behavior of the *Times* extended beyond attempts to match the *Herald Tribune*'s Lippmann. One year after Dorothy Thompson began her highly successful political column for the *Herald Tribune* in 1936, the *Times* responded by adding a column on world affairs by Anne O'Hare McCormick.)

Working in Washington over the course of almost three and a half decades (he stepped down as bureau chief in 1953 and ended his column with retirement in 1966), Arthur Krock initiated and solidified personal contacts with innumerable news sources, polished the art of the exclusive interview, and broke stories provoking countless political controversies. Among his intimates, for example, was Joseph P. Kennedy, father of the future president John F. Kennedy. It was

Arthur Krock who, upon reading John Kennedy's senior thesis for a Harvard degree, urged it be published; Krock served as copy editor and was responsible for the published work's title, *While England Slept*.

Yet, when John F. Kennedy ran for the presidency in 1960, Krock was not as enthusiastic in his support of JFK as were other Washington journalists, especially Krock's old nemesis, Walter Lippmann: "I may be getting old and I may be getting senile, but at least I don't fall in love with young boys like Walter Lippmann" (Halberstam, 1972, 26). After Kennedy's election, Krock neither sought nor received privileged access to the president. JFK preferred to use other intimates in the press to transmit his views, especially Joseph Alsop (Wicker, 1978, 101).

With other presidents Arthur Krock's personal ties had been much closer, at least up to a point. Krock described his relations with Franklin D. Roosevelt, for example, as a "cat-and-dog affair": "members loosely of the same household" who "endure each other and for periods display affection and even admiration," but "every so often nature asserts the innate conflicts of the species" (Krock, 1968, 144). Krock had met FDR when the latter was an official in the administration of President Woodrow Wilson. Their mutual displays of affection continued until Roosevelt's election as president in 1932. Their relations cooled, however, when FDR suspected that Krock was acting as a intermediary between President Herbert Hoover and the president-elect in Hoover's efforts to influence future presidential actions; FDR felt Hoover should come directly to him, not Krock, and he resented Krock's willingness to act as a go-between. Henceforth, FDR ridiculed Krock as "Lil' Arthur" and the "Tory Krock-pot"; Krock ridiculed FDR as "Br'er Fox" (Talese, 1969, 186).

Nonetheless, in spite of Lil' Arthur's opposition to Br'er Fox and New Deal domestic programs, or perhaps because of it, FDR granted Krock an exclusive personal interview in 1937 following his reelection. In it the president revealed a plan to overcome Supreme Court opposition to New Deal programs by the simple artifice of enlarging the court and appointing pro-FDR justices. Thus Arthur Krock broke the news that provoked the "court packing" controversy of FDR's second term, a major scoop for Krock that led to the award of his second Pulitzer Prize in 1938. (His first Pulitzer came in 1935 for excellence in reporting of New Deal fiscal policies.) Almost as controversial as the story itself was the granting of the exclusive interview in the first place. There was such an outcry by rival journalists at such preferential treatment given to Krock that FDR resolved never to grant such an interview again, a resolve that proved not steadfast.

However, what one president denies in public another may grant, and Arthur Krock received another exclusive interview with FDR's successor, Harry Truman. Unlike his relationship with Roosevelt, Krock's relationship with Truman never soured. Although Krock was critical of Truman in print, the president "never held it against me personally," wrote Krock, "we became friends, on his motion, and he never reproached me for any criticism or changed his friendly attitude toward me'' (Krock, 1968, 221). Krock's 1950 exclusive interview with Truman made news and sparked a conflict. Fair Deal critics jumped on Truman's assertion in the interview that as many as from 3 to 5 million unemployed was tolerable. In the end, Krock won a third Pulitzer Prize. But when a member of the Pulitzer awards committee objected, namely, Krock himself, the prize was withdrawn.

As with the FDR exclusive, Krock's privileged access to Truman brought a storm of criticism from other journalists. This, however, did not prevent Truman from using yet another exclusive interview with Krock as a conduit for getting his presidential message before the people. In 1951 President Truman and the Washington Correspondent met privately; the meeting produced another exclusive column, but it did not identify the president as the source of the ''wholly authoritative information'' (Krock, 1968, 271).

Whether calculated or not, Arthur Krock sometimes used his contacts with Washington insiders to influence the course of politics. For example, in 1933, when president-elect Franklin Roosevelt seemed to be wavering in his choice of Cordell Hull as secretary of state, Krock gave Hull a boost. Krock was always sensitive to the high society of the nation's capital. Hence, he urged Hull, who lived in a modest family hotel in Washington that was unsuited to the social obligations of a secretary of state, to move to more luxurious quarters. Hull did so and received the appointment shortly thereafter.

And, when Justice Louis Brandeis retired from the Supreme Court, Krock suggested to William O. Douglas that Douglas seek the judicial appointment; moreover, Krock brought the possibility to the attention of FDR's attorney general. Douglas got the Brandeis court seat. In 1951 Krock broke a major story in the *Times* that President Harry Truman had urged Dwight Eisenhower to seek the 1952 Democratic presidential nomination; years later Krock revealed the source for the scoop—Supreme Court Justice William O. Douglas.

By Washington's standards of the time, Arthur Krock's penchant for cementing close social relationships with newsworthy contacts yielded for him the lifestyle of a party animal. His home, both when married to his first wife, Marguerite Polley (who died in 1938), and to his second wife, Martha McCullough Granger Blair, was the venue for intimate dinner parties with political insiders from Washington and across the nation. Moreover, Krock was active in Washington ''bull sessions,'' social gatherings of Washington's political influentials. From 1925 he frequented the F Street Club, an exclusive coterie of the high and the mighty, and he routinely lunched at the Metropolitan Club with prominent lawyers and politicians. In these informal settings, the Washington Correspondent sifted out the verifiable gossip that could be authenticated for possible inclusion in ''In the Nation,'' and he picked up leads for possible *Times* stories. He encouraged *Times* reporters to emulate his news-gathering style of mixing political journalism with personal friendships.

James Reston observed that, in managing the Washington bureau of the *New York Times*, Krock did not run it; he ''presided'' over it. The bureau staff, who liked Krock, to his face called him respectfully "Mr. Krock" and behind his back an equally respectful "A. K." Krock not only recruited a competent staff, he made every effort to retain it. In 1953, when James Reston, who urged Krock to allow bureau members to be more interpretive in their reporting (Krock steadfastly refused), had an opportunity to become editor of the Washington *Post*, Arthur Krock called a staff meeting. Krock hated staff meetings; aside from this one he had held only one other, the day he became bureau chief. Krock announced that he did not want the *Times* to lose Reston, hence, "On my own motion, Mr. James Reston will become The Washington Correspondent of the New York *Times* with complete charge" (Rivers, 1965, 85). Reston introduced increasing latitude for interpretive reporting. Thus, as Arthur Krock had presided over the transition of the *Times*'s Washington bureau from a catch-as-catch-can to a routinized operation in 1932, his resignation as bureau chief paved the way for a transition from straight to interpretive reporting.

Krock continued "In the Nation" alongside Reston's column, "Washington." In content, Krock's column remained conservative in its philosophy, always suspicious of presidential power. In the Eisenhower years, Krock vacillated between criticism of the president's tentativeness and the hope that Eisenhower would act as a strong leader. During John F. Kennedy's brief presidency, Krock remained lukewarm. Many of President Lyndon Johnson's domestic and fiscal policies Krock found disappointing. In style, the prose of "In the Nation" was complicated, bordering on the obscure, with lengthy sentences in the manner of the previous century's British essayists. When Krock retired at the age of seventy-eight in 1966, Tom Wicker, the bureau chief following Reston's elevation to editor, assumed the writing of "In the Nation."

POLITICAL COMMENTARY IN TRANSITION

"He lived a disciplined life of longing, personal loyalty, and regret for a world that has gone." These words of James Reston capture a great deal of what Arthur Krock meant to the development of political commentary in the twentieth century (Reston, 1991, 133). Arthur Krock might well have longed for a world that was gone, but to the degree that the vanished world involved a specific culture of political commentary, it was a world that he both helped fashion and helped bring to an end. For Krock's standing as a professional communicator lies in the transitional role he played, across ten presidents of the United States and four major wars, in reporting politics to Americans as the Washington Correspondent of the *New York Times*.

Krock's career paralleled transitions in the *Times*' Washington bureau, in factual versus interpretive reporting, and in relations between news sources and reporters. Under Krock's management, the *Times* bureau shifted from a catch-as-catch-can operation to a smoothly running conduit of political information from the nation's capital to the nation's citizenry; and, when it came time to preserve the institution he helped father rather than lose its professional talent, Krock passed the baton in a smooth transition to his successor, James Reston. In so doing he presided over another transition, from the obsession of the *Times* with straight reporting to an increased emphasis on political interpretation.

Most important, Arthur Krock observed and participated in a major transition in the personal relationships between political officials and political journalists. Although he sought the favor of the politically powerful, he did not trade that favor for laudatory assessments of officials' performances. An easy familiarity and intimacy with news sources did not mean, for Krock, what it did for, say, Joseph or Stewart Alsop, JFK's intimates. Whereas they could write (Alsop & Alsop, 1958, 18) that "the reporter and the man in government are natural allies," Arthur Krock, Jeffersonian Democrat, remained suspicious of the intent of the "man in government."

Krock, a man of no small ego, had no illusions about the magnified egos of politicians and the folly officials could provoke because of those outsized egos. He preferred personal contacts and exclusive interviews on the grounds that press conferences were orchestrated to serve the officials' public relations ends, not provide news. Through the Kennedy-Johnson years leading up to Krock's retirement, off-the-record exclusives, "backgrounders," and "deep backgrounders" had become standard ploys of presidents and other politicians eager to serve official personal and policy interests, as much so as had Franklin Roosevelt's press conferences. In the years leading up to his retirement, Krock pointed that out in his "In the Nation," both to the *Times* general readership and to the younger members of the newspaper's Washington bureau (Wicker, 1978, 81–82).

Arthur Krock died in Washington on April 12, 1974. Perhaps, as James Reston wrote, he did so with regret for a world that has gone. Or, perhaps, it was with regret for the world that was the consequence of the transitions he had observed, even fostered: "And from these consequences I have contracted a visceral fear," he wrote in the close of his *Memoirs*. "It is that the tenure of the United States as the first power in the world may be one of the briefest in history" (1968, 416).

REFERENCES

Selected Works by Arthur Krock

"The Early Personal Journalists." In *Walter Lippmann and His Times*, edited by M. Childs and J. Reston, 83–110. New York: Harcourt, Brace, 1959.
In the Nation, 1932–1966. New York: McGraw Hill, 1966.
Memoirs. New York: Funk & Wagnalls, 1968.
The Consent of the Governed and Other Deceits. Boston: McGraw Hill, 1971.
Myself When Young: Growing Up in the 1890s. Boston: Little, Brown, 1974.

Selected Critical Works about Arthur Krock

Block, M., ed. "Krock, Arthur." *Current Biography 1943*, 407–9. New York: H. W. Wilson, 1943.

"Krock, Arthur." In *The National Cyclopedia of American Biography*, 161–62. Clifton, NJ: James T. White, 1981.

McKerns, J. P., ed. "Krock, Arthur." In *Biographical Dictionary of American Journalism*, 395–96. New York: Greenwood Press, 1989.

Reston, J. "Arthur Krock: Kentucky Gentleman." In *Deadline: A Memoir,* 129–43. New York: Random House, 1991.

Riley, S. G. "Krock, Arthur." In *Biographical Dictionary of American Newspaper Columnists*, 167–68. Westport, CT: Greenwood Press, 1995.

Schoenbaum, E. W., ed. "Krock, Arthur." In *Political Profiles: The Eisenhower Years*, 349–50. New York: Facts on File, 1977.

———."Krock, Arthur." In *Political Profiles: The Truman Years*, 291–92. New York: Facts on File, 1978.

Selected General Works

Alsop, J., and S. Alsop. *The Reporter's Trade*. New York: Reynal, 1958.

Childs, M., and J. Reston, eds. *Walter Lippmann and His Times*. New York: Harcourt Brace, 1959.

Halberstam, D. *The Best and the Brightest*. New York: Random House, 1972.

———. *The Powers That Be*. New York: Alfred A. Knopf, 1979.

Kluger, R. *The Paper: The Life and Death of the New York Herald Tribune*. New York: Vintage Books, 1989.

Rivers, W. L. *The Opinionmakers*. Boston: Beacon Press, 1967.

Steel, R. *Walter Lippmann and the American Century*. Boston: Little, Brown, 1980.

Talese, G. *The Kingdom and the Power*. New York: World Publishing, 1969.

Wicker, T. *On Press*. New York: Viking Press, 1978.

FULTON LEWIS, JR.

(April 30, 1903–August 20, 1966)

The Political Commentator as Personal Crusader

History abounds in ironies. In 1945 Harry Truman became one of America's accidental presidents: accidental in part because Truman's elevation to the office from the vice presidency was by virtue of the unexpected death of Franklin D. Roosevelt; also accidental because a year earlier few political observers would have given Truman a chance even to be a vice-presidential nominee, let alone a president. About all this bespectacled U.S. Senator from Missouri had to distinguish himself was his reputation as a vigilant watchdog, the chair of a special Senate subcommittee investigating the national war program. Yet, his committee had exposed padding of contracts, excess profits, waste, and bottlenecks; the committee uncovered wasteful Lend-Lease procedures that required shuffling papers through twenty government agencies; also revealed was a gauntlet of interagency rivalries that delayed meeting the war needs of U.S. allies for more than six weeks. It was those exposés that recommended Truman, who had a reputation for being "feisty" to Roosevelt's advisers and to the president himself, as a vice-presidential candidate in 1944.

Ironically, four years later, when Truman sought reelection in his own right, his candidacy was roundly criticized by a national figure who also had a reputation for being "feisty," and who also had made his reputation for exposing waste, corruption, and governmental bungling before, during, and after World War II. He was the popular political commentator of the Mutual Broadcasting Network; his voice reached a radio audience of 10 million listeners. He was Fulton Lewis, Jr. It was not the first time Lewis opposed a Democratic presidential ticket. Four years earlier, Lewis had predicted the Republican landslide victory of Thomas Dewey over Franklin Roosevelt; he even appeared on the rostrum of the Republican National Convention in 1944, his arms around an embarrassed former president Herbert Hoover, who did not share Lewis' taste for such public displays.

Lewis' prediction in 1944 was wrong, but he felt his leanings were correct; he thought so again in 1948. The radio critic of the *New York Herald Tribune* took a different view of Lewis' wearing his partisan preferences on his sleeve. Lewis, wrote John Crosby, was no commentator at all but, rather, a campaigner whose nationwide, five-nights-a-week newscast on Mutual should "be paid for and so listed by the Republican National Committee" (Chester, 1949, 75). There are campaigners and there are campaigners. To place Fulton Lewis, Jr. in the matrix of the twentieth-century's pioneering political commentators, one needs to look closely at the type of campaigns Lewis waged.

TO THE MANOR BORN, TO THE MANNER CALLED

The pitches of carnival barkers and mass advertisers, the pep talks of athletic coaches and politicians, the bromides of patent medicine hucksters and political candidates, the charm and guile of con artists and propagandists, the dispassionate analyses of college professors and news pundits—in their ways, they are all forms of persuasive campaigning. So too is the crusade. Crusading exploits religious fervor, moral indignation, and, sometimes, strident outrage to overturn the status quo. In contrast with the zeal of the missionary bent on educating the wavering to become lifelong adherents to a cause, for example, Elmer Davis' (q.v.) mission on behalf of free expression, the political crusader recalls, or foresees, an Edenic time. In that time, political ills do not exist; but for the presence among us of a serpent, a causal agent, Eden could be restored and all set right with the world. If the missionary seeks salvation through education, the crusader seeks it through purgation and purification (Burke, 1984; Jensen, 1980).

Fulton Lewis, Jr., was born in an Edenic setting. In fact, he was to the manor born. He was a fifth-generation Washingtonian, born in the national capital on April 30, 1903; there he resided until his death on August 20, 1966. He was the son of a wealthy attorney, the maternal grandson of Abraham Lincoln's U.S. treasurer, and a direct descendant on his father's side of a key financier of the American Revolution. He was Washington to the bone marrow—a member of the Association of Oldest Inhabitants—whose parents brought him up in a mansion in Georgetown and a summer house on the site of the grounds of the National Cathedral.

He was both monied and politically connected, not only on his parents' side but also on his wife's. With the wife of President Herbert Hoover; the vice president, Charles Curtis; and numerous U.S. senators, congressmen, and justices of the Supreme Court in attendance as guests, Lewis married Alice Huston in 1930. She was the daughter of a millionaire who already had a fortune in her own name. Her father was also the chair of the Republican National Committee (Fang, 1977). Such a background and connections with high society hardly betoken the heritage of a future crusader against the status quo unless enemy forces threaten the established Eden of one's youth, even replace it with a darker world. If so, the threat demands purgation so that comfortable values can be restored. In his career as a political communicator, Fulton Lewis, Jr., uncovered numerous threats to the manor.

Lewis' earliest interests scarcely included the art of politics; rather they were the musical arts—piano, voice, harmony, and composition. Before his 1920 graduation from Western High School, Lewis had written scripts and scores for two musical comedies. And, at one point, he had his own dance band. During two tenures at the University of Virginia (1920–1921, 1922–1924), music was a source of added income. For instance, Lewis, who had never played the organ in his life, duped a Charlottesville theater manager into giving him a job as a theater organist. And, for the princely sum of $25, Lewis composed the University of Virginia "Cavalier Fight Song." Lewis did not actually graduate from the university, but the fight song remained his legacy. He also did not graduate from the George Washington University School of Law in spite of an early resolve to become an attorney.

In 1924 Fulton Lewis, Jr., turned his back on both musical and legal careers (he also quit a job in banking), and he became a reporter for the *Washington Herald*. Although he wrote national news, his special niche at the newspaper was as its fishing columnist. (He remained an avid angler throughout his life.) By 1927 Lewis had become city editor of the newspaper. The following year, he departed the *Herald* to become assistant manager, then manager for nine years, of the Washington bureau of William Randolph Hearst's Universal News Service. From 1933 to 1936 he also wrote a column syndicated to sixty newspapers by Hearst's King Features called "The Washington Sideshow." Writing the column of commentary and gossip gleaned from Washington insiders was excellent training for his future investigative crusading as a radio commentator.

During his days at the *Herald*, Lewis had from time to time performed a task required of members of the paper's staff—to broadcast headlines on radio. Moreover, he read his fishing columns on the radio. He continued to take a turn reading headlines after departing the *Herald* staff until, in 1936, he had an opportunity to fill in for a vacationing newscaster's fifteen-minute program. Lewis' innovative style so impressed the station manager that the young journalist received, in 1937, a job offer as a broadcaster. The Mutual Radio Network (later the Mutual Broadcasting System) was founded in 1934. By 1937 Mutual was in the midst of filling out its public affairs programming. Fulton Lewis, Jr., became the network's national news commentator, and broadcast his "Top of the News" from the network's Washington affiliate WOL five nights a week at 7:00 P.M. EST.

Lewis was the first radio commentator on any network to broadcast as a Washington-based newscaster. The first radio commentator, H. V. Kaltenborn (q.v.), was broadcasting from New York, then for CBS and later for NBC; CBS' nightly newscaster, Lowell Thomas (q.v.), was also based in New York. From the time of his first broadcast on November 27 until his death almost thirty years later, Mutual broadcast Lewis' crusading voice coast to coast, eventually on as many as 150 stations.

Although there were periods when Lewis also wrote a syndicated column, "Fulton Lewis, Jr., Says," and a weekly column, "Washington Report," radio was the ideal forum for his distinctive style as a political communicator. In part, it was a mocking style. For example, when criticizing the Fair Deal of the Truman administration, Lewis would mimic the chief executive by falling into the president's use of slang, salty language, and colloquialisms. Or, Lewis would mock political leaders by stringing together a series of hyperincendiary adjectives about them or their policies, spoken with such machine-gun-like rapidity that the cadence itself poked fun at the target: "I'm an American who can't sit by self-indulgently twiddling his thumbs while a bunch of drooly-mouthed fellow-traveling rats gnaw at the vitals of government'' (Schroth, 1995, 295).

He also employed ridicule in several forms. One was to quote a political nemesis as though he were taking the politician's remarks seriously, then chuckle in pretended disbelief (as if Marc Antony not only said, ''Brutus is an honorable man,'' in ironic tones but then laughed at the very thought). If the chuckle warned listeners after the fact that the quoted source was lying, other ''Lewisisms'' ridiculed by warning listeners in advance that whatever comment he was about to make, based on a politician's claim, should be taken with a grain of salt. Typical signals were ''purports'' and ''so-called'' as, for example, in describing liberal commentator Elmer Davis as one ''who purports to be a great factual reporter'' or Davis' ''so-called factual reporting'' (Fang, 1977, 209). Lewis also ridiculed by pretending to misspeak himself; for example, he linked convicted perjurer Alger Hiss with Democratic presidential candidate Adlai Stevenson by saying, ''Alger Steven . . . , I mean Adlai Stevenson said tonight.''

Lewis' ''free-wheeling and free-hitting style of broadcasting'' (Chester, 1949, 80) also exploited the technique of introducing denial followed by a sweeping generalization. In one breath Lewis would deny, for example, any desire to personalize a dispute with another commentator, say Edward R. Murrow (q.v.); he would then claim, almost without pause, that Murrow's criticism of Senator Joseph McCarthy was nothing more than an ''intellectual lynching.''

Lewis could pose as the inside-dopester as well, often with considerable justification. He knew that among his listening audience were key members of Congress, business leaders, and military leaders. Like political columnist Arthur Krock (q.v.), Fulton Lewis, Jr., was prominent on the Washington social circuit. Many of these same members of his audience were also his key news sources: close personal congressional friends, who would provide inside tidbits; conservative businessmen (he was once paid $1,000 by the National Association of Manufacturers for originating his broadcasts at war plants); and friends in the ''Colonel's Clique,'' Pentagon officials who leak information in order to promote a favored weapons system or protect a pet project from budgetary cutbacks (Nimmo, 1964, 168–69).

With Washington insiders as both his listeners and his sources Lewis could, with considerable credibility, refer to these insiders, ''as Senator so-and-so told me,'' or ''my views are shared by Pentagon leaders.'' Identifying with such groups, in fact, is the very essence of the inside-dopester: ''Politics, indeed, serve the inside-dopester chiefly as a means for group conformity. He must have acceptable opinions and where he engages in politics he must do so in acceptable ways'' (Riesman, Glazer, and Denny, 1955, 214).

Lewis' mocking, ridiculing, denying, sweeping generalization, inside-dopester style was carefully crafted. Each fifteen-minute broadcast was the product of Lewis' telephone contacts with key sources, staff members' investigations (half of Lewis' income subsidized such efforts), and daily consultation with staff members in roughing out each evening's newscast. Like other key political communicators in the electronic media, such as Eric Sevareid (q.v.) or Lowell Thomas, Lewis delayed writing the actual script for his broadcast until the last possible moment before airtime. When he did, he wrote to sound—he vocalized the script as he typed it in order to assure that each nuance of tone and diction would receive its proper emphasis. *What* Lewis broadcast and *how* he did it intermeshed (Fang, 1977, 210).

THE GREAT CRUSADES

Born to the manor but crusading in manner, Fulton Lewis, Jr., started tilting at windmills early in his career. His first crusade took place in 1930 and 1931. Through his sources, he uncovered the fact that Eastern Airlines received a $2-per-mile subsidy for carrying mail between New York and Washington, a substantial increase over the 42-cent-per-mile of other airlines. He also uncovered an insider-trading plot in conjunction with sales of airline stock. By persistent probing of contacts, some made via Lewis' wealthy bride, he identified officials of the U.S. Post Office who were involved in the price rigging. When his own news organization, Hearst's service, refused to publish the scoop, Lewis turned to other contacts, namely, U.S. Senator Hugo Black (later a Supreme Court Justice). Lewis' revelations to Black helped spawn, in succession, a senate investigating committee, the cancellation of existing airmail routes, and a reorganization of the airlines.

Moreover, when Lewis revealed that U.S. Army Air Corps planes assigned to move the airmail had poorly trained pilots, a new training program was instituted based on Lewis' revelations. Lewis pulled off one other major coup prior to moving full-time to radio. In 1936, as a result of a Lewis investigation, in which the journalist acted as an undercover FBI agent, Lieutenant John Farnsworth was convicted of passing naval secrets to the Japanese in exchange for money to support an alcohol dependency. When Farnsworth offered to sell his story to Lewis, the journalist agreed, but he turned the officer over to naval authorities. Although Lewis was not above the criticism of some of his journalistic colleagues for using his position for duplicitous purposes, his bylined story made him appear to be a patriot in print.

Once having become a radio commentator, Fulton Lewis, Jr., took on a crusade of a different sort. This one pleased journalistic colleagues, at least those in radio. For a century, the press galleries of the U.S. House and Senate restricted their membership to accredited newspaper reporters. Nonetheless, Lewis applied for membership as a broadcaster in 1939. He was refused on the grounds that only newspaper reporters were admitted. Then why, asked Lewis, are reporters of the wire services, who are not newspaper reporters per se, admitted? Over newspaper protests, radio correspondents were given press gallery membership. Shortly thereafter, White House ''press conferences'' became ''news'' conferences as radio correspondents were invited as well. Soon microphones, recorders, cameras, and other broadcasting devices were allowed at those news conferences. Thus did Fulton Lewis, Jr., change the coverage and purpose of the White House news conference. Upon its founding, Lewis was first president of the Radio Correspondents Association, the official accrediting agency for admission to congressional radio galleries.

In subsequent crusades, Fulton Lewis, Jr., became increasingly controversial. In campaigning against U.S. involvement in European affairs prior to World War II, Lewis invited Charles Lindbergh, the transatlantic aviator hero, to appear on "The Top of the News" in 1939. Lindbergh, an isolationist, warned the United States to stay out of Europe, to refuse assistance to England, and to be aware than Nazi Germany could not be defeated in any upcoming war. Isolationist listeners applauded Lewis as a patriot for airing Lindbergh's views; interventionists decried Lewis' appeasement of Germany. Lewis took another controversial position regarding America's preparedness for war. He maintained that photos of U.S. soldiers drilling with broomsticks was a hoax, that America's military was well equipped. After Pearl Harbor, the once-musical Lewis changed his tune; America, he said, had a minimal army, no navy, and no war machine.

One serpent that Fulton Lewis, Jr., repeatedly uncovered in America's Eden was governmental bungling. For example, he revealed that it was governmental bungling that prevented radar installations around Pearl Harbor from being completed on schedule in June 1941. When the Japanese attacked on December 7, the radar units had not even been uncrated. An army investigation concurred with Lewis' charges. Lewis also uncovered massive bungling in building a pipeline that would transport Canadian oil to assist in Alaska's defense. He exposed massive overspending and incompetent management in the building of the Alcan and Pan American Highway projects; he reported that, in the government's program to produce synthetic rubber, many plants wasted millions of dollars producing nothing while those capable of production were denied permission to do so; and, during and after World War II he crusaded relentlessly against the Office of Price Administration (OPA) and price controls, urging his listeners to write to their congressmen to "clean up the OPA."

In several of his crusades, Lewis developed a variation on what a noted analyst of political communication, George Orwell, called in *Nineteen Eighty-Four* (1949) the language of *duckspeak*. In Lewis' version it permitted him to voice contradictory versions of realities almost simultaneously, thus denying his views could ever be refuted. For example, contrary to the OPA prediction that if meat price controls were abolished prices would jump from 40 to 50 percent in two months, Lewis argued otherwise. Freed of controls legitimate meatpackers would undercut high black marketeer prices "which means an actual drop in prices you are paying for meat." When price controls were removed in 1946, cattle prices soared. Lewis at first pleaded the price increase would be "momentary, and they'll last very few days." Months passed and meat prices went to record heights. Lewis insisted everything was in order as he had reported (Chester, 1949).

Similarly, in 1947, Lewis launched an attack on the cooperative movement. He labeled co-ops as "super-big business," free from taxes and sacrosanct monopolies. When movement spokespersons responded that co-ops were subject to taxation and, rather than being super-big, had small shareholders like Lewis—who owned $61.01 in common stock—Lewis simply denied he was attacking co-ops; instead, he found them "an excellent thing as long as they operate as such" and they are able to "out-compete private enterprise." Yet, within weeks he again attacked the cooperative philosophy as "to tear down and to destroy the profit system." His own investment he called "involuntary"; he was going to get it back because "I don't believe in the movement." Co-op spokespersons again rebutted: if Lewis' "involuntary investment" were really involuntary, why didn't he cash it in, for he was free to do so? Moreover, since Lewis had declared he did not believe in the movement, he could simply be dismissed by the co-op from membership. Now Lewis refused to take his money and depart (Chester, 1949).

There was a method in Lewis' wrangling and series of about-faces. He wanted to keep the newsworthy confrontation alive simply for the sake of the controversy itself, thus promoting his newscast and himself. There were other instances when, on the surface, his crusade was about one issue when, beneath the artifice, his crusade was one of self-promotion. His running attack on federal programs to provide low-cost housing for veterans served a similar purpose, as did his erroneous 1949 accusation that former vice president Henry Wallace and Harry Hopkins, who had been a key aide to President Roosevelt, conspired to send uranium and classified radar equipment to the Soviet Union. Later investigation revealed that nonfissionable uranium had been sent to the Soviet Union, but that Wallace and Hopkins had not been involved; the radar shipment was part of a training program for Soviet officers when the Soviet Union was an ally in World War II.

Like any prognosticator reading the political tea leaves, Lewis was sometimes wrong, sometimes right. He was one of only 300 reporters to predict accurately that Franklin Roosevelt would carry every state but Maine and Vermont in the 1936 presidential election. In 1940 he scooped everyone with the accurate prediction that John L. Lewis, head of the United Mine Workers and longtime FDR supporter, would throw his support to Republican Wendell Willkie in the presidential contest.

Many of Lewis' crusades were avowedly partisan. From the time of Richard Nixon's first congressional campaign, Lewis supported the future senator, vice president, and president. He was also a staunch advocate of Senator Joseph McCarthy's campaign to ferret out alleged Communists in the State Department and U.S. Army. In 1954, when political commentator Edward R. Murrow devoted a thirty-minute documentary to exploring McCarthy's questionable investigative tactics, a television program widely applauded by McCarthy's critics, Lewis invited McCarthy to appear on his nightly radio commentary. It made for memorable radio. The senator charged Murrow with having been an advisor to "a Communist propaganda school" and "worried about the exposure of some of his [Murrow's] friends." Murrow, whose nightly news program on CBS followed on the heels of Lewis' Mutual newscast, was caught off guard when McCarthy's charges were brought to his attention; Murrow declined to air his "personal reaction" until a later time (Persico, 1988, 384).

A HARBINGER OF A CONTEMPORARY STYLE OF POLITICAL COMMENTARY

Fulton Lewis, Jr., was not the first political commentator to employ inflated rhetoric, personal attacks, and, if need be, invective in support of, or opposition to, favored causes. H. L. Mencken (q.v.) was an earlier master. Nor was Lewis the first to use the radio waves to air his personal or partisan views. Indeed, in the short-lived Golden Age of Radio, he was a relatively late arrival in that respect. What set Lewis apart from many other radio commentators was his investment in investigative reporting, albeit a highly personal and inside-dopester style of investigation, to support a three-decade series of crusades against the reigning status quo of what he deemed political bungling and malfeasance.

Granted, "Lewis' own crusades had little to do with the news" (Lewis in Culbert, 1976, 172), and they frequently were a vehicle for self-promotion. Other commentators also advanced their careers via exposés; Drew Pearson (q.v.) is a notable Lewis contemporary. But others took their charge to be more gossipy than quixotic, their campaigns to be more limited than unlimited in duration, quick thrusts at political malfeasance. Lewis' self-promotion came via unrelenting claims that "New Dealers never acted as they publicly claimed" (Lewis in Culbert, 1976, 172).

If, however, Fulton Lewis, Jr., made a contribution to his era as a political communicator by way of his relentless crusades, that is not what future generations of political commentators picked up on. Instead, many of them inherited and copied his style—mocking, ridiculing, full of denials, full of sweeping generalizations, and full of inside-dopesterism. Before there was Rush Limbaugh (q.v.), for example, there was Fulton Lewis, Jr. Before there was John McLaughlin (q.v.), there was Fulton Lewis, Jr. Before many of the political commentators who promote themselves via political communication for its own sake, there was Fulton Lewis, Jr. But where are the unrelenting crusaders who combine that distinctive style with tenacious devotion to causes, be those causes victorious or lost rather than merely opportunistic?

REFERENCES

Selected Work by Fulton Lewis, Jr.

Report on the Fund for the Republic. Washington, DC: Special Reports, 1955.

Selected Critical Works about Fulton Lewis, Jr.

Chester, G. "What Constitutes Irresponsibility on the Air? A Case Study." *Public Opinion Quarterly* 13 (Spring 1949): 73–82.

Culbert, D. H. "Fulton Lewis, Jr.: We Never Put 'em to Sleep!" In *News for Everyman*, 153–178. Westport, CT: Greenwood Press, 1976.

Dempsey, W. C. "A Rhetorical Analysis of the Methods of Argumentation of News Commentator Fulton Lewis, Jr., as Found in His Broadcasts from Hawaii." Master's thesis, Iowa State University, 1947.

Fang, I. E. "Fulton Lewis, Jr." In *Those Radio Commentators!*, 199–215. Ames: Iowa State University Press, 1977.

Garraty, J. and M. C. Carnes, eds."Lewis, Fulton, Jr." In *Dictionary of American Biography*, 372–74. New York: Charles Scribner's Sons, 1988.

Herndon, B. *Praised and Damned: Story of Fulton Lewis, Jr.* New York: Duell, Sloan and Pearce, 1954.

Lahey, E. A. "Bedside Manner in Radio." In *Molders of Opinion*, edited by D. Bulman, 71–81. Milwaukee: Bruce Publishing, 1945.

McKerns, J. P., ed. "Lewis, Fulton, Jr." In *Biographical Dictionary of American Journalism*, 413–15. New York: Greenwood Press, 1989.

Reisberg, S. "Fulton Lewis, Jr.: Analysis of News Commentary." Ph.D. diss., New York University, 1952.

Rothe, A., ed. "Lewis, Fulton, Jr." In *Current Biography 1942*, 509–11. New York: H. W. Wilson, 1943.

Selected General Works

Burke, K. *Attitudes toward History*. 3d. ed. Berkeley: University of California Press, 1984.

Jensen, R. "Armies, Ad Men, and Crusaders." *Public Opinion* 3 (October/November 1980): 44–49.

Nimmo, D. *Newsgathering in Washington*. New York: Atherton, 1964.

Orwell, G. *Nineteen Eighty-Four*. New York: Harcourt, Brace, 1949.

Persico, J. *Edward R. Murrow: An American Original*. New York: Dell Publishing, 1988.

Riesman, D., N. Glazer, and R. Denny. *The Lonely Crowd*. Garden City, NY: Doubleday, 1955.

Schroth, R. A. *The American Journey of Eric Sevareid*. South Royalton, VT: Steerforth Press, 1955.

RUSH LIMBAUGH

(January 12, 1951–   )

Political Commentary with the Flair of Falstaff

In the mid-1960s, on the corner of Haight and Ashbury streets in San Francisco, a musical group, the "Grateful Dead," embarked on a mission, namely, a cultural revolution. With its perky anthem to the "Hippie Nation," the Grateful Dead, led by Jerry Garcia, traveled the country performing songs about sexual freedom and alternative lifestyles. The band slowly won a following, the "Deadheads," the phalanx of a coculture in the United States with their own traditions, norms, and language. The Grateful Dead and the Deadheads were bonded through the band's music. Its tone ranged from a dark, sorrowful temperament to a jazzy, upbeat tempo; its lyrics validated free love, drug use, and cultural freedom.

The Grateful Dead's twenty-eight albums, produced over almost three decades, scarcely captured the spirit of the group's live concerts. Using recorded songs as points of entry, the band in concert improvised, embellished, and created a new sound that captured their tribute to free expression and liberalism. Jerry Garcia was a revolutionary who promulgated through his lyrics a radical reevaluation of the American value system. For Deadheads, Garcia (who died in 1995) was an innovator who inspired a sociopolitical movement—a warrior battling the forces on behalf of his people, a crusader for good and mercy. Under Garcia's direction, the Grateful Dead found a receptive audience among the adventuresome, as well as the intellectual. Garcia became a cultural icon.

When the Grateful Dead began traveling the country to foment a cultural explosion, Rush Limbaugh was a shy teenager growing up in the Midwest. Those who knew him thought him a loner. During the 1960s, a decade of rebellion and social unrest, the Grateful Dead sang of the need for peace and freedom. Rush Limbaugh learned far more conventional ideological traditions and values in his politically conservative family. Later, embarking on a radio broadcast career that has made him a beacon for conservatives, Rush Limbaugh, like Garcia, offered a message to liberate and inspire people. Although the Grateful Dead (now gone with Garcia's death) employed a different medium for their message, there are marked similarities between Jerry Garcia and Rush Limbaugh, both as leaders of cocultures and as cultural icons.

In the mid-1980s, the conservative movement, as defined by Rush Limbaugh, began on Ethan Way 'bout Arden in Sacramento, the capital of California. With his wit and playful Falstaffian humor, Limbaugh hit the airways with commentary about the perils of liberalism and the benefits of conservatism. With success in the local Sacramento market, he embarked on a national crusade as a conservative talk show host, entertainer, and political commentator. His success transformed him into a wildly controversial, vastly wealthy, and extremely influential political commentator toward the close of the twentieth century. Like Jerry Garcia, the Grateful Dead, and the loyal Deadheads, Rush Limbaugh attracted followers who labeled themselves "Ditto Heads" as a tribute to their leader. And, like Jerry Garcia, Rush Limbaugh crusades for conservative values and a reevaluation and rejection of established liberal conventions and values. He too is a cultural icon.

THE POLITICAL MATURATION OF A CULTURAL ICON

The elder of two sons, Rush Limbaugh III, was born on January 12, 1951, in Cape Girardeau, Missouri, the heart of the state's "bootheel," with strong populist and conservative traditions. Rush Limbaugh's family possesses a legacy of public service and legal careers. His mother, Millie Limbaugh, was a Republican committeewoman for many years, and his father, Rush Hudson Limbaugh, was the most prominent attorney in Cape Girardeau and the county Republican chairman for several years. In addition, his paternal grandfather was president Dwight D. Eisenhower's ambassador to India and a practicing attorney in Cape Girardeau. Rush's uncle, Stephen Nathaniel Limbaugh, is a U.S. district court judge, appointed to the federal bench by President Ronald Reagan. Rush's brother, David, is also an attorney.

Rush Limbaugh has no law degree and has not served in public office, but he certainly inherited and exploited the family heritage of being outspoken about politics, a trait he shares with a contemporary political commentator of note who also chose broadcasting over the family business of politics, Corrine "Cokie" Roberts (q.v.). He has his mother's sense of humor and his father's flair for extemporaneous oratory, and both parents' sense of conservative political values. The Limbaugh children were proudly indoctrinated at an early age into the conservative tradition; Rush Limbaugh has built a career giving voice to that tradition, even if not in the family's preferred profession of the law, but as a radio personality, Rush's ambition since his earliest days. Limbaugh recalls his childhood desire to be on radio, "I saw it as an escape from the things I didn't like. . . . My first real interest in radio can be traced to a dislike for school. My mother would have the radio on while she was fixing breakfast, and the guy on the radio sounded like he was having so much fun" (Roberts, 1993, 28).

According to Limbaugh (1992), despite the fact that he took part in social and extracurricular activities, including the football and debating teams, he was not popular in high school. His shyness resulted in an adolescence without dating; in fact, he had very few friends, male or female, in high school. When neither debating nor playing football yielded either popularity or status, Limbaugh quit extracurricular activities when he was sixteen years old and turned to other pursuits. According to his mother, Rush was uncomfortable as a child;

since age ten, he tried to act like an adult and be treated as such ("Rush Limbaugh's America," 1995).

In search of popularity and a sense of independence, Limbaugh turned to radio. He set out to obtain a radio broadcaster's license. He attended a six-week course in Dallas at the Elkins Institute of Radio and Technology, then completed an apprenticeship at KGMO, a local radio station in Cape Girardeau, in which his father, "Big Rush," had part ownership. At the close of each school day, young Rush worked at the radio station; he rose from an assistant to a full-fledged disk jockey. Millie Limbaugh recalls in a television interview that working at the radio station "gave [Rush] a feeling of superiority; [it] made him feel like King Tut" ("Rush Limbaugh's America," 1995).

In the late 1960s, while the Grateful Dead was building a following of young adults who wanted to rebel against a social system of prescribed and proscribed rules of conduct, Rush Limbaugh toed the family line. Despite his dislike for school, Limbaugh attended the local Southeast Missouri State University after he graduated from high school. In his own way, perhaps, he too was rebelling; in his fierce independence, Limbaugh failed his speech class because he refused to complete his outline assignments. He had enough of college and dropped out to pursue a radio career, much to the dismay of Big Rush. A former high school classmate does not view this as rebellion: Rush did not follow the career path his father wanted him to take, but neither did he rebel "philosophically" or "politically" as many youths did in the 1960s ("Rush Limbaugh's America," 1995).

During the 1970s Rush Limbaugh lived the nomadic life of a disk jockey, traveling from city to city, from station to station. He worked as a disk jockey, news reader, and commentator. Yet, success eluded him. After being fired from stations in Kansas City and Pittsburgh, Limbaugh decided in 1978 to end his ten-year career in radio. Like political columnist James "Scotty" Reston (q.v.), Rush Limbaugh sold his services to a major league baseball team and took a job with the Kansas City Royals, like Reston had with the Cincinnati Reds, decades earlier, in public relations and marketing.

Limbaugh spent five years working for the Royals, but the itch for broadcasting had not yet been successfully scratched. So, in 1983, he decided to try one last time to realize his dream of becoming a successful radio personality. He took a job as newsreader and announcer for Kansas City station KMBZ. Constantly searching for a distinctive style that would, as radio broadcasters understand, separate him from the static, Limbaugh interjected his own brand of humor, sarcastic and often irreverent, into news reports. But, station management found his brand of humor too controversial; Limbaugh was dismissed from yet another job in radio broadcasting.

However, the humorous news style that offended KMBZ in Kansas City attracted the attention of the management at KFBK in Sacramento. Producers there were searching for a replacement for talk show commentator Morton Downey, Jr., who had been fired for allegedly offending his own audience with racist slurs. It was a time of flux in California politics. Population growth and increased crime provoked a "Los Angeles area flight," with southern Californians seeking refuge in northern California, particularly in the Sacramento area. In 1984 California voters elected a new Republican governor, George Deukmejian, to set matters right.

Upon his arrival at KFBK Limbaugh found an audience ripe for his brand of humor: irreverent yet calculated and controlled in the manner of William Shakespeare's fictional Falstaff, the jovial companion of princes and monarchs. Although Limbaugh soon attracted an audience, station producers wanted him to invite guests and interview them on the air. Bruce Marr, a radio consultant at the station, disagreed:

> Bruce . . . was in my corner from the first day we met at KFBK. Were it not for him I would have probably lost the battle (in the early days) over whether to have guests on my show. Bruce insisted to the management that I was one of the few hosts that didn't need guests. (Limbaugh, 1992, 6)

With his format no longer in question, Rush Limbaugh proceeded to do what he does to this day: all the talking. He quickly became the outstanding radio personality in Sacramento.

The shy, awkward boy from Missouri was finally realizing his dream of being a successful radio personality and, in the process, taking on a whole new dramatic persona. After four years of success in Sacramento, Limbaugh had a unique, distinctive style that positioned him apart from other talk show hosts, one that audience members enjoyed and identified with readily. His spontaneous quips and off-color remarks attracted the attention of professional agents. In 1987 Ed McLaughlin formed EFM Management, Inc., an independent syndication company, and was in search of new talent. After learning about Limbaugh from Bruce Marr, McLaughlin traveled to Sacramento in February 1988. His initial reaction was negative; McLaughlin found Limbaugh's style abrasive. But, after meeting with Limbaugh, McLaughlin decided to sign him to a two-year contract. Conditions were set for a major breakthrough in political commentary.

GAINING POLITICAL CLOUT THROUGH COMMENTARY

In 1978 the Mutual Radio Network approached Larry King (q.v.) to be host of a nationwide, late-night program combining interviews with listeners' telephone calls. "The Larry King Show" proved to be a success and helped spawn the burgeoning trend toward radio talk show programming of the 1980s, shows covering every conceivable subject area—sports, bass fishing, home beautification, gardening, automotive repair—including politics. However, a decade later, political talk radio in national syndication, as contrasted with radio network broadcasts, had, as yet, been sporadic; shows and hosts came and went with variable success. Rush Limbaugh changed all of that. Two years after his syndication, the once unpopular high school kid from the bootheel of Missouri was popular indeed; he had a weekly audience of more than 5 million listeners (Mooney, 1991). By 1995 "The Rush Limbaugh Show" aired on more than 650 radio stations nationwide, on shortwave throughout the world, and on 250 television stations across the United States (Combs & Nimmo, 1996, 74).

With a signed contract for representation via EFM Management, Rush Limbaugh left the River City, Sacramento, and relocated to the Big Apple, New York. In the process of launching a national talk show, McLaughlin entered into an agreement with the American Broadcasting Company (ABC) to utilize ABC radio facilities and staff; in exchange, Limbaugh would not only perform his national radio show, but would also air a local radio program for New York. The deal was made, and on July 4, 1988, Limbaugh began his local broadcast on WABC radio from 10:00 A.M. EST to noon. Then, on August 1, 1988, his national show premiered from noon to 2:00 P.M. Eventually, "The Rush Limbaugh Show" expanded to three hours, from noon to 3:00 P.M., and he discontinued the local broadcast, a choice he was eager to make. The New York audience was accustomed to the combative style of Howard Stern and other local talk show hosts, not the wit and wisdom of a Midwestern voice.

As his critics contend, Rush Limbaugh enjoys being the central focus of the show. In his book, *The Way Things Ought to Be*, Limbaugh wrote, "The show is devoted exclusively to what I think . . . callers are not allowed to read someone else's opinion or even their own" (1992, 21). Rush Limbaugh began his career as a syndicated commentator discussing social issues, such as abortion, feminism, and AIDS. In his radio broadcasts, he appealed to his listeners' prejudices, emotions, and special interest in social issues. In his biting mockery of abortions, he performed caller abortions, complete with suction-like sound effects. His fans cackled with laughter; his detractors fumed. Political commentator Molly Ivins explains her criticism of Rush Limbaugh's commentary on social issues: "I object because [Limbaugh] consistently targets dead people, little girls, and the homeless—none of whom are in a particularly good position to answer back. . . . When you use satire against . . . people, as Limbaugh does, it is not only cruel, it's profoundly vulgar" (1995, 37).

In 1990, while acting as guest host of CBS' "The Pat Sajak Show," a late-night television talk show, Limbaugh confronted people who strongly disagree with him on the issue of AIDS. Entertaining questions from the audience, he was heckled and ridiculed by members of ACT UP, a gay rights activist group. Regarding ridicule and confrontations, Limbaugh wrote, "Remember how I handle them, I laugh at their outrageous statements and I ridicule their latest lunacies" (1992, 303). However, in the 1990 incident, although caught off guard by the hostility, Limbaugh did not retaliate. In fact, after the telecast, a CBS executive stated, "He came out full of bluster and left a very shaken man. I had never seen a man sweat as much in my life" (Talbot, 1993, 41). Since that time, Limbaugh has retracted his stance on many social issues, especially AIDS. The revamped rhetoric of this celebrated political communicator focuses on more partisan issues. He still occasionally mocks the homeless and remarks on the ills of homosexuality, but Rush Limbaugh has shifted his focus to become an instrumental figure in the Republican party and U.S. politics.

Very much as with Jerry Garcia and the Grateful Dead, Rush Limbaugh's essence cannot be fully understood without hearing or seeing him in action. Using news events and reports, Rush Limbaugh delivers a spontaneous litany of political commentary. In his critique of government policy or pending legislation, Limbaugh extols the accuracy and merit of conservatives' views on the issue, and he ridicules and denounces the liberal perspectives. Through skits, jokes, and gadgets, Limbaugh delivers his message, entertains far more than he informs, and preaches to the Ditto Heads far more than he converts.

As much a phenomenon as a leader in the conservative movement, Limbaugh increased his status in the 1992 presidential campaign by backing Pat Buchanan. With his endorsement of Buchanan, Rush Limbaugh began his transformation from a political commentator on social issues generally to a political communicator, and presumed force, in the Republican party. Limbaugh announced his support for Buchanan early in the 1992 campaign. The hard-line conservative, who was challenging Republican President George Bush, won 37 percent of the vote in the New Hampshire primary (Talbot 1993, 43). Buchanan's success in New Hampshire prompted Bush and his strategists to try to enlist Limbaugh as their ally. His renomination secured, Bush invited Limbaugh to spend the night at the White House and to be a guest in the vice president's box at the Republican National Convention in Houston. In return, Limbaugh denounced Ross Perot, the independent candidate. Limbaugh made special appearances with the president during the campaign as well.

Despite Limbaugh's belated efforts, Bush lost the election. Nothing, however, was lost for Limbaugh who gained a new foil for his daily political banter in the persons of President and First Lady Bill and Hillary Clinton. From 1992 to 1994, the conservatives were without a leader. Mary Matalin, former campaign strategist for George Bush, took note of how conservatives used Limbaugh's show to motivate and rejuvenate themselves following the 1992 presidential defeat. "All we had to hold us together was Rush Limbaugh . . . the only voice in that huge defeat, in the arrogance of the Clintonistras rushing into town, that really kept us collected" ("Rush Limbaugh's America," 1995).

Taking full advantage of his new status, Rush and his Ditto Heads rallied around conservative candidates in races for congressional seats in the 1994 midterm elections. Limbaugh, although scarcely gracious in accepting the mantle of conservative leadership, was certainly no longer lacking in ego as he had been during his dateless adolescence in Cape Girardeau: "Thirty years after Ronald Reagan's brilliant enunciation of conservative ideals at the end of Barry Goldwater's campaign, the torch has passed to me," Limbaugh wrote in his nationally syndicated newspaper column a month before the 1994 elections. Why? Because, he went on, he does not fear to "provide information and analysis the media refuse to disseminate—information and analysis the public craves. . . . I champion the extraordinary accomplishments of ordinary people,'' and that is "why liberals are terrified of me. As well they should be" (Limbaugh, 1994, 25 A). Presumably, "the media" who "refuse to disseminate" information are not he, but the mainstream, liberal establishment media who fear his voice.

Following the Republican victory in 1994, Limbaugh was inducted as an honorary Republican member of the 104th Congress. Freshman representatives and Republican leaders praised his efforts in rallying the conservative vote. Not all Limbaugh observers were so laudatory. Critics contend his Ditto Heads are an uneducated, angry, racist cult following. More charitable judges argue that Limbaugh is a multimedia personality who articulates and reflects the sentiments of fellow conservatives (Roberts, 1993). As one self-proclaimed Ditto Head, a mortgage banker in Atlanta, said, "I think most of us out here listening to Rush like what he says because we already think these things. He's just incredible at saying it" (Talbot, 1995, 42): Limbaugh panders to what his listeners want to hear.

Limbaugh's role in the political process keeps him in contact with the leaders of the Republican party. According to Speaker of the U.S. House of Representatives Newt Gingrich, Limbaugh and the Republican leaders have a "very loose arrangement," whereby the leaders keep Limbaugh abreast of legislation and the conservative perspective (Roberts, 1993, 28). By way of return, Limbaugh provides conservative Republicans an unrelenting voice, one that never falls silent on their behalf.

SEE, I TOLD YOU SO

Rush Limbaugh, like Shakespeare's Falstaff, is unabashed by his critics. He is no longer the shy kid; he is not about to drop his extracurricular activities and go into hiding. And extracurricular activities do indeed occupy him. In addition to his radio program, "The Rush Limbaugh Show"; his television production, "Rush Limbaugh: The Television Show"; his newsletter, "The Limbaugh Letter"; and his newspaper columns, books, and lectures, Limbaugh performs a weekend concert entitled "Rush to Excellence." With the addition of these concerts, Limbaugh has added a component to his crusade used so effectively by the Grateful Dead: traveling across the country espousing the Message. He draws upon all his Limbaughisms—he claims to serve humanity simply by opening his mouth, to execute everything he does flawlessly with zero mistakes, to make liberals tremble, and so on. As in his *See, I Told You So* (1993), he eschews modesty and proclaims his victories.

Given his rapid rise to the status of a cultural icon, conservative strategist, and "powerful mainstream media pundit" (Carlisle, 1993, 4), Limbaugh may no longer be shielded from accountability for his political commentary as a relative newcomer. Michael Harrison, newsletter editor, says Limbaugh has "reached a point of critical vulnerability" (Feldmann, 1994, 7); as Rush Limbaugh, he has to be mindful of his actions and careful about the truthfulness of his statements. For example, in 1995, a New York–based media watchdog organization, Fairness and Accuracy in Reporting (FAIR), released two studies noting the inaccuracies in factual statements made by Limbaugh on his radio and television shows and claiming that Limbaugh's errors are egregious (Rendall, Naureckas, and Cohen, 1995).

But, like trying to pin down the claims of Shakespeare's Falstaff, as far as Limbaugh's acolytes are concerned, accurate and effective commentary need not be the same thing. If accurate and effective, fine; if inaccurate and still effective, that's fine as well. For Limbaugh's performance, and his audience's appreciation of it, wit not accuracy is the key. As Falstaff said in *The Second Part of King Henry the Fourth*, act 1, scene 2:

> Men of all sorts take a pride to gird at me. The brain of
> this foolish-compounded clay, man, is not able to invent
> any thing that tends to laughter, more than I invent, or is
> invented on me: I am not only witty in myself, but the cause
> that wit is in other men. (lines 223–28)

Yet, Limbaugh watchers need also to keep in mind what Mrs. Ford said about Falstaff's truthfulness in *The Merry Wives of Windsor*, act 2, scene 1:

> I shall think the worse of fat men, as long as I have an eye
> to make difference of men's liking: and yet he would not
> swear; praised women's modesty: and gave such orderly and
> well-behaved reproof to all uncomeliness, that *I would have*
> *sworn his disposition would have gone to the truth of*
> *his words: but they do no more adhere and keep place*
> *together*, than the hundredth psalm to the tune of "Green
> Sleeves." (lines 56–65; emphasis added)

REFERENCES

Selected Works by Rush Limbaugh

The Limbaugh Letter. Monthly newsletter of the Limbaugh Institute for Advanced Conservative Studies. New York: EFM Publishing, vols. 1–5, 1991–1996.
The Way Things Ought to Be. New York: Pocket Books, 1992.
See, I Told You So. New York: Pocket Star Books, 1993.
"Liberals Fear Me Because I Am Effective." *Dallas Morning News*, October 13, 1994, 25 A.

Selected Critical Works about Rush Limbaugh

Anderson, K. "Big Mouth." *Time*, November 1, 1993, 42, 60–67.
Boyd, C. "Speaking Rushian." *ETC: A Review of General Semantics* 51 (Fall 1994): 251–60.

Carlisle, J. "Rush Limbaugh: Propagandist of the Year." *Propaganda Review* 10 (Summer 1993): 4–9.

Corliss, R. "Look Who's Talking." *Time*, January 8, 1995, 22–26.

Davis, J. B. (Novel) *The Rise of Rush Limbaugh toward the Presidency*. Norcross, GA: MacArthur Publishing, 1994.

Feldmann, L. "For Talk Meister Limbaugh." *Christian Science Monitor*, September 2, 1994, 7.

Ivins, M. "Lying Bully." *Mother Jones*, 20, May-June, 1995, 37–39.

Mooney, L., ed. "Rush Limbaugh." In *Newsmakers '91*, 246–49. Detroit: Gale Research, 1991.

"Naked News." (Television documentary) Arts & Entertainment Network, November 10, 1995, 1 hour.

Rendall, S., J. Naureckas and J. Cohen. *The Way Things Aren't: Rush Limbaugh's Reign of Error*. New York: New Press, 1995.

Roberts, S. V. "What a Rush." *U.S. News & World Report*, August 16, 1993, 26–33.

"Rush Limbaugh's America." (Video profile) "Frontline," Public Broadcasting Service, February 28, 1995, 1 hour.

Talbot, S. "Wizard of Ooze." *Mother Jones*, 20, May-June 1993, 41–43.

Selected General Works

Avery, R., D. G. Ellis, and T. W. Glover. "Patterns of Communication on Talk Radio." Paper delivered at the Broadcast Education Association Annual Meeting, Chicago, April 15, 1976.

Combs, J. E., and D. Nimmo. *The Comedy of Democracy*. Westport, CT: Praeger, 1996.

Levin, M. *Talk Radio and the American Dream*. Lexington, MA: Lexington Books, 1987.

Nimmo, D., and M. Hovind. "Vox Populi: Talk Radio and TV Cover the Gulf War." In *The Media and the Persian Gulf War*, edited by R. Denton, 89–106. Westport, CT: Praeger, 1993.

Roberts, J. C. "The Power of Talk Radio." *American Enterprise* 2 (May 1991): 56–61.

Traimer, H., and L. W. Jeffres. "Talk Radio—Forum and Companion." *Journal of Broadcasting* 27 (Summer 1983): 297–300.

Turow, J. "Talk Show Radio as Interpersonal Communication." *Journal of Broadcasting* 18 (Spring 1974): 171–79.

WALTER LIPPMANN

(September 23, 1889–December 14, 1974)

The Sage of Political Commentary

On September 8, 1931, the *New York Herald Tribune* inaugurated a column of political opinion written by a journalist who was then in midlife and in the middle of his career, Walter Lippmann. It was not Lippmann's first systematic statement of political analysis and opinion, nor was it the first political column printed. Lippmann had already established a reputation for political commentary as an author of insightful books of political analysis and as an editorial journalist. Other journalists, notably David Lawrence, had been writing columns of political interpretation for years. But it was Lippmann who earned the title of the "inventor of the syndicated political column" (Whitfield, 1981, 68). And it was his column, "Today and Tomorrow," that in large measure cemented Lippmann's stature as the "dean" of American political journalism in the twentieth century.

While he was a student at Harvard University in the first decade of the century, Walter Lippmann drew close intellectually to the leading American pragmatic philosopher of the era, William James. For James, "the meaning of a concept may always be bound, if not in some sensible particular which it directly designates, then in some particular difference in the course of human experience which its being true will make" (1925, 82). During his lifetime, Lippmann became more than flesh and blood, more than "a sensible particular." He became a "concept," one synonymous with political influence. Wrote one observer at the height of Lippmann's notoriety, "American correspondents are no longer surprised by Lippmann's influence—he has been affecting the course of government for fifty years . . ." (Rivers, 1967, 58). Lippmann's ascribed political influence extended beyond daily political events. He was judged to be "perhaps the most important political thinker in the twentieth century" (Rossiter & Lare, 1963, xi).

On the other hand, another Lippmann critic argues that the commentator's political influence during his lifetime was "assumed" more than "investigated." What, for example, were the "sensible particulars," the hard evidence of Lippmann's influence in supporting presidential candidates Al Smith in 1928, Alf Landon in 1936, and Thomas Dewey in 1948? What difference did it really make? Moreover, Lippmann's "stature as a political philosopher is likely to remain uncertain": claims for his importance have rarely been raised by philosophers themselves, his technical command of the methods of philosophic analysis were limited, his books are "crystalline" in "accessibility," and scholars have been "unable to resolve the apparent contradictions from one book to the next" (Whitfield, 1981, 71–72).

If the "sensible particulars" render a mixed verdict regarding Walter Lippmann's actual political influence however, the "particular difference," in James' phrase, "in the course of human experience" (i.e., political commentary), of Lippmann's *reputation* for influence was substantial. It is problematic whether through "Today and Tomorrow" Lippmann reshaped the course of national politics in the twentieth century; that he reshaped the course of political commentary in the mid-twentieth century is beyond question.

FROM POLITICS TO POLITICAL COMMENTARY

John Reed, committed socialist, author of the classic *Ten Days That Shook the World* depicting the events surrounding the Russian Revolution, and Harvard classmate of Walter Lippmann, once introduced his friend to a group of fellow undergraduates, "Gentlemen, the future President of the United States" (Hicks, 1936, 34). Wrote a Lippmann biographer, "There were smiles and laughs, but not of disbelief" (Steel, 1980, 28). It was testimony and tribute to Lippmann's avid political interest even as an undergraduate—president and co-founder of the Harvard Socialist Club, a founder of the Social Politics Club, a member of the Debating Club and the Philosophical Club, and a writer for the *Harvard Illustrated*, a magazine edited by classmate H. V. Kaltenborn (q.v.). It was a political interest born early. At age nine, Lippmann attended an open-air rally featuring the hero of San Juan Hill and candidate for New York governor, Theodore Roosevelt. By Lippmann's own admission, he was shaken with admiration for Roosevelt; years later, Lippmann wrote that he had "been less than just to his [Roosevelt's] successors because they were not like him" (1935, 487).

Trips to resort towns in the United States and Europe were a staple of Walter Lippmann's upbringing. He was born on September 23, 1889, in New York City, the only child of a prosperous clothing manufacturer and real estate broker, Jacob Lippmann, and his wife, Daisy Baum Lippmann. Lippmann's paternal grandfather had immigrated to the United States a half-century before Lippmann's birth. The Lippmann family, of German-Jewish heritage, placed high value on education and intellectual growth. Hence, Lippmann's introduction to the art, music, literature, and culture of the Old Country came early; his first transatlantic crossing was in 1896. That same year he enrolled in a private school, Dr. Julius Sachs' School for Boys. There he studied the classics, history, mathematics, and languages, and he developed a fascination for geography that dominated much of his political writing throughout his career.

In 1906 Lippmann entered Harvard. In addition to his political activity he was an outstanding student. He fulfilled all the requirements for graduation in a scant three years, made Phi Beta Kappa, and remained for a fourth year of study in philosophy. He cultivated the finest minds Harvard could offer—philosopher George Santayana, Irving Babbitt in French literature, Barrett Wendell in English literature, the retired William James, and others. Although he immersed himself in the humanities, languages, and social sciences, he avoided mathematics and the physical-biological sciences. He also found time to write articles and poetry for various Harvard periodicals, and in his final year at Harvard he was a cub reporter for the *Boston Common*.

While he was at Harvard, Lippmann made the acquaintance of America's foremost muckraker, a term Theodore Roosevelt popularized in 1906 as a label for journalists and other writers who made a living out of exposing scandal and corruption in politics and business. Upon his graduation in 1910, Lippmann wrote to the muckraker, Lincoln Steffens, asking for employment. He soon found himself working for Steffens' publication, *Everybody's Magazine*, doing background work and writing articles. The work appealed to Lippmann's socialist and reformist ideals. So too did his moonlighting writing articles for the socialist monthly *International*, the reformist *Call*, various tracts, and speeches. Associates predicted Walter Lippmann would have a bright future in the Socialist party, the wave of the future.

In 1912 Lippmann hoped to put his reformist views into practice when he accepted a position as secretary to the newly elected socialist mayor of Schenectady, New York. For two months the new administration cleaned up corruption in city government, but only to find that once that was accomplished citizens made it clear that a socialist government was not what they wanted. The mayor moderated his socialist programs. Lippmann urged the mayor not to turn his back on socialism, but to no avail. After four months as the mayor's secretary, Lippmann resigned. It would not be the last time that Walter Lippmann would embrace a political leader, grow disillusioned with that leadership, then withdraw his support. Every U.S. president from Woodrow Wilson through Richard Nixon suffered at the hands of Lippmann's distaste for the compromises that politics forces upon the elected official.

In part to work off the ennui provoked by his Schenectady experience, in part because he was encouraged to do so, and in part because he had always wanted to write a book, Walter Lippmann retreated to the Maine woods and put pen to paper. He had concluded that he was not suited to public office and the tedium of political life; rather, he increasingly viewed his role as that of a political critic who could best prepare citizens for social action by improving their minds. In his *A Preface to Politics* (1913), Lippmann brought to bear on politics the contemporary insights into the political animal spawned by intellectual developments in psychology, especially Freudian psychology. Among those impressed with Lippmann's analysis was Herbert Croly, a leading progressive exponent of the era. Their acquaintance resulted in the founding of the leading journal of liberal views in the progressive period, the *New Republic*, in 1914.

In articles on domestic policies, the *New Republic*'s views often coincided with those of the administration of President Woodrow Wilson. However, founded in the year of the outbreak of World War I, the magazine could not but help being caught up in America's gradually growing role in international politics. Lippmann's editorial views advocated neutrality between the parties in the European conflict. But, for Lippmann, neutrality had to have a positive meaning, something to contribute to the resolution of the conflict. He criticized Wilson for not exerting his leadership in that direction. As the war dragged on, however, Lippmann, still advocating neutrality, began to see a shared interest between Britain and America. Believing that Wilson was committed to peace, Lippmann endorsed the incumbent in the 1916 presidential election. "The Socialist turned Progressive had now become a Democrat," wrote one biographer (Wellborn, 1969, 29).

The *New Republic* grew increasingly closer to the Wilson administration. The magazine's editorial stance toward the war shifted from neutrality to sympathetic alignment for the allies, and ultimately favored U.S. entry into the war. During this time, Lippmann became acquainted with top officials in Washington, D.C. These included presidential advisor Colonel Edward M. House and Secretary of War Newton D. Baker. With U.S. entry into World War I, Lippmann accepted a position as Baker's assistant. He soon left that post to join "the Inquiry," a secret research group organized by House to accumulate geographic, ethnic, political, and cultural data preliminary to negotiating a peace settlement at the war's end.

As a member of the Inquiry in 1917, Lippmann and his colleagues, under President Wilson's instructions, redrew the map of Eastern Europe to conform to America's peace aims. The Inquiry was to grant ethnic demands for self-determination among Czechs, Slovaks, Serbs, Poles, Magyars, and so on—virtually an endless variety of overlapping ethnicities, languages, religions, races, hopes, aspirations, and ambitions—without sparking new rivalries among them. Working with rudimentary maps, piles of partial statistics, and fragmentary charts, the Inquiry recast the ethnic, religious, linguistic, racial, and geographical frontiers of the postwar world; all this laboring night and day for a scant three weeks with no direct, personal knowledge of the region and with only minimal contact with people who did. The final memo submitted to the president became the basis of Wilson's Fourteen Points. Later, with the end of hostilities imminent, Lippmann as a U.S. Army captain in military intelligence in Paris had the task of drafting a detailed explanation of what the vague original outline of the Fourteen Points meant. His explanation, written in an all-night session, became the president's peace protocol.

Walter Lippmann's work in military intelligence involved him in political commentary foreign to his instincts; he was a propagandist. He went to Europe in a dual capacity. One was as Colonel House's personal representative to co-ordinate Allied intelligence efforts with those of the Inquiry; the second was to help coordinate a program for the preparation and delivery of propaganda materials across enemy lines. In the second capacity, he quickly ran afoul of the European efforts of George Creel's (q.v.) Committee on Public Information (CPI), the Wilson administration's World War I propaganda agency. Creel believed strongly that all U.S. and allied propaganda should be coordinated centrally by the CPI, not dispersed among separate military intelligence bureaus. Frustrated by Creel's stand, Lippmann protested to Colonel House. In the end, President Wilson sided with Creel in the ensuing controversy, and a disgusted Lippmann dropped the matter. With the cessation of hostilities, Lippmann became increasingly estranged from his superiors. He resigned from the army and departed Europe for the United States in 1919. "I am glad of the whole experience," he commented, "and I am glad it is over" (Steel, 1980, 154). His flirtation with an active political and administrative life had come to an end; his political influence, however, was just beginning.

REACHING SAGEHOOD

Walter Lippmann returned to his life as a husband (he had married Faye Albertson in 1917) and editorial writer for the *New Republic*, and he accepted assignment as a correspondent for the *Manchester Guardian*. First disturbed, then disillusioned, with what he deemed Woodrow Wilson's betrayal of the Fourteen Points via compromises at the Paris Peace Conference, Lippmann and the *New Republic* broke with Woodrow Wilson and opposed ratification of the Treaty of Versailles by the U.S. Senate.

In the period following World War I, he turned to book-length and to editorial political commentary. In 1920 he left the *New Republic* to write a book, began a regular column for *Vanity Fair* that he continued until 1934, and joined the editorial staff of the crusading New York *World* in 1921. *Vanity Fair* made him a colleague of H. L. Mencken (q.v.). Although they never had a personal tie, they shared a pessimistic view about the potential of mass democracy. Wrote Mencken about Lippmann: he "started out life with high hopes for democracy and an almost mystical belief in the congenital wisdom of the masses," but reached the conclusion that the "masses were ignorant and unteachable" (Steel, 1980, 214). And Lippmann wrote of Mencken: he did "destroy, by rendering it ridiculous and unfashionable, the democratic tradition of the American pioneers" (Steel, 1980, 259). On the *World* Lippmann ran the editorial page, then served as editor. There he was associated with Arthur Krock (q.v.) in a relationship that remained cool throughout both political columnists' careers.

But it was his book *Public Opinion* (1922), followed by succeeding volumes over the next decade, that marked him with the qualities of a sage, even though he was only thirty-three years old when *Public Opinion* was published. A sage is a person famed for possessing wisdom, whose wise judgment is derived from long experience in human affairs. Whether merited or not, sagacious persons have reputations for access to special knowledge that is hidden from the eyes and ears of ordinary people. Sages are heirs to a tradition dating back to ancient sorcerers, soothsayers, and oracles; they share a reputation for revealed insights that, before advances in the natural sciences, social sciences, and theology, were reserved for alchemists, astrologers, and theosophers. Given their superior intellectual status, sages need not talk down to the less knowledgeable; indeed, to do so would threaten their mystery, as when the Wizard of Oz's curtain is pulled aside to reveal an ordinary man. Instead, sages package their insights in language difficult for initiates to grasp, yet their words and actions are accepted by followers as unquestionable truth.

Contemporary sages, although less mystical than their ancient ancestors, are taken no less seriously by rulers and ruled alike. Having studied at the feet of other sages, as did Walter Lippmann at Harvard; having occupied prestigious positions as an advisor to the powerful, as did Lippmann to the Wilson administration and numerous presidents thereafter; and yet having retained a critical air of meditative detachment, as did Lippmann in his editorial capacities at the *New Republic*, contemporary sages are revered for their superior insight every bit as much as were the oracles of Delphi. And, if the insights appear to contradict themselves from time to time, so much the better. For that too adds to the sagely reputation as a detached oracle, especially when the sage admits error, as did Walter Lippmann:

> For more than twenty years I have found myself writing about critical events with no better guide to their meaning than the hastily improvised generalizations of a rather bewildered man. . . . I should have liked to achieve again the untroubled certainty and the assured consistency which are vouchsafed to those who can whole-heartedly commit themselves to some . . . doctrine. (1937, x)

Although less so now than when it was originally published, the theme of Walter Lippmann's *Public Opinion* was novel, especially coming from a journalist. It challenged a fundamental tenet that news is objective, news is truth. Given the strength of Lippmann's argument that people receive from newspapers not political *realities* but mediated political *pluralities*, such a claim coming from a journalist suggested that Lippmann was far more than a mere journalist; he was a critical thinker of the first magnitude, a political sage in the making.

Government by public opinion, argued Lippmann, was a chimera. For public opinion was unstable and uninformed; it was not an adequate guide for policy deliberation, let alone action. There were several reasons for this. The world is too complex and contradictory for people to understand; problems demanding solutions are too technical for citizens to comprehend; and administrative guidance in problem solving demands an expertise too sophisticated to be selected through the vagaries of the electoral process. Moreover, citizens live in their individual subjective worlds which insulate them from the subtleties of their environments. There is a vast difference between the "world outside" and the "pictures in our heads" of that world (Lippmann, 1922, 3). Confronted with unknowns, people respond to symbols and stereotypes that oversimplify political complexities.

Finally, citizens have nowhere to turn for direct information about the world outside even if they could respond to it with dispassion. They no longer depend upon the primary political environment within which "political representatives could be directly observed and political problems directly confronted" (Whitfield, 1981, 72). The world is too vast to govern through an endless series of town meetings. What people know about politics is secondhand, mediated by news accounts. News, however, also "is not a first hand report of the raw material. It is a report of the material after it has been stylized" (Lippmann, 1922, 347)—in contemporary vernacular, after the material has received the "spin" of propagandists. A news account is thus not true; it is but a single droplet selected from an ocean of possible truths.

Public Opinion was a trenchant statement about a profound problem, namely, the problematic sources of intelligence in a democratic society. Although widely hailed by many critics, not every political commentator agreed with Walter Lippmann's analysis. One who did not was John Dewey (q.v.). Dewey did not accept the premise that citizens were passive, uninformed creatures entrapped by the pictures in their heads. Nor did Dewey agree that the role of the news media is merely to furnish a secondhand version of political events; journalism's responsibility is to provoke conversation among citizens and to energize their capacities to penetrate behind the shroud of mediated political realities, indeed create their own realities and the publics associated with them (Dewey, 1927).

In the end, neither the challenge laid down to democracy by the journalistic sage, Lippmann, nor the academic one, Dewey, was an obstacle in the path to the ever increasing mediation of politics in the twentieth century and the eclipse of meaningful conversations between rulers and ruled. A principal reason resided in the recognition by politicians that news was not a firsthand report of raw material but a stylized version instead; public opinion could be manipulated by manufacturing the raw material and by dictating the stylizing. Thus did the first public relations professional, Edward L. Bernays (q.v.), draw from *Public Opinion* a vital lesson: political commentary could be shaped by "crystallizing public opinion"; that is, "make news happen" through the "created event" staged purely for media coverage and publicity (Bernays, 1923, 197). Democracy would no longer be government *by* public opinion; it would be government *of* public opinion by government (Key, 1961).

Walter Lippmann continued to write provocative books on a wide variety of political subjects throughout his long career. Although his critics have commented on his tendency to contradict himself from one book to the next, this was not so when he returned to the fundamental problem raised about the relationship between the rulers and the ruled. "A remarkable line of continuity in purpose and emphasis," wrote one analyst of Lippmann's thought, "can be traced from *A Preface of Politics* to *The Public Philosophy*" (Wellborn, 1969, 44). His first book, *A Preface to Politics*, foreshadowed the problem given comprehensive articulation in *Public Opinion*. In *The Public Philosophy* (1955), Lippmann argues that the vicissitudes of an overweening public opinion must be checked by a return to a tradition of natural law—a shift from government by "the people" to a government by "The People," a partnership "not only between those who are living" but also with "those who are dead, and those who are to be born," a "corporation, an entity, that is to say, which lives on while individuals come into it and go out of it" (1955, 35).

In 1931 the New York *World* folded, and Walter Lippmann became a political columnist for the *New York Herald Tribune*, beginning with "Today and Tomorrow" appearing four times a week, then three times a week, and finally two times a week. In syndication the column reached more than 250 U.S. newspapers and more than two dozen foreign publications. In 1962 Walter Lippmann left his three-decade association with the *Herald Tribune* and accepted an offer to move his column to the *Washington Post*; it ran twice a week for eight months per year; in addition, Lippmann wrote sixteen columns a year for *Newsweek*, then a *Post* publication.

Over the years, whatever its impact on political decisions, Walter Lippmann's syndicated column wrought major changes in journalists' attitudes toward their craft. Political commentary, under the guise of what Marquis Childs (q.v.) and James "Scotty" Reston (q.v.) called interpretive reporting, became the order of the day. As a columnist, Lippmann made it clear that "I am not a reporter" (Rivers, 1967, 59). He did not cover political stories, rarely interviewed politicians, expressed minimal interest in the details of breaking news stories, and wrote his columns from his home overlooking the Washington Cathedral in the nation's capital.

> He conceives of his column, he once said, as an effort to keep contemporary events in such perspective that his readers will have no reason to be surprised when something of importance occurs. Thus, although he has no effect on news gathering, his impact on interpretive reporting is profound. Those correspondents who seek to establish the meaning of events usually look to Lippmann for a useful approach. (Rivers, 1967, 59)

In the early days of "Today and Tomorrow," Lippmann's columns revolved about the lingering economic depression of the 1930s. In the beginning, he found many things to admire in Franklin Roosevelt's leadership as president and he was a solid, though often critical, supporter of New Deal approaches to economic recovery. In 1935, when the U.S. Supreme Court declared the National Recovery Act (NRA) unconstitutional, Lippmann, who was no great advocate of the NRA, urged the president to rethink other New Deal policies to make sure that the same fate was not awaiting them. After a luncheon with FDR at the president's New York estate, Lippmann assumed he had convinced him to slow the pace of New Deal reforms. When he soon found that he had not, Lippmann broke with Roosevelt. In the 1936 presidential election, Lippmann backed Republican Alf Landon. When FDR's landslide victory emboldened him to seek reform of the Supreme Court to ensure no additional interference with the New Deal, Walter Lippmann attacked the president as "drunk with power," perpetrator of a "bloodless coup d'etat which strikes a deadly blow at the vital center of constitutional democracy" (Steel, 1980, 319).

During World War II, Lippmann employed his column to warn against a policy of isolation once victory was won. He was a staunch advocate of diplomacy and negotiated settlements as the Cold War unfolded, and his support of the Atlantic Alliance proved valuable to the foreign policy approach of the Truman administration. In a 1947 column, Lippmann laid out the essence of what later became the linchpin of Truman's Cold War European policy, the Marshall Plan. None of this, however, prevented Lippmann from favoring Republican Thomas E. Dewey over Truman in the 1948 presidential election. In 1952 Lippmann endorsed Republican Dwight Eisenhower for president, but found him wanting once elected, and endorsed Adlai Stevenson in 1956, and John F. Kennedy in 1960.

With Kennedy's assassination, Lippmann turned his support to President Lyndon Johnson's Great Society, especially civil rights legislation. He endorsed Johnson in the 1964 presidential election. Johnson sought out Lippmann's policy views and virtually made the sagely columnist a member of his inner circle. However, as had happened before, the sage and the president had a falling out. The Vietnam War occasioned the break. In 1965 Lippmann warned that for the United States to become involved in a land war in Asia would be supreme folly. President Johnson continued to be solicitous of Lippmann's views. However, as controversy over U.S. commitments in Vietnam reached a crisis point, and Lippmann did not change his views in spite of LBJ's courting, the president viewed Lippmann's opposition as a betrayal, both political and personal. This did not deter Lippmann who unflaggingly used his column to criticize Johnson's stand.

Walter Lippmann's syndicated column earned two Pulitzer Prizes, one in 1958 and the other in 1962; both citations lauded the wisdom, perception, and responsible tenor of his superior commentary. In 1967, Walter Lippmann decided to end "Today and Tomorrow"; he wrote his last column on May 25. He and his second wife, Helen Byrne Armstrong with whom he had moved to Washington in 1938 shortly after their marriage, moved back to New York City. Lippmann, who continued his contributions to *Newsweek* for four more years, wrote his last article in January 1971. "He did not intend it to be his last; there simply were not more" (Steel, 1980, 593). In 1974, nine months after Helen's death, Walter Lippmann died on December 14 of cardiac arrest.

WALTER LIPPMANN IN THE AGE OF POPULIST SAGEDOM

Walter Lippmann's sagely influence among the Washington press corps spawned the Lippmann Syndrome (Rivers, 1967, 69–70). The syndrome consisted of a style incorporating obscurity for its own sake, as if those who use it, like Lippmann, know things that other people cannot know; hence, it is useless to write down to readers for they will not grasp the essence anyway.

That, of course, was a sad misreading of Lippmann's style—sage, erudite, scholarly, and never pandering, but sufficiently clear to those who took the trouble of close reading.

Obscure writing, however, has not been the main legacy of the Lippmann Syndrome. Rather, in the age of *USA Today*, *People* magazine, and the television sound bite, pandering is more the vogue. Rather, at its worst today, the Lippmann Syndrome produces political commentary even more remotely removed from the give-and-take of the primary political environment of directly observed politicians than ever imagined in Lippmann's day. For Lippmann there was a first order of politics rarely experienced by the rank and file, a second order of politics that reaches citizens via stylized news mediation, and his own third order of politics devoted to trying to sort the "world outside" from the "pictures in our heads" put there by mediated accounts.

As Americans approach the twenty-first century, a fourth order of politics has emerged. It consists not of what politicians do, not of mediated accounts of what they do based upon direct observation, and not of political commentary that sorts the one from the other. Instead it consists of political commentators held captive by the pictures in *their* heads, analyzing one another's thoughts, talking to one another. On confrontational radio and television talk shows, on op-ed pages, on sidebars of glossy magazines, and on thirty-second snippets of airtime, they set political "expectations" for presidents, diplomats, administrators, legislators, and judicial officials, judge whether public officials have lived up to those expectations, then render a verdict for audience members presumably unprepared to know what to think, what to think about, or what to think about that which they do not think.

The exercise of fourth-order analysis is akin to Walter Lippmann's participation in the Inquiry's 1917 redrawing of the map of Europe. In spite of the Inquiry's best intentions, the redrawing had unfortunate consequences. Lippmann learned a lesson and, in the words of the Alsops (Alsop & Alsop, 1958, 6), took "pains to refresh [his] analytical powers by frequent direct contact with people and events" even though he was not a working journalist in the conventional sense; "not even the most astute analyst can possibly know what the news means by sheer mental telepathy" (Alsop & Alsop, 1958, 6). Whether a generation of contemporary, self-proclaimed sages will learn the same lessons or, instead, produce devitalizing results for political commentary equal to 1917's "war to end all wars" remains to be seen.

REFERENCES

Selected Political Works by Walter Lippmann

A Preface to Politics. New York: Macmillan, 1913.
The Stakes of Diplomacy. New York: Holt, 1915.
Liberty and the News. New York: Harcourt Brace, 1920.

Public Opinion. New York: Harcourt Brace, 1922; Macmillan, 1960.
The Phantom Public. New York: Harcourt Brace, 1925.
Men of Destiny. New York: Macmillan, 1927.
American Inquisitors: A Commentary on Dayton and Chicago. New York: Macmillan, 1928.
A Preface to Morals. New York: Macmillan, 1929.
Interpretations, 1931–1932. Edited by A. Nevins. New York: Macmillan, 1932.
"A Tribute to Theodore Roosevelt." *New Republic*, October 27, 1935, 487–88.
Interpretations, 1933–1935. Edited by A. Nevins. New York: Macmillan, 1936.
An Inquiry into the Principles of the Good Society. Boston: Little, Brown, 1937.
U.S. Foreign Policy: Shield of the Republic. Boston: Little, Brown, 1943.
U.S. War Aims. Boston: Little, Brown, 1944.
The Cold War: A Study in U.S. Foreign Policy. New York: Harper and Row, 1947.
Isolation and Alliances: An American Speaks to the British. Boston: Little, Brown, 1952.
The Public Philosophy. Boston: Little, Brown, 1955.
The Communist World and Ours. Boston: Little, Brown, 1959.
Drift and Mastery. Englewood Cliffs, NJ: Prentice-Hall, 1961a.
The Coming Tests with Russia. Boston: Little, Brown, 1961b.
Western Unity and the Common Market. Boston: Little, Brown, 1962.
The Essential Lippmann: A Political Philosophy for Liberal Democracy. Edited by C. Rossiter and J. Lare. New York: Random House, 1963.
CBS Reports: Conversations with Eric Sevareid. Boston: Little, Brown, 1965.
Early Writings. New York: Liveright, 1970.

Selected Critical Works about Walter Lippmann

Bluhm, W. T. "Conservative Immanentism: Burke and Lippmann." In *Theories of the Political System*, edited by W. T. Bluhm, 389–416. Englewood Cliffs, NJ: Prentice-Hall, 1965.

Cary, F. C. *The Influence of War on Walter Lippmann, 1914–1944.* Madison: University of Wisconsin Press, 1967.

Childs, M., and J. Reston, eds. *Walter Lippmann and His Times.* New York: Harcourt Brace, 1959.

Dam, H. N. *The Intellectual Odyssey of Walter Lippmann.* New York: Gordon Press, 1973.

Eulau, H. "From Public Opinion to Public Philosophy: Walter Lippmann's Classic Reexamined." *American Journal of Economics and Sociology* 15 (1955/1956): 439–51.

Fisher, C. "Lippmann, Ex-Liberal." In *The Columnists*, edited by C. Fischer, 69–85. New York: Howell, Soskin, 1944.

Forcey, C. *The Crossroads of Liberalism: Croly, Weyl, Lippmann and the Progressive Era, 1900–1925.* New York: Oxford University Press, 1961.

Kunitz, S. J., ed. "Lippmann, Walter". In *Twentieth Century Authors*, 587–88. New York: H. W. Wilson, 1955.

"Lippmann, Walter." In *The National Encyclopedia of American Biography*, 69–70. New York: James T. White, 1934.

McKerns, J. P., ed. "Lippmann, Walter." In *Biographical Dictionary of American Journalism*, 419–21. New York: Greenwood Press, 1989.

Moritz, C., ed. "Lippmann, Walter." In *Current Biography 1962*, 64–67. New York: H. W. Wilson, 1963.

O'Brien, J. C. "Lapsed Liberal." In *Molders of Opinion*, edited by D. Bulman, 36–47. Milwaukee: Bruce Publishing, 1945.

Riley, S. G. "Lippmann, Walter." In *Biographical Dictionary of American Newspaper Columnists*, 186–88. Westport, CT: Greenwood Press, 1995.

Rivers, W. "The Influence of Walter Lippmann." In *The Opinionmakers*, edited by W. Rivers, 57–70. Boston: Beacon Press, 1967.

Schapsmeier, E. L. *Walter Lippmann: Philosopher-Journalist*. Washington, DC: Public Affairs Press, 1969.

Steel, R. *Walter Lippmann and the American Century*. Boston: Little, Brown, 1980.

Syed, A. H. *Walter Lippmann's Philosophy of International Politics*. Philadelphia: University of Pennsylvania Press, 1964.

Weingast, D. E. *Walter Lippmann: A Study in Personal Journalism*. Westport, CT: Greenwood Press, 1949.

Wellborn, C. *Twentieth Century Pilgrimage: Walter Lippmann and the Public Philosophy*. Baton Rouge: Louisiana State University Press, 1969.

Whitfield, S. J. "The Journalist as Intellectual." *Journal of Popular Culture* 15 (Fall 1981): 68–77.

Wright, B. F. *Five Public Philosophies of Walter Lippmann*. Austin: University of Texas Press, 1973.

Selected General Works

Alsop, J., and S. Alsop. *The Reporter's Trade*. New York: Reynal, 1958.

Bernays, E. *Crystallizing Public Opinion*. New York: Liveright, 1923.

Cater, D. *The Fourth Branch of Government*. Boston: Houghton Mifflin, 1959.

Dewey, J. *The Public and Its Problems*. Denver: Alan Swallow, 1927.

Hicks, J. *John Reed*. New York: Macmillan, 1936.

James, W. *The Philosophy of William James*. Edited by H. M. Kallen. New York: Modern Library, 1925.

Key, V. O., Jr. *Public Opinion and American Democracy*. New York: Alfred A. Knopf, 1961.

Kluger, R. *The Paper: The Life and Death of the New York Herald Tribune*. New York: Vintage, 1989.

Nimmo, D., and J. E. Combs. *The Political Pundits*. New York: Praeger, 1992.

JOHN (JOSEPH) MCLAUGHLIN

(March 29, 1927–   )

Marketing the Political Commentator

Politics in a direct, town hall, model of democracy assumes a continuous series of questions and answers. True, the ideal often proves naive, but the requirements are simple enough: officeholders ask how best they can serve constituents, constituents respond, and out of the matrix of question and answer (Q&A), officeholders act accordingly, although, as Abraham Lincoln knew, politicians please all constituents only some of the time, some of the constituents all of the time, but all constituents all the time, never. Viewed from the perspective of the citizen, the ruled who seek to hold rulers accountable ask questions, rulers respond (sometimes forthrightly, sometimes evasively), and the ruled register support or opposition. In a representative democracy there is, to be sure, an intermediary; citizens' questions and officeholders' responses pass through chosen representatives—other officeholders, leaders of political parties, and so on. "Question Time" in the British House of Commons—the time set aside for the British prime minister to answer questions raised by the opposition party—is the paradigm of representative Q&A.

However, Q&A in the American political tradition privileges another intermediary, namely, political journalists, whose vocations are not elected or partisan politics, but who are working for newspapers, newsmagazines, radio, and television. Claiming that the freedom of the press clause of the First Amendment to the Constitution of the United States grants them special status to inquire on behalf of the people's "right to know," political journalists exploit an elaborate array of extraconstitutional Q&A forums. These include press conferences, exclusive interviews, access to unnamed sources, leaks, and so on. The relationship is institutionalized: professional communicators ask questions, and professional politicians, ofttimes only seemingly, respond.

The advent of electronic politics introduced a new forum for Q&A colloquy between political journalists and politicians: the radio or television panel interview. Pioneered by the Martha Rountree and Lawrence E. Spivak (q.v.) collaboration in 1947, it remains a staple of broadcast politics. A selected panel of political journalists ask selected political officials, candidates, and world leaders questions, receiving, as in the English House of Commons, carefully crafted, albeit "spontaneous," answers. Although the Spivak-Rountree "Meet the Press" is the granddaddy of interview panels, there are numerous imitators, notably "Face the Nation," hybrid offshoots like "This Week with David Brinkley," and variations such as "MacNeil-Lehrer" or "Inside Politics."

When journalists elicit answers by questioning political leaders on panel-interview broadcasts, the result is first-order political communication: there are opportunities for reporters to uncover *political* stories, for guests to promote *political* candidacies and projects, and, as a by-product for citizens to acquire *political* information. There is another Q&A format that involves second-order politics; that is, instead of directly questioning public officials, political journalists ask questions of *one another* about politics and politicians. The format dates back to Edward R. Murrow's (q.v.) annual year-end radio and television "roundups" with a panel of CBS journalists. With Murrow moderating, a panel of CBS newscasters discussed national and worldwide political developments over the preceding twelve months and speculated about the approaching year (Persico, 1988). In 1969 political correspondent Martin Agronsky undertook a weekly assessment of politics with a Q&A colloquy among a panel of journalists, "Agronsky and Company." Although the panel debated as much as discussed and argued questions as well as answered them, politics, not oneupsmanship, was the substance of the panel discussion. As with "Meet the Press," "Agronsky and Company" has had its imitators, including "Washington Week in Review" and "Journalists' Roundtable."

In 1981 a former Jesuit priest, John McLaughlin, devised a televised political Q&A that opened a novel third-order level of political communication, one in which politics is incidental to the panel confrontation. No longer is the "play the thing wherein" to "catch the conscience of the king" (*Hamlet*, act 1, scene 2, lines 633–34), as in first-order panel interviews or in second-order panel discussions. In panel confrontations, *the play's the thing wherein panelists market themselves as kings.*

PRIEST, PROFESSOR, POLITICIAN: PRELUDES TO BOMBAST

As a political commentator, John McLaughlin is an unquestioned, unapologetic, unabashed showman. He embraces a communication tradition that has less to do with sober political reflection than with marketing and promotion. McLaughlin is more McDonald's (hamburgers) than (Eugene) McCarthy. A throwback to the days of patent medicine hucksters, carnival barkers, and vaudeville, McLaughlin argues, "There's no reason on God's planet why knowledge has to be boring" (Moritz, 1988, 405); hence, "I'm not primarily interested in dignity, or tranquility, or formality" (Remnick, 1986, 88). Yet, when examining the personal and professional background of McLaughlin prior to the 1970s, one could scarcely prophesy for him the role in political commentary that he carved out for himself as the greatest showman on the political earth.

Born on March 29, 1927, into a second-generation family whose parents were Irish-American, John Joseph McLaughlin grew up in Providence, Rhode Island. With several Catholic Democratic 'pols' around, professional politics was part of family life: one uncle, Henry McLaughlin, was president of the Providence city council for several terms, and a second, physician Edward McLaughlin, was the state's health director. Neither John Joseph's father, Augustus Hugh, nor his mother, Eva Philomena (Turcotte), ever held public office, but Augustus was actively interested in behind-the-scenes wheelings and dealings.

John Joseph's youth, given the plight of his peers at the onset of the Great Depression when he was but a toddler, was one of relative economic comfort and family affection. Rare was the American teenager who, like "Andy Hardy" in the popular Hollywood films of the period, had his own car to drive to high school (LaSalle Academy), but John McLaughlin did. Yet, John Joseph possessed qualities the romanticized Andy Hardy did not. For one, McLaughlin was an avid reader, especially of historical fiction. For another, the Jesuits appealed to him; LaSalle was a Christian Brothers school and, besides, McLaughlin found the same type of romance in the Jesuit order that fascinated him in historical novels.

At the age of eighteen, John Joseph McLaughlin entered the Society of Jesus and trained for the Jesuit priesthood for thirteen years, beginning at the Jesuit seminary in Weston, Massachusetts, Weston College. Although their careers, like Mclaughlin's, would take interesting political turns in the future, neither of two of his Weston College contemporaries could have predicted how politically involved they would become: Robert Drinan, the first priest to be a voting member of the U.S. Congress, and Daniel Berrigan, a leading peace activist and protestor against the war in Vietnam.

After his seminary work, John McLaughlin received his B.A. degree from Boston College in 1951, along with an M.A. in philosophy a year later. Thereafter, he devoted the bulk of the 1950s to teaching in Jesuit schools— Cranwell in Lennox, Massachusetts, and the preparatory schools at Fairfield University in Fairfield, Connecticut. However, McLaughlin decided preparatory school teaching was not the career for him. His request to continue advanced study met with approval from Jesuit authorities, and McLaughlin received the degree of Bachelor of Divinity in 1959. In 1960 he became an ordained Catholic priest, yet he continued his advanced studies and earned a Ph.D. in 1967 from Columbia University.

Although John McLaughlin continued teaching in Jesuit schools during his advanced studies, he also worked for *America*, a Jesuit journal of opinion, from 1967 to 1970, becoming an associate editor. At *America* he learned that achieving success in one endeavor, in this case writing magazine articles of opinion, could provide an entry into others. Father McLaughlin became a much sought public speaker, and he lectured to numerous audiences, including those on college campuses. Among his most widely popular lectures were "Intimacy before Marriage," "Love before Marriage," "Intimacy outside Marriage," and "In-School Sex Education in the Seventies."

Success on the lecture circuit opened doors to additional opportunities: Father McLaughlin was a radio commentator in Stamford, Connecticut, on WSTC (1964); he served as the host of various television series, including WJAR-TV in Providence, Rhode Island, from 1962 to 1963, WNHC-TV in New Haven and WTIC-TV in Hartford in 1963, and WOR-TV in New York City in 1964; he held film seminars at Yale, Holy Cross, and Manhattenville College and judged at the American Film Festival (1969); and, in 1969, he was executive producer of *Biafra Today*, a documentary for ABC-TV.

Father McLaughlin had obviously become a priest with a gift for self-promotion. By 1970 he was prepared to employ that gift in the interests of partisan political promotion. Although coming from a family of Democratic pols and a supporter of the party's candidates for president in 1960 and 1964, Father McLaughlin broke with tradition in 1970. Conservative Democratic Senator John Pastore was up for reelection in Rhode Island. Running as a Republican in a state basically Catholic, campaigning in ecclesiastical dress, positioning himself as a "peace" candidate against Pastore as allegedly pro-Pentagon and pro–military spending, McLaughlin drove his incumbent opponent, in Pastore's word, "batty." Asked Pastore, a Catholic, "How can I debate with a man my religion teaches me to call Father?" (Moritz, 1987, 406).

"Batty" or not, Pastore defeated the priestly politician by a two-to-one margin in a campaign in which the Catholic Church's opposition to McLaughlin was even greater than the church's dislike of Pastore. The campaign, however, advanced McLaughlin's career on two fronts. On one, he worked closely with his campaign manager, Ann (Lauenstein) Dore, a Catholic divorcee he had met when lecturing at Marymount College in 1968. In 1975, after successfully petitioning Pope Paul VI for freedom from ecclesiastical control, McLaughlin and Dore married in a civil ceremony not recognized by the church. On a second front, McLaughlin drew closer to Raymond K. Price, a White House speechwriter in the presidential administration of Richard Nixon. Reverend McLaughlin had been brought to the attention of Price by Patrick Buchanan in 1969; the future CNN political commentator and two-time candidate for the Republican presidential nomination was greatly impressed by McLaughlin's article in *America* supporting Vice President Spiro Agnew's widely publicized and controversial attacks on network television news. Buchanan had written Agnew's speech of inflammatory remarks (Buchanan, 1990). After having been soundly beaten in the 1970 Rhode Island senatorial election, Mclaughlin managed to snatch victory from the jaws of overwhelming defeat by becoming a speechwriter for Ray Price.

Father McLaughlin's political rise was fast paced during Richard Nixon's presidential administration. In 1971 McLaughlin became special deputy assistant to the president. A year later he undertook assignments beyond writing speeches and traveled to Southeast Asia to report on U.S. conduct of the widening Vietnam War. In 1973 he toured Southeast Asia again for the Nixon White House. In both instances he returned with positive reports on the U.S. war efforts, indicating minimal casualties to civilians or destruction to the environment as a result of bombing missions. In Richard Nixon's 1972 reelection campaign, Father McLaughlin supported White House policy in Vietnam; after the election he reiterated that support by openly backing the mining of Haiphong harbor and American bombing raids on North Vietnam during the Christmas holidays.

When the scandal over the break-ins at the Democratic National Headquarters at the Watergate apartment complex, and the coverup of those break-ins, intensified in Nixon's second term, Father McLaughlin remained steadfast in his defense of the White House. In speeches, meetings with reporters on the White House lawn, and other public statements, McLaughlin admitted Nixon was no saint, but he argued that the president sought the truth behind the scandals and, for all his faults, had introduced a climate of charity in politics. Since few politicians, even among Republicans, lined up squarely behind the president, McLaughlin's defense gradually attracted news media attention. And, although he might be regarded as odd by some political journalists, that was precisely McLaughlin's triumph. For, here was a priest who ceased dressing like one and appeared, instead, in immaculate and expensively tailored suits; resided at the Watergate complex; seemed to be disassociating himself from the Society of Jesus and its vows of poverty; and made few apologies for the beleaguered president.

When Richard Nixon resigned the presidency in 1974, McLaughlin did not look back but moved again with a showman's aplomb to recoup his losses like a theatrical impresario forced to accept the closing of a long-running production. After a few weeks, Mclaughlin departed the administration of Gerald Ford and, relying upon the contacts he had made at the Nixon White House, began a new enterprise. McLaughlin—priest, professor, political candidate, and political adviser—set out to become a full-time professional political communicator. Upon his marriage in 1975, he and Ann McLaughlin established McLaughlin and Company, a Washington, D.C., public affairs and media consulting firm. In 1979 John McLaughlin also became host of a weekend radio talk and call-in show on Washington's WAC-AM, a role he continued through 1982, interviewing such political luminaries as Barry Goldwater, and Eugene McCarthy. He overlapped these jobs with service as an editor of William F. Buckley, Jr.'s (q.v.) *National Review*, from 1981 to 1989, writing the column "From Washington Straight" as well. Meanwhile Ann McLaughlin's career also prospered. After the election of Ronald Reagan to the presidency in 1980, she served as assistant secretary for public affairs in the Treasury Department, then undersecretary in the Department of Interior, and finally Secretary of Labor in 1987.

A CARNIVAL OF BUNCOMBE

Prior to 1982 John McLaughlin, although exploiting an array of communication forums for various ends, had done little to change them. However, when he became executive producer and host of "The McLaughlin Group," he immediately added a new genre of political programming to conventional panel interviews and panel discussions. In creating the panel confrontation, which critics sometimes label "The McGroup," McLaughlin wedded his gift for self-

promotion with a precept about politics—and commentary about politics—
voiced decades earlier by H. L. Mencken (q.v.):

> Has the art of politics no apparent utility? Does it appear to be unqualifiedly
> ratty, raffish, sordid, obscene, and low down, and its salient virtuosi a gang of
> unmitigated scoundrels? Then let us not forget its high capacity to sooth and
> tickle the midriff, its incomparable services as a maker of entertainment.
> (Mencken, 1956, xxx)

With "The McLaughlin Group," its creator found the ideal forum to soothe and
tickle, irritate and provoke the midriff of audiences dispirited by the sober setbacks of Vietnam, the long nightmare of Watergate, and the 444 days of captivity during the Iranian hostage crisis. "McGroup," or "McLaugh," proved to
be incomparable entertainment. It was what Mencken could have portrayed as
"A Carnival of Buncombe" (1956).

The Edison Electric Institute funded the pilot for "The McLaughlin Group."
After the program's debut in April 1982, it did not obtain a permanent under-
writer until General Electric signed on as such in 1986. By 1983 the program
aired on over 300 public television stations and on NBC stations in the nation's
capital and in New York, Los Angeles, and Boston; the "Group" reached 98
percent of America's households. Yet, it is not the number of stations airing the
program or even the size of its viewing audience that constitutes the measure
of the program's success. Rather it is the *type* of audience, namely, political
attentives, especially those residing or doing business inside "the Beltway" and
in the Boston–New York–D.C. corridor: "Power Washington apartments along
the Potomac; town houses in Georgetown; Tudors and ranches in Bethesda,
MacLean, and Chevy Chase; and sweetest of all, the Alpine Lodge at Camp
David" (Remnick, 1986, 80).

During the presidency of Ronald Reagan, "The McLaughlin Group" proved
to be "must viewing" at the White House and Camp David. Reagan singled
the program out for public comment, saying, at one point, it was the most
tasteful alternative to professional wrestling and, at another, the political version
of *Animal House*. Other commentators have employed different metaphors: an
early "Group" panelist, Hodding Carter, Jimmy Carter's former assistant secretary of state, compared it to Kabuki theater; Michael Kinsley, former editor
of the *New Republic* and then a member of a rival panel-confrontation show,
"Crossfire," likened the "Group" to "I Love Lucy," a show with familiar
characters in funny situations; another "Group" panelist, *Newsweek* reporter
Eleanor Clift, commenting on the show well before she became a regular, called
it "the Super Bowl of bullshit"; and *Washington Post* columnist David Broder
proclaimed that the efforts of the "Group" to make policy calls and predictions
were"bullshit" (Moritz, 1987, 408).

In addition to the scope and composition of the audience of the "Group,"
and the fact that it attracts sufficient attention to draw favorable and odious

comparisons, there is another measure of its popularity. That consists of the new programming John McLaughlin has been able to promote in its wake: in 1987 140 independent radio stations carried "Sixty Seconds," a McLaughlin creation bringing together pairs of congressional officials debating the pros and cons of issues; in 1984 McLaughlin produced "One on One," an in-depth weekly interview series featuring his Q&A with newsmakers; for CNBC cable network in 1989, the former priest began "McLaughlin," a one-hour talk show featuring him as host.

John McLaughlin has his own characterization for "The McLaughlin Group" and for the source of its success. His description of the program, carried on the electronic World Wide Web of the Internet since July 13, 1994, promotes himself and the "Group" as having "blazed new trails in the political talk show genre of television." The proof he offers of success is that the show has been satirized on "Saturday Night Live" and "In Living Color," and was chosen in 1993 as "Best Political Talk Show" by *Washingtonian* magazine—for the seventh year in a row!

Although John McLaughlin and the "Group" became, for whatever formulaic reasons, public affairs icons on television following 1982, the pilot for the show foreshadowed no such success. McLaughlin's original panel consisted of Robert Novak, a conservative political columnist; Jack Germond, a Democratic retread and political journalist for the *Baltimore Sun*; and political reporters Judith Miller of the *New York Times* and Charles Stone of *the Philadelphia Daily News*. The result was little more than a "son" of "Agronsky and Company." McLaughlin made changes. He retained panelists Novak and Germond, and replaced the other panelists with commentators reputed to be clear-cut ideologists: conservative Pat Buchanan, former liberal turned neoconservative Morton Kondracke of *Roll Call*, and, in a fifth panel seat, he rotated the liberal Hodding Carter and the conservative Fred Barnes of the *New Republic*.

McLaughlin also energized the format, breathlessly introducing an "issue," a leading question to goad a response from each panelist, then provoking confrontations. McLaughlin said, "By creating a context of pressure I can exact more conciseness, more brilliance. It's just as if coal is subjected to enormous pressure, you can get a diamond" (Remnick, 1986, 80). Although each show's introduction promised "an unrehearsed program presenting inside opinions and forecasts," the routine movement from issue to Q&A, to argument, to panelists' talking over and past one another in search of the biting putdown, to McLaughlin's closing off debate with, "The answer is," became ritual. Entertaining and comforting, perhaps, but predictable. Moreover, since each panelist has a twenty-four-hour foreknowledge of the "issues" for each show's segment, the claim of being "unrehearsed" was plausible, but in the sense that a professional wrestling match is also unrehearsed.

During its thirteen-year-plus run through 1995, "The McLaughlin Group" went through several changes in panelists. Germond, Kondracke, and Barnes remained as regulars, but Novak and Buchanan departed. (In 1995 their seats were occupied by Eleanor Clift of *Newsweek* and Clarence Page of the *Chicago Tribune*.) Perhaps that is one reason that regular viewers of the show in the mid-1980s, who hypothetically then spent a decade in a remote village without television, returned in the mid-1990s to find that what once was a battle of water balloons had become one of creampuffs. There are other factors. Political "issues" (as defined by McLaughlin's leading, rhetorical, and argumentative questions) changed as America moved from the Reagan 1980s to the Clinton 1990s. Moreover, the ritual of the "Group" is no longer unique, is often imitated, and is less appealing.

Finally, one of the major by-products of McLaughlin's "Group" has been to make McLaughlin and the show's panelists sought-after celebrities. Political journalists, who go unnoticed when they comment about politics, when they adhere to the journalistic conventions of checking with sources or authenticating evidence, are pursued for autographs when, instead, they wildly claim insider knowledge or make shoot-from-the-hip predictions in response to McLaughlin's ringmaster's whip. Wrote one critic, "Excluding Germond, the words 'I don't know' or even 'I think' were not to be found in any of the panelists' vocabulary . . . the members always seemed to have just gotten off the phone with the guy in charge" (Alterman, 1992, 111). As for the accuracy of overall "Group" predictions, a simple coin flip can match them ("The McLaughlin Group Predictions," 1990).

Television celebrity helps ease mythical journalistic poverty. In promoting the "Group" McLaughlin has found it useful to take the program on the road to Houston, Chicago, San Diego, and other cities. For a lucrative fee, corporate, political, educational, and other associations have hired the road-show version of "The McLaughlin Group" to entertain employees, trainees, and conventioneers. The sizable check received by each panelist eases the pain of being outside rather than inside the nation's political nerve center. One of the "Group" regulars, Jack Germond, is very candid about the fact that the commentary is show business and not serious analysis. He told an interviewer that the show is not something to take seriously, and that as a journalist he was not comfortable doing the "Group." However, he has been seduced by the money, a gift from heaven in making alimony payments (Kurtz, 1996).

No technique, no matter how shopworn, is ignored in promoting "The McLaughlin Group." For example, under the auspices of General Electric, the "Group" distributes promotional bookmarks through book retailers across the nation; one side of each 2-inch-by-seven-inch marker recommends "Books That Make Sense of Our Times"; the other touts the "wit and wisdom" and "opinion and commentary" of McLaughlin and his panelists. But, as with any marketing device designed to sell persona, not to explore subsurfaces; encourage people to react to one another, not to respond to audiences; goad them to perform, not to inform, and provoke cheers and jeers, not action, the formula's success depends upon keeping its content secret. (The openly published but always "secret'' formula of Coca-Cola is a case in point [Pendergrast, 1993]). The fact is, however, John McLaughlin's secret has been around since Phineas T. Barnum.

CONCLUSION: COMMENTARY'S POLITICAL BARNUM

It is in the nature of reality that no analogy is isomorphic in every respect. However, the Barnum-McLaughlin analogy possesses sufficient correspondence to warrant consideration. P. T. Barnum, renowned for a phrase he never uttered (''There's a sucker born every minute''), like McLaughlin, was a gifted self-promoter. Also like McLaughlin, Barnum was a Yankee, although he was born in Bethel, Connecticut, rather than in Providence, Rhode Island. And, like McLaughlin, P. T. Barnum failed in a run for the U.S. Congress, namely, as candidate for the House of Representatives in 1867.

Barnum's knack for promotion derived from his inexhaustible fund of ideas continually to surprise and amaze audiences. Before Barnum became king of the traveling circus, ''The Greatest Show on Earth,'' he was the impresario of Barnum's (American) Museum in New York City. Filled with quite ordinary attractions that he posed as the odd and unusual, Barnum drew audiences into his museum by placing pictures of strange creatures on the outside of the building. No such creatures were within, but the pictures alone provoked passersby to go inside to find the unknown. John McLaughlin's claims for an ''unrehearsed'' presentation of ''inside opinions and predictions'' accomplishes much the same purpose, especially when punctuated by the ringmaster's, ''Issue Number One!''

Barnum populated the many rooms in his multistoried museum with hundreds upon hundreds of items, really too many for patrons to see. He had a purpose. By inundating the customers with so much, he worked a suspension in their judgments—they could not tell the real from the fake. Yet, they kept coming back for they were entertained even if not educated. ''The McLaughlin Group'' is a replica: too many opinions, too many prognostications, uttered in response to too many rapidly fired questions in McLaughlin's museum. Viewers cannot distinguish the founded from the unfounded, the grounded from the groundless. Yet, they too keep coming back, entertained if not educated.

One of Barnum's favorite gimmicks consisted of his ''Living Curiosities'' (the politically incorrect vernacular was ''freaks''). There was the diminutive grown man, General ''Tom Thumb''; the youth with a horrid skin infection billed as ''The Leopard Boy''; the grossly overweight being, ''The Fat Man''; a hairy creature called ''J J, the Dog Faced Boy''; and ''Chang and Eng,'' Siamese twins joined at the hip who constantly quarreled over trivial matters (one even tried to strangle the other in a staged performance).

Once, to refurbish his image as an impresario of serious art, ''America's Greatest Showman'' sponsored from 1850 to 1852 a national tour of Jenny Lind, the ''Swedish nightingale.'' (She broke off the tour when she found Barnum was pocketing $5 for every $2 he gave her! Unperturbed, Barnum admitted that the only music he *really* liked was the ring of silver dollars.) Although exploited, each of Barnum's "Living Curiosities" became celebrities in their own right; all had incomes substantially beyond what they could ever earn otherwise and a few, notably Tom Thumb and the Siamese twins, raised their talent fees as a by-product of Barnum's self-promotion.

As posed on "The McLaughlin Group," the liberal-conservative growling and gnashing is less political debate than a staging of a one-person squabble between Siamese twins; as P. T. Barnum good-naturedly joked with Tom Thumb, John McLaughlin briskly smiles through his teeth at his curious panelists. Criticized in 1986 for a lack of "affirmative action" (Remnick, 1986, 82), McLaughlin found his Jenny Lind by adding Eleanor Clift as a regular panelist. Like Barnum's curiosities, McLaughlin's panelists profit financially from the promotion, commanding higher lecture fees than they would otherwise. An infrequent panelist with the "Group" noted,

> Most of the participants are fine people, and some of them have gotten rich and famous for their ability to deliver a quip under pressure. This has not been lost on others who are not yet rich and famous and know that television can make you both. That's why there are those in the fourth estate who will say almost anything on television—things they do not for a moment believe and would never put on paper. (Remnick, 1986, 88)

Ever in search of more promotion, in 1871 P. T. Barnum took his show on the road, " P. T. Barnum's Grand Traveling Museum, Menagerie, and Circus." It played to appreciative audiences as did the road appearances of "The McLaughlin Group" over a century later. There was, however, a price to pay for moving from the intimacy of the museum to the impersonality of the road. Audiences became larger, but there was little interaction between performers and audience members, and the audiences sank into passivity and ultimately ceased coming to the tents. And, although "The Greatest Show on Earth" still tours America, it is but a shell of its former self, no longer able to surprise and amaze. Perhaps if Phineas T. Barnum were still alive, he could resuscitate the spectacle. John McLaughlin, having built his political communication career on similar promotional devices, may face a similar challenge with respect to confrontation for its own sake in his remaining years.

REFERENCES

Selected Critical Works about John McLaughlin

Bethel, T. "Man in a Hurry." *National Review*, 37, December 31, 1985, 110–12.
Liebermann, D. "Item 1: John McLaughlin is (a) TV's Most Powerful Pundit or (b) the Biggest Blowhard." *TV Guide*, May 4, 1991, 14–16.
"McLaughlin, John Joseph." In *Who's Who in America*, vol. 2, 2324–25. New Providence, NJ: Marquis' Who's Who, 1993.

"The McLaughlin Group Predictions, 1989–90." *Regard's*, August 1989–January 1990.

Moritz, C., ed. "McLaughlin, John (Joseph)." In *Current Biography Yearbook 1987*, 404–8. New York: H. W. Wilson, 1988.

Remnick, D. "The McLaughlin Group." *Esquire*, 105, May 1986, 76–88.

Shales, T. "McLaughlin: The Master Immoderator." *Washington Post*, October 30, 1985, B-11.

Selected General Works

Alterman, E. *Sound and Fury: The Washington Punditocracy and the Collapse of American Politics*. New York: HarperCollins, 1992.

Bliss, M. "Read this Column and You, Too, Can Be a Pundit." *Canadian Business*, September 1993, 14–15.

Buchanan, P. J. *Right from the Beginning*. Washington, DC: Regnery, 1990.

Cohen, J., and N. Solomon. *Adventures in Wonderland: Behind the News, behind the Pundits*. Monroe, ME: Common Courage Press, 1993.

Hirsch, A. *Talking Heads: Political Talk Shows and Their Star Pundits*. New York: St. Martin's Press, 1991.

Hitchens, C. "Blabscam: TV's Rigged Political Talk Shows." *Harper's*, March 1987, 75–76.

Kinsley, M. "Mamas, Don't Let Your Babies Grow Up to Be Pundits." *New Yorker*, October 26, 1992, 53–54.

Kurtz, H. *Hot Air: All Talk, All the Time*. New York: Times Books, 1996.

Mencken, H. L. *A Carnival of Buncombe: Writings on Politics*. Baltimore: Johns Hopkins Press, 1956.

Nimmo, D., and J. E. Combs. *The Political Pundits*, 127–28. New York: Praeger, 1992.

Pendergrast, M. *For God, Country and Coca-Cola*. New York: Charles Scribner's Sons, 1993.

Persico, J. *Edward R. Murrow: An American Original*. New York: Dell, 1988.

"P. T. Barnum: America's Greatest Showman." The Discovery Channel, October 15, 1995, 3 hours.

ROBERT (ROBIN) MACNEIL
(January 19, 1931–   )
and
JAMES (CHARLES) LEHRER
(May 19, 1934–   )

Public Television's Breakthrough in Political Commentary

The year 1992 marked the twenty-fifth anniversary of the congressional act that established the Public Broadcasting Service (PBS). PBS was designed to help distribute and promote the network's programming to its members. During the ensuing quarter of a century, public broadcasting's programming has been regularly impaired by a lack of funding. Yet, one of PBS's most pioneering efforts in news broadcasting and political commentary, inaugurated in 1975, has survived the hardships and, after three decades on the air, continues as a major PBS achievement. When Robert MacNeil, attracted by an opportunity to have his own program of televised news analysis, joined New York City's WNET-television to begin broadcasting the "Robert MacNeil Report" on October 20, 1975, he did not imagine that by his retirement, two decades later, the show, now the "MacNeil/Lehrer Newshour," would attract an audience of 2.2 million. PBS' gamble on an hour of straight news, probing interviews, and extended discussion had paid off.

MACNEIL'S ALPHABET: CBC, ITN, RNS, NBC, BBC, NPACT, AND PBS

Robert MacNeil was born on January 19, 1931, in Montreal, Canada, the oldest child of Robert A. S. and Margaret (Oxner) MacNeil. "Peggy and Bob, or Bobby and Peg—as they were variously known" (MacNeil, 1989, 8) were married a scant month before the worldwide stock market crash that generated the Great Depression. For three years, the couple sought work, lost their rented flat, and survived by pure grit. All eventually turned out well. Bobby was a superintendent of the Royal Canadian Mounted Police, then a lieutenant commander in the Royal Canadian Navy during World War II, and a diplomat in the Canadian foreign service thereafter. Peggy was a resourceful, warm, nurturing mother who encouraged her elder son's love of reading and language.

Robert MacNeil and his two younger brothers grew up in Halifax, Nova Scotia, a harbor town that came to life during World War II as a crucial link in the lifeline of survival in shipments from Canada and the United States to Brit-

ain. All three MacNeil brothers had successful careers—Hugh as commander
of NATO's Atlantic standing naval force, Michael in the computer business,
and Robert as a political analyst. Prior to attending a boarding school, young
Robert was a student at Tower Road School, went through endless air raids,
grew up with a double vision of Germans (Nazi scum versus nice Germans),
and fell in love with words and how to use them.

Drawn as he was to the sea by growing up in a maritime setting, Robert
MacNeil planned to follow in his father's footsteps and pursue a career in the
navy. After his high school graduation, Robert took exams to enter the naval
college at Royal Roads, Victoria, British Columbia—all the way across the
continent. He failed the algebra exam and was rejected. "When that happened,
the bottom fell out of both my world and my father's" (Hammer, 1982, 120).
Chastened, he enrolled at Dalhousie University in Halifax and enlisted in the
University Naval Training Division. But, his dream of a career in the navy was
replaced by another when he heard the siren call of the theater: "I stopped
reading about the sea to read plays and books about the theatre. Amazingly, I
had hidden all this from myself, continuing to believe that the Navy was where
I was headed. Lord Nelson got displaced by another hero" (MacNeil, 1989,
125).

In 1950 Robert MacNeil bid college farewell. He dropped out and worked as
an actor in Canadian Broadcasting Corporation (CBC) radio productions. From
there it was but a small step to becoming a radio announcer, then a disc jockey
for CJCH-AM, a commercial radio station in Halifax. Yet, acting was now in
his blood, or so he thought. So he went to New York in hopes of building a
career in the theater. While in New York, MacNeil recalls, "I lived on grapes
and a girlfriend, who was well off" ("MacNeil and Lehrer: PBS' Winning
Team," 1987, 95). The enterprise was futile: "It was as though a voice spoke
to me out of the sky, like the voice of God, and said, 'You're a bloody fool to
think of yourself as an actor . . . What you really are is a writer' " (1987, 95).

In 1951 MacNeil returned to Canada and enrolled in Carleton University in
Ottawa, where he majored in English and worked as a radio announcer for CJCH
in Halifax. In the fall of 1952, he was offered a job at CFRA in Ottawa where
he was announcer for a classical music show, "Symphony Hall." He stayed
with CFRA for a year and a half as an announcer, control operator, and news
copy editor, his first taste of professional journalism. He departed CFRA for the
CBC, "a large organisation and to join it was a little like joining the government" (MacNeil, 1989, 200). Despite the size of the CBC, Robert MacNeil's
career flourished. When the CBC started its television service, MacNeil began
as a television announcer, but quickly moved into reporting. Promoted to host
of a weekly program designed for children, "Let's Go to the Museum," a
weekly thirty-minute show filmed at the National Museum of Canada, MacNeil
interviewed experts on archaeology, pre-Columbian culture, and various other
topics. Several "bright children" appeared as "foils." The program, which was

well received, ran twenty-six weeks, and MacNeil came away with his first training in television reporting and interviewing.

In the spring of 1955, Robert MacNeil completed his B.A. degree in English at Carleton. Once again, the siren call of the theater beckoned: he moved to England to become a playwright. Again his theatrical career was short lived. MacNeil wanted to get married, and he needed a way to support his new wife. So he put aside his aspirations to become another William Shakespeare and returned to journalism: "beyond the mere permission to witness, journalism also permits you to share the experience of many professions, to live them vicariously—historians, archaeologists . . . the list is endless" (MacNeil, 1982, 10).

MacNeil found work as a subeditor at the newly established Independent Television News (ITN) in London. In 1955 he joined the London bureau of Reuters News Service (RNS) as a writer and was a stringer for the CBC. During his five years with Reuters, he wrote stories on some of those years' biggest events: the Suez Canal crisis and the Hungarian revolution in 1956. It was a period of growing political awareness for Robert MacNeil: "My attention had never been so concentrated on politics. As a result, I was politically awakened and the basic responses I discovered in myself colored my political attitudes ever since" (MacNeil, 1982, 29). Soon he was a foreign correspondent for Reuters, a job that "heightened" his desire to travel (1982, 50).

Thus, in 1960, with a choice between working at the *Financial Times* in London, with no prospects for travel, or for NBC News, with a greater potential for travel, Robert MacNeil decided to join the U.S. broadcast network as a London-based roving foreign correspondent. While at NBC News, MacNeil covered the civil war in Algeria, the Congolese national conflict, the construction of the Berlin Wall, and the Cuban missile crisis. While covering the crisis surrounding the building of the Berlin Wall, MacNeil took pictures of Russian soldiers and tanks. East German officials sought to confiscate the photos. According to MacNeil, from this experience, he became a "much fiercer defender of civil liberties in the West," and he gained a better grasp of the roots of opposition to Soviet totalitarianism (1982, 114).

In March 1963, Robert MacNeil moved from London to Washington, D.C., as NBC correspondent to the White House to cover President John Kennedy. In July he filed reports of the March on Washington staged by leaders of the civil rights movement. As White House correspondent, MacNeil was responsible for reporting the president's reaction to the event. "Broadcast reporters do not deal with the nuance on the White House beat. The fierce competition made us errand boys, dashing from briefing to microphone with scribbled notes for fifty-second spots on the hourly news" (1982, 190). That his "sketchily prepared," nonanalytical accounts aired amazed MacNeil.

On November 21 and 22, 1963, NBC's Robert MacNeil reported on President Kennedy's ill-fated trip to Dallas and his assassination. It was a "niche into journalistic infamy" (Guly, 1995, 27). In his memoir, *The Right Place at the Right Time* (1982), MacNeil recalls the events immediately following the shots that killed Kennedy, "I ran into the first building I came to . . . it was the Texas Book Depository. As I ran up the steps . . . a young man in shirt sleeves was coming out"—Lee Harvey Oswald, the suspected gunman (1982, 208). MacNeil is unsure whether he talked with Oswald immediately following the shooting, but he characterizes Kennedy's assassination as "an incredible story," one that caused him as a journalist to learn to follow his instinct on where to be during breaking news.

In May 1965 MacNeil became anchor of NBC's expanded, sixty-minute nightly newscasts at WNBC-TV in New York, "Sixth Hour News." In September, NBC paired correspondents Robert MacNeil and Ray Scherer as anchors of the network Saturday evening news. MacNeil also broadcast news on the radio NBC affiliate and compiled several documentaries. Given his steady workload, he was unprepared in January 1967 when NBC proposed a six-month assignment as a foreign correspondent in Vietnam. He refused.

Later, Robert MacNeil's convictions against the Vietnam War, and the media coverage of the war, contributed to his analysis of journalism and its mission in the evolving world of television. He wrote, "I slowly became aware of its frequent triviality, its distorting brevity, its obsession with action and movement, its infantile attention span, and its profound lack of thoughtful analysis" (MacNeil, 1982, 239). MacNeil departed NBC in 1967 and wrote *The People Machine* (1968), a book about the structure and declining value of television news as it functioned in the 1960s. Many of the sentiments he voiced then he continued to hold almost three decades later at his retirement, namely, television journalism, in "bottom-line terms," is a disaster (Reibstein, 1995, 88).

After NBC, Robert MacNeil returned to noncommercial television. He took a position as a reporter for the British Broadcasting Corporation (BBC) on "Panorama," a BBC documentary series, which he said later, "makes *60 Minutes* look like its pale grandchild" (Moritz, 1980, 237). MacNeil traveled between Britain and the United States covering such events as Martin Luther King's assassination in April 1968, Robert Kennedy's assassination in June 1968, and the riots at the Democratic National Convention in August 1968. These events, according to MacNeil, captured a picture of the United States that exposed its spirit and its dark soul; media coverage "left each American to sort out and explain the colliding images for himself, to make them fit some subjective consistency. It was hard: even the best informed of us were baffled" (MacNeil, 1982, 246). By 1995 he found little had improved in political coverage: "American journalism has found ways to follow the crowd and to find the cheaper end of the carnival sideshow. . . . That's always been there" (Hickey, 1995, 30).

In September 1971, Robert MacNeil resigned from the BBC and returned to the United States to join the National Public Affairs Center for Television (NPACT) as a senior correspondent covering the presidential election season. NPACT, the public broadcasting's version of a network news organization, was housed at WETA-TV in Washington, D.C. According to Alfred Vecchione, director of production for NPACT, "The company was formed by the public broadcasting community to become the sole producer and distributor of national public affairs programs'' (''MacNeil/Lehrer/Vecchione,'' 1990, 95). NPACT was also in charge of the production of ''Washington Week in Review,'' PBS' weekly discussion of national news by Washington journalist-pundits (Nimmo & Combs, 1992, 124–25). Robert MacNeil became the WWR co-anchor of both ''A Public Affair/Election '72'' and, a year later, a televised newsmagazine follow-up, ''America '73.''

Robert MacNeil and the president of the Corporation for Public Broadcasting, Robert Loomis, quarreled over Loomis' plan to limit public television programming. When MacNeil's suspicions that the administration of President Richard Nixon sought to control public broadcasting and turn NPACT into a pro-Nixon propaganda administration, MacNeil resigned from NPACT in 1973. MacNeil, however, did not leave his post until the completion of PBS' televising of the Senate Watergate Hearings for which he was paired with James Lehrer as co-anchor. A year later, when the House Judiciary Committee held impeachment hearings regarding President Richard Nixon's involvement in the Watergate scandal, Robert MacNeil covered them, but for the BBC, not PBS. After Nixon's resignation, MacNeil conducted a televised interview with his successor, President Gerald Ford, on May 24, 1975. He also had the task of preparing several well-received BBC documentaries that were broadcast throughout the world.

In June 1975, ''I backed into my smartest decision yet, to take a risk on something that has proved to be the most liberating and satisfying thing I have done, *The MacNeil/Lehrer Newshour*'' (MacNeil, 1982, 298). It was, at that time, the ''Robert MacNeil Report,'' a coproduction of WNET and WETA. However, its early success promised that the newscast might be even more popular if extended to a national audience. PBS offered the broadcast to its 250 member stations, and by May 1976, the show had become the first nightly national show in the history of public broadcasting.

LEHRER'S BUS TRIP TO PUBLIC TELEVISION

James Lehrer has always been fascinated with busses. He even wrote two books about his romance with them, *We Were Dreamers* (1975) and *A Bus of My Own* (1992). He comes by his fascination naturally. Born in Wichita, Kansas, on May 19, 1934, Lehrer was the younger son of Harry Frederich Lehrer, who worked for the Santa Fe Trailways bus company until 1946. He then bought three busses of his own—Betsy, Susie, and Lena—and opened up the Kansas Central Lines. Lois Catherine Lehrer, Jim's mother, was a teacher of English and Latin, who moved to Washington, D.C., to work with the War Department, where she met Harry, then a member of the U.S. Marine Corps. Even with sons Jim and Fred working for the family business, the line failed, and the family moved to Beaumont, Texas, then to San Antonio, Texas, in 1948.

Like Robert MacNeil, James Lehrer planned to follow in his father's footsteps, but with a bus on land, not a ship at sea. However, Lehrer also heard a siren call, one that eventually captured MacNeil. It was writing. He decided to become a sports writer. He edited San Antonio Jefferson High School's newspaper, continued his interest in journalism at Victoria College in 1954, and two years later graduated with a B.A. in journalism from the University of Missouri, a school that has produced many of the most noted sports writers and broadcasters in the nation.

As with another late twentieth-century political commentator, Bernard Shaw (q.v.), James Lehrer joined the U.S. Marines Corps. Even boot camp did not stamp out his ambitions to be a journalist; instead, it encouraged them and he edited the camp newspaper. Discharged as a marine captain in 1959 after a tour in Okinawa, Lehrer joined the *Dallas Morning News* as a cub political reporter. His series of articles, "Barbecue Bolshevism," which proved that allegations of nook-and-cranny communism were unfounded, won him awards. But, when a series he wrote exposing the tactics of the conservative, anticommunist John Birch Society was killed by the *Morning News* editor, Lehrer resigned in 1959. A few months after becoming a court reporter and political columnist for the now defunct *Dallas Times Herald*, Jim Lehrer married a schoolteacher, Kate Tom Staples, now a successful novelist. In 1968 Lehrer became city editor of the newspaper. However, in his spare time, he started writing humorous novels—a sideline he continues after publishing a half-dozen successful works— and decided in 1969 to become a full-time novelist.

A year later he recanted his decision and returned to journalism, but as a broadcaster-consultant for the Dallas public television station, KERA. At KERA he had his first nightly newscast, "Newsroom." James Lehrer liked public television and, when the job of public affairs coordinator of PBS in Washington, D.C., was created, he became the first occupant. This was 1972, however, and Lehrer's plans for expanding the role of PBS fell afoul of the same cutbacks and control battles that Robert MacNeil faced. So he left his coordinator's job and joined WETA-TV in Washington as correspondent for NPACT. He also became one of the commentators on MacNeil's "America '73." MacNeil recalls his early relationship with Lehrer:

> We learned a lot from each other. I could tell him a few things about television technology, but . . . he did a great deal to improve my interview style. I painfully learned from Lehrer that some of the most effective questions are "Why," "I don't understand," and "Could you say that again?" (Moritz, 1987, 351).

Thus was added to the notable teams of political commentators Martha Rountree and Lawrence E. Spivak (q.v.), and David Brinkley (q.v.) and Chet Huntley, that of MacNeil/Lehrer.

"A RATHER QUIETER, MORE THOUGHTFUL PROGRAM"

In January 1976, the year the MacNeil/Lehrer tandem debuted on PBS nationally, Alfred Vecchione joined the newscast as the executive producer: "I thought the idea was a very sound, solid one, and I wanted to be a part of it'' (''MacNeil/Lehrer/Vecchione,'' 1990, 95). In September 1976, the ''Robert MacNeil Report'' was renamed the ''MacNeil/Lehrer Report,'' and James Lehrer joined MacNeil as coanchor. The format was designed to be a supplement, not to supplant, the commercial networks' nightly news broadcasts. Incorporating background material, panel discussions, interviews with experts, and occasional filmed segments, the report provided probing coverage and analysis of a single news story each night. The staff consisted of two anchors, assigned in New York and Washington, and a team of reporters, who briefed the correspondents on assigned areas. Topics in the early days included national politics, foreign affairs, Congress, or business and economics.

The anchors did not create a hostile environment with confrontational questions. In fact, the staff sought to avoid the cross-examination techniques that frequent other public affairs programs. ''What you have in the end product doesn't have to be labeled fact, opinion, analysis, interpretation—it is the nearest thing to making each member of the viewing public a reporter himself, able to seek out facts from the sources who know them and to discover what they mean'' (MacNeil, 1982, 311).

It took some time for its audience to warm up to the concept of the new program, but after a few years, the ''MacNeil/Lehrer Report'' was the showpiece of the PBS schedule. On September 5, 1983, the show was expanded to a one-hour format, and the name was changed to ''The MacNeil/Lehrer Newshour.'' To wield more control over the program, Robert MacNeil, James Lehrer, and Alfred Vecchione formed a production company called MacNeil/Lehrer Productions. As president of the company, Vecchione commented, ''We wanted to be a bit more in command of our own destiny'' and ''at the same time, we also thought we could veer out a little bit and start to get ourselves involved in other kinds of programs'' (''MacNeil/Lehrer/Vecchione,'' 1990, 95). The company produced several projects on a variety of topics, including contemporary life in China, learning in American schools, and health care in America. As a tool for political commentary, the ''MacNeil/Lehrer Report'' and ''Newshour'' have tackled many controversial topics, such as the environmental causes of cancer, the legalization of marijuana, white-collar crime, welfare reform, and drug trafficking. Over the years, the program has attracted a loyal audience base, and the primary agents assert that they have a demographically diverse program, which provides an open forum for intellectual discussion.

Since its inception as PBS' first national newscast, the MacNeil/Lehrer pioneering format has been through several changes in design and detail. In 1983 Jim Lehrer suffered a heart attack and underwent double-bypass surgery, and he took a leave from the''Newshour'' to recover. His return in 1984 coincided with the decision of 100 PBS affiliates to help underwrite a face-lift for the program. ''MacNeil/Lehrer'' has remained a successful newscast throughout, earning a respectable rating in most markets (''Watchdog Group Gives Poor Marks to 'Nightline,' '' 1990, 68).

One of the reasons we continue to do well each year in audience size and recognition is that, while the others are sort of flying away into more sensational definitions of what news programs are, we stay very much the same. . . . Their news departments are more and more like circus sideshows where they have to be barking outside saying, "Look, our news is better than theirs." (MacNeil in Guly, 1995, 26)

Acknowledging the power a news anchor possesses, MacNeil contends that commercial news dramatizes the national agenda, which leads to sensationalism. "MacNeil/Lehrer," by contrast, offers viewers information without censorship, except for the choice of the topic that will be discussed and the guests who will appear. Selection and preparation of guests, however, is precisely what the critics of "MacNeil/Lehrer" focus upon. Despite MacNeil/Lehrer claims of objectivity and a free exchange of ideas, critics argue that the program is mainly composed of European-American males, who provide the narrow view of the upper middle class. Fairness and Accuracy in Reporting (FAIR), a media watchdog group, reported that in a study they found the program to be male dominated, government oriented, and conservative. Moreover, FAIR's study argues that the guests on the program are "rarely balanced by members of public interest, minority or left-wing groups" ("Watchdog Group Gives Poor Marks to Nightline," 1990, 68). Other critics stress that, to be sure,

on network television, where the level of production quality tends to be higher, most interviews are preceded by lengthy "pre-interviews," in which producers find out what the interviewee will say and outline what he [*sic*] will be asked. Such predigestion is considered essential if the interview is to pass as adequate television. This process of "casting" interviews, often in search of conflict or other television values, takes place even on such hallowed ground as *The MacNeil/Lehrer News Hour.* (Rosenstiel, 1995, 26)

Neither the comoderators nor the producers of "MacNeil/Lehrer" agree with such criticism. Robert MacNeil described the mission of the "Newshour":

We take the instruments of democracy quite seriously. We don't see ourselves as a kind of opposition to the government . . . [but] as a kind of mediating influence between the government and the people. One effect of our program is to bring in various people who form various sides to discuss an issue. This allows the viewer to make a synthesis. That is different for journalism, because journalism is usually its own synthesis. (Guly, 1995, 27)

Moreover, said MacNeil, "We don't appeal exclusively to an elitist audience. In fact, one-third of our viewers have a college education or less. . . . our evenhandedness on issues is what attracts the audience, and the show offers an alternative to commercial network newscasts" (Hammer, 1982, 119).

In October 1994, Robert MacNeil announced his departure from "The Mac-

Neil/Lehrer Newshour,'' on the program's twentieth anniversary in October 1995. Characterizing his decision as "convenient," James Lehrer became anchor of the reconstituted "Newshour with Jim Lehrer." Analysts speculated that MacNeil's departure was partly due to financial reasons; the program's funding was slashed substantially in the early 1990s (Chua-Eoan, 1994, 85). MacNeil's retirement cuts the program's expenses by deleting a costly salary and expenses for running his office in New York. MacNeil denied the claim but commented, "We needed for the good of everybody to make the decision" (Chua-Eoan, 1994, 85). " 'The MacNeil/Lehrer Newshour' has been the highlight of my career . . . since I don't think anyone paused with amazement at anything I ever did in my reporting days" (Guly, 1995, 27).

> I was not born a journalist . . . but it's not given to many people to be able to create a shop with your closest friend, hire all friends and run it the way you think it should be run with almost no interference or steering from anyone else—and get away with it. (Reibstein, 1995, 88)

REFERENCES

Selected Works by Robert MacNeil and James Lehrer

Lehrer, J. *A Bus of My Own*. New York: G. Putnam's, 1992.
Lehrer, J. *We Were Dreamers*. New York: Atheneum, 1975.
MacNeil, R. *The People Machine: The Influence of Television on American Politics*. New York: Harper and Row, 1968.
———. *The Right Place at the Right Time*. Boston: Little, Brown, 1982.
———. *The Story of English*. With R. McCrum and W. Cran. New York: Viking, 1986.
———. *The Way We Were*. Editor. New York: Carroll & Graf, 1988.
———. *Wordstruck: A Memoir*. New York: Viking, 1989.

Selected Critical Works about Robert MacNeil and James Lehrer

Chua-Eoan, C. "And Then There Was One." *Time*, October 24, 1994, 85.
Guly, C. "MacNeil's Legacy: 'Smart News.' " *The Quill*, 83, June 1995, 24–27.
Hammer, J. "Newscaster Robert MacNeil Is Happy to Take a Firm Stand on Both Sides of the Issues." *People*, September 20, 1982, 119–120.
Hickey, N. "The Good, the Bad, and the 'Gloriously Boring.' " *Columbia Journalism Review* 34 (May/June 1995): 27–32.
"MacNeil and Lehrer PBS's Winning Team." *Broadcasting*, August 3, 1987, 94–95.
" 'MacNeil/Lehrer Newshour': Is It Here to Stay?" *Broadcasting*, September 3, 1984, 48–49.
" 'MacNeil-Lehrer Newshour': Where Less Is Much Better." *Television-Radio Age*, February 8, 1988, 32.
"MacNeil/Lehrer/Vecchione." *Broadcasting*, June 7, 1990, 95.
Moritz, C., ed. "Lehrer, James (Charles)." In *Current Biography Yearbook 1987*, 350–53. New York: H. W. Wilson, 1987.

————. "MacNeil, Robert." In *Current Biography 1980*, 236–39. New York: H. W. Wilson, 1980.

"News Anchors Address the Power of the Chair." *Broadcasting*, March 23, 1987, 136–37.

Nimmo, D., and J. Combs. *The Political Pundits*. New York: Praeger, 1992.

Reibstein, L. "Good Night, Robin." *Newsweek*, October 30, 1995, 88.

Rosentiel, R. "Yakety-Yak: The Lost Art of Interviewing." *Columbia Journalism Review* 32 (January/February 1995): 23–27.

"Watchdog Group Gives Poor Marks to 'Nightline,' 'MacNeil/Lehrer.' " *Broadcasting*, May 28, 1990, 68–69.

H. L. (HENRY LOUIS) MENCKEN

(September 12, 1880–January 29, 1956)

Iconoclastic Political Commentary

Iconolatry, or idolatry, the worship of icons or images, is associated with religious adoration, reverence, and veneration. The twentieth-century's emphasis on mass communication of the printed and electronic word and picture gave birth to political idolatry, an era when the pervasive worship of publicized political images and celebrities replaced the personal, face-to-face, backstage of rough-and-tumble politics characteristic of earlier times. No critic of these sacred political idols, no political iconoclast, was as vocal in denunciation of the new iconolatry during the first half of the twentieth century as was H. L. Mencken; none of his imitators in the second half have been nearly as direct, acid-tongued, and stiletto penned as Mencken. He gave political commentary an unmatched tone and style unique to the era.

To be sure, Mencken attacked Americans' all-too-ignorant homage to celebrity before "celebrity" became a household word. He turned his attention instead to America's highly visible "successes": the politics of Calvin Coolidge, the theology of William Jennings Bryan, the philosophy of democracy, the intolerance of modern-day Puritans. Both during his life and after his death, Mencken's iconoclastic writings provoked condemnation from true believers. In times of political correctness they still do. Yet, his commentary was a warning that

> the regimentation that is really to be feared in American life is not the regimentation imposed from without, by bayonets and policemen's clubs; it is the regimentation imposed from within, by adoration of "the bitch-goddess Success." Regimentation imposed from without is accepted sullenly and will be rejected at the first opportunity; but regimentation accomplished by a man's own decision to go along with the crowd is deterioration of character and likely to be permanent. (Manchester, 1962, 12)

THE MAKING OF A WHANGDOODLE

Early in his journalistic career at the Baltimore *Sun*, H. L. Mencken devoted an editorial to Colonel Henry Watterson, feisty editor of the Louisville *Courier-Journal*. Watterson figured in molding the careers of several key political commentators of the twentieth century, including Arthur Krock (q.v.) and Robert Allen, the cofounder of "The Washington Merry-Go-Round" column with Drew Pearson (q.v.). Mencken depicted Watterson astride a "galloping cayuse" (Manchester, 1962, 51). Watterson returned the compliment in his own editorial about the young Mencken, "Think of it! The staid old Baltimore *Sun* has got itself a Whangdoodle," namely, a scribbler who produces a loud, reverberant noise with the lashing, whiplike words of his typewriter (Bode, 1986, 41).

Although he was not reared to be a "Whangdoodle," scribbling and whanging were, in part, in Mencken's genes. His grandfather, Burkhardt Ludwig Mencken, who emigrated from Germany to Baltimore in 1848, was an articulate agnostic who hanged the God of his forefathers. An earlier ancestor, Johann Mencken, had been a scribbler of published satires that hanged pedants at the University of Leipzig. Born Henry Louis Mencken, H. L. was the son of Augustus and Anna Margaret (Abhau) Mencken. Following in his father's footsteps, Augustus had been a cigar maker by trade and, with his brother, founded a prosperous Baltimore factory that manufactured cigars. Augustus deemed that his eldest child, Henry Louis, should eventually be a cigar maker as well. To be sure, the most characteristic photographs of H. L. Mencken depict him with a cigar in his mouth or between his fingers, but the young Henry Louis never wanted to manufacture the product. Instead he aspired to become a writer.

Born in Baltimore on September 12, 1880, Henry Louis Mencken lived there for the whole of his life, mostly in the same row house, at 1524 Hollins Street, that the Mencken family moved to when Henry was three years old and his brother Charlie, was twenty-one months younger. On Hollins Street two other siblings were born, August, Jr., who years later looked after Mencken after H. L.'s disabling stroke in 1948, and Gertrude. Henry was a precocious child; he walked, talked, and read well before other children his age. At age six he attended the Friedrich Knapp Institute, and aside from those subjects requiring rote memorization, such as German, he did well. He became a member of the Hollins Street "gang," waging skirmishes against other street gangs, carrying the banner of the local fire engine house, and providing election-night bonfires for the neighborhood. In spite of the continuing efforts of Augustus, an avid baseball fan and part owner of a baseball club, to make an athlete of Henry, it never happened.

By age eight Henry had discovered the thrills that come from avid reading—magazines, newspapers, and books, especially the works of Mark Twain. So interested did he become in the written word that he pestered the management of a weekly newspaper to teach him the mechanics of publishing; before long, he had his own press and was printing calling cards, insignia, and a neighborhood newspaper. He even printed a business card for himself. Heretofore, Mencken had always signed himself "Henry L," but, since all his lower case "r's" were broken, he printed "H. L. Mencken" instead. He never again used any other byline.

Mencken graduated from the Knapp Institute and entered Baltimore Polytechnic Institute. Again he excelled, led his class, and gave the valedictory address on June 23, 1896. Augustus insisted that Mencken join the family tobacco firm, Aug. Mencken and Bro. Mencken insisted that he wanted to try to land a job with the Baltimore *Morning Herald*. The compromise was that Mencken would work in the tobacco firm only so long as he did not secure a writing position. So, for two and a half years, Mencken devoted his working hours to tobacco, his leisure to reading and to taking a correspondence school writing course. His work, according to the school readers, exceeded that of other students. Then, fortune intervened. Augustus died of an acute kidney infection on January 13, 1899. Mencken's mother released him from any legal connection to the family firm.

On January 16, 1899, H. L. Mencken sought employment with the Baltimore *Morning Herald*. Since he had no journalistic experience and had published nothing, all he received from the newspaper's city editor (who thought Mencken's name was "Macon") was a promise that, if Mencken kept turning up, then the paper might give him an assignment should an opening occur. For over six weeks, Mencken turned up at the *Morning Herald* daily. Then, on February 23, he received an assignment to go to a small community and report anything that was going on (the newspaper's reporter assigned to cover the village had dropped out of sight). Mencken turned up one story, a five-line account of the theft of a horse, buggy, and harness from a local stable. The newspaper ran Mencken's story the next morning. Thereafter, "Macon" received a sufficient number of regular assignments to master the news craft and to earn for himself a payroll position, a trolley-car passbook, and a beat assignment as a crime reporter. By the time he was twenty-five years old, Mencken had moved successively from police-court reporter to city hall correspondent, drama critic, Sunday editor, editorial writer (writing news "colyums"), managing editor, and, finally, editor in chief.

It was while he was serving as drama critic that H. L. Mencken learned a lesson that set the tone of his political commentary for the remainder of his long career. The paper's managing editor, the former drama critic, defined a fundamental principle of criticism:

> The first job of a reviewer is to write a good story—produce something that people will enjoy reading. If he has nothing to say he simply can't do it. If he has, then it doesn't make much sense whether what he says is fundamentally sound or not. Exact and scientific criticism is not worth trying for. . . . Don't hesitate to use the actors roughly: they are mainly idiots. And don't take a dramatist's pretensions too seriously: he is usually only a showman. (Mencken, 1989a, 111–12)

Insert "political commentator" for "reviewer," "voters for actors," and "politician" for "dramatist," and the result is Mencken's guiding orientation toward political writing.

H. L. Mencken learned something else for future reference during his early reporting career. That was the liberating influence of adhering to a strict, disciplined routine. He believed that if he ritualized his work routine so that trivial decisions were dictated by a formula, he was then freed to exercise his creativity in important matters. With few exceptions he remained steadfast to the work routine he fashioned in his early twenties: awaken at a reasonable hour, eat a light breakfast, trolley to the newspaper, prepare his copy, break for daily lunch at the same cafe, complete his work, return to Hollins Street, dine, excuse himself, tread up to his third-floor workroom, read a wide variety of materials, settle behind his battered typewriter, compose his project of the evening (stopping to wash his hands vigorously from time to time), break off at 10:00 P.M., meet one or more friends for a drink (beer or a ginger beer-gin-lime) at his favorite bar, return home, and retire.

As his career progressed, the nature of his nocturnal writing projects changed. In the early days he supplemented his reporter's income by ghostwriting business and travel brochures, advertising copy, short stories, even poetry. Later he wrote reviews for, then edited, the *Smart Set*; edited the *American Mercury* and other magazines; and wrote more short stories (forty in all) and his proliferating books from the attic on Hollins Street. Only on weekends, or when traveling on out-of-town work, did the routine change. Those times, and one other. That occurred in 1904 when he covered the Baltimore fire that began on the evening of February 6 and leveled much of the city in the ensuing days. The *Morning Herald* offices were destroyed, and the staff was forced to work out of publishing plants in Washington, D.C., and Philadelphia.

Although the newspaper continued publication for another two years, it never recovered from the disaster and closed in June 1906. With it went Mencken's job, but not for long. Passing up offers that would have forced him to leave his beloved Baltimore, including one from the *New York Times*, Mencken joined the Baltimore *Sun*. With only brief interruptions he remained at the *Sun* for the rest of his life. After five years of editing and editorial writing, H. L. Mencken began a daily bylined column designed by him, and the *Sun*, to satisfy two criteria: be "irresponsible and readable" (Manchester, 1962, 78). During its run from 1911 to 1915, the column remained steadfast to both requirements. No icon was immune to Mencken's mischievous, rude, humorous, witty, mocking, irreverent, and refreshing style: democracy, direct primaries, prohibition, blue laws, taxation, political reformers (the "Uplifters"), prominent leaders ("Honorary Pallbearers"), and all forms of Puritanism and puritanism. By contrast, he defended such social and political pariahs as prostitutes, alcohol, and the divorced. "The Freelance" was outrageous, appealingly so to its defenders, damningly so to its detractors—none of its many readers were on the fence. The column made H. L. Mencken one of the foremost polemical writers of the day, and it was the blueprint for his later political commentaries.

In 1908 Mencken became the literary editor and reviewer for the *Smart Set*. (He became coeditor in 1914.) The literary monthly gave Mencken a monthly forum, a 5,000-word column evaluating books, to critique the American social scene, especially politics, in any fashion he chose. His reviews over the course of fifteen years made him not only a literary critic of considerable stature, but a political force as well. When he founded the *American Mercury* with George

Nathan in 1924, Mencken left the *Smart Set*, and his articles in the *Mercury* moved him to the center stage as an iconoclastic critic with "the largest following ever had by a publicist in that position (Cairns, 1982, xxi). The Whangdoodler had reached his zenith.

MENCKEN'S CRITIQUE OF DEMOCRACY

H. L. Mencken deemed himself a realist. The only way a society could cope with reality, he believed, was by basing action on verifiable, factual knowledge generated through scientific inquiry. Philosophy, religion, trial and error, and other forms of so-called knowledge were, for Mencken, mere superstition and prejudice. His faith in scientifically based knowledge grounded his view of politics. Democratic theory and practice, he argued, derived from untested, unverifiable assumptions. The chief of these untenable prejudices, he claimed repeatedly, was that human beings are capable of the rational action essential to self-government: "If x is the population of the United States and y is the degree of imbecility of the average American, then democracy is the theory that $x \times y$ is less than y" (Mencken, 1956, 621). Citizens are a "booboisie," an ignorant, prejudiced, and superstitious lot easily bamboozled and not to be trusted with political power (Mencken, 1926). Hence, "Democracy is the art and science of running the circus from the monkey-cage" (Mencken, 1956, 622).

Were Mencken's views more verifiable, hence, more realistic than those of conventional democratic theory, or were they simply more pessimistic? When he first began voicing them, as early as his commentaries in "The Freelance," Mencken had precious little empirical evidence, beyond recounting the "buffooneries" he found in the daily democratic practice, to draw upon. However, rather naively, when the U.S. military began using mental tests during World War I to gauge the intellect of soldiers, finding that almost two-thirds of those tested had the mental ability of a thirteen-year-old, Mencken delighted in the discovery. By the time regular, systematic studies of voters began to be compiled in the 1940s, Mencken was no longer writing a great deal about public affairs. Had he been he would have taken delight. He would have relished the seeming confirmation that few citizens take an active interest in politics, know anything about electoral candidates other than their party label, barely know who their elected representative are, and have minimal knowledge of even the most highly publicized issues. The romanticized citizen of democratic theory, it appeared, did not exist; the "booboisie" was real (Combs & Nimmo, 1996).

Mencken's realism, however, did not extend to an outright rejection of democracy. For one thing, democracy's buffooneries supplied him with endless copy for his columns: "I confess, for my part, that it greatly delights me. I enjoy democracy immensely. It is incomparably idiotic, and hence incomparably amusing" (Mencken, 1956, 168). Another was that he realistically assessed that democracy's alternatives—monarchy, authoritarianism in its many guises, and totalitarianism in its—were no better, and certainly were far less amusing.

Moreover, a few of democracy's principles—in the rare cases when it was actually practiced—recommended the governmental form. One was equality before the law, essential in light of Mencken's acceptance of the natural inequality of human beings. Another was limited government:

> The Fathers of the Republic, who seem to have been men of suspicious minds, apparently foresaw that the theory of democracy might develop along such lines [all power to politicians], and they went to some trouble to prevent it. Their chief device to that end was the scheme of limited powers. Rejecting the old concept of government as a kind of primal entity, ordained by God and beyond human control, they tried to make it a mere creature of the people. So far it could go, but no further. (Mencken, 1995, 49)

And, the principle of free speech should be inviolate, no matter how disturbing, profane, subversive, or insensitive the utterance. But, asserted Mencken, such "liberty and democracy are," in reality, "eternal enemies"; for "a democratic state may profess to venerate" freedom, "and even pass laws making it officially sacred," yet "to prevent the wildest anarchy in thought and act, the government must put limits upon the free play of opinion" (Mencken, 1995, 35). And, as Mencken demonstrated time and time again, government does.

H. L. Mencken was no respecter of politicians. If his father's favorite sport was baseball, Mencken's favorite pastime was, instead, "damning politicians up hill and down dale" as "rogues and vagabonds, frauds and scoundrels" (Mencken, 1956, 148). Of President Ulysses Grant, he wrote that "intelligence has been commoner among American Presidents than high character, but Grant ran against the stream by having a sort of character without any visible intelligence whatever." Of President Warren Harding he penned, "No one on this earth has ever heard Hon. Mr. Harding say anything intelligent." President Calvin Coolidge he called a "mannequin in a cloak and suit atelier" (Mencken, 1995, 33–34). Woodrow Wilson Mencken dismissed as a Puritan and Libertine (no compliment); Theodore Roosevelt as a might-have-been, but wasn't; and Franklin Roosevelt as a preposterous practitioner of political quackery (Manchester, 1962).

No political venue sparked Mencken's urge to deflate pretensions and pompous egos as did those of the quadrennial gatherings of the nominating conventions of the national political parties. Starting in 1904, H. L. Mencken could be seen regularly in the press gallery—hair flattened on his head and parted in the middle, in a wilting seersucker suit, chomping at a cigar—absorbing the buffooneries of the nation's political elite: "the imbecile paralogia of the speeches; the almost inconceivable nonsense of the platform; the low buffooneries of the Southern delegates, white and black; the swindling of the visitors by the local apostles of Service; the bootlegging and boozing; the gaudy scenes in the hall"

(Mencken, 1980, 75). Written about the Republican National Convention, Mencken's words could apply, excluding the reference to bootlegging, to almost any convention in the twentieth century.

Mencken's assessments of the prospects of various candidates were sometimes accurate, sometimes off the mark. Yet, they were always entertaining. For example, he erroneously estimated Franklin Roosevelt's chances, immediately after nomination, of defeating Herbert Hoover in 1932, as unlikely. Roosevelt, wrote Mencken, impresses beholders as "shallow and futile" with a "Christian Science smile" with "tenor overtones in his voice" (Mencken, 1980, 256). By contrast, Mencken's observations of the transformations in American conventions wrought by the arrival of broadcasting were acute. In 1932 he exposed the backstage maneuvering for radio time among Democrats: "The evening session, in fact, had been postponed to nine o'clock to get a radio hookup and every fourth-rate local leader in the hall, male or female, tried for a crack at the microphone" (Mencken, 1959, 207). In the year of his last convention reporting, 1948, Mencken devoted a column to the meticulous stage managing of the Republican convention and the removal of individuality and spontaneity to take advantage of a new medium, television.

FDR was the favorite target of HLM. Mencken detested the New Deal as unwarranted interference in the economic and political spheres, and as a threat to individual freedom. His published critique of the Roosevelt administration, however iconoclastic, lacked the bite and venom readers had come to expect. Instead his columns were cerebral and driven by logic, not invective. As a result of his persuasiveness and logic, he emerged as the foremost advocate of America's old order in the face of tumultuous change. Mencken did not, however, set aside wit and humor in attacking the New Deal. He exploited the comic; for example, of the New Deal he wrote, "If there is something you want but can't get, it will get that something for you. And, contrawise, if there is something you want and have got, it will take it away" (Mencken, 1995, 48).

It was FDR, however, who got the last laugh, at a Gridiron Dinner in Washington, D.C., on December 8, 1934. Both Mencken and the president were speakers. Mencken spoke first, acknowledged the press, but scarcely mentioned the New Deal. For his part, Roosevelt provided a copious listing of criticisms of the press. He spoke of the "stupidity, cowardice, and Philistinism of working newspaper men." The journalist is a "romantic" who aspires to high ideals, but succumbs to be a "jackass" in search of success. And, he continued, "A Washington correspondent is one with a special talent for failing to see what is before his eyes. I have beheld a whole herd of them sitting through a national convention without once laughing." At the end of the address, FDR played his trump card: all of the criticisms were direct quotations from his "old friend Henry Mencken" (Bode, 1986, 310–11). Riotous laughter filled the room leaving H. L. Mencken humiliated.

MENCKEN'S LEGACY IN THE AGE OF POLITICAL CORRECTNESS

Although certainly no causal factor, the beginning of H. L. Mencken's decline in popularity as a political commentator coincided with the ribbing he took at the Gridiron Dinner. There were several reasons for the decline. For one, he began to lose interest in reporting public affairs, especially after the death of his wife of only five years, Sara Haardt, from meningitis. For another, he was turning his attention to other pursuits. In 1933 he retired from the *American Mercury*. He resumed revising a three-volume study of the American language, began work on an autobiography, first serialized in *The New Yorker*, and undertook the editing of materials that were posthumously published as *A Mencken Chrestomathy* (1956) and *A Second Mencken Chrestomathy* (1995). At the outbreak of World War II, Mencken ceased his regular column for the Baltimore *Sun*, but he remained with the paper as a consultant and member of the board of directors.

H. L. Mencken returned to political commentary one last time when he covered the presidential election campaign of 1948. It was almost like the old days, especially at the convention of Henry Wallace's Progressive party. He was delighted when the Maryland delegation offered a motion of censure against him for "contemptible rantings which pass for newspaper reporting" (Mencken, 1976, 19). A week following the November election, Mencken wrote his final news column. Two weeks later he suffered a crippling stroke. Although he survived, his days of reading and writing had come to an end. H. L. Mencken died on January 29, 1956.

As the twentieth century drew to a close, Mencken's legacy to political commentary had become increasingly hard to assess. The reason lay in the publication of his diary and volumes of correspondence. A new generation of critics claimed to find in them intolerable examples of bigotry, chauvinism, misanthropy, homophobia, paternalism, class bias, and sexism. Free speech surely could not tolerate the intolerable. Thus did the critics confirm an oft-repeated sentient view of Mencken: "There are no institutions in America: there are only fashions" (Mencken, 1956, 622).

> I am, it may be, a somewhat malicious man: my sympathies, when it comes to suckers, tend to be coy. What I can't make out is how any man can believe in democracy who feels for and with them, and is pained when they are debauched and made a show of. How can any man be a democrat who is sincerely a democrat? (Mencken, 1926, 212)

Alistair Cooke wrote that H. L. Mencken was "devoid of malice" but also of "puritanism" (1959, x). One would think that any political commentator that contemporary critics can label in so many dreadful ways must surely be a person of malice or puritanism. Let it suffice to allow Mencken to have the last word: "When I mount the scaffold at last these will be my final words to the sheriff: Say what you will against me when I am gone, but don't forget to add, in common justice, that I was never converted to anything" (Mencken, 1995, 491).

REFERENCES

Selected Politically Relevant Works and Compilations by H. L. Mencken

(For an extended bibliography see B. Adler, *H. L. M.: The Mencken Bibliography*. Baltimore: Johns Hopkins University Press, 1961.)

Notes on Democracy. New York: Alfred A. Knopf, 1926.

Making of a President: A Footnote to the Saga of Democracy. New York: Alfred A. Knopf, 1932.

A Mencken Chrestomathy. New York: Alfred A. Knopf, 1956.

H. L. Mencken Speaking. Audio tape. Library of Congress no. R58–147. New York: Caedmon, 1957.

The Vintage Mencken. Edited by A. Cooke. New York: Vintage Books, 1959.

Mencken's Last Campaign: H. L. Mencken on the 1948 Election. Edited by J. C. Goulden. Washington, D.C.: New Republic Book Co., 1976.

A Carnival of Buncombe: Writings on Politics. Chicago: University of Chicago Press, 1980.

The American Scene. Edited by H. Cairns. New York: Vintage Books, 1982.

The Days of H. L. Mencken. New York: Dorset Press, 1989a (Single vol. ed. of Mencken's three autobiographical vols.: *Happy Days*, 1940; *Newspaper Days*, 1941; and *Heathen Days*, 1943.)

The Diary of H. L. Mencken. Edited by C. A. Fecher. New York: Alfred A. Knopf, 1989b.

A Second Mencken Chrestomathy. Edited by T. Teachout. New York: Alfred A. Knopf, 1995.

Selected Works about H. L. Mencken

Bode, C. *Mencken*. Baltimore: Johns Hopkins Press, 1986.

Boyd, E. *H. L. Mencken*. New York: R. M. McBride, 1925.

Cairns, H. Introduction. In *H. L. Mencken: The American Scene*, edited by H. Cairns, ix–xviii. New York: Vintage, 1982.

Cooke, A. An Introduction to H. L. Mencken. In *The Vintage Mencken*, edited by A. Cooke, v–xii. New York: Vintage Books, 1959.

De Casseres, B. *Mencken and Shaw*. New York: S. Newton, 1930.

Goldberg, I. *The Man Mencken*. New York: Simon and Schuster, 1925.

Kunitz, S. J., ed. "Mencken, Henry Louis." In *Twentieth Century Authors*, 658–59. New York: H. W. Wilson, 1955.

Manchester, W. *H. L. Mencken: Disturber of the Peace*. New York: Collier Books, 1962.

McKerns, J. P., ed. "Mencken, Henry Louis." In *Biographical Dictionary of American Journalism*, 480–82. New York: Greenwood Press, 1989.

Riley, S. G. "Mencken, Henry Louis." In *Biographical Dictionary of American Newspaper Columnists*, 212–14. Westport, CT: Greenwood Press, 1995.

Selected General Works

Allen, F. W. *Only Yesterday*. New York: Harper and Brothers, 1931.

Combs, J. E., and D. Nimmo. *The Comedy of Democracy*. Westport, CT: Greenwood Press, 1996.

Klingaman, W. *1919: The Year Our World Began*. New York: St. Martin's Press, 1987.

Lippmann, W. *Men of Destiny*. New York: Macmillan, 1927.

Manchester, W. *The Glory and the Dream: A Narrative History of America*. 2 vols. Boston: Little, Brown, 1973.

RAYMOND (CHARLES) MOLEY

(September 27, 1886–February 18, 1975)

Educator, Privy Councillor, Editor, and Columnist

Political journalists—reporters, broadcasters, editors—frequently retire to the quiet repose of academe after their days of chasing politicians are over. Propagandists—public relations counsels, media consultants, pollsters, and others—accept college lectureships and share the mysteries of their craft with young pioneers of a new generation of persuaders. And, many political and communication scientists, hopeful of raising their status before academic administrators, eagerly enlist on the rolodex of political pundits routinely used by news organizations equally eager to put a gloss on their political coverage.

Far more rare is the political commentator who rises to prominence as both jack-of-all-trades and master of each—educator, political adviser, political columnist, and editor. Raymond Moley was such a rarity. In his eighty-eight years of unceasing activity, Moley was a distinguished scholar of constitutional law, a councillor and speechwriter to one of the nation's greatest presidents, an editor and political columnist for a mass circulation newsweekly, and a prolific author of scholarly and polemical books. And, if that were not enough, Raymond Moley also sandwiched into his career a stint as mayor of a small town and membership on two statewide crime commissions. It was a full life indeed for a political commentator who possessed "the makings of a good political boss" ("Privy Councillor," 1934, 328).

A PROFESSOR GOES POLITICAL

Up until a week before his death, Raymond Moley had been writing a volume of his memoirs that traced his political origins back to the presidential election of 1896. Although a Republican, William McKinley, was victorious, that presidential election of 1896 foreshadowed a growing force in American politics. The defeated Democratic candidate, William Jennings Bryan, had been the nominee of the Populist party in 1892—an upstart group of agrarian radicals seeking economic and political reform. Bryan's 1896 nomination by the Democrats swallowed up the Populists and, in the process, made the Democratic party more progressive and reform minded than it had been since the Civil War. Granted, McKinley's victory in 1896 in what political scientists are fond of calling a "critical election" (Key, 1955), drew attention away from reformers' demands. "The impulse to national reform was not dead, however, and it was to rise again within a decade in a second and more powerful wave of social change and liberalism,'' and triumph in the election of Woodrow Wilson in 1912 (Kelly & Harbison, 1948, 574).

The defeat of William Jennings Bryan in 1896 left a lasting impression on ten-year-old schoolboy Raymond Moley. So too did the victory of Woodrow Wilson in 1912 leave an impression on Moley, then a twenty-six-year-old teacher deliberating on his future. Moley had inherited from his father the belief "that it was right and just to belong to the Democratic party" (Moley, 1980, 5). Moley was still a youngster in Berea, Ohio, when he absorbed news of William Jennings Bryan's campaign in the Cleveland *Press*, of which Moley was a "steady reader" by his own account. He learned quickly that there was a difference between the carefully constructed campaign persona of Bryan and the actual man.

The public image was of "a relatively unknown country lawyer who dabbled in politics" and became a "dark horse" nominee by sweeping the 1896 Democratic convention off its feet with an "improvised oration," the "Cross of Gold Speech." The fact was that Bryan had already run for president before (although few voters seemed to know it), had sought the Democratic nomination for years, and had "meticulously, lovingly constructed bit by bit on scores of platforms" his "Cross of Gold" oration. "It was my great good fortune to learn my first lessons in national politics during a campaign of such commanding public interest," wrote Moley (1980, 6) in the first of his memoirs. The principal lesson he learned, that a campaign persona is a product of meticulous propaganda, would serve him well years in the future.

From Woodrow Wilson's victory in 1912 Moley learned another equally valuable lesson. Moley had been impressed with Wilson from the time of Wilson's election as governor of New Jersey in 1910. At that time, Moley was trying to decide on a life's work. Learning that Wilson had been a professor of jurisprudence, Moley decided that he too would turn to public law: "I had been amazed at the time that somebody could get paid for teaching politics" (Moley, 1980, 58). The lesson Moley learned in 1912 was that teachers upon occasion belie the old aphorism that "Those that *can* do, those that *can't* teach, and those that can't do *either*, administer." As Wilson's example demonstrated, a college professor could succeed in the rough-and-tumble world of politics and even rise to the land's top administrative position, *if* capable of crafting and communicating a strong, forceful message to political audiences. Like Woodrow Wilson, Raymond Moley would also become a professor who would be political. Albeit not as a governor or president, but as a political adviser, Moley would do, teach, and administer.

Moley, born on September 27, 1886, was the son of Felix James Moley, who owned a "gent's furnishings" store, first in Berea, then in Olmsted Falls, Ohio, and Agnes Fairchild Moley, whose family came from Massachusetts. In spite of his father's business setbacks in the financial panic of 1893, Raymond Moley spent his youth in comfortable, although not lavish, surroundings. Early on young Raymond developed a passion for political communication derived from a "preoccupation with classical oratory" that gave him a feeling for words and practice in oral composition. As a youth Raymond fantasized about orating to crowds, an appropriate use of the imagination for one who would later put words into other politicians' mouths by writing their speeches.

Moley attended a small, two-floor public school, and he performed well enough to be promoted from the first floor to the second floor, that is, from fifth grade to seventh grade, without being in the sixth. With the stimulation of one of his instructors, plus an instinct for politics, Moley resolved to become a lawyer. That, however, was not to be. After graduation from the public school, Moley worked briefly for a Cleveland manufacturing plant and a stone quarry in Michigan. Financially the best he could do was to enroll in Baldwin University in Berea (later merged with Wallace College to become Baldwin-Wallace College). Although he took time out from his college studies to teach students aged six to sixteen in a stereotypical Midwestern one-room schoolhouse outside Olmstead Falls, Raymond Moley persevered in his studies and graduated in 1906 from Baldwin-Wallace in a class that numbered only five students.

Thinking that, in lieu of law, an exciting career would be to write about politics for a newspaper, Moley tried unsuccessfully to land a job with newspapers in Cleveland. His failure took him back to Olmstead Falls and, as he quotes the words of Samuel Johnson, "the universal refuge of educated indigents," teaching (Moley, 1980, 47). Moley taught, at $45 per month, seventh through tenth grades, and with a $25 per month raise a year later, he became the school superintendent, a position he held until 1910.

Olmstead Falls also gave Raymond Moley a brief taste of active politics. At the age of twenty-one, Moley won an election as town clerk; four years later, he was elected mayor. Moley's original desire to become a lawyer continued to compete with his journalistic aspirations. In the summer of 1909 he attended the University of Michigan where he took courses in the law school and also in English drama, the latter in pursuit of ambitions to become a drama critic. At summer's end, however, Moley took a professor's advice and decided to stick to law.

The demands of balancing the duties of school superintendent, town clerk, and taking law courses were taking their toll. Moley came down with a moderately advanced case of tuberculosis; in those days the only treatment was a year's exile to a sanatorium, for Moley, one in New Mexico. When Moley asked his doctor about the possibilities of recovery, the blunt response was anything but heartening; he was a physician not a prophet, replied the doctor. Moley resigned all of his offices, educational and governmental, and moved to New Mexico.

The medical treatment successfully arrested Moley's tuberculosis. He returned to Ohio intent on continuing the study of law. It was 1912, the year of Woodrow Wilson's election as U.S. president. Reinforced in his admiration for the professor cum political leader by Wilson's victory, Moley decided to follow his example and become a political scientist. While teaching at West High School in Cleveland, Moley also enrolled for graduate work at Oberlin College. The next year Moley earned a master's degree in political science. The topic of his thesis, the innovative approach taken to organizing the Cleveland Municipal Court, left him with a continuing interest in the topic of criminal justice; moreover, an article published in a professional political science journal yielded for him the modest beginnings of a reputation for expertise in the area that would prove pivotal in his later career.

At the urging of one of his Oberlin professors, Raymond Moley took a leave of absence from his high school teaching and enrolled in graduate study at Columbia University. There he encountered the influence of such scholarly luminaries as Charles Beard in constitutional history, William Dunning in political theory, Thomas Reed Powell in constitutional law—all of whom were in the vanguard of the fledgling discipline of political science. Beard, for example, was in the process of formulating a highly controversial reinterpretation of the origins of the U.S. Constitution; and Dunning was setting the tone for research in political theory which would last for decades (Easton, 1953). Moley's original interest in law, the positive reception of his thesis at Oberlin, and the influence of the political science faculty at Columbia all directed him toward the specialty of public law. In 1918 Moley received his doctorate.

In 1916 Raymond Moley had married Eva Dall and, like any other newly wed graduate student in any era, had worried about how to make ends meet. (His marriage to Dall ended in divorce after the couple had two sons; Moley remarried and with his second wife, Frances, had a daughter.) The doctoral candidate became an instructor in political science at Western Reserve University and, in 1918, after receipt of his doctorate, an assistant professor. That same year, the last year of the Great War, the "war to end all wars," Raymond Moley became director of Americanization activities for the Ohio Counsel of Defense. "Americanization" consisted of preparing immigrants for citizenship through instruction in the English language and in American government and providing legal counsel for those immigrants requiring it. As part of his Americanization activities, Moley prepared a citizenship training pamphlet which, reprinted in ten editions over the ensuing decade and a half, became the model for use in other training programs.

James M. Cox, who would also befriend another aspiring political commentator, James "Scotty" Reston (q.v.) in the formative period of Reston's career, was governor of Ohio. Moley's office as Americanization director was near that of the governor. Cox was preparing a run at the 1920 Democratic party nomination for president; Moley helped him as a speechwriter by setting up in the governor's office "a large map of Europe and from that instructed him to distinguish between the Yugoslavs and the Czechoslovaks, etc." But, "when it came to voting in 1920 when he [Cox] ran against Harding, I decided to skip the candidates for President" (Moley, 1980, 104–5). The experience served Moley well, for it prepared him for a similar role in advancing the political ambitions of Franklin Roosevelt a decade later.

The following year Raymond Moley undertook a project that brought him to the attention of national political figures. As head of the Cleveland Foundation, Moley undertook a five-year study of organized crime in the city. The survey contributed to Moley's major role in reforming the administration of criminal justice, resulted in his role as a consultant for crime surveys in seven other states, and landed him the position of associate professor of government at Columbia University in 1923. (He became professor of public law in 1928, a position he held until his retirement in 1954.)

Perhaps Raymond Moley did not know it at the time, but by 1928 he was on the threshold of being, like his idol Woodrow Wilson, a professor active in partisan politics. In 1926 Moley served Alfred E. Smith, then New York's governor, as director of research on the New York State Crime Commission. Moley's work there, and his scholarly study of magistrates' courts, attracted the attention of Louis Howe, the chair of the National Crime Commission, and Howe retained Moley as a consultant. Howe was also a close advisor to Franklin Roosevelt, who had run for vice president of the United States on the Democratic ticket with Cox in 1920 and was elected governor of New York in 1928. In 1930 Moley helped draft a model parole system for the state of New York; subsequently, Roosevelt appointed Moley as the governor's representative on the New York State Commission on Administration of Justice.

In 1932 another top Roosevelt aide, Samuel Rosenman, urged Roosevelt to recruit, in support of FDR's presidential candidacy, a group of academic scholars to advise in the selection of campaign issues and help prepare campaign materials. Rosenman suggested that Raymond Moley assemble appropriate university professors and serve as an unofficial leader. Roosevelt did so. In a short time Moley moved to center stage where he played a key role in the political commentary that would close out the first half of the twentieth century.

PRIVY COUNCILLOR AND POLITICAL COLUMNIST

It was Louis Howe who, partly out of derision, coined the term "Brain Trust" (sometimes referred to as "Brains Trust") to refer to the collection of academics that Raymond Moley had gathered together to advise Franklin Roosevelt. Among Moley's notables were Rexford Guy Tugwell, Adolph A. Berle, Felix Frankfurter, Hugh Johnson, and numerous others. The principal problem facing the nation in 1932 was economic. The advice of the Brain Trust was for FDR to reject both laissez-faire and conventional reforms to spur economic recovery; instead, government and business should enter into a partnership to revive the economy. Moley conceived the phrase "New Deal" after Roosevelt's election to promote the program of social and economic change embodied in such measures as the Banking Act, the National Recovery Act, the Agricultural Adjustment Act, the Public Works Administration, and the Tennessee Valley Authority.

As a political adviser, Raymond Moley made significant contributions to the

New Deal beyond giving it its name. He played a major role in drafting the president's speeches and fireside chats. In that capacity, he practiced the lessons of classical political oratory he had borrowed from William Jennings Bryan's 1896 campaign. Moley possessed a knack for taking a hastily thrown together rough draft of an address and transforming it into a style and cadence that perfectly matched Roosevelt's natural way of speaking. He also had a gift for devising capsule phrases that would have made him a much sought source for television journalists in the age of the sound bite. Moley's coinage included, in addition to New Deal, such tropes as "the Forgotten Man" (borrowed from William Sumner), which was adapted to sound like FDR's own creation.

In 1933 the U.S. Department of State was housed in what is now the Executive Office Building next door to the White House. Because of the proximity, President Roosevelt appointed Raymond Moley assistant secretary of state. For the sake of physical convenience for Moley as a trusted aide, the appointment was inspired; for the sake of Moley's continued tenure in the New Deal, it was a disaster. By being close to FDR in the administration's "First 100 Days," Moley was a conduit of access to the New Deal officials. So powerful was his influence over the flow of information that White House wits developed a parody on a religious hymn: "Moley, Moley, Moley. Lord God Almighty!" One of FDR's friends of long standing reputedly asked the president to arrange an appointment with Moley on the friend's behalf!

The negative side of Moley's appointment as assistant secretary of state was that it put him at odds with the secretary, Cordell Hull, who resented having a subordinate both not of the secretary's own choosing and, in addition, one who had the president's confidence more than did Hull. The tension between Moley and Hull was exacerbated by Moley's quick temper, blunt and outspoken manner, and lack of tact. It was a style calculated to result in enemies of anyone as powerful as Moley, and it did, especially Cordell Hull and Louis Howe.

It all came to a head during the London Economic Conference of June 1933. Moley had been influential in persuading FDR to abandon the gold standard early in the New Deal. He attended the conference, an international gathering to reach an agreement on how to cope with the worldwide economic depression, as FDR's liaison to the American delegation. That delegation's head was Cordell Hull. When the British delegation turned to Moley as the president's spokesman, rather than to Hull, the die was cast. Moley urged that FDR favor other nations' delegations by simply asserting an eventual restoration of the gold standard; when FDR refused, in a public communique, to sanction any declaration pledging U.S. cooperation with currency stabilization, it was a defeat for Moley and a victory for Hull, and it foreshadowed Moley's resignation as assistant secretary of state.

Although Raymond Moley left the New Deal, he continued to employ his communication skills on its behalf. For one thing, Moley commuted frequently to Washington from Columbia in 1934 and 1935. He continued as a key FDR speechwriter, drafted legislative bills, and advised on appointments to the Securities and Exchange Commission. Moley also became a political journalist. He started writing a syndicated column for McNaught Newspaper Syndicate in June 1933. Shortly after his departure from the Roosevelt administration, however, he began a communication project of far more import: "In the many years after his service to Roosevelt, Moley was proudest not of his role as a presidential adviser or as a political science professor, but rather as a journalist" (Freidel, 1980, 194).

Moley became editor of *Today* (later merged with *News-week*) and, until he quit doing so at the age of eighty-one, as a political columnist for *Newsweek*, contributed "Perspective," an opinion column featured on the closing page of each issue. Before he made a final break with the president at the end of FDR's first term, Raymond Moley editorially supported New Deal measures: the Securities Exchange Act of 1934, the Gold Reserve Act of 1934, the Public Utility Holding Company Act of 1935, the Banking Act of 1935, and the National Labor Relations Act of 1935. *Today* was so supportive of New Deal measures at this time that it was regarded as the unofficial mouthpiece of the presidential administration. As editor of *Today* Moley also pushed the magazine in the direction of confronting controversial issues such as pure food and drugs, Father Charles Coughlin's vociferous oratorical and radio attacks on the New Deal, and the relationship of the Supreme Court to the New Deal. The merging of *Today* with *News-Week* in 1937 converted the weekly news digest into a periodical of news and opinion.

As the end of FDR's first term approached, however, Moley became increasingly critical of the president's policies. While working both as a magazine editor and as a professor at Columbia University and Barnard College, Moley began to drift away from the president. With advisers surrounding the president who urged tighter restrictions on business, Moley grew uncomfortable in his visits to the White House. His last contribution to the president was a draft of FDR's 1936 acceptance speech. Moley became particularly incensed at the "court-packing plan," an FDR proposal to make the Supreme Court more supportive of New Deal policies by enlarging the number of members on the court, then appointing sympathetic justices. Moley appeared before a committee of the U.S. Senate to speak against the proposal. The professor, councillor, and columnist made public the particulars of his opposition to the Roosevelt administration in his book, *After Seven Years* (1939).

Following the final rupture with the New Deal, Raymond Moley continued as a professor of public law, writing scholarly analyses, and as a political journalist, with "Perspective" on the last page of each *Newsweek* issue and, in 1941, a thrice-weekly syndicated column distributed through Associated Newspapers to sixty-four newspapers. For six months in 1945 he also served as a radio commentator for the American Broadcasting Company, concluding, with a refreshing candor that one scarcely finds among the contemporary generation of radio and television talk show hosts, that there simply was not enough to talk about on the air.

Raymond Moley's political awareness sprang to life in 1896 and he became a staunch Democrat. But, when Franklin Roosevelt ran for a third presidential term in 1940, Moley shifted his allegiance. He supported the Republican candidate, Wendell Willkie, endorsed him in *Newsweek*, and campaigned on his behalf. In subsequent presidential campaigns, Moley advised and wrote speech drafts for Thomas E. Dewey in 1944 and 1948 and for Dwight Eisenhower in 1952 and 1956. He backed Barry Goldwater in 1964. Moley was particularly helpful to Richard Nixon when the defeated 1960 presidential candidate and 1962 California gubernatorial candidate returned to New York to begin his successful political comeback.

In 1970 President Richard Nixon honored Moley with the Medal of Freedom as ''A man of thought and a man of action'' who ''has not only studied and analyzed the history of our times, but also helped make it'' (Moley, 1980, 196). Although Richard Nixon would later resign the presidency in disgrace, Raymond Moley confessed that, while not condoning the acts that led to that resignation, he still respected the former president. An uncompleted page of memoirs dealing with Nixon was in Moley's typewriter when the professor-adviser-columnist died on February 18, 1975.

OUTGROWING THE PROGRESSIVE MOVEMENT

Raymond Moley came of political age in the active climate of the progressive movement—one of dissent, reform, and controversy: ''Everywhere it seemed to take the form of a revolt against the traditional party alignments'' and ''generalized a public opinion which held politics to be a more or less dirty business, and politicians a species to live under a dark cloud of suspicion'' (Moley, 1980, 187). The cure for the ills of democracy, urged progressives, was more democracy—direct primaries to make political parties accountable, as well as popular initiatives and referenda to make politicians accountable. The result was a conception of government that required no delegation of popular sovereign power, only direct popular action.

But, progressives, wrote Moley, were wrong. Theirs was a romantic, almost naive belief that citizens were ''capable of more intelligence in political affairs than the facts warranted'' (Moley, 1980, 188). Contrary to romantic notions, the sovereign populace must delegate governing functions. That, argued Moley, not the extension of the progressive movement, is what was at the heart of the *early* New Deal—''a creation of many minds and many ideas'' (1980, 190) derived from popular delegation not direct popular action. The New Deal began to fail when constructive reform was replaced by propaganda *about* reforms and actions that were either unwarranted or dangerous (i.e., an unhealthy fettering of business initiative or the court-packing scheme).

As a political commentator, Raymond Moley exploited the professor's tools of lectern and scholarly books, the councillor's confidential advice, and the journalist's editorial commentary to convey a vision of the realities and illusions of government on which politicians could act. He was the first spectacular example of what was unique for his time, and now is commonplace, an emerging kind of expert essential in American politics: the trained professional academic equally proficient in classroom, public service, and mass communication who is the repository of the citizens' delegated powers. Therein reside both his frustration with the New Deal and his legacy thereafter.

REFERENCES

Selected Works by Raymond Moley

Our Criminal Courts. New York: Hinton, Balch, 1930.
Tribunes of the People. New Haven, CT: Yale University Press, 1932.
After Seven Years. New York: DaCapo Press, 1939.
27 Masters of Politics. New York: Funk and Wagnalls, 1949.
How to Keep Our Liberty. New York: Alfred A. Knopf, 1952.
The American Century of John C. Lincoln. New York: Duell, Sloan and Pearce, 1962.
The First New Deal. New York: Harcourt, Brace and World, 1966.
Realities and Illusions, 1886–1951. New York: Garland Publishing, 1980.

Selected Critical Works about Raymond Moley

Rothe, A., ed. "Moley, Raymond (Charles)." In *Current Biography 1945* 407–9. New York: H. W. Wilson, 1946.
Freidel, F. "Epilogue." In *Realities and Illusions, 1886–1951*, edited by R. Moley, 194–96. New York: Garland Publishing, 1980.
Olsen, J. S., ed. "Moley, Raymond." In *Historical Dictionary of the New Deal*, 332–34. Westport, CT: Greenwood Press, 1985.
"Privy Councillor." In "Unofficial Observer" in *The New Dealers*, 324–39. New York: Literary Guild, 1934.
"Raymond Moley, Roosevelt Aide, Dies; Brain Trust Leader Coined 'New Deal.' " *New York Times*, February 19, 1975, 38.

Selected General Works

Easton, D. *The Political System*. New York: Alfred A. Knopf, 1953.
Freidel, F. B. *Franklin D. Roosevelt: Launching the New Deal*. Boston: Little, Brown, 1974.
Kelly, A. H., and W. A. Harbison. *The American Constitution*. New York: W. W. Norton, 1948.
Key, V. O., Jr. "A Critical Theory of Elections." *Journal of Politics* 17 (February, 1955): 3–18.
Leuchtenburg, W. E. *Franklin D. Roosevelt and the New Deal, 1932–1940*. New York: Harper and Row, 1963.
Louchheim, K. *The Making of the New Deal: The Insiders Speak*. Cambridge, MA: Harvard University Press, 1984.
Schlesinger, A. M., Jr. *The Coming of the New Deal*. London: Heinemann, 1960.
———. *The Politics of Upheaval*. London: Heinemann, 1961.

BILL (BILLY DON) MOYERS

(June 5, 1934–)

The Documentary Interview, Religious Fervor, and Political Commentary

Unquestionably, Bill Moyers has been the most prolific source of political commentary via the televised documentary to appear before American audiences, and perhaps audiences worldwide, since that form of television communication was pioneered by Edward R. Murrow (q.v.) and Fred Friendly following World War II. In 1984 the National Academy of Television Arts and Sciences named Moyers' "A Walk Through the Twentieth Century," which was telecast on the Public Broadcasting Service (PBS), the outstanding information series of the year. In many respects the title of that one-hour sequence of documentaries serves as a metaphor for Moyers' career as a political commentator. In political roles as diverse as deputy director of the Peace Corps, presidential assistant, White House press secretary, newspaper publisher, television commentator, and television documentarian, Moyers' life has epitomized a key dimension of what politics in the United States became during "America's Century," the twentieth century (Steele, 1980).

THE FASHIONING OF A POLITICAL CONSCIENCE

"Serving a president, he became known as the conscience of the Johnson administration. Battling a network, he was called the conscience of television. Now, preaching the gospel of good values, he is on his way to becoming the conscience of America." So wrote Mimi Swartz (1989, 98) in her critical appraisal of "the mythic rise of Billy Don Moyers." Conscience of America or not, Bill Moyers acquired a self-professed "specialized" missionary zeal for public affairs early in life, a zeal reinforced in his multifaceted career: "Just as a doctor specializes within the general field of medicine, I've 'specialized' in government, publishing, and broadcasting—all branches of public affairs" (Moritz, 1977, 274). However, before government, publishing, or broadcasting for Bill Moyers, there was religion. Although he may not list it as one of his current specialties, the moral conscience acquired in his youth figures prominently in the contemporary style and substance of Moyers as a political commentator.

Billy Don Moyers was born on June 5, 1934, in the small town of Hugo, located in southeastern Oklahoma, in the "Little Dixie" of the state. Within a few months, the Moyers family, father Henry and mother Ruby, along with older brother James, moved from depression-ridden Little Dixie to Marshall, Texas. There, Billy Don Moyers attended public schools, worked on the high school newspaper, was a cheerleader, played in the band, and graduated fifth in his high school class of 143. There, too, he formed religious convictions: his father was a Baptist deacon, and Billy Don was a member of a Baptist youth group. Sunday school, Sunday evening youth group meetings, Wednesday evening prayer meetings—a pattern of unblemished attendance—combined with his parents' devout faith, inclined Moyers toward a career in the ministry. Although that was not to be, the early ingrained religious views that salvation comes through sacrifice and that duty is one's highest honor have informed his political and social commentary for a lifetime. It is no small wonder that in 1990 the accolade of "Communicator of the Decade" was bestowed on him by the Religious Communication Conference.

In "Marshall, Texas; Marshall, Texas," an early program in the "A Walk Through the Twentieth Century" series, Moyers reported vignettes about his youth. One concerns an experience that would prove, along with his "good child" conduct in school and church, formative in the evolution of Moyers as a political commentator. While still in high school, Moyers followed his brother James' lead and went to work for the local newspaper, the *Marshall News Messenger*. Here Moyers won the attention, praise, and affection of one of three key mentors in his career—Millard Cope, the newspaper's editor. Impressed by Billy Don's unflagging work ethic in covering general assignments, from school board meetings to jury trials, Cope made Moyers, a high school sophomore, editor of the sports page. No longer was he "Billy Don"; as a byline, he used "Bill D.," then simply "Bill Moyers."

Cope's influence did not cease after Moyers graduated from Marshall High. Even after he enrolled at North Texas State College (now the University of North Texas), Moyers continued to spend summers as a *News Messenger* reporter. At North Texas, Moyers remained the indefatigable "good child Billy Don" no matter what his byline: in his two years there, majoring in journalism, he was elected class president twice, chosen outstanding class student twice, wrote editorials for the school newspaper, worked in the college publicity department, was a student senate officer, and was a member of the Baptist Student Union. And, he found time to write Mother Ruby every day.

At the close of Moyers' sophomore year, 1954, Millard Cope urged his protegé to seek summer employment with the majority leader of the U.S. Senate, Lyndon Baines Johnson. Moyers did. His mentor Cope wrote to soon-to-be mentor Johnson on Moyers' behalf: "He's a top boy, Lyndon" (Swartz, 1989, 212). Johnson was pleased to comply with the request of a trusted political ally like Millard Cope. Moyers went to Washington. But unlike Jimmy Stewart's fictional character, Jefferson Smith, in Frank Capra's 1939 film, *Mr. Smith Goes to Washington*, who fought the Senate establishment, "Millard Cope's friend" would someday became a confidant of the nation's power brokers under the tutelage of the senate majority leader. Although Moyers' work was largely menial, as befits a summertime employee, Johnson, like Cope before him, took the journalism major under his wing, often holding forth to Moyers as an audience of one long after the senator's office had closed for the evening.

When summer ended, Moyers married Judith Suzanne Davidson, a college classmate at North Texas. And, as he had when summer began, Moyers again took a mentor's advice, this time mentor Johnson. Instead of returning to North Texas, Moyers did as Johnson suggested and transferred to the University of Texas at Austin. There he became an honors journalism student; an assistant news director at a radio station owned by Lady Bird Johnson, the senate majority leader's wife; and a lay preacher for two Baptist churches on alternate weekends. Thus, by graduation in 1956, Bill Moyers had met all three of what he would later call his specialties in public affairs—publishing with Cope, government with Johnson, and broadcasting with LBJ's wife.

Still, he had not as yet turned his back on his first specialty—religion. Indeed, when he received his B.A., it appeared that religion would be his career choice. He devoted the next academic year to the study of ecclesiastical history at the University of Edinburgh in Scotland. In 1957 he enrolled in the Southwestern Baptist Theological Seminary in Fort Worth, Texas, where he earned his B.D. (with honors) in 1959. His first, and it would prove his only, pastorate was in the farming community of Brandon, Texas, where he served a flock of 121 for $35 a week. He also accepted an academic position at Baylor University where he lectured in Christian ethics. However, when Lyndon Johnson invited Moyers to rejoin the majority leader's staff, plans for the ministry and an academic life were not simply put on hold, they ceased. Politics and religion, Moyers had once thought, were divergent, yet similar. Having first committed himself to religion, he departed it for politics. Thus began a penchant for coming and going that would mark much of Moyers' later career as a political commentator.

Johnson's invitation to Moyers coincided with the senator's bid for the 1960 Democratic presidential nomination. Moyers rose in the Johnson entourage from personal, to special, to executive assistant. When John F. Kennedy won the presidential nomination, and selected Johnson as a running mate, Moyers scheduled LBJ's appearances, wrote speeches, and coordinated the vice-presidential campaign with that of JFK. Following the victory of the Kennedy-Johnson ticket, Moyers left the newly inaugurated vice president's staff to become the associate director for public affairs of the Peace Corps. With mentor Johnson's assistance, Moyers helped lobby the Peace Corps through Congress and win public support for the agency. When the Peace Corps became a fact, Moyers became the deputy director.

In November 1963, JFK's aides asked Moyers to travel to Texas to help mend political fences on the president's behalf. Moyers was in Austin on November 22 when he received news that Kennedy had been assassinated in Dallas. Moyers chartered a plane to Dallas, arriving as Lyndon Johnson was taking the oath of office as president. Moyers contrived to get a brief note to President Johnson: "I'm here if you need me." Apparently Johnson did, for Moyers soon rejoined his mentor as a special assistant. From the vantage point of the White House,

Moyers would quickly expand exponentially his grasp of power and politics in twentieth-century America.

For the next three years, Bill Moyers served LBJ in several capacities—speech writer, policy adviser, and troubleshooter. As a domestic affairs adviser, he was instrumental in formulating the Great Society programs dealing with health care, model cities, environmental pollution, federal aid to education, and so on. At later points in his broadcast career the expertise and contacts he acquired while dealing with Great Society areas would provide topics and themes for television interviews and documentaries. As White House chief of staff, he was the administration's point man in dealing with racial crises; in foreign matters, Moyers joined others in dealing with a threat to democracy in the Dominican Republic and in confronting the widening war in Southeast Asia. As a campaign adviser, Moyers had a hand in coordinating Johnson's 1964 contest against Barry Goldwater; he quickly learned the persuasive benefits, and dangers, of televised political ads. Especially noteworthy was his involvement in helping fashion the now-fabled "Daisy Girl" commercial.

In 1965, when Moyers became LBJ's press secretary, he reoriented Johnson's direct dealings with the news media by limiting televised news conferences (in which the president was uneasy). As an alternative he organized small gatherings for LBJ with reporters in the Oval Office, and arranged private interviews in which Johnson could confront his journalistic critics and give them the infamous "Johnson treatment." Moyers also curried favor with the political media—for himself as well as the president—through adroit leaks to reporters. Moyers became the prime source of White House news and a media celebrity who appeared on the covers of both *Time* and *Newsweek*.

Over the years, however, relations cooled between Moyers and his presidential mentor. For his part, Johnson was not always pleased with "Millard Cope's friend." Moyers' growing celebrity status seemed a betrayal; the more Moyers won media acclaim, the less he needed LBJ, and the more LBJ needed him. "Deep down, he [LBJ] knew he needed Moyers," said George Christian, Moyers' successor as press secretary (Swartz, 1989, 214–15). Johnson's Vietnam policy was a source of a rift. Although Moyers was not forceful in his opposition to the war, he did not support those advising wholesale escalation. That too vexed Johnson.

As for Moyers, the restlessness that had prompted his departure from the ministry to politics when called by LBJ in 1959 reasserted itself in another form in 1966. Once the life of a small-town pastor had become restrictive; now the life of a press secretary left Moyers unfulfilled. He sought other offices, perhaps the post of national security advisor, or of undersecretary of state. Moyers' 1963 message, "I'm here if you need me," seemed now to translate to LBJ as "I'm here; you need me." But Johnson was having none of it. Moyers received no new post.

In 1966 Moyers' brother, James, committed suicide after having developed stomach cancer. Moyers accepted responsibility for his brother's wife and children. His $28,000 per year salary as press secretary was insufficient. Moyers' restlessness, a family crisis, and a cooled relationship with his once-mentoring president led him to walk away from the White House. He resigned as press secretary to become the publisher of *Newsday*, a Long Island daily with the largest surburban circulation in the nation. The move afforded opportunity to supplement powerful political contacts in the nation's capital with powerful economic ones in the nation's financial capital. In the process Moyers exchanged one mentor, LBJ, for another, Harry F. Guggenheim, the owner of *Newsday* and the daily's retiring publisher.

For three years Guggenheim supported Moyers' efforts to refurbish the editorial policy of *Newsday*—hiring investigative reporters and respected columnists, adding an international desk, replacing soft news with news analysis, even moving the editorial stance of the daily toward the left and away from Guggenheim's own traditional conservatism. Although the editorial shifts brought the newspaper numerous awards, including two Pulitzer Prizes, by 1969 Guggenheim too had become vexed with Moyers—over *Newsday*'s editorial support of peace marches, antiwar demonstrations, and citizens' rights to dissent. The retiring and ailing publisher sold *Newsday* to a publishing conglomerate after turning down a purchase bid from Moyers that would have brought more for the controlling interest, and, in the deal, insisted that the Moyers tie to *Newsday* be terminated.

Yet, again, Moyers was left to depart from a public affairs specialty—government, then broadcasting, in 1956; religion in 1959; government once more in 1966; and publishing in 1970—or, so it seemed. In fact, he was about to give government, publishing, and broadcasting "the largest pulpit of all. Television" (Swartz, 1989, 217).

THE MOLDING OF A COMMENTATOR STYLE: PUBLIC VERSUS COMMERCIAL TELEVISION

In the summer of 1970 Bill Moyers undertook a small project that was to foreshadow his distinctive style of political commentary. Packing a notebook and a tape recorder, Moyers set out on a 13,000-mile bus tour across the country, an electronic age Alexis de Tocqueville. He wanted to learn what America was about and who Americans were, allowing them to speak for themselves, reporting their words without cant or editorializing, eliciting their feelings through a tactic of self-effacing, deferential interviews. What he found was that ordinary Americans, be one a labor organizer, a civil rights worker, a small-town doctor, a conscientious objector, a lathe operator, or whatever, found salvation by serving the needs of society and social change. The book that resulted from the project, *Listening to America* (1971), sold well and won critical acclaim.

In 1971 Bill Moyers joined the staff of New York City's public television station, WNET-TV. His first project, the production and editing of "This

Week,'' a weekly public affairs program, exploited a documentary style reminiscent of *Listening to America*, which he would later label "ideas television." It would reappear in other public affairs series: "Bill Moyers' Journal," "A World of Ideas," "Bill Moyers' Journal International Report," and "God and Politics." The style consisted of lengthy, polite, deferential interviews with people from all walks of life, but people who were making a difference in America—poets, physicists, historians, economists, religious scholars, geneticists, philosophers, filmmakers, pastors, communication scholars, media analysts, and so on. It was a style of an ordinary American, Moyers, sitting in a room with a VIP, innocently asking seemingly naive questions and eliciting quotidian responses. It was a style that would later reach its perfection in Moyers' patient questioning of comparative mythologist Joseph Campbell in the six-part PBS series, "The Power of Myth."

Early on Moyers combined extended interviews with the historical documentary—tracing, for example, the evolution of public relations from its beginnings with Ivy Ledbetter Lee before World War I to the present using probing interviews with one-time historian and 1972 presidential candidate George McGovern and with the first public relations consultant, Edward L. Bernays (q.v.); or exploring propaganda techniques in World War II through nonjudgmental interviews with Nazi Germany's Franz Hipler and U.S. filmmaker Frank Capra. The wedding of easygoing, seemingly spontaneous, conversational interviews with a rich historical probing via the documentary is apparent in "The Power of the Past: Florence," "A Walk Through the Twentith Century," and "The Public Mind."

In a manner reminiscent of another groundbreaking political commentator, Edward R. Murrow in the 1950s, Moyers announced in 1974 that he planned to take a sabbatical from television, in part to consider future television projects. Hence, once more he departed a specialty, broadcasting, albeit briefly. In fact, he would seek to combine two of his public affairs specialties, publishing and broadcasting. As part of his sabbatical year, he agreed to write a regular column for *Newsweek*. However, in 1975, with a return to weekly PBS-TV, in "Bill Moyers' Journal International Report," his ambitious schemes for the series consumed so much time that he departed *Newsweek* in September. The "International Report" added a new stylistic wrinkle to the interview documentary, namely, "issue forums" on such topics as the global environment and human rights.

Although Moyers had clearly found, in the early 1970s, to use Theodore Roosevelt's phrase, his "bully pulpit" for commentary in television, and graced it with an innovative style as well, it would not consistently remain public television. In a fashion that recalls his earlier pendulum-like movements from politics to the ministry and back, Moyers' television career has oscillated between commercial and public sectors: departing PBS for the Columbia Broadcasting System (CBS) in 1976, CBS for PBS in 1978, PBS again in 1981 for CBS, and CBS again in 1986 for PBS. His flirtations with commercial television,

like those with mentors LBJ and Harry Guggenheim, embroiled him in controversy on more than one occasion. Each contributed to the maturing of his style
and substance for televised political commentary.

Moyers' first commercial television stint was with CBS from 1976 to 1978.
A staple of CBS public affairs programming since the era of Edward R. Murrow
was "CBS Reports," a documentary series that garnered critical acclaim but
too few viewers to be competitive in the television marketplace. In 1974 CBS
tried to heighten the series' viewer appeal by appointing a "star" correspondent
to carry on the once popular Murrow tradition. Dan Rather (q.v.) left his position
as CBS White House correspondent to assume the "CBS Reports" role. Just as
Rather was making a success of the effort, however, CBS shifted him again,
this time to be the third correspondent on CBS' rating success, "60 Minutes."
While fishing about for a replacement for Rather, the CBS vice president in
charge of documentaries learned from Bill Moyers' agent that Moyers was growing "disenchanted" with PBS. In April 1976, Moyers succeeded Rather as heir
to the Murrow legacy.

Moyers got off to a rocky start. One of his first "CBS Reports" was "Born
Again," a documentary epitomizing Moyers' PBS style and building upon one
of his specialties, his religious background. The documentary treated the growing social and political force of fundamentalist Christians. Among its various
themes, Moyers included material about his own religious upbringing, admitting
that his own commentary style—cadence, speech rhythms, and choices of metaphors—reflected that religious background. CBS executives found the program
unsuitable: "I want to tell you," the vice president for documentaries said of a
prescreening, "that was a lousy show" (Boyer, 1988, 166).

The incident did not diminish Moyers' stature with "CBS Reports," but it
was an irritant, along with the network's failure to schedule Moyers' programs
in a regular time slot and, when they aired, to schedule them in unfavorable
time periods—opposite the Oscar awards or World Series on other networks.
Irritants notwithstanding, "CBS Reports" returned as a critical, if not ratings,
hit. The executive producer of the irregular series was Harold Stringer. Moyers
adopted Stringer in a fashion similar to his own adoption by mentors in the
past. The Moyers-Stringer tandem revived the Murrow-Friendly tradition for
"CBS Reports," which resulted in such politically influential documentaries as
"The CIA's Secret Army" and "The Battle for South Africa."

Moyers' first association with commercial television, and CBS, came to an
end when he refused to adopt a newsmagazine format for "CBS Reports," a
format similar to that of the popular "60 Minutes." In proposing that "CBS
Reports" be converted into a television magazine, network executives gave
Moyers a commitment for a regular monthly time slot. According to one report,
Moyers' view of the trade-off was summed up in a nonpious, but colorful,
metaphor: "Bullshit" (Boyer, 1988, 169). In 1978 Moyers departed CBS to
return to PBS.

Moyers' first foray into commercial television revolved around an attempt to restore the Murrow legacy to documentaries at CBS. It lasted two years. His second foray was longer (1981 to 1986). It too derived from the network's desire to restore a tradition, in this instance, the role of commentary on the "CBS Evening News." Since the retirement of Eric Sevareid (q.v.) in 1977, news commentary at CBS had languished. As the president of CBS News, Bill Leonard, was himself nearing retirement, he learned from Howard Stringer that Bill Moyers was again disenchanted at PBS. In November 1981, Leonard, CBS, and Moyers reached an agreement: Moyers would come back to CBS for commentaries two or three evenings a week; moreover, CBS would make a good-faith effort to give Moyers a regularly scheduled series of his own. It would be not "Bill Moyers' Journal" but more similar than dissimilar (Leonard, 1987).

Moyers' commentaries on the "CBS Evening News" apparently helped recapture the popular appeal lost following the replacement of Walter Cronkite (q.v.) with Dan Rather. Again, however, there was controversy. The tradition of news commentary heretofore had been for the analyst to appear in a scholarly pose, a "talking head" in the manner of a bust of Pericles, a tradition founded by commentator Eric Sevareid. True to his documentary-interview style, Moyers made radical changes. He took to the field with camera crews, filming visuals and reactions to illustrate his studio analysis. Moreover, he sometimes drew from his personal political background in framing his views. The style raised objections from many CBS affiliates concerned both with the visual immediacy and the rhetorical punch of the commentary.

To meet such objections, CBS executives opted to have Moyers explain the "burden of the commentator" in the "struggle to be fair" at meetings with affiliates: "The simple honesty of that statement struck a chord among the affiliates gathered in the auditorium that day. Like the Baptist preacher he'd once been, Moyers was both honest and inspirational." Here the affiliates received a "firsthand glimpse of the best side of Moyers, a man who understands the power television gives to a handful of people and feels the burden of that responsibility" (Joyce, 1988, 139).

Other controversies were not so easily surmounted, either by CBS executives or Moyers. They centered, again, upon the issue of a regularly scheduled series for Moyers at the network. In 1983 Moyers undertook a half-hour summer series, "Our Times," that considered several topics in a tight time frame—tensions in the Philippines, the Westernizing of China, a prescient prediction of AIDS as an epidemic. With summer's end, however, the series ceased as well. Negotiations for a replacement centered on "American Parade," with a magazine format. Moyers was implacable in his opposition. In a letter to Ed Joyce, then president of CBS News, he wrote, "The fact is that "American Parade" is not my kind of journalism. I don't believe in it and I can't do it. It's that simple" (Joyce, 1988, 291).

"American Parade" later aired, but without Moyers. It failed. There were hurt feelings on all sides. Andy Lack, producer of the successful "Our Times," summarized the controversy in words recalling Moyers' much earlier breakup with Lyndon Johnson. Lack said that the CBS executive who had lobbied for "American Parade" over Moyers' objections, Van Gordon Sauter, failed to understand Moyers: "Van never came to him and said, 'I need you,' and you can't work with Bill Moyers and not say, 'I need you' " (Boyer, 1988, 176). Accurate appraisal or not, Moyers concluded that CBS News had no serious interest in producing documentaries, and perhaps no interest in him.

Moreover, after a subsequent incident surrounding his role as a commentator on "CBS Evening News," Moyers hinted that he would leave CBS at the end of his contract in 1986. He had written a commentary about a pro-Arab radio political commercial, a spot several stations in New York refused to broadcast. The executive producer of the "Evening News" refused to air Moyers' commentary. Moyers declined to return to his role as commentator for months. The rift was patched up, but the bitterness remained. Moyers resigned from CBS in September 1986 and returned to PBS, where he resumed his documentary-interview programming.

THE CONSCIENCE OF A POLITICAL COMMENTATOR

From *Listening to America* through his numerous PBS and CBS documentary-interview series, CBS commentaries, and public appearances, critical themes emerge in the career of Bill Moyers as a political commentator. It is a career marked by often conflicting temptations, each temptation tried, found wanting, then tried again, sometimes repeatedly: between private, moral duty, and public affairs; between dependence upon, then independence from, mentors; among government, publishing, and broadcasting occupations; and between public and commercial television.

However, beneath the surface of these approach-avoidance pendulum swings there has emerged a recurring, consistent theme in the content of Moyers' political commentary. It too is a theme of conflicting temptations. It lies in his repeated recognition of the deep split in the modern and post-modern world, on the one hand, between the value-embedded moral behavior of a *civic* polis and, on the other hand, the increasingly uncivil, and uncivilizing, reign of *mediated* politics. For Moyers a civic polis brings people together in small, face-to-face groups. Here, to use the titles of his documentaries, is "a gathering" recognizing the "power of myth," yet exploring "a world of ideas," using the "power of the word" and "the language of life" in "facing evil," and "in search of [a] constitution" by accepting "god and politics." The civic model might be Moyers' nostalgic, sanitized recollections of Marshall, Texas, or, possibly, 1959 Brandon, Texas—121 souls gathered in the First Baptist Church.

Opposed to the civic polis is another temptation, "the public mind." Here is a mediated polis where "in politics, in business, in journalism, the visual media have taken center stage, shaping the public mind with powerful tools of fiction that both please and deceive"—dramatic "visual effects, synthetic dreams, counterfeit emotions, preconceived spontaneity." It is "public life" as a "media show'' (''The Public Mind,'' ''Consuming Images,'' 1989). This, Toto, is not Brandon, Texas; it is LBJ's Washington, Guggenheim's *Newsday*, CBS' lowest common denominator for programming. In the mediated polity, as Moyers repeated often in ''The Public Mind,'' citizens are no longer rational, involved beings; they are passive ''consumers'' for whom the political ad is the ''communion wafer of the market place''; representative democracy is merely the ''representation of democracy.''

In a mediated polity, how can Americans restore the civic polity? How can they escape the temptations of political fictions that ''please and deceive?'' The answer is Moyers' evolved technique, the documentary interview. Probing documentaries expose deception. Probing interviews with the world's ''value shapers'' before small, informed PBS or ''CBS Reports'' audiences expose the truth. It is the truth of Moyers' religious background: salvation comes not in pleasure, but in sacrifice. Or, as Moyers emphasized at the close of the four-part series, ''The Public Mind,'' ''Reality is fearsome, but as we've learned in this series, experience tells us more fearsome yet is evading it.''

REFERENCES

Selected Documentary Series by Bill Moyers on Video Cassette

''Creativity.'' Washington, D.C.: PBS Video, 1982.

''A Walk Through the Twentieth Century.'' Washington, D.C.: PBS Video, 1984.

''CBS Reports.'' ''One River, One Country: The U.S.-Mexican Border.'' New York: Carousel Films, 1986.

''In Search of the Constitution.'' Chicago: Films Incorporated, 1987.

''The Secret Government: The Constitution in Crisis.'' New York: A. H. Perlmutter, Inc., and Public Affairs Television, 1987.

''God and Politics.'' New York: Public Affairs Television, 1988.

''Joseph Campbell and the Power of Myth.'' New York: A. H. Perlmutter, Inc., and Public Affairs Television, 1988.

''A World of Ideas: Season 1.'' Alexandria, VA: PBS Video, 1988.

''The Power of the Word.'' Alexandria, VA: PBS Video, 1989.

''The Public Mind: Image and Reality in America.'' Alexandria, VA: PBS Video, 1990.

''Amazing Grace with Bill Moyers.'' Alexandria, VA: PBS Video, 1990.

''A Gathering of Men.'' New York: Mystic Fire Video, 1990.

''A World of Ideas: Season 2.'' Alexandria, VA: PBS Video, 1990.

''Hate on Trial.'' New York: Mystic Fire Video, 1992.

''Listening to America.'' Alexandria, VA: PBS Video, 1992.

''The Moyers Collection.'' Princeton, NJ: Films for the Humanities & Sciences, 1994.

''The Language of Life.'' Alexandria, VA: PBS Video, 1995.

Selected Written Works and Compilations by Bill Moyers

Listening to America: A Traveler Rediscovers His Country. New York: Harper's Magazine Press, 1971.

Joseph Campbell: The Power of Myth. Edited by B. S. Flowers. New York: Doubleday, 1988.
A World of Ideas. New York: Doubleday, 1989.
The Secret Government: The Constitution in Crisis. Cabin John, MD: Seven Locks Press, 1990.
A World of Ideas II. New York: Doubleday, 1990.

Selected Critical Works about Bill Moyers

Moritz, C., ed. ''Moyers, Bill(y Don).'' In *Current Biography Yearbook 1976*, 274–76. New York: H. W. Wilson, 1977.
Nimmo, D., and J. E. Combs. ''Is the Political Picture Fulfilling? The Critic as Cultural Psychologist.'' In *The Political Pundits*, 155–58. New York: Praeger, 1992.
Swartz, M. ''The Mythic Rise of Billy Don Moyers.'' *Texas Monthly*, November 1989, 94–98, 211–19.

Selected General Works

Boyer, P. J. *Who Killed CBS?* New York: Random House, 1988.
Gates, G. P. *Air Time: The Inside Story of CBS News.* New York: Harper and Row, 1978.
Halberstam, D. *The Powers That Be.* New York: Alfred A. Knopf, 1979.
Joyce, E. *Prime Times, Bad Times.* New York: Doubleday, 1988.
Leonard, W. *In the Storm of the Eye: A Lifetime at CBS.* New York: G. P. Putnam, 1987.
Metz, R. *CBS: Reflections in a Bloodshot Eye.* Chicago: Playboy Press, 1975.
Slater, R. *This . . . Is CBS: A Chronicle of 60 Years.* Englewood Cliffs, NJ: Prentice-Hall, 1988.
Smith, S. B. *In All His Glory: The Life of William S. Paley.* New York: Simon and Schuster, 1990.
Steele, Ronald. *Walter Lippmann and the American Century.* Boston: Little, Brown, 1980.
Westin, A. *Newswatch.* New York: Simon and Schuster, 1982.

EDWARD (EGBERT) R. (ROSCOE) MURROW

(April 25, 1908–April 27, 1965)

Political Commentary's Romantic Legend

Physicians hail Hippocrates as the Father of Medicine. Lawyers revere Blackstone as touchstone. Engineers honor Patrick; working men, Joseph; and huntsmen, Hubert, as their patron saints. Broadcast journalists have Edward R. Murrow—their Founder, Standard Bearer, Guardian, and Epic Hero. No other political reporter and commentator ever garnered the awe, esteem, and professional praise from his broadcast colleagues that Murrow received in his career, which covered a quarter of the twentieth century; nor does any other three decades after his death. In a televised Columbia Broadcasting System (CBS) commentary eulogizing Murrow on the evening he died, Eric Sevareid (q.v.) summarized the past and foreshadowed the future of a romantic legend:

> There are some of us here, and I am one, who owe their professional life to this man. There are many working here and in other networks and stations who owe to Ed Murrow their love of their work, their standards and sense of responsibility. He was a shooting star and we will live in his afterglow a very long time. ("CBS Evening News with Walter Cronkite," April 17, 1965)

APPRENTICING THE LEGEND

Hollywood films often capture in a single scene what generations of historians, social scientists, and philosophers labor to discover and rediscover. A case in point is the 1962 Paramount film, *The Man Who Shot Liberty Valance*. Valence (played by Lee Marvin) is a gunfighter and bully who terrorized the Western town of Shinbone. He meets his death in a shootout with a stumbling young lawyer, Ranse Stoddard (Jimmy Stewart). Or so the townspeople believe. Actually Valance was killed by Tom Doniphon (John Wayne) over the love of a woman that he has lost to Stoddard. Doniphon insists that the secret be kept, that Stoddard get the credit for killing Valance. As "the man who shot Liberty Valance" Stoddard is lionized, leads the territory into statehood, and becomes a U.S. senator. Years later Senator Stoddard returns to Shinbone. In an interview Stoddard reveals the truth behind the myth surrounding him—that he was *not* the man who shot Liberty Valance. The reporter listens to Stoddard's tale politely, then tears up the notes he has taken. Stoddard puzzles, "You're not going to use my story?" The reporter replies, "No, sir. As our late and great editor

Dutton Peabody used to say, 'It ain't news. This is the West. When the legend becomes fact, print the legend.' "

There is much surrounding the career of Edward R. Murrow as a political commentator that is fact-cum-legend. For example, legend has it that Edward R. Murrow almost single-handedly invented radio journalism during his ten days of broadcasting from Vienna during Nazi Germany's 1938 *Anschluss* in Austria. Yet, it is more accurate to say that Murrow's contribution was more stylistic than substantive, that H. V. Kaltenborn (q.v.), William L. Shirer, and other correspondents reported the political and diplomatic news of the event while Murrow narrated background and human interest accounts (Rudner, 1981). Also, Murrow's 1954 "See It Now" broadcast denouncing Senator Joseph McCarthy's methods for uncovering alleged Communist sympathizers in government receives justifiable praise. Yet, the legend that Murrow produced McCarthy's decline receives scant confirmation in historical analyses of the era (Baughman, 1981). Or, as a final example, biographers frequently picture Murrow's departure from the political scene as a radio and television commentator as a martyr burned at the stake of corporate greed. Less fanciful depictions point out that Murrow's time had passed because his style, as he was well aware, no longer matched the demands of television technology as it moved out of its infancy (Merron, 1988).

Murrow assuredly sought no legendary status. As Sevareid remarked, "Himself, he often doubted" (Schroth, 1995, 366). Yet, at least in minor ways, Murrow did contribute, from the very beginning of his career, to the mixing of fiction and fact, the factoids that are the stuff of romantic legend. For instance, it was as a college student tiring of jokes about his birth name, Egbert (hence "Egg"), that he renamed himself "Edward." And, it was Murrow who, when seeking employment with CBS at the age of twenty-seven, claimed he was thirty-two. Moreover, instead of listing the fact that he was a speech major in college, Murrow claimed political science and international relations. His alma mater, Washington State University, he replaced with the University of Washington. And, he never attended Stanford, yet Murrow claimed an M.A. from that university. Finally, although Murrow was fully qualified for the prestigious academic honor of Phi Beta Kappa, because of the objections of a faculty member, he never became a member (Persico, 1988, 59). Nevertheless, many biographical profiles have routinely printed legend as fact: he "graduated a member of Phi Beta Kappa in 1930" (Culbert, 1976, 181) or he "graduated with a Phi Beta Kappa key" (Fang, 1977, 306).

Legend-cum-fact notwithstanding, the essential contributions of Edward R. Murrow as a political commentator are there for all to witness: a style that reported politics through factual commentary, his molding of a distinctive news organization comprised of talented reporters, an unmatched performance as a commentator during World War II, a major force in adapting a documentary format to television, and a polished advocate of news as information and education.

Egbert Roscoe Murrow was the third son born to a family that, even by the standards of the time (April 25, 1908), lived under conditions of chronic rural poverty. Yet, the family did not think so. His father, Roscoe, was a large, hard-working, affable man whose efforts to scratch out a successful existence as a farmer went unrewarded. His mother, Ethel Lamb, was a small, fretful, asthmatic, devout woman who, by all accounts, cared for her sons in a loving way. The home of this family of Quakers in Polecat Creek, North Carolina, had none of the modern advantages slowly pushing their way through America. Edward R. Murrow, who would exploit electronic technology as no broadcaster before him, spent his earliest years in surroundings with no electricity, no telephone, no indoor plumbing, and no automobile.

At the behest of relatives, the Murrow family resettled in Blanchard, Washington, in 1914. When Roscoe could find no work other than as a farmhand, the Murrows lived in a tent. When Ethel's asthma became a problem again, the family temporarily moved back to Polecat Creek. But their return did not improve their lot and it was back to Blanchard where the family remained until Egbert, now Edward, was twenty-one years old and the Murrows moved to Olympia, Washington. Roscoe found work as a railway brakeman, then as a locomotive engineer. While he was growing up Ed worked as a farmhand, in logging camps, as a schoolbus driver, and at assorted other jobs. From the age of six through fourteen, he attended school in a two-room shack; he did well in social studies, not so well in arithmetic. At Edison High School, five miles from his home, he played baseball and basketball, played the ukulele in the orchestra, sang in the glee club, and was chosen the "best debater" in a statewide competition.

Two teachers had a profound impact on Edward R. Murrow and on his future. The first was Ruth Lawson, his high school English teacher and debate coach. From Ruth Lawson, Ed learned to overcome his stage fright. She taught him to conquer his fear of people staring at him when he spoke, urging him to think about what he as a speaker was doing *for* them. She urged him to remember, "They are here because they are eager for knowledge, and I am giving them knowledge," or, "they are here to be entertained, and I am entertaining them" (Persico, 1988, 29). These two gifts, knowledge and entertainment, he would later provide to nationwide television audiences through "See It Now" and "Person to Person," respectively.

The second teacher who significantly influenced Ed Murrow was Ida Lou Anderson, who taught public speaking and drama at Washington State University during Ed's days there as an undergraduate, from 1926–1930. Professor Anderson took Murrow under her wing and became a longtime mentor. She urged that Murrow not copy a style from any other speaker, but develop his own universal, not parochial, way of addressing audiences. Years later, in 1939 London, when Edward R. Murrow was groping for an opening for his nightly CBS broadcasts back to America, Ida Lou Anderson contributed one in a letter.

First used on September 22, Murrow's spoken words, "This is London," became his signature (later "This is the news" after World War II). Anderson not only provided the words, she provided the powerful enunciation, "THIS is London."

Ed Murrow excelled at Washington State. He was cadet colonel of the Reserve Officer Training Corps, student council president, a key figure in the leadership of student councils of colleges and universities in the region, and president of the Pacific College Association. This led to his becoming president of the National Student Federation of America (NFSA). Shortly after his college graduation, Murrow moved to New York City as NFSA president where for two years his job was to lecture, act as an advocate for student groups across the nation (he was instrumental in NSFA's act to remove all racial bars to membership), and arrange group tours to Europe. He also set up the first international debates between students of American and European universities. When, in 1930, he applied for a passport to travel to Europe, his mother submitted an affidavit as proof of date and place of birth; on the affidavit she wrote the "Edward" that he had renamed himself rather than the Egbert to whom she had given birth. Thus, for legal purposes, Edward R. Murrow was officially born.

As NSFA president Murrow received minimal pay, but he profited from extensive travel and the accumulation of influential contacts. One such contact was especially fortuitous. Through NSFA work he met a student leader from Mount Holyoke College, Janet Huntington Brewster. They were married in 1934. Also through his NSFA responsibilities Murrow met the founder of the International Institute of Education (IIE). The IIE encouraged student exchange programs among the world's nations. In 1932 Murrow became assistant director of the IIE. Among his duties was to help scholars displaced from Nazi Germany find employment, a responsibility that added to his growing knowledge of behind-the-scenes international relations.

One of Murrow's other activities at the IIE was to help provide speakers knowledgeable about public affairs to appear on radio broadcasts. Radio was no longer a novelty but still very much in its infancy. There was a continuing search for programming to fill the available broadcast time. Murrow had been especially helpful in supplying speakers for CBS' "University of the Air" program while he was still at NSFA, and he continued his cooperation at IIE. When CBS executives sought a full-time "director of talks," a title used by the British Broadcasting Corporation (BBC), to develop radio programming, it was Edward R. Murrow they approached. At Washington State Murrow had developed an interest in broadcasting. He took one of the first college courses in broadcasting offered in the nation and worked as a sports announcer. In 1935 Murrow accepted the CBS position and began an affiliation with the network that lasted for more than a quarter of a century.

PRINTING THE LEGEND

As CBS Director of Talks, Edward R. Murrow's job was to fill airtime with speakers who attracted listeners. This he did by falling back on his debating experience. He recruited speakers with contrasting viewpoints. For example, when Italy invaded Ethiopia, Murrow arranged via shortwave relay a talk by Italian dictator Benito Mussolini followed by another from Ethiopia's crown prince. During the 1936 presidential campaign, Murrow was not content to present speakers from the two major parties; he also scheduled a talk by the secretary-general of the Communist party. In guidelines he prepared for his speakers, Murrow urged them not to orate, but to approach the radio microphone as though each were standing by a fireplace, elbow on mantel, softly addressing six or eight close friends gathered in the room.

On Christmas Eve in 1936, Murrow made his first appearance as a CBS broadcaster, an unscheduled one. CBS newscaster Robert Trout and Murrow had attended a party celebrating the holiday. Trout became giddy from the alcohol, then remembered he had a broadcast scheduled. Murrow accompanied Trout to the studio. When Trout prepared to go on the air, Murrow took the script and suggested that his own state of sobriety was better suited to the broadcast than Trout's. Aside from finishing the program forty-five seconds too early, Trout judged Murrow's legendary performance as precise, monotonic, and letter perfect—nary a hint of having imbibed (Sperber, 1986).

At this point in the history of radio, each U.S. network airing broadcasts from Europe stationed a "representative" overseas to line up programs, coordinate facilities, and direct local network operations. In 1937, with considerable reluctance, Edward R. Murrow became the CBS European representative. His trepidation derived from his view that it was a job without advancement; its responsibilities were the type CBS executives did not deem important. Nonetheless Ed and Janet Murrow moved to London. Upon their arrival, the head of the BBC inquired what it was CBS expected of Murrow. Murrow replied that he did not really know. The BBC chief expressed the hope that Murrow would make CBS programming "intellectual." Murrow responded that, on the contrary, he intended CBS programs to be anything but intellectual, preferring, he said, to give listeners what they like: the down-to-earth vernacular of the street, broadcast from pubs if necessary, to catch that flavor. Murrow was merely following the tutelage of Ida Lou Anderson, formulating a style that was Edward R. Murrow's own distinctive contribution to political commentary in the twentieth century.

Political events moved rapidly in Europe. In March 1938 Murrow received word that Adolf Hitler's Nazi Germany was on the verge of *Anschluss* with Austria, an annexation forbidden by the terms ending World War I. Tensions ran high. Murrow flew from Warsaw, where he was coordinating arrangements for an upcoming CBS "School of the Air" program, to Vienna to cover Hitler's triumphant entry. From the moment of his ten-day coverage of the *Anschluss*, the Murrow career as a reporter-commentator and the Murrow legend were born. Until the end of World War II, he broadcast to America covering breaking events; acted as a correspondent for CBS' "The World Today," a daily, fifteen-minute roundup of news; and aired a weekly program of his own on CBS.

The hallmark of the new commentary style created by Edward R. Murrow during the years of World War II was what rhetorical critic Kenneth Burke called the "representative anecdote" (1969a, 59–61): a specific description of human motivation in a situation cast in language that represents the yearnings of all people confronting similar situations. Murrow was not a newspaperman; he had never been a cub reporter. He was not a slave to the representative story line of the working journalist, that wire service convention that dictated that the who, what, why, where, and how of a reported event must be contained in the opening paragraph, followed by unfolding details in the remaining body of the account. Nor was Murrow chained to the view that authoritative, representative news sources consisted solely of political or military leaders; the eyewitness experience of the man or woman in the street also held insights. Thus, Ed Murrow eschewed the iconoclastic debunking of the popular mind exploited by H. L. Mencken (q.v.), the urge to pander to popular taste of Walter Winchell (q.v.), the inside-dopester style of Fulton Lewis, Jr. (q.v.), and the posture of advisor and confidant to the high and mighty that marked the commentaries of Walter Lippmann (q.v.). In Murrow's unique way, he smoothly harmonized the experience of what both democratic leaders and citizens suffer in common during trying times.

Murrow first fashioned his version of the representative anecdote in his coverage of the *Anschluss*. To his CBS colleagues, Murrow left the task of reporting and commenting upon the political, diplomatic, and military significance of the events in Austria in 1938. He described happenings from the vantage point of the Viennese—descriptions of their mood, the resigned acceptance of the crowds, the absence of talk between German soldiers and rank-and-file residents, the imagery of resounding thuds of hobnailed boots on Viennese pavements, and the ridicule leveled at Jews forced to clean up the glass shattered in their shop windows. Six months later, Ed Murrow polished his style during the Sudetenland/Munich crisis that put Europe on the precipice of war. In his reports from London during the news roundups moderated by H. V. Kaltenborn in New York, Murrow gave listeners an eyewitness account of the "tight, strained look about the eyes" of Londoners riding in buses, talking with cab drivers, visiting with hotel doormen, and drinking at pubs. His representative anecdote was the documentary expression of the victims of fear (Rudner, 1981, 100).

The impact of CBS' coverage of the tense prelude to war in 1938 and 1939 was striking. For one thing, Murrow's broadcasts changed the nature of news. Instead of a chronicle of who, what, when, where, and how—even why—by reporters reading printed scripts, it conveyed sound images of a threatened war, then the "phoney war" that preceded the Battle of Britain. Murrow's voice and microphones captured Londoners trying on gas masks, air-raid sirens wailing, soldiers fortifying the Maginot Line, and other scenes far removed from the lives of people in Polecat Creek, or Blanchard, or even New York City. Murrow's reports positioned CBS radio as a serious rival to the National Broadcasting Company (NBC), not only for the ear of American listeners but also for status among U.S. and European political leaders.

To keep the momentum CBS had gained, network officials urged Murrow to "Give us this day our European sensation" (Fang, 1977, 310). To do so Murrow built a superlative news staff comprised of craftsmen skilled at reporting whether they were experienced in broadcasting or not: William L. Shirer, Eric Sevareid, Charles Collingwood, Larry LeSueur, Bill Downs, Howard K. Smith, Richard Hottelet, Winston Burdett, Cecil Brown, Edgar Ansel Mowrer, and others. His overture to Walter Cronkite (q.v.), then a wire service reporter, was rejected; Cronkite felt the demands of broadcasting would be too restrictive for a correspondent who preferred to report from the combat front. Years later, when Cronkite joined CBS News and became anchor of the network's nightly newscast, Murrow's opinion of Cronkite changed: he thought Cronkite, like Kaltenborn, "talked too much" (Schroth, 1995, 326).

On August 15, 1940, the first Nazi bombs fell on England. From that date Edward R. Murrow established himself as a foremost war correspondent, political commentator, and stylist. Describing the war from street corners, roof tops, air-raid shelters, bombed-out buildings, and the rural countryside; describing debates in the House of Commons, air raids over London and Germany (he went on a bombing mission and recorded the sounds and his impressions), a demolition squad sifting rubble for victims, and his tortured entry into the concentration camps of Buchenwald, Ed Murrow reported the first "living room war" well before the Vietnam conflict earned that label in the television age.

In substance, Murrow's commentaries expressed sympathies that were as much those of a Briton as an American. He sought to convince his American listeners that the tie between the two nations was consubstantial, that the two peoples shared a "way of life" in "an *acting together*; and in acting together, men have common sensations, concepts, images, ideas, attitudes that make them *consubstantial*" (Burke, 1969b, 21; emphasis in original). The CBS reporter-commentator made it his task to convey to Americans those concepts, ideas, and attitudes shared with the British. That both nations were in the same boat together was his message.

As a stylist, "Murrow was actually a sensitive musician of the spoken word" (Culbert, 1976, 185). His sense of timing and time compression was superb. In air segments rarely of more than two minutes in duration, Ed Murrow employed a speaking emphasis and cadence that matched each trope he chose to exploit. For example, he conjured up jarring contrasts: "I had tea in a big department store. . . . It seemed a little strange to see antiparachute [*sic*] men leaning their rifles against chairs as they sat down to tea" (Murrow, 1941, 111). Or, there was ironic humor, this based on a visit to an air-raid shelter: "A man wanted to smoke his pipe; the warden wouldn't allow it. The pipe smoker said he'd go out and smoke it in the street, where he'd undoubtedly be hit by a bomb and then the warden would be sorry" (1941, 149). And, there was the immediacy of war, even in a radio studio: "The air raid is still on. I shall speak rather softly, because three or four people are sleeping on mattresses on the floor of this studio" (1941, 167).

On the day after Murrow's death, political commentator James "Scotty" Reston (q.v.) paid tribute to "Brother Ed" and called him the "voice of doom" (1965, 14). It was a perception so widely shared that the U.S. Civil Defense Agency could think of no commentator better to narrate a film simulating an atomic attack on the United States, *One Plane, One Bomb* (1954), than Ed Murrow. Yet, it is more accurate to say, certainly in his coverage of the Blitz, that he was a voice of resurrection—measured, subdued, terse, detailed, and personal. The message was gloomy, to be sure, but it was a message about a Phoenix he was confident would rise from the ashes of the relentless bombing. It would rise *if* Americans understood that they too must rise and assist the effort.

In 1941 Murrow returned to the United States for a short stay. At a banquet in Murrow's honor, poet Archibald MacLeish described the commentator's overriding message of resurrection. Reviewing the London venues from which Murrow had reported, MacLeish said, "But it was not in London really that you spoke. It was in the back kitchens and the front living rooms and the moving automobiles and the hotdog stands and the observation cars of another country that your voice was truly speaking" (Address, December 2, 1941; in MacLeish, 1941, 7–8).

With the war's end, Edward R. Murrow returned permanently to the United States. From 1946 to 1947 he was a CBS executive, the vice president and director of public affairs. It was a job that he heartily disliked. Yet, he took advantage of the freedom to develop innovative programming. He formed the CBS Documentary Unit, developed a program of commentary on the United States as seen through foreign eyes, and instituted a year-end roundtable discussion that brought together CBS correspondents from around the world to interpret the year's events. He remained restive and, in 1947, Murrow returned to on-air broadcasting with a nightly fifteen-minute newscast, "Edward R. Murrow with the News," at 7:45 P.M. EDT. In an ironic bit of programming Murrow's show aired opposite NBC's program of news and comment with H. V. Kaltenborn.

Although more to Murrow's liking than sitting at an executive's desk, his news broadcast was not altogether his mien. The news portion of the program was the product of newswriters rather than vintage Murrow. A six-minute closing segment, or tailpiece, which usually incorporated interviews with political leaders, was written by Murrow. Yet, from the opening, "This is the news," to his farewell, "Good night and good luck," the combined newscast and analysis often lacked the bite of his wartime efforts.

For one reason, Ed Murrow was gradually turning to other broadcast pursuits and had a decreasing amount of time to spend on writing radio commentaries. In 1947 he met Fred W. Friendly, who had a plan to produce an album of recorded history covering the years from 1933 to 1945. Murrow joined the project as coproducer and narrator of *I Can Hear It Now*. The album sold well, and the result was a Murrow-Friendly partnership that produced a one-hour weekly radio documentary, "Hear It Now," then in 1951 television's documentary "See It Now." With "See It Now," Edward R. Murrow had for the next seven years a far more influential medium for news, analysis, and commentary—and for enhancing the Murrow legend—than network radio, then beginning its decline, could ever have provided (Friendly, 1968).

The debut of "See It Now" (November 18, 1951) came at a crucial, early point in the Cold War. Through use of "the little picture," representative anecdotes that pictured a microcosm of general situations, Murrow again exploited the technique that had won him fame during World War II. Not every half-hour documentary in the series, airing regularly at 10:30 P.M. EST on Tuesdays, derived from Cold War tensions, but the most notable certainly did, for example, "Christmas in Korea" (December 28, 1952) and from controversial telecasts, including "The Case of Milo Ridulovich" (October 20, 1953). However, no program was more notable and controversial than the "Report on Senator McCarthy" (March 9, 1954). Like Ed Murrow's reports of the Blitz on London, the "Report" provides the sinew of legend.

A portion of the Murrow legend rests on the belief that the "Report" was the first all-out attack on McCarthy and his methods. It was not. Political columnists, such as Marquis Childs (q.v.) and Walter Lippmann, had criticized the Wisconsin senator in severe language; political broadcasters, such as Elmer Davis (q.v.) and Drew Pearson (q.v.), had done the same. It is more accurate to say that the "Report" was the first attack on the senator from one of Murrow's nationally celebrated status. Nor was the "Report," contrary to legend, the catalyst for McCarthy's demise. McCarthy's troubles before and after the airing of the "Report" did that. It is fair to say, however, that the Murrow-Friendly documentary focused criticism on the senator in a vivid, dramatic, even ironic way (Rosteck, 1989).

Through indirect, ironic expression, the "Report on Senator McCarthy" used pictures and words to convey meaning at two levels—one a literal meaning that implied Murrow was permitting McCarthy to have his day in court through a straightforward, objective report of the senator; the other, a deeper meaning, that implied because of McCarthy's antics the prospects for preserving civil liberties were dark indeed. As Rosteck's analysis demonstrates, "while this *See It Now* is built from the raw material of McCarthy's own words and actions, the text ironically redirects the connotation in the McCarthy footage," with an "ironic layering of another sense over the 'objective' footage that partly depends upon our assent to the 'actuality' of what we see" (1989, 287–88).

McCarthy's staunch supporters claimed that the "Report" was a hatchet job. In a reply prepared by McCarthy and aired on "See It Now" on April 6, the senator himself offered a counterlegend to the romantic image of Murrow. Mc-Carthy proclaimed Murrow to be "a symbol, the leader and the cleverest of the jackal pack . . . always found at the throat of anyone who dares to expose individual Communists and traitors" (Friendly, 1968, 55). McCarthy's heavy-handed response lacked both the solemnity and subtle indirectness of Murrow's style and, although the "See It Now" staff feared reprisals, the "Report" did not jeopardize the series, contrary to those aspects of the Murrow legend that suggest that the long knives were out to silence the commentator's outspoken ways.

One reason "See It Now" survived until 1958 was Edward R. Murrow's celebrity. That celebrity was built not only on the legend of an acclaimed voice of information he inherited from World War II, but via Murrow's appeal as an entertaining interviewer of other celebrities on the highly popular "Person to Person." Before there were such interviewers of political and entertainment celebrities as Larry King (q.v.) and Bill Moyers (q.v.), there was Edward R. Murrow.

The Friday 10:30 P.M. EST CBS program was decidedly not political commentary, although an interview with a young Massachusetts senator, John F. Kennedy, and his wife, Jackie, in 1953 certainly helped promote the future president's career. "Person to Person" consisted of two segments, each an interview with a celebrity originating from the guest's home. Murrow conducted the interview from a studio, but he did so as if he were the guest in the celebrity's home. More people watched "Person to Person" than "See It Now," a fact that made it possible for Murrow to use his leverage as an entertainer to convince CBS executives to keep "See It Now" as a means of exploiting the Murrow celebrity (Merron, 1988).

Eventually, however, audience ratings for "See It Now" no longer justified keeping it on the schedule, and it was canceled in 1958. Murrow undertook a new public affairs project, "Small World," that featured conversations with distinguished people in a variety of fields, including politics, moderated by Murrow. Yet, with his nightly radio newscasts that were still airing on CBS, "Person to Person," and "Small World," Murrow was tiring of the grind; he was bored and as restive as he had been earlier in an executive capacity. The search by television networks for ever larger audiences rendered Murrow's personal brand of journalism and analysis unappealing to corporate executives with an eye to the financial bottom line.

Moreover, Murrow's style, once the source of his success and acclaim, was losing its popular appeal. On the one hand, a younger generation of television journalists were striving for a more affable approach, some through wit like David Brinkley (q.v.), others with the folksy, grandfatherly style of Walter Cronkite, and still others with sheer blandness (Baughman, 1981). On the other hand, Murrow's distinct approach to news stories, both in his radio commentary and his "See It Now" documentaries, which used dramatic narratives to depict events from the vantage point of rank-and-file citizens, was no longer novel; indeed, it was old hat.

Murrow declined an effort to get him to run for the U.S. Senate from New York in 1958. Shortly thereafter he took a year's leave of absence from CBS. Upon his return he undertook special projects, party convention and election night broadcasts, and a new venture with Fred Friendly narrating a "CBS Reports," "Harvest of Shame." Increasingly disillusioned by the corporate values that were driving the broadcast industry, and frequently at odds with CBS management, Edward R. Murrow left the network that had been his home for his entire broadcast career to become director of the United States Information Agency (USIA) in the presidential administration of John F. Kennedy.

Murrow's approach to the USIA was the same as that of his close friend, Elmer Davis, to USIA's World War II predecessor, the Office of War Information. Murrow argued USIA's role should be to portray, in a factual and informative manner, America in all its diversity, good and bad, to the world. Unlike an even earlier predecessor, George Creel's (q.v.) World War I Committee on Public Information, the USIA should not serve as a propaganda agency. Critics pilloried Murrow's successor, Carl T. Rowan (q.v.), charging he used the USIA to advance President Lyndon Johnson's Vietnam policy. When yet another political commentator, John Chancellor (q.v.), became director of the USIA's sister agency, Voice of America (VOA), in the Johnson administration, it was Murrow's, not Creel's, model he followed in defining the VOA's task.

INSTITUTIONALIZING THE LEGEND

For a political commentator who made irony one of the tools of his craft, there was a final irony. On two occasions "See It Now" devoted programs to the linkage of cigarette smoking and lung cancer. Ed Murrow, a heavy smoker himself, smoked three packs of cigarettes a day. The lighted cigarette had sustained him during the blackouts of the London Blitz; the cigarette's "small dull red glow," he said in one broadcast, "is a very welcome sight" (Persico, 1988, 157). On both "See It Now" and "Person to Person," a cigarette was his constant on-air companion and prop. Yet, in his "See It Now" reports on smoking and cancer, he approached the story head on, detailing the risks of smoking, and treating the tobacco industry with a critical voice. In 1963 surgery removed one of Murrow's lungs; on April 27, 1965, at the age of fifty-seven, Edward R. Murrow died of cancer.

One function of a legend is to rationalize contradictions. In romantic legends the contradictions between the protagonist's foibles or weaknesses and the superhuman qualities are swept aside. Or, if simply irreconcilable, a deficiency appears as an Achilles heel, a minor inconvenience but ultimately destructive. Edward R. Murrow, as befits a legend, was a man of contradictions—a man of impeccable professional integrity with a puffed-up resumé, a masterful reporter who never worked for a newspaper, an apostle for factual detail and a musician of verbal allusions, a man who was digital in thinking and analogical in style, an advocate of informative programming who won celebrity as an entertainer, a realist in reporting danger but a Pollyanna in courting it, an insatiable talker given to moods of dark silence, and a company man who departed the company. Yet, as the legend written as early as World War II said, he was "the only foreign correspondent who could play a foreign correspondent in the movies and give the role the glamour Hollywood wants"; he was the one with the "ultimate romantic touch" (Block, 1943, 618). H. V. Kaltenborn was arguably the father of broadcast political commentary. Edward R. Murrow remains its legend.

REFERENCES

Selected Printed Works by Edward R. Murrow

This Is London. New York: Simon and Schuster, 1941.
This I Believe. Edited by E. Morgan. New York: Simon and Schuster, 1952.
See It Now. New York: Simon & Schuster, 1955.
"A Broadcaster Talks to His Colleagues." *Reporter*, November 13, 1958, 32–6.
In Search of Light. Edited by E. Bliss, Jr. New York: Alfred A. Knopf, 1967.

Selected Radio and Television Broadcasts by Edward R. Murrow

"I Can Hear It Now." Audio phonograph recording in three volumes. With F. W. Friendly. New York: Columbia, 1949.
"One Plane, One Bomb." Public information film. Washington, DC: U.S. Department of Defense, 1954.
"Edward R. Murrow: Reporting Live." Audio tape recording. New York: CBS News Archives, 1986.
"The Edward R. Murrow Collection." Video tape in five volumes. Terre Haute, IN: Columbia House and CBS Inc., 1992:
    Vol. 1: "This Reporter"
    Vol. 2: "The Best of See It Now"
    Vol. 3: "The McCarthy Years"
    Vol. 4: "Harvest of Shame"
    Vol. 5: "The Best of Person to Person."

Selected Critical Works about Edward R. Murrow

Baughman, J. L. "*See It Now* and Television's Golden Age, 1951–58." *Journal of Popular Communication* 2 (Fall 1981): 106–15.
Block, M., ed. "Murrow, Edward R." In *Current Biography 1942*, 618–20. New York: H. W. Wilson, 1943.
Culbert, D. H. "Edward R. Murrow: The Foreign Correspondent as Broadcaster." In *News for Everyman*, 177–200. Westport, CT: Greenwood Press, 1976.
Fang, I. E. "Edward R. Murrow." In *Those Radio Commentators!*, 305–25. Ames: Iowa State University Press, 1977.

Friendly, F. W. *Due to Circumstances beyond Our Control*. New York: Vintage, 1968.
Garraty, J. W., ed. "Murrow, Edward (Egbert) Roscoe." In *Dictionary of American Biography*, 565–67. New York: Charles Scribners' Sons, 1981.
Kendrick, A. *Prime Time: The Life of Edward R. Murrow*. Boston: Little, Brown, 1969.
MacLeish, A., ed. *In Honor of a Man and an Idea*. New York: CBS Inc., 1941.
McKerns, J. P., ed. "Murrow, Edward (Egbert) Roscoe." In *Biographical Dictionary of American Journalism*, 500–502. New York: Greenwood Press, 1989.
Merron, J. "Murrow on TV: *See It Now, Person to Person*, and the Making of a 'Masscult Personality'." *Journalism Monographs* 106 (July 1988): 1–36.
Persico, J. *Edward R. Murrow: An American Original*. New York: Dell, 1988.
Reston, J. "Washington: Farewell to Brother Ed." *New York Times*, April 28, 1965, 14.
Rosteck, T. "Irony, Argument, and Reportage in Television Documentary: *See It Now* versus Senator McCarthy." *Quarterly Journal of Speech* 9 (1989): 277–298.
Rudner, L. S. "Born to a New Craft: Edward R. Murrow, 1938–1940." *Journal of Popular Communication* 2 (Fall 1981): 97–105.
Smith, R. F. *Edward R. Murrow: The War Years*. Kalamazoo, MI: New Issues Press, 1978.
Sperber, A. M. *Murrow: His Life and Times*. New York: Freundlich, 1986.

Selected General Works

Burke, K. *A Grammar of Motives*. Berkeley: University of California Press, 1969a.
———. *A Rhetoric of Motives*. Berkeley: University of California Press, 1969b.
Gates, G. P. *Air Time*. New York: Berkeley, 1979.
Hosley, D. H. *As Good as Any: Foreign Correspondence on American Radio, 1930– 1940*. Westport, CT: Greenwood Press, 1984.
Metz, R. *CBS: Reflections in a Bloodshot Eye*. New York: New American Library, 1975.
Paley, W. S. *As It Happened*. Garden City, NY: Doubleday, 1979.
Reston, J. *Deadline: A Memoir*. New York: Random House, 1991.
Schroth, R. A. *The American Journey of Eric Sevareid*. South Royalton, VT: Steerforth Press, 1995.
Smith, S. B. *In His Glory: The Life of William S. Paley*. New York: Simon and Schuster, 1990.

(ANDREW) DREW (RUSSELL) PEARSON

(December 13, 1896–September 1, 1969)

Political Commentary in the Muckraking Tradition

In the mid to late 1970s, journalism educators witnessed a remarkable increase in the number of college undergraduates eager to train themselves for careers as investigative reporters. Among the proffered rationales for the sudden attraction to journalistic careers, scarcely deemed a lucrative way to make a living, was the romantic myth surrounding investigative reporting conjured by the sudden celebrity of two *Washington Post* reporters who had pieced together the enthralling story behind one of the greatest political scandals of the twentieth century, Watergate. The revelations that the White House of President Richard Nixon was involved in a criminal coverup of massive proportions made the names of *Post* correspondents Bob Woodward and Carl Bernstein household words. The success of their 1974 best-seller, recounting the bizarre events of Watergate, *All the President's Men*, and the popularity of the 1976 film of the same name, starring Robert Redford as Woodward and Dustin Hoffman as Bernstein, made investigative journalism an irresistible draw to aspiring college students.

Although no scandal had ever forced the resignation of a U.S. president as Watergate had forced Nixon's, the tradition of investigative journalists exposing the corruption of American politicians dates back well before Woodward and Bernstein. In fact, as the twentieth century was getting under way, journalistic "muckraking" was already a key part of the nation's political communication. "Muckraking," a term once confined to the odious task of cleaning, gathering, and spreading moist animal dung and vegetable matter as manure, entered the political vernacular to describe the work of journalists bent upon searching out and exposing political and economic corruption. Crusading muckrakers, including Lincoln Steffens, who revealed the corruption of urban political machines; Ida Tarbell, who exposed the evils of American business, especially the Standard Oil Company; Ray Stannard Baker, who took on America's railroads; and Upton Sinclair who penned a graphic portrait of the slaughterhouse production line—predated "Woodstein" by decades (Hofstadter, 1955).

Across the century, however, few journalists have focused the muckraking tradition on America's national politics in such an enduring way as did Drew Pearson from the 1930s through the 1960s. First working with Robert Allen, then alone, and finally with Jack Anderson, Pearson turned journalistic muckraking into an art form. If he was the descendent of Steffens, Tarbell, Baker, and others, he was the progenitor of "Woodstein," the *National Enquirer*, and "Hard Copy." That the muckraking tradition became unrecognizable along the way is in large measure both because of, and in spite of, Drew Pearson.

A MOST UNLIKELY DIPLOMAT

One of Drew Pearson's prized possessions was his farm located on the Potomac River, a half-hour's drive from Washington, D.C. It was no mere showplace as are the homesteads of so many successful politicians, political journalists, and bureaucrats fleeing from the hurly-burly world of the nation's capital. For Pearson it was also a working farm. So much so that two of his farm products earned him $150,000 a year. One was bags of Pearson's Best Manure ("All Cow, No Bull"); the other was bags of mud reclaimed from an old canal by "Drew Pearson, the Best Muckraker in the U.S."

Andrew Russell Pearson, born in Evanston, Illinois, on December 13, 1896, did not set out to be a journalist, let alone an investigative one. As a young man he had his sights set on becoming a member of the diplomatic service. It is just as well that his ambitions were stillborn. It is difficult to imagine what fortunes and misfortunes the United States would have experienced with one so controversial as Andrew R. Pearson always pouring oil over troubled waters. In fact, although Andrew might seem a likely name for a stylish ambassador or consul, it was not after a diplomat that Drew was named; rather, he was named after another public figure with less than diplomatic ways, President Andrew Jackson, via a great-grandfather on Drew's father's side, Andrew Jackson Cameron.

Drew's father, Paul, was a professor of English and elocution at Northwestern University at the time of his son's birth. Paul's family members were Kansans; Paul was a graduate of Baker University and a Methodist minister. Drew's mother, Edna Wolfe, was from a Jewish family. When Paul first asked Edna to marry him she refused. Paul gave up preaching, departed his and Edna's native Kansas, and headed for graduate work at Northwestern. When again he asked for Edna's hand in marriage, she accepted. Four years after Drew's birth, Paul started additional study at Harvard University. Upon accepting an offer to join the faculty of Swarthmore College, a Quaker institution, Drew's father made yet another religious shift, this time joining, as did Edna, the Society of Friends. As a result Drew, brother Leon, and sisters Barbara and Ellen grew up as Quakers.

From his Kansas grandparents, Drew Pearson acquired a love of farming (and, presumably, experience at real muckraking); from his elocutionist father, he acquired a gift for lecturing and theatrical performance that would later serve him well in a different form of muckraking. Paul Pearson made a success of organizing a Chatauqua circuit in Pennsylvania and surrounding states. After he graduated from Phillips Exeter Academy, Drew Pearson went on to Swarthmore. True to his background, he played the lead in the senior play, won a state oratorical contest, and graduated Phi Beta Kappa. Also true to his background, he spent his summers working on relatives' farms in Kansas.

After leaving Swarthmore in 1919, Drew Pearson, partly to gain experience relevant to a future in the diplomatic service, partly out of his religious convictions, took a position directing a post–World War I relief mission in the Balkans for the American Friends Service Committee. His work was concentrated in Serbia, Albania, and Montenegro. One of the walled towns where he labored was temporarily renamed Pearsonavatz in honor of his efforts. When he returned to the United States in 1921, Pearson found, as many military personnel returning from Bosnia in 1996 discovered, that few people cared about his Serbian mission. His plans for a diplomatic career ended when he realized that the entrance standards for the American Foreign Service were so high, and the pay so low, that only the sons of the wealthy need apply. After a brief effort to organize a slide show–lecture preliminary to a career as a Chatauqua lecturer and a year teaching industrial geography at the University of Pennsylvania, Drew Pearson set out on an around-the-world adventure.

In a fashion that, with far greater success, propelled Lowell Thomas (q.v.) to prominence, Drew Pearson found employment as a lecturer and freelance journalist. He secured a six-month booking for a lecture tour in Australia. Combining the lecture contract with an assurance that a few newspapers would publish his freelance reports from abroad, Pearson shipped out as a seaman in a vessel headed for Asia. After debarking in Yokohama, Pearson walked away from his seaman's job and subsequently filed freelance dispatches from Japan and Siberia (where he interviewed a Russian general later shot on Josef Stalin's orders). Pearson worked his way down the Chinese coast, through the Philippines, to Australia. There he lectured and wrote feature articles for local newspapers. Upon resumption of his odyssey, Pearson reached India where he hoped to interview Mahatma Ghandi, only to find Ghandi in jail. Finally, while traveling to the Mediterranean region, Pearson received an offer of $2,000 from an American news syndicate for a series of interviews with ''Europe's Twelve Greatest Men'' (Great Britain's Lord Balfour, Italy's Benitio Mussolini, and so on.). By the time Pearson arrived back in the United States after his sojourn, he had $714 in his wallet, $14 more than when he had departed a year and half earlier.

Encouraged by his achievement as a freelance reporter, Pearson sought to repeat his success as an interviewer of great personages, this time such notables as Luther Burbank, Thomas Edison, and Henry Ford. Even though he published his material, however, no steady journalistic work came his way. Once again he returned to the classroom to teach geography, but his stint as an instructor at Columbia University in 1924 was brief; soon he was off again to the Orient— Japan, China, and Tibet.

During the days when Drew Pearson had diplomatic ambitions, his father had urged him to marry and settle down. At the time Drew joked in response that as a diplomat he would need a rich wife, but no rich bride would ''have him'' (Pilat, 1973, 64). However, in 1925, a young woman with wealthy connections,

Countess Felicia Gizycka, did have him—although she had previously rejected his proposals on several occasions. The marriage lasted only three years, but it was enough time to have a daughter, Ellen, and for Drew to cement his relationship with his mother-in-law, Eleanor Medill (Cissy) Patterson. Cissy had powerful journalistic connections; she was a cousin of Colonel Robert McCormick, the publisher of the *Chicago Tribune*, and the sister of Joseph Patterson, the publisher of the New York *Daily News*.

Through his close relationship with Cissy Patterson, Drew Pearson received a boost that lifted him out of freelance journalism and launched him toward a career as one of America's most influential investigative reporters. In 1926, after a honeymoon trip through China, Mongolia, Siberia (where he filed the first documented account of the imperialistic moves being made by the Soviet Union), and India, Pearson joined the *United States Daily* as foreign editor. The *Daily* (now the newsweekly *U.S. News & World Report*) was a project of David Lawrence, one of journalism's first political columnists. Cissy Patterson was a major financial backer in Lawrence's enterprise. It was she who urged Lawrence, in strict confidence, to hire her son-in-law. Four decades later, Lawrence confirmed the secret arrangement that without Cissy's intervention would not have been made: "I was not taken then or later with Drew Pearson," Lawrence told a Pearson biographer (Pilat, 1973, 81).

As foreign editor of the *Daily*, Pearson had a full-time journalistic post, yet he retained the option, at his own expense, of covering international conferences on a freelance basis. In his capacity as a *Daily* reporter and stringer for the Tokyo *Jiji* and Japan *Advertiser*, Pearson filed one of his first notable investigative scoops from the 1927 Geneva Disarmament Conference. He revealed that an imposter, posing as a reporter of the New York *Daily News*, filed false reports designed to sabotage cooperation between the United States and Great Britain in limiting naval armaments. Pearson's story provoked a U.S. Senate investigation that revealed the imposter was in the pay of U.S. shipbuilding companies. It was the first in what would become numerous revelations of political corruption that marked Pearson's investigative reporting over the next four decades.

Drew Pearson added to his *United States Daily* duties the job of diplomatic correspondent of the Baltimore *Sun*. Working with the accreditation of the *Daily* and the *Sun*, Pearson became an intimate of U.S. Secretary of State Frank Kellogg while he was covering the negotiation of the Kellogg-Briand Pact in Paris in 1928. That same year, he also accompanied Kellogg on a trip to Dublin. Thus, in 1930, he attended the London Naval Conference, not as the diplomat that the youthful Drew had aspired to be, but as the diplomatic correspondent his travels, lectures, reporting, and contacts had prepared him to be.

During his 1928 trip to Paris, Pearson became reacquainted with an Irishman he had met earlier during the 1927 Geneva Disarmament Conference. As a result, Pearson was contacted a year later, through diplomatic channels, and offered the job of Western Hemisphere director of the Irish Hospitals Sweepstakes, a lottery designed to help balance the Irish national budget, fund selected charities, and turn a profit for its managers. The offer was for $30,000 per year for five years plus a chauffeured limousine. Pearson wrestled, albeit briefly, with his conscience. The Society of Friends opposed all forms of gambling; moreover, use of the mails for conducting lotteries, selling tickets, or otherwise promoting games of chance was illegal. Nonetheless, Drew Pearson accepted the offer and embarked on running an international, illicit gambling operation involving mass ticket sales, money laundering, questionable bookkeeping, and the flaunting of postal regulations.

His sudden boost in income and the limousine Pearson explained as payment for confidential "public relations" work. The scam proved remarkably successful. Sales of lottery tickets in New York City under Pearson's management eventually exceeded sales in Ireland! Throughout his five-year stint as sweepstakes director, and for decades after it ended, Pearson contrived to skirt any public connection with the illegal enterprise. The lessons Drew Pearson learned in avoiding publicity of his own scandalous behavior he capitalized on as an investigative reporter to expose corruption in the behavior of others.

THE WASHINGTON MERRY-GO-ROUND

In spite of his divorce from Felicia, Drew Pearson remained close to his mother-in-law. Through her and her friends, as well as the political and social contacts he made through diplomatic reporting, Pearson grew intimate with the people in Washington, D.C., who "counted," particularly those to be counted upon to provide him with insider information, gossip, and tidbits that hinted at what was really going on in politics in contrast to what the press generally reported. In addition to enlarging his network of political and social news sources, Pearson sought out other reporters who shared his desire to report the Washington that resided behind the published accounts. Thus did he make the acquaintance of Robert S. Allen, then Washington bureau chief of the *Christian Science Monitor*.

Robert Allen was almost three years Drew Pearson's junior (born on July 14, 1900), but he could best Pearson in journalistic experience and match him in overseas adventures. A native of Kentucky, Allen was only thirteen years old when he began as a copyboy for the Louisville *Courier Journal*, a newspaper that bred many political commentators, most notably Arthur Krock (q.v.), the first "Washington Correspondent."

When World War I began, Allen lied about his age and joined the U.S. Army. He served in George Pershing's expedition to Mexico, then in France. He returned from the war with the bars of a second lieutenant on his shoulder, joined the Wisconsin National Guard, enrolled in the University of Wisconsin, and reported crime for the Madison *Capital Times*. Upon graduation he worked for the Wisconsin *State Journal* and the Milwaukee *Journal*. As a reporter, he exposed the fact that several key officials in Wisconsin were Ku Klux Klan members, information he obtained by posing as a Klan member himself.

In 1923 Allen enrolled for graduate work at the University of Munich. He was in Munich the next year when Field Marshall Erich von Ludendorff and a relatively unknown Adolf Hitler attempted their unsuccessful beer hall putsch. It was via Allen's accounts—reported to the *Christian Science Monitor*—that Americans learned of the overthrow attempt, its failure, and the trial of Adolf Hitler. Allen gave up his academic ambitions and remained in Europe as a roving *Monitor* reporter. After returning to the United States, Allen handled publicity for Robert LaFollete's presidential campaign, worked briefly for United Press, then joined the Washington bureau of the *Monitor* in 1925, becoming bureau head five years later.

Along with his bureau reporting for the *Monitor*, Allen also wrote contributions to *The Nation*. When the *Monitor* objected to the moonlighting, Allen contributed unsigned political profiles for H. L. Mencken's (q.v.) *American Mercury*. These were so well received that Allen conceived the idea for a book devoted to exposing the secret politics hidden behind Washington's facade. When a potential publisher urged that Allen seek a collaborator and combine social and political chatter about behind-the-scenes goings-on with exposure of documented scandal, Allen agreed.

Robert Allen felt that reporters in the 1920s too often stood in awe of elected politicians: "Nothing calculated to shock or alarm was permitted in their dispatches. The tales they told their friends never reached the wires" (Fisher, 1944, 230). For his part, Drew Pearson had become convinced "that even the so-called liberal papers in the United States are increasingly controlled by their cash registers and one of the few outlets to free journalism is through the medium of books" (Block, 1941, 660). It was no surprise, then, that when he called Pearson about a joint project, the latter accepted. Each working separately, Robert Allen in his basement and Drew Pearson in a study that once had served as slave quarters, they hammered out the anonymously written book *Washington Merry-Go-Round* (1931).

By the standards prevailing at the end of the twentieth century, *Washington Merry-Go-Round* would pass for bland, almost civil, political commentary. To political audiences in 1931, however, it was a revelation. The anonymous authors spared no one, not the incompetence of President Herbert Hoover, the pomposity of Vice President Charles ("Egg Charley") Curtis, the ineptness of Congress, the sanctimonious Supreme Court, the double-dealing secretary of the treasury, the giddiness of Washington high society, or the overstuffed, easily gulled Washington correspondents. Although it took weeks for Washington insiders, some amused and some shocked, to uncover the identity of the authors of *Washington Merry-Go-Round*, the truth finally came out. Robert Allen lost his job with the *Christian Science Monitor*, caught on with the International News Service, then lost that job as well. Drew Pearson retained his *Daily* and *Sun* jobs, but only temporarily. Publication of a sequel, *More Merry-Go-Round* in 1932, which contained several backstage tidbits about Cissy Patterson, resulted in Pearson's termination as well.

However, the pens and voices of Allen and Pearson were not so easily stifled. The two journalists approached news syndicates about the idea of a regular column. The United Features Syndicate agreed to a daily newspaper column, "Washington Merry-Go-Round." Although the column began in late 1932 with only a half a dozen newspaper subscribers, that number rose to 18 by early 1933, 270 a year later, 350 by World War II (when Allen ceased writing the column to return to the U.S. Army where he reached the rank of colonel), and over 600 subscribers and 20 million readers by the war's end. The success of the column produced lucrative side ventures—a "Merry-Go-Round" game; "Merry-Go-Round" toys; a comic strip, "Hap Hooper," about a crusading investigative reporter; and radio shows, "News for the Americas" on the National Broadcasting Company (NBC) and a weekly Sunday night version of "Washington Merry-Go-Round" on the NBC Blue network (later the American Broadcasting Company, or ABC). Pearson and Allen also collaborated on a book-length critique of the Supreme Court, *The Nine Old Men* (1936).

However, it was the daily column, "Washington Merry-Go-Round," that made Drew Pearson, working with Robert Allen, alone, and later with Jack Anderson, one of the twentieth-century's most controversial, influential, and innovative of political communicators:

> Whatever its record of accurate prophesy and interpretation, the Merry-Go-Round is a production of some historic importance in American journalism. It was one of the great factors in the change in the coverage of national politics which began with the New Deal. . . . The Merry-Go-Round was the first Washington column in the sense in which such compositions are regarded today. . . . It was, certainly, the first to deal in murderous candor, the first to merchandise the deplorable facts of American public life. (Fisher, 1944, 214)

As composed by Pearson and Allen, "The Merry-Go-Round" was a collaborative column written in the absence of face-to-face contact. In writing the column, each journalist worked apart from the other. In their earliest days of collaboration, Pearson and Allen shared an office, but because Pearson preferred to work out of his home, the common office soon fell into disuse. Instead, each reporter gathered his own material from his own sources; then the two conferred by telephone, agreed on the principal item for a day's column, wrote separate contributions, and left it to the syndicate office to fashion a common voice. Working as they did in a pre-fax, pre-E-mail era, the column was prepared well in advance of its being supplied to subscribers. Hence, there was always a risk that today's scoops would be old news by the time of publication. More often than not, however, Pearson and Allen were well ahead of the game and had no fear of being scooped themselves.

Although both journalists relied upon conventional sources to some degree, each developed his own unique network of informants. Moreover, both cultivated leaks, official and unofficial. Allen was a journalist of the old school; he preferred direct, face-to-face confrontations with officials. Unlike many Washington correspondents, especially James "Scotty" Reston (q.v.), who made his typewriter an extension of his telephone, Allen eschewed the telephone, did most of his legwork himself, and, when it came to personal friendships, kept his sources at a distance. By contrast, Pearson was a party animal. He mined receptions, dinner parties, and social gatherings for his nuggets of news. If legwork was necessary, Pearson hired assistants, principally his brother, Leon, in the early days, and, notably, Jack Anderson after World War II.

The "Washington Merry-Go-Round" was conceived as a column of opinion, but opinion derived from documented facts, at least as Pearson and Allen understood documentation. The journalists specialized in scoops, controversy, and, as a result, in defending themselves against lawsuits. Yet, rarely did the journalists—be they Pearson and Allen, Pearson alone, or Pearson and Jack Anderson—lose a legal challenge to their writings: "Without doubt, the successful record of 'Merry-Go-Round' writers during the past half century in defending press freedom through court involvement is a saga unmatched by any other American syndicated columnists" (Anderson, 1980, 262).

There were a few occasions when the columnists of the "Washington Merry-Go-Round" resorted to extralegal action in the face of serious legal threats. One case involved General Douglas MacArthur, a favorite bête noire of Pearson and Allen. The columnists were especially damning of MacArthur's tactics when, as the army's chief of staff in 1932, he routed a spontaneous gathering of 15,000 unemployed World War I veterans (the "Bonus Army") who had marched and hitchhiked to the nation's capital demanding economic relief. Under the instructions of President Herbert Hoover, MacArthur's troops forcibly removed the marchers from their makeshift quarters. Hoover's successor, Franklin Roosevelt, vexed at Pearson and Allen for other reasons, sympathized with MacArthur's grievances against the controversial duo and hinted that the general would do the nation and the commander in chief a service by eliminating the "Merry-Go-Round." Thereafter, MacArthur filed a $1.75 million lawsuit against Pearson and Allen.

Although *Washington Merry-Go-Round* had sold 90,000 copies, neither of its authors could afford to lose a lawsuit of the proportions contained in MacArthur's demands. Pearson's dinner table news gathering saved the day. At a soiree attended by MacArthur's ex-wife, Pearson learned that the general had dropped his Eurasian mistress, leaving the girl penniless. Pearson worked his sources, found the girl, and obtained a packet of letters detailing the general's affair. Through a series of Pearson's ruses, MacArthur learned what the columnist knew of the liaison and of the damning evidence he had. Without explanation MacArthur withdrew the legal action, paid the columnists' legal defense fees, and offered other considerations in exchange for the packet of incriminating letters. Although MacArthur was a bachelor at the time, he apparently feared for his reputation if there were a public scandal; more important, the chief of staff did not want his mother to learn about his long-term affair with a Eurasian woman (Pilat, 1973).

AN INSTITUTION HITS, MISSES, AND SURVIVES

One of the chief subscribing newspapers of the "Washington Merry-Go-Round" was the *Washington Times-Herald*, owned by Pearson's former mother-in-law, Cissy Patterson. In 1936 Pearson was married a second time, to Luvie Abell, the divorced wife of an old friend. Cissy Patterson was pleased and even hired Luvie Pearson as a film critic for her newspaper. However, as close as the bond between Pearson and Patterson was, it was not impervious to the strains put upon it by the fact that Pearson and Allen supported the New Deal and Patterson did not. Patterson began editing the "Merry-Go-Round" to right the column's liberal tilt. This did not please Robert Allen. When the column's renewal with the *Times-Herald* expired, Allen, with Pearson's assent, moved the joint venture to Patterson's Washington rival, the *Post*. Patterson was not a good loser, and she criticized Pearson and Allen in her own newspaper. As a result, the close association with her former son-in-law and protegé ended.

By that time, however, the "Washington Merry-Go-Round" had become a Washington and national institution. The column's reputation for scoops, near-scoops, and nonscoops had made it "a brand new and enormously diverting view of politics—a scene wherein great men were full of human fumbling, and statesmen had not only feet of clay but, occasionally, heads of mush as well" (Fisher, 1944, 215). With Allen as a collaborator, the column's notable coups included reporting that the Roosevelt administration would extend diplomatic recognition to the Soviet Union, that a black publisher would be named special assistant to the attorney general in the New Deal, that there were power struggles among key New Deal officials, that Roosevelt would divert public works funds to battleship construction, that the President would exchange American destroyers for bases in the Western Hemisphere held by Britain, that Franklin Roosevelt would win reelection in 1936 by carrying all but three states, and that England and France would not support Czechoslovakia's territorial integrity against Hitler's land grab in the Munich Crisis of 1939.

But, the columnists had their misses as well. For example, they predicted, in June 1941, that the Soviet Union could not hold out against Nazi Germany's invading army for more than a month. And, there was their all too trivial, yet major goof reporting that President Roosevelt's favorite song was "Home on the Range." It was not. In fact, he could scarcely abide it. Instead, it was the favorite of FDR's secretary. That error stuck in Roosevelt's craw throughout his presidency since, at every public appearance, a band would break out with the strains of the detested melody. (FDR was no happier when the columnists reported that his favorite breakfast was Danish pastry; his aides insisted on "breakfast rolls." But the columnists revealed their source—the bakery shop that supplied the daily ration of Danish.)

Although their column was controversial, it often appeared mild in comparison with another feature of the "Washington Merry-Go-Round" as an institution: the Sunday evening radio broadcasts. Pearson and Allen shared the program, taking turns reading news items. Later, the duo added a final program segment, "Predictions of Things to Come," a forerunner to John McLaughlin's (q.v.) "The McLaughlin Group" penchant for a "Predictions" segment. The accuracy rate of the predictions was kept artificially high by prophesying, on Sunday night, items already contained in news releases scheduled for distribution on the following day or during the coming week. The columnists shamelessly used the radio broadcasts to hype their column and vice versa. An opening announcement informed listeners how many newspapers subscribed to the column, thus adding import to the broadcast; Pearson and Allen then increased the number of subscribers by offering the column to newspapers cut rate, thus ever raising the number reported on the air.

A week prior to the Japanese attack on Pearl Harbor, a "Washington Merry-Go-Round" item reported that the Japanese naval fleet had sailed in secret. When the United States entered World War II, Robert Allen left the collaboration with Drew Pearson never to return. During the war he served with General George Patton's forces in Europe and lost an arm in the fighting. In a sardonic twist of fate, it was Drew Pearson in 1943 who broke one of the most controversial human interest stories of the war. General George Patton had slapped a war-weary soldier; all the correspondents traveling with Patton's army knew it, but did not report it. Pearson reported the facts of the case in a radio broadcast, including the reprimand given Patton and the general's apology to the soldier and his unit. Pearson, however, did not leave it at that. He went on to predict that Patton would never again receive a major military assignment, a grossly erroneous prognostication.

Soldiering on without Allen, Pearson not only kept the "Washington Merry-Go-Round" going, he made it prosper. In 1944 he moved the column to the Bell-McClure syndicate and ultimately became a key owner of the group. He continued to break stories other correspondents missed, making revelations along the way that "sent four Members of Congress to jail, defeated countless others, and caused the dismissal of scores of government officials" (Rivers, 1967, 115). He made intimates of successive presidents, from FDR to Lyndon Johnson (but not John F. Kennedy), then in some way riled them with his revelations. FDR labeled him "a chronic liar," and Harry Truman called him an "S.O.B."

And, he made notable enemies. When numerous Washington correspondents were hamstrung by conventions of "objective" reporting in covering U.S. Senator Joseph McCarthy's dismissal of the Bill of Rights in a frenzied search for Communists in government, Drew Pearson, who traded in opinions as well as facts, labeled McCarthy a fraud. It earned Pearson a loss of sponsorship for his radio broadcasts (Adam Hats) and a physical assault by McCarthy at a swank Washington club, a melee broken up by Vice President Richard Nixon. That earned McCarthy more investigative scrutiny and Pearson's charge that Mc-

Carthy's aides were seeking preferential treatment by the U.S. Army. The resulting Army-McCarthy U.S. Senate hearings hastened the senator's ultimate demise.

In the late 1950s, Drew Pearson began to share his column byline with a long-term assistant, Jack Anderson, and he gave Anderson his own byline in 1965. Anderson inherited the institution that was the "Washington Merry-Go-Round" when Pearson died from a heart attack on September 1, 1969. In fact, it was Anderson who had been doing the bulk of Pearson's investigative reporting since he arrived in Washington in 1947. For example, Anderson was key to Pearson's revelations that friends and advisers to President Harry Truman were given mink coats and deep freezers by lobbyists. Specifically identified in the "five percenter" scandal (i.e., those who traded commercial favors for 5 percent of the action) were a Truman buddy, John Maragon, a former bootblack and bootlegger, and the president's military adviser, General Harry Vaughan. It was the attacks on Vaughan that earned Pearson the Truman "S.O.B." designation.

Anderson later uncovered the fact that the top assistant to President Dwight Eisenhower, Sherman Adams, had accepted gifts from a wealthy industrialist in exchange for favorable political access. Anderson was also the Pearson aide who discovered that Democratic Senator Thomas Dodd was diverting campaign contributions to personal uses. These revelations led to Dodd's formal censure by the U.S. Senate. It was also Anderson who doggedly researched the story that Congressman Adam Clayton Powell was using taxpayers' money to lead a lavish lifestyle; the exposé resulted in Powell's being the lone congressman ever expelled from the House of Representatives. Although Pearson and Anderson were recommended for the Pulitzer Prize in 1967 as a result of the Dodd and Powell exposés, the Pulitzer trustees overruled the prize committee and gave the award to two reporters for the *Wall Street Journal*. (Anderson won the Pulitzer Prize for National Reporting in 1972 for revelations that the administration of Richard Nixon was covertly siding with Pakistan in a dispute with India over Bangladesh.)

When Drew Pearson assumed full control of the "Washington Merry-Go-Round" with the departure of Robert Allen, he made the enterprise, column and radiocast, more flamboyant and more opinionated, and he focused on insider politics. This suited Pearson's Washington style as a member of Washington's high society. Anderson was a Mormon and, unlike Pearson, avoided the Washington cocktail circuit and social scene. He instructed his staff to do the same. Anderson deemed that there were other ways to get behind-the-scenes political information than via the Washington night life. He relied on transcripts of closed-door government meetings leaked to him by congressional, presidential, and bureaucratic officials. If Pearson's style was that of the snoop, "Jack Anderson, by contrast, was almost purely a newspaperman. . . . He was perhaps the most resourceful reporter in Washington. 'Drew was more of a reformer,' Jack would say. 'I think I'm more of a reporter' " (Hume, 1974, 9).

FROM MUCKRAKING TO MUCKMAKING?

The "Washington Merry-Go-Round," chiefly because of Drew Pearson, with and without the collaboration of Robert Allen and Jack Anderson, created and institutionalized a unique style of political communication and commentary. Walter Winchell (q.v.) had introduced the gossip column to American journalism, but it was not until the success of Pearson and Allen that Winchell turned his columns and broadcasts toward political audiences. Larry King (q.v.) is a direct descendent of that tradition.

But, under Pearson, the "Washington Merry-Go-Round" was more than backstage reporting. Pearson was, as Jack Anderson said, a reformer. Like Lincoln Steffens, Ida Tarbell, Upton Sinclair, and the muckrakers that ushered in the twentieth century, Pearson sought to reveal the seamy side of society and politics in order to change them. He not only got under the skin of presidents, congressmen, and administrators, he drove many of them from office. More often than not, he did so by buttressing his reformer's zeal by reporting evidence of wrongdoing. He raked and mined muck more than he manufactured it. "Pearson makes a fetish of exact quotations, and when he does not have them, he re-creates them" but not by fabrication, for his "report was accurate in substance" (Rivers, 1967, 118).

There are many contemporary fabrications of the "Washington Merry-Go-Round"—the *National Enquirer*, "Hard Copy," and a host of paparazzi tabloid reports. However, it is most problematic that, unlike Pearson's muckraking, they can fairly be labeled as "accurate in substance."

REFERENCES

Selected Works by Drew Pearson

Washington Merry-Go-Round. With R. S. Allen. New York: Liveright, 1931.
More Merry-Go-Round, by the Authors of Washington Merry-Go-Round. With R. S. Allen. New York: Liveright, 1932.
The American Diplomatic Game. With C. Brown. Garden City, NY: Doubleday, Doran, 1935.
The Nine Old Men. With R. S. Allen. Garden City, NY: Doubleday, Doran, 1936.
The Case against Congress. With J. Anderson. New York: Simon and Schuster, 1937.
Nine Old Men at the Crossroads. With R. S. Allen. Garden City, NY: Doubleday, Doran, 1937.
U.S.A.—Second Class Power? With J. Anderson. New York: Simon and Schuster, 1958.
Diaries, 1949–1959. Edited by A. Tyler. New York: Holt, Rinehart and Winston, 1974.

Selected Critical Works about Drew Pearson

Anderson, D. *A "Washington Merry-Go-Round" of Libel Actions*. Chicago: Nelson-Hall, 1980.

Block, M., ed. "Pearson, Drew (Andrew Russell); Allen, Robert (Sharon)." In *Current Biography 1941*, 658–61. New York: H. W. Wilson, 1941.

Carney, W. P. "Washington Gadfly." In *Molders of Opinion*, edited by D. Bulman, 107–20. Milwaukee: Bruce Publishing, 1945.

Fang, I. E. "Drew Pearson." In *Those Radio Commentators!*, 217–43. Ames, IA: Iowa State University Press, 1977.

Fisher, C. "Pearson and Allen Go Round." In *The Columnists*, edited by C. Fisher, 210–48. New York: Howell, Soskin, 1944.

Hume, B. *Inside Story*. Garden City, NY: Doubleday, 1974.

Klurfeld, H. *Behind the Lines: The World of Drew Pearson*. Englewood Cliffs, NJ: Prentice-Hall, 1968.

Kunitz, S. J., ed. "Pearson, Drew." In *Twentieth Century Authors*, 764–65. New York: H. W. Wilson, 1955.

Lichtenstein, N., ed. "Pearson, Drew (Andrew) (Russell)." In *Political Profiles: The Kennedy Years*, 406–7. New York: Facts on File, 1981.

McKerns, J. P., ed. "Pearson, Andrew Russell 'Drew.' " In *Biographical Dictionary of American Journalism*, 551–53. New York: Greenwood Press, 1989.

Pilat, O. P. *Drew Pearson: An Unauthorized Biography*. New York: Harper's Magazine Press, 1973.

Riley, S. G. "Pearson, Andrew Russell." In *Biographical Dictionary of American Newspaper Columnists*, 243–46. Westport, CT: Greenwood Press, 1995.

Rivers, W. L. "TIME and Pearson: The Influence of the 'Outcasts.' " In *The Opinionmakers*, edited by W. L. Rivers, 110–28. Boston: Beacon Press, 1967.

Schoenebaum, E., ed. "Pearson, Drew (Andrew) (Russell)." In *Political Profiles: The Eisenhower Years*, 478–80. New York: Facts on File, 1977.

Selected General Works

Hofstadter, R. *The Age of Reform*. New York: Alfred A. Knopf, 1955.

Woodward, B., and C. Bernstein. *All the President's Men*. New York: Simon and Schuster, 1974.

DAN RATHER

(October 31, 1931–   )

From Political Commentary to Political Celebrity

In his widely acclaimed novel, *Celebrity* (1982), the author Thomas Thompson depicts a conversation between a wily, grizzled old newspaper editor and an inexperienced, ambitious cub reporter. It is early in the tenure of the reporter on the paper and each journalist tries to size up the other. "What do you want to be?" asks the editor. "Good? Or famous?" Perplexed, but without hesitation or reservation, the tyro responds, "Both." The editor barely manages a grin, "That's illegal. It's bigamy. And it's hardly possible" (167).

When a made-for-television movie based on *Celebrity* aired, a few critics speculated that the television depiction of the young journalist, who proved the editor correct by starting out as a good reporter, then growing worse with each step toward fame and fortune, reminded them of Columbia Broadcasting System (CBS) correspondent, nightly news anchor, and political commentator Dan Rather. Faced with the Faustian choice of being good or famous, what had Rather done? The answer to that question is a matter of opinion. However, if there is a quality of Dan Rather that makes him one of the key political commentators of the twentieth century it is his status as a transitional figure. Dan Rather represents a generation of political communicators in post–JFK America who, unwittingly or not, departed the hallowed and honored tradition of broadcast commentary pioneered by Edward R. Murrow (q.v.), Elmer Davis (q.v.), and Eric Sevareid (q.v.) and, instead, became political celebrities of such starlike stature that as broadcasters they, not politics, became the story of the moment wherever they went. The tradition of Larry King (q.v.), John McLaughlin (q.v.), and Corrine "Cokie" Roberts (q.v.) was born.

THE CONTEXT FOR TRANSITION

As the people on this planet, in the era of the 1960s through the 1980s, became increasingly connected via technology and, thereby, potentially informed, they grew more sophisticated and, perhaps, more blasé about political happenings. Events that, in earlier eras, were sensational, astonishing, or horrifying became almost routine. Moreover, the capability to travel at high speeds safely encouraged tourism, scholarship, and commerce between nations.

These broadening experiences helped the nation with a superior means to do so, namely the United States, to share its ideas with people from other countries. The accessibility of world travel not only benefited people in general, but also helped U.S. media organizations to create a new market. Global unrest and warfare may result in refugees fleeing to safer places, but it also provides the media with a captivating news story. The media follow these people and track their accomplishments and their failures, all the while making money by attracting an audience of readers, listeners, and viewers.

In the cross fire of a political war, defiance, fear, and integrity are at stake. Reporting on the events and movements of political figures has been described as walking a thin line between the interests of the news agency and upholding the integrity of the U.S. governance system. Some political commentators, like Noam Chomsky (q.v.), argue that the line is not thin but nonexistent.

In the 1960s, gathered behind the stately Eric Sevareid in the CBS Washington, D.C., news bureau were more than a dozen other correspondents. Among those trying to move ahead of the group to make a name for themselves with CBS executives was Dan Rather. In January 1964, Rather was named the White House correspondent, and was assigned to cover the Lyndon Johnson administration. From this assignment, Rather earned the reputation of being a hard-nosed, tough reporter, who often challenged the political system rather than enhancing its aims. Rather continued his challenge through the tumultuous presidency of Richard Nixon. Despite his confrontations with Lyndon Johnson, Richard Nixon, and later with President George Bush, Dan Rather does not view himself as a gutsy reporter. When compared to Edward R. Murrow, Rather insists there is no comparison. For instance, in an interview about the famous "See It Now" segment in 1954 on the clash between newsperson Murrow and Senator Joe McCarthy, Rather told an interviewer, "We're not even in the same cosmos, . . . I'm not as good. I'm not as brave. I don't have the tools Murrow had. Or the intellect. Or the guts. I'd like to have them" (Shister, 1994, SC7).

The late 1960s and early 1970s were, for Dan Rather, a composite of both the makings of a great career, and the potential for demise. His success was tempered by the knowledge that some of the confrontations he engaged in could lead to his dismissal at CBS. His aggressive style and tenacious coverage of Nixon made him a popular, yet controversial figure. His political commentary was more in tune with Murrow's style of journalism than with the tradition of the dispassionate news anchor, as, for example, Walter Cronkite (q.v.). Even though he was taking a risk in the late 1960s and 1970s, Rather knew if he survived this tumultuous time, he could have fame. He was "a gambler by nature," and the prize was worth the risk (Gates, 1978, 289).

SEEKING FAME VIA ENTERPRISE, BIG BREAKS, AND CONTROVERSY

The long road to the "CBS Evening News" anchor position began in Texas. The son of a pipeline worker, Irwin "Rags" Rather, and a former hotel cafe waitress, Byrl, Dan Rather was born on Halloween, October 31, 1931, in Wharton, Texas. During his early childhood, the family traveled often as his father followed the oil pipeline construction crews across Texas. The Rathers settled in Houston when Dan was a year old. They lived in a house in an increasingly depression-poor neighborhood, "The Heights." It was short of poverty, but scarcely affluent. In Houston came Dan's first taste of politics. When he was still in primary school his father took him to Democratic party precinct meetings; it was an introduction to the tumultuous arena of Texas politics which he never forgot.

The Rather family were all hard working, mainly blue-collar employees. But Dan Rather, by the time he reached adolescence, knew he wanted more than the oil fields of East Texas. His mother supported his ambitions. And, upon his graduation from Reagan High School, his mother cashed in two of the family's $25 U.S. savings bonds, bought during World War II for $18.75, for less than face value. The money helped get her son enrolled in Sam Houston State Teachers College in Huntsville. That was the extent of his parents' financial assistance. Dan decided to try out for the college football team in hopes of landing an athletic grant. The hopes proved forlorn; his physique, weight, and minimal skills, despite his high school experience, did not prepare him for competitive college football. Rather was devastated when he did not win a football scholarship.

All, however, was not lost. His source of money for continuing his college tuition was a journalism professor, Hugh Cunningham. Cunningham was impressed with Rather's work at Sam Houston State, encouraged him to be a journalist, and helped Dan obtain a part-time job as a writer and sportscaster at KSAM, the local radio station. So, as with other noted CBS political commentators before him, such as Edward R. Murrow and after him, Bill Moyers (q.v.), a mentor played a key role in Rather's choice of journalism as a career. The job at the radio station was not only his chief source of income while in college, but it was also a valuable apprenticeship. During his time in college Rather learned the craft, techniques, and characteristics of a good journalist from Cunningham, and the part-time job provided him with a place to practice and refine his skills. He was a favorite on the Sam Houston campus as well—junior class president, host of the Bathing Revue, and winner of the "Frontier Days" beard growing contest.

Throughout his college days, Dan Rather followed a pattern very similar to the one followed by another college undergraduate who someday would become a nemesis, and ticket to success, for the aspiring journalist—Richard Nixon. Rather, like Nixon, having little money, determined to work harder than anyone else, accomplish more than anyone else, and become more successful than anyone else. And, like Nixon, Rather expressed a distrust of big government and politicians. But whereas Nixon drifted toward the Republicans, Rather tilted Democrat, writing anti-Republican and anti-McCarthy articles during the 1952 campaign when Richard Nixon was championing both.

In 1953 he completed his B.A. degree in journalism. He enlisted in the Marines for a brief tour of duty (Gates, 1978) before returning to Houston where for a few months he worked briefly for the United Press International (UPI) and the *Houston Chronicle*. Then he moved to the radio station KTRH, the CBS affiliate in Houston, where for four years he was a news writer, reporter, and news director. His terse, no-nonsense style of broadcasting earned him plaudits, awards, and a reputation as a young man of promise. By 1961 Rather had shifted media, and he became news director and anchor for the CBS affiliate in Houston, KHOU-TV. He quickly became a skilled and polished reporter, particularly as a field reporter; being on the scene meant digging and searching for information, a task he relished as had his contemporary political commentator at NBC, John Chancellor (q.v.), as a cub reporter.

Yet, in television journalism there are legions of camera-ready, hard-working, smooth-talking reporters. Success, notoriety, and celebrity demand that an ambitious journalist break out of the clutter. Often that is a matter of luck, of being at the right place at the right time, seizing the moment, and showcasing talents before a national audience: the Big Break. Big breaks came often to Dan Rather in his career. The first was in the fall of 1961. In September Rather and his news crew were marooned on Galveston Island when Hurricane Carla, one of the most devastating in decades, barreled down on them. In dramatic footage of the hurricane, including scenes from the eye of the storm, Rather reported on events and conditions live and on tape for three days for the CBS-TV network. He even managed to rescue a horse from drowning in a flooded stable. It was the first time he reported an event in a manner that would later mark a distinctive aspect of Rather's career: he was not the reporter of news but the news itself. Rather's coverage of Hurricane Carla thrust him into the national spotlight. Walter Cronkite, an intrepid, on-the-scene reporter long before he was anchor and commentator, said of Rather, "We were impressed by his calm and physical courage" (Gates, 1978, 290).

As a result of his Carla coverage, Rather was elevated to a coveted position with CBS News, a network correspondent's job, first in Washington, D.C., for a six-month initiation and training run on CBS operations, then reassignment in a regular correspondent's role. It proved a difficult transition for Rather, particularly because he had not reported from outside of Texas. But he adapted and, as luck would have it, CBS decided to open two new bureaus in the South to handle expanding coverage of the civil rights movement. So in the spring of 1962, Rather returned to Texas to open the CBS bureau in Dallas; CBS correspondent Hughes Rudd opened the bureau in Atlanta.

The 1960s were a volatile time in the United States, particularly in the South. The civil rights movement happened at a time when television news was just hitting its stride. Videotape made it possible to record footage of breaking news and broadcast it to other parts of the country quickly. In previous decades, newspapers and photographs lessened the immediacy of the events due to time delays and fuzzy film imagery. Rather's experience with Hurricane Carla had taught him the value of reporting a sense of immediacy. So, he again seized the opportunity, and once again his enterprise was successful. His youth and determination helped him outhustle Rudd to cover key events; Rather searched for unique angles on stories, and he quickly recognized the importance of making news visual as well as oral in content. By the spring of 1963, Rudd voluntarily transferred to Chicago, and the network consolidated the Dallas and Atlanta bureaus into a single bureau in New Orleans with Dan Rather as bureau chief.

Rather's star was on the rise. Nothing pushed it to its peak, not coverage of Carla or the civil rights movement, as much as Rather's coverage of the events surrounding President John F. Kennedy's visit to Texas in November 1963, a trip Kennedy had undertaken to soothe factional strife in that state's turbulent politics. On November 22, 1963, Dan Rather was transformed from a regional correspondent to a national television persona. It was Dan Rather who seemed to CBS television viewers to be on the screen continuously reporting and an-choring the coverage of the four-day drama of Kennedy's assassination, the swearing in of a new president, the arrest of the alleged assassin, the murder of that assassin, and the unrelenting atmosphere of confusion and outpouring of grief that changed forever the nature of television news and commentary. Rather's flawless journalistic style, emphasizing details and accuracy, seemed to herald the birth of what many critics felt was the arrival of a new CBS Ed Murrow.

During the coverage of the Kennedy assassination and its aftermath, Dan Rather's enterprise was endless, creative, and courageous. For example, Rather informed the executive producer of "CBS Evening News" of an 8-mm film depicting the actual moments of JFK's being shot. Rather was the only television journalist invited to witness a closed screening of the film. The producer urged Rather to attend. In spite of the fact that, at that time, airing reports of the film's content might bring a lawsuit from the film's owner (who was peddling the film at a price), Rather "responded with . . . journalistic aggressiveness, bolting out of the room right after seeing the film to run back to CBS and describe, on live television , what he had just witnessed" (Bianculli, 1992, 96).

With Texan Lyndon Johnson now president, and since Dan Rather supposedly understood Texas politics better than most other CBS reporters, he was pro-moted ahead of many more accomplished correspondents to the coveted position of White House correspondent. The luck of being in the right place at the right time, and making the most of the opportunity, had again supplied Dan Rather's Big Break. Naturally there was resentment by personnel in the Washington bu-reau, but Rather managed to muddle through and believed that he was making progress. So he was quite surprised to learn that he would be transferred to the London bureau and would not remain in the United States to cover Johnson's presidency following the 1964 election.

Rather's transfer to London was the CBS news executives' way of giving their diamond in the rough extended training. He benefited immensely from it. While in the London bureau, he worked with several veterans from the Murrow era, such as the suave Charles Collingsworth and the streetwise Alexander Ken-drick. Rather was conscious of his deficiencies in both areas and, hence, utilized the assignment to master the fine art of elegance combined with a touch of noblesse oblige befitting a popular broadcaster.

Dan Rather's eagerness to sit at the feet of, by his own definition, "mentors," has led some critics to question whether his claims of being close to his senior colleagues at CBS during his formative years are accurate or are the stuff of myth. For example, in the fall of 1965, Rather requested and was granted a transfer to Saigon. He spent the next several months in Vietnam. Rather claims that, during a visit to Vietnam by CBS political commentator extraordinaire Eric Sevareid, the Grey Eminence took the untutored Rather under his wing. Sevareid became, in Rather's phrase, his "guru in television" (Boyer, 1988, 296). Rather's version of the Saigon lesson is that Sevareid urged him to take a year off from reporting and bone up on the works of the classic thinkers and philosophers to have a well-rounded analytical perspective—writers Rather had never read such as Plato, Aristotle, Machiavelli, and Herodotus. When he returned to the United States and discussed the possibility with his wife Jean (Goebel), whom he had married in 1957, Rather decided that a year away from reporting was not financially feasible. Instead, Rather bought the fifty-four-volume *Great Books of the Western World* and allegedly digested the contents. Moreover, Rather claimed that, on Sevareid's advice, he always carried a pocket copy of a classic book on writing style. Sevareid, in turn, claimed he had no recollection of the Saigon mentoring (Schroth, 1995) and, of the primer on writing style, "I've never read the book in my life" (Boyer, 1988, 237).

Be that as it may, in his years abroad, Rather learned several valuable lessons about reporting. He took those lessons and a renewed sense of self-confidence back to his post as White House correspondent in the summer of 1966. Upon his return, Rather established a firm command; he used the White House office staff members, elevator operators, even food service personnel, to provide him with inside tips. Such sources, he contends, are privy to compelling and telling situations, and, as a journalist, he is obligated to work every angle.

Although he could scarcely claim CBS and American Broadcasting Company (ABC) political commentator Elmer Davis as a mentor, as Edward R. Murrow did, Rather did take a lesson from a Davis dictum, "Don't let the bastards scare you" (Gates, 1978, 290). This sentiment, although difficult to stand by, is one Rather has adhered to throughout his career. He had major confrontations with presidents Lyndon Johnson and Richard Nixon while serving as White House correspondent, but he did not run scared. Rather's coverage of the Vietnam War infuriated Johnson; his adversarial questioning of Nixon during the Watergate scandal fueled the dissension. Rather, according to his supporters, was not anti-LBJ or anti-RMN, but instead "a diligent and aggressive reporter who refused to be intimidated by the various attempts to coerce and control him" (Gates, 1978, 298).

CELEBRITY

From 1968 through the summer of 1974, Dan Rather's career as a television journalist was on the upswing. He was the highly visible bête noir of an increasingly unpopular president, Richard Nixon. And, even though some executives of CBS affiliates protested that Rather's Watergate coverage was too politicized and that he should be removed as White House correspondent, he retained the post. He also worked on CBS prime-time news specials and was the anchor of the "CBS Sunday News." There was little question that CBS was grooming him for bigger and better things, perhaps even as a replacement for Walter Cronkite as anchor of the "CBS Evening News" should the respected and avuncular Cronkite retire. To be sure, there were rivals among CBS colleagues for network promotion. The chief one was CBS congressional correspondent Roger Mudd. Mudd, like Rather, had covered the Watergate demise of Richard Nixon and had also won a popular following in the process.

On the evening of Richard Nixon's televised address in 1974 resigning the presidency, Walter Cronkite anchored CBS' postaddress coverage. It was a testing time for political commentators and analysts of all ilks. John Chancellor, of the National Broadcasting Company (NBC), for instance, boiled his thoughts down to a single word, "Well." But that would not suffice at CBS. Eric Sevareid pontificated briefly as part of CBS' coverage. Then, it was Rather's turn. Given Rather's strong performance in covering the breaking story of Watergate, it was a time and place for Rather to take full advantage of his celebrity. This time he did not capture the moment. Although Nixon had made no apology for the Watergate break-in or cover-up, or for his own complicity, Rather all but forgave him everything. With historical hindsight, said Rather, the resignation address would possibly be Nixon's "finest hour"; the president had displayed a "touch of class—more than that a touch of majesty." By contrast, Roger Mudd found the speech unsatisfactory, pointedly remarking that the president had explained nothing and had taken blame for nothing (Boyer, 1988, 235).

Whether Rather's commentary on Nixon's resignation derived from a sense of fair play toward a fallen nemesis or from a desire to reassure CBS affiliates that Rather as a potential anchor of "The Evening News" would not be threatening, one cannot say. But, as the grizzled editor in Celebrity said, being good and being famous are not necessarily compatible. Rather certainly had become famous. Now, after long consideration, Dan Rather decided to leave his post as chief White House correspondent. Speculation was that he was being moved to less sensitive assignments in response to earlier affiliates' demands. Following the CBS announcement of August 22, 1974, he departed Washington and moved to New York, where he began his work as the host for "CBS Reports," a documentary program. Although it removed him from the day-to-day coverage of breaking news in the nation's capital, it was an opportunity to continue conducting in-depth commentary regarding political issues, political officials, and events.

His "permanent" assignment with "CBS Reports" proved to be relatively brief. In the fall of 1975, Rather made another shift in his career, one that helped him cement his later appointment as Walter Cronkite's replacement anchoring "The Evening News." When "60 Minutes" moved to a new time slot on

Sunday, December 7, Rather joined the program as a regular correspondent. It was a fortunate reassignment. The popularity of full-blown documentaries such as "CBS Reports" was on the wane, particularly among CBS executives, as political commentator Bill Moyers learned. On "CBS Reports" Rather had worked hard to create a specific and strong identity, but a lack of continuity in airtime, as the program was shifted from time slot to time slot, frustrated his efforts. The show was scheduled to air only once a month, and it was often in a weak time. This also hampered the development of a regular audience. As a journalist, Rather was accustomed to more visibility.

However, past experience with resentful correspondents made Rather uneasy about his switch in assignments. Dan Rather and Mike Wallace (q.v.), the leading correspondent of "60 Minutes," had similar styles. Wallace assured Rather that he would be a welcome addition to the show (Wallace and Gates, 1984, 348). So, with the approval of Wallace, Rather joined the "60 Minutes" team and began to reinvent his image once again. He had established himself as a hard-hitting and critical journalist, but the controversy from the Nixon era still haunted him. As a correspondent on "60 Minutes," he was able to display a warmer, more friendly persona, while still providing informative and carefully edited journalistic segments.

COVERING THE NEWS VERSUS BEING THE NEWS

Rather continued his work on "60 Minutes" until 1981 when he left to take on the challenge of assuring the loyal viewers of the "CBS Evening News with Walter Cronkite" that there could still be life in the *Evening News* without Walter Cronkite. In his fifteen years as the anchor of the "CBS Evening News," Rather has brought more life than generations of Cronkite watchers might have liked, and less energy than others might have expected. In many instances, both Rather's on- and off-the-air persona has generated as much, if not more, news than he either reports or submits to comment. In 1987 "60 Minutes" became the third-longest-running program ever rated in the top ten and the first such news show. The "CBS Evening News," by sharp contrast, was not performing very well—it was mired in third place among the three networks' evening news programs. As a means of correcting the imbalance, a proposal circulated to move popular CBS news correspondent Diane Sawyer from her "60 Minutes" role to co-anchor of the "Evening News." However, CBS decided to stay the course and retain Rather as sole anchor.

Then, on September 11, an angry Rather stalked off the set of the "Evening News" leaving the newscast with a blank screen for six minutes. He did it while CBS was airing, during the evening news time slot, the completion of a women's semifinal match in the U.S. Tennis Open. No sooner had he left the set than the match ended. When the evening news aired there was no Rather; he had to be found and rushed back to the set. Although Rather denied he walked off the set in protest of the airing of the match, Walter Cronkite was not forgiving. Asked what he thought of Rather's conduct he said, "I can answer that in five words: I would have fired him" (Slater, 1988, 319). Rather's noncoverage of news was now news.

In January 1988, Dan Rather made news for being a newsman rather than failing to be one. He was conducting a live interview on the "Evening News" with Vice President George Bush, who was then seeking the 1988 Republican nomination for president. When Rather endeavored to turn the topic of the interview toward an arms-for-hostages controversy that had dominated the previous year's headlines and, apparently, toward Bush's knowledge of the Reagan administration's role in it, tensions mounted. Bush challenged Rather's style and, by implication, his motives in questioning, and Rather became momentarily speechless. Rather insisted that he was attempting to "get the record straight"; Bush insisted that it was unfair to judge "my whole career by a rehash on Iran." The exchange made news: an example of a liberal anchor ambushing a Republican candidate. Countless, and perhaps pointless, journalistic and scholarly investigations suggest the *real* story was one of a presidential candidate endeavoring to shed a wimpish image by ambushing an unsuspecting news anchor and political commentator who, according to public opinion surveys, was the most suitable anchor target (Goldberg & Goldberg, 1990, 238–41).

Whatever the authentic account, it was but another in a long line of newsworthy controversies surrounding the celebrated Rather. Even in his private life he made news: once, he was allegedly "kidnapped" by a Chicago taxi driver; on another occasion, he was mugged by assailants on the streets of New York City. Rather summed it up in 1996, "I've got all these bullet holes, stab wounds, spear hurts and self-inflicted wounds. Holy mackerel. I'm still here. That's pretty amazing" (Bark, 1996, C8).

Operating in an era where market shares dictate the content and style of a program had become a new reality for old-time television journalists, especially those who worked for CBS News. In former times the network prided itself on in-depth coverage and extensive research teams, but the new age of television in a competitive market meant combining thrift with quality. Rather has commented that were one of many idols in his pantheon, Edward R. Murrow, in the contemporary news business, "He'd be the biggest name in the business." But with the cutthroat ratings war, "He'd feel much greater pressure today than when he left" (Shister, 1994, SC7).

The pressure for ratings and a larger market share led the network to add Connie Chung as coanchor on the "CBS Evening News" in 1994 (Endrst, 1994, E7; Hall, 1995, F1); "the fervor over Rather and Chung is a well-known secret: the news anchors' jobs are much more about great ratings than great reporting" (Goodman, 1995, H28). Rather commented, "The adventure of working with and as a coanchor has made it possible for me to undertake more adventures" (Endrst, 1994, E7). After a decade of anchoring a national news program, the addition of another person possibly provided Rather with more adventures than he had anticipated, for following the initial novelty, the duo did not boost ratings; in fact, the newscast dropped to third place (Hall, 1995, F5).

More than ratings, however, were at issue. Rather was staunch in advocating a journalistically sound nightly newscast. As far as he was concerned, his reportorial skills had not diminished, and he expected the correspondents and his coanchor to uphold *his* standards and display *his* skills. When CBS News sent Chung to anchor the signing of the Middle East peace accord, Rather was miffed but claims he did not oppose the decision, "That's pretty big and important turf, (but) I did not oppose her going" (Hall 1995, F5). When, in the wake of the April 19, 1996, bombing of the Alfred P. Murrah federal office building in Oklahoma City, CBS News sent Chung alone to cover the breaking story, it proved a mistake. Chung did not perform well; indeed, she earned the criticism of rescue workers who claimed her demands to be on-site hampered their emergency efforts. She also earned the criticism of her coanchor; Rather requested changes in the newscast. "I told them, I can't go through this again," Rather said (Hall, 1995, F5). Chung announced her departure from CBS shortly thereafter, coincidentally, the day Dan Rather was delivering a commencement address at the University of Texas on the virtues of a free and unfettered press.

Although Rather is a respected reporter, his criticism of contemporary journalism as being too much advocacy, too little straight reporting, is difficult for his critics to accept, particularly from one who achieved celebrity by exploiting controversy. Rather's defense is vehement. In the Murrow tradition, Rather wants the news to be informational, and the reporter to offer a contextual analysis of the facts. But even there he has erred and, in the erring, made news. While on assignment in Haiti, Rather reported the dropping of parachutes as a possible attack by a large military force (Kurtz, 1994, A11). In fact, the parachutes contained leaflets and portable radios. Critics denounced Rather's actions, citing him in violation of the principle he advocates: avoid sensationalism. Rather retaliated, "Whatever mistakes I made, real or imagined, at least I didn't make them sitting in a windowless room on the Westside of Manhattan" (Kurtz, 1994, A11).

After a decade and a half as anchor of the "CBS Evening News," and more recently as the host of "48 Hours," another CBS newsmagazine program, Dan Rather remains a controversial political commentator. In an industry where change is the order of the day, survival alone is a mark of success for some. Yet, at the age of sixty-five, Rather retains an influential presence in the world of telejournalism. He claims still to enjoy the search for information and the reporting of breaking news to the public along with an analysis of what it all means. To that end he keeps his reportorial skills honed by working on occasional field assignments and documentary segments. Yet, he long ago transcended his origins as a reporter and analyst of events; as a celebrity, he *is* the event.

Few aspects of the transition wrought in political commentary during Dan Rather's lifetime are as telling as how three of the most widely known CBS commentators referred to themselves at the end of their careers. When Ed Murrow departed CBS, he referred to himself simply as a "reporter." When Walter Cronkite wrote his reminiscences of his career, he called himself simply a "photojournalist." The subtitle of Dan Rather's memoirs labels him a "television journalist," perhaps not quite an oxymoron but surely as close as "military justice."

REFERENCES

Selected Works by Dan Rather

The Palace Guard. With G. P. Gates. New York: Harper and Row, 1974.
The Camera Never Blinks. With M. Herskowitz. New York: William Morrow, 1977.
I Remember. With P. Wyden. Boston: Little, Brown, 1991.
The Camera Never Blinks: The Further Adventures of a Television Journalist. New York: William Morrow, 1994.

Selected Critical Works about Dan Rather

Bark, E. "Rather Remarkable." *Dallas Morning News*, March 17, 1996, C1, C8.
Goldberg, R., and G. J. Goldberg. *Anchors: Brokaw, Jennings, Rather*. New York: Birch Lane Press, 1990.
Goodman, W. "Twinkle, Twinkle, Network News Stars." *New York Times*, May 28, 1995, H28.
Hall, J. "Dan and Connie: He Says, She Says." *Los Angeles Times*, May 23, 1995, F1, F5.
Kurtz, H. "Dan Rather Stands by Haiti Report." *Washington Post*, September 17, 1994 A11.
Moritz, C., ed. "Rather, Dan." In *Current Biography 1975*, 337–40. New York: H. W. Wilson, 1976.

Selected General Works

Bianculli, D. *Teleliteracy*. New York: Simon and Schuster, 1992.
Boyer, P. J. *Who Killed CBS?* New York: Random House, 1988.
Endrst, J. "At CBS, a Weary Eye on the News." *Sacramento Bee*, November 23, 1994, E7.
Gates, G. P. *Air Time: The Inside Story of CBS News*. New York: Harper and Row, 1978.
Halberstam, D. *The Powers That Be*. New York: Alfred A. Knopf, 1979.
Joyce, E. *Prime Times, Bad Times*. New York: Doubleday, 1988.
McKibben, B. *The Age of Missing Information*. New York: Random House, 1992.
Schroth, R. A. *The American Journey of Eric Sevareid*. South Royalton, VT: Steerforth Press, 1995.
Shister, G. "CBS Reports Examines Murrow, McCarthy Clash." *Sacramento Bee*, June 15, 1994, SC7.
Slater, R. *This . . . Is CBS*. Englewood Cliffs, NJ: Prentice-Hall, 1988.
Thompson, T. *Celebrity*. Garden City, NY: Doubleday, 1982.
Wallace, M., and G. P. Gates. *Close Encounters*. New York: William Morrow, 1984.

JAMES (BARRETT) "SCOTTY" RESTON

(November 3, 1909–December 6, 1995)

A *Political Commentator for His* Times

Throughout the 1950s television increasingly eroded the dominance of newspapers and radio as sources Americans turned to for information about politics. There was no major land shift, merely a gradual wearing away at the surface of political communication until, in the 1960s, many newspapers vanished, network radio all but disappeared, and television served as the cultural loam within which political messages took root and flourished. Yet, one newspaper in particular not only fought off the erosion, it was the substructure that supported other news organizations at the political surface. That was the *New York Times*.

The *Times* had long been influential in political circles, avidly read by policy officials, political insiders, and America's political intelligentsia. There is, for example, an apocryphal account of a State Department official who, when asked in an interview whether he could add anything to a *Times*' dispatch on a vital negotiation, replied, "Heavens, no! Where do you think we've been getting our information?" (Rivers, 1967, 76). With its reputation for straight and accurate factual reporting, pipeline to political insiders, and *the* newspaper of record, the *Times* possessed a stature not easily diminished by television's rising popularity.

Before the 1950s the *Times* had already attracted more than its share of working journalists who contributed to the evolution of twentieth-century political communication in major ways. For example, Elmer Davis (q.v.) was a *Times*man long before he achieved a controversial reputation as a radio commentator and director of the Office of War Information during World War II; and Arthur Krock (q.v.) was covering breaking news stories as the *Times* Washington correspondent in the 1930s and 1940s. Yet, in many respects, with the appointment of James "Scotty" Reston as chief of the *Times* Washington bureau in 1953, the organization enhanced its standing as a political force many times over. Reston largely reinvented the *Times* as a political institution through his reporting, thrice-weekly columns, and managerial style. At the close of the 1950s, one seasoned political journalist, Douglass Cater, summed up the Reston influence:

> Under the leadership of James Reston, the traditionally stodgy *New York Times* bureau has achieved new standards of capable and reliable reporting. . . . *Times* reporters . . . operate with the happy certainty that they have the latitude and, equally important, the space to tell a story the way it deserves. The *Times*

bureau occupies a position of almost frightening ascendancy in the reporting of Washington. (Cater, 1959, 175)

President Dwight Eisenhower put the thought in less praiseworthy terms when he allegedly exploded after reading one of Reston's critical commentaries about his administration, "Who does Scotty Reston think he is, telling me how to run the country!" (Rivers, 1967, 72).

FROM SPORTSMAN TO *TIMESMAN*

With Scotty Reston the *Times* made the man; the man answered in kind and made the *Times*. James Reston first joined the staff of the *New York Times* on September 1, 1939—the day World War II began—after three decades of a tumbleweed-like existence in his personal and professional life. He was born in Clydebank, Scotland, on November 3, 1909. When Scotty was two, the Reston family—his father James, mother Johanna, an older sister, Joanna, and James Barrett—immigrated to Dayton, Ohio. It was a brief stay; before 1911 was out, the family returned to Scotland because of Johanna's desire to go home. Back in Scotland James Barrett attended the Vale of Levan Academy, an impressive name for what was a village school. Had the family remained in Scotland the future *Times*man, influenced by the strict Scottish Presbyterian regimen of his mother, might have become a preacher. However, in 1920, the family again immigrated to America where James Reston worked as a machinist for the Delco division of General Motors.

James, Jr., attended Huffman Grade School, Stivers Manual Training High School, and Oakwood High School. Among several odd jobs, he caddied at a local golf club after school and on weekends. Every weekend Reston caddied for James Cox, a newspaper publisher who had been the Democratic candidate for U.S. president in 1920 and, coincidentally, had given a helping hand to the career of another of the twentieth-century's key political commentators, Raymond Moley (q.v.). At Cox's urging, James, Jr., learned the game of golf and became skilled at it: he won the state high school golf championship, a district tournament, and the Ohio Public Links title. Through golf, Reston became friends with sportswriters, hung out at the *Dayton Daily News*, and wrote short accounts of high school basketball games. After high school graduation, Reston, through his sports contacts, got a full-time job editing the Delco Remy house organ, "Delco Doings."

In 1928 James Reston entered the University of Illinois where he majored in journalism. By his own account, Reston was an "indifferent student" (1991, 29). He captained the golf team, played soccer, and worked for the university's sports publicity office. As a sports publicist, his job was to write profiles of the university's football players, profiles more colorful than true: "It was there that I learned to be skeptical of press agents, a talent that came in handy when I got to Washington" (1991, 30). He also fell in love with Sally Fulton, who became his wife on Christmas Eve, 1935. When the University of Illinois suffered financial setbacks as a result of bank failures during the Great Depression, Reston too faced a financial crisis for the bank on which Reston's tuition check had been written was one of those that closed. Reston appealed to James Cox; Cox wrote out a check for the younger man's tuition and suggested there might be a job at one of the Cox newspapers for him upon graduation. The publisher made good on the promise. After receiving a B.S. degree in 1932, Reston landed a job as a sportswriter with the *Daily News* in Springfield, Ohio.

However, by 1933, Reston was restless. He moved to Columbus, Ohio, to work in sports publicity for Ohio State University. Shortly thereafter Leland MacPhail, whom Reston had met through golf, sought Reston's advice. Desirous of selling the Cincinnati Reds baseball team to Powell Crosley, a manufacturer of household appliances and radios, MacPhail wanted to convince Crosley that team ownership would sell appliances and radios. Reston's proposal was inspired: name the Reds' ballpark "Crosley Field," thus obtaining free advertising in newspaper sports pages every time sportswriters mentioned the ballpark in newspaper stories. The tactic worked: Crosley bought the Reds, MacPhail became general manager, and Reston got a job as traveling secretary and publicity director for the Reds.

The fortuitous aspect of Reston's job with the Reds was that it took him to New York when the team played the New York Giants or Brooklyn Dodgers. While he was in New York during the 1934 season, Reston used his spare time trying to land a job with a New York newspaper. He was rejected everywhere, most notably by the *New York Times*. But, there was another stroke of good fortune. One of Reston's friends from Stivers Manual Training High School days, Milton Caniff (later the creator of the hugely successful "Terry and the Pirates" and "Steve Canyon" comic strips), introduced the aspiring *Times*man to the editor of the Associated Press Feature Service. The AP needed a sports reporter. Reston jumped at the opportunity and impressed the AP editors so much that, shortly after he joined the service, he was writing not only sports, but also a nationally syndicated column, "A New Yorker at Large," which appeared six times a week.

By 1937 James Reston was on the move again, this time to London. Although his principal assignments involved sports, Reston also covered the British Foreign Office for AP. The latter assignment brought him into contact with the political events in Europe leading to World War II. It also brought him in contact with the foreign correspondent of the *New York Times*. As the war drew closer, the *Times* correspondent requested additional staff from the home office to cover breaking news; he proposed hiring Reston. It was thus that sportswriter Scotty Reston, approaching his thirtieth birthday, become a *Times*man. It was an affiliation that lasted half of the twentieth century, until Reston's eightieth birthday on November 3, 1989.

In his memoir, *Deadline* (1991), James Reston cites three influences that dominated his life: the "stern" teachings of his parents, who respected the Scottish Calvinist way of life; the love and intelligence of his wife, Sally; and "the influence of the integrity of the *New York Times*" (1991, xi). So dominant was the fifty-year influence of the *Times* that observers often viewed Reston and the *Times* as one and the same: "Reston's whole stance seemed so intertwined with the *Times*, his idealism and character so in keeping [with the institution] that to question James Reston would be to question the *Times* itself" (Talese, 1969, 22).

This joining at the hip between *Times* and *Times*man began soon after Reston joined the organization. In spite of suffering through the Battle of Britain with what was finally diagnosed as undulant fever, Reston persevered at his *Times* reporting: "All I could do was write inadequate accounts each day or so of some human incident in the hope that these vignettes would gradually illuminate the larger tragedy" (1991, 90). Shortly after the Blitz ended in 1940, Reston returned to New York. When he was offered the opportunity to take over the Boston bureau of the *Times*, Reston suggested an alternative assignment, namely, the Washington bureau. The bureau chief, Arthur Krock, who was over-staffed with reporters whose European bureaus had been closed by the Nazis (like "running a damn displaced persons' office," grumbled Krock), reluctantly agreed to accept Reston only when the *Times* publisher, Arthur Hays Sulzberger, urged it (1991, 98). Thus began a mutually acrimonious, yet mutually admiring, relation of long standing at the *Times* bureau.

In Washington, Reston was assigned to cover the U.S. Senate and various foreign embassies. In addition, based upon his wartime experience, James Reston wrote a book, *Prelude to Victory* (1942), which helped boost his career. When the United States entered World War II in 1941, Elmer Davis, a former *Times*man and the director of the Office of War Information (OWI), requested that Sulzberger give Reston a leave of absence. In 1942 Reston returned to London, not as a correspondent, but as an OWI propagandist attached to the U.S. Embassy. In that capacity, Reston learned the art of the planted story and, incidentally, how to guard against being conned by it as a Washington journalist. His task was to counter Nazi anti-American lies, rumors, and gossip commu-nicated to Britons via Nazi shortwave broadcasts. For each fabrication, Reston prepared a factual response and arranged through British officials to have a question asked in the House of Commons about the Nazi claim. The reply given to the question by the British foreign minister, based on Reston's response, received sufficient publicity to rebut the Nazi charges.

The U.S. ambassador to England, John Winant, praised Reston's propaganda efforts to Arthur Hays Sulzberger when Sulzberger visited the U.S. Embassy in 1942. As a result Sulzberger brought Reston back to New York as an assistant to the publisher following his stint with OWI as a propagandist. A correspondent acting as a publisher's assistant bears a heavy burden. When Arthur Krock assisted Joseph Pulitzer on the *New York World* back in the 1920s, it earned for him the derogatory label of "spy" among his colleagues. Reston used the same term to summarize his duties as Sulzberger's assistant (what Sulzberger called his "s.o.b. administrative man" [Rivers, 1967, 86]). Reston's duties were to scrutinize the *Times*, identify its accuracies and inaccuracies, and report them to the publisher each day: "The editors were seldom amused by these inquiries and blamed them all on the new 'spy' " (Reston, 1991, 122).

Reston did not enjoy his colleagues' resentments nor did he enjoy criticizing his colleagues. The *Times* in his judgment was too important to let petty quarrels get in the way. Hence, he lobbied to be reassigned correspondent duties, preferably in Washington. After a brief stint as interim bureau chief in London, Reston rejoined the Washington bureau of the *Times* in 1944.

THE MOST INFLUENTIAL NEWSMAN

Over the course of next two decades, from 1944 to 1964, James Reston, known to colleagues, public officials, and friends as "Scotty," became "the most influential newsman in Washington" (Rivers, 1967, 71). He got off to a quick start with a series of stories, certainly scoops by any standard, reporting the behind-the-scenes negotiations of the Dumbarton Oaks Conference, held in August 1944, to plan the United Nations Organization. Reston obtained from a Chinese delegate a full set of each nation's secret position papers. Each day of the conference, the *Times* published a different nation's position on key issues, timing publication to coincide with the nation's public pronouncements but in far more detail. Although the "you are there" message to *Times* readers drew protests from *Times* rivals and several delegations, Reston argued that the citizens had a right to know the broad outlines of policy and continued with daily disclosures. The Dumbarton Oaks series won Reston a prestigious Pulitzer Prize in 1945. (His second Pulitzer Prize came in 1957 for a series of five articles on the disposition of executive power in the event of presidential disability.)

In the following years, Scotty Reston borrowed from the Dumbarton Oaks experience and devised a news-gathering technique that set him apart from other Washington correspondents. The technique eschewed a news-gathering source dear to the hearts of other reporters, especially Arthur Krock: being in the forefront of Washington social life and working dinner parties for news tidbits (Wicker, 1978). It was also not a technique that placed great stock on officials' news conferences, for Reston, like Krock, believed them to be little more than official exercises in news orchestration, management, and manipulation. Instead, Reston worked his magic with the telephone. Reston would begin by placing himself in a governing official's position, imagining what should be, and therefore rightly could be expected to be going on in government councils. Reston called it "amateur speculation" that consisted of "a few general assumptions" about what was happening, based on the principle that news lies not at the center of politics but at the fringes, where anonymous officials plan what higher officials do:

> By imagining that we were running the State Department, we could guess that
> the secretary of state would have to react to the latest outrage . . . , so we would

call up officials at State on the assumption that they had already reacted. . . . we were often wrong, but it was remarkable how many times our guesses were right and how often we got ahead of the competition with this device. (Reston, 1991, 205)

On the telephone with sources Reston was aggressive, but not demanding; he used long pauses, seemed never to be in a hurry, pretended that he knew far more than he did, and conned the source to believe that the reporter was in possession of precisely the information he actually was trying to elicit. Reston knew "how to take a tiny chunk of information and make it grow and add small bits to it until they were finally a piece" (Halberstam, 1979, 222). In an interview with *Newsweek*, Reston said, "I think I know where the brains are in this town. I pick 'em. When I pick enough of them I can write an analytical piece about whatever the problem is" (quoted in Moritz, 1981, 334).

In 1953 the publisher of the *Washington Post* tried to lure Scotty Reston by offering him the position of editor of the *Post*. Reston was tempted to take the offer. The path to advancement appeared to be blocked at the *Times* Washington bureau by Arthur Krock, who had been bureau chief for two decades and showed no signs of yielding the post. Moreover, although Krock and Reston respected one another, they did not see eye to eye. Krock demanded straight, factual reporting, and Reston argued for an interpretive analysis; Krock insisted that bureau correspondents' assignments should be restricted, and Reston wanted a more free-floating approach; Krock preferred reporters who were generalists, and Reston wanted specialists.

Hence, it came as a surprise to Reston when Krock, in order to keep Reston with the *Times*, stepped down as bureau chief and appointed Reston as his successor in 1953. Reston was even more astonished when Krock left him a note: "I have known many of the reporters of my time who were called great. I have worked against some of them, and unworthily directed the services of others, but in my opinion, none has been your superior" (Reston, 1991, 199).

As bureau chief James Reston made major changes. Some were apparent on the surface, including the addition of his own column, "Washington," which was placed on the editorial page, sometimes with Krock's venerable "In the Nation" column. Whereas Arthur Krock did not hold staff meetings, Reston instituted what were almost daily meetings to plan *Times* coverage of politics collectively. One particular task of these daily sessions was to derive questions to be asked in news conferences that would counter officials' efforts to manage the news. This was especially true of presidential news conferences: "Each question would be planned, not only in its substance but for the actual phrasing that would most likely elicit a useful answer" (Wicker, 1978, 91).

Other changes were more subtle, but key. For one, Reston set out to recruit the most promising young journalists in the nation—Tom Wicker, Neil Sheehan, Anthony Lewis, David Halberstam, Russell Baker, and Hedrick Smith, were a few of them. Each was a specialist; for example, Anthony Lewis in legal matters and John Finney in science reporting. Each correspondent was given considerable latitude to generate stories and to write interpretive pieces. What Reston insisted on was that correspondents' stories be well written, concise, and accurate. As a result, *Times*' reports from the nation's capital were now written in a livelier, lighter style.

The bureau's copy editor would frequently take a newly recruited correspondent's efforts through as many as ten revisions to attain the proper style. In this and other respects, under Reston, the *Times* bureau was an educational institution—*Times* stories would educate readers, mentoring by *Times* colleagues would educate younger correspondents. When Reston first became a *Times* correspondent in 1939, one problem he encountered was that he "agonized over every paragraph" and had problems meeting deadlines. The *Times* bureau chief in London advised Reston, "Think about it as if you were writing a letter to a friend back home" (Reston, 1991, 78). Reston practiced that the remainder of his career. He not only practiced it, he preached it. After David Halberstam, a Pulitzer Prize winner, joined the *Times* Washington bureau, he told an interviewer in 1961: "I remember what Reston said to me, the first thing he said to me when I came. I guess he knew I was probably a little bit taut, and he called me in and said, 'Write these things like you were writing a letter home to somebody in Nashville' " (Halberstam, 1961).

Through his unique news-gathering techniques as a reporter, managerial tactics as a bureau chief, and mentoring as an educator, Scotty Reston enhanced the stature of the *New York Times* among its principal readership, "the people who have influence": government leaders, diplomats, business executives, and university thinkers, and "the saving remnant" of citizens who seek "knowledge and wisdom" (Reston, 1967a, 105). These people of influence learned that the *Times* would not stand for "debasement of news coverage" (Kluger, 1989, 410), that the *Times* treated "the news with care and will probably write their obituaries. This opened a lot of doors" (Reston, 1991, 201). It not only opened doors; it made James Reston one of those "people who have influence."

As the "most influential newsman in Washington," there were numerous instances when his political communication not only reported politics but changed it. Even before he became bureau chief, Scotty Reston's influence was on the rise. For example, Reston and Walter Lippmann (q.v.) were instrumental in convincing Senator Arthur Vandenberg, chair of the Foreign Relations Committee, that an isolationist foreign policy, which Vandenberg had been promoting, was hopelessly outmoded. Vandenberg was convinced, and Reston and Lippmann drafted a speech for Vandenberg to deliver on the floor of the U.S. Senate calling for an internationalist policy. Then, in a *Times* article, Reston hailed the speech as wise and statesmanlike, thus promoting as commentator a speech he had written as political adviser stating a political position Reston advocated personally (Steele, 1980).

In his years as *Times* bureau chief, and later as executive editor, James Reston typically exerted political influence not as he had with Vandenberg—through direct contact—but indirectly by swaying "the people who have influence" through the analyses in his "Washington" column. During the presidential administration of John Kennedy, for example, one of Kennedy's aides described the process: "Reston writes a column about Kennedy losing the liberals in the Democratic party. A week later you see two others writing the same story, and ten days later, six correspondents are saying the same thing" (Rivers, 1967, 82). As agenda setter for other journalists, Reston's political priorities and views as espoused in "Washington" had a multiplier effect; politicians and the public taking their cues from the news were indirectly responding to Reston's influence in shaping that news.

The content of the "Washington" column was unique to its author. It was less cerebral than those of Walter Lippmann, less ponderous than those typical of Arthur Krock, less doctrinaire than those of David Lawrence, less Cassandra-like than those of Dorothy Thompson (q.v.), less pretentious than those of George F. Will (q.v.), and less streetwise than Georgie Anne Geyer (q.v.). Reston was at his most persuasive when he true to his skills as a working journalist gathering, reporting, and analyzing news. His column leads, often summarizing the whole of the column in a single opening sentence, were legendary. "Washington" was least persuasive when its author wrote like what he had once aspired to be, a preacher. His rigid Calvinist nature rendered his tone solemn and moral, especially near Christmas and Easter. Reston drew upon his knowledge of baseball to liken writing a column to the working of a major league pitcher—the fast ball cannot be used all the time, there must be a change of pace. But, also like the sportswriter he had once been, in columns on foreign affairs, Reston was "reluctant to condemn the home side, even when it made errors, or to concede that the local heroes also played dirty sometimes when they had to to win" (Talese, 1969, 8–9).

Reston was well aware that his regular *Times* column was vital to his political influence and that it made him a confidant of presidents and world leaders, first among his journalistic peers, and a powerful figure in the internal politics of the *Times*. During the 114-day strike by a printer's union that halted publication of major New York dailies in 1962, Reston was unable to publish a column lamenting the action. Undaunted, he read the column on television instead. Moreover, in 1964, when James Reston turned over the reins of the Washington bureau to Tom Wicker, he kept writing his thrice-weekly "Washington" column. Four years later, upon becoming executive editor of the *Times*, Reston moved to New York on what he thought would be a temporary basis. "Washington" moved with him; Reston later wrote wryly, "I insisted on continuing my column three days a week, because while there was no noticeable demand for my opinions, I wanted to go back to the column when the great transition was over" (Reston, 1991, 352). When, after leaving the editorial position, he returned to Washington, his insistence on retaining the column proved prescient; he continued writing it as a *Times* vice president and member of the board of directors from 1969 to 1974.

REDEFINING POLITICAL NEWS

Upon retirement Scotty and Sally Reston concentrated on the operation of their family weekly, the *Vineyard Gazette* of Martha's Vineyard, Massachusetts. Looking back from the vantage point of the 1990s to the decades of the 1950s, 1960s, and 1970s, when James Reston was the most influential political commentator in Washington, it is difficult to appreciate the changes he wrought in affecting the attitudes of politicians, political journalists, and politically aware citizens regarding the flow of political information between politicians and the news media. His dispute with Arthur Krock, for instance, over straight versus analytical reporting, now seems quaint, like quarrels over the proper style of waistcoats in Victorian England. Interpretive journalism has come to pass with a vengeance. Contemporary political journalism is typically laden with opinion: facts are not inherently neutral, speeches and sound bites convey impressions, politicians and journalists compete as spinmeisters. Similarly, Reston's effort to broaden the nature of the news fit to print in the *Times* has become commonplace. "Mood pieces," "the news of the mind," and probes of causal trends residing under the surface of "the fertility of people, the creativity of scientists, the techniques of engineers and economists, and the discoveries of physicians" (Nimmo, 1967, 520) are accepted practices in a world of satellite communication, computerized interactive networks, and conversational webs. Reston's "modest proposals" for redefining news to include political commentary of educators, artists, scientists, and others outside conventional political venues, thus making punditry respectable, are now entrenched customs. Whether it is respectable one cannot judge, but the innovative is now the conventional; all manner of nonpolitical pundits offer political opinions on op-ed pages, in newsmagazines and opinion magazines, and on radio and television talk shows.

In assessing Reston's contributions to political communication one must bear in mind that what is apparent in the postmodern world was not so apparent in postwar America. When, for example, Reston coined the term "news management" in 1955, he unmasked news practices of the presidential administration of Dwight Eisenhower that superficially appeared informative but were actually deceptive. Today, after the lessons of Vietnam, Watergate, and Iran-contra, Reston's alarm may seem understated and antiquated. It was not four decades ago when he sounded it. Indeed, the very reason the alarm now rings with boring dullness lies in part with Scotty Reston. For, in 1971, when the *Times* published the Pentagon Papers, a set of secret documents that revealed serious discrepancies between the stated public American aims in Vietnam and the aims that were actually being pursued, it was with the strong prodding of James Reston.

Toward the end of his career, James Reston had his detractors. Critics pointed out tendencies in Reston's columns to harp repeatedly upon pet themes, become a Johnny-One-Note, draw upon a small set of news sources, identify increasingly with Washington insiders, present established policies rather than critique them, and view "the press more as a natural ally than as a neutral observer" (Chapman, 1980, 23). To the degree such criticism was justified there is an irony. They are the same rebukes James Reston leveled at journalists for his half-century as a *Times*man: "We will have to become more detached, more disinterested, more forehanded and farsighted if we are going to report accurately and criticize effectively in this kind of mixed-up world" (Reston, 1967a, 94–95). Perhaps that is the prime achievement of James "Scotty" Reston, who died on December 6, 1995, as a political commentator: a reformer of established political journalism whose reformation became *the* establishment.

REFERENCES

Selected Works by James Reston

Prelude to Victory. New York: Alfred A. Knopf, 1942.
"The Job of the Reporter." In *The Newspaper and Its Making*, no editor, 92–108. New York: Charles Scribner's Sons, 1945.
Walter Lippmann and His Times. Coedited with M. Childs. New York: Harcourt, Brace, 1959.
The Artillery of the Press: Its Influence on American Foreign Policy. New York: Harper and Row, 1967a.
Sketches in the Sand. New York: Alfred A. Knopf, 1967b.
Washington. New York: Macmillan, 1986.
Deadline: A Memoir. New York: Random House, 1991.

Selected Critical Studies about James Reston

Chapman, S. "James Reston." *New Republic*, 182, April 19, 1980, 19–25.
Lichtenstein, N., ed. "Reston, James B(arrett)." In *Political Profiles: The Kennedy Years*, 424–25. New York: Facts on File, 1981.
Moritz, C., ed. "Reston, James (Barrett)." In *Current Biography 1980*, 332–36. New York: H. W. Wilson, 1981.
Nimmo, D. "Mr. Reston's 'Modest Proposals.' " *The Virginia Quarterly Review* 43 (Summer 1967): 517–20.
Nykoruk, B., ed. "James ("Scotty") Reston." In *Authors in the News*, vol. 2, 233. Detroit: Gale Research, 1976.
"Reston, James Barrett." In *The National Cyclopedia of American Biography.* Vol. 1, 1953–59, 210. New York: James T. White, 1960.
Riley, S. G. "Reston, James Barrett." In *Biographical Dictionary of American Newspaper Columnists*, 264–65. Westport, CT: Greenwood Press, 1995.
Rivers, W. "James Reston and the New York *Times*" In *The Opinionmakers*, edited by W. Rivers, 71–91. Boston: Beacon Press, 1967.

Selected General Works

Cater, D. *The Fourth Branch of Government.* Boston: Houghton Mifflin, 1959.
Halberstam, D. Personal Interview by D. Nimmo. Washington, D.C. May 15, 1961.
Halberstam, D. *The Powers That Be.* New York: Alfred A. Knopf, 1979.

Kluger, R. *The Paper: The Life and Death of the New York Herald Tribune.* New York: Vintage Books, 1989.
Steel, R. *Walter Lippmann and the American Century.* Boston: Little, Brown, 1980.
Talese, G. *The Kingdom and the Power.* New York: World Publishing, 1969.
Wicker, T. *On Press.* New York: Viking Press, 1978.

(MARY MARTHA) CORRINE COKIE ROBERTS

(December 27, 1943–   )

Considering "All Things Considered"

During the 1920s, noncommercial radio stations, usually funded by educational institutions, began broadcasting. When commercial broadcasting established its place in the economy, commercial stations purchased many of the noncommercial outlets. Public, noncommercial broadcasting almost faded away from the airways. However, in 1945, with the coming of frequency modulation (FM) broadcasting, several points on the FM dial were set aside for the exclusive use of educational or noncommercial broadcasting stations. This action produced a rebirth of interest in noncommercial radio stations, and in 1970, National Public Radio (NPR) emerged as an alternative, albeit underfunded, presence in broadcasting.

NPR is one of two radio networks that serve noncommercial stations in local markets. With its inception, Anglophiles, either weaned on shortwave newscasts of the British Broadcasting Corporation (BBC), or caught up in hope that political information and commentary could be broadcast unfettered by the interference of commercial advertisers or government regulation, looked forward to a feast of public affairs programming, news, and analysis.

NPR supporters argue that, despite momentary lapses, the commercial-free alternative has grown into a respected radio service that offers news and insightful commentary on the economy, lifestyles, and politics. Critics are not so certain. Neoconservative critics find NPR news offerings tilted to the liberal side (Barnes, 1986); other critics claim that in NPR's efforts to win ever larger audiences and grow closer to established political interests of both left and right, NPR has sacrificed lucidity for pandering (Porter, 1990).

To more than 14 million listeners weekly, NPR offers a lengthy presentation of the day's news, including a discussion of the meaning surrounding the events and related issues. In its infancy, NPR lacked the financial resources to purchase equipment and hire staff to cover breaking news stories, and many of its correspondents were outside the inner circle of journalists. The noncommercial network had a small staff of reporters who filled the airtime with news reports and a series of programs produced and announced by amateurs. By the mid-1990s, the network provided newscasts seven days a week and had a host of correspondents stationed around the world. Douglas Bennet, who became president of NPR in 1983, commented, "This may have begun as an experiment, but we're way beyond that now; we're in the big leagues. . . . People are now relying on us for the news, and this creates a whole new accountability to live up to'' (Porter, 1990, 27).

In the closing decade of the twentieth century, NPR became a showcase for political commentary. The network won awards for its two most popular shows, ''Morning Edition'' and ''All Things Considered''; several of the news correspondents on the two programs had personal connections to the national journalistic and Washington political establishments. Four of the most prominent NPR political correspondents were women: Susan Stamberg, the original cohost of ''All Things Considered,'' which debuted in 1971; Linda Wertheimer, who joined NPR in 1972 and excelled in campaign coverage; Nina Totenberg, who came to the airways in 1975 and became a widely known voice; and Cokie Roberts, an award-winning journalist and senior news analyst for NPR who joined in 1978. All four have ''been indispensable in making [NPR] distinctive,'' but Roberts moved NPR to celebrity status (Powers, 1990, 154). Bob Edwards, anchor of NPR's ''Morning Edition,'' said, ''What she brings to coverage can't be duplicated. . . . Can you think of anyone who knew more about government at [age] five? This woman was bounced on [famed House Speaker] Sam Rayburn's knee. [President] Lyndon Johnson and Lady Bird danced at her wedding'' (Mooney, 1993, 429).

FROM THE BOGGS' TO THE ROBERTS' FAMILY BUSINESS

Few of the twentieth century's most celebrated political commentators have been born into and reared in the estates of power in the nation's capital. A few have come from economically depressed backgrounds, such as Edward R. Murrow (q.v.) and Carl T. Rowan (q.v.). Most have sprung from America's vast middle class, including Walter Cronkite (q.v.), Elmer Davis (q.v.), Georgie Anne Geyer (q.v.), Paul Harvey (q.v.), and Larry King (q.v.). Few have been born to the power elite (Mills, 1957) and successfully used it as a springboard to fame in political commentary. Fulton Lewis, Jr. (q.v.) was an exception. And, most certainly, so is Mary Martha Corrine Morrison Claiborne Boggs, a celebrity political commentator known popularly as Cokie Roberts and ''a quintessential Washington insider to the 14.7 million Americans'' who listen to NPR (Graham, 1994, 40). Born in New Orleans on December 27, 1943, she was given the nickname Cokie by her brother, Thomas, who could not seem to pronounce his younger sister's most frequently used given name, Corrine. Cokie's father was the late Louisiana Democrat and majority leader of the U.S. House of Representatives, Hale Boggs, who served for thirty-two years before his presumed death in an air crash occurred in Alaska in 1972. Her mother is former congresswoman Lindy Claiborne Boggs, who took over her husband's seat in the House when his plane disappeared (Hale Boggs' body was never found). After completing her husband's term, Lindy Boggs was reelected to fill the seat, and she remained in Congress until 1990, serving her district for seventeen years.

Cokie's husband since 1966, Steven V. Roberts, has been a political writer for *U. S. News & World Report* and for the *New York Times*, and he has been a panelist on "Washington Week in Review," a program of political commentary airing on PBS. She and her husband shared the rearing of two children, then the writing of a syndicated column of political opinion.

That Cokie Roberts' political connections, via heritage and marriage, are strong is clear. Before finishing her husband's term after his death, Lindy Boggs had been Hale Boggs' campaign manager during much of his political career, helped set up his congressional office in Washington, D.C., coordinated inaugural receptions and dinners for two presidents (John F. Kennedy and Lyndon B. Johnson), and was an active participant in every phase of Hale Boggs' political career. The Boggs' children grew up privy to conversations about the civil rights movement, Vietnam, the economy and other political issues—a hands-on lesson in American politics. "Politics is our family business" (Mooney, 1993, 429). Cokie's brother, Tom, became a lawyer and lobbyist in the nation's capital, and her sister, Barbara Sigmund, became a mayor of Princeton, New Jersey. Barbara died of cancer in 1990, which was a major loss to Cokie's mother, Lindy, and to Cokie, who helped care for her sister during her terminal illness.

As a child of a politically charged family, Roberts marks time by political campaigns: "I find that I date my life by campaigns, which is probably not a good way to do it. But it is how I remember things" (Roberts, 1994, 9). She credits much of her political understanding to her mother, an astute political player even before she ran for political office. By watching her mother, and without realizing it, Cokie acquired a grasp of how the political process works and how politicians manage and manipulate people and issues.

Hence, having a legacy of politics, Roberts said there was a "sense that I was going over to the other side, when I, somewhere along the line, chose this trade [journalism]" (Roberts, 1994, 10). Hale and Lindy Boggs met, however, while they both worked at a newspaper, the *Tulane Hullabaloo*; Hale was editor in chief and Lindy was the "Newcomb editor, the highest position a woman could achieve" (Roberts, 1994, 10). Moreover, Hale worked at a newspaper while he was a college student, and he aspired to be a journalist until the editor of the *Picayune*, now the *Times Picayune* in New Orleans, told Boggs to attend law school as a necessary requirement for remaining with the paper. Boggs did go to law school, but his profession pointed him not back to the *Picayune* but to politics.

So, when Cokie also expressed journalistic aspirations, both parents accepted, reluctantly, and indulged her wish not to stay in the "family business." The dues were too high and she did not want to pay them, she said later: "I want to go home at night and not have the interruptions of constituents who demand your time and have the right to demand your time . . . it never ends. I want my day to end" (Mooney, 1993, 429).

Roberts attended Catholic girls' schools and was editor of her high school's newspaper. After graduation from high school, she matriculated at an elite school, Wellesley College in Massachusetts; she graduated (B.A., 1964) with a major in political science. Where better for an aspiring journalist with political connections and a political science degree to pursue her ambitions than in Washington, D.C.? Nowhere. Hence, Cokie Boggs' first job was at WRC-TV; she was host of a weekly television public affairs program called the "Meeting of Minds."

The path was opened to a career in broadcast journalism, but if the Boggs' family business did not attract her, the Roberts' family business did. When Cokie Boggs became Cokie Roberts and Steven Roberts a correspondent for the *New York Times*, she moved with her husband to New York. In New York, outside the Washington milieu, Roberts could find a job in journalism only as a typist. She spent eight months calling on magazines and television stations in hopes of finding an opening. Her perseverance finally paid off when she got a job as a reporter and editor for Cowles Communications in 1967. The next year, she landed a position with WNEW-TV in New York City as a producer. But, a year later, Steven Roberts' career took the couple to Los Angeles; Cokie worked there as a producer with Altman Productions until 1972, then as a producer for KNBC-TV, the National Broadcasting Company (NBC) affiliate, until 1974, producing "Serendipity," an award-winning children's program.

Again her husband's career intervened, and the family was off to Athens, Greece, where Cokie worked as a stringer for Columbia Broadcasting System (CBS) News. The move to Greece proved fortuitous. Roberts reported a story in 1977 that captured national attention in the United States. A coup d'état that toppled the Greek regime began while she was riding by the presidential palace. Her report of the events was the opening segment on a telecast of the "CBS Evening News with Walter Cronkite." Again, a career as a broadcast journalist beckoned. Yet, despite the acclaim for her coverage of the Greek coup, Cokie Roberts had not yet made a firm commitment to a separate professional life. She recalls that her values were conventional: tag along where Steven's work took him and raise a family. Her journalistic success evolved without forethought on her part, she maintained years later (Dreifus, 1994).

Cokie Roberts' claims about her career's unexpected advancement, however, are a little disingenuous. In 1977 Cokie Roberts and her family returned to Washington. Conveniently, Cokie and Steven Roberts purchased her parent's home in Bethesda, Maryland. The locale made it possible for her to accept a broadcast role with National Public Radio: "When I came in for an interview Linda [Wertheimer] and Nina [Totenberg] were there, greeting and encouraging me. . . . NPR was a place where I wanted to work because they were there" (Roberts, 1994, 41). Nina Totenberg, also a Wellesley alum, knew that the Robertses had returned to Washington and she contacted Steven Roberts, who supplied Totenberg with Cokie Roberts' resumé. Totenberg recalls, "I was the one who drafted Cokie for NPR" (Dreifus, 1994, 15).

MORNING RADIO VERSUS EVENING TELEVISION

Frank Mankiewicz, then head of the service, hired Cokie Roberts for National Public Radio. Roberts relates a backstage account of her introduction. "Cokie," he said, was "a little too flip" for NPR; he urged Roberts to sign off her reports with her full name. After learning what her seven-name sign-off would be, undoubtedly something that would please NPR's most upscale listeners but few others, Mankiewicz conceded that "Cokie" would suffice (Mooney, 1993, 429).

On joining NPR Cokie Roberts became the organization's congressional correspondent. Although her mother, a member of a Washington law firm, Patton, Boggs & Boggs, with extensive lobbying activities before Congress, took great care to avoid any conflict of interest between the firm's work and Cokie's, the old ties to the Boggs' family business certainly enhanced NPR's congressional coverage. Cokie Roberts, for example, had a solid rapport with Tip O'Neill, speaker of the House of Representatives and longtime colleague of Hale Boggs in that body. Her work at NPR attracted the attention of the Public Broadcsting Service (PBS) executives, and in 1981 Roberts became cohost of "The Lawmakers," a national weekly public television program about Congress. The show was a collaboration between public radio and public television, and the program covered congressional committee hearings and debates from the congressional floor, as well as profiles on individual members of Congress.

Cokie Roberts does not deny that her family connections proved an asset. She recalls not being able to walk down the street with her father without being stopped at every step; her celebrity and connections made it the same for her own movements on Capitol Hill. Roberts quickly earned the reputation of being both an influential figure covering the news of influential people and, on behalf of average listeners of NPR, an analyst clarifying issues that she believed they would want to know more about. According to Roberts, her positions as reporter and political commentator allow her to uncover what constituents' elected representatives are doing and how officials' acts and failures to act affect the lives of citizens (Dreifus, 1994).

In 1984 Cokie Roberts became a contributor to the "MacNeil/Lehrer Newshour," coanchored by Robert MacNeil and James Lehrer (q.v.). She appeared as a correspondent from 1984 to 1987. Also during that time she was a guest panelist on "This Week with David Brinkley." In 1988 she joined the Sunday public affairs show as a biweekly panelist, and in 1992 she became a regular weekly panelist.

Alongside George F. Will (q.v.) and Sam Donaldson, Cokie Roberts joins what host David Brinkley (q.v.) has called "uninhibited, free-for-all discussions" following the departure of interrogated guests (Hirsch, 1991, 41). The program's format encourages the panelist commentators to express their opinions. Cokie Roberts thrives on the format. Brinkley has paid her tribute:

> Cokie Roberts, our newest club member, brings a fresh view that no male could
> ever match or would try to match. . . . In my opinion she knows more about
> the Congress than any of its members. On the air or off, I've never asked her
> a question about the nuts and bolts of complicated issues before the Congress
> that she did not answer quickly and clearly. The truth is that the members often
> seek her advice. (Brinkley, 1995, 238)

No-holds-barred political commentary, of course, frequently puts Brinkley's panelists in harm's way. For example, on January 12, 1991, the U.S. Congress approved a resolution authorizing President George Bush's use of force to remove Iraqi occupation troops from Kuwait. Brinkley asked Donaldson, Roberts, and Will how each would have voted on the resolution. Will and Donaldson favored the resolution, but Roberts quickly voted no. The whole exercise raised the ire of several journalists, most notably, Robert Pierpoint. Pierpoint had been a CBS correspondent of long standing; he was covering Congress when Cokie Boggs was a schoolgirl and well before her father, Hale, became Democratic majority whip or leader in the House. In a letter to the *Washington Journalism Review*, Pierpoint spoke for many observers who have witnessed the decline in political commentary from the era when commentators analyzed without opinions, expressed opinions without judgments, but did not judge for judgment's sake: He was "troubled," he said, by those "who allowed themselves to be quoted on their personal opinions about the war. Let's leave that sort of *indulgence* to the columnists and stick to tough questions and hard analysis" (Pierpoint, 1991, 9; emphasis in original).

ABC News, the network of "This Week with David Brinkley," hired Cokie Roberts in 1988 to be a political correspondent for "World News Tonight" with Peter Jennings. She also became the regular substitute for anchor Ted Koppel (q.v.) on ABC News' "Nightline." Hence, Cokie Roberts, who had expressed ambivalence about a career in journalism since 1966, little more than two decades later was an influential political commentator on all the major political media—radio, television, newspapers, opinion magazines, and the lecture circuit.

Given her numerous commitments, a few critics have pondered Cokie Roberts' tendencies to sacrifice the quality of her analysis for the opportunity to court celebrity. She responds that she has her priorities in order. She enjoys the work she does at NPR and would not leave to fulfill the other commitments. In fact, when ABC News chief Roone Arledge recruited Roberts, she initially resisted the offer because she preferred her role at NPR. Through a compromise, however, she managed a change in her schedule at NPR to accommodate her work for ABC News. Instead of continuing to file reports on both NPR's "Morning Edition" and "All Things Considered" in the afternoons, Cokie Roberts cut back almost exclusively to reports for the "Morning Edition," thus allowing her time to fulfill her various evening television assignments.

Cokie Roberts' commitment to NPR has its rewards, namely, the freedom to ask interviewees probing, follow-up questions, a luxury afforded by noncommercial radio to commentators who seriously wish to serve the information needs of readers, listeners, or viewers. In a speech at Harvard University, she certainly recognized that responsibility as a political commentator:

> Any citizen can get information at the same time people in government do now. Same time we in the mainstream press do. And it promotes a sense of, I know as much as those guys do. What do I need them for? That attitude is very much reinforced by the Ross Perots of the world, talking about a national town meeting, where the voters get to decide what government does. And it sounds so fair. (Roberts, 1994, 16)

She maintains steadfastly that such conditions do not promote an effective democratic government, but instead a government with more bureaucracy. Roberts explains her solution, ''We need to do a better job explaining the institutions of government'' (Roberts, 1994, 17), which surely is the task being attempted by NPR journalists.

However, television also apparently has its separate rewards. Although Roberts' work for NPR provides her with an audience of millions, her work on television has brought her nationwide fame. Roberts' role as a political commentator on television results in people's ascribing to her credibility, television's version of trust: ''People accord me more weight, they treat me more seriously.'' Granted, television may stifle quality news commentary: ''The drawbacks of television journalism include rampant 'soundbite-itis,' particularly from newer members of Congress.'' Thus, although Cokie Roberts endeavors to order her priorities, there come times when they must still be juggled. For those occasions when she is completing two assignments for competing organizations, Roberts had a line installed into her home that permits her to do so by broadcasting from her residence, if necessary, as she puts it, in a nightgown (Mooney, 1993, 430).

Much of Cokie Roberts' fame and credibility resides in her image as a rough-and-trouble woman capable of giving as good as she gets in the equally rough-and-tumble world of male-dominated politics. She says, ''All this is very nice. You know, men come up to me on the street and say, 'We like your common sense on the Brinkley show.' '' But women view it from a different perspective; they ''say, 'We love that you don't let them interrupt you, and that you hand it right back to them.' I get the feeling that the country is full of women who've never gotten a word in edgewise when men talk about politics'' (Mooney, 1993, 430). If she is correct, Cokie Roberts may have hit upon the same formula for success in contemporary political commentary that Phil Donahue (q.v.) has exploited for years.

During the 1992 presidential campaign, Cokie Roberts managed to book Ross Perot, who was jumping in and out of the race during the campaign, to appear as a guest on "Nightline," a program that has built a reputation for dealing directly with complex issues—demanding simplified, no-conditions-attached answers to either-or questions from regular host Ted Koppel. Unaware that the tone and demeanor of Cokie Roberts as host would be no different from Koppel's, Ross Perot agreed to appear. He was totally unprepared for aggressive questions posed by Roberts. During the interview, Perot was openly furious. Cokie Roberts later described the incident with Perot:

> I had written an op-ed piece that talked about why he was having the effect he was having . . . his organization (thought) that this was the best description of the phenomenon. . . . But then I had him on *Nightline*. . . . The whole interview became unbelievably testy and it just got ruder and tenser and awful. (Dreifus, 1994, 17)

Ross Perot, said Roberts, commented that he no longer wanted to be interviewed by female reporters because "they're all trying to prove their manhood" (Dreifus, 1994, 17).

Cokie Roberts' aggressive approach to news gathering and commentary has occasionally produced controversy. Robert Pierpoint's plea for commentators to cease indulgence and return to analysis is a case in point. Another occurred in 1994. Cokie Roberts drew a reprimand from ABC News for staging the scene of a news report. In a January 26 report, she appeared on television to be originating her broadcast from Capitol Hill. In fact, she was not at her old stomping grounds at all. She was in a studio, dressed in a coat to appear as though outdoors, standing in front of a video background of Capitol Hill. An ABC producer, who allegedly requested Roberts to stage the scene without the knowledge of ABC "World News Tonight" anchor Peter Jennings, was reprimanded as well (*Facts on File*, 1994, 196).

WILL NPR REMAIN ALL THINGS ROBERTS CONSIDERS?

Observers of both politics and the news media have speculated that Cokie Roberts' career as a political journalist and commentator will be increasingly celebrated before it ends. For example, nightly television network news has continuously searched for a woman news anchor or coanchor who would provide the breakthrough for female journalists in prime time. For various reasons, promising candidates, such as Barbara Walters with ABC or Connie Chung at CBS, have had relatively short tenures in news anchor positions (Sanders & Rock, 1988). Cokie Roberts may change that trend. Or, should Ted Koppel, who insists he will remain on "Nightline," depart, Cokie Roberts may be his replacement.

Although she left the family business of politics for her own business of family and journalism, one should not rule out a return. Noted political commentators have frequently been urged to run for political office; Walter Cronkite,

Chet Huntley, and Edward R. Murrow, to name a few, resisted the urge. But times are changing. Both in 1992 and 1996 commentator Pat Buchanan of Cable News Network's "Crossfire" did seek the Republican nomination for U.S. president. Cokie Roberts' celebrity status outmatches that of commentators who have turned down opportunities to run for political office and those who have run. Certainly her celebrity, combined with her stock of political acquaintances, contacts, and know-how, make her a formidable contender for any office.

Whatever the course of her future career, Cokie Roberts has established herself as a permanent fixture in the world of political commentary and celebrity. She is the first political commentator to mesh roles on commercial and noncommercial radio and television. In a nation where the dispensing of political information is dominated by, and often at the mercy of, commercial interests, that sets her career as a political commentator apart from her peers at the close of the twentieth century.

REFERENCES

Selected Works by Cokie Roberts

"Politics and the Press: Clashing Cultures." The Theodore H. White Lecture, John F. Kennedy School of Government. Cambridge, Massachusetts: Harvard University, November 17, 1994.

Critical Works about Cokie Roberts

"People." *Facts on File*. 54 (#2781, 1994): 196.

Dreifus, C. "Cokie Roberts, Nina Totenberg, Linda Wertheimer." *New York Times Magazine*, January 2, 1994, 14–17.

Graham, J., ed. "Roberts, Cokie." In *Current Biography* 55, 40–43. New York: H. W. Wilson, 1994.

Mooney, L., ed. "Cokie Roberts." In *Newsmakers*, 428–31. Detroit: Gale Research, 1993.

Selected General Works

Barnes, F. "All Things Distorted." *New Republic*, October 27, 1986, 17–19.

Brinkley, D. *David Brinkley: A Memoir*. New York: Alfred A. Knopf, 1995.

Hirsch, A. *Talking Heads: Political Talk Shows and Their Star Pundits*. New York: St. Martin's Press, 1991.

Mills, C. W. *The Power Elite*. New York: Oxford University Press, 1957.

Pierpoint, R. "Too Much Flag-Waving." Letter to the editor. *Washington Journalism Review* 13 (May 1991): 9.

Porter, B. "Has Success Spoiled NPR?" *Columbia Journalism Review* 29 (October 1990): 26–32.

Powers, R. "The Ladies of the Club." *GQ*, December 1990, 146–54.

Sanders, M., and M. Rock. *Waiting for Prime Time: The Women of Television News*. New York: Harper and Row, 1988.

MARTHA ROUNTREE

(1916–   )

and

LAWRENCE E. SPIVAK

(June 11, 1900–March 9, 1994)

Pioneering the Electronic Forums of Political Commentary

Aside from mandating an annual message to be given by the president of the United States on the state of the union, the U.S. Constitution is remarkably silent about when and how public officials should report their goings-on to the citizenry, or to one another, or be questioned about their political actions. The extraconstitutional convention of presidential press conferences, often erroneously likened to Question Time in the British Parliament, involves only one official who has the discretion to submit to such questioning or not. Press conferences with other officials are also held at the discretion of the political leaders, not members of the Fourth Estate.

However, following World War II in the mid-1940s, two enterprising individuals, one a male magazine publisher and the other a female journalist and broadcast producer, invented novel formats for broadcasting political exchanges. In collaboration, Martha Rountree and Lawrence Spivak devised ways of placing politicians at the disposal of inquiring journalists, pairing opposing leaders who responded to questions by notable citizens, and conducting debates between leaders of contending political parties. To them, politics owes the origin of the electronic modes of political news gathering and commentary that are now institutionalized forums, so taken for granted that Americans forget they are of relatively recent origin.

FROM THE *AMERICAN MERCURY* TO "MEET THE PRESS"

In the 1920s today's electronic political "empire of the air" was but a beachhead on a vast continent of print (Lewis, 1991). Radio's broadcasting of the Republican and Democratic national nominating conventions in 1924 was, to be sure, an advance. By the same token, however, President Calvin Coolidge, in the first sound bite ever solicited by an interviewer sticking a microphone in the presidential face, provided more of a retreat. Asked what message he had for Americans as he departed on a long rail trip, "Silent Cal" lived up to his reputation and replied, "Goodbye."

If radio was devoid of political commentary, aside from the editorial pages, political commentary was not the norm of the newspaper either. Whatever political columnists there were in the 1920s, such as David Lawrence, Mark Sullivan, and Frank Kent, "were reporters and inside dopesters rather than analysts" (Steele, 1980, 281). Analytical political commentary did not begin in column form until Walter Lippmann (q.v.) began "Today and Tomorrow" for the New York *Herald Tribune* in 1931. Instead, it was the intellectual magazine that was the forum of informed political commentary in the 1920s. And, among the most notable of those was the monthly magazine *American Mercury*, founded in 1923 by political critic H. L. Mencken (q.v.). *American Mercury* attacked the nation's political foibles in analytical rather than the ideological tones of its competitors. *Mercury*'s iconoclasm, almost a revolutionary savagery, was remarkably influential and, for the era, far reaching. The magazine's circulation surpassed 100,000, a substantial number for the 1920s (Tebbel & Zuckerman, 1991).

When Mencken tired of the magazine in the late 1920s, he sold it. By 1939 the *American Mercury* had passed into the hands of yet another owner, Mencken's former business manager for the magazine, Lawrence E. Spivak. Spivak, who was born on June 11, 1900, was the first of four children, and only son, born to Sonya (Bershad) Spivak, the wife of William Benjamin Spivak, a manufacturer of nurses' uniforms and ladies' apparel. Son Larry grew up in Brooklyn, graduated from Boy's High School in 1917, and then majored in history and English at Harvard University where he graduated cum laude in 1921. He married Charlotte Beir Ring in 1924.

As a young man, Larry Spivak was a boxer; he lost only one of his many fights—to a fighter who later was in the Olympic Games. Spivak was also attracted to journalism; while still in high school, he worked for the Brooklyn *Daily Eagle* during a period when another future political commentator of note was at the newspaper, H. V. Kaltenborn (q.v.). Upon his graduation from Harvard, Spivak decided to give the publishing as well as the reportorial side of journalism a try. He became business manager of *Antiques* magazine and also a reporter for the Boston *American*, managing the magazine as a day job and reporting for the newspaper at night. By 1930 he had had enough of the toil and became an assistant publisher for *Hunting and Fishing* and *National Sportsman* magazines.

In 1934 Lawrence Spivak became the business manager of the *American Mercury*; five years later, he purchased the monthly and became the publisher. Under Spivak's editor, Eugene Lyons, the *American Mercury* became "the leading anticommunist publication in the country" (Tebbel & Zukerman, 1991, 214). Although strongly Republican in its views, the monthly took a staunch prointerventionist view prior to U.S. entry into World War II in 1941. After the attack on Pearl Harbor, the *Mercury* features stressed how the backward state of U.S. air power had contributed to the debacle in the Pacific and lobbied in an unrelenting fashion for a buildup of the army air corps. Over the opposition of a truculent naval elite at the time, the *American Mercury* influenced congressional officials to step up appropriations for the heavy-bomber building program. Toward the end of World War II in 1944, Lawrence Spivak became editor as well as publisher of the *Mercury*.

During his association with the *American Mercury*, Lawrence Spivak had other publishing interests as well. He was president and publisher of Mercury Publications. The firm published mystery novels, science fiction novels and magazines, and magazines devoted to portraying "true crimes." In 1954 Spivak sold out his financial interest in the publishing firm to concentrate on producing a radio-television property he had developed in collaboration with Martha Rountree.

In 1946 Martha Rountree, than a freelance reporter and radio producer, submitted an article to the *American Mercury*. From 1947 to 1954 she was a roving editor for the *American Mercury*. Rountree, born in 1916 and a native of Columbia, South Carolina, became hooked on writing at the age of nine when she penned a short story. When her father, a real estate and automobile salesman, died, Martha Rountree was sixteen years old and still in high school. In order to pay her way to the University of South Carolina, she worked for the Columbia *Record*. The taste for journalism, and the need for financial support, won out over her desire to finish a college degree; she left the university and took a position at the *Tribune* in Tampa, Florida. There she worked as a general reporter and eventually became a sports columnist, a rare newspaper assignment for a female journalist in those days. In 1938 she left Tampa and moved to New York City as a freelance writer, selling material to magazines and writing advertising copy.

The same year that Lawrence Spivak bought the *American Mercury*, Martha Rountree joined her sister, Ann, in the formation of a production company, Radio House. One of the Rountrees' ideas led to the production of a Mutual Broadcasting System (MBS) radio program, "Leave It to the Girls," in 1945. The program utilized a panel format—one male joined women celebrities to answer questions submitted by listeners. The radio program, which proved a success, was later adapted for NBC-TV in 1948. Substitute questions from a live audience for those submitted by listeners, and "Leave It to the Girls" was the basic format exploited so successfully by Phil Donahue (q.v.) and others in the final decades of the twentieth century.

Because of Rountree's work in radio production, Lawrence Spivak sought her advice in 1945. Spivak was using a radio program to promote the *American Mercury* (Campbell, 1976). He sponsored a series that dramatized *Mercury* feature articles. Spivak asked Rountree's opinion of the program. Her view was bluntly critical. So the two created a format for an alternative program. The result was "Meet the Press." It made its debut on the Mutual Broadcasting System in June 1945, and it has been a weekly staple of radio and television political commentary for more than half a century.

"MEET THE PRESS" AND BEYOND

In its inception, ''Meet the Press'' simply adapted the format of Martha Rountree's ''Leave It to the Girls.'' A panel of several journalists, usually from two
to four, including Lawrence Spivak as permanent panel member, asked questions
of a prominent politician, eliciting commentary from the guest, often offering
commentary themselves via questions. Although the panel members thoroughly
briefed themselves on each political guest's background and public views, the
program was unrehearsed; neither the specific questions asked by panel members
nor the guest's response was known in advance. Journalists appearing on ''Meet
the Press'' were paid; the guest was not. In addition to the panel and guest,
Martha Rountree served as moderator of the thirty-minute give-and-take.

After its debut, with Eric Johnston, president of the U.S. Chamber of Commerce, as a guest, ''Meet the Press'' evolved into the most influential forum of
news making, commentary, and manipulation on the airways: ''The show's early
prominence . . . came from Spivak's uncanny knack for snaring newsmakers
while they were hot, and from the tough questions he threw at them once they
were on the air'' (Campbell, 1976, 110). In 1948 ''Meet the Press'' moved to
television, on NBC-TV, while the radio broadcast remained on MBS for several
years before it also moved to the National Broadcasting Company (NBC). (In
addition, the program reached overseas through the Armed Forces Radio and
Television Services.)

In its news-making role, ''Meet the Press'' derived from the dogged efforts
of its journalists, especially Spivak's, at interrogation. Under questioning by
such noted journalists and political commentators as Marquis Childs (q.v.), Carl
T. Rowan (q.v.), and James ''Scotty'' Reston (q.v.)—to name a few—it was
on ''Meet the Press'' that several notable news stories broke. For example, it
was a ''Meet the Press'' scoop, and an accurate prophesy, in 1950 that two-
time presidential candidate Thomas E. Dewey would not seek the nomination
in 1952 but would urge General Dwight Eisenhower to do so. It was also on
''Meet the Press'' that Eisenhower's 1952 Democratic opponent, Adlai E. Stevenson, first expressed public interest in running for president. Among other
U.S. politicians making news on ''Meet the Press'' were Harry Truman, Henry
Wallace, Richard Nixon, Robert Taft, and Joseph McCarthy. (''Are you sug-
gesting J. Edgar Hoover [knows] a spy in the State Department and [has] done
nothing?,'' Lawrence Spivak chided McCarthy.)

In the earliest days of the program, before politicians adjusted to exploiting
broadcasting rather than being threatened by it, guests approached ''Meet the
Press'' with trepidation. George Meany, politically powerful kingmaker and
president of the American Federation of Labor and Congress of Industrial Organizations, complained after an appearance of the program, ''A half hour on
that show can age you ten years'' (Campbell, 1976, 110). Yet, as Spivak said,
''Men in public office live by the voters they attract, and it is therefore hard for
any politician to refuse to appear on a program that attracts an audience in the

millions—and makes important news across the country the next morning" (Candee, 1956, 51).

As "Meet the Press" evolved, politicians became increasingly adept at exploiting the program for making news as they wanted to make it, and at evading intense interrogation through the fine art of giving answers to questions that were not asked, or simply not answering them at all. In 1954 a young Massachusetts senator, John F. Kennedy, used the show to charm not only the panel members and moderator, but millions of viewers as well. After Kennedy was elected president, Spivak recalled JFK's eight performances on "Meet the Press": "Brief, clipped, forceful. From the beginning he knew how to handle a press conference and you didn't expect for him to say anything he didn't want to say" ("Question Man," 1962, 68). By contrast, a rival of Kennedy's for the 1960 Democratic presidential nomination, Lyndon Johnson, exasperated Spivak by not answering a single question as a guest on a "Meet the Press" program. Spivak said later that he could barely restrain himself from demanding of Johnson, "Now that we're off the air, will you tell us if your name is Lyndon Johnson" (Rivers, 1967, 167).

Because of the frequency with which politicians started to use "Meet the Press" as a forum for self-promotion rather than the spontaneous give-and-take of interrogation and analysis, Spivak and Rountree had their critics. One was Edward L. Bernays (q.v.), a founder of public relations who knew whereof he spoke regarding matters of promotion. In 1946 U.S. Senator Theodore Bilbo of Mississippi, suspected at the time of being a member of the Ku Klux Klan, accepted an invitation to appear on "Meet the Press." While sharing a compartment on a train from New York to Washington, D.C., with Spivak and Rountree, Bernays questioned the wisdom of giving Bilbo nationwide exposure to air his racist sentiments. Spivak agreed that there was a risk, but he argued that, as a U.S. senator, Bilbo already had a visible platform for racist views. But, said Bernays, "Larry thought exposure would hang Bilbo; the public would be antagonized by the answers Bilbo made to his interviewers' questions" (Bernays, 1965, 688). Spivak proved to be correct. On the August 9, 1946, edition of "Meet the Press," Bilbo admitted being a member of the Klan. As a direct result of the admission, a U.S. Senate investigation led to an attempt to unseat Bilbo, an effort thwarted only by the senator's death.

The success of "Meet the Press" gave rise to imitators: in the early days of television, to Columbia Broadcasting System's (CBS') "Face the Nation," later David Brinkley (q.v.) and his "This Week with David Brinkley," and Cable News Network's (CNN's) "Newsmaker Saturday" and "Newsmaker Sunday." Compared to the "Meet the Press" of Spivak and Rountree, however, the clones differ in key respects. For one, the "grilling" on "Meet the Press," although thorough, was always understated, civil, and courteous. Confrontation for the sake of sensation or audience building had no place.

Second, the panel members on "Meet the Press" accepted their roles as getting and analyzing the news. Panelists on imitative programs are not always so restrained. For instance, Sam Donaldson and Corrine "Cokie" Roberts (q.v.) on "This Week with David Brinkley" are not only irreverent in interrogating guests, they frequently go beyond getting the story to becoming "the story" themselves (Hirsch, 1991). Contemporary members of interview panels reflect what social commentator Alan Bennett said about political analysis in writing about David Frost: His "rise as a political commentator is in direct proportion to the decline of respect for politicians" (1996, 35).

In 1950 Lawrence Spivak sold *American Mercury* because of the financial losses the magazine, in spite of its considerable political influence, was suffering. And, in 1953 Martha Rountree sold her share of "Meet the Press" to her collaborator, closing her six-year job of moderator on November 3. (Ned Brooks replaced Rountree as the show's moderator from 1954 through 1965.) In 1955 Spivak sold "Meet the Press" to NBC but retained his post as a producer and panel member. From 1966 to 1975 Spivak served as moderator of "Meet the Press" before he retired to become a consultant to NBC. Lawrence E. Spivak died on March 9, 1994, one year before "Meet the Press" celebrated its fiftieth anniversary. It is the longest running program in television history.

"Meet the Press" was not the only pioneering political forum generated by the Spivak-Rountree collaboration. In 1951 they produced "Keep Posted" (which was later changed to "The Big Issue"), a show originating from the nation's capital and viewed on the DuMont television network. The format foreshadowed contemporary political commentary programming, such as CNN's "Crossfire." Two political guests on opposite sides of a controversial issue responded to questions from a panel of citizens with expertise on the topic. In another joint creation, this one presaging the forums common to contemporary presidential nominating contests, Spivak and Rountree presented U.S. senators from rival political parties arguing points of view on controversial issues. The show, "Washington Exclusive," also aired on the DuMont network.

Under the terms of her sale of "Meet the Press" and other collaborative efforts to Lawrence Spivak in 1953, Martha Rountree was prohibited from developing competing properties for a two-year period. In 1956 she returned to commentary with "Press Conference," "a no-holds-barred, give and take between a roomful of reporters and a top drawer, noteworthy [guest] subject" (Candee, 1957, 42). "Press Conference" aired originally over NBC-TV but soon moved to ABC-TV. The similarity of confrontational interview shows developed in the 1980s to the "Press Conference" format, such as "Evans and Novak," the "Capitol Gang," and "Crossfire," is not coincidental. In 1952 Martha Rountree entered her second marriage; her first, from 1941 to 1948, was to Albert N. Williams, Jr., a magazine and radio writer. Oliver Presbrey, a former account executive with a leading advertising agency, became her second husband. He joined Rountree and political commentator Robert Novak in 1956 as partners in Rountree Productions, the producers of "Press Conference." Novak took Rountree's concept of a no-holds-barred encounter and, as a journalist, made a career of exploiting the adversarial relationship between commentators and politicians, on confrontational television.

THE LEGACY OF SPIVAK AND ROUNTREE

Aside from the production team of Edward R. Murrow (q.v.) and Fred Friendly in developing the documentary as a form of political commentary at CBS, no other joint enterprise has left its mark on broadcast politics as that of Martha Rountree and Lawrence Spivak. With virtually no models to follow, the two producer-journalists created forms of political commentary that have endured to the approach of the twenty-first century. In one form or another, the panel interview in all its variations is the most pervasive staple of syndicated and cable television, not only in politics but in all areas of televised entertainment. That it may have become as abused as it is used, certainly the contention of many critics (e.g., Kurtz, 1996), is not the fault of its two creators.

Separately, Spivak and Rountree each made a distinctive contribution to the development of twentieth-century political commentary. Spivak's was in using both magazine publishing and commentary to wield influence over policy officials. Both the *American Mercury* and ''Meet the Press'' not only covered political news via news and commentary, under Spivak's prodding, both became vehicles for making news and setting the agenda of public commentary as well.

Rountree's contribution was in demonstrating, at a time when the female's presence in television production and in television news was routinely dismissed as unfeminine, that there is not only a niche for the female broadcaster; there is also potential for quality in any commentary regardless of gender of the commentator and the forum of its presentation. Mrs. William Randolph Hearst once called Rountree ''a diesel engine under a lace handkerchief'' (Taft, 1986, 294); Rountree described her niche in more generic, less gender-oriented ways: ''a blunt-speaking, down-to-earth television news reporter and I'm proud of it'' (Taft, 1986, 294).

In spite of her notable contributions to the development of political commentary, biographical data concerning her life and career are sketchy. For example, entries in biographical directories (e.g., Candee, 1957; Taft, 1986) record only the year, but not the month or date of her birth. Moreover, NBC News, the TV network home of ''Meet the Press'' for almost half a century, 1948 to date, also has no record of Rountree's date of birth.

It is all the more surprising, that one of the singular pioneers of women in political broadcasting, Martha Rountree, has been largely ignored by the very women of television news for whom she paved the way. Thus, for example, television political journalist Marlene Sanders in her exhaustive survey of women in television news, from the period after World War II to the 1980s, makes no mention of Martha Rountree (Sanders and Rock, 1988). If the reminiscences of political commentator David Brinkley are any indication, the slight to a pioneer like Rountree may well lie in a perception that her off-the-air views simply did not set well with those of the Washington establishment. Brinkley dismissed Rountree in an almost snide manner as "a fervent admirer of Joe McCarthy. She said to me one day, leaning against the mantel in somebody's living room, 'When you're trying to save America as I am, you have to take some chances" (Brinkley, 1995, 235).

Nevertheless, well before the contemporary generation of women in political broadcasting, who have too often overlooked Rountree's pathbreaking presence, and long before Brinkley's panel-interview series, "This Week with David Brinkley," arrived on the scene, there was Martha Rountree. She was a force to be reckoned with then and, for those taking the trouble to become aware of her contributions, should be for many generations to come.

REFERENCES

Selected Works and Television Specials of Lawrence E. Spivak

The American Mercury Reader. Edited with C. Angoff. Boston: Blakiston, 1944.
"Meet the Press International: Dean Rusk." Produced and moderated by Lawrence E. Spivak. Aired April 2, 1967, NBC-TV .
"Meet the Press International: Delegates to the Pacem in Terres Conference." Produced by Lawrence E. Spivak. Aired May 28, 1967, NBC-TV.
"A Day for History: The Supreme Court and the Pentagon Papers." Edited and produced by Lawrence E. Spivak. Aired June 30, 1971, NBC-TV. Emmy Winning Report on a Current Controversy.

Selected Works about Martha Rountree and Lawrence E. Spivak

Bernays E. "Senator Bilbo." In *Biography of an Idea: Memoirs of Public Relations Counsel Edward L. Bernays*, 686–93. New York: Simon and Schuster, 1965.
Candee, M. D., ed. "Rountree, Martha." In *Current Biography* (February 1957):40–42.
———. "Spivak, Lawrence E(dmund)." In *Current Biography* (May 1956): 49–51.
Downs, R. B., and J. B. Downs, eds. "Lawrence E. Spivak." In *Journalists of the United States*, 324. Jefferson, NC: McFarland, 1991.
"Question Man." *Newsweek*, September 3, 1962, 68.
Severo, R. "Lawrence E. Spivak, 93, Is Dead: The Originator of 'Meet the Press.' " *New York Times*, March 10, 1994, D 21.
"Spivak, Lawrence Edmund." Obituary. *Facts on File*, 196. New York: Facts on File, 1994.
Taft, W. H. "Rountree, Martha." In *Encyclopedia of Twentieth-Century Journalists*, 293–94. New York: Garland Publishing, 1986.
———. "Spivak, Lawrence Edmund." In *Encyclopedia of Twentieth-Century Journalists*, 323. New York: Garland Publishing, 1986.

Selected General Works

Bennett, A. "The Diary of Alan Bennett." *Weekly Telegraph* (London, England) issue 235, January 24–30, 1996, 35.
Brinkley, D. *David Brinkley: A Memoir.* New York: Alfred A. Knopf, 1995.

Campbell, R. *The Golden Years of Broadcasting*. New York: Charles Scribner's Sons, 1976.
Hirsch, A. *Talking Heads: Political Talk Shows and Their Star Pundits*. New York: St. Martin's Press, 1991.
Kurtz, H. *Hot Air: All Talk, All the Time*. New York: Times Books, 1996.
Lewis, T. *Empire of the Air*. New York: Harper/Collins, 1991.
Nimmo, D., and J. E. Combs. *The Political Pundits*. New York: Praeger, 1992.
Rivers, W. *The Opinionmakers*. Boston: Beacon Press, 1967.
Rose, B. G., ed. *TV Genres: A Handbook and Reference Guide*. Westport, CT: Greenwood, 1985.
Sanders, M., and M. Rock. *Waiting for Prime Time: The Women of Television News*. New York: Harper and Row, 1988.
Steel, R. *Walter Lippmann and the Twentieth Century*. Boston: Little, Brown, 1980.
Tebbel, J. and M. E. Zuckerman. *The Magazine in America: 1741–1990*. New York: Oxford University Press, 1991.

CARL T. (THOMAS) ROWAN

(August 11, 1925–   )

Commenting on Politics Inside and Out

"Washington is a very wicked city," wrote nationally syndicated columnist Carl Rowan in 1974 ("The Leak Game," 14). He was discussing the perfidious tactic of the news leak used by Washington insiders to advance their political interests at the expense of others. But he could have been commenting on virtually any other device used by Washington politicians to gain an advantage—friendships with journalists, invitations to dinner soirées, exclusive interviews, promises of appointments to high places for the ambitious, and so on.

Rowan knew whereof he wrote. He witnessed Washington from the outside for decades as an African-American journalist working on white-dominated newspapers, covering the civil rights movement and politics from inside the beltway. His later syndicated political commentary covered not only the American civil rights movement but also the Cold War, the Vietnam War, and the economic policies of a succession of U.S. presidents. He also witnessed it from the inside, as deputy assistant secretary of state for public administration, director of the United States Information Agency, and U.S. ambassador to Finland. Yes, both from outside and inside, Carl Rowan knew Washington as a "very wicked city."

BREAKING THROUGH POVERTY

In an interview with his biographer in 1974, Carl Rowan passed along to her a lesson from a college instructor that Rowan had taken to heart and never forgotten: "Make no little plans. They have no power to stir men's blood and probably themselves will not be realized" (Bynum, 1975, 1). Born as he was in poverty in Ravenscroft, Tennessee, on August 11, 1925, before most white Americans knew about economic depression, let alone were victims of it, Carl Thomas Rowan could have been justified in setting his sights low. He did not. When he was an infant, his parents, Thomas Davis and Johnnie B. (Bradford) Rowan, moved the family to McMinnville. The small town had job opportunities for blacks in nurseries, lumberyards, and livestock stables. Certainly the Rowans could not forecast the economic hardships that were to befall them and other families shortly after their move to McMinnville.

The stock market crash of 1929 and the Great Depression that followed were economic disasters for many Americans, but the despair was particularly devastating to blacks living under Southern Jim Crow laws. Thus, Carl Rowan, along with his brother and three sisters, not only grew up in poverty, they faced the discrimination meted out in a segregated South. Thomas Rowan struggled to support his family on a meager salary, $2 for ten hours on a "good day," earned from stacking sawmill lumber. Rowan's mother occasionally took in laundry to help earn money for the family.

In his memoirs, Carl Rowan recalls the difficulty in obtaining food, and the different avenues his family found to survive. He wrote, "When there was no lumber to stack, when times were really rough, my father would ask me to go hunting with him. . . . They called him [Thomas Rowan] Two-Shot Rowan. . . . Tom Rowan might miss a rabbit with the first barrel, but never with the second" (Rowan, 1991, 11). The family survived the depression by eating beans and rabbits. In order to help financially, Carl worked at various menial jobs for the white community, including washing dishes, shoveling snow, and mowing grass. Economic and social conditions in McMinnville provoked Rowan and his friends to illegal, dangerous risks: "The question of the early 1940s is still the question today. How do deprived, poorly educated kids escape temptation and deprivation, survive foolish and often unlawful escapades, and get anyplace close to an even chance in the race that privileged Americans like to call 'the pursuit of happiness' " (Rowan, 1991, 29).

Education proved to be Carl's route to economic freedom. It was his opportunity to exploit his talents and escape the despair of poverty. Rowan describes the luckiest thing to happen to him: his going to live with his grandparents in Nashville during his seventh and eighth grade years. While living with them, Rowan learned a lesson in indoctrination. Being devout Seventh-Day Adventists, his grandparents enrolled Carl in a school run by the church. He learned discipline and an appreciation for a commitment to a higher being that induced, out of fear of the consequences of disobedience, moral and legal conduct in the once recalcitrant Carl.

After two years at a church-run school, Carl Rowan elected to return to McMinnville for high school rather than attend a larger public school in Nashville. During his elementary education, Rowan's mother worked extra jobs to ensure that the children had books for classes. She worked with him by candle light to help him complete his homework. The efforts of Carl's mother, coupled with the Nashville experience, prepared Rowan for high school. But it was the guidance of several teachers who challenged him to dismiss peers who tried to belittle him for speaking standard English. The chiding from his classmates was hard on Carl because he wanted to be on the high school football team; popularity was important to Rowan during his teenage years.

Upon his return to McMinnville, he studied with teachers who stressed the values of education and persistence as the way to confront the obstacles of segregation and economic oppression. According to Rowan, his mother, who had an eleventh-grade education, "displayed an innate understanding that parental support and praise" raised a child's sense of self-worth and encouraged a yearning for knowledge (Rowan, 1991, 17). One high school teacher in particular, Bessie Taylor Gwynn, known as "Miss Bessie," offered Rowan sound advice for his life on how to demonstrate gumption: "Refusing to lower your standards to those of the dumb crowd. It takes guts to say to yourself that you've got to live and be somebody fifty years after these football games are over'' (Rowan, 1991, 31). Upon her death in 1980, Rowan dedicated a column to this woman, who smuggled books for him out of the all-white library in McMinnville so that he could excel. Rowan recounted the important message imparted to him by Miss Bessie: "If you don't read, you can't write, and if you can't write, you can stop dreaming" (1991, 33).

Carl Rowan heeded his mother's and teachers' advice and did well throughout school. He developed an interest in writing and, as a proud thirteen-year-old, had his poem read before an audience on his school's stage. He graduated from all-black Bernard High School as class president and valedictorian in 1942. After graduation, Rowan spent the summer working to earn money to attend college in the fall. However, instead of saving his money, he squandered it and returned to Nashville with only seventy-seven cents in his pocket and hopes of entering Fisk University on a football scholarship. Those hopes were illusions; he was not accepted at Fisk. He moved in with his grandparents and worked as an attendant at the hospital where his grandfather was employed, earning $30 a month for his college expenses.

In 1942 Rowan entered Tennessee Agricultural and Industrial State College, an all-black college and, later, Tennessee State University. While there Carl Rowan once again met professors who encouraged and challenged him to excel. In 1943 one of Rowan's professors urged Rowan to take an entrance exam for the U.S. Navy's officer training program. Rowan passed the exam and was assigned to Washburn University in Topeka, Kansas, as one of the first fifteen blacks in U.S. Navy history to achieve officer status. Rowan later attended Oberlin College in Ohio as part of the program, and then the Naval Reserve Midshipmen School in Fort Schuyler, the Bronx. There he was in the same battalion with Howard Baker, who later become a U.S. senator from Tennessee, a Senate majority leader, and the White House chief of staff. At sea Rowan excelled as deputy commander of the communications division.

In 1946 Rowan's naval duties ended, and he returned to McMinnville. But his time in the navy led him to set new goals in his life. He had "outgrown my raising. . . . When you are plucked out of a totally Jim Crow environment at age seventeen and thrown into a totally white environment where more is at stake than your personal life, you mature rapidly" (Rowan, 1991, 57–61).

ENTERING THE WORLD OF POLITICAL COMMENTARY

Rowan returned to Oberlin College to complete his B.A. degree in mathematics. He came to appreciate Oberlin's reputation for egalitarianism, and it proved to be a positive experience for him. Because of Oberlin's integrated system, Rowan socialized with white students and learned to read about current events and formulate opinions on political and social issues. Most of the students, unlike Rowan, had come from families where political, economic, and social issues were discussed daily. Rowan majored in mathematics, and he earned his degree in 1947.

"Mathematics had been his means for getting ahead," writes his biographer, "but all the while his love was journalism" (Bynum, 1975, 3). He wrote for a black newspaper in Columbus simply because he knew he wanted to write. During the summer of 1947, Rowan began working as a freelance writer for the black newspaper chain, the *Baltimore Afro-American*. He was accepted to three graduate programs in journalism, but decided to attend the University of Minnesota.

When he started graduate school in journalism, Rowan worked as a northern correspondent for the *Afro-American*, and also wrote for the Twin Cities' two black papers, the *Minneapolis Spokesman* and the *St. Paul Recorder*. In August 1948 he graduated from the University of Minnesota with an M.A. in journalism. During the 1948 presidential election, Rowan conducted public opinion polling for the *Baltimore Afro-American*. The experience taught him a lesson in the ethics of his chosen craft. The results of his polls indicated that most blacks favored incumbent Harry Truman over the Progressive Henry Wallace or Republican Thomas Dewey. But the editor of the paper had made an agreement to support Dewey. The editor used headlines misrepresenting the substance of the poll findings. Carl Rowan, the twenty-three-year-old fresh out of journalism school, learned quickly to protect the credibility of his byline.

After the elections in November 1948, Rowan was hired at the copy desk of the all-white Minneapolis *Tribune*. Two years later, he became that paper's first black general assignment reporter, one of the few in the entire United States. As a reporter, Rowan recalled a conversation he had had with a white sailor he had met in the navy. Rowan had told the sailor that, if he became a writer, he would "tell all the little things it means to be Negro in the South, or anyplace where being a Negro makes a difference" (Rowan, 1991, 49). So, in December 1950, Rowan proposed to the *Tribune* management that he travel through the Deep South and report on the effects of Jim Crow discrimination laws on blacks. The *Tribune* enthusiastically agreed, and he embarked upon a 6,000-mile journey through thirteen states. From his experiences, he wrote a series of eighteen articles in 1951 entitled, "How Far from Slavery?" His work earned him the Service to Humanity Award from the Minneapolis Junior Chamber of Commerce and resulted in a book, *South of Freedom* (1952).

Rowan's objective was "to tell the American people some truths they do not know, explain some things that they clearly do not understand, and . . . fulfill every journalistic obligation that burdens any reporter of any race" (Rowan, 1991, 98). Carl Rowan was now fulfilling his reason for becoming a journalist in the first place: "When I came out of the war, I saw that all those glowing promises of the war-makers were not coming true in this society, and we had a media that wasn't much inclined to make it come true" (Oder, 1993, 445). His articles were attempts to correct that. Critics praised his writing not as bitter accounts, but as vivid stories that brought the perils faced by a group of individuals to a level that all people could understand.

Hodding Carter, a white editor of a liberal Mississippi newspaper, wrote in the *New York Times*, on August 3, 1952, that *South of Freedom* was "a vivid reminder that changes which a white Southerner thinks are swift seem snail-like and indecisive to a southerner who is not white and who suffers from color barriers"; Carter called the book a "noteworthy contribution to the sad folklore of American interracial relations" (quoted in LaBlanc, 1992, 210). Other reviewers noted that Rowan's work was profound and that it effectively chronicled the experiences of blacks in the South.

The newspaper series and the subsequent book attracted attention and, in 1954, the U.S. State Department invited Carl Rowan to travel to India and lecture on the role of a free press in a free society. Taking the opportunity to share his opinions in his newly visibly role as a political commentator, Rowan wrote a series of articles for the Minneapolis *Tribune* that earned Sigma Delta Chi awards. He extended his trip to travel to Southeast Asia where he wrote another series of articles on the political climate in the region, in addition to covering the 1955 Bandung Conference of Non-Aligned Nations, a gathering of twenty-three underdeveloped nations. In 1956 the articles were the basis for his second book, *The Pitiful and the Proud*.

After the U.S. Supreme Court's landmark 1954 case, *Brown v. Board of Education of Topeka* outlawed racial segregation in public schools, Carl Rowan traveled once more to the South. He wrote a series of articles, entitled "Dixie Divided," that discussed the slow progress in implementing the Court's ruling. This series was also highly acclaimed; Rowan now had his third book, *Go South to Sorrow* (1957). In the book Rowan covers the progression of the civil rights movement in the South, including the historic Montgomery (Alabama) bus boycott in 1955. He developed special friendships with the movement's leaders, including Martin Luther King, Jr. Rowan passed information he learned as a journalist along to the movement's leaders, giving them an opportunity to discredit erroneous information provided to the press by civil rights opponents. Rowan later wrote that his efforts were his way of "lashing out at President Eisenhower, Hodding Carter, and other gradualists who, in my view, were compromising away the freedom of America's black people" (Rowan, 1991, 145). Media observers, then and now, question whether a journalist is justified in changing the course of events by conveying intelligence acquired as a correspondent to parties involved in the event: should a reporter make as well as gather news? (Cater, 1959).

In 1956 Rowan moved from the South to become the United Nations (UN) correspondent for the Minneapolis *Tribune*. The world was undergoing twin international crises: the Suez Canal crisis in which England, France, and Israel attempted to seize the canal from Egypt, and the Hungarian uprising against the Soviet Union. Rowan's earlier coverage of unrest in Southeast Asia and the Bandung conference qualified him for the UN post; moreover, he could obtain the confidence of the various parties involved in unfolding events. His UN coverage analyzed both the Suez and Hungarian crises. Years later, Rowan reflected on those events in his memoirs, and the ironic connection they had to the civil rights movement in the United States:

> In the mentalities of our White House, our Congress, our media, there were no "troublemakers on both sides" in Hungary. The villains were the brutal Soviet rapers of innocent Hungarians who had dared to reach out for freedom. But in America the air was filled with cries, even by [President] Eisenhower and [Democratic challenger Adlai] Stevenson, for a "moderate" approach to ending segregation and a national rejection of "the extremists on both sides." (Rowan, 1991, 151)

In his assessment, the Americans who insisted on shouting the loudest about Soviet atrocities in Hungary were those who were working the hardest to dehumanize black Americans, to portray them as little more than beasts and demons in the same mold as Soviet aggressors.

During 1957 Rowan wrote a series of articles on American Indians and their status as a "forgotten people." This series met with mixed reviews. Rowan stirred discontent, provoking some American Indians to feel used and maligned. In response, Rowan pointed to the concrete improvements in the lives of American Indians in the Minneapolis area that resulted from his series. In 1960 Rowan undertook another complex writing task when he assisted in writing the autobiography of Jackie Robinson, the first black, major league baseball player. That too provoked mixed comment, but Rowan weathered the criticism.

During the 1960 political campaign, Rowan interviewed both presidential candidates, Richard M. Nixon and John F. Kennedy, for the Minneapolis *Tribune*. After the election President Kennedy offered Rowan the position of deputy assistant secretary of state for public affairs. Rowan became responsible for the press relations of the State Department and was involved in the sensitive area of news coverage of the increasing U.S. military involvement in Vietnam. He was also a part of the negotiations that secured the release of pilot Francis Gary Powers, who had been shot down over the Soviet Union in a U2 spy plane during the Eisenhower administration. When Vice President Lyndon Johnson toured Southeast Asia, India, and Europe, Carl Rowan returned to the region to accompany the vice president. In 1963 he became the youngest ambassador in the diplomatic service, and only the fifth black to serve as an envoy, when President Kennedy named him U.S. ambassador to Finland.

After Kennedy's assassination in November 1963, President Johnson named Rowan head of the United States Information Agency (USIA). With the appointment, Rowan became the highest ranking black in the federal government and the first ever to attend National Security Council meetings. He supervised a staff of 13,000 who were responsible for directing the government's communications network, including the controversial Voice of America radio system and the daily communiques to U.S. embassy personnel around the world.

Carl Rowan was not the first noted political communicator to be drawn into controversies surrounding agencies designed to provide both information and propaganda about U.S. aims across the world. Nor would he be the last. George Creel (q.v.) founded the first U.S. propaganda agency, the Committee on Public Information (CPI), during World War I. Elmer Davis (q.v.) headed the USIA's predecessor, the Office of War Information (OWI), during World War II. Edward R. Murrow (q.v.) headed the USIA for John F. Kennedy. John Chancellor (q.v.) was President Johnson's director of the Voice of America (VOA). And, William Buckley (q.v.) was a member of the supervisory board for the USIA during the presidency of Richard Nixon. To their regret, all of them found, as did Carl Rowan, that providing a factual account of U.S. domestic conditions and worldwide aims and serving the propaganda interests of U.S. presidents are not compatible (Shulman, 1990).

In his USIA position, Rowan assumed the task of developing an information program to explain U.S. interests and activities in the growing Vietnam conflict. Within the USIA, Rowan raised eyebrows for what his critics perceived as his neglect of important USIA responsibilities at the expense of the Vietnam program. Outside the USIA, opponents of the Vietnam War criticized the USIA's alleged selling of the war. In 1965, like all of his predecessors in sensitive CPI, OWI, USIA, and VOA posts, Rowan had experienced enough of the constant carping from politicians and journalists alike. He resigned from the USIA to become the Washington columnist for the *Chicago Daily News*, write a regular column of political analysis and opinion for the Field Newspaper Syndicate, and serve as a broadcast analyst airing his views in three weekly radio commentaries for the Westinghouse Broadcasting Company.

Carl Rowan reentered the world of journalism with a more focused view of the political community and its political processes, a view shaped by his experiences as an insider. He quickly became one of the nation's most vocal, and controversial, columnists and broadcast analysts. Unrelenting sociopolitical unrest and change marked the ensuing years after Rowan's departure from government. Speaking on national political and social issues, Rowan urged national leaders to take action that would facilitate a refocus of America's priorities. He did not hesitate to call for the resignation of powerful officeholders or challenge serious abuses of power or unethical or illegal conduct. In the early 1980s, when Ronald Reagan became president, Carl Rowan became a passionate critic of the administration's policies. He charged Reagan with destroying the advances in human rights made by the civil rights movement. Rowan was unrelenting in pointing out the perils that faced disadvantaged minorities as a result of Reagan administration cutbacks in social program funding.

While Carl Rowan remained throughout his career a steadfast spokesman for civil and economic rights for blacks and other disadvantaged groups, he was critical of black leaders who failed, in his judgment, to address aggressively the serious issues that affect their followers. In 1988 Rowan shot and wounded an intruder in his Washington, D.C., home. The incident made national headlines since Rowan, who is a supporter of national gun control laws, was charged with possession of an unregistered firearm. His actions in this incident drew an abundance of criticism, but Rowan utilized the incident to comment on societal woes. The charges were later dropped in court, but not until after Rowan had accused the mayor of Washington, D.C., Marion Barry, of extortion. According to Rowan, Mayor Barry had agreed to have the charges dropped only if Rowan ceased his harsh criticism of the mayor's administration in his syndicated columns.

Although he continued to criticize Barry, it was still Rowan who suffered the bulk of public criticism. He said, "I have learned over four decades as a journalist that city hall becomes more and more corrupt as more and more citizens lose the guts to fight" (Rowan, 1991, 348). His criticism of Barry, and of other minority leaders who misplaced their followers' trust, did not mark any shift in his priorities. They remained the same: "A minority group has 'arrived' only when it has the right to produce some fools and scoundrels without the entire group paying for it" (Quote of the Day, 1993).

CARL T. ROWAN: A COMPENDIUM OF "FIRSTS"

Other political commentators have been the "first" to accomplish a particular feat: Walter Lippmann (q.v.) was the first syndicated political columnist; H. V. Kaltenborn (q.v.) was the first broadcast commentator; and Edward L. Bernays (q.v.) was the first public relations counsel. Carl T. Rowan compiled several firsts in his lifetime: he was one of the first black officers in the U.S. Navy; he was the first black reporter on national assignment for a white U.S. daily newspaper; and he was the first black to be both State Department deputy assistant secretary and the USIA chief.

More important, however, than "firsts," is the consistency of aim and accomplishment in his career as an outspoken political communicator. In a 1974 letter written to Rowan's biographer, Lynn Bynum, the president of *Post-Newsweek* Stations, James L. Snyder, put the thrust of Rowan's contributions in perspective:

> We feel Mr. Rowan is enormously effective as an intelligent, courageous, experienced journalist who feels very strongly about the right and duty of the journalist in our free society to speak out with vigor for what he believes. The fact that he is black makes his performance all the more impressive to many of our viewers since there are so few black commentators and none that I know of who has been as effective as Carl. . . . He is a complete professional. (Bynum, 1975, 25)

REFERENCES

Selected Political Works by Carl T. Rowan

South of Freedom. New York: Alfred A. Knopf, 1952.
The Pitiful and the Proud. New York: Random House, 1956.
Go South to Sorrow. New York: Random House, 1957.
Just Between Us Blacks. New York: Random House, 1974.
"The Leak Game." *The Chattanooga Times*, June 26, 1974, 14.
"President Carter's Interview," "Meet the Press." January 20, 1980. Washington, DC: Department of State, Office of Public Communication, 1980.
Breaking Barriers. Boston: Little, Brown, 1991.
Dream Makers, Dream Breakers: The World of Justice Thurgood Marshall. Boston: Little, Brown, 1993.

Selected Critical Works about Carl T. Rowan

Bynum, L. *Carl T. Rowan: Journalist Extraordinary*. Bloomington, IN: Afro-American Institute, Blacks in American Journalism Series, 1975.
Candee, M. D., ed. "Rowan, Carl T(homas)." In *Current Biography 1958*, 370–72. New York: H. W. Wilson Co., 1958.
"Charges Dropped." *Time*, October 17, 1988, 65.
LaBlanc, M. L., ed. "Carl T. Rowan." In *Contemporary Black Biography*, vol. 1, 208–12. Detroit: Gale Research, 1992.
Lichtenstein, N., ed. "Rowan, Carl T(homas)." In *Political Profiles: The Kennedy Years*, 449. New York: Facts on File, 1976.
Oder, N. "Carl T. Rowan." *Publisher's Weekly*, January 18, 1993, 444–45.
Riley, S. G. "Rowan, Carl Thomas." In *Biographical Dictionary of American Newspaper Columnists*, 277–78. Westport, CT: Greenwood Press, 1995.

Selected General Works

Cater, D. *The Fourth Branch of Government*. Boston: Houghton Mifflin, 1959.
Cohen, R. "The Syndicated Columnist." *Gannett Center Journal* 3 (Spring 1989): 9–16.
Quote of the Day. Regular news feature, the Internet, August 11, 1993.
Shulman, H. C. *The Voice of America*. Madison: University of Wisconsin Press, 1990.

(ARNOLD) ERIC SEVAREID

(November 26, 1912–July 9, 1992)

Political Commentary to Elucidate Not Advocate

The twentieth century was reaching a midlife crisis; network radio was in the prime of its life; television was in its infancy. Then, on August 15, 1948, arrived a newborn, a child that would have a major effect in later years on the career of Eric Sevareid as a political commentator—as he would have a major impact on the newborn child as it came of age and, through it, on the political views of a generation. For on that mid-August evening in the dog days of summer, the Columbia Broadcasting System (CBS) gave birth to the network's first nightly television news program, "Douglas Edwards with the News." Thirty thousand viewers in five cities along the eastern seaboard welcomed the fledgling fifteen-minute broadcast; but it grew quickly as a new station joined the telecast every week until, in 1951, news reader Edwards greeted viewers with "Good evening, everyone, coast to coast."

At the time, the birth of a nightly CBS televised newscast had nothing to do with Eric Sevareid. As far as he was concerned, his broadcast career was in radio. He was one of the original "Murrow Boys" recruited to CBS news by Edward R. Murrow (q.v.) on the eve of the outbreak of World War II. His radio debut was scarcely auspicious. By nature a writer rather than a speaker, Sevareid's early journalistic career had been in newspapers as a reporter for the *Minneapolis Star, Minneapolis Journal* (from which he was fired in 1937), and the Paris edition of the *New York Herald Tribune*. While he was city editor of the *Tribune*, he was literally moonlighting as night editor of United Press when Murrow brought him to London. Sevareid shared his first broadcast (August 1939) with noted CBS newscaster H. V. Kaltenborn (q.v.), who was visiting London at the time. Kaltenborn completed his prepared text, then—as he often did—he continued to speak off-the-cuff. Sevareid was left speechless; with no time left to speak, and cursed with "mike fright," he cut material as he read (Persico, 1988, 153).

Sevareid's debut debacle proved *not* to be a harbinger of what was to come, except in one respect. In spite of the fact that he would become one of the foremost radio and television commentators of his age, his fear of the microphone became legendary. For example, in 1947 Sevareid had another debut, this time with his own fifteen-minute nightly newscast on CBS. When, at precisely 6:00 P.M. EST on the last Friday of March, he began his maiden broadcast, he froze. For the whole quarter of an hour, he could not utter a word. It never happened again. Yet, how, one wonders, had a man so intimidated by an electronic gadget come so far in radio? Moreover, how did he later become the pioneer of television news analysis?

THE RISE OF A JOURNALIST, THE FALL OF FRANCE, AND BEYOND

"The Gloomy Dane," the name Edward Murrow used to tease Sevareid (Persico, 1988, 64), came by the nickname naturally. Born of Norwegian stock on November 26, 1912, in Velva, North Dakota, he was one of three children of Alfred and Clare (Hougen) Sevareid. His paternal grandfather immigrated to the United States in the mid-nineteenth century; his maternal grandfather was a minister of the Norwegian Lutheran Synod and a pillar of the Norwegian-American community. Born Arnold Eric Sevareid, he would be called "Arnold," "Arne," or "Arnie" until he was twenty-five years old when he began to use his middle name, Eric, the wanderer in Norwegian. It was appropriate; he had wandered much of his life and would continue to do so.

Shortly after Sevareid's birth his father, an executive in a local bank, moved the family to a brown-and-white bungalow that Alfred Sevareid had built. The setting was Edenic—ideal for pheasant hunting, fly-fishing, and hiking, as well as for reading; Arnold had learned to love books from his mother. As a student, however, he was average, with poor penmanship. Yet, having acquired a desire to write and after doing odd jobs at the *Velva Journal*, a four-page weekly published by a family friend and mentor, Sevareid aspired to be a newspaperman.

The idylls of Sevareid's youth, however, were interrupted in the 1920s by the gradual onset of drought. By 1925 Alfred Sevareid's bank was ruined. The family moved to Minot for a year, then to Minneapolis. There Arnold Sevareid attended high school. He continued to aspire to a journalism career and worked on, then edited, the high school paper. When heavyweight boxing champion Jack Dempsey came to town, Arnold and a friend had the audacity to ask the champ for an interview. It was brief. "You want an interview?" asked Dempsey. "OK. Work hard, live clean. Get lots of exercise." So much for Sevareid's debut as an interviewer of celebrities (Schroth, 1995, 23).

Sevareid graduated in 1930. With a school chum, Will Port, Sevareid set out on a canoe trip from Minneapolis to Hudson Bay in Canada, a 2,200-mile journey. Before leaving Sevareid secured a promise from the *Minneapolis Star* to pay $100 for his articles about the trip. The trip was long, arduous, and dangerous. As Arnold and Will were about to set out on the first leg, they encountered a fur trapper. "Just think about the next mile you have to go, not about the one after that, and I believe you can make it" (Schroth, 1995, 334). It was valuable advice, not only for the trip but for Sevareid's career. He wrote more than 2,000 broadcast scripts for CBS in a career that spanned almost four decades, but he always remembered the immediate task: write the next *one*.

The *Minneapolis Star* liked Sevareid's feature accounts of the canoeing trip.

(He would later tell the tale in a book, *Canoeing with the Cree*, 1935). So did the *Star*'s rival, the *Minneapolis Journal*. After six weeks as copyboy he was elevated to reporter status. Sevareid worked days and attended the University of Minnesota as well. During the summer of 1933 he hitchhiked to California and took a disastrous gamble on gold mining. To return to Minneapolis he had to ride the rails as a hobo.

As a student Sevareid worked on the school newspaper, the *Minnesota Daily*. A major campus controversy involved a campaign against compulsory military drill: proponents argued it was appropriate at a land grant university supporting the Reserve Officers Training Corps (ROTC); opponents deemed drill useless and out of place in an institution devoted to a liberal education. Arnold Sevareid covered the debate for the *Daily*. In one front-page feature, Sevareid foreshadowed a style that would reappear often on radio and television . He traced the history of the debate over militarism, and how it had been sharpened by World War I. He traced the history of drill to the Morrill Land Grant Act of 1862, making it clear that military science is required to be taught at land grant institutions, but courses in it could not be made compulsory. Sevareid led his readers to several possible viewpoints, but left it up to them to reach their own conclusions. Four decades later, this very style, analytical elucidation and clarification of issues without dictating conclusions, would earn for him the lampoon, "Eric Severalsides."

Sevareid graduated from the University of Minnesota in 1935 with a major in political science and a minor in economics. His continued tenure with the *Minneapolis Journal* was short lived. Sources differ over the reason for his departure: that when the newspaper rejected one of his investigative pieces, he tried to sell it to the *Star*; that management released him rather than pay him the increase in salary to which he was entitled; that he was a victim of an economy drive; and that his views were too liberal.

In any event, he and his first wife, Lois, sailed to Europe. Their first port of call was London. One evening they visited the home of another young couple, Ed and Janet Murrow. Murrow was a CBS executive. During the evening, they stared at a glass rectangle housed in a box of wires; on the glass was a visual drama, like a movie in a furniture cabinet. "That's television," said Murrow. "That's the wave of the future, my friend" (Sperber, 1986, 113). To Sevareid, who didn't even listen to radio, it hardly seemed much of a future.

After brief studies at the London School of Economics and the Alliance Française in Paris, Sevareid landed a job as a feature writer for the Paris *Herald*. Eric, no longer Arnold, Sevareid soon had an impressive list of bylines. One series of Sevareid pieces concerned the widely publicized 1939 trial, for kidnapping and murder, of a man found guilty and executed as a modern-day Bluebeard. One avid reader of Sevareid's coverage in the Paris *Herald* was Ed Murrow. He phoned Sevareid from London and offered him a job with CBS: "I don't know much about your experience, but I like the way you write and I like your ideas" (Ferran, 1993, 581). Although Sevareid's audition left network personnel with doubts—good material, bad delivery—Murrow insisted that what he wanted was correspondents who could think and write, regardless of voice; Sevareid went with Murrow's Boys for $250 a month.

From 1939 until his retirement in 1977, Eric Sevareid worked continuously for CBS. In 1940, when the Nazi army invaded the Low Countries, then blitzed across France, Sevareid rescued his wife and newly born twin sons from a hospital in Paris and eventually got them on board a liner sailing back to the United States. When the Germans converged on Paris, Sevareid had a scoop that he was unable to report because the French censors would not let him broadcast news of the impending fall of France. Drawing upon a prearranged code, Sevareid was able to relay the news to New York. Sevareid's last broadcast from Paris, the last of any American, was on June 10, 1940, when he informed American audiences that, if they again were to hear a radio voice from Paris, "It would be under jurisdiction other than French" (Hosley, 1984, 129). Fleeing Paris ahead of the invading force, Sevareid broadcast from Tours, then from Bordeaux. In the process he reported several scoops to CBS in New York via shortwave, including the ascendancy of Marshal Petain and that, contrary to wishful thinking, Petain would not continue the fight but would capitulate and sue for peace. Shortly thereafter he escaped France in an overcrowded refugee freighter bound for London.

After joining Murrow's CBS contingent in London, Sevareid's tenure there was relatively brief—and harrowing. In September 1940, he took part in one memorable CBS broadcast during the Battle of Britain, "London after Dark." The program used correspondents to provide a varied portrayal of what it was like to be under bombardment in the English capital. As vivid as the broadcast was, however, it could not capture the experience itself. One evening, while they were standing just outside the British Broadcasting Company (BBC) building, Sevareid, Murrow, and other correspondents, following Murrow, ducked into a doorway just as a jagged antiaircraft shell casing crashed on the spot they had left a second earlier. Years later, Sevareid would say that no journalistic medium could ever really capture war: "Only the soldier really lives the war. The journalist does not. He may share the soldier's outward life and dangers, but he cannot share his inner life" (Ferran, 1993, 581).

In October 1940, Sevareid returned to the United States and worked out of the CBS news bureau in Washington, D.C., from 1941 to 1943; he also reported from Mexico and Brazil during the period. However, in 1943, he returned to being a war correspondent, this time in China. There his one-mile-at-a-time rule paid dividends as it had while canoeing with the Cree. On a flight from India to China in August, the army aircraft's engines failed. All twenty passengers bailed out into the remote jungle. Sevareid left the plane just before it crashed into a mountain; he had been too busy jotting down notes to jump any earlier.

For weeks the party struggled to stay alive, then began a 140-mile trek to safety. Throughout the ordeal, Sevareid continued to keep a diary. On a hand-cranked wireless set dropped to the party by a supply plane, Sevareid filed a story to CBS beginning, "Burmese jungle headhunters, every one a primitive killer, saved our lives" (Schroth, 1995, 218). With a boot nail wounding one foot and blisters on both, Sevareid recalled the old fur trader's advice; he didn't think of how far or how long it would take to get out of the jungle but instead of just getting to the next hill or friendly village. Finally the party emerged from the jungle to a waiting convoy of jeeps and trucks and a battery of cameras.

Sevareid continued in the Asian theater of operations, returned to the United States briefly, then set out for Europe. He reported the Italian campaign, the victorious entry into Rome, Marshal Tito's guerilla warfare in the mountains of Yugoslavia, the U.S. invasion of southern France, and the crossing of the Rhine into Germany by U.S. troops. In 1945 Sevareid returned to the United States and coverage of the United Nations' founding. From the fall of France to the fall of Nazi Germany five years later, Sevareid's live broadcasts from France, England, China, Burma, Italy, and Germany had brought the fact of war home to CBS listeners. For the remainder of his career, he would report not only the facts of war and peace, but the reasons they came to be at all.

CHISELING THE BUST OF PERICLES

In all successful endeavors, it helps to be in the right place at the right time. As a foreign correspondent, Eric Sevareid had been fortunate in that respect—reporting the fall of France, the Battle of Britain, the fall of Italy, the invasion of southern France, even his own escape from Burma. Postwar America also found him in the right place at the right time: in CBS' Washington news bureau at the height of radio's influence as a news medium. At the war's end, Edward R. Murrow returned to the United States and became the CBS vice president for public affairs. He appointed Sevareid Washington bureau chief as well as chief Washington correspondent. (Murrow always respected Sevareid's talents as a correspondent; however, he had some reservations about Sevareid's habits. Once, while boarding an airplane, Sevareid, sloppily eating a bag of popcorn, walked beside Murrow. Horrified, Murrow walked several steps ahead to disassociate himself from the "popcornism" [Halberstam,1979, 44]).

Sevareid's star was in the ascendancy. Not only was he a chief correspondent and a CBS executive, he was a successful author. His *Not So Wild a Dream* was published in 1946 to positive reviews, one of those by his newscast mentor, Elmer Davis (q.v.). Davis' review pictured the brooding, etched face and piercing eyes of "The Gloomy Dane," the soon-to-be CBS "Gray Eminence" (Boyer, 1988, 18). In addition, by 1947, Sevareid—despite his debut broadcast with fifteen minutes of silence—was becoming one of the network's celebrated radio newscasters.

During World War II the major broadcasting networks, CBS, the National Broadcasting Company (NBC) (divided into Red and Blue networks, the Blue network became the American Broadcasting Company, or ABC, in 1945), and the Mutual Broadcasting System, had each built a staff of correspondents to cover the conflict. At the war's end, each network had to reassign broadcast journalists to other duties. Many became radio commentators, a role originated and polished by H. V. Kaltenborn in the earliest days of broadcast news. In 1931 there were only a half dozen such commentators; in 1947, there were 600 (Fang, 1977). Few of these were particularly notable; fewer still survived the advent of television.

When Eric Sevareid debuted as a radio commentator on March 28, 1947, he had the same problem as any other commentator for any other network, namely, how to separate himself from the clutter. Some positioned themselves primarily as news readers akin to the style of the British Broadcasting Company; they inserted few personal views. Among them were CBS' Robert Trout and NBC's Morgan Beatty. Others distinguished themselves from their rivals as doctrinal voices, conservative or liberal, such as Mutual's Fulton Lewis, Jr. (q.v.) and ABC's Elmer Davis. A few did it via a distinctive vocal style, such as NBC's Kaltenborn or Mutual's Gabriel Heatter. Another was to become an editorial voice for an institution, such as ABC's Edward P. Morgan, who became a voice for his sponsor, organized labor. There were also the storytellers, for example, Lowell Thomas (q.v.) of first CBS, then NBC, then CBS.

Sevareid found his niche slowly but surely. In part, his approach reflected a fundamental CBS policy: "the listener, not the broadcaster, was to make the final judgment about his or her opinion on the news" (Schroth, 1995, 296). It also reflected Sevareid's background as a man considerably bookwise and street-wise in politics, one whose populist experiences of youth combined with moving comfortably in the elite culture of wartime America. It was a background admirably suited to *priestly* discourse: "rhetoric that crosses the boundaries between a particular elite subculture [in this case political leaders] and the broader social groups within which it is nested [Sevareid's listeners]" (Lessl, 1989, 184).

In fact, Sevareid grew so skilled at positioning himself as priestly that he was both criticized and feared for it. His newscast sponsor, Metropolitan Life, worried that Sevareid was "high hat" and talked "over the heads" of the insurance company's policyholders, that he was too priestly (Schroth, 1995, 301). Decades later, after Sevareid had moved his priestly commentary to television, an aide to President Richard Nixon (a president Sevareid questioned) noted that the White House never fought back because Sevareid "looked and dressed like God" (Ferran, 1993, 581).

For himself, Sevareid did not refer to his commentary as priestly. His term was *elucidation*: "I was more interested in elucidating than advocating" (Schroth, 1995, 328). Whatever the descriptive label, Sevareid's approach set him apart as a political commentator. It took clear form after Metropolitan Life dropped its sponsorship and Sevareid's newscast moved from 6:00 P.M. to 11:00 P.M. (April 1, 1950). A new format provided him with five minutes for what CBS called analysis and Sevareid called commentaries. In any event, they were vocal essays, think pieces in the manner of Montaigne, the French philosopher; the noted columnist Walter Lippmann (q.v.); and irascible journalist

H. L. Mencken (q.v.). In many respects, Sevareid's elucidations borrowed the style he attributed to a close mentor, Elmer Davis: "He was a boy in Indiana" and "he was a scholar of the classics," Sevareid commented after Davis' death in 1958; "And there is, therefore, in his precise and natural speech an effortless integration" (Schroth, 1995, 333). Similar words could be used to describe the sources and style of Sevareid's own broadcasting niche.

The subjects of Sevareid's radio commentaries were numerous; he endeavored to elucidate each issue in the same historical, cultural, and nondirective manner that Arnold Sevareid had used in covering the ROTC controversy at the University of Minnesota decades earlier. For example, he explained why U.S. soldiers fought in Korea as residing in Americans' unseasoned cultural belief in their country; and, that the lesson of Senator Joseph McCarthy's rise and fall was historical, that the weakness of others contributed to McCarthy's strength. Sometimes his analyses of political contexts led to prescient views, such as when he used his program on the opening day of the 1952 Democratic National Convention to predict that Adlai Stevenson would be drafted as the party's presidential candidate and not even President Harry Truman could prevent it.

Rarely did Sevareid's commentary violate CBS dictates against airing personal views. One exception proved notable. In 1955 a CBS correspondent violated a U.S. State Department prohibition against traveling to China; the reporter entered China and even broadcast reports for CBS via shortwave. When he returned to the United States, the State Department denied the renewal of the correspondent's passport. Sevareid had long been critical of the "China lobby," politicians and businessmen advocating support for overthrowing the Communist regime in China through aid to Chiang Kai-shek (Swanberg, 1972). CBS executives had paid no mind. In this instance, however, Sevareid treated the passport nonrenewal as a mistake on two grounds: first, it denied the nation opportunities to gather vital information on China; therefore, and second, withholding a passport is a form of censorship of a free press having partial responsibility to acquire information vital to Americans' interests. CBS executives killed the commentary, demanding that Sevareid comment on another topic. He refused, and the network rushed in a substitute commentator. Miffed, Sevareid gave the canceled commentary script to a U.S. senator who read it into the *Congressional Record*, an act viewed by CBS as insubordination. Sevareid was not fired, nor did he resign when he was offered an opportunity to move to NBC.

THE APOGEE OF TELEVISED POLITICAL COMMENTARY

The rift with his administrative superiors eventually lessened. Sevareid and CBS president William Paley never discussed it again (Smith, 1990, 370). Otherwise, Sevareid's major contribution as a political commentator in the twentieth century might not have been on CBS. At the time of the canceled commentary, Sevareid was becoming a major political influence. Newspapers frequently reprinted his commentaries and congressional officials inserted them into the *Congressional Record*. Moreover, since 1953, Sevareid had been delivering his nightly radio commentaries on Washington's WTOP-TV. Like other of the Murrow Boys, Sevareid in the 1940s snubbed television news as a "novelty," "not the place for a serious reporter" (Persico, 1988, 294). But all that was changing. The Golden Age of Radio was on the decline and being replaced by the Golden Age of television. Although he complained about the visual emphasis of television, Sevareid was making his peace with the box of wires he first encountered in Ed Murrow's London home on the eve of World War II. Sevareid might rather write books, but the reality was that television could pay his bills. So, he undertook a Sunday afternoon program, "State of the Nation," and, in 1954, a Sunday evening CBS program, "The American Week."

Meanwhile, in the mid to late 1950s, CBS News began to face stiff competition from rivals, especially NBC. NBC's "Huntley-Brinkley Report" debuted on October 29, 1956. With the commanding presence of Chet Huntley as anchor in New York and the droll David Brinkley (q.v.) as cohost and correspondent in Washington, the newscast was soon a ratings hit (Goldberg & Goldberg, 1990). CBS' 1948 pioneer, "Douglas Edwards with the News," found itself in a dead heat with Huntley-Brinkley by 1958; after coverage of the 1960 presidential conventions, NBC pulled substantially ahead. Eric Sevareid was about to be a beneficiary of the troubles confronting "Douglas Edwards with the News." In 1962 CBS replaced Edwards, not, however, with the now prestigious Sevareid but with a lesser known Walter Cronkite (q.v.). Sevareid was too priestly again: "There were those who felt that Sevareid had simply priced himself out of the market intellectually. Eric was too interested in analysis and opinion and thus not an entirely believable transmission belt for straight information" (Halberstam, 1979, 413).

On Labor Day the following year, CBS inaugurated the first thirty-minute nightly network newscast, "The CBS Evening News with Walter Cronkite." The added time permitted the newscast to incorporate analysis. For the next fourteen years, until November 20, 1977, Americans would witness the talking head of Eric Sevareid—some called it the Bust of Pericles—elucidating in from 400 to 800 words for two and a half minutes an evening, the pros and cons of the Vietnam War, the political and social turbulence of the 1960s, the fall of Richard Nixon, even the death of Edward R. Murrow. During his career, he would have other outlets for his analysis: a weekly syndicated column for more than 100 newspapers, magazine articles (most notably one based on the evening he spent with Adlai Stevenson on the day before Stevenson's death in 1965), public affairs television programs, books, and lectures. But, his commentaries on "The CBS Evening News" remain his legacy to political communication.

Sevareid was not the only television analyst of the time. Many of the reports of David Brinkley from Washington on "The Huntley-Brinkley Report" were commentaries as much as straight news reports. Sevareid's former CBS colleague, Howard K. Smith, had a thirty-minute weekly program on ABC, "Howard K. Smith—News and Analysis.'' By comparison, however, Brinkley's, more puckish, were less an elucidation than a point of view with bite. Smith, by contrast, favored the didactic; he had a professorial flair for blackboards, charts, and maps. In addition,

> Sevareid was a more subtle writer, perhaps more deft, and he learned to make a fierce point without seeming to be fierce, whereas Smith was a more forceful writer, using more sharp, straight, declarative sentences and very direct, and there was never any mistake about what he was saying and how he was saying it. (Halberstam, 1979, 410)

Video technology aided Sevareid considerably. By using videotape, Sevareid could overcome his fear of the microphone and camera through retakes of fluffs. He eschewed films, stills, charts, or graphics. He and his writing constituted the message. Without pomposity, he appeared reflective; without professorial demeanor, he seemed thoughtful; and with the clever use of calculated obscurity, he paraded punditry as profundity (Nimmo & Combs, 1992, 40). None of this came easy. His biographer reports that he once told novelist Kurt Vonnegut that he felt he was writing the Gettysburg Address every day (Schroth, 1995, 361). And, in spite of the ''Gloomy Dane's'' disdain for the television camera, Sevareid's tapings of his think pieces demonstrated a concern for his visual image as well as his 400 crafted words. Producers lowered the television lights to soften Sevareid's facial features to meld with the softness of his voice, providing a more authoritative image.

Given his lingering reluctance to face the microphone or camera, it is not surprising that he was an opponent of the fashionable ''instant analysis'' whereby a correspondent goes on camera after a political event or politician's utterance with a live critique. In fact, during the months leading up to President Richard Nixon's 1974 resignation, when the White House protested the ''instant analysis'' of television journalists, Sevareid agreed; not, however, because he deemed the criticism of Nixon inappropriate per se. Rather he said, in a memo to CBS president William Paley, Nixon's public utterances were too ambiguous and vague to elucidate clearly on the spot: ''We are not serving the public well,'' he wrote (Smith, 1990, 493).

In his valedictory commentary on ''The CBS Evening News,'' Sevareid stated that his office and function were ''unelected, unlicensed, uncodified''; the rules for such an office are few and ''self-imposed,'' namely, neither underestimate the intelligence of the audience or its information, ''to elucidate, when one can, more than advocate,'' to remember that no two audience members are alike, and to ''retain the courage of one's doubts as well as one's convictions'' (Schroth, 1995, 404).

After his retirement from CBS, Sevareid continued to write, to appear on television public affairs programs, and to submit to numerous interviews. His first marriage had ended in divorce in 1962; a second ended in divorce in 1972; and his third wife survived Sevareid's death on July 9, 1992.

CONCLUSION: THE PYRRHIC TRIUMPH OF POLITICAL ADVOCACY

Following Sevareid's retirement, CBS made efforts to replace him; other networks to imitate him—but all to no avail. By the end of the 1970s, analysis had vanished from television networks' nightly newscasts. Efforts to resurrect it have been sporadic and unsuccessful. Sevareid's "elucidation" has been replaced by the confrontational commentary of John McLaughlin (q.v.) and others, the endless harangues of Rush Limbaugh (q.v.) and other talk radio and television gurus, the overestimation of the public's information manifested in audience participation shows such as Phil Donahue's (q.v.), and the underestimation of the public's intelligence apparent in the gratuitous remarks of panelists on "This Week with David Brinkley"—George F. Will (q.v.), Corrine "Cokie" Roberts (q.v.), and Sam Donaldson.

What Eric Sevareid brought to political commentary that his successors, real and bogus, have not been able to match was a skill for the written word rather than the spoken or visual symbol. Another key political commentator of the twentieth century, James "Scotty" Reston (q.v.), recalled Sevareid from his days as one of the Murrow Boys during the Blitz: "Sevareid could outwrite us all" (Reston, 1991, 89). It is a fitting tribute to Sevareid and to a lost art in political communication.

REFERENCES

Selected Works by Eric Sevareid

Canoeing with the Cree. 1935. Reprint. St. Paul, MN: Minnesota Historical Society, 1968.
Not So Wild a Dream. 1946. New York: Atheneum. 2d ed., 1976.
In Our Ear. New York: Alfred A. Knopf, 1952.
Small Sounds in the Night. New York: Alfred A. Knopf, 1956.
Candidates 1960. Editor. New York: Basic Books, 1959.
This Is Eric Sevareid. New York: McGraw-Hill, 1967.
Conversations with Eric Sevareid: Interviews with Notable Americans. Editor. Washington, D.C.: Public Affairs Press, 1976.

Selected Critical Works about Eric Sevareid

Downs, R. B., and J. B. Downs. "Arnold Eric Sevareid." In *Journalists of the United States*, edited by R. Downs and J. Downs, 311–12. Jefferson, NC: McFarland, 1989.
Ferran, C. "Eric Sevareid." In *Newsmakers*, edited by L. Mooney, 581–82. Detroit: Gale Research, 1993.

McKerns, J. P., ed. "Sevareid, (Arnold) Eric." In *Biographical Dictionary of American Journalism*, 642–44. New York: Greenwood Press, 1989.

Moritz, C., ed. "Sevareid, Eric (Arnold)." In *Current Biography 1966*, 363–65. New York: H. W. Wilson, 1967.

Nimmo, D., and J. E. Combs, "Eric Sevareid: The Search for a Priestly Formula." In *The Political Pundits*, 38–41. New York: Praeger, 1992.

Riley, S. G., ed. "Sevareid, Arnold Eric." In *Biographical Dictionary of American Newspaper Columnists*, 186–88. Westport, CT: Greenwood Press, 1995.

Schroth, R. A. *The American Journey of Eric Sevareid*. South Royalton, VT: Steerforth Press, 1995.

Selected General Works

Boyer, J. *Who Killed CBS?* New York: Random House, 1988.

Desmond, R. W. *Tides of War: World News Reporting 1931–1945*. Iowa City: University of Iowa Press, 1984.

Fang, I. E. *Those Radio Commentators!* Ames, IA: Iowa State University Press, 1977.

Goldberg, R, and G. J. Goldberg. *Anchors*. New York: Birch Lane Press, 1990.

Halberstam, D. *The Powers That Be*. New York: Alfred A. Knopf, 1979.

Hosley, D. H. *As Good as Any: Foreign Correspondence on American Radio, 1930–1940*. Westport, CT: Greenwood Press, 1984.

Lessl, T. M. "The Priestly Voice." *Quarterly Journal of Speech* 75 (1989): 183–97.

Persico, J. E. *Edward R. Murrow: An American Original*. New York: Dell, 1988.

Reston, J. *Deadline*. New York: Random House, 1991.

Smith, S. B. *In All His Glory: The Life of William S. Paley*. New York: Simon and Schuster, 1990.

Sperber, A. M. *Murrow: His Life and Times*. New York: Freundlich, 1986.

Swanberg, W. A. *Luce and His Empire*. New York: Dell, 1972.

Westin, A. *Newswatch*. New York: Simon and Schuster, 1982.

BERNARD SHAW

(May 22, 1940–   )

Pioneering Round-the-Clock Commentary

Prior to the Persian Gulf War, in late 1990, the Cable News Network (CNN) and the other major networks brought in dozens of experts on topics ranging from military hardware to oil field operations to interpret the meaning of the day's events. U.S. officials placed restrictions on what information could be released to the public regarding the events occurring during the air and ground offensive against Iraq. Scholars, journalists, and military leaders debated the issue of censorship: the withholding, management, and dissemination of information (Woodward, 1993).

On January 17, 1991, the U.S. air assault against Iraq began. CNN had three correspondents—Peter Arnett, Jim Holliman, and Bernard Shaw—in the Iraqi capital, Baghdad, when the air assault started. The CNN trio, nicknamed the "Boys in Baghdad," broadcast live the opening air attack on the Iraqi capital. By bypassing the Iraqi phone system, the trio broadcast for sixteen hours before they were shut down by Iraqi authorities. CNN was the only network able to broadcast the events from inside Iraq at that time. The coverage's immediacy illustrated the impact of television broadcast news and commentary on events in a manner reminiscent of CBS' Edward R. Murrow's (q.v.) radio commentaries from London during the Battle of Britain and the Blitz during World War II (Denton, 1993; see also Carlsson, 1992).

In 1980, when Ted Turner, CNN's owner, and his executives hired journalists, they sought talented individuals suited to the challenge of launching a specialty network, a twenty-four-hour telecable news service. Critics were skeptical that a network of this type could survive. However, CNN, the world's first around-the-clock, seven-days-a-week television news operation, as evidenced by its coverage of countless events since 1980, most notably the Persian Gulf War, evolved into a viable competitor to the entrenched terrestrial U.S. networks, the American Broadcasting Company (ABC), the Columbia Broadcasting System (CBS), and the National Broadcasting Company (NBC). As CNN became a respected competitor in the news industry, CNN's nightly news anchor, Bernard Shaw, emerged as a leading reporter and analyst of news.

REACHING THE ALTAR OF INFORMATION DISSEMINATION

It is remarkable, therefore, that even as late as 1990, when the television critic of the *Wall Street Journal*, Robert Goldberg, and his father, Gerald Jay Goldberg, a professor of English at UCLA, published a widely reviewed study entitled *Anchors*, their focus narrowed to the three anchors of the nightly newscasts of the three major over-the-air television networks: Dan Rather (q.v.) of CBS, Tom Brokaw of NBC, and Peter Jennings of ABC. Although it had been a major player in bringing political news to Americans and the world for a decade, CNN and its nightly news anchor, Bernard Shaw, still received scant notice, not only from Goldberg and Goldberg, but from television critics and scholars generally. In fact, Goldberg and Goldberg did not even mention Bernard Shaw, although their book does contain a photo (opposite page 241) of Jennings, Rather, Brokaw, and "CNN's Bernard Shaw toasting their distinguished predecessor, Walter Cronkite" (q.v.).

But what critics and scholars continued to ignore, television news producers, journalists, and politicians did not. Political activists had long since recognized Bernard Shaw as one of the most celebrated political commentators in the late twentieth century. Shaw himself draws a distinction between being a celebrity and a journalist, a difference also drawn by Walter Cronkite, but not necessarily so by Dan Rather. Like those other news anchors, Bernard Shaw has access to a national audience and is a celebrity in the field of journalism. However, despite the national exposure, Shaw insists that he is not the focal point, nor should any reporter be, of a news story. "His philosophy is that the messenger shouldn't get in the way of the message," according to V. R. (Bob) Furnad, a senior executive producer for CNN in 1988 ("Bernard Shaw," 1989, 143). As an anchor and journalist, Shaw believes that the intelligence of the audience and the integrity of the news agency are served if the focus remains on the dissemination of information.

The son of Edgar Shaw, a house painter and New York Central Railroad worker, and Camilla (Murphy) Shaw, a housekeeper, Bernard Shaw was born on May 22, 1940, in Chicago, Illinois. Edgar Shaw was an avid consumer of news; hence, he toted home Chicago's daily newspapers. It was still the era when each major city had competing metropolitan dailies, so Bernard Shaw was exposed to varying news accounts of identical events in the four Chicago papers. He recalled, "My father read newspapers constantly, . . . to the point that he kept them stacked around the house" ("Bernard Shaw," 1989, 143).

Following his father's example, Shaw also developed an avid taste for journalists and their accounts of who was doing what in politics. Most notably, Edward R. Murrow, the nation's leading television news commentator during Shaw's adolescence, was one of his early role models. Shaw commented in an interview, "He [Murrow] was my idol, and I used to watch everything he did, along with the things Cronkite did" ("Bernard Shaw," 1989, 143). Moreover, "He was such a dominant force in television news when I was growing up, I said, 'I want to be like that man' " (Graham, 1995, 42).

To be sure, in the 1950s, African-American journalists were not seen on television, but this did not deter Shaw from setting his sights on becoming a television newscaster. As far as he was concerned, Edward Murrow was simply a journalist, not a white journalist. Shaw downplays the importance of race and his role as an African-American role model: "This is a cutthroat business for anybody, black, white, or green" (McCall, 1988, 46). Just as being a television celebrity may be a by-product of his profession, the fact that he is a positive image for African-Americans, wonderful though that is, does not deny the fact that he is, first and foremost, a journalist—the focus is the message and not the messenger.

As a twelve-year-old, Shaw was reading more than the Chicago papers, and he walked to the Green Door bookstore, located on the University of Chicago campus, to purchase the Sunday edition of the *New York Times*. There he struck up an acquaintance with Clifton Utley. Utley, a reporter, was a member of a family of noted broadcast journalists that included, among others, NBC's Garrick Utley. Since Shaw had a passionate desire to learn about the journalism profession, he plied Utley with incessant questions. He acquired the habit of visiting newsrooms and talking to reporters, and making it a point to go on tours of the newspaper and seek out these people ("Bernard Shaw," 1989, 143). While he was in his early teens, Shaw finagled his way into the 1952 and 1956 Democratic National Conventions, both held in Chicago (Zuckerman, 1988). Those conventions marked the reinvention of political party conventions in the telepolitical age (Smith & Nimmo, 1991). "When I looked up at the anchor booths, I knew I was looking at the altar," he told Laurence Zuckerman of *Time* (Zuckerman, 1988, 64).

Newspapers were not Bernard Shaw's only focus. He also loved baseball, like many other key political commentators of the twentieth century, including Elmer Davis (q.v.), James "Scotty" Reston (q.v.), and George F. Will (q.v.). But, like so many other aspiring major leaguers, he could not hit the hanging curve ball. Journalism appeared to be a more realistic career option. So, as a student at Dunbar High School, Bernard Shaw wrote for his high school newspaper, produced a morning broadcast for the school's public address system, announced basketball games, and was on the school's debate team. Upon graduation Shaw had aspirations to attend college, but with no funding available, he decided to enlist in the U.S. Marine Corps to earn money for his college education.

From 1959 to 1963, he served in the U.S. Marines Corps. While in the military, Shaw not only earned money to pay for his education, but he also had an opportunity to meet and talk with one of his idols. In 1961 the twenty-one-year-old corporal Bernard Shaw, stationed in Oahu, Hawaii, learned that Walter Cronkite of CBS News was coming to town to film scenes for Cronkite's CBS series, "The Twentieth Century." Shaw managed to contact Cronkite at his hotel and arrange a brief meeting (five minutes, but he stayed half an hour) to discuss a career in journalism. Cronkite offered Shaw advice that he continues to practice. Shaw remembered it years later,

"Read, read, and read." He [Cronkite] was right; he was absolutely right. You have to be interested in everything because you never know where you are going to be assigned or what you are going to cover. You have to be a vacuum cleaner when it comes to human life. You have to be interested and curious about it. (''Bernard Shaw,'' 1989, 143)

The advice from Cronkite confirmed the legacy Shaw had inherited from his father. He continued to read, read, and read, and he met Cronkite again a decade later, this time as a member of Cronkite's profession.

In 1963 Bernard Shaw was discharged from the Marines, and he enrolled at the University of Illinois, Chicago Circle, selecting history as his major. Following up on his contacts with reporters and disk jockeys in the Chicago area, which he had been cementing since his childhood, Shaw, while carrying a full college load, took an unpaid position in the wire room at a rhythm-and-blues station, WYNR-AM. Within a few months, in 1964, the station renamed itself WNUS-AM and switched to an all-news format. After the transition to the news format, Shaw convinced management to assign him to cover local stories as an anchor and a reporter. His first major story covered the visit of Martin Luther King, Jr., to Chicago to stage a civil rights rally. Shaw worked very hard to impress station managers with his skills, and he performed in a credible manner.

During the mid-1960s the civil rights movement was arguably the decade's major news story. From protests to church bombings, the events of the movement filled the evening newscast. As a journalist in radio and television, Shaw reported on major breaking stories. In 1965 Shaw became a news writer for the Chicago station WFLD-TV, his first experience in television. It proved brief; he returned to radio in 1966 as a reporter for WIND-AM in Chicago, a station owned by the Westinghouse Broadcasting Company. Shaw was working for Westinghouse in Chicago in April 1968 when Martin Luther King, Jr., was assassinated in Memphis, Tennessee. He was one of two journalists selected to chronicle the King family's transport of the slain civil rights leader's body from Memphis to Atlanta.

Riots broke out in several U.S. cities as a result of King's murder; Bernard Shaw returned to Chicago to report on riots there for WIND-AM. Shaw's coverage brought him praise and compliments from his superiors. As a consequence he was transferred to the Washington bureau as the White House correspondent for Westinghouse later in 1968. Although he was interested in the opportunities the promotion offered, Shaw was faced with a dilemma. Acceptance of the promotion would mean he would have to suspend his college education, with only a year remaining until he received his degree. Like Walter Cronkite, who faced a similar problem before completing his degree at the University of Texas, Shaw felt he simply could not afford to lose the opportunities afforded by his assignment. He moved to the nation's capital and worked for Westinghouse Broadcasting until he received a job offer from CBS News.

In 1971 Bernard Shaw joined the network his idols, Murrow and Cronkite, had made famous. CBS News offered him a job as a reporter. At that time it was the premier news organization in the profession of television journalism, and its Washington bureau was staffed with major figures in television news journalism, such as Dan Rather, Mike Wallace (q.v.), and Eric Sevareid (q.v.). Shaw served as a CBS general assignment reporter from 1971 to 1974, then as a correspondent from 1974 to 1977 covering the White House, the State Department, the Pentagon, and the Supreme Court. His most celebrated work at CBS came in August 1974. During the Watergate scandal that led to President Richard Nixon's resignation, Shaw conducted an exclusive interview with John Mitchell, former attorney general and Nixon campaign chair.

Working at CBS had been an ambition of Bernard Shaw's from the time he first tuned in to Edward Murrow's broadcasts. But by 1977, Shaw had decided that Latin America was an "undercovered" part of the world. Since he was fluent in Spanish, he requested an assignment in Latin America, but CBS News turned him down. Faced with rejection at CBS, Shaw left the network and joined ABC as Latin America bureau chief and correspondent. Based in Miami, Florida, Shaw spent the next three years in Latin America. He covered several major news stories during that time, including the renegotiation of the Panama Canal Treaty and the revolution in Nicaragua that resulted in the ouster of that country's dictator-president, General Anastasio Somoza. He also conducted an interview with Cuban president Fidel Castro.

In 1978 Shaw went to the jungles of Guyana to confirm rumors of a mass suicide in Jonestown by more than nine hundred American followers of the religious cult leader Jim Jones. In a filmed report, Shaw offered evidence from an eye witness to the tragedy, Mark Lane, an attorney for Jones' church, the People's Temple. Lane had received considerable previous publicity for his probes of alleged conspiracies behind the assassinations of President John F. Kennedy and Martin Luther King, Jr. Shaw's filmed description, using Lane's account, of events in Jonestown confirmed that Jones' last words, before his own death by suicide, were, "Mother, Mother, Mother, Mother, Mother." Shaw's report was a dramatic, sensational account of what an ABC news anchor summed up as an "incredible but true" tragedy (Nimmo & Combs, 1985, 40).

Although he found reporting events in Latin America rewarding, Shaw also regarded the experience as frightening and sad. From the assignment, Shaw learned a lesson in reporting that he might not have received at the University of Illinois. In an interview discussing the death in a air crash of an ABC colleague who was covering a story in place of Shaw when Shaw was given another assignment, Shaw said, "It was a real education about problems in that part of the world. . . . I lost a colleague, Bill Stewart. . . . I have a picture on the wall of Bill, of them bringing his body back from Panama. It reminds me of just how dangerous this business is" ("Bernard Shaw," 1989, 143).

When he returned to Washington in 1979, Shaw became ABC's senior Capitol Hill correspondent. Because of his experience in reporting international matters, Shaw had assignments reporting the developing crisis in Iran, where radicals had occupied the American embassy in Tehran and had taken the embassy staff hostage. The Iranian hostage crisis was one of the largest news stories of that time, and it was an issue in the 1980 presidential election between Democratic president Jimmy Carter and Republican presidential nominee Ronald Reagan. Shaw's vantage point as both a Capitol Hill and special assignment correspondent gave him a unique opportunity to report on the unfolding presidential contest.

ASCENDING AND COMMENTING FROM THE FOURTH ALTAR

Despite the prestige of Shaw's position and the plaudits he received for his work, he grew restive. His boyhood dream to be a television news anchor appeared to be unobtainable at ABC News. Shaw had excelled as a reporter and correspondent at the local, national, and international levels, but an anchor position at ABC News seemed remote because there was such a rich pool of talent waiting in the wings, including coanchor Peter Jennings and correspondents Ted Koppel (q.v.) and Sam Donaldson. Nor did rival networks offer any hope of Shaw's ascending to their anchor-altars: Dan Rather was to succeed Walter Cronkite at CBS; and John Chancellor (q.v.) was still presiding at NBC.

However, fortune intervened. George Watson, the former ABC News Washington bureau chief, departed the network for another project: to assist in the founding of CNN. A vexing question at the fledgling network was who had the experience and stature to anchor the prime-time newscasts. Watson knew of Shaw's ambitions and suggested him as chief anchor at CNN. Shaw was reluctant. The prospects for success of the all-news network did not appear good. Moreover, Shaw had another dilemma. ABC had offered him a new, fairly lucrative, contract to continue his regular assignment. On the other hand, he was excited about the possibility of being an anchor, and changing to CNN would afford him an opportunity to explore a new type of television.

At this crossroad in his career, Bernard Shaw reflected upon the career of Edward R. Murrow. He recalled his thoughts in an interview for *Time*. Shaw decided that, as a television reporter in the 1950s, Edward R. Murrow had been "on the threshold of the new age," and that he, Shaw, could have a similar opportunity at CNN to revolutionize journalism. "I thought that a 24-hour news network had to be the last frontier" (Zuckerman, 1988, 64). In addition to the career opportunity, CNN provided the requisite financial incentive. Shaw explains, "They made me an offer, more money than ABC was willing to offer me, and I had to consider it." But, it was Shaw's wife Linda (Allson), whom he had married on March 30, 1974, who convinced him to take the job with CNN. After watching him agonize over the decision for weeks, his wife told him, "If you don't and CNN takes off, I won't be able to live with you" ("Bernard Shaw," 1989, 143). With her approval, or threat, the soul searching ceased. Bernard Shaw left ABC News to join CNN as one of its chief anchors.

> The early days were wild. We were building something, so we worked ex-
> tremely hard. We worked on weekends. We worked whenever we had to work.
> It was exciting. We were working on something that nobody else had or had
> done, or were doing. We felt we were pioneers. That was one of the big en-
> ticements for coming to CNN. I thought CNN was the last frontier in television.
> ("Bernard Shaw," 1989, 143)

Thus does Bernard Shaw remember those first days after June 1, 1980, when CNN began to broadcast from Atlanta. Although CNN executives assembled a staff of enthusiastic and energetic employees to join the U.S.S. CNN on a Star Trek–type probe of the "final frontier of television news," critics were not impressed. They dubbed it the "Chicken Noodle Network," a little of this, a little of that, but too little of substance (Wittemore, 1990). CNN had to strive to earn respect and to develop a significant viewership. Yet, this was the dawn-ing of a new information age; viewers increasingly demanded up-to-the-minute coverage of breaking events and quick, capsulized summaries of what had happened a scant five minutes earlier. Forget history, at least for the moment, even if it had been Shaw's major in college. The staff at CNN aggressively pursued new stories poking cameras in whenever and wherever news could be generated.

The efforts paid off. By 1987 Bernard Shaw had joined the anchor elite. In a ritual once reserved for only the exalted altars of the over-the-air networks, CNN's Bernard Shaw gathered with Dan Rather of CBS, Peter Jennings of ABC, and Tom Brokaw of NBC in a nationally telecast interview with the president of the United States. The occasion was to chat with Ronald Reagan before his summit meeting with Soviet president Mikhail Gorbachev. If anyone required additional evidence that a fourth altar was now in the High Church of Television News, it came in October 1988. Shaw moderated the second presidential cam-paign debate between Republican Vice President George Bush and the Demo-cratic nominee, Michael S. Dukakis (Barnes, 1990). Still wed to Walter Cronkite's advice to a twenty-one-year-old marine corporal, Shaw devoted weeks to reading in preparation for the presidential debates.

By this point in his career, Bernard Shaw had won a reputation as a skilled interrogator, one who, like Mike Wallace, had mastered the art of rendering commentary via asking questions. He had honed his interviewing skills through his 1984 and 1988 stints as anchor of CNN's coverage of the national political party conventions. If televised convention coverage serves no other purpose, it is an opportunity for television network news departments to showcase their anchors and correspondents and outshine one another in the process. CNN's distinctive image in convention coverage relied on its claim of offering "gavel-to-gavel coverage"—as long as a convention was in session, CNN would be there. Given the fact that each party scheduled four whole days and evenings for its quadrennial promotion, this left CNN on the air continuously for long periods. With little that was newsworthy actually occurring during the sessions,

CNN sought to make news by interviewing party leaders, candidates, and other notables. Shaw, therefore, had ample time to sharpen his questioning technique. He prepared probing questions that reflected his commitment to his views and his philosophy that reporters must seek direct answers and not be lulled into acting as shills for politicians. One leading television critic, Ed Bark of the *Dallas Morning News*, complimented Shaw in 1988 as being "the toughest anchor interview." He called NBC's John Chancellor, in contrast, the "most overrated commentator" (Smith & Nimmo, 1991, 208).

As the moderator of the second 1988 presidential debate, Bernard Shaw focused on matters he thought concerned voters. For example, since popular perception appeared to consider Republican vice-presidential candidate, Dan Quayle, an unsuitable replacement should something happen to, if elected, President George Bush, Shaw asked George Bush to speak to those concerns. His most telling question, however, was for Democratic candidate Michael Dukakis, a question that evoked a response that probably did not cost Dukakis the election, but certainly left him appearing confused. Dukakis opposed capital punishment. Shaw asked Dukakis if the candidate's opinion on the issue would change if someone raped and murdered his wife, Kitty Dukakis. Dukakis groped for an answer, never managed an effective response, and struggled through the remainder of the debate.

In May 1989, CNN's Bernard Shaw and CBS' Dan Rather were the only American television network anchors reporting live from Beijing, China, on Mikhail Gorbachev's summit visit. During their stay, a group of Chinese students and workers staged a protest in the presence of the international media to publicize their demands for democracy by holding daily demonstrations in Beijing's Tiananmen Square. In early June 1989, the Chinese government sent in military troops to break up the peaceful movement. Shaw provided continuous live coverage of the confrontation that ensued.

Shaw's experience in Beijing soon paled in comparison with his landmark work during the Persian Gulf War. In mid-January 1991, Shaw was in Baghdad to conduct a second interview with Iraqi president Saddam Hussein. The Iraqi and the United States governments were in a standoff over Iraq's invasion of Kuwait. Hussein canceled the interview. Shaw subsequently commented on the evening news that he believed war could be avoided. No sooner had he signed off than he was back on CNN to report the air assaults under way on Iraq. From that point, Shaw's comments were of war not its avoidance. United States Secretary of Defense Richard Cheney and General Colin Powell, the chairman of the Joint Chiefs of Staff, praised the CNN Gulf War broadcasts. Other network news divisions also acknowledged the professional work of CNN correspondents and of Bernard Shaw.

Shaw, who once deemed his path to anchoring a nightly newscast forever closed, received an ironic compliment; he was interviewed by anchor Tom Brokaw on "NBC Nightly News." In addition, the reports made by Shaw and his colleagues from Iraq were aired "across the country by hundreds of local news directors who abandoned their own network's feed to get CNN's coverage.'' The Persian Gulf War was an opportunity for the type of coverage Shaw had long loved—no scripts, no prepared newscast, just reporter against the world: "the consummate challenge" ("Bernard Shaw," 1989, 143). In recognition of his work in Baghdad, Shaw received several awards including the George Foster Peabody Broadcasting Award.

Whether reporting breaking news stories, anchoring the news, working CNN's gavel-to-gavel coverage of political party conventions, or acting as cohost of CNN's daily "Inside Politics," Bernard Shaw appears on air as a calm, unruffled, dispassionate observer. If there is a model for his demeanor it was certainly the style of Edward R. Murrow, which he watched on television as a young boy, and the factual approach of Walter Cronkite, whom he had promised on their first meeting that he would someday be a colleague. Shaw regards journalism as serious work and not for the faint of heart. Objectivity, in the sense that the story takes precedence over the storyteller, is an utmost requirement. Objectivity, however, does not relieve journalists of a responsibility to question news makers vigorously to obtain the facts of a story. It is the reporter's duty to citizens, urges Shaw, to delve into the issues and to scrutinize the responses of all politicians. "Your viewers and listeners are keen for those kinds of reporting distinctions. . . . They want them; they expect them; they need them for perspective on the sleight of hand they are subjected to by politicians lacking in so many ways" (Brown, 1991, 28).

Bernard Shaw's role as the pioneer of political commentary on a cable network news outlet puts him in exalted company. In the 1920s Walter Lippmann (q.v.) invented the syndicated political column; many have imitated his efforts, none earned his repute. In the 1930s H. V. Kaltenborn (q.v.) was the first political commentator on radio; many imitated him as well, but none had his bravado. In the war-torn 1940s Edward R. Murrow created an entirely new style of broadcast commentary unique to his age; many also tried to emulate him, but none did. In the 1950s Murrow created a documentary news form for television that energized the medium; no one tried to copy it. In the 1960s Eric Sevareid reinvented political commentary on network television's evening news; he soon had his imitators, but when he retired, separate commentary on nightly newscasts virtually retired as well. Through the 1970s Mike Wallace and his colleagues polished a televised newsmagazine format that popularized public affairs programming and spawned numerous clones. The 1980s and beyond proved to be Bernard Shaw's. It was a period that found him no longer looking up at a trinity of altars of political commentary; he occupied his own.

REFERENCES

Selected Critical Studies about Bernard Shaw

Barnes, R. "CNN's Shaw Still Rising." *Black Enterprise* 20 (February 1990): 32.
"Bernard Shaw: CNN's Anchoring Reporter." *Broadcasting*, April 24, 1989, 143.

Brown, R. "CNN's Shaw Lam Blasts T.V. Campaign Coverage." *Broadcasting*, September 30, 1991, 28.

Graham, J., ed. "Shaw, Bernard." In *Current Biography* 55 (February 1995): 41–45.

McCall, N. "The Shaw Also Rises." *Black Enterprise* 18 (June 1988): 46.

Phelps, S., ed. "Shaw, Bernard." In *Who's Who among Black Americans, 1994–1995*. Detroit: Gale Research, 1994, 1316.

Zuckerman, L. "A New Member Joins the Club." *Time*, February 22, 1988, 64.

Selected General Works

Carlsson, U., ed. "The Gulf War in the Media." *Nordicom Review* 2 (November 1992). Goteborg, Sweden: University of Goteborg, 1992.

Denton, R. E., Jr. "Television as an Instrument of War." In *The Media and the Persian Gulf War*, edited by R. E. Denton, Jr., 27–42. Westport, CT: Praeger, 1993.

Goldberg, R., and G. J. Goldberg. *Anchors*. New York: Birch Lane Press, 1990.

Nimmo, D., and J. E. Combs. *Nightly Horrors: Crisis Coverage in Television Network News*. Knoxville: University of Tennessee Press, 1985.

Smith, L. D., and D. Nimmo. *Cordial Concurrence: Orchestrating National Party Conventions in the Telepolitical Age*. New York: Praeger, 1991.

Wittemore, H. *CNN: The Inside Story*. Boston: Little, Brown, 1990.

Woodward, G. C. "The Rules of the Game: The Military and the Press in the Persian Gulf War." In *The Media and the Persian Gulf War*, edited by R. E. Denton, Jr., 1–26. Westport, CT: Praeger, 1993.

LOWELL (JACKSON) THOMAS
(April 6, 1892–April 29, 1981)

Foreshadowing Political Infotainment

As American citizens approached the end of the twentieth century, the environment of political communication was vastly different from the one their parents and grandparents had known. For the generation that fought in World War II, and for their offspring, the task of becoming politically informed meant reading the major daily newspapers, especially the *New York Times*. And there were the newsmagazines, *Time, Newsweek*, and *U.S. News and World Report*. There were also, in the early postwar era, nightly newscasts and political commentary on radio; later came the nightly television networks' "CBS Evening News," "NBC Nightly News," "World News Tonight" on the American Broadcasting Company (ABC), and the "MacNeil-Lehrer Report" on the Public Broadcasting Service (PBS), as well as each commercial network's morning television magazines.

By the century's last decade, all that had changed. Traditional news sources for Americans were threatened, sometimes shoved aside, by "new news." The Cable News Network (CNN) supplied around-the-clock saturation with public affairs. Along came phone-in talk formats, first on radio, then on television: Larry King (q.v.), Rush Limbaugh (q.v.), G. Gordon Liddy, an all-talk cable television channel—every citizen became a political commentator, a source of information and misinformation. Audience participation formats thrived: "Donahue" (q.v.), "Oprah," "Sally Jesse," "Geraldo," and a host of competitors. Afternoon television spawned shows catering, like the "National Inquirer," to "inquiring minds"—"Hard Copy," "Inside Edition," and "Current Affair."

Slowly but surely the boundaries between what was political information and what was sheer entertainment were erased. What had once been regarded as "straight news" publications and programs took on glitzy and gossipy images; what once were fictional dramas of adventure and intrigue became daily docudramas; and the line between fiction and fact vanished in the rise of the factoid (Combs & Nimmo, 1996).

Yet, the late twentieth-century merger of show-and-tell, of political commentary that sought to be, at one and the same time, commercially successful at both entertaining and informing, was scarcely novel. It was foreshadowed in the career of a political commentator whose career spanned more than six decades and who circled the globe many, many times—Lowell Thomas.

THE ENTERTAINING ADVENTURER

If one were to judge solely by Lowell Thomas' autobiography, *Good Evening Everybody* (1976), it would be difficult to include Thomas in a volume devoted to significant political commentators of the twentieth century. For the bulk of his memoir scarcely touches upon politics in the traditional sense, that is, with politicians, issues, campaigns, elections, and policies. Instead, the volume is about Thomas the performer, the showman who captivates large audiences with accounts of adventures, tales of exotic places, remembrances of Samarkand. Although Thomas had experience as a newspaper reporter and editor, a war correspondent, and a broadcaster with the longest running, continuous news program in the century, his memoir is that of an entertaining soldier of fortune, a combination of the Stanley who found Livingstone and the personification of the *National Geographic*.

Although he was born in the same town as Annie Oakley, who was famed as a horseback rider and sharpshooter in Wild West shows, Thomas' lust for adventure should not be traced to his birth in Woodington, Ohio, alone (on April 6, 1892). Instead, his upbringing in the gold rush environs of Cripple Creek, Colorado, is a better candidate for what sparked his penchant for walking on the wild side. There his parents' nurturing gave his adventurous character a love of culture, education, and refinement. Both parents, Harry and Harriet Thomas, were teachers in Ohio. Harry Thomas went to medical school and then to Cripple Creek to establish a practice in 1900; he later served in the U.S. Medical Corps during World War I. He was a strong believer in education (even at the age of eighty-three he enrolled in Oxford), reading (his was one of the finest libraries west of the Mississippi), and precise diction (he demanded that Lowell practice elocution religiously).

Lowell had a newspaper route that took him daily to Cripple Creek's rollicking gambling houses, saloons, and red-light district. Needless to say, he encountered an endless array of fascinating characters, tellers of tall tales about real and imagined adventures in other places. Even his Sunday school teacher, who escorted Lowell to school when he was first enrolled, was remarkable; she was Texas Guinan from Waco, Texas, who later became famous as the owner of a notorious speakeasy in New York City; her greeting to customers, "Hello, sucker!," was synonymous with an America on the make. With his imagination, which was fired by even an adventuring Sunday school teacher, his attentive ear for stories, and his ever more polished diction, it is small wonder that Lowell Thomas would one day become a storyteller to millions.

Before the century's first decade ran out Cripple Creek's gold ore did. While Dr. Thomas looked for a more promising community where he could relocate his practice, Lowell went back to Ohio with his mother; there he attended high school, was an award-winning orator, and a football quarterback. Following graduation Lowell Thomas earned a four-year B.S. and an M.A. at Valparaiso University all in two years, graduating in 1911. Lowell had Dr. Thomas' drive for formal education; in subsequent years, he earned a B.A. and an M.A. from the University of Denver (1912), attended Kent College of Law in Chicago (and also taught public speaking) from 1912 to 1914, and earned an M.A. degree from Princeton in 1916 while also serving as an English instructor.

During his pursuit of college degrees, Lowell Thomas acquired experience as a journalist. In 1911, after leaving Valparaiso, he was a reporter for the *Times* of Cripple Creek, then editor of two newspapers in Victor, Colorado, the *Daily Record* and the *Daily News*. And, while he was attending Kent College, Thomas was a reporter for the Chicago *Evening Journal*. Yet, it was not as a journalist that Lowell Thomas found a unique niche as a commentator; it was as a promoter. In 1915 Thomas took a leave from the *Evening Journal* and traveled to the West Coast in a failed effort to win the hand of a woman he had met at the University of Denver. (In 1917 the woman, Francis Ryan, accepted his proposal; they remained married until her death in 1975, and Thomas married Marianna Munn two years later.) To pay his trip expenses, Thomas talked railroad officials into a deal: in exchange for transportation, Thomas would promote the West and the coming San Francisco Panama-Pacific Exposition, encouraging Midwesterners to travel by rail to California. However, when his proposal of marriage was rejected, Thomas did not return immediately to New Jersey. Instead he turned north to Alaska. He lived with the Eskimos, shot treacherous rapids, and realized his dreams of adventure.

On his return to Princeton, Thomas fashioned a public lecture about his Alaskan trip; he incorporated photos he had acquired at the time. Through his lectures he supported his Princeton studies. When summer came Thomas set out again, this time to the Grand Canyon (he crossed the Colorado River hand walking on a cable suspended 200 feet in the air); he also returned to Alaska. At summer's end Thomas had material for more public lectures that now had the added feature of movies he had taken of his adventures. It is telling that at this point Lowell Thomas ceased calling his public appearances "lectures" and billed them as "shows."

He was unaware of it at the time, but Thomas had discovered a promotional gimmick that would win him worldwide fame and fortune. In early 1917 Thomas received a letter from Frank Lane, the U.S. secretary of the interior. Lane, desirous of promoting tourism in the United States, hit upon a promotional scheme to sell Americans, who no longer could travel on vacations to war-torn Europe, on the idea of "See America First!" To kick off the promotional campaign, he organized a conference at the Smithsonian Institution to include prominent politicians, conservationists, national park superintendents, and other leaders representing all states of the union. While he was casting about for a representative from Alaska, a railroad executive recommended "Professor Thomas."

Thomas tried to make it clear that he was neither a professor nor from Alaska, but he was scheduled for a thirty-minute talk at the conference, illustrated with film, anyway. It was a talk he had already given more than 100 times, just as

William Jennings Bryan had delivered his Cross of Gold speech at numerous gatherings before it propelled him to a presidential nomination at the 1896 Democratic National Convention. As last speaker of the day, Thomas knew he needed an attention-getting opening for this gathering of notables. Although perhaps outside the boundaries of contemporary political correctness, in 1917 Thomas' introduction was effective: "Mr. Secretary, distinguished guests: I think I can tell you something about Alaska, but I confess I feel out of place in this illustrious company. You see, I grew up in a mining camp, where I got my start in an ore house" (Thomas, 1976, 92). The attention of the audience never wavered thereafter.

So effective was Thomas' presentation that the secretary of the interior asked him to take over the "See America First" campaign. Thomas agreed, but on April 6, 1917, the United States entered World War I and the campaign was canceled. Instead, Lane urged Thomas to travel with a cameraman to Europe, gather film and insights about the war, and return to promote the U.S. war effort at home. Thomas became a staff reporter and writer for the Committee on Public Information, the U.S. World War I propaganda agency chaired by George Creel (q.v.), and he traveled to the Western Front for the CPI News Division (Desmond, 1980, 370).

The adventurous Thomas quickly realized that the stagnant conflict at the front was scarcely likely to produce words or pictures that would stir young men in the United States to flock to recruiting stations (Knightley, 1975). He sought a more glamorous appeal. He and his cameraman pieced together filmed reports of British general Sir Edmund Allenby's successful campaign that drove the Turks from Jerusalem. He also was the only reporter to cover the guerrilla campaign of Lawrence of Arabia. Since Thomas, not the CPI, was paying the expenses for his war travels, Thomas alone came out of the war with major bylined scoops with his coverage of the Lawrence campaigns. Two subsequent "shows" derived from the material gathered through Thomas' war reporting: "With Allenby in Palestine" and "With Lawrence in Arabia."

Thomas had one other scoop as a war correspondent. After the armistice, journalists were forbidden to enter Germany. Nonetheless, Thomas and another journalist, after repeated failures, arrived at the Swiss border hidden in an ambulance, got through the barbed wire guarding the frontier, and made it to Basel. Although they were arrested, the U.S. consular official permitted them to board a train for Freiburg. Once in Germany, they reached and interviewed Prince Max, the last German imperial chancellor; they then traveled to Berlin, Hamburg, and back to France. Thomas thus became the first correspondent to provide an eyewitness account of the German revolution that deposed the kaiser (Desmond, 1980, 398–99).

On his return to the United States following World War I, Lowell Thomas became a celebrity. His various commercial theatrical productions—on Allenby, Lawrence, the U.S. effort in France, and the revolution in Germany—drew huge audiences in a twelve-week run at Madison Square Garden. A combined illustrated show on Allenby and Lawrence filled London's Covent Garden, Royal Albert Hall, and Queen's Hall; it played to a total audience of more than a million, including royalty, political leaders, military leaders, and T. H. Lawrence himself. Throughout the 1920s Lowell Thomas parlayed his nonstop travels, adventures, and brushes with death (a plane crash in Spain, a fall from a horse on a mountain trail in Tibet, a hotel fire in Alaska, and so on) into a commercially successful series of illustrated theatrical productions, books (he wrote fifty-five in his lifetime), and commercial films. Then, virtually out of the ether, network radio news beckoned. It was a forum for his showmanship for forty-five years.

THE POLITICAL BROADCASTER

KDKA, the nation's first commercial radio station, aired returns of the 1920 presidential election of Warren Harding's defeat of James Cox. Thus had rudimentary political commentary, which H. V. Kaltenborn (q.v.) would, beginning in 1932, make a staple of national convention coverage, first reached the U.S. airways. By 1928 the National Broadcasting Company (NBC) had Red and Blue networks; William S. Paley ventured to start another network, the Columbia Broadcasting System (CBS). Yet, there was very little broadcast news. In fact, there was only one daily network newscast on radio, the *Literary Digest*'s sponsored broadcast featuring a popular swashbuckling figure as a news reader, former war correspondent Floyd Gibbons.

Gibbons deservedly had a reputation as a two-fisted drinker; the president of *Literary Digest*'s parent company was a teetotaler. A rift was inevitable, and in 1930 the only daily newscast was in danger of being canceled unless a replacement for Gibbons was found. Bill Paley saw an opportunity to give flight to his fledgling network by finding an acceptable newscaster and wresting the newscast from NBC. As the weeks went by and no acceptable replacement for Gibbons emerged, Lowell Thomas received an invitation to visit CBS. He met Bill Paley, then found himself in front of a microphone. When Thomas asked what was going on, Paley said simply, "When you hear the buzzer start talking. Talk fifteen minutes—I don't care what about. Then stop" (Thomas, 1976, 291).

It was not Thomas' first broadcasting experience. In 1924 he had reported a few of his adventures on radio. And, in 1925, in a one-hour program over KDKA, Thomas ad-libbed an account of the first airplane flight around the globe, an eyewitness' view as a member of the party. Yet, since he did not know he was being auditioned by Paley, Thomas, ever the showman, turned to the studio musicians (always on hand lest something should go wrong), told them to play Oriental music in the background, then talked for fifteen minutes about Lawrence, India, the Khyber Pass, and Afghanistan. Paley was pleased. Only then did Thomas learn that the executives of the *Literary Digest* had been listening to his voice. To satisfy the potential sponsors that Paley had indeed found the right man, a few days later Thomas broadcast a fifteen-minute newscast, based upon a hasty reading of the newspapers, in a time slot before Gibbons' broadcast. A comparison of the two broadcasters' on-air performance clinched it (Slater, 1988).

On September 29, 1930, broadcasting on NBC to the eastern United States and on CBS to the West, Lowell Thomas became the "new voice" of the *Literary Digest*. "So far as I know, this was the only time in radio history that a single program was shared by rival networks" (Thomas, 1976, 295). For Paley it turned out to be a Pyrrhic victory. A year later Sun Oil undertook sponsorship, and Thomas' newscast aired only on NBC.

It was 1947 before CBS was able to reclaim Lowell Thomas as a newscaster. When he returned to CBS, it was a combination of factors that produced the shift. One was that, given his lifestyle, Thomas faced indebtedness in 1946. His radio sponsor, Sun Oil Company, agreed to assist him if Thomas would sign a lifetime contract with the company. He declined, ending up negotiating a long-term, but not lifetime, contract with Proctor & Gamble, whose network of choice was CBS. "CBS, in its corporate pride, ruled that Proctor & Gamble could not supply the broadcaster for its program, but the network had to do it" (Thomas, 1977, 134). Thus was Bill Paley, seventeen years after first selecting Lowell Thomas, justified in saying he had done so again. In the interim between leaving and rejoining CBS, Thomas had gained his peak audience in 1936 (20 million), continued to have 10 million listeners in successive years, and upon switching to CBS in 1947 took an audience of 8 million with him (Fang, 1977).

As a newscaster, Lowell Thomas used his showmanship to advantage. In one instance, out of necessity, realizing that news had to capture a sizable audience, he was an innovator. In the beginning, he obtained the news that he broadcast as had Floyd Gibbons: "We swiped it" (Thomas, 1976, 297). That is, Thomas simply broadcast what was in the day's newspapers. However, the newspapers' wire services, threatened by radio's popularity, denied radio access to wire service news. Thomas, through the aid of two assistants who both had worked on newspapers, turned to the telephone. By making telephone calls, they interviewed, got tips from, and picked the brains of sources involved in the headline news of the day. Thomas now had fresh and exclusive material to air. The wire services responded by establishing specialized services for radio news, thus ending the press-radio war of the era.

Thomas' role as a political commentator was not confined to radio. He continued lecturing, writing books and articles, and traveling. Along the way he became the first reporter to broadcast from a ship at sea, an airplane, a helicopter, a mountaintop, a jungle, even ski resorts (an avid passion). Moreover, he branched out into other media. One was television. On February 21, 1940, Thomas broadcast the first televised newscast, a simulcast of his radio program. Moreover, as he told his audience that evening, it was "the first sponsored program ever to go out by television" (Thomas, 1977, 18). When the United States entered World War II, however, wartime restrictions limited television's news role, as did the fact that television sets were very rare in American households (Ritchie, 1994). The television simulcast was discontinued, making Thomas, who did not want to be chained to a camera or television studio, happy.

A few years later, however, when television replaced radio as an entertainment medium, Thomas filmed successful television series that portrayed his worldwide adventures—"High Adventure with Lowell Thomas" and "The World of Lowell Thomas," and "Lowell Thomas Remembers." When the cineramic technique hit films, partly to lure people away from their televisions and back to the movie houses, Thomas capitalized on that as well. He financed *This Is Cinerama*, *The Seven Wonders of the World*, and *Search for Paradise* (Thomas, 1977, 173–85).

In 1931 Lowell Thomas had edited and produced an ill-fated venture, *The American Newsreel*. Competing with the major film studios, his project had no chance (Jacobs, 1939, 56). So, in 1932, he became the voice of Fox *Movietone News*. Before television, the newsreel was the audio/visual source of news for Americans, the nation's "visual newspaper information" (Combs & Combs, 1994, 20). Fox *Movietone News* played to 80 million moviegoers a week; considering Fox competed with the newsreels of Warner's *Pathe News*, *Paramount News*, MGM-Hearst's *News of the Day*, and Universal's *Newsreel*, the total audience for newsreels in the United States in the 1930s and 1940s was substantial (Fielding, 1972).

Overall, 500 camera personnel and thousands of stringers produced miles of raw frame from which came the ten-minute edited political realities supplied to 16,000 movie houses from coast to coast twice a week. Thomas' role was not limited to narrating the newsreels. Two times a week for seventeen years he gathered with his aides at Movietone studios and screened the film supplied by camera crews across the world. "As the night wore on, the pressure intensified," he recalled later, "especially if there was a late-breaking story due." Thomas and his aides "cut and spliced, wrote and rewrote [the narrated script], recorded and rerecorded" (Thomas, 1976, 313).

Among the memorable events transmitted to American audiences during Thomas' association with Fox Movietone were vivid portrayals of the assassinations of King Alexander and French premier Jean Louis Barthou in 1934 by Croatian terrorists, and the Japanese air attack that same year on the *Panay*, an American gunboat in China. President Franklin Roosevelt used newsreel film to refute Japanese claims that the sinking was an honest mistake and extracted an indemnity from Japan, which reinforced the enmity of its militarists for the United States.

Lowell Thomas' last nightly news radio broadcast came at the age of eighty-four, on April 30, 1976. There had been 16,800 nightly newscasts. In the last broadcast, Thomas closed by noting that his newscast had served as the longest running broadcast of any kind, not just news. He was saddened by the fact that in the 1970s the "spot news program," which consisted only of headlines, had no time for what he called, "my specialty," namely, "human interest, adventure, colorful stories from around the globe." Then, for the first time since he had first used it to close his broadcasts forty-six years earlier, he changed his signature line, "So long until tomorrow," to "Here's to all of you. So long." On April 29, 1981, he said his final "so long" with his death (Thomas, 1977, 82).

Across all media—theater productions, books, radio, television, newsreels, film—Thomas' style remained the same. He was uppermost a storyteller, a commentator who used colorful, yet spare, language to personalize abstract notions. In this he was the forerunner of such other political commentators as Paul Harvey (q.v.). Although he had political views, he regarded the commentator's task as remaining noncommittal: "He takes no sides. He never analyzes, never makes profound pronouncements, delivers no messages, sounds no alarms" (Crouse, 1961, 234). Thomas wrote in his original autobiography that it was one of his "absolute rules on the air" not "to confuse opinions with hard news or to be drawn into taking sides" (Thomas, 1976, 301). In a companion biography, he wrote that his broadcasts were "straight down the middle, without favor to either Democrats or Republicans" and the general public "may not have known what my political preferences were" (Thomas, 1977, 131).

It was a style of political commentary that many politicians, and obviously U.S. presidents, preferred. In a 1965 testimonial dinner given for Thomas, former president Harry Truman called him the "Methuselah of radio broadcasts" who "never helped me much," but "rarely, if ever, hurt me." Former president Dwight Eisenhower celebrated Thomas' "speaking and writing and exploring." Former president Lyndon Johnson observed that Thomas' "influence on tens of millions of listeners and readers cannot be measured" (all quoted by Thomas, 1977, 281).

THE FIRST POLITICAL INFOTAINER

A career as an entertaining adventurer, joined with that of a reporter, editor, war correspondent, and broadcaster, sparked in the first decade of the twentieth century in Lowell Thomas what in the last decade of that century would be called infotainment. It was a role that positioned Thomas uniquely in the world of political commentators.

The political commentator is heir to a tradition that dates back to Greek mythology, to the daughters of Zeus and Mnemosyne, who presided over forms of expression in song, poetry, art, and science. These "muses" reported, reflected, and made recommendations on weighty matters. Centuries later, a philosopher borrowed from the muses to coin a term for a way of thinking, "musement." Musement is "an agreeable occupation of the mind," "refreshing," and "involves no purpose save that of casting aside all purpose"; in fact, he wrote, "it is Pure Play" (Peirce, 1958, 360).

The political commentary of Lowell Thomas fitted this form of thought; his combination of passing along information in an entertaining way to huge audiences, never taking sides, never being judgmental, never making profound pronouncements, is the essence of political commentary as infotainment. Be it uttered by a contemporary commentator like Larry King, who calls himself an "infotainer," or much earlier by Lowell Thomas, it is musement, pure play that is devoid of purpose save to cast aside purpose. Given King's current and Thomas' lasting popularity, it appears to be a political message much in demand.

REFERENCES

Selected Works by Lowell Thomas

With Lawrence in Arabia. New York: Century Press, 1924.
The First World Flight. Boston: Houghton Mifflin, 1925.
Magic Dials: The Story of Radio and Television. New York: L. Furman, 1939.
These Men Shall Never Die. Philadelphia: John C. Winston, 1943.
History as You Heard It. Garden City, NY: Doubleday, 1957.
Good Evening Everybody. New York: Avon Books, 1976.
So Long until Tomorrow. New York: William Morrow, 1977.

Selected Critical Works about Lowell Thomas

Block, M., ed. "Thomas, Lowell (Jackson)." In *Current Biography 1940*, 796–98. New York: H. W. Wilson, 1941.
Bowen, N. R., ed. *Lowell Thomas: The Stranger Everyone Knows.* Garden City, NY: Doubleday, 1968.
Crouse, R. "Yes There Is a Lowell Thomas." *Reader's Digest*, April 1961, 232–52.
Fang, I. E. "Lowell Thomas." In *Those Radio Commentators!*, 65–83. Ames, IA: Iowa State University Press, 1977.
McKerns, J. P., ed. "Thomas, Lowell Jackson." In *Biographical Dictionary of American Journalism*, 696–98. New York: Greenwood Press, 1989.
Rothe, A., ed. "Thomas, Lowell (Jackson)." In *Current Biography 1952*, 52–54. New York: H. W. Wilson, 1953.

Selected General Works

Combs, J. E., and S. T. Combs. *Film Propaganda and American Politics.* New York: Garland, 1994.
Combs, J. E., and D. Nimmo. *The Comedy of Democracy.* Westport, CT: Praeger, 1996.
Desmond, R. W. *Windows on the World: World News Reporting 1900–1920.* Iowa City: University of Iowa Press, 1980.
Fielding, R. *The American Newsreel, 1911–1967.* Norman, OK: University of Oklahoma Press, 1972.
Hosley, D. H. *As Good as Any: Foreign Correspondence on American Radio, 1930–1940.* Westport, CT: Greenwood Press, 1984.
Jacobs, L. *The Rise of the American Film.* New York: Harcourt, Brace, 1939.
Knightley, *The First Casualty.* New York: Harcourt Brace Jovanovich, 1975.
Nimmo, D., and J. Combs. *The Political Pundits.* New York: Praeger, 1992.
Peirce, C. S. *Values in a Universe of Chance.* Garden City, NY: Doubleday, 1958.
Ritchie, M. *Please Stand By: A Prehistory of Television.* New York: Overlook Press, 1994.
Slater, R. *This . . . Is CBS.* Englewood Cliffs, NJ: Prentice-Hall, 1988.

DOROTHY THOMPSON

(July 9, 1893–January 30, 1961)

Giving Voice to Hyperpolitical Commentary

As the first of two Golden Ages of Broadcasting opened in the 1930s, radio's, the medium's typical political commentators shared common writing backgrounds, usually as newspaper correspondents; many had experience or training in public speaking; few entered radio with broadcasting backgrounds. And, they had one other attribute in common; all were male—H. V. Kaltenborn (q.v.), Lowell Thomas (q.v.), Elmer Davis (q.v.), Edward R. Murrow (q.v.), and Eric Sevareid (q.v.), and so on. Dorothy Thompson broke the mold; she too was a working journalist, a talented lecturer, and from a nonbroadcasting background. She was, however, decidedly female, a trendsetter for numerous future women who would successfully combine the talents of print and electronic journalism, including Martha Rountree (q.v.) and Cokie Roberts (q.v.).

It is interesting to note the shorthand phrases that biographers, critics, and devotees of Dorothy Thompson have used to depict her career: crusader, cosmic force, Cassandra, legend in her own time, and zealot are among them. All designate a person of energy, drive, dynamism: "an undiminishable aggressive nature, an extravagant lack of diffidence, and limitless faith in herself, her intuitions, her judgments and her place as wet nurse to destiny" (Fisher, 1944, 16). Dorothy Thompson founded a breathless, hyperpolitical commentary that set her apart from her contemporaries, one later counterfeited as the currency of many political commentators at the century's end. If Marshall McLuhan was correct in his observation that communication media were "hot" before the arrival of "cool" television, then Dorothy Thompson provides a paradigmatic case of "hot" (McLuhan, 1964, 36–45).

WARMING TO THE COMMENTATOR'S TASK

Before the contemporary era of—enlightened or benighted depending on one's view—political correctness, a young girl who behaved like a spirited boy was called a "tomboy." Today's advocates of gender-neutral language would doubtless find that label offensive. Whether Dorothy Thompson, a very liberated female, found it offensive when it was applied to her, biographical accounts do not record. But Thompson's chroniclers do so label her: she was "gawky and a tomboy," writes one (Block, 1940, 799); she "grew up a leggy tomboy," says another (Fang, 1977, 132); she was "a mischievous tomboy at fourteen," says a third (Sanders, 1973, 12).

Dorothy Thompson was the daughter of Peter Thompson, a Methodist minister and Englishman from Durham who came to America to visit a brother. In America Peter met and married Margaret Grierson; instead of returning to England, Thompson settled down to the cleric's life and its relentless transfers from one parsonage to another in upstate New York. Dorothy Thompson was born in Lancaster, New York, the oldest of three children of the marriage of Peter and Margaret. Although all accounts record the date as July 9, there is a discrepancy regarding the year. Separate biographers record the year as 1893 (Sanders, 1973, 4; Kurth, 1990, 10). However, "sometime during the 1920s, in the only truly mysterious gesture in her life," she "began to give year of birth as 1894" (Kurth, 1990, 471–72). Hence, the *National Cyclopedia of American Biography* (1938, 35) and *Current Biography* (Block, 1940, 799) list 1894, as do two other chroniclers whose profiles postdate the information supplied to the *Cyclopedia* and *Current Biography* (Fang, 1977, 132; Fisher, 1944, 32).

The precise year is itself less consequential than what it says about the factual basis of political commentary, especially when those facts are supplied by the commentator. When confronted by her brother with the family Bible that proved 1893 to be the correct date, Thompson expressed her rationale for perpetuating the inaccuracy in a letter to H. L. Mencken (q.v.), "I don't give a damn, but having stood on its being 1894 through a series of Who's Whos, I shall keep to 1894 despite my annoying brother" (Kurth, 1990, 472).

There was to have been another child born to Peter and Margaret Thompson, but when the physician failed to recognize a miscarriage for what it was, his attempts to halt the hemorrhage resulted in blood poisoning that killed Dorothy's mother. Dorothy was seven years old at the time. The death reinforced her sense of independence. She assumed the role of protector to her younger sister and brother, sometimes enlisting them in her rebellions, sometimes making them the targets. Peter Thompson had always tolerated his older daughter's independent spirit. "Punishments" for Dorothy's misdeeds were to memorize and recite passages from books in the minister's sizable library, especially passages from English poets and from biblical verses. Like the elocution lessons forced on Lowell Thomas by his father, Dorothy's "punishments" served her well; in her career as correspondent, columnist, and broadcaster, she displayed a keen memory, a rapid recitative style, and a penchant for English pronunciations and idioms.

However, two years following the death of Margaret Thompson, Reverend Peter took a second wife, Eliza. Stepmother and stepdaughter did not get along. With each passing incident of the former's scolding and the latter's rudeness, the antipathy escalated. When Dorothy drew a week's suspension from high school in Gowanda, New York, for mocking a teacher, matters worsened. Apparently convinced by Eliza that Dorothy was a severe problem, Peter Thompson sent his daughter to Chicago to live with two aunts to complete high school there. In Chicago Dorothy Thompson attended Lewis Institute where she proved to be an excellent student in English, history, and Latin, respectable in French and German, and barely acceptable in mathematics.

She regarded her most impressive teacher to be Professor Edwin Herbert Lewis, the same professor who had influenced young Arthur Krock (q.v.) a few years before Thompson was exposed to his teaching. Lewis challenged Dorothy's mastery of the English language and sharpened her argumentative skills. She was an excellent debater and basketball player. Upon graduation she entered Syracuse University as a junior, thanks to her experience at Lewis Institute. At Syracuse she continued to play basketball, sharpened her oratorical skills, and developed a keen interest in politics, particularly in the suffrage movement.

After receipt of her A.B. in 1914, Dorothy Thompson obtained a job stuffing envelopes in the Buffalo offices of the New York State Woman Suffrage party. Within a year she was an "organizer," the title bestowed on grassroots suffrage propagandists. She made countless speeches, wrote countless press releases, and orchestrated countless publicity events—all with an unmatched intensity and verve. Once, when antisuffrage campaigners tried to drown out one of her speeches with music and jeers, she resorted to hopping off the speakers' platform, running into a furniture store, buying a blackboard, returning to the platform, and writing out her speech line by line. The attention getter quieted the band and her hecklers. She later recalled, "It *was* a good show. It was the last romantic political movement this country ever had" (Kurth, 1990, 39; emphasis in original).

When the New York State suffrage movement ended in victory in 1917, Dorothy Thompson found employment in New York City writing publicity for a publisher, then as a publicity writer for a social service project, the Social Unit, first in Cincinnati, Ohio, where she also edited the unit's newspaper, and later back in New York City where she became the unit's national publicity director in 1919. After an unhappy romantic affair, Dorothy Thompson resolved, in the parlance of the 1990s, to get on with her life. Getting on meant boarding a steamship to London in hopes of finding employment as a newspaper correspondent.

Fortuitously, the ship also carried several prominent American Jews, including Supreme Court Justice Louis Brandeis and noted law professor Felix Frankfurter (who would later also sit on the Supreme Court), who were traveling to London for an international Zionist conference. By the time she arrived in London, Dorothy Thompson had managed to learn so much about Zionism that she proposed to the London bureau of the Hearst International News Service (INS) that she cover the conference as a freelance journalist. She got the job, made the most of it, and entered the world of professional political communication as a journalist.

FORTUNE, FAME, AND FLIP-FLOPS IN POLITICAL COMMENTARY

After the end of the London conference on Zionism, Thompson was able to scratch out a living as a freelance journalist by selling her pieces at space rates (i.e., per line of published material) to wire services. In the process, she built an impressive reputation for resourcefulness in scooping competing journalists. First among her celebrated coups was her interview with Terence McSwiney, Lord Mayor of Cork. It was the last interview he ever gave. Thompson sailed to Ireland to track down relatives. While there she interviewed Sinn Fein leaders, McSwiney among them. An hour after Thompson left the Irish patriot's office, he was arrested for sedition. In prison McSwiney went on a hunger strike and died within two months. Upon her return to England, Thompson casually mentioned to the INS bureau chief that she had interviewed McSwiney, unaware of the mother lode her notes constituted. "Sit down at a typewriter, girl, and write out those notes," the chief ordered (Kurth, 1990, 52). Her dispatches were published as front page stories in the United States. Thompson was also at the right place at the right time when she subsequently went to Italy; there she wrote dispatches on workers' unrest in Milan that resulted in street fighting between Fascists and Communists, the prelude to Benito Mussolini's seizure of power in Italy.

Although Thompson's freelance scoops were being published, her income scarcely covered her expenses. She took a job with the American Red Cross in Paris to supplement her finances; for writing publicity, she received ten francs a line. Postwar Paris teemed with refugees from across Europe. Among them was the wife of a key anti-Bolshevik leader in the Russian civil war. Again in the right place at the right time, Thompson interviewed the wife. This led to a published series of articles on Russian emigration, which were sold to the *Philadelphia Public Ledger*. Building on the series' success, Thompson urged the *Public Ledger*'s European news bureau chief to add a news office in Vienna and send her to staff it. The bureau chief was skeptical; he agreed to allow Thompson to use the *Public Ledger*'s credentials in Vienna and serve as a special correspondent, but without salary. She would be paid only for published articles.

Once again fortune smiled after Thompson arrived in Vienna in 1921. The once proud capital of the Austro-Hungarian empire was in decay, the empire was gone, Austria was stripped of its possessions, and Hungary was in chaos. Trying to make sense of this postwar madness, Thompson toured the former empire. Shortly after her arrival in Budapest, there was an abortive putsch to regain the Hungarian throne for the former emperor, Karl. Resourceful as always, Thompson discovered where Karl and his empress were lodged and, disguised as a Red Cross medical assistant in a nurse's uniform, she entered the emperor's castle. The intrepid correspondent interviewed both the emperor and empress and even smuggled away a note from the empress to her son. The emperor, however, met a fate similar to that of Terence McSwiney. Karl's interview with Thompson was his last; he was exiled to an island and died shortly thereafter.

Dorothy Thompson racked up other scoops, a sufficient number to land a position as a staff member of the *Public Ledger* and a position as Vienna bureau

chief. Although Margaret Fuller was probably the first female foreign correspondent, for the *New York Herald Tribune* in the 1840s (see Georgie Anne
Geyer), it is fair to say that Dorothy Thompson was the first female correspondent to achieve national, even international, fame. Her articles reached nationwide audiences through the combined news services of the *Ledger* and the *New
York Evening Post*. Many were picked up for international distribution. In 1925
she moved from Vienna to become the full-time correspondent for the *Ledger*
in Berlin. As a foreign correspondent in both Vienna and Berlin, Thompson
provided audiences with eyewitness accounts of such critical events as street
riots in Sofia, Bulgaria; the 1926 Polish revolution, following her harrowing
entry into Warsaw; and the rise of Nazi Germany.

As early as 1923, after the failed Beer Hall putsch, Dorothy Thompson had
sought to arrange an interview with Adolf Hitler. Before she could complete the
arrangements, Hitler had been imprisoned. In prison Hitler wrote *Mein Kampf*;
upon its publication, Thompson read the German version. She doubted that the
book's message—that the German people would eventually vote in a dictatorship—would succeed. Yet, by 1931, Hitler appeared to be on the brink of success. Thompson was able to arrange through Hitler's press attaché, Ernst
Hanfstaengel (a former classmate of H. V. Kaltenborn at Harvard), an exclusive
interview with Hitler. Dorothy Thompson was decidedly not impressed with
Adolf Hitler. She (as did Kaltenborn in his later interview with Hitler) found
the Nazi leader "formless, almost faceless," having the countenance of a "caricature"; he was "inconsequent and voluble, ill-poised, insecure." "He is," she
wrote in a devastating way, "the very prototype of the Little Man" (Thompson,
1932, 12–14). The interview was first published in *Cosmopolitan* magazine in
its April 1932 issue, and it was the basis for her book, *"I Saw Hitler!"* (1932).

By this time, Dorothy Thompson was not only an established correspondent
in her own right, she was also the wife of a famous novelist, Sinclair Lewis.
(She had previously been married to an international playboy, Josef Bard; Bard's
eye proved too roving for Thompson's tastes and there was a divorce.) Conse-
quently, the interview and Thompson's put-down of Hitler received wide circulation. When Thompson's book came to Hitler's attention, he was furious at
Hanfstaengel: "What have you done, you imbecile! Scram—get out of my sight!
I never want to see you again!" (Metcalfe, 1988, 57). The incident did not end
there. Dorothy Thompson had to eat her words; within two years, Adolf Hitler
was in power and by popular vote. But, as with Kaltenborn, the order of magnitude of Thompson's widely publicized misjudgment only enhanced her growing celebrity. With Hitler's success Thompson reassessed the Little Man and in
the process became aggressively anti-Nazi.

It was not the final time she reassessed her public judgments. In fact, over
the remaining years of her career, Dorothy Thompson frequently found herself
taking a public stand, then reversing it. In 1940, for instance, Thompson threw
her public support behind the Republican presidential candidate, Wendell Willkie, after having predicted that Franklin Roosevelt would not seek a third term.

However, before the campaign ended, she switched and came out for Roosevelt's effort to win a third consecutive presidential term. She accurately anticipated a European war, but she stated that the United States would not enter it; when the war began in 1939, she urged a quick U.S. entry. These and other flip-flops explain the appraisal of the 1940 entry in *Current Biography*: "There is a perpetual dualism in Dorothy Thompson's personality and mental makeup that colors her political observances" (Block, 1940, 798).

Three years after her notable interview with Adolf Hitler, Dorothy Thompson returned to Berlin as a writer for the *Saturday Evening Post*. She was promptly expelled "because of numerous anti-German references" according to Nazi officials (Desmond, 1982, 483). However, the record suggests that her critical references to Nazi Germany, especially her negative 1931 appraisal of Adolf Hitler, may not have been the principal reason for her ouster. In 1934 Thompson published a devastating review of a book written by Ernst Hanfstaengel, also known as "Putzi." In his book, Hanfstaengel printed and refuted, one-by-one, more than 100 anti-Nazi cartoons. Thompson labeled the book, "Putzi-Footing Propaganda." Putzi did not forget. Although Thompson's critical commentary in 1931 of Hitler might have figured in her 1934 expulsion from Germany, "her offense was of a more recent vintage and lodged like a poisoned arrow in the sensitive soul of Hitler's chief of the foreign press" (Metcalfe, 1988, 284).

After her expulsion from Germany, Dorothy Thompson entered into a new phase of her career as a political commentator. In 1935, at the behest of Helen Reid, the wife of the publisher of the *New York Herald Tribune*, the newspaper added Dorothy Thompson to its staff; she was to serve as the "sort of distaff counterpoint" to Walter Lippmann (q.v.). Thompson began writing in a style that "nicely contrasted with Lippmann's," she "emerged from the printed page as a very wise, warm, and caring earth mother, mourning the world's frailties, bolstering its sagging confidence, and appealing to the conscience of a time of rampant political wickedness" (Kluger, 1986, 288). Thompson's thrice-weekly column, "On the Record," ultimately reached 8 million readers through 195 newspapers. However, her contract with the *Herald Tribune* stipulated that her views must coincide with the newspaper's. Hence, when, in 1940, she supported Franklin Roosevelt's third-term bid, the news organization did not renew her contract in 1941.

By then, however, her celebrity as the nation's most influential female journalist transcended any single news organization. (Twice, once in 1937, again a decade later, Dorothy Thompson's admirers proposed she run for president of the United States.) In 1941 she had no difficulty having her three-times-a-week political column syndicated, so the *Herald Tribune*'s action was of minimal consequence. Thompson also wrote a monthly column for the *Ladies Home Journal* that reached 3.5 million readers (she continued it until her death). She was the subject of a cover story in *Time* in 1939, feature articles about her appeared in numerous mass circulation magazines, cartoonists delighted in using her for a subject, and critics either praised or damned her excessive, excited, enthusiastic style, but they never ignored her.

And, she continued to make news as well as offer professional opinions about the news. In 1939 she received worldwide publicity for heckling speakers at a German-American Bund rally in Madison Square Garden; she provoked an uproar, and the police had to keep order as well as escort Thompson to safety. Weeks prior to the U.S. entry into World War II, Thompson's fourteen-year marriage to Sinclair Lewis ended in divorce. That too was news, as was her third marriage to a Czech painter, Maxim Kopf, in 1943 (her third husband died in 1958).

At the 1936 Democratic and Republican national nominating conventions, Dorothy Thompson became a celebrity of another sort. The National Broadcasting Company (NBC) hired Thompson to provide radio commentary on the proceedings. Her broadcasts met with popular response. The following year, Thompson began a weekly radio commentary on NBC (she later moved to the Mutual Broadcasting System). Critics found her broadcasts, like her columns, vibrant and full of energy, so much so that to some they seemed breathless: "Miss Thompson talks fast," a "torrent of words" that "covers an incredible amount of ground in thirteen minutes," a "topical swing session" (Fang, 1977, 141). One sponsor for Thompson's broadcasts, in the hopes of softening what some stations found a "belligerent" tone, introduced her radio commentaries with a song, "Love Sends a Little Gift of Roses," played in the studio by Phil Spitalny's highly popular "All Girl Orchestra."

In addition to columns, broadcasts, articles, and books, public speaking was an opportunity for Dorothy Thompson to express her distinctive, hyperactive style of political commentary. Her invitations to speak were so numerous that she could accept relatively few, especially from groups no woman had been invited to speak to before—the Union League and Harvard clubs of New York, the American Manufacturers Association, and the U.S. Chamber of Commerce. In a widely publicized debate during the 1940 presidential election, Dorothy Thompson squared off with Clare Booth Luce, wife of the publisher of *Time* magazine, Thompson speaking on behalf of President Roosevelt, Luce on behalf of Wendell Willkie. But the two antagonists largely ignored the candidates and attacked one another. Since Thompson had recently visited the Maginot Line in France, Luce referred to her as the "Molly Pitcher of the Maginot Line." Dorothy Thompson gave tit-for-tat: "Miss Booth is the Body by Fisher in this campaign," a mere dilettante who had "torn herself loose from the Stork Club to serve her country in this serious hour" (Swanberg, 1972, 255–56).

Dorothy Thompson's views influenced both popular and elite opinion. When a young Polish Jew allegedly assassinated a Nazi embassy secretary in Paris in 1938, Thompson defended the boy in a broadcast. Listeners contributed $30,000 to the youth's defense fund even though she had not asked for donations in her broadcast. Also in 1938 Thompson published an article on the fate of European refugees in the influential journal, *Foreign Affairs*. President Roosevelt read the article and forthwith set about convening a thirty-nation conference on the refugee problem.

During World War II, Dorothy Thompson turned war propagandist on behalf of the Allied cause. Based upon her intimate acquaintance with the nation, she prepared materials on Nazi Germany for President Roosevelt, the State Department, and the Office of Strategic Services (OSS). She also attended meetings at the Office of War Information (OWI), which considered wartime information policies. Complaining at how the talent of American journalists was being wasted in the war effort (a view shared by OWI's director, Elmer Davis), she begged for a propaganda assignment with OWI. What she received instead was a role in a project that used the shortwave facilities of the Columbia Broadcasting System (CBS) to broadcast anti-Nazi propaganda.

Thompson undertook a weekly shortwave broadcast in German over CBS to an imaginary friend named "Hans," the alias for Count Helmuth von Moltke. The purpose of "Listen, Hans!" was to appeal to Moltke and others to rise up against Hitler and stop the mounting Nazi atrocities and to accept the inevitable Allied victory. Recalling the last time that she and "Hans" had seen one another, Thompson said in her broadcast, "I asked you whether you and your friends would ever have the courage to act" (Shirer, 1960, 1016). Like the Lord Mayor of Cork, Terence McSwiney, and the deposed Emperor of Hungary, Karl, "Hans" had little opportunity to act; von Moltke was executed in early 1945 (Sanders, 1973).

After the end of World War II, Dorothy Thompson's influence as a political commentator gradually diminished. As a result of her postwar support for the Arab cause in the Mideast, American Jews, sensing another one of Thompson's flip-flops, grew increasingly critical of her. She ended her weekly Sunday broadcasts in the spring of 1945 but continued her thrice-weekly columns through 1958, thus surviving longer as a political columnist than any journalist other than David Lawrence or Walter Lippmann.

Thompson's career, as well as her "perpetual dualism," ended on her death by a heart attack on January 30, 1961. So too did the strange dualism of her birth dates. Per her instructions the date of birth provided on her gravestone lists the year not as 1894 as she had so long insisted, but as 1893.

CONCLUSION: PRELUDE TO BOMBAST

One can scarcely disagree that Dorothy Thompson's career as a political commentator, whether as correspondent, broadcaster, or activist, was remarkable. She reminds us of the words to the Country-Western ditty, "I was country when country wasn't cool." Thompson was a feminist pioneer in political commentary when feminism wasn't cool. As a foreign correspondent, bureau chief, columnist, and broadcaster she opened professional pathways in political commentary that few, if any, women had ever trod before. Yet, she receives scant mention for doing so; for example, former ABC and CBS news correspondent Marlene

Sanders, in her tribute to the "women of television news," writes only that Thompson "didn't stay with broadcasting" (Sanders and Rock, 1988, 10).

Thompson also leaves another legacy to political commentary, albeit one corrupted by many of its current practitioners. Dorothy Thompson was not reluctant to raise her voice, right or wrong. She did it breathlessly, relentlessly, publicly, and, yes, belligerently. She did so not in the manner of a professional wrestler, an "in-your-face" athlete, a bombastic political talk show host, or a late-night television interviewer—each putting on a show simply for the sake of monopolizing the limelight. Rather, her Cassandra-like style and prophesies derived from a belief that important matters needed to be addressed, not ignored; important threats confronted, not ignored; important truths heeded, not ignored.

More than three decades following her death, there are few such political commentators. Dorothy Thompson erred, then reversed, her political observations. Granted, the prognosticating flip-flop is a polished art of contemporary political pundits, but unlike Thompson they make no apologies for their errors. So bombastic is their style that accuracy is a secondary consideration. The end of hyperpolitical commentary is not as Dorothy Thompson practiced it, not to awaken citizens to, and enlarge, the world in which they live. The message is not Thompson's Cassandra-like, "Look, look out there!," but a narrowing, self-centered appeal, "Look, look at me!"

REFERENCES

Selected Works by Dorothy Thompson

The New Russia. New York: Henry Holt, 1928.
"*I Saw Hitler!*" New York: Farrar and Rinehart, 1932.
Essentials of Democracy. Vol. 1, *The American Scene.* New York: Town Hall, 1938.
     Vol. 2, *The European Scene.* New York: Town Hall, 1938.
Once on Christmas. London: Oxford University Press, 1938.
Refugees: Anarchy or Organization? New York: Random House, 1938.
Let the Record Speak. Boston: Houghton Mifflin, 1939.
Listen, Hans. Boston: Houghton Mifflin, 1942.
Let the Promise Be Fulfilled. New York: American Christian Palestine Committee, 1946.
The Developments of Our Times. Deland, FL: John B. Stetson University Press, 1948.
The Crisis of the West. Toronto: University of Toronto Press, 1955.
The Courage to Be Happy. Boston: Houghton Mifflin, 1957.

Selected Critical Works about Dorothy Thompson

Block, M., ed. "Thompson, Dorothy." In *Current Biography 1940*, 798–801. New York: H. W. Wilson Co., 1940.
Fang, I. E. "Dorothy Thompson." In *Those Radio Commentators!*, 131–49. Ames, IA: Iowa State University Press, 1977.
Fisher, C. "Dorothy Thompson, Cosmic Force." In *The Columnists*, 16–51. New York: Howell, Soskin, 1944.

Kennedy, J. S. "Global Lady." In *Molders of Opinion*, edited by D. Bulman, 13–24. Milwaukee: Bruce Publishing, 1945.

Kurth, *American Cassandra: The Life of Dorothy Thompson*. Boston: Little, Brown, 1990.

McKerns, J. P., ed. "Thompson, Dorothy." In *Biographical Dictionary of American Journalism*, 698–700. New York: Greenwood Press, 1989.

Sanders, M. K. *Dorothy Thompson: A Legend in Her Time*. Boston: Houghton Mifflin, 1973.

Seehan, V. *Dorothy and Red*. Boston: Houghton Mifflin, 1963.

"Thompson, Dorothy (Mrs. Sinclair Lewis)." In *National Cyclopedia of American Biography*, 35–36. New York: James T. White, 1938.

Selected General Works

Desmond, R. W. *Crisis and Conflict: World News Reporting between Two Wars 1920–1940*. Iowa City, IA: University of Iowa Press, 1982.

Kluger, R. *The Paper: The Life and Death of the New York Herald Tribune*. New York: Vintage Books, 1986.

McLuhan, M. *Understanding Media*. New York: Signet, 1964.

Metcalfe, P. *1933*. New York: Harper and Row, 1988.

Sanders, M., and M. Rock. *Waiting for Prime Time: The Women of Television News*. New York: Harper and Row, 1988.

Shirer, W. L. *The Rise and Fall of the Third Reich*. New York: Simon and Schuster, 1960.

Swanberg, W. A. *Luce and His Empire*. New York: Dell, 1972.

MIKE (MYRON LEON) WALLACE
(May 9, 1918–)

The Political Commentator as Grand Inquisitor

It is late on any Sunday evening in the spring of 1957. Television viewers gaze at a dark screen illuminated only by a light shining in the eyes of someone who appears to be as uncomfortable as if he were squirming on a seat in the inter-rogation room of a local police station. Slightly off camera, barely visible in the darkened shroud, looms a seated figure, a haze of cigarette smoke curling above his head. Through the gloom the figure barks questions. Under the spotlight the "guest" fidgets for a response.

Depending upon the television viewer's point of view, the unfolding drama is "stimulating," "fresh," and "candid"; or it is "savage," "ruthless," and "humorless." It is "The Mike Wallace Interview," a controversial weekly hour of one-on-one confrontations between an interrogator and a celebrity "guest"— a film star, a U.S. senator, the head of the American Communist party, the Grand Wizard of the Ku Klux Klan, or some other hapless victim. The show, which ran for eighteen months, had healthy television ratings and made a former B-minus high school student and unseen narrator of a popular radio drama, "The Lone Ranger," America's Grand Inquisitor. Thereafter, Mike Wallace would have his ups and downs in the television industry, but he would never again go unnoticed.

FITS AND STARTS IN SHAPING A TELEVISION PERSONA IDENTITY

The 1950s and early 1960s, remembered as the Golden Age of Television, constituted a period marked by tremendous growth and innovation. The major networks clamored to produce news programs that fit the limited sound, video, and time constraints of television. In addition, diverse program genres were produced for television: dramas, Westerns, situation comedies, game shows, talk shows, television newsreels, and documentaries. The television industry was revolutionizing American life, and throughout this time, Mike Wallace was a part of the evolving new medium.

In the summer of 1939, when Wallace entered professional broadcasting, it was a world far removed from the power, glamour, and big network productions he would later come to know. All the appeal was on the older medium of radio. The Great Depression had created a larger audience for radio's free entertain-ment; the popular programs of this period reflected a need for diversion and escape. By contrast, television was viewed as nothing more than an experiment.

Even more to the point, broadcast journalism was not accepted as a legitimate profession. The networks did have regular newscasts, but these were more like brief updates read from the wire copy than full fledged reports and analysis. Television stations did not, by and large, employ full-time reporters to cover the day's news. Instead, people relied on newspapers for in-depth information on local issues and events. In September 1938, with Hitler threatening Europe, the Columbia Broadcasting System (CBS) and the National Broadcasting Company (NBC) sent broadcasts from abroad to the United States to report on the situation in Europe. While he was in Europe, Edward R. Murrow (q.v.) and his staff of reporters began to transmit eyewitness accounts of the events in World War II. But, that great pioneering effort had little impact on Mike Wallace, who had just graduated from college.

In 1939, while many Americans were concerned about the war, Mike Wallace was working at a small radio station in Grand Rapids, Michigan. The Grand Rapids' station, WOOD, hired Wallace as an announcer. According to Wallace, the citizens in the area took an isolationist view that the war in Europe would not impinge on the security of America (Wallace with Gates, 1984). So his broadcasting was more parochial—reporting community affairs, moderating quiz shows, and reading commercials. This mixing of reporting and entertainment characterized his work until 1955.

Unlike many of the major figures who provided political commentary in the twentieth century, Mike Wallace did not initially develop strong journalistic skills. He had worked on a number of different projects during his early career. While in high school, he was involved in many activities, and he worked at numerous part-time jobs to put himself through college. The trend at the time was to pursue a life involving various paths. His life lead him into a career that contained at least three phases.

Mike Wallace was one of four children of a wholesale grocer, and later an insurance broker, Frank Wallace, and Tina (Sharfman) Wallace. Born Myron Leon Wallace in Brookline, Massachusetts, on May 9, 1918, he soon was known simply as Mike Wallace. Wallace was born and grew up in a community that could be viewed as a hotbed of overachievers. In addition to Wallace, John F. Kennedy, Leonard Bernstein, and Barbara Walters called Brookline home.

While he was in high school, Wallace developed a severe case of acne, which was painful and disfiguring, that persisted into his early manhood. The acne would leave scars that later enhanced his abrasive tone and his demeanor in interviews. Critics would later characterize his face as that of a "pock marked, prize fighter" (Wallace with Gates, 1984, 12). According to Wallace, the acne was the only painful memory of his childhood, and even it served him well in the end. Wallace left Brookline with fond memories of his years at Brookline High School, where he had been involved in public speaking, the drama society, the school newspaper, and the tennis team and had carried a respectable, albeit hardly scholarly, B-minus average. He entered the University of Michigan in Ann Arbor with the intention of earning a degree in English; instead, during his sophomore year, Wallace decided that speech and broadcasting would be his emphasis. He concentrated on the fundamentals of broadcasting, and in the spring of 1939 he earned his B.A degree. This led to his job as an announcer for WOOD in Grand Rapids, a station owned by a furniture company and a laundry.

Mike Wallace left Grand Rapids after only nine months to join WXYZ in Detroit, a larger station, where Wallace took on a more ambitious role. WXYZ originated broadcasts from coast to coast, airing some of the most popular and innovative programs of that era. He was not only an announcer for the news broadcasts, he was also involved as an announcer, a narrator and sometimes an actor, with the radio entertainment programs, such as "The Green Hornet" and "The Lone Ranger." Wallace finally departed WXYZ for a brief stint at the Chicago *Sun*, did some radio acting, and narrated the most popular radio soap operas of the age: "Ma Perkins," "Road of Life," and "Guiding Light," which has survived on television to this day. He joined the U.S. armed forces in 1943, where he was trained as a communications officer, and served in Australia and in the Philippines; he was discharged in 1946 as a lieutenant junior grade (Wallace with Gates, 1984).

After service in the U.S. Navy during World War II, Wallace returned to Chicago to various jobs in radio broadcasting, from news and public affairs to soap operas and game shows. During this phase of his career, he continued to broaden his scope of activities; he worked on a program called "The Air Edition of the Chicago Sun," moderated a popular radio quiz show called "Famous Names," and read commercials for various products on such children's shows as "Super Circus."

While Mike Wallace was juggling these various jobs, his personal life was at a crossroads; by 1947, his marriage to Norma Kaplan, with whom he had two children (Peter and Christopher), was essentially over. While working on "Famous Names," Wallace met and eventually married Buff Cobb, the granddaughter of Irvin S. Cobb, the humorist. This union would guide Wallace's career farther away from journalism and more toward entertainment. He and Buff Cobb were cohosts of a radio talk show from a Chicago nightclub. In 1951 CBS-TV persuaded Wallace and Cobb to move their program to New York for a national telecast. The show, "Mike and Buff," displayed the couple's bantering and quick wit but scarcely foreshadowed that Wallace would ever become a key political communicator of his generation. The bantering turned out to be not only a part of the show, but also a part of their lives. The show, along with the marriage, ended in 1954.

Throughout the early 1950s, Mike Wallace continued to develop multiple facets in his career. He enjoyed the freedom of exploring new television ideas, a luxury during the early days of television. He was host of several television shows, "I'll Buy That" and "The Big Surprise," as well as radio ventures. One of his radio ventures, "Stage Struck," a documentary about Broadway, led to a stint as an actor on Broadway. Wallace not only had his debut on Broadway, but he, along with two friends, produced a theater comedy.

His career had given Wallace two things: an adventure and a source of income. What it had not given him was a clear sense of direction and respect as a journalist. He continued to search for a clear direction from August 1955 until September 1963. During this period, Mike Wallace met and married his third wife, Lorraine Perigord, and began his journey, although not directly, back to the world of journalism and into political commentary. Wallace joined with Ted Catt and Ted Yates to work for the DuMont television station in New York as its evening news reader. In the summer of 1956, Yates decided to replace the 11:00 P.M. newscast with "Night Beat," a hard-hitting interview program. This show was the forerunner of "The Mike Wallace Interview," which earned him the nicknames of "Malice Mike," "Mike Malice," and the "Grand Inquisitor" (Gates, 1978, 272). Looking back on the experience, Wallace writes,

> Our guests would be thoroughly, painstakingly researched and then, once we got them on the air, I'd go at them as hard as I could. If they appeared to be hiding behind evasive answers, I'd press them . . . to come clean. If, in response to pressure, they became embarrassed or irritated or sullen, I'd try to exploit that mood instead of retreating into amiable reassurance . . . that was the formula . . . candor . . . in the context of American television in the mid-fifties, this was revolutionary. (Wallace with Gates, 1984, 23–24)

Mike Wallace's boldness and candor, as he so aptly describes his formula, was highly praised at the start of both "Night Beat" and its successor. However, by the summer of 1958, his candor was labeled as sensationalism, and the American Broadcasting Company (ABC) canceled the show. Over the next four years, Wallace took a variety of jobs in television. He anchored a local New York nightly television newscast, spent time with the Westinghouse Broadcasting Company, and returned to his television celebrity role, hosting game shows and talk shows. By the early 1960s, the bulk of his income came from commercials. This would be his primary source of income until the summer of 1962.

In the desolate summer of 1962, Mike Wallace's older son, Peter, was killed when he fell while on a camping trip in the mountains. His son's death caused Wallace to pause and rethink his life. He vowed that he would renew his commitment to return to serious broadcast journalism. However, he knew that he would have to quit his lucrative job as pitchman for Parliament cigarettes. After he quit, Wallace began contacting the major networks about correspondent positions. They all refused to make him an offer. In March 1963, Wallace decided to accept a position at KTLA in Los Angeles.

In the meantime, a rumor circulated in the trade that Wallace had decided to buy up the time for his remaining commercial work to keep his ads off the air (Wallace with Gates, 1984, 85). Hearing this and viewing it as a sign of Wallace's total commitment to journalism, executives at CBS offered Wallace a position at CBS News in New York. His life was finally on course to become a "serious journalist."

UNLEASHING THE GRAND INQUISITOR

Observers familiar with Mike Wallace's broadcasting reputation met his arrival in the CBS News division with skepticism. Wallace was a forty-five-year-old television celebrity who had made his career outside the bounds of conventional journalism. The transition from entertainer to journalist would not be an easy one. Wallace spent the first few months working on modest assignments and interviewing guests on the CBS radio series, "Personal Close-Up." His performance on radio paid off; the name of the program was changed to "Mike Wallace at Large" in recognition of a job well done and his enhanced stature as a broadcast journalist (Wallace with Gates, 1984). Wallace's interview program remained a staple of CBS radio programming for over two decades.

Other assignments on radio, live reporting on breaking events, and filling in as anchor on the local New York newscast prepared Wallace for the position that would be the catalyst for his new career as a television commentator: anchor of the "CBS Morning News." The "Morning News" was the latest in a long line of CBS efforts to find a successful television formula to compete with NBC's innovative and successful "Today" show. However, all CBS efforts to gain respectable ratings against "Today" had failed—including the one to convert newsman Walter Cronkite (q.v.) into an entertainer talking to a puppet! In 1963, when CBS launched a midmorning, 9:00 A.M. EDT news program, it did not schedule it in a time slot directly opposite "Today." To attract a wide following, CBS producers flooded the "Morning News" with consumer-oriented news and features for women; moreover, the show dealt with controversial, daring topics: marital infidelity, birth control, venereal disease, menopause, and so on. Drawing on his experience from working with various types of programming, Wallace was able to fit in well, and he projected the confidence and poise of a veteran anchor (Slater, 1988).

An anchor's stature and pay are a generous cut above those of a correspondent, but in the summer of 1966, Mike Wallace gave up the stature and the pay to return to the lesser role of a CBS correspondent. He felt he had no choice. When the producer of the "CBS Morning News" departed in 1965, CBS executives attempted to capitalize on the popularity of the "Morning News" by slotting it in direct competition with "Today" at 7:00 A.M. EDT. Wallace protested, but to no avail. After a year of dismal ratings, Wallace gave up the onerous task of arising in the middle of the night to go to work; he returned to the ranks of general-assignment correspondent.

For the next few years, Wallace covered a variety of stories, including Richard Nixon's campaigns for Republican candidates during the 1966 midterm election. This was the beginning of Richard Nixon's comeback after losing the 1960 presidential and 1962 California gubernatorial elections. In the fall of 1967,

Mike Wallace was one of the few reporters who took an interest in Richard Nixon's efforts. In the winter months of 1968, Nixon was winning numerous Republican primaries, and Wallace was excited about the prospect of becoming the new White House correspondent, covering a Nixon administration. After reporting on Nixon's performance in the 1966 midterm elections, Mike Wallace had a two-month tour of duty in Vietnam and several weeks in Israel after the Six-Day War. While abroad, Wallace interviewed Nixon, thereby reaffirming his credentials on foreign policy. After he returned to the United States in the summer of 1967, Mike Wallace awaited his opportunity to travel with the Nixon campaign, which he did through the Republican National Convention and Richard Nixon's nomination.

Mike Wallace just might have replaced Dan Rather (q.v.), the political commentator who converted the job of White House correspondent into a celebrity position, were it not for CBS' creation of a novel format for political programming on television, a televised magazine. Don Hewitt, the creator and producer of the new show, "60 Minutes," who had earned his spurs working with Fred W. Friendly and Edward R. Murrow on "See It Now" in the 1950s, contacted Mike Wallace about an assignment as a correspondent on the new program. But Wallace had set his sights on the prestigious White House assignment; he had never worked in Washington and wanted to add the assignment to his list of accomplishments.

When Richard Nixon won the presidency in 1968, Mike Wallace faced a decision. However, it was not, as he thought it would be, whether to become CBS chief White House correspondent or to move to "60 Minutes" and work with cohost Harry Reasoner. Instead, it was whether to go with "60 Minutes" or accept a position offered by the Nixon administration as White House press secretary. Wallace was flattered and tempted. He sought out Don Hewitt's advice. Hewitt cut to the heart of the matter, namely, Wallace's ego: "That doesn't make any sense. You don't want to go from being Mike Wallace to being a press secretary, even a White House press secretary. It's the kind of job a nobody takes so that he can become a somebody" (Slater, 1988, 246). That sealed it; Wallace thanked the president and joined "60 Minutes."

Mike Wallace had developed a unique style of interviewing. His combative, adversarial, almost accusatory questioning was in stark contrast to that of his cohost, Harry Reasoner. Wallace displayed a rugged disposition. His thorough knowledge of the issues being debated and his moxie to force the points in interviews were his trademark. It had not been a mistake to go with the assignment of "60 Minutes." A scant six years, had Wallace remained with the president, would reveal that a job in the Nixon White House would have ruined Mike Wallace's chances of ever being a reputable, let alone a pioneering, political commentator.

The CBS public affairs program, "60 Minutes," worked its way from obscurity to one of the most respected programs on television. It made stars of its on-camera correspondents. When asked about the style that he had developed as a journalist, apropos to the "malice Mike" reference, Wallace explained in an interview, "You don't ask a nasty question in order to make somebody uncomfortable. You ask a carefully researched, perhaps an uncomfortable question because you're trying to get close to the bone, to get close to the truth" (James, 1984, 312).

According to Wallace, his style of interviewing "has probably been useful, on balance, in exploring or understanding things that [he], as proxy for the audience, wants to illuminate" (James, 1984, 312). Yet, the subjects of Wallace's interviews are often offended by his seemingly rough handling. In his quest "to get close to the bone . . . the truth," (James, 1984, 312), Mike Wallace has taken on heads of states, bureaucrats, legislators, leaders of social organizations, political celebrities, and private citizens embroiled in political or social controversies. Whether friend or foe, Wallace claims to engage in tactics designed only to reveal the truth.

For example, in an interview with Ronald Reagan during the 1980 presidential election, Wallace posed a series of controversial questions to the candidate and his longtime friend. His interrogation of Ronald Reagan did not go unnoticed by the future first lady, Nancy Reagan. Nancy Reagan and Mike Wallace had met in the early 1940s, when Wallace was working radio jobs in Chicago (Wallace with Gates, 1984, 202). Wallace met Nancy Reagan, then Nancy Davis, because he worked with her mother at the radio station. Nancy Reagan hinted, not so subtly, that her forty-year friendship with "Mike" would be threatened if Wallace posed his probing questions to Ronald Reagan in 1980, then aired the controversial answers during the lead-in to CBS' coverage of the Republican National Convention, where Ronald Reagan would be named the Republican nominee. In reflecting on the incident, Wallace wrote,

> I understood his resentment, and, in fact, after we broadcast the interview, it occurred to me that . . . I had taken a cheap shot at [Ronald] Reagan. Not that I had in any way misrepresented him; . . . (but) I realized that I could not recall any major American politician . . . who at one time or another had not said something reckless or foolish. (Wallace with Gates, 1984, 216)

Mike Wallace does not apologize for his style or his journalistic tactics. It is clearly not the gentlemanly fisticuffs practiced in an earlier era of televised question-and-answer sessions between reporters and politicians such as those viewed on "Meet the Press" created by Martha Rountree and Lawrence E. Spivak (q.v.), or even in the more contemporary manner of Phil Donahue (q.v.). Yet, it is a far cry from the mud wrestling mayhem that President Ronald Reagan once in jest attributed to John McLaughlin (q.v.). Rather, Mike Wallace is an inquisitor, a persistent, combative prosecuting attorney unwilling to let witnesses off the hook, with or without the protection of the Fifth Amendment.

To be sure, in many respects, Wallace's quest for respect as a journalist has caused him to go to extreme lengths to get a story. Several of his critics have accused him and the producers of "60 Minutes" of not always presenting both sides of an issue and not thoroughly researching a topic (Bar-Illan, 1991). Mike Wallace answers his critics by affirming that "60 Minutes" has been on the air for more than twenty-five years and "remains far and away [one of] the most watched and among the respected news series on American television" (Bar-Illan, 1991, 19). His comments are accurate; the show has gone through staff stages, and correspondents such as Harry Reasoner, Diane Sawyer, and Dan Rather (q.v.) have come and gone, but the show has remained a strong forum in political commentary. With his drive for thought-provoking and controversial coverage, Mike Wallace has helped shape public discussion on numerous po-litical issues, such as heroin addiction, biological warfare, the rehabilitation of Vietnam veterans, and drug testing.

In defense of his free expression, Mike Wallace stresses his view of the function of free speech under our system of government. He contends that the rights of free speech allow him to do his job, and according to Wallace, the principle of free speech allows for open and public debate. From this perspec-tive, dispute is a welcome and necessary element to a free world. Mike Wallace subscribes to the philosophy that the public is best served when there is a system of open debate, which creates dissatisfaction with unacceptable conditions and embraces change to renew society and its members.

THE INQUISITION CONTINUES

As the 1990s passed their midpoint and a new century loomed, Mike Wallace continued to be known for his hard, relentless interview tactics on "60 Minutes." His inquisition cum commentary is a form of unfettered political analysis that was once the touchstone of a proud CBS tradition stretching from Elmer Davis (q.v.), to Edward R. Murrow, to Eric Sevareid (q.v.), to Howard K. Smith, to Walter Cronkite.

Mike Wallace's career as a broadcast journalist surpassed a half-century sev-eral years ago. "60 Minutes," the pioneering television newsmagazine with which Wallace's name has become synonymous, has been on the air almost three decades. It is doubtful that Wallace and "60 Minutes" together will sur-vive the passing of the twentieth century. Septuagenarian Wallace, although still up to the rigors of broadcast commentary via putting impertinent questions to the politically powerful, is weary of the controversies surrounding "60 Minutes": CBS' reluctance in 1995 to air an interview with a high-ranking executive of the tobacco industry which threatened to bring a lawsuit against the network (Grossman, 1996), a reprimand by CBS News of Wallace in 1994 for secretly taping a freelance writer helping the correspondent to produce a story (Alter, 1995), and network flirtations with tabloid techniques in the face of mounting ratings competition (King, 1995).

Certainly, in the 1990s, Wallace and other "60 Minutes" correspondents have persisted in producing controversial and thought-provoking shows, covering a variety of topics. Yet, in certain respects, the once vibrant "60 Minutes" is showing signs of aging, more like seventy than sixty minutes in duration. With the loss of its ratings-building lead-in, telecasts of the National Football League, an edge has been removed from the seeming ratings invulnerability of "60 Minutes." Moreover, the television newsmagazine format is no longer novel. Imitators abound, some of which are successfully appealing to a generation of television viewers not even born when Mike Wallace grilled the nation's number one law enforcement officer, Attorney General Ramsey Clark, on September 24, 1968, on the debut of "60 Minutes." One of those, NBC's "Dateline" began a prime-time, head-to-head scheduling duel with "60 Minutes" in the 1996–1997 viewing season.

Thus, it is ironic that Mike Wallace, who made the shift from entertainer to journalist, yet never lost sight of the view that journalism should be entertaining in order to appeal to audiences, has come full circle and now faces again the same choice he has confronted so often in his career. Granted that the overlap is a fait accompli, what is the priority—to entertain or to inform? Perhaps the development of political commentary in the last third of the twentieth century has already answered the question: it is to entertain.

REFERENCES

Selected Works by Mike Wallace

The Art of Interviewing: Newsmen Discuss the Purpose and Value of the Live Interview. With C. Fandiman. Hollywood, CA: Center for Cassette Studies, 1955.
Mike Wallace Asks: Highlights from Forty-Six Controversial Interviews. New York: Simon and Schuster, 1958.
Close Encounters. With G. P. Gates. New York: William Morrow, 1984.

Selected Critical Works about Mike Wallace

Alter, J. "Blowing Smoke at CBS." *Newsweek*, December 4, 1995, 45.
Bar-Illan, D. " '60 Minutes' & the Temple Mount." *Commentary* 91 (February 1991): 17–25.
Brown, R. "Wallace Blasts Trend to Sensationalism." *Broadcasting*, 121, September 30, 1991, 73.
James, C. "The Grand Inquisitor." *Vogue*, 174, September 1984, 312–13.
Moritz, C., ed. "Wallace, Mike." In *Current Biography 1977*, 417–20. New York: H. W. Wilson, 1978.
"Wallace, Mike." *Facts on File*, 54, December 31, 1984, 1015.

Selected General Works

Boyer, P. J. *Who Killed CBS?* New York: Random House, 1988.
Gates, G. P. *Air Time: The Inside Story of CBS News.* New York: Harper and Row, 1978.
Grossman, L. K. "CBS, '60 Minutes' and the Unseen Interview." *Columbia Journalism Review* 34 (January/February 1996): 39–51.

Joyce, E. *Prime Times, Bad Times*. New York: Doubleday, 1988.

King, L. Interview with Tom Brokaw, Mike Wallace, and Barbara Walters. "Larry King Live," CNN, June 17, 1995.

Slater, R. *This Is . . . CBS*. Englewood Cliffs, NJ: Prentice-Hall, 1988.

THEODORE H. (HAROLD) WHITE
(May 6, 1915–May 15, 1986)

Chronicler of Political Campaigns

As a student at Harvard in the 1930s, Theodore ("Teddy") White studied to become a professor of history. Instead, by his good fortune, he became a chronicler of politics. He reenergized political journalism in the 1960s. But, when his good fortune ran out a decade later, White's youthful aspirations returned to haunt him. The chronicler tried to combine cultural history with political narrative. The energy drained away. Today White's contributions as a chronicler, often imitated but never duplicated, have yielded to the works of cultural critics—to the detriment of political commentary.

"I KNEW I WASN'T GOING HOME TO BE A PROFESSOR"

In 1891 the runaway son of a rabbi from Pinsk, Belorussia, arrived in Boston. David White, sixteen at the time, was among the first wave of Russian Jews to immigrate to the United States. He worked as a peddler, taught himself English, went to YMCA night school and Northeastern University. David became a neighborhood lawyer whose clients were penniless. In spite of a poverty-level income, David managed with his wife, Mary Winkeller, to rear a family of four. Their son, Theodore Harold White, was born in Boston on May 6, 1915, and grew up in the Jewish ghetto of Dorchester. From both parents, Teddy learned a lesson about the exploitive nature of capitalism; from his ambitious mother, he also learned the lesson that education is a ticket out of poverty. So, when the first lesson hit home with the arrival of the Great Depression in 1929, Teddy persevered in implementing the second and managed to get through Boston Latin School and graduated in 1932.

Harvard University accepted Teddy White for admission, but he had no funds. White sold newspapers, jumping on and off streetcars to hawk his copies to trolley riders. At the end of the trolley run, he collected the used papers, refolded them, and resold them to the distributor for a few more pennies. After two years, Harvard awarded White a scholarship; he also won a scholarship set aside for newspaper boys. To Harvard Teddy White went, but not as most students do. White was a rare commuter student; each day he came to and left the campus without the advantages that accrue from taking part in Harvard's social and intellectual life. Harvard "was a classroom and a way station, little more, often more wounding than nourishing" (Halberstam, 1979, 72).

Yet, at Harvard, Teddy White acquired a mentor, a young professor of history, John King Fairbank. Fairbank, who would later become a noted authority on

China, passed his boundless enthusiasm for Chinese studies on to White. In 1938 White graduated summa cum laude with a B.A. specializing in Chinese history and Oriental languages. In Fairbank's judgment, despite Teddy's acute intelligence and energy, there was scant likelihood that White, a Jew, could crack the diplomatic service's strait-laced demands. Instead, Fairbank advised Teddy that he would make an excellent scholar or journalist. Although White had been set on becoming a professor of Chinese history, at his graduation, Fairbank gave White an old typewriter and several letters of introduction to take with him to China.

White devoted the summer of 1938 to improving his colloquial Chinese at the University of Michigan. With a Sheldon Traveling Scholarship, an award financing deserving students to take a leisurely trip around the world, White set off and got as far as Chungking, China, in April 1939. Fairbank's enthusiasm for the country had been infectious. White resigned the fellowship and took a job with the Chinese Nationalist government's information ministry (Desmond, 1984). He freelanced for the Boston *Globe* and Manchester *Guardian* as well and earned a $50-per-month retainer as a stringer for *Time* magazine.

In September 1939, Teddy White took a leave of absence from the information ministry and "set off for the Yellow River in the north, and the province of Shansi, where a battle was going on" (White, 1978, 89). The "battle" that he provided an eyewitness account of in news dispatches was the Japanese bombing and burning of Peking where 3,000 people died: "Once I had seen that, I knew I wasn't going home to be a professor" (Moritz, 1977, 433).

White's dispatches for *Time* met with favor and, in a rarity for the magazine, many of them were published without editorial changes. Moreover, when one was published with White identified as the reporter, he became the first *Time* foreign correspondent to rate a byline: "White wrote in a manner which [*Time* publisher Henry] Luce above all could appreciate, showing the sympathy of one who loved China and was moved by the pounding the Chinese were taking" (Swanberg, 1972, 264). In 1941, after visiting Chungking and meeting Theodore White for the first time, Henry Luce put White on regular salary and took him back to New York to the magazine's headquarters. It was the beginning of a long, sometimes intimate, sometimes bitter, relationship between the powerful publisher and intelligent, energetic, passionate, and hardheaded correspondent. Through the years they moved through friendship, an acrimonious breakup, and a welcome reconciliation.

Initially, following America's entry into World War II and White's return to Asia from New York, the friendship of the publisher and the correspondent was easygoing. White covered the war for *Time* and was an eyewitness to the Japanese surrender aboard the U.S.S. *Missouri* in Tokyo Bay in 1945. In the interim, he had become chief of *Time*'s China bureau. White covered the Honan famine, the Fourteenth Air Force's flights over the "hump" of China, and the opening of the Burma Road. He flew aboard bombing raids over Hong Kong, the Hainan Islands, and Lashio; and he flew with the Flying Tigers of Claire Chennault. White won an Air Medal in 1944 as the only newsman who flew on a raid over Formosa.

Most important, White reported the internal struggles within Chiang Kai-shek's ruling Kuomingtang party (Desmond, 1984). It was White's growing disenchantment with Chiang Kai-shek's government, especially the incompetence, "bungling, corruption, and profiteering" during the Honan famine of 1942–1943, that led to a break with Luce (Knightley, 1975, 277). White rode through the province on horseback, whispering to his mount to keep moving lest starving mobs kill it for food. White later wrote, "The country is dying almost before my eyes" (Halberstam, 1979, 78). Although *Time* published White's outraged eyewitness dispatch of March 22, 1943, on the famine, editors cut the report to 750 words and eliminated the criticism. By the war's end, *Time*'s annoyed editors had taken White off political assignments.

There were, however, deeper reasons for the Luce-White break than simply Luce's admiration and support for Chiang Kai-shek's Nationalist China and White's criticism of Chiang. In what would prove to be an ironic contrast in White's later career, in the years surrounding World War II, the future chronicler of presidential campaigns believed that transcendent cultural, economic, and social forces—*not* Great Men—dominated history. Luce, however, was a hero worshiper, Chiang was his hero, and White's dismissal of Chiang was almost as big an irritant to Luce as the correspondent's criticism of the Kuomingtang leader. The smoldering differences came to a head in 1946. White knew that Luce no longer wanted him to be in China, and he asked for a reassignment. When Moscow appeared in the offing, White jumped at the chance. But Luce dashed those hopes, informing White through an intermediary that he must accept any assignment the company gave him. White resigned. Then, with former *Time* colleague and would-be sweetheart Annalee Jacoby, White wrote and published *Thunder Out of China* (1946), a best-selling critique of Kuomingtang China and U.S. support for Chiang's Nationalist regime. After White departed from *Time*, he and Henry Luce would not be reconciled for ten years, chiefly at the insistence of mutual friends. Thereafter, White contributed frequently to Luce's *Life* magazine.

FROM *THUNDER OUT OF CHINA* TO *MAKING OF THE PRESIDENT*

In 1947 Theodore White turned down an attractive offer from the *Saturday Evening Post* to serve as senior editor of the *New Republic*. The timing proved disastrous. The *New Republic* magazine had once been the voice of progressive liberals; Walter Lippmann (q.v.) was a staff member and John Dewey (q.v.) was a contributing writer. By 1948 the *New Republic* was virtually a campaign organ for Henry Wallace's Progressive party bid for the presidency, a wholly different brand of progressive politics and reform: "a magazine committed to, or dominated by, a single man, as most sectarian magazines are, is as rigidly restricted in opinion as those magazines which depend on the marketplace and profit'' (White, 1978, 267). Thus, having left *Time*, a magazine dominated by Henry Luce, White left the *New Republic*, a magazine committed to another Henry, namely, Wallace, a scant six months after joining the publication. White opted for freelance work and contributed features to several magazines: *Saturday Review of Literature*, *Harper's*, and others. He also published a second book as the editor of *The Stilwell Papers* (1948), the private papers of General Joseph Stilwell.

In 1948 Theodore White made a personal decision that enlarged the growing gulf between himself and his Jewish traditions. His collaboration with Annalee Jacoby on *Thunder Out of China* had disrupted and eventually destroyed the couple's budding romantic relationship. Two years later, White was engaged to marry Nancy Bean, a researcher he had met when he was still with *Time*. She did not want to be married in a synagogue, and he did not want to be married in a church, so they settled on a civil service. They later had a daughter and a son, who was named David Fairbank in honor of White's mentor, John King Fairbank. The marriage lasted until 1971 when the couple divorced. In 1974 White married a historian, Beatrice Kevitt Hofstadter, at a time when his career too was turning toward pursuits of cultural history.

After his marriage to Nancy Bean, he and Nancy moved to Paris. White's intention was to make Europe a stopover on his way back to China. However, the imminent birth of the Whites' daughter and their limited resources required a change in plans. White took a position as a correspondent with the Overseas News Agency only to learn that the agency was almost bankrupt. When the agency fell six months arrears in paying White's salary, he quit. The Whites lived on the proceeds of his work as the European correspondent for *Reporter* magazine and sales of *Thunder Out of China*. When that financial cache dwindled, and the Whites' son was born in 1951, White began to write another book, the story of Europe's postwar economic and social recovery. Published in 1953, *Fire in the Ashes: Europe in Midcentury* won critical plaudits and became a best-seller; it even earned White a promotional appearance on Edward R. Murrow's (q.v.) prestigious ''Person to Person'' television show.

But, as White recalled in his 1978 memoir, writing his second hugely successful book under the pressures of a hand-to-mouth existence took a toll on his marriage: ''One of the faults of my first wife, Nancy, was her strange yet happy belief that with enough yellow paper, enough typewriter ribbons and enough coddling, any man can write a successful book.'' Since White's first two books had provided the family's financial wherewithal, ''it seemed elementary to her that as soon as she could have me seated once more before the typewriter to write another, all would be well'' and the family could live ''in style''—journeying periodically with children, two servant cooks, and family to the Riviera (1978, 370–71). The another-book-in-a-pinch approach led, in part, to White's varied success as a novelist in his later years.

After his return to the United States in 1953, Theodore White began covering politics for major magazines, first, as a national political correspondent of the *Reporter*, then, as the senior national political correspondent for *Collier's*. As a political correspondent, White started making the contacts that would stand him in good stead when he undertook the project that would make a major contribution to political commentary in the 1960s and 1970s, the *Making of the President* series. However, in moving to *Collier's* the timing proved as unfortunate as his move to the *New Republic* in 1948. In the mid-1950s publishers, such as Crowell-Collier, of major mass circulation magazines were threatened by the inroads of television. In 1956 White, as part of the editorial staff, had the task of analyzing how *Collier's* could meet television's pressures. His assignment came just as he was working on an elaborate feature piece reporting the behind-the-scenes aspects of the 1956 presidential campaign. In the end, *Collier's* folded late in the year anyway and White's feature, "The Making of the President—1956" was never published.

Yet, the 1956 effort sowed in Theodore H. White the seed of an idea that would grow and flourish:

> The idea was to follow a campaign from beginning to end. It would be written as a novel is written, with anticipated surprises as, one by one, early candidates vanish in the primaries until only two final jousters struggle for the prize in November. Moreover, it should be written as the story of a man in trouble, of the leader under the pressure of circumstances.
>
> The leader—and the circumstances. That was where the story lay. (White, 1978, 471)

The reporter who had dismissed Chiang Kai-shek as less important that the cultural, economic, and social forces that move a people would now focus, instead, on "the leader," first, "and the circumstances" as "where the story lay." White planned a twenty-year project of quadrennial documentary novels; they might be called "docunovels" in the contemporary parlance of presidential campaigns. Since "History is Story" and "Politics, in the process of becoming History," is the "story of a handful of men reaching for the levers of power," White planned to write politics, story, and history all at once (1978, 488).

Although Theodore White thought he had not only the germ but a gem of an idea, publishers were not so sure. In his 1978 autobiography, where he mixes referring to himself in the first and third person, he writes, "White peddled the idea of a book . . . from publisher to publisher for several weeks" (472). His regular publisher, William Sloane Associates, thought it a dreary subject but reluctantly agreed to publish the money-losing project out of a debt of gratitude; two other publishers agreed to do so only if either could publish future White novels to make up the losses. When a friend who was beginning a new publishing firm, a Harvard classmate of John F. Kennedy, expressed enthusiasm, White closed a deal. The rest, as the saying goes, is history.

POLITICAL CHRONICLE, YES, CULTURAL HISTORY, NO

The chronicler writes a chronological record of events, that is, acts arranged in the order of time of occurrence. The result is of necessity a linear narrative, a far cry from a nonlinear portrayal such as the one that appeared in the 1994 Academy Award nominated film, *Pulp Fiction*. There is little question that Theodore White's early excursions into the political commentary genre of his creation, the docunovel, were straightforward linear reconstructions of both the on-the-record and behind-the-scenes events of the 1960 and 1964 presidential campaigns. Critics gave high marks to White's chronicles. And, because of the work's quality, the identity of the electoral victor, or both, *The Making of the President 1960* won White a Pulitzer Prize for general nonfiction in 1962.

The success surrounding White's work changed the tenor of political commentary about presidential campaigns. Once dismissed by political scientists and journalists as little more than exercises in preaching to the choir that had little impact on electoral outcomes, campaigns gradually were accepted by scholars and reporters alike as important facets of political persuasion and change. White's approach to campaign analysis gave rise to numerous imitators and to the "Teddy White syndrome" of probing the backstage lives, manipulative techniques, and speculated effects of candidates, handlers, campaign strategists, image manipulators, and journalists.

White's method in 1960 was that of the straight chronicle. It was as if he had taken to heart the words of Wilkie Collins, the noted English novelist of the mid-nineteenth century, "to go far enough back at the beginning to avoid all impediments of retrospection in its course" (*The Woman in White*, New York, Harper & Brothers, 1860, 479). As Collins advised, White was scrupulous in 1960 in not imposing the outcome of the campaign on how it actually unfolded. As he later told an interviewer, April Koral:

> The whole secret in this business is overkill. You interview everyone you can talk to and then you use what is necessary to make the story. It's like being blindfolded while you go through a basket of black and red peas trying to pick one color. If I knew at the beginning of any presidential campaign what was going to happen, I could interview only twenty people to get my whole story. But I have to interview 150, 200 or 300 people during the campaign in order to get the proper stuff. (Moritz, 1977, 434)

White's statement is revealing. He is acutely aware that a political campaign, like politics generally, is made up of numerous actors in a cacophony of simultaneous, overlapping, sometimes complementary, sometimes contradictory activities that mutually affect one another. The chronicler's task is to observe, gather, and sort, then impose *after the fact* a narrative that selectively uses "what is necessary to make the story." The docunovel is, thus, neither a true nor false account, neither comprehensive nor complete. It is a version driven by whatever tragic, romantic, didactic, comic, or other novelist's imperative dictates (Burke, 1984).

At every stage of chronicle "overkill," the docunovelist makes choices. A crucial one is what sources to access, which ones to ignore. A distinguishing feature of White's approach was his incorporation in his campaign biographies of documents, interviews, and other behind-the-scenes material not readily accessible to others. Asked in 1983 how he achieved such access, White drew an analogy between seeking information and selling magazines door to door when he was working his way through Harvard: "Don't get discouraged. If you knock on 100 doors a day and you say, 'Lady, you want to buy a magazine?' you'll find one lady who says yes." By the same token, said White, "I have found that the best way of getting things is my direct and forthright asking for it" as "one of the major political writers in the country" (Langer, 1983, 62).

However, neither one who buys a magazine nor one who offers access is like picking colors blindfolded in a "basket of black and red peas." Political sources use entrée to control information flows, manage perceptions, and manufacture images. Hence, what the chronicler discovers and uses to "make the story," while seemingly of the campaign chronicler's own choosing, runs the risk of being something else, namely, the by-product of candidates' manipulations. It was White's seeming inability to grasp this not-so-subtle possibility, along with his novelist's selectivity, that brought his series of books on The Making of the President increasingly under criticism. For example, one critic charged White with reducing politics "to mere anecdotage—a literal *reductio ad absurdum*" so that "it was what White did *not* report that was significant" (Burgess, 1989, 330–31; emphasis in original). Historian Andrew Hacker wrote, "White treats political campaigns as if they adhered to an unchanging, almost Aristotelian formula. . . . We have the inside story but not the outside one" (1965, 112).

Publication of the third volume in White's series, *The Making of the President 1968*, furnished critics with additional grist for the mill. Many found fault with White for his not fully appreciating the tidal current of social change beneath the surface of the 1968 campaign, change underscored by the aftermath of the Tet offensive in Vietnam; the assassinations of Martin Luther King, Jr., and Robert Kennedy; the populist anger surrounding the third-party candidacy of George Wallace; the trauma of the Chicago Democratic National convention; and the "new politics" of compassion of antiwar demonstrators versus the "new politics" of technique during the campaign of the "new Nixon."

Four years later, while preparing his chronicle of the 1972 presidential campaign, White encountered a writing crisis. The novelist's device of the "leader under the pressure of circumstances," which had guided his reconstruction of earlier campaigns, failed him. By the time White was ready to go to press with *The Making of the President 1972*, the "leader," Richard Nixon, faced drastically altered "circumstances" in the wake of the unraveling scandal over the Watergate break-in. The ten pages White had allotted in his docunovel could not suffice; his solution, delaying publication for several weeks to add a prologue and two new chapters on Watergate, failed to allay criticism. Reviewers judged it equivalent to placing a bandaid over a massive head wound.

Theodore White was sensitive to the reviews of each volume in his series and to the fading luster of his career as a political analyst and commentator. He adjusted in a variety of ways. One was to discontinue the series, hence, there was no volume after 1972. Another was to turn his attention to analyzing the flaws in American politics that might account for the phenomenon of Richard Nixon; this yielded White's 1975 *Breach of Faith: The Fall of Richard Nixon.* He also turned to autobiography, *In Search of History: A Personal Adventure* (1978), and to a summing-up volume, *America in Search of Itself: The Making of the President, 1956–1980* (1982).

Following the critical acclaim of his Pulitzer Prize–winning first volume in his monumental series on presidential campaigning, then increasing critical dismissal thereafter, White tried to make adjustments in each successive volume. Looking back in 1973 he said, "When I did the first one, all I had to do was follow Kennedy, Humphrey and Nixon around. With each succeeding book I've had to have my social antennae out further. Now everything is broken loose. The old structures are falling" (Arnold, 1973, 33). As incorporated into his volumes, the "social antennae" consisted of encyclopedic details regarding cultural, economic, and social changes.

In the process, the crisp, succinct, disciplined writing of White's volume about the 1960 campaign gradually vanished. The style that had made him a crack reporter for *Time* in China, a style admirably suited to the perceptive coverage of unfolding chronology, yielded to increasingly heavy sociological prose— longer, more complex passages, academic hedging, and undisciplined writing. It is as though, as in Ernest Hemingway's case, the style manual of the *Kansas City Star* that restrained *The Sun Also Rises* (New York: Scribner's, 1926) had been replaced by a Marxian tract emulated in *To Have and Have Not* (New York: Scribner's, 1937).

It was Theodore White who first used the analogy of "Camelot," based upon Mrs. Kennedy's references to the myth, in describing the presidential administration and family of John F. Kennedy following the assassination in 1963 ("The Last Side of 'Camelot,' " 1995). In White's autobiographical account of how he selected the Camelot analogy, he quotes something Jacqueline Kennedy told him following her husband's death. Mrs. Kennedy, says White, asked the president's brother, Robert Kennedy, "What's the line between history and drama?" Ironically, that was the question Theodore White wrestled with throughout his career.

Critic Kenneth Burke argued that all life is drama (1974). Accounts of life, to be comprehensive, must include all elements of drama—actors, acts, agencies, scenes, and purposes. Yet, all such accounts are inevitably partial in that they select but one or two of those elements to describe life; in other words, they privilege a few in accounting for the whole. The line between unfolding history and its dramatic reconstruction is a shifting one; it moves depending upon what element, as in the case of White's writing docunovels, a historian-dramatist privileges in a narrative. As Theodore White extended his "social antennae," he buried campaign actors (leaders) and actions (events) in lengthy accounts of scenes (cultural, economic, and social circumstances), conflicting purposes (ulterior motives of campaigners), and agencies (manipulative practices). White's problem was that scenes, purposes, and agencies do not lend themselves to the linear, cause-effect treatment that defines a chronicle; instead, they require a recognition of an "infinite regression of causes" wherein "the precise attribution of causal conditions" lies "beyond the capacity of human intellect" and narrative capabilities (Cuzzort & King, 1980, 327–28).

White's mounting difficulties in chronicling successive presidential campaigns were inevitable. The chronicle at its best reports perceptively a sequence of events; to ask that it do more and analyze change (and *change* in change) pushes it beyond its narrative capacity. A reviewer of White's *America in Search of Itself* put it thus:

> White's problem is not, as has variously been proposed, that he has burned out, or sold out, or lost interest in his subject. It is rather that he did not push hard enough with the knowledge and intuition he has. . . . One suspects that the reason for this lies not in any deficiency in White's analytical abilities but rather in the kind of myopia characteristic of those required to criticize that to which they are indissolubly attached. (Nuechterlein, 1982, 34)

POLITICAL COMMENTARY MISSES TEDDY WHITE

"At some point, fashion usually discards once-popular writers," Teddy White told an interviewer. "If I'm going to be discarded by fashion because of the way I write, so be it. But I can't change the way I write. I don't want to" (Cockshutt, 1981, 95). No, Teddy White could not change the way he wrote; he was a chronicler. But he *did* try to change; he tried to write as a cultural historian. In the process, he increasingly reduced his chronicled campaigners to creatures of circumstances, imposing on events not the model of heroic mythology critics say he abused but a set of causal cultural, economic, and social categories whose effects proved unfathomable.

By his death, on May 15, 1986, authentic chronicles of campaigns, Teddy White's chief contribution to political commentary, had been replaced by other types of "fashionable" coverage. Instead of narrating campaigns, coverage arbitrates them (Kondracke, 1995). Instead of accepting that "politics is politics, to be valued as itself, not because it is 'like' or 'really is' something else" (Crick, 1962, 12), arbitration coverage reduces politics to the sensational, trivial, negative, biased, and corrupt. It is a politics not of White's "the leader—and the circumstances" but of the Liar, the Lie, the Lied About, and the Lied To. That is why political commentary, although he is no longer fashionable, misses the Teddy White of *Thunder Out of China*, *Fire in the Ashes*, and *The Making of the President 1960*.

REFERENCES

Selected Works by Theodore White

Thunder Out of China. With A. Lee. New York: William Sloane, 1946.
The Stilwell Papers. Editor. New York: William Sloane, 1948.
Fire in the Ashes. New York: William Sloane, 1953.
The Making of the President 1960. New York: Atheneum, 1961.
The Making of the President 1964. New York: Atheneum, 1965.
China: The Roots of Madness. New York: Norton, 1968.
The Making of the President 1968. New York: Atheneum, 1969.
The Making of the President 1972. New York: Atheneum, 1973.
Breach of Faith: The Fall of Richard Nixon. New York: Atheneum, 1975.
In Search of History: A Personal Adventure. New York: Harper and Row, 1978.
America in Search of Itself: The Making of the President, 1956–1980. New York: Harper and Row, 1982.
"The Last Side of 'Camelot.' " *Dallas Morning News*, July 16, 1995, 1 J, 10 J.

Selected Critical Works about Theodore H. White

Arlen, M. "The Ancient Mariner and the Wedding Guest." *New Yorker*, 56, September 29, 1980, 102–4.
Arnold, M. "For Writers on Presidents, Watergate Meant Opening a Closed Book." *New York Times*, July 23, 1973, 33.
Burgess, P., ed. "Theodore H. White." In *The Annual Obituary 1986*, 330–31. Chicago: St. James Press, 1989.
Cockshutt, R. "In Search of Theodore H. White." *Journal of Popular Culture* 15 (Fall 1981): 86–96.
Hacker, A. Review of *The Making of the President 1964* by Theodore H. White. *Commentary* 40 (December 1965): 110, 112, 114.
Langer, H. J. "Confessions of a Second-Look Liberal." *Society* 20 (July/August 1983): 56–63.
Lichtenstein, N., ed. "White, Theodore H(arold)." In *Political Profiles: The Kennedy Years*, 535. New York: Facts on File, 1976.
McKerns, J. P., ed. "White, Theodore Harold." In *Biographical Dictionary of American Journalism*, 742–44. New York: Greenwood Press, 1989.
Moritz, C., ed. "White, Theodore H(arold)." In *Current Biography 1976*, 433–36. New York: H. W. Wilson, 1977.
Nuechterlein, J. "Liberalism & Theodore H. White." *Commentary* 74 (September 1982): 32–38.
"White, Theodore Harold." In *The National Cyclopedia of American Biography*, vol. 1, *1953–1959*, 276–77. New York: James T. White, 1960.

Selected General Works

Burke, K. *Attitudes toward History*. Berkeley: University of California Press, 1984.
———. *A Grammar of Motives*. Berkeley: University of California Press, 1974.

Crick, B. *In Defense of Politics*. Chicago: University of Chicago Press, 1962.

Cuzzort, R., and E. King. *20th Century Social Thought*. New York: Holt, Rinehart and Winston, 1980.

Desmond, R. W. *Tides of War: World News Reporting 1931–1945*. Iowa City: University of Iowa Press, 1984.

Halberstam, D. *The Powers That Be*. New York: Alfred A. Knopf, 1979.

Knightley, P. *The First Casualty*. New York: Harcourt Brace, 1975.

Kondracke, M. "Journalists Should Narrate Campaigns, Not Arbitrate Them." *Dallas Morning News*, October 1, 1995, 5 J.

Swanberg, W. A. *Luce and His Empire*. New York: Dell, 1972.

GEORGE F. (FREDERICK) WILL

(May 4, 1941–   )

Political Commentary with a Philosophical Flair

In the American setting, political commentary draws much of its character and style from a rich journalistic tradition of firsthand observations of politics and politicians. Political analysis undertaken from a more theoretical nature has been more likely to be the province of the intellectual housed in the academic venues of the college or the university. To the degree that the professorial stance has invaded the popular press, it has been via intellectuals who have made their reputations as scholars well before undertaking political activity. Even as political commentators they retained their status as members of the academic community. Noam Chomsky (q.v.), John Dewey (q.v.), and Raymond Moley (q.v.) are noteworthy examples of this pattern. Exceptions have been notable because they were exceptions; for example, John McLaughlin (q.v.) fled the classroom altogether to become a full-time commentator, and so did George Frederick Will.

Unlike McLaughlin, however, George Will departed the academic profession but neither the academic style or substance departed George Will. The old proverb, "You can take the boy out of the country but you can't take the country out of the boy," applied to Will in a different way; he took the boy out of the academy but not the academy out of the boy. The unique mix has marked George Will's career as a political commentator with an academic flair ever since.

PRIVILEGED CLASSICAL BEGINNINGS

George F. Will is, on the one hand, a passionate fan and student of what was once "America's favorite game," baseball, and, on the other, a passionate advocate of the classical tradition of politics and education. The subject of both passions have much in common. Will proclaims of baseball:

> Proof of the genius of ancient Greece is that it understood baseball's future importance. Greek philosophers considered sport a religious and civic—in a word, moral, undertaking. Sport, they said, is morally serious because mankind's noblest aim is the loving contemplation of worthy things, such as beauty. ... Winning is not everything. Baseball—its beauty, its exactingness—is an *activity* to be loved [and] loving is a form of participation. (Will, 1990, 2–4, emphasis in original)

About the classical virtues of civic activity, Will proclaims:

> I think the defining, distinguishing characteristic of the United States is the care taken for public education from the word ''go.'' Even when the American state was a light and gossamer thing, it was intruding itself into this sphere, saying, ''If you're going to be citizens of the free society, that has certain prerequisites, and it is the civic authority's responsibility to see to the civic prerequisites. (Clapp and Spring, 1984, 24)

As the twentieth century comes to an end, both baseball and civics, as *active* participation in the contemplation and creation of beauty, are rapidly eroding away. No longer is baseball America's number one game. No longer do civics engage the eager efforts of the citizenry. Twin classical traditions are vanishing. America is not the better for it.

Both Will's passions for the traditions of baseball and for the civic polity derive from his upbringing in Champaign, Illinois. He became a fan of the Chicago Cubs at the age of seven and has remained so all his life. He delights in his occasional stints as a celebrity radio and television analyst of Cub games on Chicago's Superstation, WGN-TV, Channel 9. In the 1995–1996 season George Will served a term as commissioner in baseball's minor leagues with the fledgling Texas-Louisiana League. His book, *Men at Work: The Craft of Baseball* (1990), is a loving homage to baseball's leading managers, pitchers, hitters, and glovemen. The basic premise of the book, George Will explains, is achieving excellence. He stated in an interview, ''In almost any field, excellence comes down to the same virtue: discipline, caring, attention to detail . . . which is how to do things right'' (Staggs, 1990, 54). Here ''right'' translates into the classical way of doing things.

As he grew up a baseball fan so too did he grow up with a philosophic flair for political analysis. He was born on May 4, 1941, the son of a philosophy professor at the University of Illinois, Frederick L. Will, and a high school teacher and editor of a children's encyclopedia, Louise Will. Classical teachings were as much a part of his youth as a glove and a bat. As far as his early schooling was concerned, Will described his high school as follows: ''I went to a small university-run high school composed of anemic, nearsighted faculty children like me'' (Wallace, 1983, 106).

After his high school graduation, George Will entered Trinity College in Hartford, Connecticut. While he was at Trinity College, he was more interested in sports, as the sports editor of the school's newspaper, than in academics and politics. That interest continued until his senior year, when he took over the helm as editor of the newspaper. Will states, ''The spark didn't hit the kindling of intellectual life until the time between my junior and senior years in college'' (Staggs, 1990, 54). His political ideology was liberal at that time, and he reportedly quit his fraternity because it refused to admit blacks. During his undergraduate years, he was also the cochairperson of the Trinity Students for Kennedy in 1960.

In 1962, after graduating with a degree in religion from Trinity College (Wallace, 1983), George Will enrolled at Oxford University in England. There he met a group of students who advocated a free market economy, scarcely a mainstream view in the welfare state era of post–World War II America and England. Shortly he became an "ideological capitalist" (Wallace, 1983). Will explained his ideological shift in an interview for *Publishers Weekly*: "I met some disciples of Milton Freidman and Friedrich von Hayek, and became interested in free-market economics," but soon learned that "the social energies of a society [Britain] suffocated by too much statism" (Staggs, 1990, 54).

In 1964 George Will returned to the United States and entered graduate school at Princeton University, where in 1967 he received a doctorate in political science. In his studies for his doctorate, Will tempered his views regarding the promise of a free market economy. He reached the conclusion that those who subscribe to unfettered capitalist economics do not fully understand the vital role of politics in society. According to Will's evolving philosophy, political institutions ensure justice, whereas the strictly free market ensures only greed. In an interview he once stated, "We all respect the market, a marvelous allocator of wealth and opportunity, but that's rough justice, and politics is to take the roughness out of it" (Clapp and Spring, 1984, 24).

After graduation from Princeton, George Will and his wife Madeleine (Marion) Will, whom he married in 1967, moved to East Lansing, Michigan, where he began teaching political science at Michigan State. The 1960s witnessed a rapid enlargement in enrollments on college campuses and the expansion of university faculties to meet the need. It was not unusual for newly credentialed instructors and assistant professors to jump from one institution to another in search of improved teaching and research opportunities. At first, Will appeared to be one of these carpetbaggers; the Wills' stay in Michigan was brief, for the next year, they moved to Canada, where George Will taught at the University of Toronto.

But Will's career as a professor turned out to be very brief. If one accepts the view of one of his critics, David Bromwich, Will had set his eyes from the time of his Ph.D. work on being not a classroom teacher, but an "opinion-maker" whose influence would extend to policy officials, not undergraduates (1992, 58). In 1970 U.S. Senator Gordon Allot, a Colorado Republican and chair of his party's policy committee in the Senate, recruited George Will to write speeches and conduct research. He departed the academic community, but only after absorbing from it his father's love of ideas and his own penchant for philosophical discourse.

While he was working for Allot, Will rekindled his passion for political writing that had been sparked at Trinity College. He began submitting columns to the *Washington Post* opinion-editorial page and to a conservative opinion journal, the *National Review*. At the *Post* the deputy editor of the editorial page was Meg Greenfield. Greenfield, who would, like Will, later become a regular political columnist and commentator for *Newsweek*, respected Will's acerbic writing style. "Her own pungent writing unquestionably affects the national debate more than any other editorial voice in the country,'' wrote critic Roger Piattadosi (Taft, 1986, 138). Her enthusiastic reception of George Will's unsolicited contributions helped pave the way for Will to acquire a similar influence.

The *National Review* was under the leadership of another of America's foremost political commentators of the late twentieth century, William F. Buckley, Jr. (q.v.). He too liked Will's stiletto-like writing probes. Moreover, he liked Will's conservative commentaries as well. Buckley not only published George Will's contributions to *National Review*; when, despite Will's efforts, in the 1972 election, Gordon Allot lost his seat in the U.S. Senate, making George Will unemployed effective January 1973, Buckley hired Will as the Washington editor for the *National Review*. He held that position until 1975.

Combining his own talents with the promotion derived from the assistance of Greenfield and Buckley, George Will's career as a political commentator began to flourish. In September 1973, the op-ed column he had been writing for the *Washington Post* was syndicated nationally; in January of the following year, it began appearing twice a week in cities across the country and soon built a syndication of more than 300 newspapers. Two years later, *Newsweek* hired Will as a contributing editor; in that capacity, he started writing a biweekly column of political opinion that is now in its third decade. The column, ''The Last Word,'' which appears in the hallowed space on the back page of the magazine where Raymond Moley's column was placed during his career, alternates each issue between the byline of George Will and Meg Greenfield.

PHILOSOPHIC COMMENTARY WITH A LIVELY JOURNALISTIC STYLE

For social change to occur among any people, at least two preconditions must be met. First, popular perceptions of the values and ideals of the prevailing social order must be incongruent with the benefits promised by the new order. Second, the outline of the new alternative must be crafted to convince the populace of the positive conditions of change. In the United States in the late 1970s, it had become clear that the number of citizens who believed in the sonorous vacuities of the Democratic party's claims of economic recovery was declining. Democratic party rhetoric had come to mean little in the presence of economic stagnation and hardship. In times like those of the resultant political disharmony of the 1970s, it was the task of advocates of change to expose the weaknesses of the status quo and argue for, first, political renewal, then economic reform.

In the classical tradition of political rhetoric, the wisdom of a natural aristocracy and the principles of noble virtue guide citizens, via precept and law, toward social affection, moral decency, and a dedication to the common good. Although liberals might think that challenges to basic precepts and laws are the hallmarks of an ''open society,'' they are not—at least, not according to George Will. Wise basic guidelines are the foundation of the conservatism that George Will has espoused since his days as a graduate student at Princeton. These guidelines constituted the foundation of his dissertation, "Beyond the Reach of Majorities: Closed Questions in the Open Society." "A specter is haunting American liberals," he paraphrased Karl Marx (a technique of parody he would perfect in his years as a commentator), "the specter of confident politics . . . the kind of open mind the liberal favors is a political menace" (Bromwich, 1992, 59).

In the late 1970s, the ideals of conservatism were no longer a faint voice in the distance, but they were instead a growing cheer of the crowds at political rallies across this country. Americans' memories of a conservative in the White House included Dwight Eisenhower, Richard Nixon, and Gerald Ford. Despite their presence, however, the nation's political thought remained liberal, even when the political party in power veered to the right, and in spite of the best efforts of such political commentators as William Buckley, Paul Harvey (q.v.), and John McLaughlin.

The Iranian hostage crisis of 1979–1980 signified for many Americans the country's weakness abroad; combined with the impact of inflation and economic repression, it provoked citizens to question the liberal policies and ideology of the times. The shift in the American conscience allowed citizens to heed the tone of a new rhetoric—the conservative rhetoric. Any rhetoric that brings about social change possesses several characteristics. First, it contains methodically selected words to motivate the audience members, and second, it includes guidelines for action, insinuating the course of action. In the late 1970s, the stage was set for social change. The ideals of the current order, liberalism, were revealed as incongruent with the benefits of the new social order, conservatism. The rhetoric of the new order had been crafted to illuminate the positive conditions of change, and George Will was a major agent in the process of creating that new rhetoric. A new direction of political thought had begun.

By the late 1970s, George Will was "America's first true hope(s) for intellectual, but popular 'political commentators' since Walter Lippmann" (Clapp and Spring, 1984, 22). His syndicated columns gave him an extended audience who were excited and inspired by his ideas. Sometimes they infuriated and inflamed both liberals and conservatives, but, in the tradition of Walter Lippmann, they taught and rewrote history as well (Aron, 1959).

In 1977 George Will received a Pulitzer Prize for distinguished commentary, which affirmed his stature in the ranks of political commentators. Yet, even an award-winning political commentator is not without critics. The reasons for both the criticism and the praise bear exploration. George Will claims that the social unrest and liberalism of the 1960s were an "assault" on the state and produced a reaction in the "conservative intellectual cadre of the 1980s" (Staggs, 1990, 55). As a member of this conservative cadre, George Will led the way at the pinnacle of the intellectual shift of ideas during the 1980 election of Ronald Reagan.

A controversy arose over Will's conduct during the campaign on behalf of Reagan's conservative triumph. The Reagan campaign team invited several reporters and political commentators to participate in a rehearsal for Reagan's sole presidential debate with incumbent Jimmy Carter. During Will's participation in the rehearsal, the columnist learned that the Reagan team had acquired a copy of President Jimmy Carter's campaign strategy book. The fact that Will, who was also hired by the American Broadcasting Company (ABC) to be a commentator on the political election, had knowledge of the Carter campaign book led critics to claim that Will should have declined the offer to participate in Reagan's debate rehearsal and refused the role of ABC political pundit. Instead, not only did George Will participate in the rehearsal, with knowledge of the contents of the purloined strategic intelligence, he also, during a broadcast of ABC's "Nightline," proclaimed Reagan the superior debater. Some journalists and several news organizations openly criticized Will for what has been deemed his unethical behavior in participating in the campaign process and then commenting on the performance of his favored candidate (Griffith, 1983, 57).

With the same confidence and fervor he extols in his columns, George Will defended his actions, stating that he is a commentator, and this should be judged by a different set of standards than those for other journalists. Will's political philosophy, which calls for collaboration instead of competition, was evident in his response to his critics. He stated in an interview where he discussed the incident,

> I think that the rules are different, have to be different for someone who's a straight news reporter and someone who . . . is paid to be opinionated. And I really regret the idea that social friendship among journalists and politicians should somehow be forbidden. Because the tendency then is to treat politicians as abstractions, not flesh and blood men and women, but as embodiments of political ideals. ("Ethical Debate Ensues over Conduct of George Will," 1983, 45)

The incident had no lasting negative impact on George Will's popularity or his career as a political commentator. Yet, some critics still argue the hypocrisy of Will's actions in this case. One such critic, David Bromwich, writes of the Carter-Reagan debate controversy,

> What it ought to cost him [Will] is some part of the reputation he holds for personal probity and public virtue. For, if this act of collusion was unscrupulous, even by the standards of the Reston-Safire insider tradition, it was beyond conceiving by the standards of a tradition Will affects to cherish more dearly. (Bromwich, 1992, 82)

The incident apparently did teach Will to be protective of his public persona. In 1986 cartoonist Garry Trudeau ridiculed Will in one of his "Doonesbury" strips. By that time Will had added to his popularity as a political commentator by becoming a television celebrity, first, as a regular panelist on "Agronsky and Company" on public television, then, even more notably as a panelist along with Cokie Roberts (q.v.) and Sam Donaldson on ABC's Sunday weekly program, "This Week with David Brinkley." After the appearance of Trudeau's cartoon, and during a rehearsal run-through prior to the airing of David Brinkley's (q.v.) show, George Will forbade Sam Donaldson to make any reference to the cartoon during the live broadcast. No panelist mentioned it (Hitchens, 1987).

WILL'S PHILOSOPHICAL TOUCH

Being a political commentator involves providing one's opinion. In rendering one's opinion, a commentator, such as Will, exposes himself or herself to criticism in return. George Will understands this and does not linger on the criticism by either his opponents or his proponents. As a passionate baseball and politics fan, he is well aware of the celebrated Babe Ruth's fabled put-down of his critics, "I don't care what they write about me, as long as they spell my name right" (Dickson, 1991, 379). Will commented in an interview, "True. Politics is a passionate activity. It attracts the passionate. It ought to" (Clapp and Spring, 1984, 25).

During his tenure as the nation's leading conservative political commentator since William Buckley, Will continues to sell his vision of a new form of conservatism. One observer of his work writes, "Will anchors his belief in the pursuit of virtue in the concept of natural law, and he calls for the dispensation of the American pursuit of self-actualization" (Nuechterlein, 1983, 41). In his writings, George Will calls for a reform of American ideals and a return to the classical tradition.

The ancient philosophers believed that their gods were the ultimate rulers of the state and that those who held power over them had received their authority directly from the gods. They accepted the idea of a natural order, without question. They believed that all the laws they lived by were given to their ancestors by the gods. This, in turn, meant that the laws could not be questioned. George Will's political philosophy, like that of the ancient philosophers, hinges on citizens' acceptance of a government system led by the wise, referring to the natural aristocracy. According to Will, one of the major problems with the American political system is that self-interest controls decision making, causing an irrational sense of excessive individualism and an inadequate sense of community. Moreover, "Will's comments on the failings of an uninstructed populace proceed from the perfectly reasonable supposition that inside every civilized individual, perhaps including George Will, lurk uncivilized passions, and that virtue, personal or collective, is a difficult and precarious endeavor" (Burner & West, 1988, 25).

George Will's resounding rhetoric was credited with a key shift in social order in the 1980s. The change in the balance of power from liberalism to conservatism, as a result of the 1994 midyear elections, has also been attributed to the rhetoric of Will and other conservatives such as Rush Limbaugh (q.v.). The success in 1994 was not instantaneous, according to Will. He traces its origins back to the 1950s when William F. Buckley, Jr., started the conservative *National Review*. George Will told the *Christian Science Monitor* that the conservative success in 1994 "was not a wave that rose out of a flat sea, but the completion of a conservative transformation of the country" (Lamb, 1994, 13).

Regardless of the substance and content of George Will's political commentary, there are features of his style and manner that also win plaudits from his admirers, as well as guffaws from his critics. For example, Bromwich notes that

> mannerisms are an index of character, and Will's writing from the first has been notable for two: the ventriloquized gruffness of a downright Oxford slang . . . and the studding of his text with the names of learned authorities, whom Will brings forward as an *arriviste* displays silverware, to dazzle, stagger, oppress, and sicken the visitor to his study. (1992, 75)

A recent case of "ventriloquized gruffness," but one of many, was Will's commentary on the American labor movement and the leader of the AFL-CIO, John Joseph Sweeney: "Sweeney occupies an eighth-floor office in the house of labor on 16th Street, looking down on the White House. (Doesn't everybody seem to nowadays?)" (Will, 1995c, 98). Thus Will gave a Bronx cheer to the "native Bronx," Sweeney, as well as the more lowly U.S. president, Bill Clinton.

Ever the authority dropper, Will peppers his commentaries with references to luminaries—T. S. Eliot, Evelyn Waugh, Mark Twain, Dante, and every ancient Greek philosopher ever born. Sometimes he combines gruffness and source courting; for example, consider his lead in a column criticizing the nefarious consequences of the Voting Rights Act of 1965 on its thirtieth anniversary:

> When Sir Arthur Stanley Eddington (1882–1944), the astrophysicist, was asked how many people understood his theory of the expanding universe, he paused, then said, "Perhaps seven." That may be more than fully understand how we got from the Voting Rights Act of 1965 to the notion that racial gerrymandering is not only virtuous but also mandatory under that Act. (Will, 1995a, 64)

Will has been compared to the key columnist-commentators of the twentieth century, especially Walter Lippmann (q.v.). Operating under the assumption that ideas are to be shared and explored, Will "has injected an entire political tradition . . . into everyday American political discourse" (Carlin, 1985, 422). Will's purpose is no less than to reshape American political culture. He advocates a more positive attitude toward politics in general and the political role of state governments specifically. From Will's perspective, politics allows for justice to be attained, and whereas the free market theory can stifle the cohesiveness of a society, a welfare state builds a consensus for the common good (Rozell, 1992, 52).

According to Will, government officials have no major impact on change in society. In an interview, Will stated, "Change is actually driven by industry and innovations" (Smith, 1993, 5). He criticizes government officials who proclaim that they are agents of change. In fact, he argues that the role of the politician is overrated. Will comments, "Prior to [Woodrow Wilson's personal delivery of the State of the Union address in Congress] the state of the union address was just sent to Congress" (Smith, 1993, 5). Will offers the assessment that the role of the president has been inflated since the days of Woodrow Wilson, and that the exaggeration of the role is a hindrance to democracy. Presidents who make grandiose claims to the contrary, like President Bill Clinton's about a balanced budget or welfare programs, are "neither bad nor dangerous, just silly" (Will, 1995b, 94).

Detractors declare that George Will's criticism of the modern world leaves the United States with museums to worship rather than contemporary lives to lead. Others argue that Will's call for new conservatism is actually a cover for his liberal underpinnings, a critique that stems, in part, from the commentator's independence to speak against policies of the Republican party that he feels violate the tenets of true conservatism. George responds, "Conservatism is a stance of intellectual humility in front of the complexity and unknowability of the future. . . . One of the reasons for being a conservative is that we don't know the future" (Lamb, 1994, 13).

George Will's contribution to political thought via commentary is that he challenges both conservatives and liberals to seek a means by which the state's protection of individual interests and material items enhances the citizen's affection for and allegiance to the political community. His view on free market versus big government, and his argument that the basic decision is between injustice and justice, has been criticized as extreme polarization. Will, however, views the continuum he operates on as continous in nature rather than nominal, giving consideration to incremental degrees, not polar opposites. According to Mark Rozell, a Will critic who agrees with him on this point, "The question is not simply whether we want justice or injustice, but rather who we want to regulate the distribution of society's scarce resources (1992, 54).

In his book *Statecraft as Soulcraft* (1983), Will responds to the bulk of his detractors by declaring that capitalism encourages the development of self-interest, and part of the "soulcraft" of the state is to be noble and enrich the lives of its citizens, even if that means embracing a welfare state that Will's fellow conservatives consider anathema. His conservatism is undoubtedly a complex perspective built on the philosophy of the classical traditions. In his books, columns, television appearances, and lectures, George Will challenges modern conservatives to consider the major assumptions of their public philosophy. Whether one agrees with his political philosophy is, for him, not the point. As with most political commentators, the purpose of an opinion maker is to challenge citizens to think, read, and seek understanding of the political system in this country. Will, donning the mantle of the baseball observer, has written, "The instructions to umpires include seven lyrical words to live by: 'Keep your eye everlastingly on the ball' '' (1996, 78). Agree with him or not, George F. Will everlastingly keeps his eye on the political ball.

REFERENCES

Selected Politically Relevant Work by George F. Will

"Beyond the Reach of Majorities: Closed Questions in the Open Society." Ph.D. diss., Princeton University, 1968.

Press, Politics and Popular Government. Washington, DC: American Enterprise Institute, 1972.

The Pursuit of Happiness and Other Sobering Thoughts. New York: Harper and Row, 1978.

The Pursuit of Virtue. New York: Simon and Schuster, 1982.

Statecraft as Soulcraft: What Washington Does. New York: Simon and Schuster, 1983.

The Morning After: American Success and Excesses, 1981–1986. New York: Free Press, 1986.

The New Season: A Spectator's Guide to the 1988 Election. New York: Simon and Schuster, 1987.

Suddenly: The American Idea Abroad and at Home. New York: Free Press, 1990.

Restoration: Congress, Term Limits and the Recovery of Deliberative Democracy. New York: Free Press, 1992.

The Leveling Wind: Politics, The Culture, and Other News. New York: Viking, 1994.

"The Voting Rights Act at 30." *Newsweek*, July 10, 1995a, 64.

"A Weird Sincerity." *Newsweek*, November 13, 1995b, 94.

"Arise, Ye Prisoners . . ." *Newsweek*, November 27, 1995c, 98.

"Baseball's Rule of Law." *Newsweek*, April 1, 1996, 78.

Other Selected Work by George F. Will

Men at Work: The Craft of Baseball. New York: Macmillan, 1990.

Selected Critical Works about George F. Will

Broder, D. *The Changing of the Guard.* New York: Simon and Schuster, 1980.

Bromwich, D. *Politics by Other Means.* New Haven, CT: Yale University Press, 1992.

Burner, D., and T. R. West. "George Will: Community and Chauvinism." In *Column Right: Conservative Journalists in the Service of Nationalism*, edited by D. Burner and T. R. West, 17–38. New York: New York University Press, 1988.

Carlin, D. R. "The Machiavellian Will." *Commonweal*, 112, August 9, 1985, 422–23.

Clapp, R., and B. Spring. "The Convictions of America's Most Respected Newspaper Columnist." *Christianity Today*, 28, July 1984, 22–27.

"Ethical Debate Ensues over Conduct of George Will." *Broadcasting*, July 18, 1983, 45–46.

Griffith, T. "The Danger of Hobnobbery Journalism." *Time*, August 8, 1983, 57.

Lamb, G. "George Will: Conservative Pundit Displays an Independent Bent." *Christian Science Monitor*, 87, December 15, 1994, 13.

Moritz, C., ed. "Will, George F(rederick)." In *Current Biography 1981*, 443–46. New York: H. W. Wilson, 1982.

Nuechterlein, J. "George Will and American Conservatism." *Commentary*, 76, October 1983, 35–43.

Riley, S. G. "Will, George Frederick." In *Biographical Dictionary of American Newspaper Columnists*, 349–50. Westport, CT: Greenwood Press, 1995.

Rozell, M. J. "George F. Will and Contemporary American Conservatism." *Modern Age* 35 (Fall 1992): 51–60.

Smith, B. "George Will on America's Changing Political Mood." *HR Focus* 70 (August 1993): 5.

Staggs, S. "George Will." *Publishers Weekly*, March 16, 1990, 54–55.

Wallace, C. "George and Madeleine Will Have the Government Cornered: He Writes about It and She Serves in It." *Publishers Weekly*, 21, September 19, 1983, 103–107.

Selected General Works

Aron, R. "The Columnist as Teacher and Historian." In *Walter Lippmann and His Times*, edited by M. Childs and J. Reston, 111–25. New York: Harcourt, Brace, 1959.

Dickson, *Baseball's Greatest Quotations*. New York: Edward Burlingame Books, 1991.

Goldman, A. I. "Epistemic Paternalism: Communication Control in Law and Society." *Journal of Philosophy* 85 (1991): 113–131.

Hirsch, A. *Talking Heads: Political Talk Shows and Their Star Pundits*. New York: St. Martin's Press, 1991.

Hitchens, C. "Blabscam: TV's Rigged Political Talk Shows." *Harper's*, March 1987, 75–76.

Mankiewicz, F. "From Lippmann to Letterman: The Ten Most Powerful Voices." *Gannett Center Journal* 3 (Spring 1989): 81–96.

Nimmo, D., and J. E. Combs. *The Political Pundits*. New York: Praeger, 1992.

Shaw, D. "Of Isms and Prisms." *Columbia Journalism Review* 30 (January/February 1991): 55–57.

Taft, W. H. "Greenfield, Meg." In *Encyclopedia of Twentieth Century Journalists*, edited by W. H. Taft, 138. New York: Garland Publishing, 1986.

WALTER WINCHELL
(April 7, 1897–February 20, 1972)

Political Information as Apocryphal

As the twentieth century wound down in the 1990s, serious observers fretted over the frivolous direction of political discourse. Reasoned discussion, it seemed, had been displaced by showmanship; the Zeus-like oratory of Franklin Roosevelt or John Kennedy yielded to the whirl of politicians parading their candidacies and programs on late night television, trading quips with comics Jay Leno or David Letterman, or making guest appearances on "Murphy Brown" and other sitcoms. In a decade of televised political spots, sound bites, and scripted one-liners it was no longer clear where politics began and show business ended (see Altheide & Snow, 1991; Lichter, Lichter, & Rothman, 1994).

Forgotten in much of the handwringing and anguish was a political commentator who was also a former vaudevillian. In the 1940s this commentator sat in front of a radio microphone, shirt collar open, fedora tilted back on his head, one hand beating out meaningless sounds on a telegraph key, while breathlessly pouring out over 200 words a minute in a stream of political half-truths and opinions to an audience of 25 million listeners—13 percent of the nation's total population. If mass communication about politics has indeed been reduced to show business, it is the crowning legacy of Walter Winchell.

"THE COLUMN": APOCRYPHA OF CELEBRITY GOSSIP, RUMOR, AND INNUENDO

In 1947 two social scientists published a seminal study of the nature and psychology of rumor (Allport & Postman). In it they reported a "rumor intensity formula"—a measure of the intensity of a rumor and the importance and ambiguity of the subject of any rumor. In the formula, $R = i \times a$, R designates rumor, i is intensity, and a is ambiguity. Hence, the amount of rumor in circulation varies with the importance of the subject to people, multiplied by the ambiguity of the evidence available on the topic of the rumor. Thus, given the multiplicative nature of the relationship, if either the perceived importance of the rumor or the ambiguity of evidence surrounding it is zero, there is no rumor. Walter Winchell's position as the most popular political commentator of the mid-twentieth century rested on his talent for making rumors, or gossip, *seem* important, and for shrouding politics in clouds of ambiguity.

There was no ambiguity about Winchell's popularity. For example, one audience rating scheme for 1946 gave Winchell an 18.9 rating. That far outdistanced any other political commentator, including Lowell Thomas (q.v.), second with 11.0; H. V. Kaltenborn (q.v.), at 9.3; Drew Pearson (q.v.), at 8.3; and Fulton Lewis, Jr. (q.v.), 4.9. Given his popularity, "The Jergens Journal," Walter Winchell's 9:00 P.M. EST Sunday night fifteen minutes of news and commentary, was a windfall for his sponsor, a hand lotion manufacturer. In exchange for paying Winchell from $500 to $1,500 per minute to broadcast, Winchell rewarded his sponsor with surveys that indicated over one-half of the audience members who listened to Winchell every week used the advertised hand lotion (Fang, 1977).

Although not overly interested in politics, and certainly not politically informed, Walter Winchell created a political persona that treated political leaders and show business figures as one and the same. By equating politics and entertainment, he made politics popular with vast numbers of Americans who otherwise were not politically attentive; by the same token, he foreshadowed the trivializing of politics so rife in the radio and television talk show formats of the 1990s. To understand how Winchell reduced politics to the cult and culture of celebrity, one must examine his, or his time's, unique approach to the character of political information (Gabler, 1994).

In common vernacular the words "rumor," "gossip," and "innuendo" evoke negative connotations. Dictionary synonyms for rumor, defined as information of uncertain origin, are gossip or hearsay. Dictionaries define gossip as groundless, trifling rumor or chat, and a gossip monger as one who passes rumors along. Innuendo involves subtle, indirect, oblique derogatory reference. Scholarly studies generalize that rumors, gossip, innuendo, and the like are inaccurate, or untrue. Sociologists call the rapid, emotional spread of such inaccuracies by rumors, fads, and gossip "social contagion."

Generally, therefore, the gossip or rumor monger possesses the image of a deceptive and deceitful manipulator; for example, William Shakespeare's portrait of a diabolical *Richard III* (act 4, scene 2, lines 50–60) who resorts to gossipy intrigue:

> Rumor it abroad,
> That Anne, my wife, is sick, and like to die;
>
> . . . .
>
> About it; for it stands me much upon,
> To stop all hopes whose growth may damage me.

Political leaders, columnists, commentators, and analysts, claiming they deal in communicating only *authenticated* information, are loath to trade in rumor, gossip, and innuendo. Yet, as the studies of Chomsky (q.v.), Shibutani (1966), and other scholars suggest, the line between political information and rumor is not easily drawn. In the 1980s, President Ronald Reagan routinely used persuasive parables to illustrate his rhetorical claims, parables that had no basis in fact. And, toward the end of the twentieth century, "factoid" journalism, the assertion of facts with no evidentiary base when facts were not available, was commonplace (Pratkanis & Aronson, 1991).

Ignoring that there is a vast residue of political communication that derives from gossip, rumor, innuendo, fads, and factoids is to deny much of politics itself. If apocryphal communications are actually false, why are they taken seriously, why do they play a key role in political communication? What Walter Winchell grasped was that the seductive appeal of political apocrypha lies not in its being false, but in the possibility that it may be true. Apocrypha—assertions of questionable authorship or authenticity—seduce precisely because (1) it is about important matters, (2) the supporting evidence is highly ambiguous, yet credible, and (3) it challenges political authorities to disprove its authenticity.

A key feature of apocrypha, namely, that its authenticity is rejected by constituted authorities, is what gives apocrypha populist appeal. For example, during World War II, Nazi propagandist Joseph Goebbels waged "whispering campaigns" (*Mundpropaganda*) against the British by planting rumors with respected foreign citizens who, he knew, would pass the disinformation along. Goebbels thereby avoided any responsibility for proving the rumors true; instead, he challenged the English to disprove the fictive claims (Baird, 1974). In a democracy, just as in a dictatorship, gossip, rumor, hearsay, and other apocryphal claims are a *populist* challenge to political authorities' claims that rulers, not the ruled, have the right to define what is important to speak about, and what to say about those matters when they do reach the public agenda (Kapferer, 1990). This insight, which Walter Winchell exploited, was the key to his popularity as a political communicator. It was also his legacy to political communication in the 1980s and 1990s.

Whether his insight derived from Winchell's impoverished upbringing, or perhaps in spite of it, is problematic. Winchell's own posthumous autobiography (1975) is replete with apocryphal musings. Moreover, many biographies of Winchell, often written by his former scriptwriters (Klurfeld, 1976), nemeses (Lyle, 1953), or promoters (Thomas, 1971), have their own apocryphal axes to grind. For example, in part due to Winchell's numerous efforts to con press agents, there is considerable confusion regarding his birth name: "Winchel," "Lipschitz," "Hirshfield," "Weinshield," or "Bakst" (Bakst was his mother's maiden name).

In any case, born on April 7, 1897 (although Schoenebaum, 1973, claims 1894), Walter Winchel (one "l") was a child of the tenements of turn-of-the-century Harlem. The battle for the right-of-way on Harlem's streets in Winchel's youth pitted horse-drawn carriages, trolleys, motor cars, and children's sleds against one another. Walter got his name in the newspaper for the first time when he lost one of those encounters; he was injured when his sled collided with a horse-cart and knocked him into the gutter at Lenox Avenue and 116th Street. Both the young Walter and his hunger for publicity survived.

Walter's grandfather, Chaim Winechel (the first "e" was later dropped) was a rabbi and cantor. Walter's parents, Jacob and Janet Winchel, immigrated to the United States in 1893 in search of the American Dream. Jacob was a sales-man and silk store owner; when he was unsuccessful at both, he sought refuge in gambling at pinochle. That left Janet the task of paying the rent and providing food and clothing for Walter and his brother, Al, from her meager earnings as a seamstress. Jacob and Janet fought a great deal and, eventually, Jacob simply deserted the family. With the help of relatives, Janet soldiered on until she, too, left, moving with Al to Virginia and leaving Walter to grow up with his grand-mother. Walter, who grew up streetwise, survived by charging pennies for walk-ing people home in the rain under his umbrella from the subway station, or by selling newspapers and magazines on Harlem corners.

Although Walter's mother preached the virtues of a formal education, he paid no heed to her (perhaps because it was difficult for him to accept the advice of a mother who routinely tied his left hand behind his back to break his left-handedness). For whatever reason—boredom, rebellion, being burdened with odd jobs, or spending too much time after class in nickelodeons—Walter did poorly in school. Unable to conquer long division, he failed math in the sixth grade; unwilling to repeat the class, Walter quit Public School 184 at the age of thirteen. From then until his death on February 20, 1972, Walter Winchell remained blissfully ignorant of the matters he purported to inform his nationwide readership and 25 million radio listeners about: he read few books and no serious articles or government documents; he avoided public lectures; he eschewed se-rious discussions of public affairs; and he rarely traveled. Instead, he traded being book wise for being a street-smart brain-picker; he picked the brains of entertainment and political celebrities and their press agents and publicists.

As a teenager, Walter joined two friends, George Jessel (who would become one of America's most popular entertainers) and Jack Weiner (who would be-come a successful theatrical agent), to form "The Little Men with the Big Voices," also dubbed "The Imperial Trio." They ushered and led sing-alongs at theater intermissions (Fisher, 1944, 105). The trio auditioned for a vaudeville production and signed a contract to go on tour. Walter soon found himself traveling with the Newsboy Sextette (Eddie Cantor was also a member) in a musical revue, "School Days," on the vaudeville circuit. Although he never became a great stage performer, Walter learned from vaudeville how to put on an act, how to con and charm an audience, and how to rub elbows in the culture of celebrity (Gabler, 1994).

> In myriad playhouses, he learned from audience reactions, getting the feel of crowds, to know what people wanted, what excited them, and what trick or style manipulated them. Almost by osmosis he learned about the mob, the public—the conglomeration of humanity he was later to enthrall. He learned how to quicken the imagination, developing a subtle and mysterious power that can come under the heading of "showmanship." (Klurfeld, 1976, 12)

In 1914 Walter Winchell (now with an added "l," the result of a misspelling of his name on a Chicago theater marquee) departed the "School Days" revue.

To take advantage of the patriotic fervor provoked by the outbreak of the World War I, Winchell put together a flag-waving act in 1915. He sang (one song was his own creation, "The Land I Love"), danced, and gave a tearful patriotic oration. The act had several bookings, but the popularity of the war theme produced successful rivals. In 1916 Winchell joined Rita Green (whom he would later marry, then divorce) in a boy-girl act that toured the Midwest and the West Coast. The act proved a hit but, like so many other vaudeville acts in the period, was a victim of U.S. entry into World War I, which closed numerous theaters.

In 1917 Walter Winchell enlisted in the navy. His assignment was as a receptionist (Winchell would later claim he was a cloak-and-dagger agent) for an admiral stationed at the New York Customs House. From this service, Winchell concocted an apocryphal tale he told often. His duties called for him to handle the admiral's mail—open it, seal envelopes with wax, stamp them, and so on. Allegedly, one day while melting sealing wax with a candle, Winchell tried to eavesdrop on a conversation between the admiral and other officers in an adjoining room. Forgetting that he was wearing a bandage over a nose blister, Winchell got too close to the candle flame, ignited the bandage, and burned his nose. Supposedly this was the first time Winchell stuck his nose into other people's business and got burned, his trademark as a communicator. Once, when asked by a biographer if it all really happened, Winchell gave a revealing reply: "Never spoil a good story by trying to verify it" (Klurfeld, 1976, 18).

After the war ended, Winchell and Green teamed up again in a song-and-dance act. After their marriage ended, Winchell wed another vaudeville performer, June Aster; the couple had a daughter, Walda, and a son, Walter. When he was not performing in vaudeville, Winchell composed a bulletin of backstage gossip that he pinned up on the theater call-board, "The Newsense," pronounced "nuisance." The bulletin, which caused controversy, earned him a black eye from a target of Winchell's gossip. When a copy of "Newsense" was published in *Vaudeville News*, an antiunion throwaway competing with *Variety*, Winchell landed a job in 1922 with the *News* publisher, selling advertising in exchange for favorable news about the advertiser. In a short time, Walter Winchell's two throwaway gossip columns, "Merciless Truth" and "Broadway Hearsay" proved so popular that *News* publishers started charging a nickel a copy. In 1924 Walter Winchell joined the staff of the New York *Evening Graphic*, a sensationalist newspaper. In addition to writing a weekly column, "Broadway Hearsay," he was drama critic and editor, reported stories from Broadway, and sold amusement advertising.

He did not know it at the time, but Walter Winchell was inventing the bread and butter of the lasting mark he left on political commentary in the twentieth century: the gossip column (and, by extension, gossip broadcast). His early columns for the *Graphic* consisted of news, musings, jokes, and poetry. Any gossip he picked up on his beat he merely gave to the newspaper's city desk. In one instance, however, Winchell passed along gossip that the city editor did not print. A rival newspaper, the New York *Daily News*, managed to scoop the competition by publishing a tip that was similar to the one discarded by Winchell's editors at the *Graphic*. This provoked Winchell into including gossip in his weekly Monday column, soon retitled "Your Broadway and Mine." Winchell continued with the *Graphic* until a falling out with editors led him to shift to the New York *Daily Mirror* where his syndicated column (in over 800 newspapers) ran for thirty-four years from 1929 to 1963. The *Graphic* claimed that Winchell's column accounted for over 20 percent of the newspaper's circulation; it went out of business shortly after Winchell's departure.

By the time Winchell had perfected his invention, and thus reinvented himself from vaudeville entertainer to journalist, his gossip column was little more than a series of from twenty to fifty snippets and tidbits of information, misinformation, and disinformation about popular, newsworthy celebrities. His literary one-liners purported to be intimate, confidential revelations garnered as a result of private snooping. Winchell's "snooping" tactics were legendary. One consisted of regular appearances at his reserved Table 50 at the Stork Club, a popular New York City night spot frequented by celebrities. There he circulated, made contacts, and picked up news tips.

The Stork Club was his private preserve, but he roamed elsewhere as well and "covered Broadway from midnight to sunup seven nights a week" writing about "mainly illiterates . . . gangsters, playbores, chorines, show gels, Prohibition Agents and society youths" (Winchell, 1975, 50). One popular speakeasy that was a key source of gossip was the nightclub of Texas Guinan. She was a devoutly religious woman—she had walked Lowell Thomas to Sunday school in her younger days in Colorado—but she was someone who loved to gossip. Guinan revealed to Winchell the goings-on of her nightclub clientele:

> *Guinan:* "Mrs. Vanderbilt is going to have twins!"*WW:* "Who?"*Guinan:* "Mrs. Vanderbilt! One of the most famous ladies in the world!"*WW:* "Oh."*Guinan:* "I just gave you a heckuva scoop. . . . Why don't you make a note of it for the column, you fool?"

Winchell, suspicious that anyone could predict the birth of twins, nonetheless incorporated the item in his column. Weeks later Mrs. Vanderbilt had "twinfants" (Winchell, 1975, 51).

Another gossip-gathering technique was the careful cultivation of press agents. Winchell agreed to "plant an item in Winchell" favorable to an agent's client in exchange for news tips—for each item an agent got printed in Winchell's column, the columnist charged five news tips. The promotional items Winchell published for agents often had considerable influence—saving a broadway show threatened with closure, promoting books for little known authors, keeping entertainment teams together who were about to break up, splitting up happy marriages and cementing shaky ones.

During the height of his popularity, Winchell fancied himself an on-the-scene reporter as well as a gossip columnist. The New York City Police Department permitted Winchell to snoop about the city, from crime scene to crime scene, in an auto equipped with a red light, siren, and police radio. The investigative Winchell joined in police chases, sometimes arriving at the scene of a crime before the police. (Once police found the intrepid columnist being held at bay by a bandit holding a gun.)

Although Walter Winchell's byline apeared on his columns, he relied upon press agents and his staff writers to write items in "Winchellese." Winchell then edited, tightened, and condensed each item to give it a sharp, biting focus. So successful was he that, during his lifetime, "Winchellese" was regarded as more of a contribution to communication than the gossip column itself. Winchellese consisted of coining words, often compound words—Winchell's version of American slang. H. L. Mencken (q.v.) in *The American Language* (1936) singled out Winchell's linguistic euphemisms for critical analysis. There were such Winchell inventions, for example, as "Joosh" for "Jewish"; "shafts" for "legs"; "middle-aisled," "merged," or "lohengrined" for "married"; "fooff" for a pest; "making whoopee" for any manner of illicit affairs; "giggle-water" for liquor; "storked" for having babies; and "the idyll rich" for the frivolous uppercrust. These coinages were not merely affectations. They also served as a protective code Winchell used to report confidential items and avoid getting sued for libel. Unlike the gossip column, however, few of Winchell's "contributions" to American language survived his passing.

It was not as an investigative reporter, such as Drew Pearson, or language connoisseur, like Mencken, that the young Winchell took most pride. It was in his column: "When Winchell says something about "The Column" it is as if he were discussing an immutable force which he had miraculously unleashed but scarcely understood. It seems sometimes as though he regards his professional self as an overmastering creation, whom he can only serve and revere" (Fisher, 1944, 103).

THE POLITICAL BROADCAST: THE APOCRYPHA OF POWER

Prior to the 1930s, Walter Winchell's interest in politics was marginal, and his influence as a political communicator was nonexistent. When Winchell enlisted in the navy in World War I, "politics or philosophy had nothing to do with it," he said (Klurfeld, 1976, 17). As late as 1932, he wrote, "I don't care whether Roosevelt wins or Hoover loses. I know too much about politics to care" (Fang, 1977, 263). However, his interest in politics began to emerge at about the time he added radio listeners to his newspaper readers as part of his devoted national following. Winchell first started broadcasting a gossip series, entitled "New York by a Representative New Yorker," over a network of forty-two stations of the Columbia Broadcasting System (CBS) in 1929. The sponsor was a women's hair tonic. Then, the American Tobacco Company signed Winchell for a thrice-weekly gossip program as part of its "Lucky Strike Hour" on the National Broadcasting Company (NBC).

By 1933 Walter Winchell's forum, broadcast content, and political interests had changed. The "Jergens Journal," a weekly fifteen-minute program on Sunday evenings on CBS, combined entertainment news and gossip with political commentary and rumor. For a short time, Winchell was on both CBS and NBC; when NBC's Blue network became the American Broadcasting Company (ABC), that was Winchell's radio home until 1955. In 1955 Winchell quarreled with ABC and left the network of 365 radio and forty-five television stations and a $16,000-per-week salary to join the Mutual Broadcasting System where he stayed until he retired from broadcasting and his column in 1969; he returned to ABC for a brief six weeks as a television news broadcaster in 1960. For almost four decades, Americans heard some version of Walter Winchell's signature broadcast sign-on: "Good evening, Mr. and Mrs. North [sometimes South] America and all the ships at sea. Let's go to press!"

Walter Winchell's approach to politics was like that of his newspaper column: a flurry of machinegun-like "news items" mixing fact, fiction, and factoid. It was an approach that, no matter how popular and seemingly intimate or confiding, could only trivialize politics, reducing the communication of complex political phenomena to the banality of entertaining one-liners, sound bites, and trivia that it had become by the approach of the year 2000. For instance, a typical World War II Winchell column or newscast might, almost in the same sentence or breath, denounce American fascists or racists, confide that a famous actress visited the Stork Club, reveal that a wartime industrialist and his younger wife were about "phfft" (about to divorce), and report that General George Patton was training a "secret" force of special troops outside London. In such an information hodgepodge, the Battle of the Bulge was of equal importance to actress Marlene Dietrich's stroll down Fifth Avenue, the outcome of revolution in China equal to an aging Hollywood star's successful face-lift.

In Winchell's column he used "departments" as punctuation: "Manhattan Murals," "Memo from Girl Friday," or "Orchids to . . ." The Sunday evening broadcast employed catch phrases as punctuation: "The Washington Ticker," "Around the World in a Minute," "A Reporter's Report to the Nation," or "Now for Some Tips to Reporters." But, the punctuation did little to alleviate the impression that all news is homogenous, all reports born equal. Winchell's aim was not serious commentary, in-depth analysis, or the "elucidation" of Eric Sevareid (q.v.). Rather Winchell's aim was to shock and hold an audience for a fifteen-minute broadcast or the time it took to read his column, then to *move* listeners and readers to buy an advertised product, attend a promoted play, or listen to a singing group that Winchell plugged in exchange for a news tip.

One of Winchell's most notable coups as a broadcaster derived less from his snooping than from sheer necessity. When radio news began to compete with U.S. daily newspapers in the early 1930s, newspapers and wire services responded by forbidding radio newscasts to use published items (see Lowell Thomas). Winchell dealt with the ban by hiring a former newsman to monitor foreign newspapers for hot tips to put on the air. Winchell's foreign spotter concluded from a reading of the British press that the Prince of Wales, who had not yet been crowned Edward VIII, would probably abdicate his kingship to wed a commoner. Although Winchell thought it unlikely that the prince would surrender the kingship once crowned, he aired the gossip on a broadcast. When Edward VIII abdicated in 1936, after barely a year as king, Walter Winchell's reputation as a seer soared.

As one of Winchell's chroniclers points out, "To say that Winchell was none too careful about his facts is not quite correct. He just did not distinguish fact from rumor" (Fang, 1977, 255). Not making that distinction made him the target of libel suits, but he managed to finesse those by using language that worked by innuendo, not by direct assertion. More important, in political reporting, it made Walter Winchell a tool of politicians shrewd enough to use "confidences" leaked to Winchell as means of self-promotion—politicians who could become his staunchest advocates or worst enemies.

Among the most notable politicians who played Walter Winchell like a drum were Franklin D. Roosevelt, J. Edgar Hoover, and Joseph McCarthy. Winchell was a strong advocate of FDR. The president, often his own press agent, frequently met privately with Winchell and used the columnist-broadcaster as a channel for leaking news items in FDR's interests. In the president's bid for an unprecedented third term in 1940, Winchell's support for breaking the no-third-term tradition proved valuable in isolating FDR's opposition and in winning the election. In the buildup to World War II, Winchell's ridicule of Adolf Hitler as a homosexual, along with unrelenting Winchellese references to "Hitlerooters," "swastinkas," and "Ratzis" (one of FDR's favorite coinages), was instrumental in feeding anti-Nazi sentiment in the United States and in fostering popular support for giving aid to the Allies. For his efforts, Winchell had FDR's backing in becoming a lieutenant commander in the U.S. Navy when the United States entered the war. His duties? Promote the navy in his columns and broadcasts.

Winchell's support of J. Edgar Hoover, director of the Federal Bureau of Investigation, not only resulted in a continuing hyping of the Hoover myth, it also made Winchell an unofficial FBI agent. For example, in 1938, Hoover recruited Winchell's assistance in the case of Louis "Lepke" Buchalter. On Hoover's behalf, Winchell contacted Lepke and informed the gangster that capital punishment could be avoided by surrendering to Hoover. Winchell then arranged a meeting for himself, Hoover, and Lepke. Hoover made the arrest and Winchell broadcast the scoop. Lepke, who was tried and found guilty for murder, was executed in spite of Winchell's arranged "deal" (Powers, 1983).

After World War II, Winchell was one of the first to sound the alarm about a potential Communist conspiracy to conquer the world through domination by the Soviet Union. He opposed any appeasement of the Soviets: "When Communists say it with flowers, it's because they expect a funeral" (Schoenebaum, 1973, 614). Hence, it was not surprising that, in 1950, Winchell lent his support to U.S. Senator Joseph McCarthy's crusade to ferret out Communists in positions of authority in the U.S. Department of State, the Department of the Army, news organizations, and American colleges and universities. Winchell became one of McCarthy's most reliable conduits for leaking rumors about Communist infiltration to the press.

Not all politicians could abide Walter Winchell as readily as FDR, the FBI director, and McCarthy. To his credit, Winchell often crossed congressmen from Southern states whom he labeled as racist and bigoted; the congressmen, in turn, attacked Winchell as a "Jewish kike" and "Nigger-Lover." During World War II, Winchell brought other congressmen down on his head when he not only made his radio broadcasts in tailored navy uniforms but also appeared in New York nightspots as a lieutenant commander. Because of congressional opposition, Winchell was put on the inactive naval list and forced to forego wearing the uniform.

With the death of FDR in 1945, Walter Winchell's access to the White House ended. President Harry Truman considered Winchell's news style of gossip and innuendo repulsive. He was highly critical of attacks made by Winchell and Drew Pearson on James Forrestal; he even blamed the defense secretary's suicide on the unrelenting and unfair charges leveled by the broadcasters. Furthermore, he was furious at a Winchell-mongered rumor that Margaret Truman, the president's daughter, had undergone a nose bob in her aspirations for an acting and singing career. Winchell responded by supporting the Republicans during Truman's relection bid in 1948, attacking liberal Democrats (once Winchell's allies), and joining Joseph McCarthy's anticommunist witch-hunts.

AN AMERICAN ORIGINAL?

Walter Winchell's popular appeal began to wane in the mid-1950s for several reasons. One was that his political turnabout and support of McCarthy rankled former friends and allies; when McCarthy's star fell, so did Winchell's. Another was that Winchell, the lifelong purveyor of gossip, became a victim of gossip himself: gossip that Winchell had sparked racial discrimination against a popular African-American female singer and gossip that Winchell had been behind a blackjack beating of the author of an uncomplimentary biography of the columnist (Lyle, 1953). His publication of a series of twenty-four articles in the New York *Post* provoked a lawsuit and a public apology by Winchell in print and on the air to the editor of the *Post* for calling the newspaper the New York *Compost* and the *Postitute*. Publicized feuds with other popular columnists and broadcasters—including Ed Sullivan, Westbrook Pegler, Drew Pearson, Arthur Godfrey, and Jack Paar—tarnished Winchell's image, making him look small and tawdry.

Finally, there was the advent of television, a medium that exposed Winchell's news broadcast style as corny and its content as uninformative and opinionated. Winchell responded by marketing himself as an entertainer as the host of a variety program, "The Walter Winchell Show" on NBC; the host of a crime show, "The Walter Winchell File"; and the narrator of "The Untouchables" on ABC. Even counting the four-year run of "The Untouchables," Winchell's television success was minimal. Two years before his 1969 retirement, Winchell ran a full-page ad in *Variety* urging newspaper editors across the land to audition his column for a month; at the age of seventy, the millionaire who invented the gossip column and had been America's most popular news commentator had no takers. The curtain was falling on the vaudeville act.

"Walter Winchell was an original. There was no one like him before or since" (Fang, 1977, 247). He was more than an original; he was an originator, the creator of an apocryphal news style now institutionalized in the factoid journalism of *USA Today*, the opinionated renderings of such radio and television talk show hosts as Rush Limbaugh (q.v.), and unconventional broadcasters as Phil Donahue (q.v.), who have aired such topics as "politicians who stop cheating on their wives and start cheating the taxpayers." True, there was no one like Walter Winchell before his time, but in political commentary at the end of the twentieth century, his clones are ubiquitous.

REFERENCES

Selected Work by Walter Winchell

Winchell Exclusive. Posthumous autobiography. Edited by E. Cuneo. Englewood Cliffs, NJ: Prentice-Hall, 1975.

Selected Critical Works about Walter Winchell

Block, M., ed. "Winchell, Walter." In *Current Biography 1943*, 832–36. New York: H. W. Wilson, 1944.

Fang, I. E. "Walter Winchell." In *Those Radio Commentators!*, 245–73. Ames, IA: Iowa State University Press, 1977.

Fisher, C. "Winchell Likes Privacy." In *The Columnists*, 87–135. New York: Howell, Soskin, 1944.

Gabler, N. *Winchell: Gossip, Power and the Culture of Celebrity*. New York: Alfred A. Knopf, 1994.

Goss, I. B. "A Study of Walter Winchell's Sunday Evening Broadcasts Made in the Summer and Fall of 1948." Master's thesis, Miami University, 1951.

Kennedy, J. S. "A Bolt from the Blue." In *Molders of Opinion*, edited by D. Bulman, 155–66. Milwaukee: Bruce Publishing, 1945.

Klurfeld, H. *Winchell: His Life and Times*. New York: Praeger, 1976.

Lyle, S. *The Secret Life of Walter Winchell*. New York: Boar's Head Books, 1953.

McKelway, St. C. *Gossip: The Life and Times of Walter Winchell*. New York: Viking Press, 1940.

McKerns, J. P., ed. "Winchell, Walter." In *Biographical Dictionary of American Journalism*, 752–54. New York: Greenwood Press, 1989.

Mencken, H. L. *The American Language*. 4th ed. New York: Alfred A. Knopf, 1936.

Nimmo, D., and J. E. Combs. "Walter Winchell: Bard of Print and Radio." In *The Political Pundits*, 60–64. New York: Praeger, 1992.

Riley, S. G. "Winchell, Walter." In *Biographical Dictionary of American Newspaper Columnists*, 186–88. Westport, CT: Greenwood Press, 1995.

Schoenebaum, E., ed. "Winchell, Walter." In *Political Profiles: The Truman Years*, 614–15. New York: Facts on File, 1973.

Thomas, B. *Winchell*. Garden City, NY: Doubleday, 1971.

Weiner, E. H. *Let's Go to Press*. New York: Putnam, 1955.

Selected General Works

Allport, G., and L. Postman. *The Psychology of Rumor*. New York: Henry Holt, 1947.

Altheide, D. L., and R. P. Snow. *Media Worlds in the Postjournalism Era*. New York: Aldine De Gruyter, 1991.

Baird, J. *The Mythical World of Nazi War Propaganda, 1939–1945*. Minneapolis: University of Minnesota Press, 1974.

Kapferer, J. N. *Rumors: Uses, Interpretations, and Images*. New Brunswick, NJ: Transaction Publishers, 1990.

Lichter, S., L. Lichter and S. Rothman. *Prime Time: How TV Portrays American Culture*. Washington, DC: Regnery Publishing, 1994.

Powers, R. G. *G-Men: Hoover's FBI in American Popular Culture*. Carbondale: Southern Illinois University Press, 1983.

Pratkanis, A., and E. Aronson. *Age of Propaganda*. New York: W. H. Freeman, 1991.

Shibutani, T. *Improvised News*. Indianapolis, IN: Bobbs-Merrill, 1966.

SELECTED BIBLIOGRAPHY

Alterman, E. *Sound and Fury: The Washington Punditocracy and the Collapse of American Politics*. New York: HarperCollins, 1992.

Barnouw, E. *Documentary*. New York: Oxford University Press, 1974.

Bernays, E. *Biography of an Idea: Memoirs of Public Relations Counsel Edward L. Bernays*. New York: Simon and Schuster, 1965.

Boyer, P. J. *Who Killed CBS?* New York: Random House, 1988.

Bulman, D., ed. *Molders of Opinion*. Milwaukee: Bruce Publishing, 1945.

Burlingame, R. *Don't Let Them Scare You*. Philadelphia: J. B. Lippincott, 1961.

Burner, D., and T. R. West. *Column Right: Conservative Journalists in the Service of Nationalism*. New York: New York University Press, 1988.

Carey, J. W. "The Communications Revolution and the Professional Communicator." In *The Sociology of Mass Communications*, edited by P. Halmos, 23–38. Staffordshire, England: University of Keele, 1969.

Childs, M. "The Interpretive Reporter's Role in a Troubled World." *Journalism Quarterly* 27 (Spring 1950): 134–40.

Cohen, R. "The Syndicated Columnist." *Gannett Center Journal*, 3 (Spring 1989): 9–16.

Creel, G. *Rebel at Large: Recollections of Fifty Crowded Years*. New York: G. P. Putnam's Sons, 1947.

Culbert, D. H. *News for Everyman*. Westport, CT: Greenwood Press, 1976.

Dewey, J. *The Public and Its Problems*. New York: Holt, Rinehart and Co., 1927.

Fang, I. E. *Those Radio Commentators!* Ames, IA: Iowa State University Press, 1977.

Fielding, R. *The American Newsreel, 1911–1967*. Norman, OK: University of Oklahoma Press, 1972.

Fisher, C. *The Columnists*. New York: Howell, Soskin, 1944.

Geyer, G. A. *Buying the Night Flight: The Autobiography of a Woman Foreign Correspondent*. New York: Delcorte Press/Seymour Lawrence, 1983.

Goldberg, R., and G. J. Goldberg. *Anchors*. New York: Birch Lane Press, 1990.

Halberstam, D. *The Powers That Be*. New York: Alfred A. Knopf, 1979.

Hirsch, A. *Talking Heads: Political Talk Shows and Their Star Pundits*. New York: St. Martin's Press, 1991.

Hosley, D. H. *As Good as Any: Foreign Correspondence on American Radio. 1930–1940*. New York: Greenwood Press, 1984.

Kaltenborn, H. V. *Fifty Fabulous Years*. New York: G. P. Putnam's Sons, 1950.

Kluger, R. *The Paper: The Life and Death of the New York Herald Tribune*. New York: Vintage Books, 1986.

Knightley, P. *The First Casualty*. New York: Harcourt Brace Jovanovich, 1975.

Krock, A. *Memoirs*. New York: Funk & Wagnalls, 1968.

Kurtz, H. *Hot Air: All Talk, All the Time*. New York: Times Books, 1996.

Lippmann, W. *Public Opinion*. New York: Harcourt Brace, 1922; Macmillan, 1960.

Mankiewicz, F. "From Lippmann to Letterman: The Ten Most Powerful Voices." *Gannett Center Journal* 3 (Spring 1989): 81–96.

McKerns, J. P., ed. *Biographical Dictionary of American Journalism*. New York: Greenwood Press, 1989.

Mencken, H. L. *A Carnival of Buncombe: Writings on Politics*. Baltimore: Johns Hopkins Press, 1956.

Moley, R. *After Seven Years*. New York: DaCapo Press, 1939.

Nimmo, D., and J. E. Combs. *The Political Pundits*. New York: Praeger, 1992.

Persico, J. *Edward R. Murrow: An American Original*. New York: Dell, 1988.

Rai, M. *Chomsky's Politics*. London: Verso, 1995.

Reston, J. *Deadline: A Memoir*. New York: Random House, 1991.

Riley, S. G. *Biographical Dictionary of American Newspaper Columnists*. Westport, CT: Greenwood Press, 1995.

Rivers, W. *The Opinionmakers*. Boston: Beacon Press, 1967.

Sanders, M., and M. Rock. *Waiting for Prime Time: The Women of Television News*. New York: Harper and Row, 1988.

Schroth, R. A. *The American Journey of Eric Sevareid*. South Royalton, VT: Steerforth Press, 1995.

Steel, R. *Walter Lippmann and the American Century*. Boston: Little, Brown, 1980.

Talese, G. *The Kingdom and the Power*. New York: World Publishing, 1969.

Westin, A. *Newswatch*. New York: Simon and Schuster, 1982.

White, T. *In Search of History: A Personal Adventure*. New York: Harper and Row, 1978.

INDEX

Page numbers in **boldface type** indicate location of main entries.

About the Authors

DAN NIMMO is visiting scholar in the department of political science at Baylor University. He is author and/or editor of numerous books on politics and the news media, political campaigning, and American government, including *The Comedy of Democracy* (Greenwood, 1996), *The Political Pundits* (Praeger, 1992), and *Cordial Concurrence: The Orchestration of National Party Conventions in the Telepolitical Age* (Praeger, 1991).

CHEVELLE NEWSOME is assistant professor of communications at California State University, Sacramento. In addition to her teaching and research interests in political communication, she has conducted research in women's attitudes toward female political office-holders.

ISBN 0-313-29585-9

90000>

EAN

9 780313 295850

HARDCOVER BAR CODE

DATE DUE

HIGHSMITH #45115